Oxford Archaeological Guides

General Editor: Barry Cunliffe

Rome

Amanda Claridge is currently a research associate of the Institute of Archaeology, Oxford, and Lecturer in Archaeology at St John's College, Oxford. Assistant Director of the British School at Rome from 1980 to 1994, her wider archaeological activities include fieldwork in Rome, elsewhere in Italy, North Africa, and Turkey, and the study of Roman marbles and sculptural techniques, on which she is a noted authority.

Barry Cunliffe is Professor of European Archaeology at the University of Oxford. The author of over forty books, including *The Oxford Illustrated Prehistory of Europe* and *The Ancient Celts*, he has served as President of the Council for British Archaeology and the Society of Antiquaries, and is currently a member of the Ancient Monuments Board of English Heritage.

'We have long needed what no one before Claridge has provided: a synthesis, balanced and user-friendly, of all [the] recent scholarship, one that sets Roman monuments in their proper urban and historical contexts, and accurately describes what is currently known or thought about them. …[T]ravellers … will welcome a synthesis so balanced, intelligent and well informed, and will find Amanda Claridge a fine companion on their archaeological walks in Rome.'
JOHN H. D'ARMS
Times Literary Supplement

Oxford Archaeological Guides

Rome

An Oxford Archaeological Guide

Amanda Claridge

with contributions by
Judith Toms and Tony Cubberley

OXFORD
UNIVERSITY PRESS

OXFORD
UNIVERSITY PRESS

Great Clarendon Street, Oxford OX2 6DP

Oxford University Press is a department of the University of Oxford.
It furthers the University's objective of excellence in research, scholarship,
and education by publishing worldwide in

Oxford New York

Athens Auckland Bangkok Bogotá Buenos Aires Calcutta
Cape Town Chennai Dar es Salaam Delhi Florence Hong Kong Istanbul
Karachi Kuala Lumpur Madrid Melbourne Mexico City Mumbai
Nairobi Paris São Paulo Singapore Taipei Tokyo Toronto Warsaw

with associated companies in Berlin Ibadan

Oxford is a registered trade mark of Oxford University Press
in the UK and in certain other countries

Published in the United States
by Oxford University Press Inc., New York

British Library Cataloguing in Publication Data

Data available

Library of Congress Cataloging in Publication Data

Data available

ISBN 0–19–288003–9

7 9 10 8 6

Designed by First Edition, London
Typeset by Best-set Typesetter Ltd., Hong Kong
Printed by Book Print S. L.
Barcelona, Spain

Series Editor's Foreword

Travelling for pleasure, whether for curiosity, nostalgia, religious convic-
tion, or simply to satisfy an inherent need to learn, has been an essential
part of the human condition for centuries. Chaucer's 'Wife of Bath' ranged
wide, visiting Jerusalem three times as well as Santiago de Compostela,
Rome, Cologne, and Boulogne. Her motivation, like that of so many
medieval travellers, was primarily to visit holy places. Later, as the Grand
Tour took a hold in the eighteenth century, piety was replaced by the need
felt by the élite to educate its young, to compensate for the disgracefully
inadequate training offered at that time by Oxford and Cambridge. The
levelling effect of the Napoleonic Wars changed all that and in the age of
the steamship and the railway mass tourism was born when Mr Thomas
Cook first offered 'A Great Circular Tour of the Continent'.

There have been guidebooks as long as there have been travellers.
Though not intended as such, the *Histories* of Herodotus would have been
an indispensable companion to a wandering Greek. Centuries later
Pausanias' guide to the monuments of Greece was widely used by travelling Romans intent on discovering the roots of their civilization. In the
eighteenth century travel books took on a more practical form offering a
torrent of useful advice, from dealing with recalcitrant foreign innkeepers
to taking a plentiful supply of oil of lavender to ward off bedbugs. But it
was the incomparable 'Baedekers' that gave enlightenment and reassur-
ance to the increasing tide of enquiring tourists who flooded the
Continent in the latter part of the nineteenth century. The battered but
much-treasured red volumes may still sometimes be seen in use today,
pored over on sites by those nostalgic for the gentle art of travel.

The needs and expectations of the enquiring traveller change rapidly
and it would be impossible to meet them all within the compass of single
volumes. With this in mind, the Oxford Archaeological Guides have been
created to satisfy a particular and growing interest. Each volume provides
lively and informed descriptions of a wide selection of archaeological sites
chosen to display the cultural heritage of the country in question. Plans,
designed to match the text, make it easy to grasp the full extent of the site
while focusing on its essential aspects. The emphasis is, necessarily, on
seeing, understanding, and above all enjoying the particular place. But
archaeological sites are the creation of history and can only be fully appreciated against the *longue durée* of human achievement. To provide this,
each book begins with a wide-ranging historical overview introducing the
changing cultures of the country and the landscapes which formed them.
Thus, while the Guides are primarily intended for the traveller they can be
read with equal value at home.

Barry Cunliffe

Acknowledgements

This book would not have happened without the generous input of friends and colleagues: Tony Cubberley, whose original idea it was, did a lot of the initial groundwork and also provided bibliography and quotations; Sheila Gibson's unmistakable hand is not only responsible for many of the more familiar illustrations but also many new ones. Mark Wilson Jones donated his masterly drawings of the orders of Rome's Corinthian temples; Janet DeLaine put me straight on the Baths of Caracalla and much else; Margareta Steinby kindly let me see the articles in her new *Lexicon* in advance of publication. Finally, and just as importantly, Judith Toms rescued a continually slipping schedule by writing the section on Catacombs and contributing the bulk of the Museums section. For other help and advice I am indebted to Lucos Cozza, Nicholas Purcell, Robert Coates-Stephens, Chrystina Häuber, the participants in the annual Summer Schools of the British School at Rome during the 1980s, the staff of the British School, especially Maria-Pia Malvezzi and Valerie Scott, and the Ashmolean Library, Oxford.

Amanda Claridge
Oxford, December 1997

Contents

Note

★★ Major sites, commonly on easy access
★ Other readily visible or accessible sites

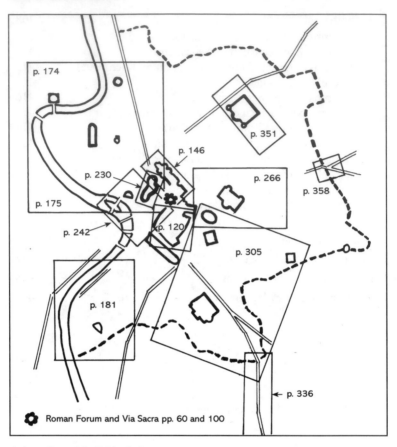

p. 174

p. 351

p. 146

p. 230

p. 266

p. 358

p. 175

p. 242

p. 120

p. 305

p. 181

p. 336

Roman Forum and Via Sacra pp. 60 and 100

▲ Location of individual site maps

How to use this Guide

The city and its archaeological monuments are divided into nine main areas, each accompanied by an area site map; further maps are to be found in the 'Other Sites' section. An overall plan of the areas covered by the site maps is provided opposite.

Sites not within designated archaeological zones have their addresses given beneath their name and are on open view unless otherwise indicated:

> * designates a site with fixed hours of opening, usually requiring a ticket (see p. 422)
>
> † designates a site normally closed to the public, requiring a special permit by application to the authority concerned. Some may be open for short periods on a regular basis on one or two days a week (see p. 422).

Starred Sites

** major sites, commonly on easy access
* other readily visible or accessible sites

Scales to plans and elevations are often given in Roman Feet (RF) as well as metres. 1 RF = 0.296 metres (9 mm. shorter than the English Foot). 1 Roman mile = 1481.5 metres.

For a glossary of building types and materials and other terminology see pp. 37–59, and also consult the Index.

Introduction

Writing guide-books to the antiquities of Rome has been going on for centuries and all those that have ever been written have steered a similar course, between fact and fiction, or rather, between two different kinds of reality. On the one hand, to a degree unmatched anywhere else in the world, Rome's physical past has continued to be woven into the fabric of its present, with buildings now well over 1,500, some well over 2,000 years old still standing (some even still functioning) as part of the modern city. Three thousand years of continuous occupation have produced one of the most deeply stratified and complex urban sites in existence. Up to 20 metres of deposits overlie the street levels of the C6 AD, which in their turn frequently represented a rise of about 2 metres compared with the imperial city of the C2 AD, and in places the C2 level is at least another 4 metres above that of the republican city—and so on back to the huts and cemeteries of the end of the Bronze Age. The sites appear in groups or in isolation, within designated 'archaeological zones' or on the side of a busy street, in a deep pit in the ground or in the middle of a traffic roundabout. Their survival has rarely had to do with their original purpose; that can only be said of the city walls, first laid out in AD 271–5, and continuously operative until breached for the last time by Garibaldi's forces on 20 September 1870. The other structures which have never been buried have usually survived by being converted (in varying states of decay) into churches, monasteries, fortresses, and palaces; some are massive concrete buildings, immune to natural elements and beyond most human means to destroy until the age of dynamite; later generations merely built into, around, or over them as if they were part of the bedrock. Some have been 'liberated' on various occasions from their later encumbrances; there was a rash of that during the French occupation of Rome in 1809–14 and again under the Fascist regime of 1921–44. In the late C19 concerted archaeological excavations were undertaken with the express purpose of rediscovering the Roman Forum, but they are the exception; practically every other site which has been dug up afresh came to light by chance in the course of redevelopment—and whether they have then been allowed to remain visible has been less a question of their archaeological importance, and more a question of their perceived historical significance.

For the second reality is that nowhere else is the archaeological record supplemented, at times overwhelmed, by quite so much historical evidence. Not only was Rome the stage for countless famous episodes (such as Horatio defending the Sublician bridge against the whole Etruscan army; Julius Caesar being murdered on the Ides of March in the curia of the porticus of Pompey and Mark Antony's speech in the forum;

Nero fiddling in the Gardens of Maecenas while the city burned), but a lot of general Roman history is couched in terms of buildings. Ancient Rome was a place where every temple, basilica, arch, road, or aqueduct was potentially a political act: it mattered a great deal who built what, and when. They were celebrated on the coinage, listed in public calendars, satirized or lauded by contemporary poets, and chronicled with criticism or praise by generations of historians. On more than one occasion the physical extent of the city was recorded in stone, incised on marble in the form of a great map. Numerous fragments of one such map have survived. As a result, the study of Roman topography has been a popular pursuit among archaeologists and historians since the late C15, devoted to reconstructing the vanished city from the written or graphic record in association with the scatter of actual remains.

A third reality is that the ancient city was very large, measuring 3–5 km. from side to side in any one direction—far larger than its medieval and Renaissance successors. It did not become as large again until the C20. While the buses and the Metropolitana of the C20 are very good for longer journeys, there are many parts of the city that they do not (or cannot) reach, and for most shorter distances it is generally quicker to walk. That means that archaeological tourists rarely move around the city's monuments in a chronological or typological order; it is much easier to see as many sites as possible in a given area and then start again elsewhere. Since ancient Rome was not a single undifferentiated mass, this approach can be organized to positive advantage, as this guide tries to do, biting off manageable daily portions which also make sense in terms of the ancient city. Starting in the centre, there is a monumental, political Rome composed of three distinct zones (the Forum, the Palatine, and the Imperial Forums); on the inner periphery there are five more or less equally well-defined units (the Field of Mars, the Capitoline hill, the Cattle Market, the valley of the Circus Maximus, and the Valley of the Colosseum). Then there are the predominantly residential quarters on the hills and the area on the right bank of the Tiber (modern Trastevere). Much of the archaeology in these peripheral regions is of the fictional variety; it exists on paper but not in the flesh, or exists in reality but no normal visitor can expect to see it. For this reason, the Aventine and the Quirinal hills and Trastevere have not been included here.

The first part of this guide traces the fortunes of the city from its origins to the end of the C6 AD, placing the visible sites and monuments within a chronological narrative. Subsequent introductory sections provide notes on the various documentary sources, and glossaries of Rome's local stones and other building materials, building techniques and decoration, and the main building-types.

Historical Overview

NOTE: visible sites and monuments covered by this guide are named in the text and listed at the end of each section in SMALL CAPITALS. For further references please consult the index.

Early Rome

With the transition from the Bronze Age to the Iron Age in the C10 BC, the population of central Italy was on the increase; large nucleated settlements began to develop, mostly located on hilltops, and Rome was one of them. The Tiber river, wide and easily navigable from the sea as far as 100 km. upstream, wound through meadows and marshes full of wildlife, beyond which to either side lay rolling plains of highly fertile volcanic soils. At the particular point where Rome grew, 20 km. inland, the natural amenities were combined with a series of 'hills' from whose lower slopes issued fresh water springs and whose heights made convenient refuges from floods,

▼ **Fig. A.** The site of Early Rome

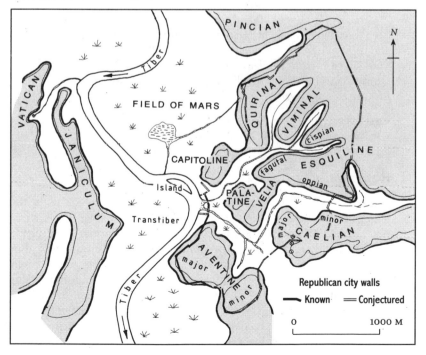

summer heat, and animal and human predators. The hills were in reality irregularly shaped ridges or spurs created by tributary streams running down the edges of the larger valley which had been cut through the plains by the river.

The Anglicized Latin names for the four main spurs, clockwise from the north, are the **Quirinal** (*Quirinalis*), ESQUILINE (*Esquiliae*), CAELIAN (*Caelius*), and the **Aventine** (*Aventinus*). Each ended in a larger knoll or series of knolls which had separate hilly identities: the CAPITOLINE (*Capitolium*) at the end of the Quirinal, the PALATINE (*Palatium*) and **Velia** at the end of the Esquiline. The Caelian and the Aventine ended in parts simply called major and minor, large and small. Between the Quirinal and the Esquiline was a lesser spur, the VIMINAL (*Viminalis*). Various parts of the Esquiline were also sometimes distinguished as 'hills'—the **Cispian** (*Cispius*), the **Oppian** (*Oppius*), the **Fagutal** (*Fagutalis*). The Quirinal had several specific heights—*Latiaris*, *Mucialis* or *Sanqualis*, and *Salutaris*. Beyond the deep valley on the north side of the Quirinal lies a further high ridge, the **Pincian** (*Pincius*), which in earlier days went by the name *Collis Hortulorum* ('Garden heights'). On the right bank, running more or less parallel with the river, is a massive ridge called the **Janiculum**, from which a small promontory (now occupied by S. Pietro in Montorio) projects towards the river roughly in line with the Capitoline hill. To the north-west of the Janiculum, the hill at the end of a second parallel ridge was called the **Vatican** (*Vaticanus*).

Traces of iron-age huts and cemeteries dating from the C9–C7 BC have been found principally in deep-level excavations on the Palatine (p. 125) and Esquiline and in the valley between (p. 108), but many other sporadic finds suggest that if similar excavations were possible on the Capitoline, Quirinal, Aventine, and Caelian early settlement would prove to have included them as well.

- **PALATINE**
- Palatine Museum
- Forum Antiquarium
- L. Pigorini Museum (EUR)

Romulus' city (C8–C6 BC)

Later Roman tradition dated the foundation of Rome to 753 BC, at the hands of a man called Romulus, who became its first 'king'. Whether or not the tradition was invented, it may not be far from the mark. During the C8–C7 BC there emerged three geographically distinct groupings within central Italy as a whole, one on Rome's side of the Tiber to the south (Latium), one to the north (Etruria), and one in the Apennine mountains to the east (Samnium). The peoples in each area spoke a different language (Latin, Etruscan, or Oscan respectively) and had rather different religious and funerary practices but socially and politically their systems were similar; the individual settlements were separate units, each with a

Seven Hills?

Everyone knows that Rome is built on the magical number of seven hills but even the ancient Romans had difficulty deciding which hills to count. In the late C1 BC an annual festival on 11 December was called the *Septimontium* (normally translated as seven hills, but perhaps a corruption of *saepti montes*, enclosed or fortified hills), when each of the '*montes*' made sacrifices followed by a feast, but the participants were eight: the Palatine, Velia, Fagutal, Subura, Cermalus, Oppian, Caelian, and Cispian, two of which (Subura and Cermalus) are not generally considered to have been hills at all, whereas no mention is made of the Capitoline, Aventine, Quirinal, and Viminal. Later lists suggest that efforts were made to define a new seven, in keeping with the city as it had developed by the early Empire. A statue set up in the Roman colony of Corinth (in Greece) towards the end of the C1 AD showed the goddess Roma seated on seven hills and six are labelled: Palatine, Esquiline, Aventine, Caelian, Quirinal, Viminal. The seventh was probably the Capitoline (but could also have been the Janiculum). The Regionary Catalogues of the early C4 AD made yet another selection: Caelian, Aventine, Tarpeian (i.e. Capitoline), Palatine, Esquiline, Vatican, and Janiculum.

'king' or small ruling elite chosen by birth or competition from a larger aristocratic class of warrior-landowners. Although independent, they regularly formed alliances or leagues with one another and there was considerable mobility between the members of one local aristocracy and another; even the 'kings' could be exchanged. All were in increasing contact not only with Greeks who had colonized parts of Southern Italy as far north as the bay of Naples, but also, via Greek and Phoenician traders, with most of the wider Mediterranean. Etruria especially, by virtue of the superior wealth generated by rich mineral resources, made early advances in agriculture and urbanism, draining large areas for new farmland and building cities with stone architecture on the Greek model. Latium was less well-endowed with mineral wealth and its centres developed more slowly, generally on a smaller scale, but Rome was soon an exception. Her position on the Tiber, combining excellent port facilities for traffic up and down the river itself with the river crossing of a main land route, enabled her to take particular advantage of the opportunities provided by trade.

In the course of the C6 BC, traditionally the period during which her 'kings' included at least two who muscled in from Etruria (the Tarquins, Priscus and Superbus, whose family had earlier emigrated to Etruria from Greece), Rome grew into a major power. Her Temple of Jupiter on the Capitoline hill was to be the largest in the Italo-Etruscan world (see p. 237), land drains and culverts made the hillsides and valley bottoms habitable (pp. 62, 267), large aristocratic houses were constructed of stone

(p. 111). Like her neighbours, she built a circuit of defensive walls, but her walls probably enclosed 426 hectares (see Fig. A), larger than any other city in Italy, and she held sway over a considerable area of Latium, ranging as far as 100 km. to the south (Circeo and Terracina).

- **TEMPLE OF JUPITER** podium (Palazzo dei Conservatori)
- Terracottas from archaic temple at **S. OMOBONO** (Capitoline Museums)

- Villa Giulia Museum
- Vatican Museums (Gregoriano Etrusco)

Capital of Italy (C5– C3 BC)

Towards the end of the C6 BC (traditionally 510–509), Rome took a momentous step and abolished her regal system, instituting a new political order, the **Republic**, wherein the king was replaced by two consuls and a range of lesser magistrates, elected annually by the whole male citizen body. The consuls chose an advisory council, the Senate, at first ad hoc, later according to well-defined qualifications (of landed wealth, military and political service). The consuls led the army in times of war and had executive legislative powers in most other matters. Army service was a duty of citizenship but it was also a privilege for which only the wealthier (who could supply their own equipment) were eligible. Soon a small group of aristocratic families, the patricians, managed to gain a virtual monopoly on the consulship and most other civic and priestly offices, but in the late C5 this was challenged by the rest, the plebeians, who formed their own alternative state within the state, and fought successfully in the course of the C4 to win equal rights. A large part of the solution relied on further territorial expansion, to acquire more land which was then allocated among the plebians. Veii, a major Etruscan rival a few kilometres north of Rome on the other side of the Tiber, was the first conquest, in 396 BC, after which Roman armies moved against the rest of Latium and up into the mountains of Samnium, making treaties by threat or outright war until the whole of central Italy was under Roman control. Etruria and Umbria to the north, Campania and the Bay of Naples to the south soon followed, then Lucania and the Greek cities of southern Italy; the last Greek stronghold at Taranto was captured in 272 BC.

Archaeologically, the only visible features of the Rome of the C5– C4 BC are various parts of its **city walls**, rebuilt in massive fashion around 378–350 probably on the line of the earlier C6 circuit. The rest is currently still a blank except for the first phase of the **twin temples at S. OMOBONO** and the knowledge that the great houses of the C6 on the north side of the Palatine (p. 111) remained in occupation. But we know from written sources that at least ten important temples were built, including the two on the Forum (**SATURN** and **CASTOR**), the first of the major **aqueducts** were led into the city (the Appia in 312 BC, the Anio Vetus in 272 BC), and the first of Rome's famous **roads**, the Via Appia, was put in hand: the main route south to the new territories, it was metalled as far as Capua around 312 BC, extended to Venosa in 291, and all the way down to Taranto in 272.

Capital of the Mediterranean (C3 – C2 BC)

Once started, the process of conquest was difficult to stop. Rome's way of obtaining and maintaining power in Italy had been to make her enemies into allies and co-opt them into her own military machine, offering them a share of the booty in return for more fighting men to go on more campaigns. And the greater the prize, the more ambitious the machine became. After peninsular Italy, the next step was to move over to Sicily in 264 BC, which brought war with Carthage (near modern Tunis), whose great trading empire ranged from the coast of North Africa over western Sicily, Sardinia, and southern Spain. Sicily was annexed as the first overseas province in 241 BC, then Sardinia and Corsica (238). The temporary defeat of Carthage itself in 202 brought parts of Spain with it and the temptation to conquer the rest of the Iberian peninsular (largely achieved, after horrendous bloodshed, in 133 BC). By 175 BC Rome also held northern Italy and the Po Valley; in 146 BC Carthage was razed and a new province of Africa created. Southern France (Provence) was taken over in 125–121 BC. The eastern Mediterranean was collapsing apace; in 200 BC Roman troops invaded the Balkans and by 100 BC Greece, most of the Aegean, and large parts of Asia Minor and central North Africa came under direct Roman rule; treaties of one kind or another bound those which were not.

For the city of Rome the C3–C2 BC were revolutionary, especially once the eastern victories got under way. Spain brought a flood of silver bullion, slaves, and other riches, but Greece and Asia brought the best of contemporary Hellenistic Greek culture and its practised exponents (philosophers, poets, playwrights, doctors, teachers, mathematicians, astrologers, every kind of specialist craftsmen) together with innumerable works of art: paintings, tapestries, furniture and table ware, and statues in stone, bronze, fine woods, ivory, and precious metals. The art objects came from all sorts of places and contexts; many were of considerable antiquity, in styles familiar to Rome from her own older past, others were like nothing yet seen in the city. First-hand experience of the more spectacular cities of the East (Athens, Corinth, Ephesus, Pergamon, Rhodes) must also have been a revelation to the thousands who formed the armies of conquest.

Public building in Rome down to the end of the C3 BC, when not concerned with redoing the city walls, consisted mainly of **temples**, set up to honour the gods who it was hoped would look after the Roman people in times of war or other trials, or who had already done so. The

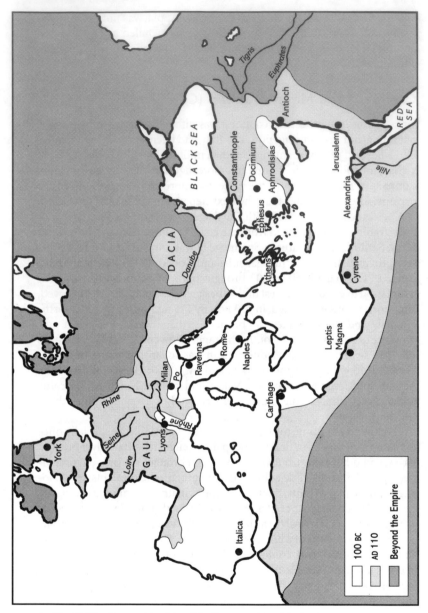

▲ **Fig. B.** The Roman Empire, with sites mentioned in text

right to vow and choose the site of a temple as an individual act was given only to the magistrates with *imperium* (supreme command on behalf of the people in war and other matters) i.e. the generals of her armies. During the C3 it was a right which practically every general exercised in the event of victory. Their *imperium* also allowed them to decide their own share of war booty, so they could not only vow the temple but easily afford to pay for it themselves, thereby gaining additional prestige for themselves and future generations of their family. Some forty such **victory-temples** (an average of one every two years) are listed in the written sources. Fragments of six are actually visible, though altered or rebuilt at later dates (TEMPLE OF VICTORY on the Palatine; TEMPLES A AND C IN THE LARGO ARGENTINA; all three at S. NICOLA IN CARCERE).

It was the C2 BC when things really began to move. Within the first three decades, while temple building went on unabated, two new forms of monumental public building made their appearance in the city, the **porticus** and its close relative the **basilica** (see pp. 53, 57). New Tiber **docks and port facilities** were constructed (p. 368), including the PORTICUS AEMILIA (174 BC). The main **drainage systems** were reviewed in 184 BC and **street paving**, first heard of in 238 BC, was introduced on a wide scale from 174 BC. Architects and engineers sought out better quality **building stone**—compact tufas from the Anio and Monteverde, the hard *peperino* of the Alban hills and Gabii, the white **travertine** limestone from the plain below Tivoli (see p. 38). They also began to explore the possibilities of **concrete** (p. 42). By the end of the 140s BC the first temple was being built completely of **white marble**, imported all the way from Greece (pp. 38–9). Two **new aqueducts**, the Marcia (140 BC) and the Tepula (125 BC), greatly augmented the supply of spring water.

In later years the Romans liked to play up their self-image of simple farmer-soldiers to whom art and fine architecture in any other context except the worship of the gods was a luxury, even a crime, but the exaggeration had an element of truth. The culture shock was unsettling to many and an inspiration to others: the period is full of contradictions.

- TOMB OF THE SCIPIOS (C3–C2 BC)   - PORTICUS AEMILIA (174 BC)
- S. OMOBONO

Civil Wars (90–31 BC)

In the space of just two centuries the city of Rome had gone from being a city state among many others of its kind, albeit a fairly important one, to being mistress of her whole known world. Alexander the Great, from Macedonia in northern Greece, had jumped the gun some sixty years earlier, when his armies swept over the whole of the Near and Middle East as far as India in only seven years (334–327 BC). But he died shortly after, and his empire dissolved into a set of smaller states. Rome's empire, by contrast, was to grow larger still and to last for five centuries; much of its eastern half endured for a millennium. What kept it going is just as interesting as why it eventually declined, for in the beginning there were lots of reasons for it not to succeed.

As soon as the pace of constant warfare and conquest abroad slowed down in the late C2 BC, things started to come apart at home, fuelled by various rebellions and counter-attacks in the new territories. The republican-style army and powerful negotiating skills had achieved an empire but were not really capable of running it. The first thing needed was a professional, long-service army, which the state could deploy quickly and at will, and it was achieved in 107–100 BC simply by abolishing the old property qualification and enlisting and training a proletariat force. However, since the command of the army was also an executive political office, this was a risky initiative, for unscrupulous generals could make their armies a personal weapon (by promises of previously unobtainable rewards, principally land) and take that force directly into the political arena. The best part of the C1 BC was taken up in a series of military dictatorships (magistrates given supreme powers to deal with emergencies) and terrible internal wars as the system struggled to find its feet. First the Italian allies aided and abetted by opposing Roman generals Marius and Sulla took up arms against Rome in the so-called Social War (90–88 BC), winning the right of citizenship and other concessions; then Marius and Sulla fought it out between each other (in 88–82 BC), then Pompey, Crassus, and Julius Caesar (49–45) and ultimately Mark Antony and Octavian (44–31) variously conspired and battled, with terrible loss of life.

For Rome the era was hardly conducive to sustained investment in civic resources. Sulla paved the Forum square and added various other embellishments to its political fixtures and fittings when trying to carry out constitutional reforms in 81–80 BC. In 55 BC Pompey made a major flourish by building the first permanent theatre (p. 214). **Julius Caesar** during his brief ascendancy to total power in 48–44 BC had great ambitions for himself and the city, including diverting the course of the Tiber so that the flood plain to the north of the city (the FIELD OF MARS) could be developed as housing. He set about major replanning and reconstruction in the Forum, building a new basilica (the JULIA, p. 89), moving the Senate house and the speakers' platform, and opening up a whole new Forum square to the north (p. 148). Otherwise, what we hear about most are the wealthy endowing their own homes with new luxuries, such as monolithic columns and veneer in brightly coloured imported stones (p. 39–42). An extraordinary form of illusionistic wall painting (the so-called Second Style, p. 49) came into vogue, decorating the main halls, dining rooms, and bedrooms of aristocratic houses in a variety of architectural schemes, some evoking the exotic temporary architecture erected

for the theatrical games and public banquets which accompanied Rome's
bulging calendar of religious festivals.

- **'TABULARIUM'** (100 BC?)
- **ROUND TEMPLE** by Tiber (c.100 BC)
- **TEMPLE OF PORTUNUS** (c.80 BC)
- **FABRICIUS' BRIDGE** (62 BC)
- **TIBER ISLAND PROW** (C1 BC)
- **TOMB OF BIBULUS** (early C1 BC)

- **TOMB OF EURYSACES** (mid-C1 BC)
- **ARISTOCRATIC HOUSES** on the
  north slope of Palatine
- **HOUSE OF 'LIVIA'**
- **HOUSE 'OF THE GRIFFINS'**
  (Palatine)

Augustus and the Imperial System (31 BC–AD 14)

Octavian (C. Octavius) was born in 63 BC at Velitrae (Velletri) near Rome.
His mother was Julius Caesar's niece and Caesar adopted him in 45 BC, at
the age of 17, making him his heir. When Caesar was murdered six months
later, Octavian reacted with precocious skill to establish himself with
Caesar's friends and forces and manœuvred doggedly for the next thirteen years to eliminate all possible rivals. His final victory came with the
naval battle against the forces of Mark Antony off Actium (NW Greece) in
31 BC. Unchallenged leader of the whole Roman world, he set about
reshaping the republican institutions of Rome as the core of a new world
order, with himself as '*princeps*' ('first citizen or leader amongst equals'),
an astutely judged political compromise between military dictator and
senatorial rule. In 27 BC the senate gave him the title '**Augustus**'
(reverend), which became the customary form of address for all later
emperors. He matched his new position with a wide-ranging programme
of reforms in the army (which would owe its allegiance henceforth to its
only legitimate commander-in-chief, the ruling emperor), and reorganiz-
ing the taxation and administration of the provinces. Yet further military
campaigns were undertaken to consolidate natural boundaries and
increase revenue, doubling the size of the provincial empire, and a fifth of
the population of Italy was resettled in overseas 'colonies'—new towns on
the revised Roman model. Augustus ruled with increasing authority for
forty-four years and by the time he died, although the question of the
succession was not properly resolved (and was to remain a problem for
ever after), the 'imperial system' he had instituted endured for the next
three centuries.

With Augustus, the city of Rome as we know it starts to take shape
(Fig. C), in the same crafty blend of tradition and innovation that charac-
terized his government. He first restored dozens of old temples throughout the city but at the same time set up his own **HOUSE ON THE PALATINE**
in direct association with a new **TEMPLE** and cult **OF APOLLO**, his particular god, promoted as the equal of Jupiter on the Capitoline. He gradually
remodelled the old centre of political life, the Forum, into an Augustan
version of its older self (p. 63), while building a completely new Forum on

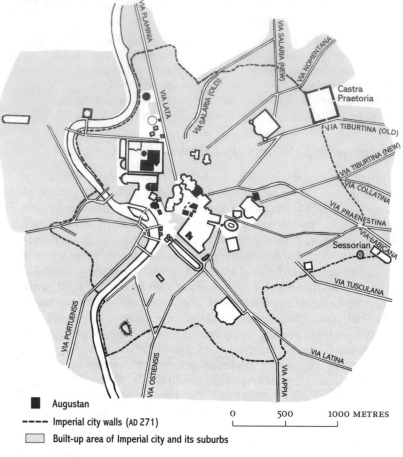

■　Augustan

- - - -　Imperial city walls (AD 271)

▢　Built-up area of Imperial city and its suburbs

0　　　　500　　　1000 METRES

▲ **Fig. C.** The Imperial City

a different site (p. 158) to which he then transferred many of the ceremonies of state. On the Field of Mars (the low-lying plain in the bend of
the Tiber north of the city centre), he and his trusted deputies did the
traditional thing and built temples, porticoes, theatres, and an amphitheatre in the vicinity of the CIRCUS FLAMINIUS, hub of republican military
triumphs, but they also transformed its wider amenities into a luxury
public resort, with a great lake, baths, gardens, a calendar-sundial; all
under the watchful eye of Augustus' gigantic dynastic tomb (p. 181).

The lives of the general populace came in for the same dynamic reorganization; Rome by now was easily the largest city in the ancient world,
its population having probably quadrupled in size since the C2 BC to
around 1,000,000 or more (the actual figure is unknown but in 2 BC there

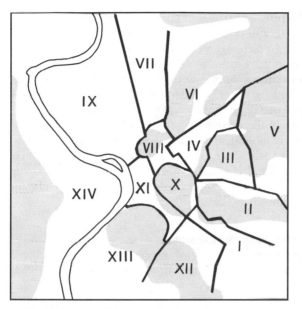

Key

I	Porta Capena
II	Caelimontium
III	Isis et Serapis
IV	Templum Pacis
V	Esquiliae
VI	Alta Semita
VII	Via Lata
VIII	Forum Romanum
IX	Circus Flaminius
X	Palatium
XI	Circus Maximus
XII	Piscina Publica
XIII	Aventinus
XIV	Transtiberim

▲ **Fig. D.** Augustus' Fourteen Regions

were some 200,000 households receiving a monthly ration of grain). It was desperately overcrowded, dangerous, under constant threat of famine, floods, and fires. The old city within its C4 BC walls had been divided into four districts (*regiones*); Augustus in about 7 BC replaced those by fourteen new regions, eight covering the area inside the old walls, six outside using the main roads leading out of the city as boundaries (see diagram, Fig. D). Some of the gates of the old city wall came in for a facelift as a result (pp. 299, 312). Each region had its own magistrates (aediles and tribunes) elected annually, and was subdivided into many smaller units called *vici* (*vicus* = street or neighbourhood), each with their own four elected officials (*vicomagistri*) whose duty it was to look after the 'compital' shrine (see p. 300). The regional magistrates oversaw the enforcement of new building regulations, (for a while) the distribution of the public ration, and the organization of seven fire brigades (which also served as a sort of police force/night watch). The four old aqueducts were reconditioned and two new ones built (the Julia and the Virgo, p. 58); the bed of the Tiber was dredged, its banks cleared and demarcated with boundary stones to avoid further encroachments.

　　Increasingly all public building in Rome, while requiring the Senate's approval, was almost exclusively the prerogative of the emperor and, with his sanction, other members of the imperial family. In art and architecture, no less than in the writing of history, poetry, and drama, there emerged an unmistakably Augustan 'court' style, and the emperor and his

circle remained the principal arbiter of taste thereafter. Augustan architects and craftsmen became obsessed with the Classical Greek style, technical refinement and the formulation of rules (it is no coincidence that the
one Roman architectural treatise we have, by Vitruvius, was addressed to
Augustus); the Corinthian column was singled out for special attention,
canonized as the Roman 'imperial' order, together with a repertory of
ornamental motifs based on the spiny-leafed acanthus plant which char-
acterized its capital. In the decoration of private houses the exuberant
'Second Style' of the republican aristocracy went abruptly out of fashion,
replaced by the relative delicacy and restraint of the 'Third' (p. 49). As their
competitive political life declined, the town houses of the aristocracy
became of less importance; a new phenomenon developed, the elegant
suburban residence known as 'Gardens' (horti) (p. 55).

- MAUSOLEUM (28 BC)
- TOMBS OF THE 'SERVILII' and CAECILIA METELLA on the Via Appia
- PYRAMID OF GAIUS CESTIUS
- FORUM OF AUGUSTUS
- SUNDIAL OBELISK
- THEATRE OF MARCELLUS
- TEMPLE OF APOLLO MEDICUS SOSIANUS
- PORTICUS OF GAIUS AND LUCIUS, BASILICA PAULLI, TEMPLE OF CASTOR, TEMPLE OF CONCORDIA AUGUSTA on the Roman Forum, and the FORUM PAVING
- ESQUILINE, CAELIAN CITY GATES
- 'AUDITORIUM' OF MAECENAS
- Farnesina frescoes (Palazzo Massimo Museum)

Tiberius to Claudius (AD 14–54)

Augustus had done so much that his successors Tiberius, Caligula, and
Claudius had a relatively easy time. They repaired the odd public building
here and there, and undertook further work on the Tiber, Rome's lifeline
to the sea (under Tiberius a special magistracy was set up to supervise a
permanent body of maintenance staff; Claudius created a new sea port
north of the river mouth, called Portus). In AD 21–3 Tiberius was
persuaded to draw the Praetorians (imperial guard), hitherto quartered in
and outside the city, together in one large fort, the *Castra Praetoria*.
Originally sited well beyond the city limits, the castra were later incorporated into the late C3 defences, forming the rectangular projection at the
NE angle of the circuit, now bounded by the Viale del Policlinico. In
AD 38–52 Caligula started and Claudius finished another two copious
aqueducts (the Claudia and New Anio). Otherwise, they concentrated
most of their attention on the imperial palaces and other residences.
However, a major problem was looming in the number of major fires
which raged in the tightly packed residential quarters, with their narrow
streets and high-rise timber blocks. The fires of AD 15, 27, 31, 36, 38, and

53/4 were bad enough to become matters of official record; there were presumably hundreds of lesser incidents.

- **TEMPLES IN THE VEGETABLE MARKET** (AD 17)
- **CARCER** (AD 39–42)
- **DOMUS GAI** (AD 40–4)
- **AQUA VIRGO ARCADES** (AD 46)
- **AQUA CLAUDIA/ANIO NOVUS** at Porta Maggiore (AD 54)
- **UNDERGROUND BASILICA** (c. AD 20–40)

Nero and the Great Fire of AD 64

During the first ten years of his reign, which began when he was not quite 17, Nero lavished yet more money and resources on the Palatine palaces but also made at least two popular additions to the city—a large public market somewhere on the Caelian hill, and a new set of public baths on the Field of Mars—and was greatly liked for his gifts of money, banquets, and games. All that changed, however, with the fire which started in the early hours of 19 June AD 64 in some shops beside the CIRCUS MAXIMUS. The flames swept through the circus itself and into the area of the Cattle Market, destroying the ancient altar of Hercules, then jumped up on to the Aventine (destroying an ancient temple of Luna) and to the Palatine (burning the imperial palaces and the houses on the north slope, including that of the Vestal Virgins). It was stopped at the foot of the Esquiline by demolishing a wide area of housing (including a palace extension that Nero had just built), but intermittent fires kept going for several more days. Nero was blamed for not intervening soon enough (he was out of Rome in his villa at Anzio and only came back to town when it was clear the fire was going to be serious), for apparent indifference to the human suffering (he had gone into his palace theatre and sung to his lyre about the fire of ancient Troy, comparing the two calamities), and then, once it was clear what the aftermath was to bring, he was accused of starting the fire in the first place to further his own grand schemes. Gods and oracles were beseeched for an alternative explanation, but when nothing was forthcoming he found convenient scapegoats among the Christian sect, already suspect on other counts, ordering them to be burned alive in fit retribution for their crime.

The fire had lasted nine days, leaving three regions razed to the ground, another seven severely damaged; only four escaped unscathed. Disaster that it was, it gave an unprecedented opportunity to rebuild whole quarters of the city on completely different lines and Nero was quick to seize the moment. Streets were to be made wider, with large open squares; buildings were to be of limited height and use as little wood as possible and to be protected by outer walls of Alban or Gabine stone (hard *peperino* tufa); imperial funds paid for porticoes along the façades of the new apartment blocks, so that firefighters could have swift access to upper floors; new checks were instituted to cut down on the amount of public water being diverted into private hands, so that more flowed in public places. There were those who complained that the new developments let in too much sun, the apartments boiled in the summer heat—the old high buildings and narrow streets had been cooler and shadier; but generally the city was going to be a safer and healthier place. Unfortunately Nero included himself in his desire to improve everyone's lot and alienated many of the aristocracy by confiscating huge tracts of their property in the city centre to create his own GOLDEN HOUSE. Conspiracies followed and his rule deteriorated, ending with his suicide in June AD 68, which also ended the Julio-Claudian monopoly on the principate.

Architecture and interior decoration under Claudius and Nero began to throw off the somewhat stifling classicism favoured by Augustus and to experiment with other styles, materials, and techniques, especially after the Great Fire. Concrete walls were commonly faced in brick (considered more fire-resistant than soft tufa). Concrete vaulting became more adventurous. Window glass, cast in sheets, came into widespread use, transforming ideas of space and light. 'Fourth style' wall painting (p. 49) made its appearance, but painting in general was losing status, replaced by more exotic and permanently coloured schemes in stucco-work, glass mosaic, and marbles.

- **TEMPLE OF CLAUDIUS PLATFORM** (AD 54–6)
- **DINING SUITE** under Palace of Domitian (AD 60)
- **ESQUILINE WING** of Golden House (AD 64–8)
- **NYMPHAEUM** (AD 64–8)
- **CAELIAN AQUEDUCT** (AD 64)

The Flavians (AD 69–96)

After three other contenders had briefly held the throne in quick succession, in AD 69 Titus Flavius **Vespasianus** restored stability for the next twenty years between his own reign and those of his sons **Titus** and **Domitian**. Of relatively modest birth, from Reate (Rieti) in the Sabine hills, Vespasian had made a very successful career in the army in the AD 40s (commanding a legion in the invasion of Britain in AD 43), was stand-in consul in AD 51, and governor of Africa in the early 60s. He acquired the status which brought him to imperial power as the general sent by Nero to suppress the rebellion in the province of Judaea.

The Flavians inherited and continued Nero's programme of urban renewal but dismantled most of the Golden House, not returning its confiscated lands to their original owners but converting them mainly to public use. Vespasian celebrated his victory in Judaea with three great monuments in the republican manner: the TEMPLE OF PEACE, the amphitheatre (COLOSSEUM), and a rebuilding of the temple of Jupiter on the Capitoline. The Capitoline temple had almost immediately to be rebuilt again, after a major fire in AD 80 which also struck the Field of Mars (one of the areas least affected in AD 64) and destroyed pretty well all its central Augustan monuments. In the rebuilding, Domitian added a STADIUM, odeum, and a porticus in honour of his father and brother—and went on to yet grander projects, almost completing one new forum (p. 156) and at least beginning the site for another (p. 161), as well as a huge reconstruction and expansion of the palaces on the Palatine (p. 134). The blatant autocracy that coloured his later rule led to plots against him, and eventually his murder by members of his own entourage, his wife Domitia possibly among them.

By the AD 90s imperial ownership and operation of the principal quarries was providing ever greater supplies of fine quality marbles and other stones; concrete architecture became increasingly ambitious in scale and decoration.

- COLOSSEUM (AD 80)
- LUDUS MAGNUS (c. AD 80)
- META SUDANS (89–96)
- House and horrea under S. CLEMENTE
- HORREA ON THE VIA SACRA
- TEMPLE OF VESPASIAN AND TITUS
- ARCH OF TITUS

- PALACE OF DOMITIAN
- RAMP AND HALL at NW angle of Palatine
- FORUM TRANSITORIUM (of Nerva)
- STADIUM (Piazza Navona)
- PORTICUS IN VIA DEI CALDERARI (c. AD 90–100)

The High Empire: Trajan, Hadrian, and the Antonines (AD 96–180)

The ninety-odd years from the death of Domitian to the accession of Commodus were an age which even before it had ended Romans were calling 'Golden'. By chance none of the emperors involved had sons living at the time they had to hand over power, with the result that their successors were chosen on ability and experience. **Nerva**, who was chosen to succeed Domitian, was elderly and childless; in AD 97 he adopted as his co-emperor **Trajan**, born at Italica in Spain c. AD 53 and a long-serving officer in the army, who had already been consul in 91. Trajan ruled in exemplary fashion (even to the Senate's satisfaction) for almost twenty years, largely by launching the Roman army on further wars of conquest, taking the empire to its widest extent. He personally commanded the conquest of Dacia beyond the Danube (annexed as a new province in 109) which brought military glory and huge amounts of new wealth, both to himself and the city of Rome, manifest in the number of surviving monuments. He completed the projects left unfinished by Domitian, built a huge FORUM and BASILICA, endowed the residents of the Esquiline hill with the largest PUBLIC BATHS yet seen in the city, and led in Rome's tenth aqueduct, the Traiana, to serve the Transtiber. The TIBERSIDE DOCKS at the emporium were rebuilt to a new design (p. 368) as was the harbour at the Tiber mouth (Portus).

- **CIRCUS MAXIMUS** (AD 103)
- Imperial **BATHS** and **CISTERN** on the Esquiline (AD 104–9)
- **FORUM OF TRAJAN** (AD 112)
- **BASILICA ULPIA** (AD 113)
- **COLUMN OF TRAJAN** (AD 113)
- **LIBRARY** (AD 115)
- **'TRAJAN'S MARKETS'** (AD 106–11)
- Rebuilding of the **TEMPLE OF VENUS GENETRIX** and **FORUM OF CAESAR** (AD 106–13)
- Rebuilding of the **HOUSE OF THE VESTALS** (*c.* AD 113)

Trajan died suddenly in late AD 117 while returning from campaigns against the Parthian empire in the Middle East. One of his younger commanders, **Hadrian** (born AD 76) also from Italica and distantly related, stepped swiftly into the breach, despite some doubts that Trajan had actually intended him to be his successor. Hadrian's rule also lasted for twenty years and made a major impact both on the empire and the city of Rome. On the imperial front, he retracted some of Trajan's expansions and took the first steps to fix the frontiers (Hadrian's Wall in northern Britain being one), with the army deployed in permanent positions, recruiting locally. He travelled widely, especially around the Greek cities in the East (for whose language and culture he felt a particular affinity), and introduced numerous measures to raise provincial morale and encourage disaffected local aristocracies to aspire to high positions in the imperial system.

In Rome there is hardly any part of the city which has not produced evidence of new building during Hadrian's reign. Growing prosperity permitted the urban architectural models which had emerged from the fire of AD 64 to be pursued to the full, and the public projects Hadrian sponsored in person were many: raising the ground level and rebuilding in the central Field of Mars; an extension of Trajan's Forum with a great temple and precinct in honour of the now deified Trajan and his wife Plotina, the equivalent of a new forum on the Velia (**TEMPLE OF ROMA AND VENUS**), the rebuilding of the adjacent Baths of Titus. He also built a great **MAUSOLEUM** to rival that of Augustus (with whom he confidently identified himself) and carried out improvements and extensions to the imperial palaces and other residences around the city, though he lavished most of his efforts in that regard on a **great villa outside Rome, near Tivoli**. Many other wealthy senatorial families followed suit. A skilled amateur architect himself, the architecture of Hadrian's age is full of **new departures in forms and materials** (including new varieties of coloured stones from Greece, Asia Minor, and Spain). Life-size and larger

figurative statuary in huge variety came into vogue, much of the architecture designed specifically to display it to decorative and programmatic effect.

- **PANTHEON** (AD 118–25)
- **SAEPTA JULIA** (118–25)
- **'BASILICA OF NEPTUNE'** (AD 118–25)
- Column and capital of **TEMPLE OF DEIFIED TRAJAN** (c. AD 128)
- **TEMPLE OF ROMA AND VENUS** (AD 121–41)
- **MAUSOLEUM** (AD 123–39)
- **AELIAN BRIDGE** (pre-AD 134)
- Sculpture collections in the Capitoline and Vatican Museums

In AD 138 Hadrian died, having adopted as his successor the 52-year-old **Antoninus Pius**, born T. Aurelius Arrius Antoninus, at Lanuvium (SW of Rome), who was to rule for another twenty-three years, his reign a byword for peace, prosperity, and tranquility, in fact one of the dullest figures in Roman political history. He hardly moved out of Italy, a man devoted to his family, a careful manager of imperial wealth and resources, conservative in person and taste. He built practically nothing public in Rome except a temple for Hadrian, and another for his wife Faustina, who died and was deified in AD 140, dedicated in their joint names on his own death in 161. It was an age of domestic, cultured luxury for the aristocracy: the elegant and extensive 'Gardens' on the hilltops became ever more elegant and the suburban villas of the imperial family and their peers, set in a ring around the city, came to resemble small towns.

- **TEMPLE OF HADRIAN** (AD 145)
- **TEMPLE OF FAUSTINA** (AD 140)
- **MONTE TESTACCIO**
- **VILLA OF QUINTILII** on the Via Appia
- **SS. GIOVANNI E PAOLO INSULA**

Marcus Aurelius, aged 40, had already been adopted by Antoninus Pius as his successor on Hadrian's instructions in AD 138 and the transfer of power in AD 161 went without incident. However, Marcus' reign was anything but tranquil, troubled by continuous emergencies on the northern and eastern frontiers of the empire which took him on campaign, accompanied by his wife Faustina, for years on end. Despite his absences he evidently felt no need to exert his authority in Rome by great buildings. He erected a **monumental column** in association with an **altar** on the Field of Mars, to mark the **deification of Antoninus Pius**, and in due course one or more **triumphal arches** celebrated military victories in the frontier struggles.

- **BASE** of column of Antoninus Pius (Vatican Museums)
- **PANEL RELIEFS** from one or more triumphal arches (Palazzo dei Conservatori and Arch of Constantine)
- **BRONZE EQUESTRIAN STATUE** (Piazza del Campidoglio/Capitoline Museum)

Rome's run of luck ended when Marcus Aurelius handed over to his real son **Commodus** in AD 180. Born in the year of his father's accession, Commodus was only 18 when he succeeded and his grasp on power was shaky from the beginning, not helped by a series of unscrupulous advisers, growing increasingly unstable as he also became mentally unbalanced, wanting to fight as a gladiator, to be worshipped as a form of Hercules and associating himself with eastern sun-gods, the equal of Jupiter. He was hopeless at finance, given to extravagant largesse, constantly ordering confiscations and proscriptions to get the money he needed. After several assassination attempts he was eventually strangled in 192. As far as Rome is concerned, most of his benefactions took the ephemeral form of games and other gifts or crises, but he was presumably responsible for the great column in honour of his parents which still stands on the Field of Mars, and he built a large temple, probably to Jupiter, within the Palatine palace (p. 141). Written sources record his name also in connection with a set of *thermae* (large public baths) erected in AD 183. In the last year of his reign **a major fire** destroyed Vespasian's TEMPLE OF PEACE, the nearby 'Pepper Halls' (horrea Piperataria), the TEMPLE OF VESTA, and parts of the Palatine.

- COLUMN OF MARCUS AURELIUS AND FAUSTINA
- PORTRAIT BUST OF COMMODUS AS HERCULES (Palazzo dei Conservatori)

The Severans (AD 193–238)

The year after Commodus' death was like that after Nero's; five army generals made bids for power with the support of their troops, the victor being **Septimius Severus**, governor of Pannonia (Bosnia) at the time, who marched on Rome with sixteen legions backing him, was accepted by the Senate, and then set about eliminating his rivals, a process that went on until AD 197. Born in AD 145 of a wealthy family of Leptis Magna in Tripolitania (western Libya), Severus had acquired senatorial rank under Marcus Aurelius and been consul in 190. His wife Julia Domna came from Emesa (Homs) in Syria, daughter of a family of hereditary priests of the local sun-god Elagabalus. They had two young sons **Caracalla** and **Geta**. In 195, in one of various efforts to validate his constitutional position, Severus declared himself the adopted son of Marcus Aurelius and brother of Commodus, and renamed his son Caracalla Marcus Aurelius Antoninus, giving him the title of Caesar (junior emperor, heir designate). Julia Domna was hailed as 'Mother of the Camps'. In 198, at the age of 10, Caracalla was made co-emperor, his younger brother became Caesar. The years 197–202 were spent first campaigning against the Parthians in the East and then on prolonged visits to Egypt and Syria, and Tripolitania.

Reluctantly recognizing the need to establish themselves in Rome, the family stayed in Italy during 203–8, having set in train an almost manic programme of repairs and new building. In 204 Severus and Caracalla presided over Secular games (p. 181) and the term *Urbs Sacra* or **Holy City** came into currency. The damage of the fire of AD 191 was reversed: the Temple of Peace and the Temple of Vesta rebuilt, the Palatine palaces restored together with the addition of some huge extensions and the Septizodium, a sort of dynastic billboard (p. 144). A massive new temple dedicated jointly to Hercules and Bacchus, patron gods of Caracalla and Geta, was installed on the flank of the Quirinal hill, approached by an enormous flight of steps (the foundations are preserved in terracing of the gardens of the Palazzo Colonna and the Pontifical University). New stations (*excubitoria*) were constructed for the city's seven fire brigades (p. 311); additional barracks were built for an enlarged imperial cavalry guard (p. 306). Some of their restorations, such as those to Hadrian's PANTHEON (p. 201) and the TEMPLE OF VESPASIAN AND TITUS (p. 79), may have been conducted more in spirit than kind.

In AD 208, supposedly to stop Caracalla and Geta constantly quarrelling, Severus took the family on campaign in Britain, where there was some trouble with the Caledonians, and settled in Eburacum (York). There he died in 211, leaving Caracalla and Geta joint emperors. Back in Rome, Caracalla had Geta killed, instigated a purge of all his other perceived enemies, extended the citizenship to all freeborn inhabitants of the empire (so as to raise new taxes), gave orders for a new set of Baths to be built, and then set out on a series of frontier wars, becoming increasingly paranoid and dangerous, with a fixation that he was Alexander the Great. Opellius Macrinus, praefect of his imperial guard finally murdered him at Carrhae (in Mesopotamia) in 217 and took control, only to be challenged and deposed by Caracalla's Syrian relatives, who proclaimed the youth Varius Avitus Bassianus, subsequently known as Elagabalus, to be Caracalla's son and successfully persuaded the army to back him instead. Bassianus came to Rome in 219 and, holding the family priesthood of the sun god **Elagabalus**, declared that he and the god were one and the same, building himself a temple on the Palatine and laying out a new palace, later called the **'Sessorian'**, with its own circus and amphitheatre, on older imperial property in the south-east sector of the city (S. Croce in Gerusalemme). He further scandalized Roman opinion by marrying a Vestal Virgin and lasted only three years, assassinated by his family and replaced by his cousin, who was renamed Marcus Aurelius Alexander for the occasion, subsequently adding the further name Severus. **Alexander Severus**, aged 13, was essentially the instrument of his mother Julia Mamaea (niece of Septimius Severus' wife Julia Domna), who managed to instil a degree of popular support, setting up an advisory council of sixteen elderly senators, and undertaking various public works. The BATHS started by Caracalla were completed and those of Nero on the Field of Mars were reconstructed and enlarged, fed by a new aqueduct, both taking Alexander's name. The adjacent Stadium was renovated at the same time, standing in for the Colosseum, which was also undergoing major repairs after a fire in AD 217. In 234, however, major problems on the German frontier took Alexander and his mother to Mainz, where they were murdered in an army mutiny in 235.

- **ARCH OF SEPTIMIUS SEVERUS** on the Forum (AD 203)
- **TEMPLE OF VESTA**
- **HALL OF THE MARBLE PLAN** (AD 204)
- **ENTRANCE TO THE PORTICUS OF OCTAVIA** (AD 203)
- **ARCH OF THE ARGENTARII** (AD 204)
- **BATHS OF CARACALLA** (AD 211–16 and later)
- **LOGGIA** (S. Martino ai Monti)
- **BATHS OF NERO** (Thermae Alexandrinae)
- **NYMPHAEUM OF ALEXANDER SEVERUS**
- **MITHRAEUMS** (near **CIRCUS MAXIMUS**, under **S. CLEMENTE**, under **BATHS OF CARACALLA**)

The Later Third Century

With the death of Alexander Severus and Julia Mamaea all hell broke loose; the next fifty years saw at least eighteen emperors and hordes of usurpers try their chances; peoples on the fringes of the empire seized the opportunity to invade (the Sasanids of Persia moved against the eastern frontiers, the Goths against Asia Minor and the Balkans); the period was one of constant warfare in one part of the world or another. Some emperors were homegrown, from the senatorial aristocracy of Rome, such as the Licinii, Valerian and Gallienus, who held sway over the central empire from AD 253 to 267 (tolerating usurper kingdoms in Gaul and the East); many more were career army officers from the northern provinces (especially the Balkans). Few succeeded in holding power for more than a couple of years and it became an accepted fact that separate parts of the empire might be ruled by different emperors, in collaboration, not conflict with one another. Out of this emerged the solution known rather inaccurately as the **Tetrarchy** (rule of four), whereby the empire was formally divided into two halves, with one emperor in each. The deviser of the scheme was **Diocletian**, from Dalmatia (Croatia), who achieved outright power in AD 285 and installed his comrade **Maximian** as emperor in Italy and the West, while he took responsibility for the East. In 293 they each adopted a junior emperor (Caesar) to be their designated successor, **Constantius** in the West, **Galerius** in the East.

In Rome, the local magistrates had continued to perform their curatorial duties throughout the period and for all their other preoccupations some emperors did their duty by the city. In AD 249–51 the emperor **Decius**, in origin a senator from Pannonia who took the name Trajan in emulation of his famous predecessor, endowed the Aventine hill with a set of public baths and may also have carried out restorations to the Colosseum. The locally-born emperors Valerian and Gallienus (AD 253–67) were not so conscientious; they took the opportunity principally to improve their own family 'Gardens' on the outer Esquiline, in association with which the ESQUILINE GATE was reinscribed in their honour. Most impressive of all was the huge new circuit of CITY WALLS which **Aurelian**, emperor in AD 270–5, ordered to be erected to protect the city in the event of barbarian invasions of Italy (it was expected that the German tribes who had been harassing Gaul and northern Italy would keep on trying). Aurelian, who came from the Danube region, lived for a while in the Gardens of Sallust, favourite retreat of Vespasian and other earlier emperors, which occupied both sides of the valley between the Pincian and Quirinal hill, building a mile-long porticus in which he would exercise on horseback. In 273, somewhere in region VII (at the foot of the valley, beside the Field of Mars), he also built a magnificent temple to the oriental sun-god Sol, celebrating a triumph in the old republican fashion, for victories he had won in the East.

Diocletian visited Rome only once, in 303, to celebrate the twentieth anniversary of his accession, but kept a watchful eye from afar through Maximian. Parts of the Roman Forum and the Forum of Caesar that had been badly damaged by fire in AD 283 were rebuilt, remodelling the space in monumental style; a great set of imperial BATHS was constructed on the Viminal hill. Aurelian's walls had enclosed an area of 1,370 hectares, by no means the whole city, whose population was probably still well over a million (1,280,000 is one estimate, not counting slaves).

- AURELIANIC WALLS (AD 271–5)
- 'MINERVA MEDICA' (c. AD 300)
- SENATE HOUSE (after AD 283)
- SHRINE OF IUTURNA
- BASILICA JULIA (restored after AD 283)
- BATHS OF DIOCLETIAN (AD 298–306)

Maxentius, Constantine, and the Fourth Century

Diocletian's system was short-lived. In AD 305 he abdicated and forced Maximian to do the same, handing power over to the junior emperors Constantius and Galerius, who in their turn chose two new juniors; this was the plan, but things did not work out. The Western emperor Constantius died in 306 and his junior, Severus, was challenged by Maximian's son **Maxentius**, who seized control of Rome and, recalling Maximian from retirement to help him, was able to force Severus first to abdicate, then to his death. In 308 Maximian and Maxentius then quarrelled and Maximian took refuge with Constantius' son **Constantine**, who in the meantime had been manœuvring to become emperor of the West himself. Constantine's opportunity came in 312, after Galerius had died and the two alternative emperors that he had officially recognized, Licinius in the West and Maximinus in the East, were at loggerheads.

Maximinus supported Maxentius, so Constantine invaded Italy on Licinius' behalf, routed Maxentius' northern army at Turin and Verona, and marched on Rome, defeating vastly superior forces and killing Maxentius, to be hailed as emperor by the Senate.

For six years Rome had been the focus of Maxentius' imperial ambitions, which he had expressed in the traditional way, investing huge energy and resources in public and dynastic projects. He concentrated on the area near the entrance to the Palatine palace: a rebuilding of Hadrian's Temple of Roma and Venus (damaged by fire in AD 307); a new basilica and an elegant vestibule connected with a hall in the Temple of Peace; new baths in the imperial palace itself. He also started a mausoleum and a circus outside the city on the Via Appia. All except the last were taken up and finished off by Constantine, who in addition ordered a set of imperial baths on the Quirinal; his mother Helena, who settled in Rome together with other members of Constantine's family, paid for the rebuilding of public baths in the vicinity of the Sessorian palace, which was her favoured residence.

- VESTIBULE TO THE TEMPLE OF PEACE ('TEMPLE OF DIVUS ROMULUS')
- TEMPLE OF ROMA AND VENUS
- NEW BASILICA
- AMPHITHEATRE AND BATHS IN THE PALATINE PALACE
- CIRCUS-MAUSOLEUM ON THE VIA APPIA
- HONORARY COLUMNS on Roman Forum
- ARCH OF CONSTANTINE
- ARCH OF JANUS IN THE VELABRUM

Constantine and **Licinius** (who saw Maximinus off the scene in 313) divided the empire uneasily between them for ten years, with Constantine in the West (basing himself in Milan rather than Rome) and Licinius in the East, until Constantine took the offensive in 324, forced Licinius to flight and suicide, and executed his heirs, becoming sole emperor, henceforth the 'Great'. Licinius' headquarters, the ancient city of Byzantium on the Bosphoros, was taken over and in 330 with much ceremony refounded as **Constantinople** and proclaimed as the 'New Rome'. Though always declared subordinate to the old one in status, the move was symptomatic of a radical change taking place in imperial thinking, a search for new solutions.

In his early drive to obtain power Constantine had already become well aware of the difficulty of achieving any sort of unity within the empire unless the followers of **Christianity** were made part of it. The monotheistic Christian sect had made considerable advances in the course of the troubles of the C3, notably at Rome, where the huge dependent population offered a lot of scope for charitable works, previously the prerogative of emperors. We hear in the mid-C3 AD of 1,500 widows and orphans being looked after by seven *diaconia* (welfare centres run by Christian clergy). Growing numbers of the Roman aristocracy converted to Christianity and began to make political mileage out of benefactions in the name of the church, while refusing to participate in the rites of polytheistic religion which traditionally underpinned the state.

Diocletian and Galerius had attempted to eradicate the conflict by drastic persecutions, but in a world already drained by internal violence that was clearly not a very sensible policy. Since Christianity was by definition exclusive of all other beliefs, owing allegiance to Christ before the emperor, the alternative was for the empire and its emperor to become Christian. In 312 Constantine declared that his victory over Maxentius had been due to the Christian god and announced that persecutions were to end, Christian property was to be restored, and clergy given privileges. Christianity became a state religion. He made numerous benefactions, endowing a great **basilica, baptistery,** and **residence** for the bishop of Rome (the Pope) at the **Lateran** (p. 346), and helping to build several enormous **funerary basilicas** associated with martyrs' graves in the Christian cemeteries on the outskirts of the city: **St Peter's** at the Vatican, **St Sebastian** on the Via Appia (p. 412), **St Lawrence** on the Via Tiburtina. Other members of his family followed suit: his mother **Helena** built a church for a relic of the cross on which Christ had been crucified, within the grounds of the Sessorian palace; she also built a funerary basilica and a mausoleum on the Via Labicana. Constantine's daughter **Constantina** did the same somewhat later, erecting her MAUSOLEUM AND CIRCUS-BASILICA on the Via Nomentana.

A large proportion of the Roman senatorial aristocracy, however, remained unpersuaded of the attractions of Christianity, resentful of the favours being granted to Christians at court, and deeply resistant to any idea of change. Constantine's desire to make a fresh start elsewhere is understandable. His definition of being Roman, like most of those born in the provinces, no longer saw Rome as one city with an empire. It represented an ideal of universal government, a model for life itself, everywhere within the emperor's domain was equally part of Rome; wherever the emperor went, Rome went with him. Old Rome was cherished and revered, pandered to and indulged, but imperial priorities were now set by circumstances over which the Senate of Rome had no control.

Constantine died in 337, succeeded by three sons: **Constantius II** in the East, **Constantine II** in Gaul, Britain, and Spain, and **Constans** in Italy, Africa, and Illyrium. Constans eliminated Constantine II in 340 but was deposed by a usurper Magnentius in 350. Constantius suppressed Magnentius, and in due course (355) nominated a cousin, **Julian**, as western Caesar, who won over his local army and was proclaimed Augustus (senior emperor) in 361; Constantius died soon after and Julian's rule was confirmed. A highly educated man and gifted philosopher, although brought up in Christian circles he was concerned that traditional Greek and Roman culture should not suffer; he openly advocated the restoration of equal opportunities for non-Christians, positively discriminating in their favour, reinstating priesthoods and ancestral cults, even planning to rebuild the Jewish Temple at Jerusalem. At Rome, his wishes are manifest in the rebuilding of the TEMPLE OF SATURN and perhaps the **colonnaded enclosure at S. MARIA IN COSMEDIN**. Julian died too soon for his measures to take any real effect and although his successors Valentinian (364–75) and Valens (364–78) were similarly tolerant of most non-Christian beliefs, attitudes hardened under Valentinian's son **Gratian** (375–83), to become downright intolerant with the appointment of **Theodosius**, from Cauca (Coca) in Spain, who ruled as Gratian's co-emperor in the East from 379, with his own narrow definition of Christianity very much in evidence. From one state religion among several, it became the only state religion. In 382 the Senate in Rome was instructed to abolish the altar of Victory (p. 70) which had presided over its meetings for more than 400 years and although temples were not officially closed down, they were not protected in the event that fanatical Christians wished to destroy them; in 390 sacrifices and other public and private ceremonies of non-Christian cults were prohibited, and in 394, the Vestal Virgins—an institution as old as Rome itself—were ordered to disband. Theodosius subsequently took control in the West too, from 387 until his death in 395, when he handed over power to two feeble sons, 17-year-old **Arcadius** in the East, 10-year-old **Honorius** in the West.

Rome in the C4 AD must have been an amazing place to live. Its local aristocracy, Christian and non-Christian alike, were still immensely wealthy, with estates all over the Mediterranean. They sent their sons to be educated in the best philosophical and rhetorical schools in Africa and the East; they dreamed of founding a major university in Rome. Although few emperors after Constantine ever did anything more than make brief visits, the city continued to enjoy many of its privileges, its Senate and popular magistracies, its free distributions of food, its games and festivals. Praefect of the city of Rome, an office which had been instituted by Augustus, grew in significance. In effect the post was that of deputy emperor, who presided over the Senate, had his own court of justice, and was responsible for keeping order and overseeing the magistrates in charge of public works and water and food supply.

Architectural monuments were matters of great and justified pride, the ultimate expression of a once universal political power which it was always hoped, by many more than the citizens of Rome, might yet be restored. When Constantine's son **Constantius II**, emperor of the East, **visited the city for his first and only time in 357**, the event was chronicled by an eye-witness. He headed straight for the Forum and the speakers' platform, where he greeted the populace in the midst of a forest of columns bearing statues of his family. He then set off on a tour of the rest of the city: up to the **Temple of Jupiter** 'beside which everything else is like earth compared to heaven', to the great **public baths** 'as big as provinces' (two of them built by his father and grandfather), the **Colosseum** 'that massive pile of travertine that is the amphitheatre', the **Pantheon** 'like a self-contained district under its high and lovely dome', the **Temple of Roma and Venus**, the **Forum of Peace**, the **Theatre of Pompey**, the **Odeum**, the **Stadium**, and best of all, the **Forum of Trajan**, 'the most singular structure in the whole world'. Amongst its other marvels were the 'House of Romulus', a hut of wood and straw, to be seen on the Palatine (p. 125), and a shipshed on the Field of Mars housing an ancient wooden ship in which Rome's other founding hero, Aeneas, was believed to have sailed over from Troy.

And for a long time, although neither Constantius nor any of his successors contemplated moving the capital back there, the imperial administration made **regular attempts to preserve state monuments**. In 364 the emperor Valentinian instructed Symmachus, the City Praefect, that within the city of Roma aeterna—Eternal Rome—no magistrate was to be allowed to waste resources on building anything new ... the city was more than adequately provided with everything it could possibly need ... but anything that fell into disrepair was to be restored. In 376 the orders were repeated, with the rider that if people did want to build something new, they were to provide their own materials, not to do it by despoiling temples or other ruinous public monuments.

- TEMPLE OF SATURN
- PRECINCT OF THE HARMONIOUS GODS
- S. MARIA IN COSMEDIN COLONNADE
- BASILICAL HALLS: VIA IN SELCI
- 'LIBRARY OF AGAPETUS'

Rome and the Goths (C5–C6 AD)

In AD 376, displaced by the Huns from Mongolia who were piling into south-east and central Europe, groups of Goths from the northern Black Sea region crossed the Danube and started to make themselves at home in the Roman Empire, by a mixture of force and negotiation. In 378 as much to their own surprise as that of the Romans, they defeated the Roman army in pitched battle not far from Constantinople, killing the emperor Valens. In 382 Theodosius signed a treaty with them, reckoning that they would be a lesser evil than the Huns hovering behind them. The Roman army had long been full of Goths—and many other types of barbarian auxiliaries—recruited beyond the imperial frontiers, but it was the first time that barbarian peoples were allowed to settle within the imperial boundaries, ruled by their own chieftains, and it was not long before further concessions were expected. Federated under one particularly charismatic leader **Alaric** (*c.*395–411), the Goths moved down into

Greece, where Honorius' regent, the tough general **Stilicho** (p. 84) crossed over from Italy to stop them in 395 and 397 but was forced to withdraw. In 401–2, as Alaric set seige to Milan, Honorius created a new northern Italian stronghold at **Ravenna** (on the Po delta) and also set about doubling the height of Rome's defensive walls. Stilicho drove Alaric out but another lot of Goths, with hordes of German tribesmen, came back in 405 and although they too were repulsed, they joined forces with Alaric to become the Visigoths (the West Goths) who returned in 408 (following the dismissal and execution of Stilicho) to try to do a deal with Honorius. When Honorius refused, Alaric blockaded Rome, where the Senate bought him off with 5,000 pounds of gold, 30,000 of silver, and 3,000 of pepper (!) and a promise to intercede with the emperor. In the event Honorius still refused, so Alaric avenged himself and his army by **sacking the city in 410** (to the shock of Romans everywhere) and then went on to occupy Sicily, but died the year after. In 418 the Visigoth threat was solved by settling the majority in Aquitaine, where the wealthy Gallic aristocracy apparently welcomed them.

The next crisis did not emerge until 455, when Valentinian III (who had succeeded Honorius at the age of 4 in 423 and whose reign was mostly managed by his mother Galla Placidia until her death in 450) was assassinated. His replacement, Petronius Maximus, of an old Roman senatorial family, was a disaster, opening the door to the Vandals (another barbarian group displaced by the Huns who had crossed the Rhine in 406 and moved across Gaul to Spain and thence to North Africa, taking Carthage in 439). Their king Gaiseric moved into Sardinia and then sacked Rome, killing Maximus and subsequently marrying his son to a daughter of Valentinian III. The situation was taken in hand by a trusted military commander at Rome, **Ricimer**, a German, who in the course of 456–72 saw off first Eparchius Avitus (a candidate sponsored by the Gallic nobility and their local Visigoths), then a fellow army officer called Majorian, and finally Anthemius, an appointee sent by the eastern emperor Leo. In 472 a senator called Olybrius was proclaimed emperor with the support of the Vandal Gaiseric and Ricimer, but both the new emperor and Ricimer died within a year. The nomination passed to Julius Nepos, a Dalmatian general, who marched on Rome, where he was acclaimed in 474 but soon ousted by Orestes, one of his subordinate officers, who placed his own child Romulus Augustulus ('little Augustus') on the throne. Named for Rome's first king, Romulus was destined to be Rome's last emperor. The army (mostly composed of Germans) mutinied, demanding land, and when their claims were denied, they elected **Odoacer**, a fellow German officer, as their king. Odoacer exiled Orestes and Romulus to the bay of Naples and set about ruling Rome and Italy with fair success; the Roman Senate accepted him and though he was never officially recognized by the eastern emperor he was tolerated for many years, until the emperor Zeno sent **Theodoric, king of the Ostrogoths**, against him in 489.

Theodoric had been a hostage in Constantinople as a child, educated as a Roman, serving as consul in 484. He overthrew Odoacer's government as instructed, but then ruled in his place, again not recognized but tolerated *de facto* by the East, for thirty years from 495 to 526.

For much of the C5, somewhat incredibly, civic life in Rome went on almost as normal. The population had surely begun to diminish, but was still substantial (we have no real figures) and there was an immense amount of new building, not by the emperors but by the local aristocracy and the papacy: **palatial town houses, large churches,** and other ecclesiastical structures (**monasteries, oratories, hostels**) including some extraordinary projects such as that of S. STEFANO ROTONDO. Many older public buildings, especially the baths, were still in common use, and were dutifully repaired in the event of damage or decay. The City Praefect of 443 **renovated the Baths of Constantine,** by then over a century old; the 400-year-old amphitheatre (Colosseum) was repaired in *c.*450 and again in 484 and 508. By 458 the realities of the situation were beginning to tell; private individuals were still not allowed to lay hands on public buildings and temples, but the latter could be recycled by the city authorities if they had fallen into such a state as to be impossible to repair. A policy of selective salvage came into play. In 500 Theodoric addressed the people of Rome from the speakers' platform in the Forum, pledging that he would uphold the Roman civil administration. Bricks with his name stamped on them attest to building work (not only repairs) in the **Forum** and the **New Basilica,** the **Palatine palace, Baths of Caracalla** and of **Constantine,** the **Tiber wharves** and **bridges,** and the **Castra Praetoria**. He also made considerable improvements to the Aurelianic Walls.

- S. CLEMENTE (lower church)
- S. STEFANO ROTONDO
- SS GIOVANNI E PAOLO
- LATERAN BAPTISTERY
- S. Sabina (Aventine)

The Ostrogoths got on well with the local aristocracy and were evidently keen to maintain the image of old Rome, but unfortunately the Byzantine emperors of the East could not leave well alone. In 526 Theodoric handed over to a 10-year-old grandson Athalaric, but really to the boy's mother Amalasuntha. When Athalaric died in 534, supposedly of drink, Amalasuntha married a second husband Theodahad as his successor, who promptly deposed and killed her. This gave the eastern emperor **Justinian** (527–65), spoiling for the reconquest of Italy, the excuse he was looking for. His general **Belisarius** entered Rome unopposed in 536. The Ostrogoths (operating from Ravenna) dropped Theodahad and substituted Vitigis, who attempted to beseige Belisarius in Rome in 537 but the

Byzantine held out until reinforcements arrived and when Vitigis withdrew, moved his army up to Milan, whose people threw out the Gothic garrison and happily surrended. Vitigis counter-attacked, lost, and agreed that the Goths would retrench north of the Po river. Belisarius then took him captive and occupied Ravenna but was recalled in 540 to Constantinople. The Ostrogoths came back on the offensive, electing a new king Ildebad, then one called Eraric, and eventually found a great leader in **Totila**, who waged war for the next ten years, recapturing Rome in 546, invading Sicily in 550. At that point Justinian sent a new army, under the eunuch Narses, and the tide turned; Totila was defeated and killed in 552 and so was his successor Teias. Narses went on to retake the whole of Italy south of the Alps, ruling it from Rome until his death in 573. By then the **Lombards** (Germanic peoples who had settled in Pannonia but were now being driven out of there by the Avars) were migrating in force to northern Italy, carving out a kingdom and several duchies. Italy was fragmenting, devolving into separate enclaves, Rome among them. Nominally the city came under the jurisdiction of the Byzantine exarchy at Ravenna, attested by 584, but in practice the popes took over more and more of the secular administration and authority, finding suitably powerful leaders in Pelagius and Gregory the Great. The Roman Senate is last mentioned in 580; Rome was on the way to becoming a **papal state**— and the next 1,400 years of its history are another story.

Documentary Sources

In addition to the evidence on the ground a vast amount of supplementary information concerning the archaeology of Rome is available in various forms.

I. Antiquarian and Architectural Drawings and Maps. Many buildings that have since completely disappeared were drawn by artists and architects in the C16 and C17 with considerable care, and even those still with us frequently benefit from the extra information provided by such older records. Several are included in this guide, notably two examples (Figs. 59, 80) of the work of Etienne Du Pérac (*c*.1525–1604), a French antiquarian, painter, and architect combined, who came to Rome in the 1550s and stayed thirty years in the city making many drawings of its ancient monuments in their actual state. His book of thirty-nine engravings *Vestigi dell'antichità di Roma* (Remains of the Antiquity of Rome) was published in 1575, with eight subsequent editions, and is a continuing source of delight and otherwise unobtainable information. He also made a map of the whole city, both in its actual state and as it had been in antiquity, in this much influenced by the work of his older contemporary, the Neapolitan architect and antiquarian Pirro Ligorio (*c*.1513–83) (see Fig. 141). Other architects whose notebooks and measured drawings are particularly valuable are those made by members of the Da Sangallo family (Giovanni, Antonio) in the late C15 (see Fig. 6) and Andrea Palladio (1508–80), who was especially interested in bath-buildings and is our main authority for the plans of the Baths of Agrippa, Titus, and Trajan (Fig. 138).

II. Marble Plan. Map incised on the wall of a hall in the Temple of Peace *c*. AD 203–11, at a scale of 1 : 240 (see p. 153). Many of the buildings have their names incised as well, making it an exceptional document. Unfortunately only about 10 per cent survives, in about 1,000 fragments, a huge jigsaw puzzle of which less than 160 pieces have actually been put in place.
    Fragments of several other ancient stone maps and plans of buildings have been found.

III. Coins. A peculiarity of the coinage of ancient Rome, first appearing in the early C1 BC but becoming very common under the emperors, are the reverses with minute representations announcing or commemorating new buildings in the city, a clear indication of the status such public works enjoyed. The images are often highly schematic but can generally be relied on to give the basic character of the structure, and are sometimes remarkably accurate.

IV. Reliefs. In addition to examples such as that from the tomb of the Haterii (p. 142, Fig. 58), detailed representations of buildings, presumably meant to be recognizable, appear in the background of scenes showing the emperor riding in triumph through the city, sacrificing at temples, or engaged in other public duties (e.g. p. 238, Fig. 110). Like the coins, they have to be used with caution.

V. Inscriptions. The Roman 'epigraphic habit' is not only an immense help in having left a variety of labels on or in association with the surviving buildings but also provides a great deal of information about others. Over 50,000 inscriptions found over the ages in and around the city, cut in stone or bronze, include dedications and other references to many other buildings.

VI. Regionary Catalogues: two editions, one called the *Notitia* (catalogue) dating from about AD 354, the other the *Curiosum* (inventory) of AD 375, of a description of Rome according to the 14 city-wards (*regiones*) drawn up in the reign of Constantine (AD 312–37). For each region major buildings and other landmarks are first listed separately, followed by a count of the total numbers of different types of buildings (apartment blocks, houses, baths, warehouses, etc.). At the end a summary gives the overall totals for the whole city.

VII. Other classical texts. Hardly any ancient Latin writer does not make some reference relevant to the archaeology of Rome; numerous Greek authors did so too. The main ones are, in order of the time they were writing:

Plautus (*c.*250–184 BC), comic playwright from Umbria. Twenty of an alleged 130 plays survive, with varied plots often involving references peculiar to contemporary Rome.

Ennius (239–169 BC), poet, from South Italy. His epic *Annals* in 18 books chronicled Roman history down to his own day. Only 600 lines extant.

Polybius (*c.*200–after 118 BC), Greek historian of Rome's rise to world power in the period 220–146 BC. In 40 books, only 5 and parts of others extant.

Varro (116–27 BC), from Rieti, polymath author of 600 books. Those surviving are 'on farming', part of 'on the Latin language', and fragments of 'Menippean satires', critical sketches on Roman life.

Cicero (106–43 BC), Roman orator and statesman, contemporary and enemy of Julius Caesar, whose extant works include numerous political speeches, philosophical works, and letters to family and friends.

Sallust (86–35 BC), Roman historian from Amiternum, who wrote vivid accounts of the Cataline conspiracy (62 BC) and Jugurthine War (118–104 BC) and a history of the years 78–67 BC (fragments).

Catullus (*c*.84–*c*.54 BC), Roman poet from Verona; 116 poems on very varied subjects survive including episodes from daily life and lampoons on contemporary politics.

Vergil (70–19 BC), Roman poet born near Mantua, author of the pastoral Eclogues, the Georgics ('husbandry'), and the *Aeneid*, which celebrates the origins and growth of Rome through the adventures of Aeneas, the Trojan hero.

Horace (65–8 BC), Roman poet from Venosa in south Italy, patronized by Maecenas; his Odes, Epistles, *Ars Poetica*, and Satires have all survived, the Satires containing many references to the Rome of the 30s BC.

Diodorus Siculus (fl. *c*.60–30 BC), Greek historian from Sicily, author of *Bibliothecae Historica*, a world history focused on Rome in 40 books (15 survive in full, the rest in fragments) compiled from many sources.

Augustus (63 BC–AD 14), first Roman emperor, who wrote his own account of what he had accomplished in his lifetime, the *Res Gestae*, which was published at his death, copies being inscribed on the many temples erected in his honour throughout the empire.

Livy (59 BC–AD 17), Roman historian, from Padua, who wrote a history of Rome from its legendary foundation down to 9 BC, in 142 books, 35 fully extant; all but two of the rest are known in epitomes and short abstracts.

Ovid (43 BC–AD 17), Roman poet from Sulmona, educated at Rome, and a leading figure in Augustan literary circles. Of his numerous surviving works, the *Fasti* are the most relevant to Rome, being a poetical calendar of the Roman religious year with its archaic legends and festivals.

Strabo (64 BC–after AD 24), Greek geographer from Pontus (Asia Minor), who visited Rome in 44 BC and several times afterwards, completing his *Geography* in 17 books, covering most countries of the Roman world, in about 7 BC.

Dionysius of Halicarnassus (d. 7 BC), who lived in Rome from 30 BC. His *Roman Antiquities* covered the history of Rome down to 264 BC, but the surviving books (11 out of 20) stop at 441 BC.

Vitruvius (*c*.80–*c*.18 BC), Roman engineer and architect from Fano who served in the army of Julius Caesar and Augustus in c.50–26 BC and wrote a treatise *On Architecture* in ten books, which all survive.

Velleius Paterculus (*c*.19 BC–after AD 30), Roman historian who wrote a compendium of Roman history down to AD 29 in two books, especially useful for its biography of the reigning emperor Tiberius.

Valerius Maximus (early C1 AD), author of *Memorable Deeds and Sayings*: historical anecdotes, many concerning Rome, for the use of orators.

Verrius Flaccus (fl. late C1 BC), tutor to the grandsons of Augustus, author of a book 'on the meaning of words', preserved in an abridged form in the lexicon of **Festus** (C2 AD); lots of incidental information on Roman toponyms.

Persius (AD 34–62), satirical poet from Volterra (Etruria), author of six *Satires* on life in Rome during the reign of Nero.

Calpurnius Siculus (fl. *c.* AD 50–60), Latin poet, author of seven *Eclogues*, the seventh including a description of a wild beast show in the amphitheatre.

Lucan (AD 39–65), poet from Cordoba, educated at Rome, favoured by Nero; his only surviving work is *Pharsalia*, the story of the civil war between Caesar and Pompey.

Juvenal (late C1–early C2 AD), satirical poet from Aquinum (Latium) who wrote 16 *Satires*, published around AD 110–27, the third of which gives a famous picture of life at Rome in the late C1 AD (reign of Domitian).

Josephus (AD 37–after 93), Jewish historian, who moved to Rome after the fall of Jerusalem in AD 70; author in Greek of a history of the Jewish Wars.

Statius (*c.* AD 45–*c.*96), Roman poet from Naples, author, among other works, of the *Silvae*, which describe various parts of Rome in the reign of Domitian.

Tacitus (AD 56/7–after 117), Roman historian, possibly from Gaul, whose major works, the *Annals* and the Histories, covered much of the C1 AD with numerous details about Rome.

Suetonius (*c.* AD 70–after 122), lawyer, secretary at the imperial palace, and biographer, best known for his twelve gossipy 'Lives of the Caesars' (from Julius Caesar to Domitian).

Pliny the Elder (AD 23–79). From Como, educated in Rome, he pursued a successful military career which ended abruptly in the eruption of Vesuvius; author of the encyclopaedic *Natural History* in 37 books, including much information about buildings and works of art in Rome.

Pliny the Younger (AD 61–113), nephew of the elder, Roman lawyer specializing in inheritance, a magistrate, and administrator (in AD 100–3 he was in charge of the Tiber banks), who published ten books of *Letters* and a panegyric of the emperor Trajan, full of circumstantial detail about life in Rome and the duties of emperors.

Plutarch (*c.* AD 46–*c.*120), Greek biographer and moralist who lived most of his life at home in Boeotia but travelled in Egypt and Italy, teaching and lecturing in Rome. His *Parallel Lives* (of twenty-three Greek soldier-statesmen for whom he found suitable Roman counterparts) and *Roman Questions* show considerable knowledge of Roman antiquities.

Martial (*c.* AD 40–103/4), Roman poet from Bilbilis (Spain), who moved to Rome in AD 64, living in a small house on the Quirinal. His *Book of*

Shows celebrated the opening of the Colosseum in AD 80, and a collection of over 1,500 *Epigrams* provide endless sidelights on cosmopolitan Roman society of the time.

Frontinus (*c.* AD 30–*c.*104), consul in AD 73 or 74 and then served as governor of Britain. Appointed curator of Rome's water supply in AD 97 he wrote a manual for his successors *On the Waters of Rome*, describing the history of the aqueducts, the technical specifications of each, and the regulations governing their administration.

Aulus Gellius (*c.* AD 130–180?), Roman essayist whose *Attic Nights*, in 20 books, cover a huge variety of topics, among them many notes and quotes concerning Rome.

Dio Cassius (*c.* AD 150–235), Roman historian from Bithynia (Asia Minor), twice consul at Rome and governor Africa and Dalmatia, who wrote (in Greek) a *History of Rome* from Aeneas down to AD 229 in 80 books, 27 of which (covering 68 BC–AD 46 and AD 217–20) are more or less extant; the rest are known in C11/C12 summaries.

Appian (fl. *c.* AD 160), from Alexandria, practised law at Rome and wrote in Greek a *History of Rome* down to AD 69 in 24 books, 9 and some fragments of which survive, those covering 170–146 BC being especially useful.

Tertullian (*c.* AD 160–*c.*225). Born at Carthage, he was given a traditional Roman education, but had converted to Christianity by AD 197 and produced many important works on theology. His anti-gladiatorial tract *On Shows* is the main work of relevance to Rome.

Solinus (fl. *c.* AD 200), author of the *Polyhistor*, largely an epitome of Pliny's *Natural History* and other encyclopaedic sources.

Herodian (fl. *c.* AD 230), of Syria, wrote (in Greek) a *History of his own Time*, in 8 books, from AD 180 to 238.

Historia Augusta, a collection of biographies of Roman emperors and other figures from Hadrian (AD 117) to Numerianus (AD 284), missing 244–59. Possibly written by six different authors or a clever forgery, of uncertain date and doubtful veracity.

Eusebius (*c.* AD 264–*c.*340), bishop of Caesarea (Palestine), who wrote the first history of the eastern Greek Church and the *Chronicle*, a major source for events and dates in Greek and Roman history.

Chronographer of AD 354, also called the Calendar of 354, an illustrated almanac compiled from a variety of sources, including a list of Roman emperors and their buildings in Rome.

Eutropius (fl. *c.* AD 370), Roman historian, who wrote a ten-book survey of Roman history from Romulus down to AD 364, the last part from his own experiences.

Ammianus Marcellinus (*c.* AD 330–95), from Antioch but settled in Rome in 378 and wrote in Latin a *History of Rome* from the reign of Nerva (AD 96) to the defeat of the Romans by the Goths in AD 378.

Macrobius (fl. *c.* AD 400), probably Praetorian prefect of Rome in 430, author of *Saturnalia*, a dialogue set at a dinner party of non-Christian intellectuals in Rome during the Saturnalia festival in AD 384.

Claudian (fl. AD 395–404), from Alexandria, court poet to the western emperor Honorius. His *On the Gothic War* celebrated the victories of the general Stilicho. A bronze statue was erected to him in the Forum of Trajan.

Sidonius Apollinaris (*c.* AD 430–82), Latin poet and bishop in Gaul, who wrote many *Letters* which give many insights into late Roman society.

Zosimus (late C5 AD), Greek historian who wrote a *History of the Decline of the Roman Empire*, from Augustus down to AD 410.

Cassiodorus (*c.* AD 490–583), from southern Italy, consul in 514, retired in the 540s to a monastery and published letters and other works important for the history of Rome in the C6.

Procopius (*c.* AD 500–after 562) of Caesarea (Palestine), Byzantine Greek historian, who accompanied the general Belisarius on his campaigns in Africa and Italy and wrote a *History of the Wars of Justinian*.

Glossary

Rome's Building Materials

From the C6 BC onwards most major building in Rome used solid blocks of stone if at all possible and finely dressed masonry is an immediate clue to a building of high status. Even when the whole structure is not made of stone, when concrete substituted for the bulk, the concrete is commonly made with stone aggregate and faced with stone in the form of nodules, pointed cubes, or small blocks.

TUFA. Until the end of the C2 BC, the only general purpose stones available were the local volcanic conglomerates, called **tufas**, of which there are different varieties, characteristic of particular periods:

Cappellaccio. Grey tufa of relatively poor quality (soft and friable) quarried from the hills of Rome during the C7–C5. For the great projects of the C6 BC (terracing, drains, city walls) huge networks of caverns were mined under the Palatine, Capitoline, and Quirinal hills.

Grotta Oscura (18 km. up the Tiber, right bank, various localities near Prima Porta). Yellowish, rather porous tufa, much used in the C4 BC (after the defeat of Veii in 396 brought the whole territory under Roman control) but occasionally used before then. Quarrying declined at the end of the C2 BC as better alternatives opened up (Monteverde, Anio, and Peperino).

Fidenae (16 km. up the Tiber, left bank, at Castel Giubileo). Yellowish tufa with large black inclusions, much used from the later C5 to C2 BC, then gives way to Monteverde and Peperino.

Monteverde (behind the Janiculum ridge and 10 km. downriver at Magliana). A light greyish brown tufa peppered with white and darker (red and black) inclusions. Quarrying began in the C2 BC and continued until modern times.

Anio (up the Anio, a tributary of the Tiber, 8 km. west of Rome near Tor Cervara). Reddish brown tufa. Quarried from the mid-C2 BC, characteristic of the C1 BC and C1 AD.

Peperino, *Lapis Albanus* (20 km. SE of Rome in the Alban Hills, near Marino). Ashy blue-grey in colour, even-textured, hard, and compact. Some already being used in Rome for sculpture and other stone artefacts in the C4 BC but appears as a high-quality building stone from the C2 BC onwards. It is harder to work than the normal tufas but weathers better, often being employed on the outer face of a building, whereas the internal work could be of softer tufa. Another peperino, *Lapis Gabinus* came from Gabii (16 km. west of Rome, beside the Via Praenestina, near Osteria dell'Osa). Very similar to the Alban but rather coarser texture, introduced towards the end of the C2 BC.

BASALT, *silex* (Italian 'selce'). Used in large polygonal blocks for paving streets and main roads, came mainly from old lava flows from the volcanoes of the Alban hills which outcrop near Frattocchie, Acqua Acetosa, Borghetto (Frascati) and closer in, beside the Via Appia antica (near the tomb of Caecilia Metella). A flow from the Bracciano volcano north of Rome was also tapped, near S. Maria di Galeria.

TRAVERTINE. The hard white limestone found in deep beds on the plain between Rome and Tivoli (currently enjoying a great revival in modern architecture). More durable than any of the volcanic stones, and takes a strong edge and sharp detail far better. Roman quarrying probably started in the C2 BC, but its use in buildings was very selective until the early C1 BC; thereafter an excellent substitute for white marble in public architecture and widely employed for paving, steps, thresholds, doorframes, keystones and springers of arches, stone corbels, well-heads.

WHITE MARBLE. The earliest recorded marble buildings in Rome are a temple to Jupiter Stator vowed in 146 BC and a decade later one to Mars, both commissioned by triumphing Roman generals from a Greek architect Hermodorus of Salamis and both presumably employing marble (and marble workers) shipped in from Greece or the Aegean. Such practice became the hallmark of the capital city, the physical embodiment of its empire and the capacity of the imperial regime literally to move mountains. White or greyish white marble, metamorphosed crystalline limestone, had been the traditional medium for fine architecture in the eastern Greek world for generations, and by common consent there was nothing better. If Rome was to have the best, it had to have marble, but there is none worth speaking of in central or southern Italy; the closest sources lie in the Apuan Alps 350 km. to the north (modern Carrara), which had hardly been touched before the Romans got there in the C2 BC and which they did not begin to exploit until the mid-C1 BC. Even then, although Italian quarries were able to furnish the bulk of supplies, without which marble architecture on the scale achieved in Rome would have been unthinkable, great quantities of white marble were regularly imported from elsewhere, together with a whole range of coloured stones: where they came from was as important as the purity of their tone or the vividness and variety of their colouring—and (at least for the emperors' projects) long-distance transport was no object. From the early C1 AD until well into the C3 the emperors kept direct control of all the major sources, employing their own officials to run the quarries and oversee supplies (rather than contracting out).

    Parian. Pure, highly translucent white marble from the island of Paros in the Cyclades, rated the best of all marbles by the Greeks. It was quarried from the C6 BC or earlier until late antiquity, in two qualities, one with fine, the other medium-coarse crystals; the coarser stone also came in a greyish white variety. From the very beginning

Parian was accustomed to travel, being shipped with or without the necessary sculptors to execute commissions all around the eastern Mediterranean and sometimes further afield. The Romans were able to plug into an existing system and Parian, together with Pentelic, constituted the mainstay of supplies to the city during the C1 BC.

Pentelic. The white marble of Athens, quarried on Mount Pentelikon and Mount Hymettos since the C5 BC. Like Parian, during the C4–C2 BC it had been exported together with its sculptors quite widely among the Hellenistic kingdoms, and was an early import to Rome. Finely crystalled and translucent, the beds exploited during the Roman period were of variable quality, often full of greenish, pink, or grey micaceous faults and a general tendency to split along bedding lines. Employed for both architecture and statuary at all periods, especially during the reign of Domitian (AD 81–96) and in the early C4 (perhaps using older reserves).

Luna. A very stong, fine grained white marble, often slightly grey and rather dull compared with the Greek, from the Apuan Alps of Italy, north of Pisa (modern Carrara), shipped to Rome through the port-colony of Luni (hence its name). Large-scale quarrying probably started around 50 BC, promoted by Julius Caesar for the great projects he planned in Rome, and continued under imperial control until at least the C3 AD. A range of variegated light-medium greys with streaks or veins of white and dark grey were much sought out for column shafts and veneer in the C2–C3 AD.

Docimium. From the highlands of Phrygia in central Turkey, 500 km. from the sea and without a navigable river; one of imperial Rome's maddest enterprises, instigated by the emperor Augustus. The quarries produced both a fine crystalled, translucent white, very similar to Pentelic, and the particularly desirable Phrygian purple (see below).

Thasian. A brilliant white with coarse, shimmering crystals, from the island of Thasos in the northern Aegean, where it had been quarried since the C6 BC. At Rome it was generally favoured for veneer but is also found in architecture and statuary, especially in the C2 AD and C4–C5.

Proconnesian. From the island of Marmara (ancient Proconnesos) in the sea of Marmara in NW Turkey. Medium crystalled, translucent, greyish white or strongly marked horizontal bands of grey and white. Although quarried for local regional use ever since the C6 BC it does not appear at Rome much before the end of the reign of Hadrian (AD 130s) but is then employed in huge quantities, especially under the Severans in the first half of the C3.

COLOURED MARBLES AND OTHER HARD STONES. Although the Romans took their lead in the matter from the Hellenistic kings of the C2 BC, especially the Ptolemies of Egypt, they developed a passion for coloured stones in architecture and interior decoration that far outstripped anything seen before. The first signs are found in the early C1 BC, when the consul for

78 BC Marcus Lepidus caused a stir by installing thresholds of yellow stone from Numidia (North Africa) in his own house, and four years later the consul L. Lucullus shipped in a black/red marble from Asia Minor which thereafter took his name; M. Aemilius Scaurus had 38-foot monolithic column shafts of it in his house by 58 BC. Other colours were also beginning to come in from Greece by the 40s BC, such as green from Carystos and red from Cape Tenaros, and the choice blossomed when Egypt, the heartland of polychromatic stone architecture and sculpture, was taken over by Rome in 31 BC to be run as the emperors' private estate. The Nile valley and the eastern desert are rich in white and brightly variegated red, yellow, and brown alabasters, black, pink, grey, and green granites, green gabbro-diorites, dark green and black basalts. Imperial surveyors not only checked out all the existing sources, but in the first decades of the C1 AD identified many which had not been previously worked, especially far off in the eastern desert, including the deep red porphyry which was to become synonymous with imperial power. The Egyptian quarrymen (with practice born of generations) were particularly adept at extracting huge monoliths for column shafts up to 50 and even 60 Roman feet (15–18 m.) long. Their other specialities were enormous stone tubs and basins for Rome's imperially sponsored public baths. In due course new stones were also identified and brought into production in Greece, Asia Minor, Mauretania (Algeria), Spain, and Gaul (Pyrenees), many of them operated by local entrepreneurs both for local use and export. It is not clear to what extent imperial ownership and administration was intended to keep certain stones in the imperial gift or simply ensured adequate supplies for imperial projects with any surplus being available for sale. Certainly 'imperial' marbles regularly ended up in non-imperial circles.

Vast quantities of the coloured stones brought into the city during the Roman period are still around, but are rarely to be seen in their original settings, having been recycled, over and over, into the decoration of churches, palazzi, and other monuments right down to the present day. Consequently a whole subculture of stone appreciation exists, with its own Italian nomenclature distinguishing hundreds of different types, mostly by the characteristics of their colouring, occasionally by reference to a location in Rome. However, since modern studies have been able to determine what parts of the empire many of the stones came from, a new terminology is coming into use, which tries to place appropriate weight on provenance. The following are those most frequently encountered in this guide and some others it is useful to know about (the old Italian names are given in square brackets):

Numidian yellow [giallo antico]. From Chemtou (Tunisia), first quarried by the local kings of Numidia, attested in Rome by 78 BC. Plain yellow crystalline limestone of varied intensity, brecciated red and yellow, and brecciated yellow and white. The same source could also produce a strong black and a pale green limestone. Used for columns, paving, and veneer.

Lucullan black/red [africano]. From Teos, on the coast SW of Izmir (western Turkey). A breccia of red, fleshy pink, white and grey marble in a black (tending to dark green) matrix, it took its name from the Roman general L. Lucullus, who first brought it to Rome in 74 BC. Columns, paving, and veneer.

Phrygian purple [pavonazzetto]. From Docimium (see under white marbles, above). White marble strongly variegated with purplish blotches and veins. Columns, paving, veneer, basins, table supports, and statuary.

Chian pink/grey [portasanta]. From the island of Chios, eastern Aegean. Under imperial control by the mid-C1 AD but already being imported to Rome in the late C1 BC. Columns, paving, veneer, basins, and table supports.

Carystian green [cipollino]. From Carystos, on the island of Euboea (Greece). Strongly marked streaks of green, with veins of grey and white, its Italian name likens the effect to a sliced onion. Cut on the bias the streaks form wave patterns. Columns, paving, and veneer.

Tenaros or Iasos red [rosso antico]. From Cape Tenaros (southern tip of Mani, Greece) and similar beds near Iasos (SW Turkey). Some veneer but primarily used for edging strips and quarter mouldings. The burgundy-wine colour inspired some exotic imperial commissions for statues of satyrs, companions of the wine-god Bacchus.

Red porphyry [porfido]. From Mons Porphyrites in the eastern desert of Egypt. Discovered by AD 18 and exploited down to the C5, a deep red/purple evenly sprinkled with tiny pink or white flecks, the quintessential imperial stone. Columns, paving, veneer, basins, sarcophagi, statuary.

Grey Egyptian granite [granito del foro]. From Mons Claudianus in the eastern desert, grey flecked with white and black. The name implies that quarrying began in the reign of Claudius (AD 41–54) and the stone is found in the veneer of imperial buildings soon afterwards. Its large-scale use for columns is characteristic of Trajan and Hadrian. Another very similar granite was obtained from the Troad (Kozani, NW Turkey).

Pink Egyptian granite [granito rosso]. Rose pink speckled with black and white quartz from Aswan, along the banks of the upper Nile, quarried by the Pharoahs since 1800 BC; most really large obelisks are made of it. Came into widespread use at Rome in the late C1 AD, very popular in the late empire. Columns, paving, veneer, basins, some Egyptianizing statuary.

Green porphyry [serpentino]. From near Sparta, southern Greece. Dark green with tiny mid-green or yellow rectangles. Its ancient name was the Lacedemonian stone. Exported to Rome from mid-C1 AD. Paving and veneer, small columns and capitals, rare statuary.

Thessalian Green [verde antico]. Found in various parts of Thessaly (northern Greece), the main quarries at Kastri and in the Larissa valley. Pale green limestone breccia with white marble and black flecks/veins. Under imperial control by the early C2 AD, when imported to Rome in quantity; still being exploited by the emperors in the C5–C6 for projects in Constantinople and occasional gifts elsewhere.

Spanish breccia [broccatello]. From the Ebro valley, near Tortosa. Golden yellow with dark purplish-red blotches and shelly incusions. Characteristic of the C2–C4 AD, in floor and wall veneer.

Celtic black/white [bianco e nero antico]. From Aubert, near St Girons at the foot of the Pyrenees. Principally exploited in the C4–C6 AD.

CONCRETE. A combination of lime mortar and rubble aggregate at first used only as infill in structures whose main load-bearing elements were made of stone, but developed in the course of the C2 BC into a major building material which could do everything stone could do—and more. Its success was largely due to the particular qualities of the mortar, made with the volcanic sand (*pozzolana*), which occurs in plentiful deposits in and around Rome, and lime, generally obtained by roasting limestone and gypsum, which had to come from further afield, brought by river from the Sabine hills behind Tivoli, Mount Soracte 30 km. up the Tiber, or Terracina 120 km. down the coast. Between them the two main ingredients produced a very strong and durable mix which had excellent hydraulic properties (capable of hardening even under water).

Unlike modern concretes Roman concrete was not poured but laid in courses, the aggregate usually consisting of recycled offcuts of tufa, peperino, and/or brick (but chunks of travertine, marble, wall plaster and stucco, amphora handles, pegs, rim and body sherds would do) carefully graded to suit the job in hand.

From the C1 BC concrete constituted the normal general purpose material for foundations and walls but could also be used to construct vaults and roofs. In the latter, the aggregate might consist of lumps of pumice (another volcanic product in good supply), to lighten the structure. The lime-pozzolana mortar mix could be refined by sieving the sand to make a smooth coating for finishing work.

BRICK. The Tiber basin has deep deposits of alluvial clays suitable for shaping and firing ('terracotta') into roof-tiles, plaques and bricks, some good sources being the valleys on the right bank very near Rome, just behind the Vatican and the Janiculum ridge. In the early days the bricks were simply sun-dried, but by about 100 BC, as every other aspect of Roman building practice was being revolutionized, the kilns began to fire bricks as well and from the early C1 AD fired brick became one of the principal materials for facing concrete. During the C2 AD brickyards were operating to supply the city's needs from as far away as Narni, 100 km. up the Tiber valley.

The standard form was nothing like a modern brick but a large flat slab—a *bipedalis*—two Roman feet (59 cm.) square and an inch to two inches (2.5–5 cm.) thick. Some were used whole, for the roofs and floors of drains, to cap off concrete foundations, or form levelling courses at intervals higher up a concrete wall. Most were sawn or split into smaller triangles (18 from one brick), for the wall facing. Smaller slabs, of 1½ feet (*sesquipedalis*) and 8 inches (*bessalis*) square were made for lining the underside of vaults. Circular bricks were also produced, to be cut into quarters or smaller segments for building columns, and other preformed shapes could be supplied which combined to make cornices and other decorative mouldings.

Brickstamps (Fig. E). Stamping, though not unknown elsewhere (the army often did it), is a particular feature of brick production in the Rome area. The large numbers of contractors and subcontractors involved in the business often found it necessary to be able to distinguish their products from someone else's. During the C2 AD and occasionally later, probably by imperial decree, the stamps were actually dated (in the normal Roman fashion by the names of the consuls for the year) and as a result the dating of a brick building can be equally precise.

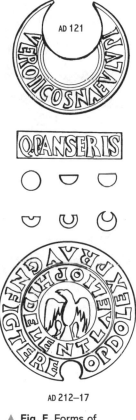

AD 212–17

▲ **Fig. E.** Forms of brickstamps

COCCIOPESTO (*opus signinum*). A mixture of lime, pozzolana, and crushed brick or pottery (hence its Italian name), general purpose waterproofing for heavy duty floors, pavements, concrete roofs, lining cisterns and bathing pools.

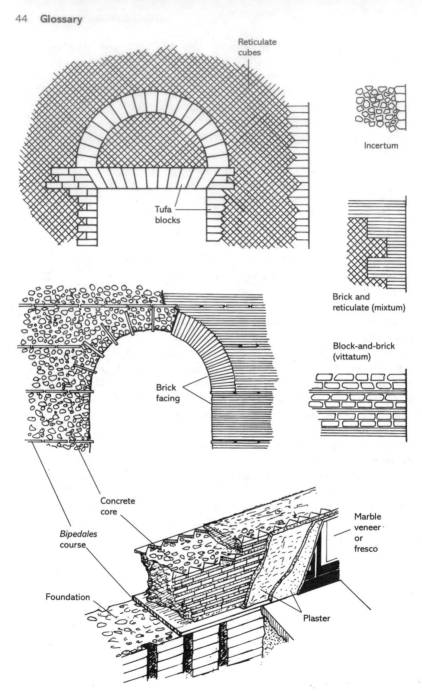

▲ **Fig. F.** Roman concrete walls

Building Techniques

Ashlar Masonry (*opus quadratum*)

Squared blocks of stone, usually laid without mortar, kept in place by their own weight and a tight fit, fixed with dowels and clamps. By the C2 BC tufa blocks were quarried to a standard $2 \times 2 \times 4$ Roman feet ($60 \times 60 \times 120$ cm.). When building walls the blocks were laid in alternate courses of 'headers' and 'stretchers', two parallel rows of blocks laid lengthwise, followed by a row where they are all laid crosswise.

In travertine masonry the blocks vary in size, to minimize waste and extra labour, since the quarrying followed the natural bedding faults; when tufa walls were reinforced with travertine piers (as in the Colosseum) the tufa had to be dressed into equally varying sizes to match the travertine.

Marble masonry was rarely used on its own except in very small buildings. Anything of any size tended to combine marble and travertine or marble and tufa, putting the marble only on the outside.

Concrete Construction

Concrete buildings are far more widespread in and around Rome, and are on the whole far more ambitious there, than in the Roman world at large. This was not just because the city was so much larger than its nearest rival and the focus of continual imperial attention, but because not many other places were able to make the right sort of strong concrete.

WALLS. The thickness of a concrete wall and the depth of its foundations was determined as in a stone building by the projected height and the type of roofing. Walls as thin as 18 cm. and as wide as 6 m. were possible, with every gradation in between, though tending to follow simple dimensions in Roman feet. Major foundations were formed by setting a series of wooden posts into the ground at regular intervals to mark out the shape of the foundations required, to which wooden shuttering would be fixed to contain the concrete, planks and posts being removed once it had set. Numerous examples are visible on and around the Palatine. The same technique could have been used to build the elevation of the wall as well but it never was (though it was used for vaults, see below); instead the wooden shuttering was laboriously substituted by an outer facing of stone and/or brick which rose in tandem with the concrete core. Materials and techniques employed for the facings changed in the course of time (Fig. F), providing useful clues to dating:

Tufa nodules (*opus incertum*). Small, irregularly shaped lumps (average 6–10 cm. across) roughly smoothed on one side to form a flat outer face. C2–C1 BC.

Tufa reticulate (*opus reticulatum*). Pyramid-shaped nodules 6–12 cm. square at the base and about 8–14 cm. in depth; the point stuck into the concrete, the base formed the outer facing on the wall, set on its diagonal in a net-like pattern (hence the name). Edges, corners, door and window frames made of squared blocks, 8 × 8, 20–24 cm. long. Characteristic of the mid-C1 BC to the late C1 AD.

In the mid-C1 AD horizontal bands comprising 1–3 courses of brick began to be inserted at intervals and brick replaced the tufa blocks for the edging, in a **mixed technique** (for which the modern latinism is *opus mixtum*). In the course of the C2 reticulate is gradually phased out in favour of fully brick, or block-and-brick facings.

Brick. Used as a facing on its own is occasionally found in the later C1 BC but rare until mid-C1 AD, after which it becomes increasingly common and continues until the Middle Ages. The bricks are generally isosceles triangles, or vaguely so, with the long side to the fore. Differences in the relative thickness and colour of the bricks, and the amount of mortar set between courses, can be used (with varying degrees of reliability) as criteria for dating.

Tufa block and brickwork (*opus vittatum*, Italian 'opera listata'). Alternates one or two courses of brick and one or two courses of small tufa blocks. The blocks are rectangular on the outer face (*c.*10–14 × 4–6 cm.) but tapered to the rear. The technique is introduced to Rome around the middle of the C2 AD (having been long used in other parts of Italy) but becomes especially popular in the C4.

VAULTS. Solid caps of cast concrete in a variety of arched shapes (Fig. G). starting with the barrel, cross, and semicircular dome and moving on to the more elaborate curvilinear and multifaceted forms. Required immensely strong timber framing to construct them: essentially they built the profile of the vault in negative inside the space to be covered, then laid the concrete on top and let it set. By the C3 AD flat vaults over 6 m. wide were being cast by the same technique. Actually there was often no need for the arched shapes, which were a habit born of stone construction. The concrete was an inert mass, as if a huge block of stone had been hollowed out and lowered into position. It exerted mainly downward, little outward pressure on the walls which supported it and could bear the stress of its own weight far better

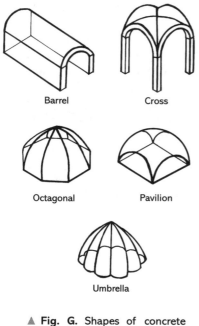

Barrel Cross

Octagonal Pavilion

Umbrella

▲ **Fig. G.** Shapes of concrete vaulting

than stone. Empirical experience gradually led to vaults of increasing span, the imperial palaces and the great bathing halls of the imperial *thermae* providing the main opportunities to experiment. The largest single vault is that of the Pantheon at 44 m. (150 Roman feet) but that is a dome; there was clearly felt to be a limit of about 80 RF (25 m.) for cross-vaulted shapes (Baths of Caracalla, p. 319 and Diocletian, p. 352; New Basilica p. 115).

Exterior Finishings

Of all the materials described above, only marble, travertine, and peperino were regularly left in their natural state in the finished building. Decorative finishes in their case consisted of finely **drafted channels** emphasizing the joints between blocks, an effect often reproduced in moulded stucco (see below). In peperino and travertine masonry the stone between the drafted margins might be '**rusticated**', left in rough relief to catch the light; a very exaggerated version is found on buildings associated with the emperor Claudius (pp. 198, 312, 358).

The softer tufas, when used externally, were always coated with white plaster to protect them from the weather (intense heat being as damaging as rain and frost); peperino did not need it on practical grounds but might be rendered white for aesthetic effect (to resemble marble). Odd though it seems, the precisely worked and often highly decorative effects produced on concrete by brick and tufa facings generally also got covered over with lime-plaster both inside and out.

The plaster was preferably **stucco**, an extremely hard and durable lime plaster made from calcined gypsum (plaster of paris) and fine washed sand; the best quality was blended with marble dust. Depending on the status of the building and its builder, such coatings were either left plain white, or painted (in red, black, yellow) or both moulded in relief and painted, in various schemes imitating ashlar masonry (Fig. H). The Senate House on the Forum (p. 68) still preserves traces of such treatment. In the C2 AD, as colour crept into the exteriors of temples and other prestigious public buildings in the form of monolithic columns in coloured stones, a fashion developed lower down the scale for polychrome brickwork, made to be seen. The pilasters framing doorways and arches were executed in extra finely shaped deep red brick, with hardly any mortar in the joins. The façade of Trajan's Markets is a fine example (p. 170).

Painted **terracotta panels and friezes** enlivened many exteriors, in the old days only on temples and aristocratic houses, but in the C1 AD they are found on apartment blocks and warehousing. By that time, prestige architecture had graduated to marble, bronze, ivory, and gold: the panels and friezes were sculpted in **marble** or worked in **bronze**, marble and bronze statuary stood in, around, and on top, doors were sheathed in ivory or gold, or both, and roofs tiled with **gilded bronze**.

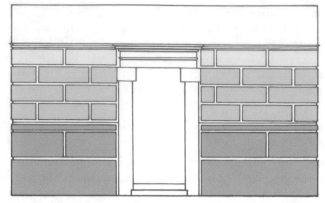

First 'Masonry'

Second 'Architectural'

Third 'Closed'

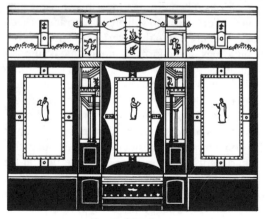

Fourth 'Fantastic'

Interior Decoration

In contrast to the preponderance of white on the outside Roman interiors were frequently a riot of colour. Walls, ceilings, and floors were rarely if ever left bare and their finishing could take a wide range of forms.

WALLS. The stucco **masonry** treatment employed on the outside of walls (see above) could also be applied to the inside, painted in bands of colour corresponding to zones within the masonry scheme (black, red, and white). Some schemes were richly painted in imitation of alabasters and other exotic stones, which apparently reflect real versions of elaborate stone panelling first devised for royal palaces at Alexandria and other late Hellenistic kingdoms. They soon had their real versions in Rome, too, and marble panelling remained at the top of the scale (used in temples, basilicas and porticoes, public baths, palatial halls, and churches) down to the C6 AD and beyond.

In the C1 BC and C1 AD, however, before marble became available in suitable quantity, wealthy patrons experimented with many other forms of wall decoration. **Wall painting** (in a mixture of fresco and tempera techniques) had a long history in central Italy, though principally in temples and tombs rather than domestic interiors, but around 100 BC it appears on the Roman scene in a particularly ambitious form (for which the modern term is '**Second Style**'), aimed at creating the illusion of elaborate architectural settings (Fig. H). Some are relatively simple effects of colonnades and garlands in front of panelled walls of masonry type; others are much more complicated, presenting temples and sanctuaries, whole cityscapes; some look like theatrical stage sets or picture galleries. All may be presumed to be making specific statements about the culture of the people who commissioned them, but quite what their terms of reference were is rather obscure. Some may be intended to evoke the luxury temporary architecture which was erected to host the pageants and banquets that greeted military triumphs in the C2 BC. Although some houses kept their Second Style paintings for the rest of their existence, another style came in fashion at the end of the C1 BC (c.15 BC), promoted by the new imperial court of Augustus. **Third Style** (Fig. H) closes the wall off as a flat screen, and was of short-lived currency, soon giving way (by the AD 50s) to more florid schemes of many different individual tastes, all broadly classified as '**Fourth**' in which the architectural element returns, though not in any very logical sense and probably far from any real models (Fig. H). The style was interpreted in many different media, in moulded stucco, in glass mosaic. A room in a wealthy (probably imperial) residence on the Esquiline even interpreted it in real jewels, semi-precious stones, and gilded bronze.

◀ **Fig. H.** Styles of Roman wall decoration

CEILINGS were generally plastered and painted, or stuccoed in extensions of the designs found on walls. Pumice stone, shells, and mosaic might be used in wealthy dining rooms, and are also attested in the great public baths. The ultimate luxury was coffering lined with gilded sheet bronze.

FLOORS. The simplest form of decoration in the early days was to set a scatter or simple geometric pattern of small chips of white, black, or coloured stone in a **concrete of crushed pottery and tile**. Overall surfaces of **mosaic**, in white and black tesserae, became popular in the C1 BC and remained in widespread use for domestic and commercial spaces down to the end of the C3 AD. The designs were mainly geometric, favouring endlessly repeatable motifs which could be adapted to any shape or size of floor. **Pictorial mosaics**, in coloured tesserae, are also found—in settings of more pretensions, inlaid as panels in larger mosaic or marble floors. **Polychrome mosaic**, in large tesserae made of coloured marbles, is occasionally found in the C3 AD and became very popular in the C4–C6. From the end of the C1 BC onwards **marble** on floors swiftly worked its way down the socio-economic scale from public halls and aristocratic houses to almost every kind of interior. As on walls, it was laid in the form of veneer, in slabs of different shapes and sizes and different ranges of colours depending on the context. The great majority of patterns were based on squares within squares, simple geometric designs which took their individual character from the particular marbles chosen. Almost from the beginning, such floors were designed to be recycled, the shapes from one floor readily being recombined to form another. Those who could not afford proper shapes simply used offcuts and scraps. Floors in basilicas or similarly prestigious public and imperial buildings were generally distinguished by the use of much larger dimensions.

Architectural Orders and Dimensions

Corinthian is the commonest and most typically Roman order, especially favoured for major temples (see pp. 79, 91, 107, 159). Its columns are of slender proportions, with the height of the shaft being 8 times its lower diameter, and ⅚ of the total height of the column. The **base** consists of a rectangular plinth on top of which is a circular element (the base proper) in either of two forms: the 'Attic' type has two cushion-like convex mouldings (*torus*) separated by a concave channel (*scotia*); the other is more ornate, with two *scotiae* in the middle separated by one, or more usually two, bands of half-round moulding (*astragal*). The **shaft** can be composed of two or more blocks (called drums) or a single block (monolith), either decorated with 24 vertical grooves (fluting) or left plain, and is normally given a tapered profile (*entasis*), rising straight for the first third of the height and then narrowing towards the top. The Corinthian **capital** takes the form of an inverted bell set in the midst of an acanthus plant. Two rows of alternating short and tall acanthus leaves cover the lower half of the bell, and a pair of stalks rises in the centre of each of the four faces. Each stalk sprouts two tendrils curving in opposite directions, the outer ones to form large spirals (volutes) at the angles. On the top of the capital is a flat square slab (*abacus*) with an acanthus flower in the centre of each side. Although the basic design developed in the C4 BC in Greece, early versions produced in Italy took their leaf-form from the soft rather shaggy local acanthus (*a. mollis*). The spikier leaf of the eastern Mediterranean species (*a. spinosus*) makes its appearance in Rome with the arrival of eastern Greek architects in the C2 BC (for example Round Temple by the Tiber, p. 256). A sort of compromise between the two forms emerges when the Corinthian order was taken up by Augustan architects as the hall-mark of the imperial style. The spikier versions found in Rome in the later C2 and C3 AD came in with new waves of eastern Greek influence and the use of Proconnesian Greek marble.

Composite. An ornate form of **capital** invented during the Augustan period as an alternative to the Corinthian in public buildings other than temples (notably the imperial palaces, baths and triumphal arches). It is a hybrid of the Roman four-sided Ionic (see below) and Corinthian acanthus leaves. The shaft and base are the same as for Corinthian. Most of the examples found in Rome are from the Flavian period and later. In the late C3 AD a simplified (presumably more economical) form came into widespread use in domestic architecture and is also found in early churches.

Ionic has an 'Attic' base, a (usually fluted) shaft of similar slenderness to the Corinthian and a low capital consisting of a flat cushion with scrolled ends overhanging the shaft to either side. Essentially two-sided, with limited scope for elaboration, it was a major order in the Greek world and is found in temples at Rome down to the C1 BC (for example

Portunus, p. 254) but relatively rarely thereafter, though a four-sided version with diagonal volutes was available. It continued to be employed in other kinds of buildings, such as colonnaded garden porticoes and columnar screens, and in superimposed 'engaged' orders on monumental facades (for example the Colosseum, p. 276). A particular type in imported Thasian marble came back into vogue in the C4 and C5 AD.

Doric/Tuscan, in use by the C6 BC, are the plainest of the orders, closely related to each other, with a similar form of capital: a circular cushion (*echinus*) below a low square plate (*abacus*). According to Vitruvius the Tuscan was essentially an Italian version of Doric with an unfluted shaft and a circular base (as reconstructed on the first Capitoline Temple of Jupiter, Fig. 109, p. 237), but no examples now survive in Rome. The Greek Doric (used for the south temple at S. Nicola in Carcere, p. 249) has no base and the shaft is normally divided into 20 shallow flutes meeting in sharp edges (arrises); in its Roman interpretations the capital was often given a decorative collar at the top of the shaft and a single torus base, while the shaft was often unfluted. Like Ionic, it is not common in temples after the C1 BC, but was used for colonnaded porticoes and as pilasters in more utilitarian contexts.

Entablatures consist of a lintel (**architrave**) on top of the columns followed by an intermediary zone (**frieze**) capped by a projecting cornice. Some colonnades had only an architrave. In the Greek world each order was associated with a particular type of entablature: the Doric is distinguished by a frieze of alternating tripartite vertical elements (triglyphs) and roughly square panels (metopes) over a low plain architrave, the Ionic and Corinthian by a decorative frieze crowned by a series of small blocks (dentils) over a stepped architrave. Roman architects were far less conventional, often combining elements from the different orders together. The official Roman Corinthian in the late C1 BC developed a more standardized entablature, well illustrated by the examples in this guide, incorporating elaborate scrolled brackets (modillions) supported by acanthus leaves; at the same time no two buildings follow precisely the same scheme.

Dimensions. The Roman mind was always ready to be impressed by size, and was greatly attracted by simple geometrical proportions. Both were even more satisfying if they could be expressed in round numbers of feet based on multiples of 12 and 10. As far as we know, the ideal was to design buildings whose architectural orders were related dimensionally as well as proportionately to the overall size and shape of the structure. Such mathematical relationships often extended to the pattern on the floor and the decorative schemes on the walls.

Building-Types

ARCHES as free-standing monuments became a particular feature of the Roman scene from the early C2 BC onwards, generally sited across roads and resembling city gates (perhaps intentionally the Triumphal Gate through which triumphal processions entered the republican city walls). They were erected by or for a specific person, either in celebration of a military triumph or more generally in their honour, bearing their statue or other insignia. Only four are still standing but over fifty are known to have existed, mainly along the triumphal route, but also in and around the Forums and on main roads leading in and out of the city.

ATRIUM. Term which could be applied to a hall where one of the public magistracies had their offices, the residence of the Vestal Virgins, maintained at public expense, and the front hall of an aristocratic house (see *domus*), whose function was also primarily public. It is possible that, at least early on, all shared a similar architectural form, a broadly rectangular hall with alcoves or rooms down the sides.

BASILICA. A large public building whose principal function was to house law courts, the first recorded in Rome being the Basilica Porcia built near the Forum by the censor of 184 BC, followed in 179 and 170 by two others (Fulvia and Sempronia). The name basilica apparently derived from the Greek: stoa *basileios* or 'Royal stoa', and early versions may have been architecturally indistinguishable from a large porticus (see below). Surviving examples, the Paulli (p. 67), Julia (p. 89), and Ulpia (p. 162), reflect the type as it had developed by the late C1 BC, a huge rectangular hall whose interior space was divided by rows of columns to form a central nave with narrower aisles on all four sides (double aisles in the case of the Julia and Ulpia). Both the nave and the aisles were two storeys high, and the aisles were floored at first storey height, providing upper galleries. One of the long sides, colonnaded for its full length as in a porticus, formed the main entrance; the other long side was usually a solid wall with doors. The apses at either end of the Ulpia were a new departure.

Some much smaller buildings could also be called basilicas and may have served as more general purpose communal meeting and/or commercial halls. The Regionary Catalogues list three (all of unknown location): Vestilia, Vascellaria, and Floscellaria, whose names might refer to clothing, metal table ware, and flowers respectively. The Basilica Hilariana, built in about AD 150 by one M. Poplicius Hilarus, a dealer in pearls, was partly excavated in 1987–9 in the grounds of the military hospital on the Caelian (inaccessible). It was associated with a college of priests (the 'Tree-bearers of the Great Mother') and is similar to a large basilica in plan, with nave and double side aisles, but apparently the nave was not roofed. Another example, the Basilica of Neptune on the Field of Mars (p. 207), if correctly identified, shows another plan type altogether.

In the C4 AD large public Christian churches started to be called basilicas. They had colonnaded interiors but their plan was different again, based on a type of large reception/audience hall common in imperial palaces and aristocratic houses of the period. The entrance colonnade was on one short side, the aisles only down the long sides, and the longer central nave ended in a large semicircular apse. The aisles did not normally have upper floors and the outer walls were solid.

BATHS. Introduced to the Romans by their conquest of Greek southern Italy and Sicily in the C3 BC, social bathing in specially designed bath-houses became the single most characteristic feature of Roman culture. The bath-houses were called either *balneum* (singular), or *balnea* (plural), more rarely *lavacrum(-a)*, or *thermae* (always plural). The terminology was to some extent interchangeable, but plurals tend to imply institutions of greater size and complexity. The basic formula established by the C2 BC required a changing room (*apodyterium*), an unheated room with cold pool (*frigidarium*), a warm room with or without a tepid pool (*tepidarium*), which might draw its heat indirectly from a strongly heated room (*caldarium*), which had a hot pool and a separate water basin on a stand (*labrum*). The particular kind of heating system which developed *c.*100 BC had a Greek name, *hypocaust*, but was a considerable advance on older Greek methods. It burned wood in a furnace connected to voids under the floor (which was raised on small piers) and, where extra heat was desired, to terracotta pipes embedded in the walls. Thereafter, almost as many individual solutions were devised as there were baths built, depending on their context and the level of patronage. The invention of window glass in the C1 AD provided further sources of thermal power and encouraged the development of many intermediary grades of heat and atmosphere. With increasing supplies of water from aqueducts cold and hot swimming-pools were added to the repertoire.

According to the Regionary Catalogues by the C4 AD Rome had 856 **balnea** and numerous names appear in documentary sources suggesting that many were owned and operated by private individuals, or as part of the social clubs of affluent *collegia* (professional associations), but extraordinarily few examples have been found. There are some in private houses (see p. 112), one in a smart insula block (p. 317). The C4/5 church of S. Pudenziana on the Via Urbana took over one hall of what must have been a substantial complex dating from the early C2 AD, and the Lateran baptistery lies within the area of another of the C3 (p. 347). The larger baths called **thermae** were often the object of public benefaction, and given a greater degree of axial symmetry in expression of their higher status. In this respect the **imperial thermae** of the C2–C4 constitute a class unto themselves, all following a very similar pattern. Only Trajan's (p. 288), Caracalla's (p. 319), Alexander Severus' (p. 208), and Diocletian's (p. 352) are known in detail but something of the plans of those of Titus (actually Hadrianic), Decius, and Constantine can be supplied from C16 drawings. Two named after Commodus and Septimius Severus are only briefly mentioned in written sources.

COLUMNS, HONORARY. Monuments in the form of a single free-standing column with a statue on top erected to honour a public benefactor had a long history in Rome. One may have been set up as early as 439 BC, in gratitude to one L. Minucius for ensuring the grain supply; certainly there was one by 318 BC, and others are recorded in 260 and 255. The latter were 'rostrate': bristling with the sharp bronze prows of captured Carthaginian warships; the earlier ones too, judging by representations on coins, took some exotic shapes and the custom continued under the empire, though only three are standing today, Trajan (p. 164), Marcus Aurelius (p. 193), and Phocas (p. 84).

FORUM. A public square, more or less architecturally enhanced, normally a market place. Rome's original forum lost its market function and became a primarily political space, to be repeated in the great imperial forums (p. 147), but market-type forums are recorded in various parts of the city, many specializing in particular staples: Boarium (cattle) and Holitorium (vegetables) beside the Tiber port (p. 247–52), Suarium (pigs) on the east side of the Via Lata (Field of Mars), Gallorum et Rusticorum (chickens and wildfowl), Pistorum (flour) perhaps in the Transtiber.

HORREA (the singular **horreum** denotes a small version). Specialized storage buildings originally designed for public granaries but employed for many other similar purposes: a series of rooms on two or more floors evenly distributed around an open courtyard, enclosed within an outer wall of (hopefully fire resistant) tufa. Wide entrances allowed carts direct access into the court from the street and ramps rather than staircases facilitated transport of heavy loads to upper floors. Those intended for storing grain had the ground floor raised on piers to reduce damp. Particularly huge versions, where two or three courtyards were placed back to back, were located down by the docks, run by the State and other large importers. Others were to be found in all regions of the city (the Regionary Catalogues of the C4 AD list 290). Some acted as general safe deposits, rentable by anyone who needed to store anything. Some have names suggesting that they stored (and probably sold) only one particular commodity, such as wax (*candelaria*), paper (*chartaria*), pepper (*piperataria*), or grass-fodder (*graminaria*). Others around the foot of the Palatine palaces are named after emperors or members of the imperial family and were perhaps more like elegant shopping arcades.

HORTI. In origin and in the singular (*hortus*) the word simply means a vegetable garden. Early Rome was probably full of them, spreading in a ring close around the outskirts like modern suburban allotments, where the inhabitants of the city would grow much of their own food. In the

C3–C2 BC as the powerful political elite acquired immense wealth and built themselves ever more palatial town houses in which they exercised their public duties, they started buying up the vegetable gardens, not only to feed their expanding households but to provide pleasant retreats where they could take their leisure (*otium*). After the end of the C1 BC, when public political life declined, many made their horti into their main residence, embellished with lavish architecture.

HOUSES. The Regionary Catalogues of the C4 AD distinguish only two kinds of housing in the city, *domus* and *insula*, of which there were only 1,790 of the former compared with 44,300 of the latter. **Domus** was the traditional town house of old Rome, occupied by a single wealthy family with their retinue of servants, containing an atrium in which the master of the household would receive clients and friends, generally at least one peristyle garden, and other courts. **Insula** can be broadly interpreted as a multi-storey apartment block accommodating several families or single individuals, the natural response to enormous influxes of population in the C2 BC.

Both might be built by speculators and rented out for profit and ground-floor street frontage was frequently given over to shops or small workshops. Only fragments of either type are to be seen in the city (domus: pp. 128, 284; insula: pp. 232, 315), but Ostia has many different examples, several preserved to the third floor. Insulas twelve storeys high are mentioned in Rome in the C1 BC, but a limit of 70 Roman feet (21 m.) was imposed on the height of new buildings by the C1 AD, further reduced in the early C2 AD to 60 (18 m.) signifying 4–5 floors at the most. The limit applied to the street front; there could be higher floors to the rear (and given Rome's hillside sites there probably were). As in present-day Rome, the quality of the accommodation could vary from crowded tenements stacked up back to back to spacious, well-appointed apartments laid out around a communal courtyard.

The Marble Plan and other sources bear out the Regionary Catalogues in indicating that during the C1–C3 AD domus-type houses although comparatively rare were fairly evenly distributed in the residential areas of the city, either in small groups or on their own, with about one domus for every twenty-five tenement apartment blocks. Some areas may have been more desirable to live in than others but they were generally not monopolized by one social class, except during the late Republic when many senators clustered in the immediate vicinity of the Forum, the centre of their political life. It is not until the C4–C5, as the population was declining, that particular aristocratic enclaves can be identified on the Esquiline and the Caelian.

MITHRAEUM. Modern term for the meeting place of followers of the cult of Mithras, an Indo-Iranian god who became very popular in the Roman west in the C2–C3 AD, in association with a mystery religion about which hardly anything definite is known. Organized in autonomous cells, the sect was exclusively male, its initiates ranked in a hierarchy of seven grades. Their own word for the places where they met was *spelaeum*: a 'cave', usually a long dark chamber at or below ground level, provided with platforms on either side where the participants would recline to eat a communal meal. In addition to those treated in this guide, there is an important example under the church of S. Prisca on the Aventine.

PORTICUS. A long building, one or two storeys high, with one long side made of piers or columns to allow open access, the other long wall and the ends predominantly closed, the interior divided by a second parallel row (sometimes more) of piers or columns to support the roof. The rear half (or third in the case of wider versions) could be divided into rooms. The basic form is the same as the Greek *stoa*, a covered hall erected on the margin of a temple precinct or the public market square (*agora*) to provide large crowds with shelter from the wind, heat, or rain. Introduced at Rome in the early C2 BC, isolated or single buildings of the sort were soon relatively rare; the noun is usually plural, signifying a matching pair down opposing sides of a forum (p. 148) or temple precinct (p. 224), or three around the large open space behind the stage building of a theatre. Four could constitute a separate public building altogether, a monumental version of the domestic courtyard garden (p. 303). Apparently the oldest Roman building called **porticus**, dating from 196 BC, was a very different and utilitarian affair, set up beside the Tiber docks (see p. 368).

TEMPLES. Houses built for specific gods, whose statues were placed inside. The proper Latin term was *aedes*, not *templum*, which referred to the ground on which the temple was built, which had been 'inaugurated' by the augurs. Most temples in Rome were rectangular and stuck to the central Italian tradition whereby it was customary to raise a temple up on a high platform (*podium*) with access restricted to a single frontal staircase. Sometimes the podium contained cellars for the safe keeping of valuables. In its simplest form the temple building on top was a square or rectangular room, the *cella*, under a pitched roof which projected forward supported on columns to form a porch in front of the door. The gable end of the roof formed a triangular pediment (*fastigium*). Larger temples of the sort might have four columns in the entrance, smaller ones only two. A fancier version made a vestibule under the porch in the Greek manner (*pronaos*), projecting the cella walls forward, in which case the width of the podium and roof was often increased so that the colonnades could continue down the outside of the cella as in a Greek temple, sometimes around the back as well (a *peripteros*), more commonly stopping at the sides (*peripteros sine postico*). The columns of such lateral colonnades could be 'engaged', built in half-round relief as part of the cella walls. The larger porches might have more than one row of columns across the front.

The size, the order (Doric or Tuscan—its local Roman version, Ionic, or Corinthian), the number of columns and their spacing, the materials and workmanship were matters for the patron and architect to decide depending on resources and the intended location, and occasionally the particular deity.

Major Public Works

Aqueducts

Appia (312 BC), from the 7th to the 8th milestones Via Praenestina, 16 km. long mostly underground, entered Rome at the Porta Maggiore (called 'ad Spem Veterem': Ancient Hope), then along Caelian to Porta Capena, thence across Aventine and down to the Cattle Market beside the Tiber. Delivered 73,000 cubic metres of water a day.

Old Anio (272 BC), from springs up the valley of the Anio river at Vicovaro-Mandela, 63 km. Entered Rome at the Porta Maggiore and along Esquiline to Viminal. 176,000 cubic metres a day.

Marcia (144–140 BC), tapped a series of springs up the Anio valley at Arsoli-Agosta, 91 km. distant. Carrying 187,000 cubic metres a day 80 km. of its course ran underground, but also required 9.5 km. of arches. From Porta Maggiore ran over Esquiline to the Viminal, thence a branch to the Capitoline. Remained in use into the C10 AD.

Tepula (126–125 BC), from the Alban hills near Marino, 18 km. long. Its name means warm and its capacity was quite small: 17,800 cubic metres; from 33 BC its waters were combined with the Julia.

Julia (33 BC), from same area as the Tepula, near 12th milestone of the Via Latina, Squarciarelli (Grottaferrata) both joined in the same channel, 23 km. long from source to distribution tank, capacity 48,000 cubic metres; inside the city it followed the same route as the Marcia.

Virgo (19 BC), from same area as the Tepula-Julia, but brought underground right round the city to the north of the Pincian ridge, then to the Field of Mars. Delivered 100,000 cubic metres a day.

Alsietina or **Augusta** (2 BC), from Lake Alsietinus (Martignano), 22 km. north of Rome, 33 km. long, kept on the right bank of the Tiber, and entered the city from the Janiculum. Not drinking water, apparently built primarily to supply the arena (naumachia) for mock sea-battles which Augustus built somewhere in the Transtiber, possibly where the church of S. Cosimato is now. Produced 16,000 cubic metres a day, two-thirds for the emperor's use.

Claudia (AD 38–52), from same area as the Marcia, 68 km., 16 km. on arches. Its arches formed the Porta Maggiore. 184,000 cubic metres. Nero led a high-level branch off it along the Caelian (over the same route as the Appia).

New Anio (AD 38–52), built at the same time as the Claudia and followed much the same course. 86 km. long, the largest capacity of all, 190,000 cubic metres.

Traiana (AD 109), from Vicarello on the north side of Lake Bracciano, 32.5 km. from Rome. It entered the city at Porta S. Pancrazio, drove water mills on the hilltop before descending to the Transtiber.

Antoniniana (AD 210–15), a branch of the Marcia supplying the Baths of Caracalla.

Alexandrina (*c.* AD 226), from 22 km. out along the Via Praenestina, to the Porta Maggiore and then passed underground down on to the Field of Mars, to supply Alexander Severus' rebuilding of the Baths of Nero.

Fortifications

Republican walls. A circuit of 11 km. (7½ Roman miles), enclosing 426 ha. (see Fig. A), probably established during the C6 BC, built of the local cappellaccio tufa. When rebuilt in the early C4 BC using a mixture of the old blocks and new ones of tufa from Grotta Oscura, the walls were over 4 m. thick, and in places over 10 m. high. Across the level ground between the Esquiline and the Quirinal they were reinforced by an earthen rampart behind, and a deep ditch in front. The longest visible stretch is beside Termini railway station (Fig. 174); another is on the Viale Aventino, at Piazza Albania, where the walls formed a re-entrant to protect a gate, the *porta Raudusculana*. Although large parts of their course remained a feature of the urban landscape, by the end of the C1 BC the city had spread far beyond them and remained essentially unwalled for the first three centuries of the Empire.

Aurelianic walls. A circuit of almost 19 km. (13 Roman miles), enclosing 1,372 ha. (see Fig. C), in brick-faced concrete 3.5 m. thick, 8 m. high, with a square tower every 100 Roman feet (29.6 m.). Built incredibly quickly, in the five years AD 271–5. Thirty years later Maxentius heightened the parapets, then the whole upper elevation was substantially remodelled by Honorius in AD 401–3, doubling the height. Further work was done in the C6, by which time the circuit had 383 towers, 7,020 crenellations, 5 posterns, 116 latrines, and 2,066 large external windows.

Best-preserved stretches: (1) Muro Torto (Villa Borghese) to Corso d'Italia to Castro Pretorio; (2) Porta S. Giovanni to Porta Ardeatina (Sangallo Bastion); (3) Porta Ostiense to the Tiber; (4) Porta S. Pancrazio (on the Janiculum).

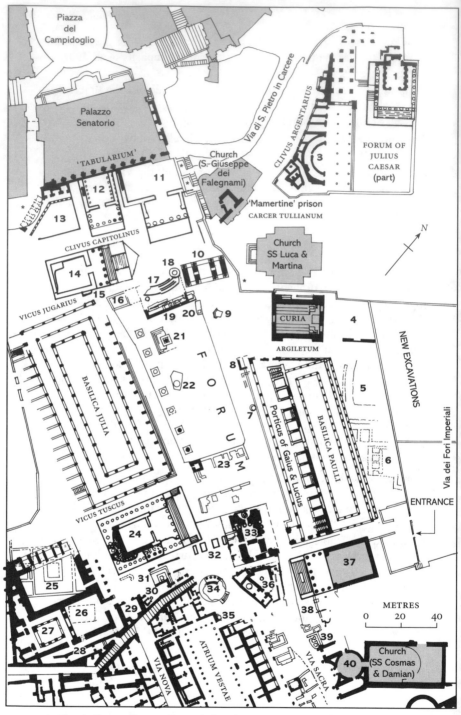

▲ **Fig. 1.** Roman Forum. General site plan

The Roman Forum (Map: Fig. 1)

*Piazza del Foro Romano (at junction between Via Cavour and Via dei Fori Imperiali). *State. The Forum and Palatine count as a single site. There is another public entrance from the Via di S. Gregorio.*

Good general views over the Forum square and the monuments at its Capitoline end can be had from either side of the back of the Palazzo Senatorio ('Tabularium'), at the foot of the Via del Campidoglio, and from the staircase behind the Arch of Septimius Severus. It's a good idea to get your bearings from one or both of these points before going into the site. The lower terrace in front of SS Luca e Martina gives the best closer view (but for that reason can be very crowded). Once up on the Palatine, it is also possible to look down from the terrace at the NW angle, above the House of the Vestal Virgins.

There is no more historic place than the Roman Forum. By the time it was remodelled after a disastrous fire in AD 283, it was a thousand years old. For the Romans themselves it had acquired the status of a museum and a monument to their increasingly remote past, a talisman which protected against an increasingly uncertain future.

Key to Fig. 1

 1 Temple of Venus Genetrix
 2 'Basilica Argentaria'
 3 Large public latrine
 4 South corner of Forum of Caesar
 5 South end of Forum of Nerva (part)
 6 Part of Temple of Peace
 7 Shrine of Venus Cloacina
 8 Arch of Janus (?)
 9 Black Stone
10 Arch of Septimius Severus
11 Temple of Concordia Augusta
12 Temple of Vespasian and Titus
13 Precinct of the Harmonious Gods
14 Temple of Saturn
15 Arch of Tiberius (?)
16 Lacus Servilius (?)
17 Caesarian Rostra
18 Umbilicus Urbis
19 Augustan Rostra
20 Decennalia base
21 Column of Phocas
22 Lacus of Curtius
23 Late Imperial Rostra

24 Temple of Castor
25 Domitianic Hall/*Domus Gai* (?)
26 Forecourt (S. Maria Antiqua)
27 Atrium (S. Maria Antiqua)
28 Covered ramp to Palatine
29 Oratory of the 40 Martyrs
30 Shrine of Juturna
31 Lacus Juturnae
32 Arch of Augustus
33 Temple of Divus Julius
34 Temple of Vesta
35 Shrine
36 Regia
37 Temple of Divus Antoninus and Diva Faustina
38 Archaic burials
39 Basement of a Late Republican house
40 'Temple of Divus Romulus'

It had started life as an open area with a stream running through the middle, at the head of a marshy inlet from the Tiber (the Velabrum) between the Palatine and the Capitoline hills, overlooked from further afield by the Quirinal, Viminal, and Esquiline. By the C5 BC it was the political, constitutional, and symbolic centre of the republican city-state, a general purpose open public space for political assemblies (and riots and rallies), committee meetings, lawsuits, public funerals (and their associated gladiatorial and/or theatrical games), and public feasts. The stream had been sent underground in the Great Drain (*cloaca Maxima*) and the square was surrounded by aristocratic houses intermingled with stalls selling all sorts of foodstuffs and goods, beyond which were larger markets both further down and further up the valley—cattle and vegetables in the Velabrum near the river; fish and spices in the Argiletum.

Then, during the last two centuries BC, as Roman armies blazed their way around the eastern Mediterranean, they brought back in triumph not only piles of booty and slaves, but also an ideal of civic life and public building modelled on the cities of the Hellenistic kings. The buildings around the Forum became the show-pieces of a new form of political competition. One after another, victorious generals converted their military successes into public office and embarked on costly projects, not just rebuilding temples, shrines, and fountains, as had long been the custom, but introducing ambitious new building types. The shops (*tabernae*) and larger houses (*atria*), the traditional settings for all sorts of public and private business, were transformed into colonnaded porticoes and basilicas. Few physical traces of these are to be seen today; their names are known from ancient writers and some appear in miniature in the coinage.

The Forum we encounter is a radically different one, which was set in train by Julius Caesar and developed further under the emperors from Augustus to Constantine. A lot of the imperial buildings and the ideologies behind them preserved the aura of earlier Republican precedent, but in effect the space was recast into a monument to Julius Caesar and the dynastic principles on which imperial authority rested. In 29 BC the **Temple of the deified Julius Caesar** was erected at the eastern end, opposite the new Rostra that Caesar had set up at the western end, estab-

▼ **Fig. 2.** Basilica Julia. Reconstruction of Forum façade

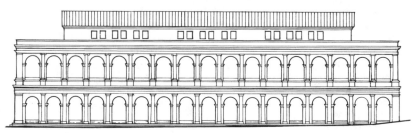

Characters around the Republican Forum c.200 BC

For perjurers, try the Comitium. Liars and braggarts hang around the Shrine of Cloacina: rich, married ne'er-do-wells by the Basilica. Packs of prostitutes there too—but rather clapped-out ones. In the Fish-Market members of dining-clubs. In the Lower Forum respectable, well-to-do citizens out for a stroll; in the Middle Forum, flashier types, along the canal. By the Lacus Curtius, you'll find bold fellows with a tongue in their head and a bad intent in their mind—great slanderers of others and very vulnerable to it themselves. By the Old Shops, the money-lenders—they'll make or take a loan. Behind the Temple of Castor, there are men to whom you wouldn't entrust yourself. In the Vicus Tuscus are men who sell themselves. In the Velabrum you'll find a baker or a butcher or a fortune-teller—or men who will do a turn for you or get you to do a turn for them. (Plautus, *Curculio* 470–82)

lishing a new axis down the length of the Forum. Soon, with the opportunities provided by major fires which ravaged the area in 14 and 9 BC, the **Temple of Castor** and the **Basilicas** on the north and south sides were rebuilt and dedicated to the glory of the Julian house, their hundred-foot-high marble façades, together with that of an equally **new Senate House**, turning the Forum square into a monumental precinct. **Triumphal arches** linked the Temple of Julius to the Temple of Castor and the Temple of Saturn to the Basilica Julia. In AD 10 the finishing touch came with the placing of a **Temple of Concordia Augusta** (Harmony in the Imperial House) at the foot of the Capitoline hill but directly in line with the Temple of Julius Caesar.

For the next two hundred years the whole installation stayed more or less untouched, gradually filling up with honorary statues, under the porticoes, on and beside the Rostra, and in the middle of the Forum square. The basilicas continued to be used for lawsuits, for which imperial Rome had an ever burgeoning passion, and both they and other Forum

▼ **Fig. 3.** Porticus of Gaius and Lucius. Reconstruction of Forum façade

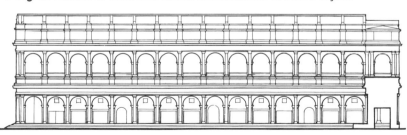

buildings provided niches for numerous branches of the imperial admin-istration—the *fiscus* (imperial purse) and office of weights and measures in the podium of the Temple of Castor; the *tabernae* in the Basilica Julia housed archives to do with the Province of Asia; a building near the Rostra housed the secretaries to the curule aediles. Otherwise, the Forum's prin-cipal ceremonial function was State funerals and such new buildings that appear on the scene are temples for deified emperors. The large temple erected for Augustus in AD 37 was located on the fringes, somewhere close behind the Basilica Julia, and in the AD 40s Caligula played with the idea of appropriating the Temple of Castor to his own cult. In AD 80, the Flavians squeezed a **Temple for the Deified Vespasian and Titus** between Saturn and Concord. In AD 140 a **Temple for the Deified Faustina**, joined later by her husband the Deified Antoninus Pius, was neatly inserted across the street from the Regia. The first significant inter-vention in the inner space was the great **Arch of Septimius Severus**, set across the Via Sacra in AD 203, and in line with it an extension to the angle of the Porticus of Gaius and Lucius. Severus also made repairs to the Temple of Vespasian and Titus, so the opportunity might have been provided by a fire.

It was certainly a great fire, in AD 283, which occasioned a really substantial restructuring of the Forum, undertaken by the emperor Diocletian. The emphasis shifted away from the Temple of Divus Julius to the **Basilica Julia** and the **Senate House**, which were both rebuilt in fine style. The Forum square was shortened to coincide with the eastern end of the Basilica, marked by a **new Rostra** or tribunal. The old Rostra at the western end was embellished with a set of five **honorary columns** and seven more were installed along the edge of the square in front of the

▼ **Fig. 4.** The Forum in Late Antiquity

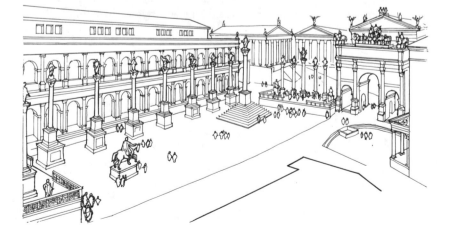

Basilica. The placing of the **single column (of Phocas)** indicates that the main approach was from the Argiletum.

This **Late Antique Forum** gathered its own host of monuments around it, in an alternation of pagan and Christian initiatives, including the rebuilding of the **Temple of Saturn** and the refurbishment of the **Precinct of the Harmonious Gods** in the second half of the C4. Honorary dedications were still being made throughout the C5 and into the C6. The latest known is that to Phocas in the early C7 but it need not have been the last. Though in AD 630 the Senate House was converted into the **church of St Hadrian,** the people of Rome were still being called to assembly in front of it in AD 767. By then, however, the population of Rome may have numbered less than ten thousand and was distributed in small pockets; most were living on the other side of the Capitoline hill, in the direction of the Vatican. There were simply not the resources to maintain the monster structures on the Forum, and as they decayed from neglect and earthquakes they must have become very dangerous. In AD 790 the Temple of Concordia Augusta, which had served as the diaconia (welfare centre) for the church of St Sergius and St Bacchus, at the back of the Rostra, had to be evacuated because it was starting to collapse. Today the area looks as though hit by a bomb, but the worst devastation occurred during the C15–C16, when the ruins were systematically plundered for materials with which to build and decorate the churches and palaces of papal Rome.

Archaeological excavations began in the early C19 as a series of separate holes, one around the Arch of Septimius Severus in 1803, another around the Column of Phocas in 1811–16, partly financed by the Duchess of Devonshire. Others followed, by the temples of Saturn and Castor and in the Basilica Julia, but only after 1870 did matters really get underway. In six years the Basilica and the central Forum square as far as the Temple of Julius were laid bare. Then there was a pause while the upper Via Sacra was cleared to the Arch of Titus and the exploration of the House of the Vestals began, but from 1898 to 1910 the operation in the Forum continued to the present limits of the site. During 1980–8 there was a major programme of study and conservation, in association with which many areas of the old excavations were reopened and some new excavations made (such as that in the Domitianic Hall and behind the Temple of Saturn). In 1996 work started in depth on a completely new sector, where the Argiletum led out of the Roman Forum to connect with the imperial forums of Caesar, Augustus, and Nerva.

Visit: The order followed in this visit to the Forum assumes that you enter from the Via dei Fori Imperiali.

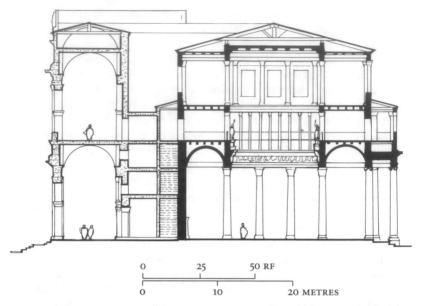

▲ **Fig. 5.** Porticus of Gaius and Lucius (*left*), and Basilica Paulli (Aemilia). Reconstructed cross-section (NE–SW)

▼ **Fig. 6.** Porticus of Gaius and Lucius. Remains on the north side (?) in a drawing by Giuliano da Sangallo (*c.* 1475)

Porticus of Gaius and Lucius and the Basilica Paulli (Aemilia) ★

To the right of the slope leading down to the ancient level are two long buildings, one behind the other: the Basilica Paulli at the back, fronted along the Forum square by a monumental gallery or *porticus*. Their main upstanding feature is the (heavily restored) wall of tufa blocks which lay between them.

The **basilica**, once two storeys high, was entirely supported on colonnades, open on three sides. It was first started in 55 BC by Lucius Aemilius Paullus and finished in 34 BC by his son Lucius Aemilius Lepidus Paullus, replacing the Basilica Fulvia (a building of 179 BC, partly excavated under the canopy at the far NE end). After only twenty years the new basilica burned down, together with the row of shops between it and the Forum and the two elements were rebuilt in tandem. The shops were transformed into the grand two-storey porticus, probably that dedicated in 2 BC in the names of Augustus' grandsons and heirs apparent at the time, Gaius and Lucius Caesar. (A loose fragment of a large and beautifully cut dedicatory inscription naming Lucius can be seen at the SE angle). The reconstructed basilica, although actually paid for by Augustus and other friends, was dedicated in the name of an Aemilius Paullus, and a certain M. Aemilius Lepidus is recorded seeking senatorial sanction for further embellishments in AD 22. For a while it could rank as one of the most magnificent buildings in the Roman world, though a considerable stretch of the imagination is required to appreciate this now.

The two short sections of entablature reconstructed in the NE corner of the site belong to the upper and lower orders respectively. The one with a frieze of acanthus is the upper, and had acanthus-scroll pilasters to match. The frieze of the lower order, still being painstakingly recomposed from thousands of tiny pieces, was carved with episodes from the legendary history of Rome (those displayed are casts and show the Rape of the Sabine Women). Somewhere at the same level stood statues of barbarians, larger than life-size and carved alternately in Numidian yellow and Phrygian purple marble. The surviving column shafts from the inner colonnades on both levels are of 'Lucullan' black/red breccia from the west coast of Turkey. The shafts in the two further colonnades on the side away from the Forum were of Carystian green. The outermost colonnade, which formed little more than a shallow porch, was largely walled up in the late C1 AD when the Temple of Peace (Fig. 1: 6) and the Forum of Nerva (Fig. 1: 5) were built hard against it. The paving in the side aisles is of variegated grey Italian marble; in the central nave it is composed of huge slabs of Numidian yellow, Carystian green, Phrygian purple, 'Lucullan' black/red, and the pink/grey from Chios. The marble veneer on the south wall was restored in antiquity, perhaps after the fire of AD 283.

▲ **Fig. 7.** Porticus of Gaius and Lucius (?). Reconstructed elevation

The **porticus**, with three and then four steps descending to the Via Sacra, contained a row of shops. Staircases at each end led to an upper storey. A reconstruction of its arcaded Doric façade, based on the various fragments lying around on the ground and Renaissance drawings, shows that it will have completely masked the basilica from the Forum side, though three doors led between the two buildings.

In the early C5 the basilica was gutted by a fierce fire, which reduced the 'Lucullan' columns to the ugly stumps we see now and also accounts for the bright green stains on the paving towards the NW end, where a scatter of late bronze coins melted into the marble. The site was levelled over the destruction debris and a brick wall with seven niches replaced the façade towards the Argiletum. Part of the porticus was also rebuilt, possibly using a set of sixteen red granite columns on white marble pedestals found in the area: three have been re-erected at the SE end, though none is in place. In the C6 a substantial building with high quality *opus sectile* floors was installed at the SE end, to be devastated in the great earthquake of AD 847.

Beside the steps towards the other end of the porticus, is a small circular plinth in white marble, the **Shrine of Cloacina** (Fig. 1: 7), on the original line of the great drain with which she shares her name. Representations on coins show a small enclosure containing an altar and two statues (Cloacina was also identified with Venus). The cult was traditionally associated with the Sabine king Titus Tatius and the ancient course of the Velabrum, the stream in the bottom of the Forum valley later canalized as the *cloaca Maxima*, which marked the boundary between the early Romans (on the Palatine) and the Sabines (on the Quirinal).

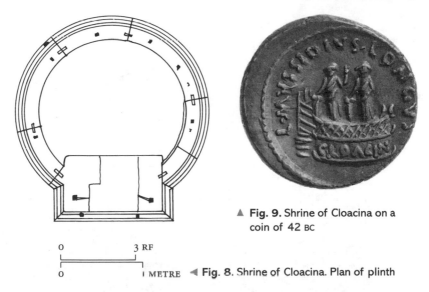

▲ **Fig. 9.** Shrine of Cloacina on a coin of 42 BC

0   3 RF

0   I METRE   ◀ **Fig. 8.** Shrine of Cloacina. Plan of plinth

Another ancient territorial landmark in this area was the shrine of **Janus Geminus** (double Janus), a small arched passage with doors at both ends which were closed only in times of peace. It appears on Imperial coins celebrating peace and was constructed or clad in bronze. Its precise location has not been identified. The little brick building now adapted to a custodians' hut and masked by a tree (Fig. 1: 8) has been suggested as a possible candidate but that is actually part of a larger structure of unknown purpose built over the porticus steps in the late C2 or C3 AD. An alternative is to place it further up the Argiletum, perhaps at the far corner of the Basilica Paulli or inside the precinct of the Forum of Nerva.

▼ **Fig. 10.** Arch of Janus Geminus. Coin issued by Nero in AD 65

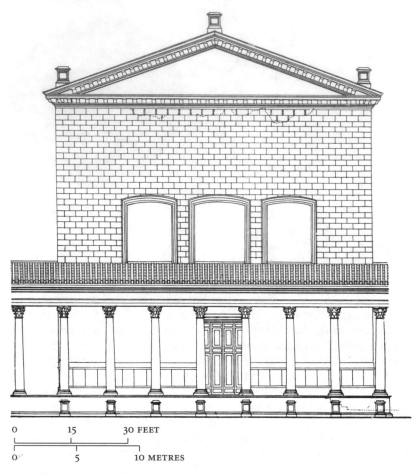

0   15   30 FEET

0   5   10 METRES

▲ **Fig. 11.** Senate House. Reconstruction of façade

Senate House (*Curia*)   ★

†Interior frequently closed

The present building, 31.6 m. (105 RF) high to the gable of its restored
roof, belongs to the reconstruction of the Forum after the fire of AD 283. It
reused the foundations of its predecessor, adding only the four solid
buttresses at the corners, and seems to have resembled the earlier building
quite closely. The previous senate house was planned by Julius Caesar as
part of his new Forum and completed by Augustus in 29 BC. It had a
Winged Victory on a globe crowning the pediment at the front, and there
was another statue and an altar of Victory inside. The description fits a
building shown on coins of 28 BC. A similar colonnade across the front
of the Diocletianic building is suggested by the squarish sockets below

the windows, which are part of the original construction and presumably supported a low pitched roof. Up to that level the exterior brickwork was once revetted with white marble; above, it was coated in fine white stucco to imitate marble. Remnants of the stucco-work can be seen just below the pediment. The bronze doors are modern replicas. The originals, somewhat enlarged and decorated with Chigi stars, can be seen at St John Lateran, where they form the main doors of the church, transferred there by Pope Alexander VII (Chigi)

▲ **Fig. 12.** Senate House. Coin of 28 BC

in 1660. A coin of Domitian (AD 81–96) was found in their core when they were being adapted to their new setting.

Inside, the walls are stripped and stark but the **marble floor** is one of the finest surviving examples of C4 *opus sectile*: stylized rosettes in squares alternate with opposed pairs of entwined cornucopias in rectangles, all worked in green and red porphyry on backgrounds of Numidian yellow and Phrygian purple. The three broad steps on either side, paved in Phrygian purple, could have accommodated five rows of chairs, for a total of about 300 senators. At the far end, between the two doors leading to the Forum of Caesar and preceded by a large slab of red porphyry, is a low platform, which will have borne the presiding statue and altar of Victory. You have to imagine the walls veneered in marble for two-thirds of the height, with painted stucco or mosaic above that, and the ceiling richly gilded. The lowest zone, against which the back row of chairs were placed, was relatively plainly clad in large panels of Phrygian purple with countersunk frames of white, but above head level there was an elaborate architectural scheme, starting in three-dimensional form with the three niches, which were framed with brightly coloured alabaster columns supported on brackets carved with acanthus leaves and spread eagles. The upper zones, partly surviving until 1562, had Corinthian columns and pilasters in flat relief framing lozenge and other geometric panel designs, in white and grey marble and red and green porphyry. The old Augustan interior had been further enlivened by two antique Greek panel pictures donated by the emperor: an encaustic wax painting signed by Nikias (fl.

▼ **Fig. 13.** Senate House. Lost marble wall panelling (C4 AD)

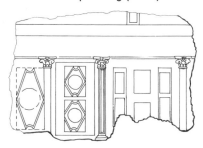

▲ **Fig. 14.** Marble balustrade with relief scene set in the Roman Forum

332 BC) commemorating a victory at the Nemean Games and a portrait by one Philocares, of a father and son, whose family likeness was skilfully enhanced by their difference in age.

In AD 630 the Senate House was converted by Pope Honorius I into the church of St Hadrian, almost all trace of which vanished in 1935–8 when the present restoration was carried out. The long horizontal slots on the façade, blocked with cement, once contained medieval burials (note the correspondingly higher ground level) and some fragments of medieval frescoes survive in the interior.

The two **marble balustrades** or parapets (*plutei*) now housed in the Senate House were found not far away, on the Forum square, where they had been mounted in the Late Empire on two rough travertine plinths (Fig. 27: 4). Their backs each show the same scene of a sow, ram and bull being led to sacrifice (the *suovetaurilia*), the fronts bear a composite scene of imperial benefaction set in the Forum, divided in two halves. In one half the emperor (headless and thus anonymous) stands at the left addressing a crowd from the Rostra in front of the Temple of Divus Julius; the Arch of Augustus appears in the background followed by the façade of the Temple of Castor; then, after a gap (the vicus Tuscus), there comes the arcaded façade of the Basilica Julia, in front of which is a figure seated on a tribunal, with a fig tree and a statue of Marsyas behind him. The same tree and statue appear at the left side of the other panel, with the Basilica Julia continuing in the background. In front a line of porters carry books (records of public debtors) to be burnt at the right end, in front of the imperial Rostra. Behind is the Ionic façade of the Temple of Saturn (the public treasury) and the Temple of Vespasian and Titus. They are usually dated on style to about AD 120 (late Trajanic/early Hadrianic) but could be later.

The Comitium and the Black Stone. Fig. 1: 9

The area in front of the Senate House was called the Comitium. In Republican times it had been the chief place of elected political assembly,

▲ **Fig. 15.** Marble balustrade with relief scene set in the Roman Forum

an inaugurated space delimited towards the Forum by a series of ritual pits, whose positions were still carefully recorded in the early imperial paving of the square (see Fig. 27: 9). Seven successive pavements have been identified beneath the present surface, the earliest dating back to the late C7 BC. By the beginning of the C3 a large circular arena surrounded by steps for the assembled citizens to stand or sit on had been laid out on axis with the old Senate House. Although those and other major elements of the Comitium—the tribunal, the Rostra, the foreigners' gallery—were moved or abolished in the course of time, certain features remained fixed, one being an area of ill-omen called the **Black Stone** (*lapis niger*), which can still be seen in front of the Arch of Septimius Severus, protected by metal railings. It consists of an irregular patch of bluish-grey limestone

▼ **Fig. 16.** 'Black stone'.
A. Plan of structures beneath. B. Plan at forum paving level

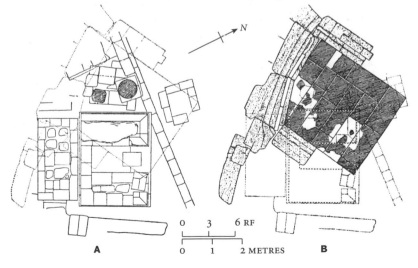

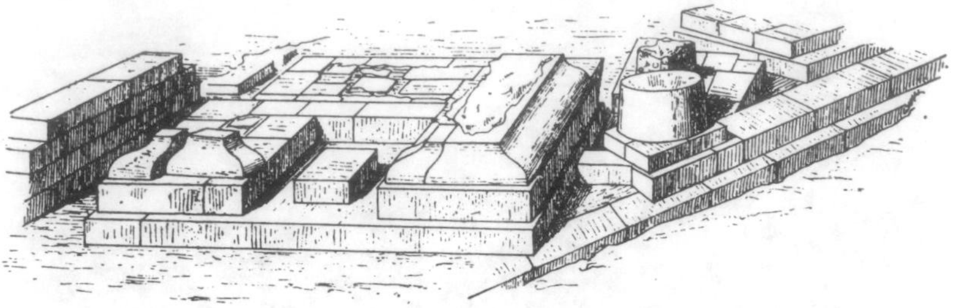

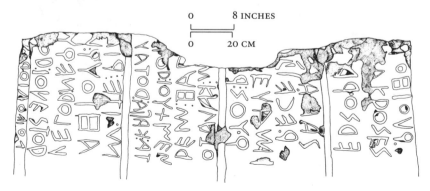

▲ **Fig. 17.** 'Black stone'. Axonometric view of structures beneath: *(left)* altar, *(right)* circular pedestal with inscribed pillar behind it

paving at a lower level than the surrounding white travertine and set off from that by upright slabs. Excavations underneath the paving (in 1899 and 1955) discovered that it overlies a gap in the circular steps which in its turn coincided with a group of three monuments: a U-shaped altar of the late C4 BC, a column base of the early C3, and an inscribed tufa block dating from the mid-C6 if not earlier. All had been truncated and buried in the early C1 BC when the Comitium was repaved and the Black Stone set to mark the spot. They were originally located on the edge of a pool, apparently an early cult site to which the inscribed block refers. Written in very early Latin with the lettering running vertically up and down in alternate directions, nobody knows quite what the text on the block says. It seems to be a set of regulations for a religious rite, in which the king (or high priest) and his herald perform various duties involving yoked animals. Most Romans probably couldn't read it either, and by the time the assemblage vanished beneath the black stone, Late Republic tradition was firmly convinced that it marked a grave: either that of Romulus, legendary founder of Rome, or his shepherd foster Faustulus, or Hostilius, grandfather of the third king of Rome Tullus Hostilius.

▼ **Fig. 18.** 'Black stone'. Inscriptions on the four sides of the rectangular pillar

Arch of Septimius Severus. Fig. 1: 10 ★

Towering 21 m. (70 RF) above the Comitium, the **triple arch** is sited on the triumphal route just before that turned hard left in front of the Temple of Concordia (Fig. 1: 11) to ascend to the Temple of Jupiter on the Capitoline hill. The road ran through the central passage only; the side passages were approached by steps. The inscription on both faces of the attic tells us that it was awarded to the emperor Septimius Severus and his sons Caracalla and Geta in AD 203, for having 'restored the Republic and expanded the dominion of the Roman people'. They had seized power ten years previously, following the assassination of the last Antonine emperor Commodus, and in the process of eliminating a rival contender in the East, had made an attack on Parthia (modern Iran). There they captured the capital city Ctesiphon in AD 197 and annexed a new province of Mesopotamia in AD 199. The gilded bronze lettering of the inscription has been robbed, revealing that the dedication was altered after Caracalla murdered Geta in AD 212: traces of earlier dowel holes show that *et* (and) was removed from the end of line 3, and line 4 *optimis fortissimisque principibus* (excellent and strongest princes) replaced *P. Septimio L. fil. Getae nobiliss(imo) Caesari* (most noble Caesar Geta).

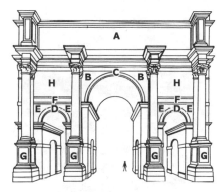

Key:
A. Dedicatory inscription
B. Flying figures of Victory carrying trophies, with personifications of the four seasons at their feet
C. Principal keystone carved with figure of Mars, God of War
D. Lateral keystones carved with lesser deities (one was Hercules)
E. Figures of river gods
F. Frieze showing booty and captives being displayed in the triumphal procession
G. Roman soldiers escorting Parthian prisoners
H. Panel reliefs relating episodes from the Parthian campaigns:
Forum side (left), lower zone: army leaving camp; *middle zone:* battle; *upper zone:* Septimus Severus addressing the troops and the liberation of Nisibis
Forum side (right), lower zone: Roman siege machines before the city of Edessa, which surrenders; *middle zone:* peoples submitting to Septimus Severus; *upper zone:* council of war being held in a fortified camp (at right), starting a new campaign (at left)
Capitoline side (left), lower half: attack on the city of Seleucia, on the Tigris river, and rout of the Parthians; *upper half:* fall of Seleucia and submission of the Parthians
Capitoline side (right), lower half: siege of Ctesiphon; *upper half:* the emperor addressing his army in front of the fallen city

▲ **Fig. 19.** Arch of Septimius Severus

▲ **Fig. 20.** Arch of Septimius Severus on a coin of AD 210

The eight free-standing composite columns and all the exterior facing of the arch are of the banded grey/white Proconnesian marble so beloved of C2 and C3 Rome, but much of the core of the structure, like the uppermost courses of the foundations which have been exposed at its feet, is of travertine. The attic interior is hollow, with a concrete vault supporting the roof, which coins show us was crowned with a forest of gilded bronze (or silver) statuary: in the centre the emperor and his sons riding in triumph in a chariot drawn by six horses, with foot-soldiers to either side and a cavalryman at each of the outer corners. More ornament was originally supplied by bronze appliqués (trophies and garlands) on the plain surfaces around the inscription panel. A staircase in the south pier, its door placed some 5 m. above ground level for security, leads up to the attic chamber and out to a walkway on top of the second cornice, and also up to the roof. These features made it an attractive candidate for a fortress in the Middle Ages, when towers were erected on top, and it bears the scars of other later structures erected around and within its massive shelter. At some time a sculptor or stonemason set up shop in the central passage, etching profiles on the walls, and stalls still occupied the side aisles until the early C19. This accounts for some but not all of the extensive damage to the richly carved decoration, which has suffered further from modern atmospheric pollution. The worst damage was caused by the original builders who (perhaps having to make do with limited supplies of stone) ignored the natural horizontal bedding of the marble. As a result, several of the column shafts have split vertically, large chunks of the figured reliefs have fallen away, numerous other projecting or isolated elements of the design have been lost, and artistically, the Arch's reputation is low. Actually, the carving was not at all bad. The figurative reliefs, very similar in style and technique to those on the Column of Marcus Aurelius (see p. 195), are three-dimensional interpretations of the painted panel pictures which Severus, as Roman generals had done ever since the old Republic, sent back to show the Senate how the campaigns were going and to be displayed in the triumphal procession.

Temple of Concordia Augusta. Fig. 1: 11

The mound of concrete behind the Arch of Septimius Severus belongs to the great temple–museum of Concordia Augusta (Harmony in the Imperial Family), one wing of which is still trapped under the adjacent terraces and staircase. The threshold of the cella survives in place, composed of two huge slabs of pink-grey Chian marble, and a section of the richly carved entablature is installed in the gallery of the 'Tabularium' above. There are also two column bases and a Corinthian capital from the interior order, with leaping rams instead of volutes at the angles, which can be seen in the Forum Antiquarium. Coins and the reports of various ancient authors tell us what we are missing.

Dedicated by Tiberius in AD 10, it replaced an **earlier temple** of Concord, which had been struck by lightning or otherwise burned down in 9 BC. The earlier building, whose podium has been identified within that of the later structure, was a conventional rectangular temple *peripteros sine postico* of 41 × 30 m. (140 × 100 RF) built by the consul Lucius Opimius in 121 BC. It had celebrated the victory of the aristocracy over democracy, the defeat of the reforms sought by the Gracchi. The **new temple** conveyed a very different message. It was laid out with the cella crossways, the entrance on the long side through a narrower porch at the top of a tall flight of steps, to either side of which stood statues of Hercules and Mercury, symbolizing respectively the security and prosperity of the Augustan regime. Inlaid in bronze on the threshold was Mercury's wand (*caduceus*), an emblem of peace. On the apex of the pediment statues of three female deities linked arms, presumably Concord herself, with either Pax (Peace) and Salus (Health)—or Securitas (Security) and Fortuna (Good Fortune). Beside them stood two soldiers holding spears, Tiberius and his brother Drusus, in whose name the temple was dedicated, paid for by their share of the booty from their German triumph in 7 BC, represented by the figures of Victory at the outer angles.

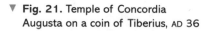

▼ **Fig. 21.** Temple of Concordia Augusta on a coin of Tiberius, AD 36

The cella, a vast hall of 45 × 23 m. (150 × 80 RF) and often used for Senate meetings, was designed to display a fine collection of Greek works of art: a statue of Hestia, the Greek goddess of the domestic hearth (Roman Vesta) which Tiberius requisitioned from the people of Paros, five two- and three-figure

bronzes by Greek sculptors of the C4 and C3 BC, and panel paintings by Zeuxis, Nikias, and Theoros. Augustus gave four elephants carved in obsidian (black volcanic glass) and Livia a famous sardonyx gem said to be that which the pirate ruler Polycrates of Samos (*c.*540 BC) had thrown into the sea to Fortune, only to have it miraculously returned to him in the belly of a fish.

For the 'Tabularium' see p. 239.

▼ **Fig. 22.** Temple of Vespasian and Titus. Reconstructed façade

Temple of Vespasian and Titus and the Precinct of the Harmonious Gods

The three columns forming an angle immediately to the left of the Temple of Concord belong to the **Temple of Vespasian and Titus** (Fig. 1: 12), which was squeezed in between Concordia and the front of the Temple of Saturn in the 80s AD. In the process it blocked the foot of a staircase which originally led out from underneath the 'Tabularium'. The emperor Vespasian, builder of the Colosseum, died at his country estate near Rieti in July AD 79 with the immortal words, 'Pity, I think I'm turning into a God.' His son Titus succeeded him and made arrangements for his deification but then died himself soon after, in AD 81, and it was left to his younger brother Domitian to complete the temple, dedicating it to Titus as well. The letters ESTITUER on the architrave at the front come from the last word of an inscription put on the temple by Septimius Severus and Caracalla after they restored it (*restituer[unt]*) in the early C3 AD. What was restored, apart from the dedicatory inscription, is not evident; the surviving architecture, in white Italian marble, is all Flavian work (*c.* AD 80–85). The order is Corinthian, 48 RF (14.2 m.) high, with an **elaborately decorated entablature** including a striking frieze of bulls' skulls interspersed with the implements of sacrifice (helmet, knife, axe, plate, jug).

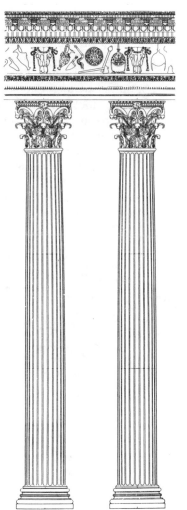

▼ **Fig. 23.** Temple of Vespasian and Titus. Corinthian order

The next building along the line (Fig. 1: 13) was built, or rebuilt, at the same time. It consists of a **trapezoidal platform**, once paved in marble, raised on seven vaulted chambers. Eight other chambers open off the platform to the rear. The portico of twelve fluted Corinthian columns in Carystian green marble (the five shafts in white travertine are modern), their capitals decorated with trophies, probably dates from the reign of Hadrian (AD 118–38), but the inscription on the architrave records that the whole precinct and its statues (DEUM C)ONSENTIUM—of the Harmonious Gods—were repaired by Vettius Agorius Praetextatus, who was the city prefect in AD 367 and a determined pagan in an increasingly Christian world. The cult had probably been introduced to Rome in the late C3 BC at the time of the Second Punic War against Hannibal, and was a Roman version of the Athenian Twelve Gods (six male paired with six female): Jupiter and Juno, Neptune and Minerva, Mars and Venus, Apollo and Diana, Volcanus and Vesta, Mercury and Ceres. It was closely connected with the cult of Saturn (the Roman equivalent of the Greek Kronos), whose large temple lies close by on the opposite side of the road.

Temple of Saturn. Fig. 1: 14

The façade of eight Ionic columns on a tall footing of travertine blocks belongs to the **Temple of Saturn**. The inscription on the architrave reads SENATUS POPVLVSQVE ROMANVS | INCENDIO CONSVMPTVM RESTITUIT (Destroyed by fire, restored by the Senate and People of Rome). The restoration took place in about AD 360–80—another significant manifestation of pagan revivalism amongst the politically disgruntled senators of late C4 Rome. The cult of Saturn was very old, the first temple having been dedicated on this site at the beginning of the Republic (probably in 497 BC), and precisely what sort of deity Saturn was is obscure. Unusually for a god, his images show him veiled, and he holds a pruning knife or sickle; in some respects he was related to the Greek Kronos. His feast day was 17 December, the *Saturnalia*, when the feet of the cult statue in the temple, normally tied together with wool, were released. It was the day when slaves were allowed to do what they liked, family and friends exchanged gifts and there was general merry-making (by the C4 AD the festival was already moving closer to the New Year, eventually to become Christmas). From the earliest times the temple had also housed the public treasury, and it continued to do so (in the more limited sense of the municipal treasury of Rome) under the Empire; some of the rooms beneath the Precinct of the Harmonious Gods possibly served as treasury offices.

▼ **Fig. 24.** Image of Saturn from the Calendar of AD 354

The temple steps have disappeared, except for part of one of the vaults in their substructures, where the treasury itself may have been located. Most of the podium to the rear has also gone, but the **remnants of the façade** are an excellent example of *spolia* (recycled elements from older buildings). Only the Ionic capitals, carved in brilliant white Thasian marble in the latest Late Antique style, were new. All the other material was reused. The column shafts are all in Egyptian granite, the six across the front in grey (Mons Claudianus), the two side ones in pink (Aswan), but they derive from several different colonnades. Only three are monoliths, the others have been made up by joining two broken lengths together. The architrave blocks, with a frieze of acanthus leaves and palmettes on the inner face, are datable to about 30 BC and were probably salvaged from the previous temple building, which had burned down. That, shown on the *plutei* relief (Fig. 15), was also Ionic. Vowed and paid for by Lucius Munatius Plancus with the booty from his Alpine triumph of 43 BC, it had been one of the last great temples financed by private individuals before the Imperial monopoly set in. Four of the column bases in the present building probably came from the same source; the other four are a miscellany, two of C4 workmanship, two from two other different buildings, one perhaps of the C3.

Vicus Jugarius

The street leading from the Forum, beside the Temple of Saturn, along the flank of the Capitoline hill down to the Forum Holitorium and southern Campus Martius is of great antiquity. It was originally much longer, starting from the Quirinal hill, and its name may predate the customary sense of 'yoke' and signify only 'high road' as opposed to low road. In the Imperial period it started beside the Basilica Julia, near a fountain called **Servilius' pool**, which might be identified with the concrete foundation (Fig. 1: 16) or with a basin recently excavated at the SW corner of the Basilica. The remnants of a substantial brick arch (Fig. 1: 15) wedged between the Temple of Saturn and the Basilica Julia, may be the **Arch of Tiberius**, erected in AD 16 in celebration of the recovery of the legionary standards lost by Varus to the Germans in AD 9.

Rostra (Orators' Platform). Fig. 1: 19

A platform for public speeches in this commanding position on axis with the Forum square was part of Julius Caesar's grand scheme of 46 BC, replacing one which had been located somewhere on the outer edge of the old circular Comitium. Initially, the replacement appears to have copied the form of its predecessor: the rear of the present structure (Fig. 1: 17) consists of a concrete core with a curved front, faced with coloured marbles (panels of pink-grey from Chios and vertical bands of black-red from Teos), reproducing the curved segment of the Comitium wall, approached by a bank of (perhaps straight) steps behind. After Caesar's

▲ **Fig. 25.** Rostra. Reconstruction

death, Augustus adjusted the steps appropriately and extended the platform a further 30 RF forwards into the rectangle we see today. The front wall, 80 RF long, 12 RF high, is mostly restoration (1904) but some of the original tufa blocks survive at the NE end. The marble moulding at the foot once supported a marble facing, capped by a heavy marble cornice. The vertical slots with large dowel holes presumably held the **rostra**, the sharp bronze prows taken as trophies from captured enemy warships, which it had been customary to mount on public speakers' platforms, hence the name, ever since the C4 BC (the first recorded instance followed Rome's victory over the Latins at sea off Antium (Anzio) in 338 BC). Many statues, honorary columns, and other dedications clustered on and around the rostra platform in the course of the Empire. Somewhere at the back was the *milliarium aureum* (the Golden Milestone), set up by Augustus in 20 BC, and the *umbilicus Urbis* (the Navel of the City), perhaps to be identified with the cylindrical brick structure (Fig. 1: 18).

A set of five honorary columns was erected on the rostra itself in AD 303, when the emperor Diocletian visited Rome for the first time to celebrate the twentieth year of his reign, which was also the tenth year of the Tetrarchy (the four-emperor system he had instigated in 293). The column shafts (lying in fragments on the ground to the north of the custodians' hut) were all monoliths of rose-pink Aswan granite, the middle one 40 RF high, carrying a statue of Jupiter; the others 36 RF high, bearing the four reigning emperors. One of their Proconnesian marble pedestals, the **Decennalia base**, was found in 1547 and is displayed close by (Fig. 27: 2). Carved in relief on the front side are two winged Victories holding up a shield on which one has written CAESARUM DECENNALIA FELICITER (Happy Tenth Anniversary of the Caesars). The reliefs on the other three sides represent the vows for another happy decade. On the left side is a procession of Roman senators wearing the ornately folded togas which symbolized their rank; on the right side a bull, ram and pig are being brought to sacrifice, and on the back is the scene at the sacrificial altar, where an emperor, with the toga-clad Genius of the Senate behind him, is being crowned by a little winged Victory. Mars looks on from the left, Roma (headless) is seated at the right, with the sun-god Sol Invictus hovering behind her. The plinth on which the Decennalia base has been

▼ **Fig. 26.** Decennalia base. The Emperor sacrificing

placed (Fig. 27: 1) was the **base of an equestrian statue**. Although nameless, it is aligned not with the Rostra but with the Via Sacra and the Arch of Septimius Severus and probably carried a large bronze statue of Severus or some later emperor. On the other side of the road in front of the other side passage of the arch is another large equestrian statue base, whose inscription fortunately survives to tell us it was dedicated in AD 352/3 in honour of Constantius II.

In the later C5 a small brick extension to the Rostra was built at its NE end, in front of the Arch of Septimius Severus. Fragments of its cornice blocks are inscribed with the name of Junius Valentinus, Urban Prefect in AD 455–76, possibly honouring the emperors Leo and Anthemius for repelling a Vandal attack on Rome in AD 472. Earlier in the century the threat had been Alaric and the Goths (who succeeded in sacking Rome in AD 410) and several monuments were set up in this vicinity lauding the imperial army of Arcadius and Honorius. Only one survives, the tall marble pedestal (actually an old equestrian statue base set on its end) perched on a travertine block (Fig. 27: 3). A fifteen-line inscription on the side facing the street says that it was set up by Pisidius Romulus, city prefect in AD 405, on behalf of the Senate and People in celebration of the 'fidelity and valour of the most devoted troops' in a battle against the Goths won under the command of a general whose name has been chiselled off. He was Stilicho, who defeated Alaric's Goths at Pollentia (Pollenza) and Verona in AD 402 and Radagaisus' Ostrogoths at Fiesole in AD 403 but was executed in AD 408 and his memory erased. All that is left of the statue which the pedestal supported are the sockets for his feet, facing the Arch of Septimius Severus.

Column of Phocas. Fig. 1: 21

The **fluted Corinthian column** of Proconnesian marble, 50 RF (14.8 m.) high, rises on a pedestal of marble blocks at the top of a pyramid of steps to an overall height of 75 RF (22.2 m.). On the north side of the marble pedestal is an inscription: 'To our best, most gracious, most pious lord Phocas, supreme commander in perpetuity, crowned by God, triumphant, emperor for ever. Smaragdus, previously praepositor at the Palatium, patrician and exarch of Italy, devoted to his Grace because of the innumerable benefactions of his piety, the peace brought to Italy and liberty preserved, placed this shining statue of his Majesty on top of this sublime column to his perennial glory, on 1 August AD 608.' Phocas was actually a brutal centurion in the Byzantine army who had usurped the throne in 602 by assassinating the emperor Maurice and his five sons, and was himself deposed and tortured to death in 610. As the careful wording indicates, Smaragdus only placed Phocas' statue on top, he did not claim to have built the column monument itself, which belongs to the C4, in its turn recycling an earlier monument taken from elsewhere. The style of the

Corinthian capital is typical of the mid-C2 and the seven drums composing the shaft have their joins faintly countersigned with letters (A-A, B-B, etc.) so that they could be reassembled in the new location. The location seems odd until you realize that it is on axis with the Argiletum but also calculated to fit in with the line of honorary columns along the south side of the Forum. The spreading outer base measures 50 by 50 RF but is not quite square, each side apparently taking its alignment from the nearest adjacent monument. The marble steps, preserved only on the south side, were made by cutting rectangular frieze blocks across the diagonal and are supported on an assortment of tufa blocks piled up around an inner base of brick-faced concrete, visible on the north side, which was demolished in 1903 to find the end of the Surdinus inscription in the Forum paving (Fig. 27: 6).

The Forum Pavement. Fig. 27

Much of the travertine paving in the centre of the Forum has been robbed or removed to permit modern excavations. What is left is a horizontal palimpsest, endlessly patched and adjusted, invaded and overlaid, in which the ghosts of at least twenty individual monuments can be detected (Fig. 27). Only the more evident or significant are mentioned here. The bronze inscription (Fig. 27: 6) almost 13 m. long near the Column of Phocas has been restored as L. NAEVIUS L.[F. SURD]INUS PR(aetor), the name of a man who was in charge of the mint several times between 23 and 9 BC. The size and placing of the inscription suggests that it relates to a repaving (overseen by Surdinus, probably after the fire of 14 BC) of the whole Forum square, whose present level is therefore essentially that of the Augustan period, which then remained fixed thereafter. This could easily happen, because in the Augustan period the Forum ceased to serve as an amphitheatre. Forum fixtures and fittings, previously kept low or movable, were replaced by more substantial monuments, and there was less and less scope for any radical change. While the streets around it rose, the level in the Forum square stayed where it was, eventually set off by high kerbstones.

The unpaved area (Fig. 27: 5) was planted in 1956 with a fig, vine, and olive in the belief that it was the grove where the statue of Marsyas stood, but seems rather to have been the site of the praetor's tribunal (the statue, a fig-tree and the tribunal are shown on the *plutei* (Fig. 14)). Over to the right the trapezoidal area with low roof (Fig. 27: 10) is the **lacus Curtius** (Curtius' pool), missing its surrounding parapet wall. Two phases of paving are visible within its boundaries, the lower one in tufa dates from the early C2 BC, by which time the Romans were already confused about who Curtius had been and what his dried-up 'pool' signified. He was either a Sabine knight, Mettius Curtius, who fell into a marsh when fighting against Romulus; or a Roman knight Marcus Curtius who sacrificed

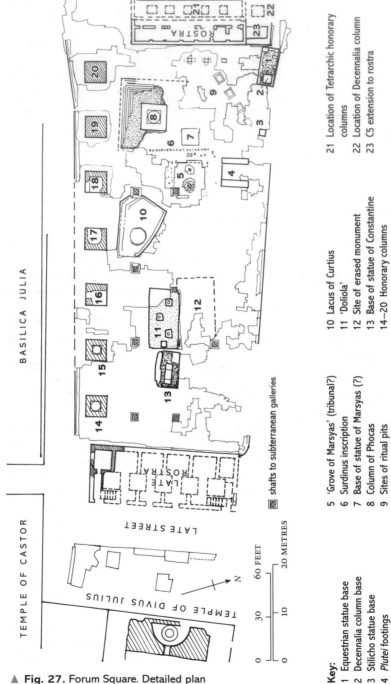

▲ **Fig. 27.** Forum Square. Detailed plan

Key:

1 Equestrian statue base
2 Decennalia column base
3 Stilicho statue base
4 *Plutei* footings

5 'Grove of Marsyas' (tribunal?)
6 Surdinus inscription
7 Base of statue of Marsyas (?)
8 Column of Phocas
9 Sites of ritual pits

10 Lacus of Curtius
11 'Doliola'
12 Site of erased monument
13 Base of statue of Constantine
14–20 Honorary columns

21 Location of Tetrarchic honorary columns
22 Location of Decennalia column
23 C5 extension to rostra

▨ shafts to subterranean galleries

▲ **Fig. 28.** Relief from the Lacus of Curtius

himself and his horse to save the city by leaping into a chasm which
opened in the Forum; or he was Gaius Curtius, consul in 445 BC,
who consecrated a site which had been struck by lightning. The low
roof at the eastern end protects the crumbling remains of a twelve-sided
base enclosing a circle of tufa blocks with a hole in the middle, into
which in Augustus' day people used to throw coins for good luck. At the

▼ **Fig. 29.** Lacus Curtius. Plan

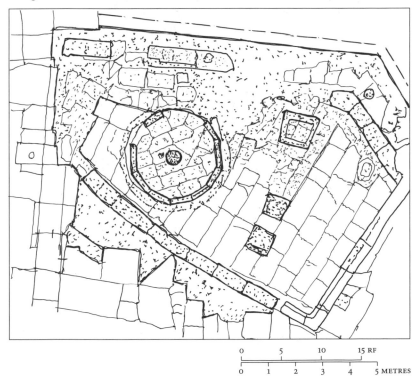

```
0        5        10        15 RF
|————————|————————|————————|
0    1    2    3    4    5 METRES
```

western end stood two (previously three) votive altars or statue bases and possibly set somewhere in or on the parapet was a relief now in the Palazzo dei Conservatori Museum (Fig. 28). The next large gap in the paving (Fig. 27: 11) was made in 1903–4 to uncover a yet greater enigma: the '**doliola**', 400 cubic metres of concrete over 5 m. thick, with several travertine blocks set in its upper surface. The top of each block has a square cutting, in which traces of bronze and carbon were found; one set lower down in the concrete had a lid and contained a group of pottery dating from about 675–650 BC. Since the concrete is evidently centuries later, the explanation offered by the excavators was that in digging the foundations for whatever the concrete mass was meant to support, the builders came across an ancient tomb, whose grave goods they then religiously redeposited in the base of the new structure. (That such surprises could lurk in the subsoil of this part of the Forum was demonstrated by a sounding just to the south, which encountered at a depth of 6 m. the skeletons of a man, woman, and child, apparently bound together and drowned as human sacrifices at some remote period.) The concrete rectangle was once capped with large blocks which would have brought it up to the level of the present paving or just above. It used to be interpreted as the base of a huge equestrian statue of Domitian, known to have been set up in the centre of the Forum in AD 91, but that is probably represented by a large rectangular patch in the paving immediately to the north (Fig. 27: 12). What else it might be is anyone's guess; the three travertine blocks are symmetrically arranged. The cuttings in their tops could be the bottoms of sockets which continued upward through the missing stone topping, perhaps to support large poles on which to display trophies or for other shows. There is a complicated sequence of large rectangular footings in this general area for, until the Late Imperial Rostra intervened to cut off the eastern end in front of the Temple of Divus Julius, it was the centre of the Forum. Some of the rectangles could indeed be equestrian statues, but they could also be arches; two were buildings. The latest of the series is Fig. 27: 13 (three blocks poised on a pile of concrete flanked by a broken Numidian yellow column), possibly the base of an **equestrian statue of Constantine** the Great. It is on axis with the centre of the **Late Imperial Rostra** to the east (inadvertently demolished as medieval by the C19 excavators and now marked by the large patch of grass).

Honorary Columns. Fig. 27: 14–20

Spaced at equal intervals along the southern edge of the Forum square are seven enormous brick pedestals, in varying states of preservation: they were originally faced with marble and had cores of *peperino* stone which made them attractive targets for stone robbers. The first two at the eastern end (Nos. 14, 15) have been restored but the Phrygian purple shaft on No. 15 ought to be on No. 14 and the grey granite column on No. 14 may not belong at all, having been found some way away to the east (the holes for metal attachments to its shaft are interesting; it may have been a *columna rostrata*, a column commemorating a naval victory, decorated with the bronze prows of ships). The columns on bases 18–20 had shafts of rose-pink Aswan granite, like those of Diocletian's five-column monument of AD 303 on the Rostra. Stamped bricks used in their construction indicate a similar date, at the end of the reign of Diocletian, though they could be later, for the same bricks are found in buildings of Maxentius (AD 306–12) and early in the reign of Constantine (AD 313–33). Both the latter emperors are perhaps more likely than Diocletian to have wished to erect another seven statues (and possibly an eighth if we count the Phocas Column). Either way, the result was to create a great columnar façade in front of the Basilica Julia, to which the Forum square, shortened by the new Rostra at the east end, now became a forecourt, to be approached from the Argiletum (hence the significance of the placing of the Phocas Column).

Basilica Julia

The **Basilica** (for plan, see Fig. 1) is now mainly reduced to its vast floor, 107 m. (360 RF) long by over 61 m. wide, approached on the Forum side by a flight of steps which increase in number from one end to the other to accommodate the slope between the Temple of Saturn and the Temple of Castor. The site was previously occupied by a row of shops and the old Basilica Sempronia, which had been built by Ti. Sempronius Gracchus in 169 BC. Excavations under the floor at the eastern end in the 1960s found part of the earlier basilica and the large aristocratic house that it had replaced. The name Julia comes from Julius Caesar, who dedicated the first version while it was not yet finished in 46 BC (in company with his new Forum and the temple of Venus Genetrix). It was completed by Augustus but burned down soon afterwards and took another twenty years to rebuild, being dedicated once more in AD 12, this time in the names of Augustus' deceased heirs Gaius and Lucius Caesar. The later title did not catch on, perhaps because of the possible confusion with the porticus of the same name on the opposite side of the square. The front was made entirely in marble; the one standing pier is a reconstruction by Pietro Rosa who excavated the building in the 1850s (see also Fig. 2, on p. 62). The internal piers were originally of travertine with a white marble veneer. The outer aisles, paved in white marble, were two storeys high, with an upper gallery at first floor level (the staircases must have been located in the rooms along the south side of the basilica).

The basilica was the seat of the Court of the Hundred (the *centumviri*), a special civil court which generally dealt with matters of inheritance and actually numbered 180 judges when they all sat together at an important trial. Pliny the Younger describes the scene at one where he pleaded on behalf of a senatorial lady suing her 80-year-old father, who had disinherited her ten days after he took a new wife. In addition to the judges the place was packed with onlookers. Both parties had brought in large numbers of seats for their supporters, behind which were rows of people standing as far as the outer walls, and the crowd spilled upwards to the galleries, hanging over the rails in their efforts to hear the proceedings. The front steps and the paving in the aisles are covered with **gameboards** made by the many who idled away their days around the Forum courts.

When the basilica was rebuilt following the fire of AD 283, many of the travertine piers were replaced in brick-faced concrete and the side aisles were vaulted in concrete (segments of vaults with stuccowork coffering were found in the excavations of 1852 but destroyed in 1872). The central nave was paved with Numidian yellow, Phrygian purple, and 'Lucullan' black (the present surfaces composed of marble fragments are modern) and soared three storeys high to be lit by windows over the tops of the side aisle roofs. Its own roof, spanning 16 m. (54 RF), is likely always to have been of wood. In the Late Empire Gabinius Vettius Probianus, urban prefect in AD 377 or 416 carried out restorations and embellishments to the building, transferring some ancient Greek bronze statues into its shelter. The plinths of three survive, with labels declaring them to have been respectively the work (*opus*) of Praxiteles, Polyclitus, and Timarchos. The latter two and the pedestal of Probianus' own statue recording his deeds are mounted on the steps towards the centre of the façade.

The side away from the Forum has not been fully excavated but seems to have been lined with large *tabernae*, which could have housed the court secretaries, public scribes, and perhaps other branches of the public administration, as well as some bankers or money-changers, the *nummulari de basilica Iulia*, who are recorded in an inscription (*CIL* VI 9709).

Somewhere in the area beyond was a commercial sector called the *Graecostadium* (possibly meaning market for Greek slaves) and also the great Temple of Divus Augustus, on the site of the first house he had lived in before he entered public life. Vowed by the Senate on his death in AD 14 but not completed until AD 37, the temple was destroyed by fire and rededicated by Domitian in AD 89/90, to be restored again by Antoninus Pius in the late 150s.

At its east end the basilica opened on to the **Vicus Tuscus** (Street of the Etruscans), which ran along the higher ground at the foot of the Palatine hill to the Circus Maximus. It was famous as the route for processions during the Roman Games (*Ludi Romani*), when statues of the gods were paraded on wagons down from the Capitol to the Circus. During the Republic it was lined on both sides with wealthy houses and shops, mostly replaced in the course of the Empire by specialized commercial buildings (*horrea*).

Temple of Castor. Fig. 1: 24

Readily recognized by its three standing columns which have been a landmark for centuries, the surviving structure was a rebuild contemporary with the rest of the major Augustan monuments on the Forum. Tiberius dedicated it in AD 6, in his own name and that of his brother Drusus. All the marble revetment and the tufa blocks have been removed from the outside of the podium, leaving only the concrete core, but it once measured 108 × 168 RF (32 × 50 m.) and was 23.5 RF (almost 7 m.) high. Twenty-five small chambers are incorporated into its design, interspaced with the foundation piers of the temple colonnade. Most were probably occupied in connection with the temple's function as the office of weights and measures and a banking centre but (judging by finds from the drains) one was apparently used by a dentist.

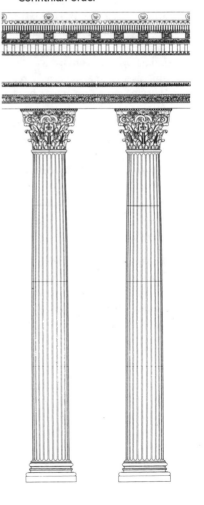

▼ **Fig. 30.** Temple of Castor. Corinthian order

The temple proper, in white Italian marble, a *peripteros* with eight columns at the front and back and eleven down the sides, was of the Corinthian order, 50 RF (14.8 m.) high. The entablature added a further 12.5 RF (3.8 m.) for a total roof height of perhaps 100 RF—as high as the Basilica Julia. The front of the podium was originally designed, like that of the adjacent Temple of Julius Caesar, to provide a tribunal or speakers' platform, approached by lateral staircases, but by the early C3 AD that arrangement had been changed into a single frontal flight. The building may have been in a state of disrepair by the C4 AD, though the cult endured long thereafter.

Castor and his twin brother Pollux were demi-gods and semi-mythical cavalry heroes. The sons of Jupiter, they were equivalent to the Greek Dioscuri, Pollux born immortal, Castor mortal. Their cult is attested in the Greek areas of south Italy already in about 570–530 BC, spreading to Latium soon after; the temple in Rome was founded only a generation or so later. Tradition had it that two young men on white horses appeared in the Roman ranks at the height of the battle of Lake Regillus on 15 July 499 or 496 BC, and were seen later that same day watering their horses at the spring of Juturna beside the Forum, telling of Roman victory. The battle marked Rome's defeat of the Latins and the first temple, vowed by the victorious general Aulus Postumius, was dedicated in 484 BC. Bits of the original temple podium have been traced within the later; it was on the same huge scale. In the following centuries Castor became increasingly important as a symbol of Roman military success, favoured especially by the Roman knights (*equites*). Restorations were made to the Forum temple in the first half of the C2 BC, perhaps by L. Aemilius Paullus in celebration of his victory over the Macedonians at Pydna in 168 BC, and then again in 117 BC, even more substantially, by Lucius Caecilius Metellus after his victories in Dalmatia. Not long after, another victorious Caecilius Metellus built a second temple near the circus Flaminius. A great cavalry parade was held each year on 15 July commemorating the initial victory at Lake Regillus. As many as 5,000 young men took part, carrying spears and shields and wearing olive wreaths and purple robes with scarlet bands, led by two youths on white horses, representing Castor and Pollux. Under Augustus, taking advantage of the rebuilding required after the fire of 14 or 9 BC, the Forum cult was 'imperialized': a new feast day was instituted, on 27 January, and the heavenly twins were associated with the Imperial heirs-apparent Gaius and Lucius Caesar. In the event, both princes died before the new temple was ready and the association passed instead to Tiberius and his brother Drusus (who had died on campaign in 9 BC after falling from a horse).

Domitianic Hall—Ramp—S. Maria Antiqua

The huge buttressed walls in brick-faced concrete immediately behind the Temple of Castor started life under Domitian in the early 90s AD. They eliminated an atrium-like structure with a peristyle court, whose razed remains have been partly excavated and tentatively identified with the *domus Gai*, built as an adjunct to the Palatine palaces by the mad emperor Caligula in the 40s AD. Domitian apparently had an even larger scheme, to extend and restructure the whole of this corner of the Palatine hill, including the ramp of steps and the House of the Vestals, but the work may not have got very far before he was assassinated in AD 96. Fronting onto the Vicus Tuscus (perhaps directly opposite the Temple of Divine Augustus) was the great **hall** (Fig. 1: 25), its back wall even now rising 26 m. high, almost on a level with the palace on the hill behind. The façade has been lost (if ever built, it was probably composed mainly of arcades or columns). The interior was apparently intended to be lined with elaborate marble architecture framing the tall niches in the walls, but was never finished. Whether the space was meant to be roofed (if so, the roof will have been of wood) and what its function was to be, we do not know. Although connected by a side passage to a common portico which runs along the northern flank, it seems to have been otherwise independent of the structures behind it (the two rectangular openings in the back wall were clearly part of the original construction but are low and probably only temporary). Under Hadrian in the early C2 AD the shell was converted into a *horreum*, with storerooms and offices along the long walls and a paved courtyard down the middle, complementing the adjacent *horrea Agrippiana* or *Agrippiniana* (named after Marcus Agrippa or Agrippina), which extend between it and the church of S. Teodoro to the south (see map, p. 242). The short brick walls on the street side belong to this phase. The many holes and horizontal and diagonal cuttings higher up the interior bear witness to various later adaptations, down to the C19.

Behind the great hall the axis of the original building turns through 90° to open on to the area east of the Temple of Castor. Tucked in against the hillside at the end of the northern portico is the entrance to a tall **covered ramp** (Fig. 1: 28), which substituted for the lower section of the stairs which had for many years run down from the NW corner of the Palatine to a point between the Temple of Vesta and the spring of Juturna. In Domitian's plan the lower stretch only served the House of the Vestals; his new ramp led off above the junction with the western end of the Via Nova and probably continued upward to connect directly with the Imperial palace itself. To allow light into the corridors the roof level in the space between the ramp and the great hall was kept low. There, in line with the Lacus Juturnae (Fig. 1: 31), a wide entrance through the northern portico leads first into a square hall or court (Fig. 1: 26), a smaller version of the great hall, with niches all around the walls. From that a yet wider doorway allows a clear view into a peristyle atrium (Fig. 1: 27), on the far side of which is a rectangular chamber, flanked by two smaller ones. The axiality of the arrangement suggests some ceremonial purpose focused on the innermost chamber. That and the atrium (whose concrete vaults were reconstructed in 1986 to protect the interior) owe their present configuration to the **church of S. Maria Antiqua**, installed in the middle or second half of the C6, perhaps during the papacy of Justin II (AD 565–78). By then Belisarius had recaptured Rome from the Goths and a Byzantine governor had taken up residence on the Palatine, to which the Domitianic ramp may have already become the principal entrance, with the buildings at the foot as its guardroom/vestibule. Few structural changes were involved, except for the four granite columns and their capitals, which replaced earlier brick piers, but the marble and mosaic pavements and the decorations on the walls are all early medieval. In the mid-C9 the church had to be abandoned, probably because of the earthquake of AD 847, and its cult functions (including a famous icon of Mary to which the epithet *antiqua* referred) were transferred to S. Maria Nova. During its short life, it had been richly endowed with wall-paintings, notably by the C8 popes John VII (705–7), Zacharias (741–52) and Paul I (757–67). In the left-hand aisle are paintings on three registers, the upper two illustrating the Old Testament stories of Jacob and Joseph, the lower one showing Christ with nine Greek saints to the left and eleven Latin saints to the right, all in

▼ **Fig. 31.** S. Maria Antiqua. Icon of Mary (now in S. Francesca Romana)

rich Byzantine costumes and all with their names written in Greek. On the wall to the right of the apse is an extraordinary palimpsest of paintings from the early C6 to C8. Out in the forecourt, which must have been given some sort of roof and was full of burials, the wall-niches contain patches of further Christian wall-paintings. Most have been removed to safety in the church but in the niche to the right of the outer entrance are C9 images of Saints Agnes and Cecilia, with identifying labels written in Greek. Other paintings belong to later redecorations, when the inner church had been destroyed but the forecourt continued in use as a church of St Anthony, associated with a monastery, and was not abandoned until the late C11 or early C12.

The apsidal hall (Fig. 1: 29), called the **Oratory of the Forty Martyrs**, takes its name from the wall-paintings in the apse, which depict the forty Christian soldiers who were martyred in Armenia during the persecutions of AD 303, frozen to death in an icy lake. They date from the C8 or C9, when the hall was presumably part of the larger complex of S. Maria Antiqua. Another painting on the right-hand wall may represent St Anthony the hermit, and the roughly-made floor of marble fragments is also medieval. The main construction, however, is contemporary with the ramp (started by Domitian, completed by Trajan in the early C2 AD). Placed in line with the western end of the Via Nova, it could have supported an upper storey, or a terrace, at the higher level, but what its original function was at ground level is not known.

The Spring (*fons*) and Pool (*lacus*) of Juturna

The reconstructed white marble shrine backing on to the Oratory of the Forty Martyrs at an oblique angle marks the spring of Juturna, a primary source of fresh water to which a route had led down from the Palatine from time immemorial. The shrine is a late rebuild after the fire of AD 283, but reused the architectural elements as well as the foundations of its predecessor, including the architrave inscribed IVTVRNAE S[----], to be completed as *sacrum* (sacred to Juturna), or SPQR (to Juturna from the Senate and People of Rome). In front of the shrine is the cast of a marble well-head (*puteal*) which was found in place, covered in inscriptions dedicating it to Juturna by one M. Barbatius Pollio, *aed[ilis] cur[ulis]* (a city magistrate) in the 20s BC. The altar mounted beside it was a stray find and may not belong. Its figures of an armed man and a woman with a lance are generally identified as either Juturna and Turnus or Mars and Venus. Juturna is a complex figure; a Latin goddess (a 'nymph') of spring water and of good health, mythical wife of the god Janus, daughter of the river Volturnus, mother of Fons, she also appears in the Trojan legend as the sister of Turnus, king of the Rutuli whom Aeneas had to defeat on his way to found Rome (Vergil, *Aeneid* Book 12). In the late C3 the curators of Rome's water supply made numerous votive dedications to the spring,

▲ **Fig. 32.** Shrine of Juturna. Reconstruction (1953–5)

having perhaps transferred their office here from the Campus Martius (where there was another temple of Juturna, see pp. 218–9).

Ten metres to the north of the shrine and aligned instead with the Temple of Castor, is the **water basin** at which Castor and Pollux are supposed to have appeared watering their horses after the battle of Lake Regillus. Its complicated sequence of structures were first excavated around 1900 and have recently been re-excavated. The basin was first 'monumentalized' about the middle of the C2 BC, probably in 168 BC, when L. Aemilius Paullus is recorded as having adorned it with marble statues of the twins holding their horses in celebration of his victory over the Macedonian Greeks at Pydna (fragments of the four statues have been found and are reconstructed in the Forum Antiquarium). In its earliest phase the basin was rectangular, 7.5 m. by over 9 m., lined simply with waterproof concrete, with an edging of tufa blocks. In the later C2 BC (possibly at the same time that Metellus rebuilt the adjacent Temple of Castor in 117 BC), the long sides were shortened to form a square and a pedestal was constructed in the middle (which could have held the statue group). In a third phase, again likely to be associated with a rebuilding of the Temple of Castor, this time by Tiberius in AD 6, the basin was reduced to about 5 m. square, with a ledge running round the inside, lined and edged in white marble. Alterations to the lower part of the ramp in the early C2 included a series of *tabernae* which encroached on the area from the rear. The largest of these, located directly behind the pool, has a small rectangular niche for a statue in the back wall, on axis with the pedestal in the pool. In Late Antiquity further structures were erected on all sides and a wall (perhaps a staircase) was carried over the eastern end of the pool on a brick arch.

Temple of Divus Julius. Fig. 1: 33

When Julius Caesar was assassinated in 44 BC he was given a public funeral. His body was carried to the Forum on an ivory couch and set up on the Rostra in a gilded shrine modelled on the Temple of Venus Genetrix (see p. 150). Mark Antony delivered his famous speech and so moved the crowd that they took over the funeral. Instead of proceeding in the traditional rite to the Campus Martius where the pyre had been prepared, the body was actually cremated at the other end of the Forum, in front of the Regia, which had been Caesar's headquarters as chief priest (*pontifex maximus*). An altar and a column of Numidian yellow stone, inscribed *Parenti Patriae* (to the founder of the nation), were briefly erected on the spot for the cult of the dead dictator, but abolished almost immediately by the anti-Caesar camp. However, Caesar's supporters soon struck back, and in 42 BC Mark Antony, Octavian (Augustus), and Lepidus decreed that a temple should be built, instituting official games and a new priest to look after the cult. It was not the first time that a mortal hero had been turned into a god, even during the hero's lifetime. The practice was common enough in the Greek East, where the honour had been conferred on various Roman generals. Individual aristocratic households in Rome were long accustomed to honour their worthier ancestors with something of the sort, and charismatic political leaders such as the Gracchi had been venerated with altars and sacrifices at least for a while after their death. But the official public cult created for Caesar was a major innovation. Caesar himself had paved the way by actively promoting the concept of his own divinity during the last year of his life, when he was to be called *Juppiter Julius*. *Divus Julius* was a milder alternative, which became the norm for all the emperors who were deified thereafter.

The temple was dedicated by Augustus on 18 August 29 BC and survived to Late Antiquity. In the C16, however, most of it vanished into the papal building yards and limekilns. Nothing remains of the super-structure except a column base, fragments of a Corinthian pilaster-capital and small sections of a frieze and cornice (Forum Antiquarium). The podium has also been robbed—both inside and out—of practically all its cut stone blocks of tufa and travertine, leaving only parts of the concrete infill. An approximate idea of its area is given by the marble kerbs: an almost square platform 24–25 m. across, 27 m. (perhaps longer) from front to back. It was at least 5.5 m. (18 RF) high, but dropped to 3.5 m. at the front. There it actually invaded the Forum space, forming a second tribunal, the *rostra Julia*, to match that at the other end, and was decorated with the symbols of Augustus' own victory—the prows (*rostra*) of the ships captured in the Battle of Actium in 31 BC, when he defeated Mark Antony to gain absolute power. It became the favoured venue for Imperial funeral orations. In (or under) the platform is a semicircular recess, later blocked in, containing a round monument, probably an altar replacing that which had marked the site of Caesar's funerary pyre, possibly a refuge, since the temple was endowed with rights of *asylum*. It appears beside the temple on a coin struck in 36 BC, which also shows the cult statue of Divus Julius, wearing the toga and holding an augur's staff.

▼ **Fig. 33.** Temple of Divus Julius on a coin of 36 BC

▼ **Fig. 34.** Temple of Divus Julius and adjacent arch on a coin of Hadrian, AD 125–8

Neither the coin nor the standing remains show us how the steps to the tribunal were arranged, or how the rest of the temple worked in elevation, but the odds are that it was consciously modelled, as the shrine made for his funeral had been, on the Temple of Venus Genetrix in the Forum of Caesar (see p. 150). A later coin, issued by the emperor Hadrian in AD 125–8, suggests a peripteral design with columns along the sides like the Venus temple. Fragments of a pilaster-capital indicate that the order was Corinthian, and Vitruvius tells us it was 'picnostyle' (i.e. the columns were spaced at intervals equal to one-and-a-half column diameters). Given the known dimensions of the podium, the temple therefore had six columns across the front, 40 or 42 RF (11.8–12.4 m.) high.

Arch of Augustus

Spanning the gap between the Temple of Castor and the Temple of Divus Julius, are the footings of a **three-way arch** (Fig. 1: 32), of Augustan date but uncertain identity. It is most likely to be the arch dedicated at the same time as the Curia and the Temple of Divus Julius in 29 BC, celebrating Augustus' victories in Dalmatia, Egypt, and at Actium, but it could be another, of 19 BC, commemorating the return of the legionary standards and prisoners which had been taken by the Parthians during the war with Rome (50–20 BC). Both are shown on coins as triple arches, differing slightly in elevation. A few marble fragments found in the area are thought to belong to the arch, including an elaborately decorated Doric capital (now in the Forum Antiquarium) and parts of a Doric entablature.

Some also believe that the fragmentary lists of triumphs and consuls (the *Fasti*) to be seen in the Capitoline Museums (see p. 384), came from this arch. The fragments were salvaged from a monumental stone structure, perhaps an arch, which was demolished somewhere in this vicinity in 1546. However, it has been argued equally forcefully that they could come from an arch at the crossroads on the other side of the Temple of Divus Julius, to be identified as the Arch of Fabius (*fornix Fabianus*). An old theory, currently out of fashion but still worth bearing in mind, is that they came from the Regia.

▼ Fig. 35. Arch of Augustus on a coin of 29 BC

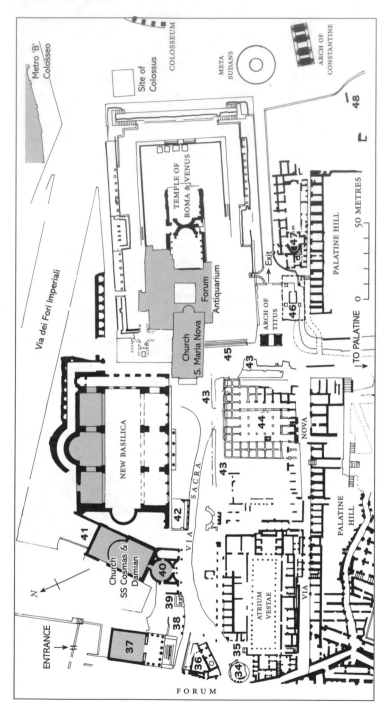

FORUM

ENTRANCE →

N

Church
SS Cosmas &
Damian

NEW BASILICA

Via dei Fori Imperiali

Metro 'B'
Colòsseo

Site of
Colossus

COLOSSEUM

META
SUDANS

ARCH OF
CONSTANTINE

TEMPLE OF
ROMA & VENUS

Church
S. Maria Nova

Forum
Antiquarium

VIA SACRA

ARCH OF
TITUS

Exit

PALATINE HILL

50 METRES

0

TO PALATINE

NOVA

VIA

PALATINE
HILL

ATRIUM
VESTAE

37

40

41

42

43

43

43

43

44

45

46

47

48

38

39

34

35

36

The Upper Via Sacra (Map: Fig. 36)
(N. slope of the Palatine Hill)

The Forum proper ends more or less at the back of the Temple of Divus Julius; on the rising ground behind the temple, originally on the edge of the Forum area, is a cluster of buildings dating from Rome's earliest days: the Temple of Vesta, the House of the Vestal Virgins and the Regia. Beyond them, the Via Sacra (Sacred Way) runs uphill, with the terraces of the Palatine on the right and the Velia in front, to where the Arch of Titus marks the top of the ridge between the two hills. Down to the great fire of AD 64 both sides of the street were lined with large aristocratic houses, and several streets branched off to the left.

Temple of Vesta. Figs. 1 and 36: 34

Another victim of Renaissance quarrymen, the marble superstructure of the temple was stripped in 1549, leaving only a round mound of concrete surrounded by a few courses of tufa blocks. The outer diameter, estimated at 14.8 m. (50 RF), was the same as the round temple by the Tiber (p. 255). With the aid of assorted fragments found in the vicinity during the excavations of 1877–1901, and lots of modern travertine, a short section of its outer elevation has been reconstructed (in 1930) on the western side of the mound. The architectural style and workmanship suit a date in the late C2/early C3 AD, when Julia Domna, wife of the emperor Septimius Severus, is known to have carried out restorations. The entrance was on the east side, towards the House of the Vestals, with which you have to imagine it bound by a walled enclosure. The large **shrine** (Fig. 36: 35) beside the entrance to the House of the Vestals, has one angle of its Ionic order reconstructed from various original fragments in white marble (the

◀ **Fig. 36.** Upper Via Sacra. General site plan

Key:

34	Temple of Vesta	42	Medieval porticus
35	Shrine	43	Foundations of Neronian porticus
36	Regia	44	*Horrea* of Vespasian
37	Temple of Divus Antoninus	45	Steps to precinct of Temple of Rome
38	Archaic burials		and Venus
39	Basement of a Late Republican house	46	Unidentified monument
40	'Temple of Divus Romulus'	47	*Insula* building (s. Maria de Metrio?)
41	Hall of the Marble Plan of Rome	48	Late Roman house

▲ **Fig. 37.** Temple of Vesta and the six vestals on a coin of Julia Domna, AD 207–9

travertine shaft is modern, as is the brick pier supporting the other angle) and contains a marble statue base. The inscription on the entablature says that the Senate and People of Rome paid for it out of public funds (*pecunia publica*), but it is otherwise anonymous. Stamped bricks found in the podium and the elegant lettering of the inscription indicate a date in the Hadrianic period (*c.* AD 120). A reasonable suggestion is that it could have housed a statue of Vesta, since she could not be portrayed in the temple; others see it as a compital shrine to the Lares Augusti (the guardians of the Imperial household), of which hundreds were erected at crossroads all over the city, but the site is within the precinct of Vesta, not a crossroads, nor even on a street.

Vesta was the goddess of the household hearth, a figure of great importance in early royal ritual. Under the Republic she became the hearth goddess of the Roman state. Her temple appears on coins of the C1 BC as a flimsy hut-like structure with a statue at the apex of a conical roof and dragons' heads on the eaves. It was not a temple in the strict sense of an inaugurated space, and there was no image of Vesta inside, but a fire which was the sacred duty of the Vestal Virgins, the handmaidens of Vesta, never to let go out. The ashes were ritually disposed of once a year, on 15 June, by throwing them into the Tiber. The Vestals lived in convent-like conditions in a house nearby, on a relatively modest scale until the fire of AD 64, after which their accommodation was radically redesigned on a new orientation and eventually enlarged on a massive scale.

A Vestal Virgin is accused of being too smart

Postumia, a Vestal Virgin, was tried for incest, a charge on which she was found not guilty, but suspicion had been aroused by the fact that she was always got up rather prettily, and that she had a wit that was too loose for a Virgin. Delivering judgement on behalf of the Board of Priests, the Chief Priest told her to stop making jokes and, in her dress and appearance, to aim at looking holy rather than smart. (Livy 4. 44. 11)

House of the Vestal Virgins (*Atrium Vestae*)   ★

There were six Vestals at any one time, appointed by the *pontifex maximus* (the chief priest, who under the Empire was always the reigning emperor). Only girls aged between 6 and 10 with both parents living were eligible, usually of patrician or plebeian birth but by the Empire they could be the daughters of freed slaves. They had to serve 30 years, after which they were released from their vows and free to marry, but if they broke the vow of chastity before then they were buried alive outside the Colline Gate. Their duties included not only tending the sacred fire and safeguarding various sacred objects on which the survival of Rome depended (such as the 'palladium') but making salt cake to sprinkle at sacrifices and numerous other rituals and ceremonial appearances at public games. Their official dress was old-fashioned and heavy, and their hairstyle a complicated arrangement of braids and bands which other women only wore on their wedding. In return they enjoyed various special privileges; any injury to them was punishable by death; they could own and administer their own property (many were given a substantial dowry from the emperor); when they went out they were preceded by a *lictor* and had complete right of way on the streets; they could even drive in carriages within the city limits (otherwise only permitted to empresses).

The peristyle **garden court** and the **buildings** which surround it on four sides were all completed in about AD 113, during the reign of Trajan, probably finishing a scheme begun by Domitian, which in turn had been made possible by Nero's redevelopment of the valley following the fire of AD 64. Prior to that the House of the Vestals had shared the same cardinal

▼ **Fig. 38.** House of the Vestal Virgins, temple of Vesta, and the ramp to the North corner of the Palatine hill. Restored view as of c. AD 150

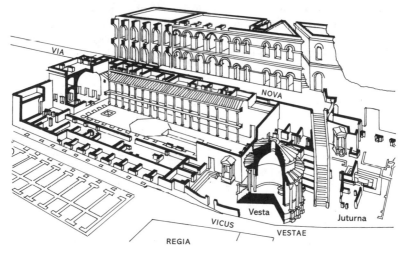

alignment as the Temple of Vesta and the southern side of the Regia and for most of its history had been confined to the western end of the site. Traces of its earlier floors and walls, dating from the C2–C1 BC, can be seen at a lower level under the bridge inside the main entrance. The eastern end of the site was previously occupied by the *Domus Publica*, the residence of the chief priest (*pontifex maximus*), which Augustus donated to the Vestals in 12 BC when he took over the priesthood and moved the official residence to his house on the other side of the Palatine hill. In the expanded structure the western end remained linked closely to the temple while the accommodation for the Vestals (and their numerous servants and slaves) ranged along the south and north. The colonnades around the garden were two storeys high, with columns of Carystian green marble below and variegated red/white limestone (*breccia corallina*) above. The north-facing position, overshadowed further by the massive platforms of the Palace on the corner of the hill above, was probably rather gloomy and damp. The lower levels of the south wing (which was itself four or five storeys high) were insulated against the hillside by hollow walls, and included a bath-suite whose heating system was extended to heat the floors of other rooms in the wing. In the centre of the east wing is a large barrel-vaulted room approached by four steps, with three smaller rooms down each side, rather like the bedrooms in a traditional atrium-style house. Although surely not the Vestals' normal bedrooms (the rest of the house is big enough to give each Vestal a sizeable apartment to herself), the design probably embodies some symbolic or ceremonial function, perhaps a formal dining hall. The inscribed marble base beside the entrance once bore a statue honouring Flavia Publicia, Head Vestal (*v[irginis] V[estalis] maximae*) in AD 247–57, which was donated by two court couriers (*deputati*) in gratitude for her help, presumably in advancing their careers.

The statues lined up along the north side of the garden were found in a pile at the west end of the court; there is no knowing what their original positions were, nor do the inscribed bases necessarily belong with the statues presently set on them, but they too are all Head Vestals, dating from the C3 and C4 AD.

▼ **Fig. 39.** Regia. C16 reconstruction of south face of south wing

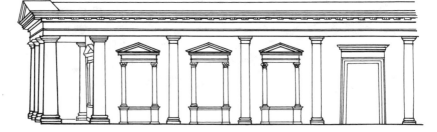

Regia. Fig. 36: 36

The wedge-shaped area between the House of the Vestals and the Temple of Antoninus Pius and Faustina is the site of the **Regia**, meaning 'Royal Palace', which tradition attributed to Numa, the second king of Rome (715–673 BC). Although *regia* denotes a residence, it was actually a *templum*, a sacred, inaugurated space. The chief priest (*pontifex maximus*) and his college of pontiffs held official meetings there, and stored their records in its archive (*tabularium*) but they lived elsewhere. A shrine of Mars within its precincts housed the shields (*ancilia*) and the spears of Mars, which generals embarking on a war rattled before setting off (if they rattled of their own accord it was a bad omen requiring an expiatory ceremony). Another shrine, which only the Vestal Virgins and the *pontifex maximus* were allowed to enter, was dedicated to Ops (goddess of plenty, wife of Saturn) Consiva ('she who sows'). Two sacred bay trees grew in the courtyard.

Excavations in depth have proved that there was certainly a building resembling a **noble Etruscan-style residence** on the site by the C7 BC: a

▼ **Fig. 40. Regia.** Plan, actual state, with indication of two earlier phases

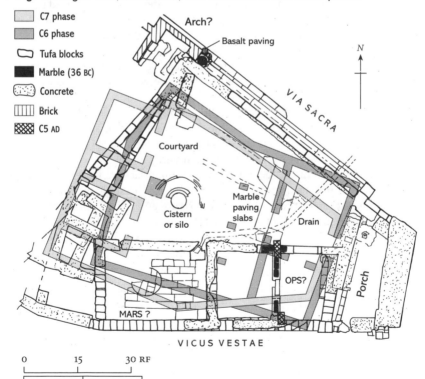

courtyard with a pair of rooms preceded by a columned porch, decorated with painted terracotta plaques. Before the end of the C6 BC it had already been rebuilt at least three times, with a different layout each time. From the beginning of the Republic onwards, however, the basic plan stayed the same, despite at least three more rebuildings, all after fires, one in 210 BC, another in 148 BC and the third in 36 BC. This last, paid for by the general Cnaeus Domitius Calvinus out of the spoils of his victory in Spain in 39 BC, had solid marble walls and thick marble floors on foundations capped with travertine. It seems to have been proof against the fires of AD 64 and 191, but (judging by the brick walls which still stand here and there on the site) had suffered considerable damage by the C4 or C5 AD. Abandoned by the C9, its ruins were completely despoiled in 1543–6, when every usable block of marble and travertine was carried off for papal building projects and the rest burned for lime.

In ground plan, which is almost all there is to see, Calvinus' marble building of 36 BC was a polygon consisting of a rectangular wing along the south side joined to a roughly triangular courtyard on the north. The rectangular wing (whose longer axis has the same east–west alignment as the Temple of Vesta and the older phase of the House of the Vestals/*domus Publica*) was divided into three rooms of different sizes, all paved in white and grey marble. The largest room, at the west end, is commonly identified as the shrine of Mars, the smaller one at the east as the shrine of Ops; the room between them served as a vestibule to both, with a door to the courtyard (and perhaps one to the *vicus Vestae*). The east wall of the vestibule is delineated by the metal fence between the brick pier labelled Regia and the pier which clasps five courses of white marble blocks, cracked by fire, at its NE corner. Something of the original quality of the architecture can be seen in the blocks, despite the damage. Their external faces have finely drafted margins in the Greek manner. Out in the courtyard, which was also paved in white and grey marble and may have had a colonnade on the inside of its northern boundary wall, there was a conical underground cistern or grain silo. Part of a threshold marks a doorway through the short east wall of the courtyard and a fragment of entablature with an oblique angle suggests that this end of the building was furnished with a small columnar porch. The opposite (west) side, facing the Forum, may also have had a small porch or shrine at the southern corner and perhaps a staircase up to another door into the courtyard.

At the NW corner of the site, the fluted column of green Carystian marble on a red granite base is a typically Late Roman combination and probably belongs with the brick wall behind it. This has been interpreted as a late repair to the pier of a monumental four-way arch which spanned the adjacent crossroads, possibly the triumphal arch of Fabius Maximus, dating from 121 BC but rebuilt in 57. Nearby, a small patch of basalt paving marks the level of the Via Sacra by the C2 AD.

Temple of Divus Antoninus Pius and Diva Faustina

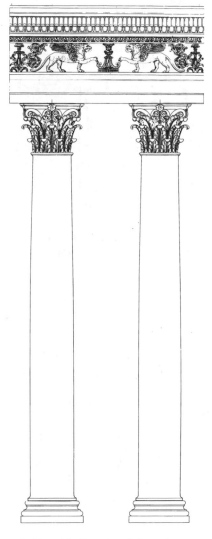

The temple is readily identified by its façade of Carystian green marble columns, six across the front, two more at the sides, behind which rears the baroque pediment (1602) of the church of S. Lorenzo in Miranda, installed in the cella of the temple since the C7 or C8. The entablature still bears the ancient dedicatory inscriptions: the second line came first DIVAE FAUSTINAE EX S.C. (To Deified Faustina, by decree of the Senate). The temple was built by Antoninus Pius for his wife Faustina, who was deified after her death in AD 140. When Antoninus Pius died and was deified twenty years later, the frieze above Faustina's inscription was chiselled off and his name added: DIVO ANTONINO ET (To Deified Antoninus and...). The architectural order is top quality Imperial Corinthian, 48 RF high, with 40 RF shafts. Its beautifully sculpted frieze, of griffins and acanthus scrolls and candelabra, is still well-preserved along the sides. The original roof has gone, together with most of the upper cornice and the rear wall of the cella, dismantled in the C14 to provide stone for rebuilding the Lateran palace. The grooves below the necks of the column shafts were made to attach

▲ **Fig. 41.** Temple of Antoninus Pius and Faustina. Corinthian order

a makeshift roof over the portico, possibly in 1430, when the church was given over to the guild of apothecaries. The podium and cella walls of dark grey *peperino* tufa are pockmarked with holes made by medieval blacksmiths in search of the iron and lead from the clamps and dowels which pinned the blocks together. The blend of marble and tufa was not the intended final effect; the podium was once faced with white marble slabs,

▲ **Fig. 42.** Temple of Antoninus Pius and Faustina. Restored view

▼ **Fig. 43.** Temple of Antoninus Pius and Faustina. Coin

with matching marble mouldings at top and bottom (only the latter have not been robbed). The marble facing probably continued some way up the cella walls before changing to stucco. The front steps, partly reconstructed in modern brick, were originally of marble and ran the full width of the façade with an altar in their midst. A coin shows how they were fenced off from the street below and bore statues on pedestals at either side above. The seated figure between the columns is Faustina, whose colossal statue will have stood inside the cella, joined later by one of Antoninus Pius. Fragments of both statues, dug up in front of the temple, are displayed in the porch.

What, if anything, occupied such an important location before the temple was built is unknown; it is possible that the eastern end of the basilica Paulli previously faced an open square rather than a street, which allowed wider access to the area behind (and subsequently also the Temple of Peace). Excavations on the eastern flank of the Temple of Antoninus and Faustina in 1902, behind the travertine footings of a colonnade or arcade along the side of the Via Sacra, exposed an expanse of marble paving, partly invaded in the Late Empire (?C4/C5) by a **bath building**, and then came straight down onto an **archaic cemetery** (Fig. 36: 38), with burials ranging in date from the C9 to the early C6 BC. The excavations have been filled back in, but the positions of some of the graves are marked in the grass. Cinerary urns and other finds are displayed in the Forum Antiquarium. The brick walls to the rear of the cemetery area belong to the late bathhouse, which once extended also over the tufa structure to the right (Fig. 36: 39): part of the **basement of an aristocratic house** of the C3 or C2 BC, with narrow corridors of slave cells like those found higher up the street (Fig. 45). The rest of the house presumably lies under the next building along, the 'Temple of Divus Romulus', which reflects the same alignment.

'Temple of Divus Romulus'. Fig. 36: 40 ★

The little round building, constructed of brick-faced concrete, is a gem of Late Roman passage architecture dating from the early C4 AD. A fragmentary inscription recorded on the façade in the C16 included the name of Constantine the Great. Its circular hall, 50 RF in diameter with a concrete dome, was flanked by two long apsidal halls which projected forward to open directly off the street (as the exposed drains and foundations demonstrate, the present street level is much too low; in the C4 it was 1–2 m. higher). The vaults of the side halls have long since collapsed and the left-hand hall has mostly disappeared; the right-hand one survives, with the two columns of its tall porch still standing: the 24-RF Carystian green marble column shafts, like the majority of the other architectural marbles used in the façade, were *spolia* taken from earlier buildings; the Corinthian capital on the left-hand column was made in the Flavian period (*c.* AD 90); the topmost cornice block is Severan (early C3 AD). Probably only the pedestals and intermediary entablature block were new. The recessed entrance to the circular hall between the two side halls was initially planned as a simple rectangle; the curving walls were a later refinement, and included two rows of statue niches, set in architectural frames (*aediculae*) to either side of the central door. The various components of the **doorway** were dismantled in 1632 to be reset in a new door at a higher level, and only returned to their old position in 1879. Missing is a pair of consoles between the capitals and architrave, an unusual feature of the design which was lost in the previous move and compensated for by the C17 architect by adding travertine plinths to the pedestals. However, the rest of the assembly is genuine. The **bronze doors** and their surrounding marble frame came from a Severan building (*c.* AD 200). The cornice over the lintel is in four blocks, the middle two dating from the C1 and early C2 AD, the outer two made up by the C4 builders. The red porphyry column shafts are of slightly different lengths, adjusted by a marble spacer at the neck of the left-hand one; their Corinthian capitals are Flavian. The architrave with its elaborate plant scroll decoration was originally carved to be viewed vertically, on one side of a richly decorated door frame, dat-able to the early C1 AD. The uppermost cornice is composed of three blocks, two from an Augustan building, filled in with C4 work. Sockets in the top surface suggest a pediment. In overall effect the façade will have resembled a triumphal arch or a city gate.

Inside, the **circular hall** connected with the halls on either side and a wide door in the rear wall opened on axis with the centre of the great rectangular hall behind (Fig. 36: 41), which in its turn led to the Temple

▲ **Fig. 44.** Coins of Maxentius issued in memory of Romulus, c. AD 310

(by the C4 called Forum) of Peace (see p. 153). The most evident intention was to provide monumental access to the latter, a pivot between its differing alignment and that of the new basilica further up the Via Sacra. Other possible purposes are much discussed. The long-standing association with Romulus, deified son of the emperor Maxentius, who died at the age of 4 in AD 309, is based on the evidence of some coins issued by Maxentius in AD 310–12 in memory of Romulus and other recently deceased members of the family. They represent, with considerable variations, a domed building with a columnar façade, in some cases looking not unlike the Via Sacra building, which it is therefore argued might first have been dedicated in the names of Maxentius' deified relatives, subsequently rededicated in honour of Constantine. Alternatively, because the building on the coins shows two statues of nude youths standing in the wings with their legs crossed and holding sceptres or spears, attempts have been made to identify it with a temple of the Penates (Roman household gods who protected the family larder in private domestic cult, but who were also worshipped with Vesta and the Lares in a public form on behalf of the whole community). A separate temple is known to have been located somewhere on the Velia and was restored by Augustus but is not heard of thereafter and possibly perished in the fire of AD 64. It is not impossible that Maxentius wished to revive the cult as part of his general revival of Rome's ancient traditions and that the new vestibule was put under their protection. However, it should be stressed that the resemblance to the coins in question is more generic than specific and all may refer simply to the mausoleum on the Via Appia (see p. 336).

In the wedge-shaped gap to the east of the 'Temple of Romulus', between it and the SW corner of the New Basilica can be seen the **paving** of the street which once branched off the Via Sacra towards the neighbourhood called the Carinae ('the Keels'). It ran along the back wall of the Temple of Peace and was densely lined with shops; when the New Basilica was built, a tunnel was incorporated into the foundations to keep the passage open but the first stretch of the old street was converted to some other use, for a wall continued from the adjacent corner of the New Basilica, with a large doorway, in front of which the arcaded portico (Fig. 36: 42) was constructed in the Middle Ages.

At this point the basalt paving of the present Via Sacra you are walking on bends off to the right but that is its old route prior to AD 64. After the great fire, when Nero redesigned the whole area on the Palatine side and rebuilt it at a higher level, the street was raised and straightened to run parallel with a huge colonnade along the edge of the Palatine redevelopment. Across the way from the 'Temple of Romulus' the massive foundations of the colonnade can be traced intermittently running uphill (Fig. 36: 43) to a point beside the front steps of the church of S. Francesca Romana (S. Maria Nova), where they turn at a right angle towards the Palatine. In the 80s AD Domitian abolished Nero's scheme and replaced it with large specialist markets: the *horrea* of Vespasian on the right (Palatine) side and the *horrea piperataria* (pepper halls) on the left (Velia) side. The latter burned in the fires of AD 191 and again in 283 and were then replaced by the great New Basilica.

Horrea Vespasiani—Etruscan and Republican Houses. Fig. 36: 44

The *horrea Vespasiani* (Vespasian's markets) seem to have endured with only minor alterations until the C5 or later.

New excavations have been able to go deep below the imperial levels to explore the earlier history of the site, and although they have mostly been reburied, the principal discoveries are worth knowing about. Right at the bottom, cut into bedrock, is what the excavators have called the **Wall of Romulus**, a short stretch of a fortification running along the slope. Its first phase is contemporary with the traditional date for the foundation of Rome in the middle of the C8 BC. Rebuilt twice on a larger scale, the wall was destroyed towards the end of the C6 BC, when the slope behind it was terraced and laid out with large aristocratic houses. The ground plans of two of these, the first finds of their kind, although very fragmentary, can be reconstructed. They measure some 60 × 40 m., with shops on the street front, between which a passage led to a central courtyard (beneath which was a cistern). To the rear of the courtyard were another three large rooms. The layout can be closely paralleled in Etruscan tombs but is also clearly related to the atrium-style houses of the later Roman tradition. Both houses stood, hardly changed, for the next 400 years until the region was devastated by fire. The new houses which

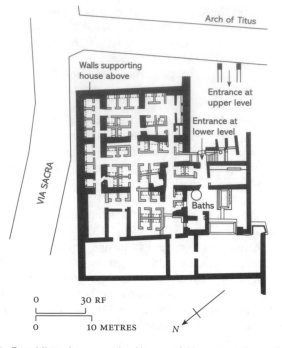

▲ **Fig. 45.** Republican house under Horrea of Vespasian. Plan of basement level

replaced them (Fig. 45) occupied smaller plots but were probably several storeys high. They were raised on basements packed with individual cells just large enough to contain a stone bench for a bed. One relatively well-preserved basement at the east end of the site (under the protective roofing) had fifty such cells, corresponding to the number of slaves which ancient writers tell us were needed to run a noble Roman household, and it also contained a small bath-house. Unfortunately, the ground floor of the house is only scantily preserved, but its location and various phases make it an attractive candidate for the house created in 58 BC by M. Aemilius Scaurus, considered scandalously luxurious because it had columns of black-red 'Lucullan' marble 38 RF high in the atrium (they were removed in 17 BC to decorate the Theatre of Marcellus). In 53 BC it changed hands for 14.8 million sesterces. Among the neighbouring properties were possibly those once owned by P. Clodius Pulcher, M. Tullius Cicero, and other famous men of the last years of the Republic. The whole quarter perished in the fire of AD 64.

Temple of Roma and Venus (Church and Monastery of S. Francesca Romana—S. Maria Nova)

In Nero's scheme after AD 64 the straightened Via Sacra led up to the entrance to his new house on the Esquiline (his Golden House (*Domus Aurea*)) and on the summit of the ridge he placed the Colossus, a bronze statue of himself in the guise of the sun-god Helios (see p. 271). After Nero's death Vespasian had the head of the statue changed to that of Helios but left it where it was. The real change came in the C2 AD when the site was taken over by the emperor Hadrian for a magnificent Temple of Roma, set back-to-back in a single structure with a Temple of Venus. Vowed in AD 121 the project took at least until AD 135, and may have been finished off by his successor Antoninus Pius in the early 140s. Hadrian designed the double temple himself, in characteristically Greek style, on a low stepped podium, with ten columns at both ends and twenty down the sides. The order was Corinthian, 60 RF high, with fluted columns of white

▼ **Fig. 46.** Temple of Roma and Venus. C4 AD plan

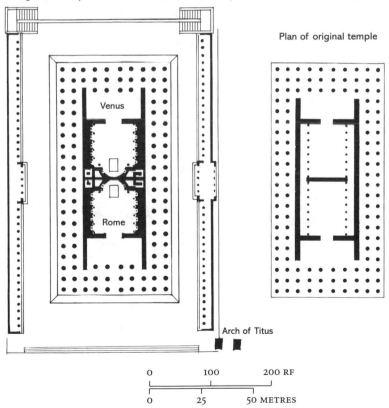

Plan of original temple

Venus

Rome

Arch of Titus

0   100   200 RF

0   25   50 METRES

(Proconnesian) marble, taking the temple roof about as high as the bell-tower of S. Francesca Romana. Much of what survives today, largely hidden beyond the cloister behind the church (the Forum Antiquarium), is the result of a rebuilding by Maxentius after a fire in AD 307, in which the wooden roof was replaced by coffered concrete vaults: the cellas now met in two opposed semicircular apses and their walls were doubled in thickness to take the extra weight, enlivened on the inside in prime Maxentian taste with niches flanked by red porphyry colonnettes on white marble brackets, in front of which ran a larger colonnade of red porphyry columns. The most that is readily visible on the Forum side are the marble steps (Fig. 36: 45) between the side of the church of S. Francesca Romana and the Arch of Titus which belong to the western edge of its great rectangular precinct. Covering an area of 1.5 hectares and lined with colonnaded porticoes of grey Egyptian granite down the long sides, the precinct was to all intents and purposes Hadrian's Forum, a monumental route between the old Forum valley and the Amphitheatre. The lateral colonnades ended in staircases which led down to the Colosseum level, where Hadrian set up the Colossus on a new base, the site of which is marked by a grass square. An excellent view of the platform and the cella of the Temple of Venus is to be had from the upper level of the Colosseum (see p. 281).

Roma had not previously been worshipped at Rome as a goddess in her own right (though she frequently appeared in company with the

▼ **Fig. 47.** Temple of Roma and Venus. Reconstruction of eastern (Colosseum) façade

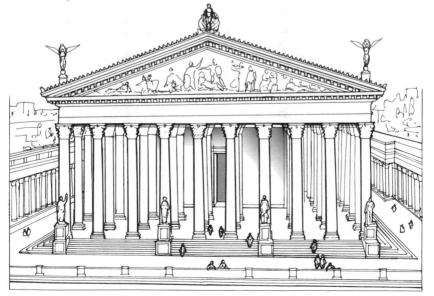

emperors in state reliefs) and the coupling of her cult with that of Venus carried a potent new message. The particular Venus is Venus Felix, hitherto unknown, goddess of fertility and prosperity; in AD 176 an altar was set up in her part of the precinct at which all newly married couples in the city were expected to sacrifice. In their adjacent cellas the cult statues, as shown on coins, sat back-to-back in very similar form. Roma, called Roma Aeterna, was seated on a curule chair holding a spear in her left hand and the Palladium or a Victory. Venus Felix was seated on a throne, a spear in her left hand and a winged Cupid or Amor (which is Roma spelled backwards) in her right. Between them the new deities exalted the Golden Age which was generally believed to have begun with Trajan; an era which stressed the power of Rome and the Empire rather than the power of individual emperors, and the temple went on to become the most enduring of the city's pagan monuments. Maxentius' rebuilding, and indeed his choice of location for the New Basilica, emphasized its continuing significance in the Late Empire. Its annual festival in celebration of the birthday of Rome (21 April) was still significant among Christians in the C5. It was not until the early C7 that permission was granted to remove the bronze tiles from its roof. In the mid-C8 a church to St Peter and St Paul, patron saints of Rome, was built in the vestibule of the Roma side, replaced a century later by one to the Virgin Mary (called S. Maria Nova to distinguish it from the other 'Antiqua'), now called S. Francesca Romana.

New Basilica (Basilica Nova)

You can enter the basilica at the SE corner and stand in the **central nave**: the three arcades with coffered barrel vaults 25 m. high constitute its north aisle; the rest probably fell during the great earthquake of AD 847. The project was started in AD 306 by Maxentius and finished off by Constantine after 313. Measuring 96 × 65 m. (325 × 220 RF), the New Basilica was actually slightly smaller than the Basilica Julia (which had just been rebuilt at about this time) but was entirely roofed in concrete, employing a design previously used only for the central halls of the great Imperial baths (see Baths of Caracalla and Baths of Diocletian). The central nave, 25 m. wide, was spanned by three cross vaults springing to a height of 35 m. (120 RF) above the floor, supported on concrete brackets braced by flying buttresses on the roofs of the side aisles. A restored view of the interior shows how the nave roof will have appeared like a billowing canopy tethered to the Corinthian columns around the sides. The columns were 60 RF high, with 52 RF monolithic shafts of Proconnesian marble. One, removed in 1614, stands (with an alien capital) in Piazza S. Maria Maggiore. The floor was paved in Numidian yellow, Carystian green, red and green porphyry, and Phrygian purple marble set in a geometric pattern of squares and circles in 12-RF squares; the marble

▲ **Fig. 48.** New Basilica. Reconstruction of interior

panelling on the walls can be inferred from the clamp holes in the brickwork. Both ends of the building were massively reinforced, on the west by an apse and walls almost 5 m. thick, on the east (towards the Colosseum and the Temple of Roma and Venus) by the addition of an outer porch. There were entrances on both long sides, but the approach from the Via Sacra was made especially grandiose by a wide flight of steps leading up to a porch of four red porphyry columns in front of the central bay. Both the porch and the large apse on axis with it in the north wall, elaborately decorated with niches, are Constantinian modifications to the original Maxentian plan (which foresaw only the apse on the west). With the alteration the western apse became the setting for a gigantic seated statue of Constantine, almost 15 m. (50 RF) high, whose white marble head, hands, and feet are now in the courtyard of the Palazzo dei Conservatori.

Arch of Titus ★

The southern corner of the precinct of the Temple of Roma and Venus is built hard against the Arch of Titus, which had been set up in AD 81–2 at the point where the road leading up from the Colosseum valley met the Via Sacra. (Once again, the exposed foundations of the arch, of rough concrete capped with travertine blocks, show that you have mentally to restore the present road surface to a higher level especially on its Forum side.) The inscription on the east face (towards the Colosseum) is original and reads 'The Senate and People of Rome, to Divus Titus, son of Divus

▲ **Fig. 49.** Arch of Titus. East side

Vespasian, Vespasian Augustus'. The title *Divus* signifies that the arch was erected (or completed) after Titus' early death (aged 50) in AD 81, and indeed his deified figure appears, riding heavenwards on the back of the eagle, in the centre coffer of the coffering on the underside of the archway. The **reliefs** carved on the archway walls illustrate two scenes from the triumph which he had celebrated with his father Vespasian in AD 71, the procession travelling over this very spot on its circuitous route from the Campus Martius to the Capitoline hill. The scene on the south side shows the procession as it approached the Triumphal Gate at the beginning of the route. The gate, with two chariot-groups on its roof, is at the right; the booty from the Great Temple at Jerusalem, sacked in the Jewish War which the triumph was glorifying, is displayed on wooden stretchers: on the first are the golden table and silver trumpets; on the second, the seven-branched candlestick (*menorah*), all subsequently deposited in Vespasian's new Temple of Peace. The placards held up in the background probably had painted inscriptions giving the names of the cities and peoples defeated in the war. The scene on the north side is dominated by Titus riding in his chariot drawn by four horses, with the goddess Roma holding on to the bridle of the leading horse. To the left, and in the background, marked by their long sacrificial axes (*fasces*) are the lictors, who preceded the emperor. To the right, Victory is holding a wreath over Titus' head and the figure with the nude torso represents the People of Rome; the one wearing the toga represents the Senate. The theme continues on the outside of the arch, where the frieze of the middle entablature shows the whole procession in miniature, but carved in such high relief that it is readily visible. The spandrels below are filled with flying Victories, with their feet on globes, carrying Roman banners, trophies, laurel wreaths, and palm branches; the keystones have little figures of Roma and the Genius of the Roman People.

It will be noted that much of the arch, originally constructed entirely of Pentelic marble, has been restored in travertine, one of the earliest and most successful exercises of the kind. Having been incorporated into a medieval fortification wall which saw heavy fighting in the C12–C13, the arch was in a dire state by the early C19, mainly kept up by houses built to either side. When these were demolished the architects Stern and Valadier actually dismantled the arch altogether and reassembled it, integrating the missing pieces as they went, but carefully distinguishing the old from the new, not only by the material but also surface effect.

Just beyond the Arch of Titus the Via Sacra is joined by a road coming from the right, the Via Nova (New Way), which runs the length of the terrace at the foot of the Palatine palace, behind Vespasian's *horrea* and the House of the Vestals, to the Forum. Despite its name the New Way was in origin a very old street and its earlier, winding route round the hillside survives higher up the slope, retained within the later terracing as part of a complex network of underground or covered passageways which ran round the outside of, and interconnected with, the various sectors of the palaces on the summit.

The Palatine (Map: Fig. 50) ★★

The Palatine hill (latin *Palatium*) rises 32 m. above the present city (51 m. above sea level) and measures over 2.25 km. in circumference, a vast archaeological maze, much of it still unexcavated, in which even the more visible fragments do not always make sense. The first thing to take on board is that the brick-faced concrete ribs and tall **vaulted chambers** exposed around the edges of the hill (especially impressive at the north corner overlooking the Forum and on the south side towards the Circus Maximus) are not buildings as such, but massive substructures. Their primary function was to support extensions to the hilltop palaces, though many included lower terraces which accommodated all manner of lesser houses, apartments, warehouses, workshops, and stores. Another thing is that the summit itself developed upwards as well as outwards. For all the trees and green grass, the present profile is entirely man-made, one set of buildings replacing another in a great pile, ending up in places 15 m. above the natural rock. And because of stone-robbing and more recent excavations, two or three different phases in this build-up may be seen at once.

In Roman tradition the Palatine was where Rome began, the original city founded by Romulus in 753 BC on the site of a pre-existing settlement, and indeed, excavations at the top SW corner, matched by the new finds on the north slope (see p. 111), have encountered a continuous sequence from the C9 BC onwards. Although only small pockets of the older levels have been explored elsewhere, all suggest increasingly dense occupation down to the late C1 BC. Then, in the course of the C1 AD, the summit was taken over by the emperors as their sole domain, their official residence and the ceremonial centre of Imperial authority (with the result that the name *Palatium* changed its meaning, entering the language to become our word 'palace').

The principal phases in the Imperial takeover, in so far as they are manifest on the ground, are keyed on the general site plan (Fig. 50) in numerical order. The process started in 36 BC when Octavian, the future emperor Augustus, flush with victory over his rival Sextus Pompey, gave up the house he had beside the Forum in favour of another which he had bought a few years before, near the **Precinct of Victory** (1), the goddess who was to be a cornerstone of his Imperial ideology. He then purchased an adjoining house and used part of the site for a great **new temple** to his other favourite deity, Apollo (2). The location was triply fortunate because Octavian was to be seen as the new Romulus, the founder of a new Rome, and the SW corner of the hill was where Romulus and his twin brother Remus were said to have been reared by the shepherd Faustulus and his wife Acca Larentia. Other members of the Julio-Claudian family set up

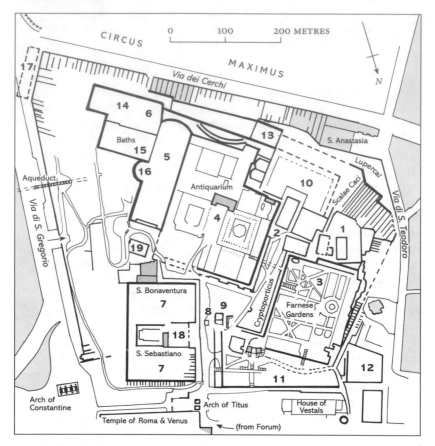

▲ **Fig. 50.** Palatine. General site plan

Key:

1	Temples of Victory and Great Mother	12	Ramp and hall (Domitian)
2	Temple of Apollo/House of Augustus	13	Extension: *Schola Praeconum* (early
3	Platform: '*Domus Tiberiana*' (Nero)		C2 AD)
4	Domitian's Palace	14	Platform (Trajan–Hadrian–Severans)
5	'Hippodrome' garden (Domitian)	15	Baths (Severans)
6	Baths (Domitian)	16	Exhedra (Severan rebuild)
7	Platform (Domitian)	17	*Septizodium* (Severans)
8	Arch: Palatine Gate (Domitian)	18	Temple (late C2–C3 AD)
9	Temple (Domitian rebuild)	19	Baths (Maxentius)
10	Library court (Domitian rebuild)	20	Late Roman house
11	Extension to platform 3 (Domitian)		

house nearby, including Augustus' stepson and successor Tiberius (AD 14–37), perhaps at the southern end of the **great platform** (3), which generally goes by his name (*Domus Tiberiana*) though it was actually constructed by Nero after the fire of AD 64. The fire wrecked all the earlier palace complex, including a new wing (the so-called *Domus Transitoria*) that Nero had just built in the area east of the Temple of Apollo. Nero's rebuilding in AD 64–9 (as part of his even larger *Domus Aurea*) probably extended over the rest of the eastern hilltop, but most of those works were immediately obliterated by the Flavian emperors Vespasian (AD 70–9) and his son Domitian (AD 81–96), nos 4–12. The core of **Domitian's palace** (4) consisted of two suites of immensely tall reception/dining halls flanked further to the east by the '**Hippodrome**' garden (5) and a set of **baths** at the south corner (6). A **platform** extending to the NE (7) apparently supported further gardens, perhaps incorporating a temple in the middle (though the surviving podium dates from the 170s). A matching **extension** (11) brought the front of (3) into line with it, between them framing the main approach up the Via Sacra. The entrance to the new palace was marked by a **monumental arch** (8), set beside a large pre-existing **temple** (9), probably dedicated to Jupiter Stator, rebuilt for the occasion. Flavian remodelling also involved the area of the houses of 'Augustus' and 'Livia', and included a **new precinct and libraries** at the Temple of Apollo (10).

Trajan and Hadrian in the early C2 made substantial changes to both ends of platform (3), carried out repairs and some internal improvements to the rest of the Domitianic palace (Hadrian installed heating under the floor of its great dining hall) and developed the core of a further terrace beyond the baths (6). The C2 also saw the systematic terracing and redevelopment of the outer fringes of the hill on the south (Circus Maximus) and the east (Caelian) side, which were crowded with shops, commercial buildings (*horrea*) and apartment blocks (*insulae*) in symbiosis with the palace on top. Under the Severan emperors in the early C3 the **exhedra** (16) on the east of the sunken garden, although a feature of the original Domitianic layout, was partly rebuilt at the same time as a large set of **baths** (15) and a substantial **new wing** (14) were added at the south corner. The additional area looks relatively modest in plan but actually represents a typical Severan extravagance. The platform is entirely artificial, raised over 40 m. high to reach the same ground level as the rest of the palace, and the structures it supported will have risen a futher 25–30 m. The initial idea could have been even more ambitious, to extend to the far corner, where the *Septizodium*, a gigantic freestanding façade (17), was constructed in AD 203, dominating the approach from the Appian Way.

Maxentius (AD 306–13) is likely to have had some suitably grandiose plans for the northern sector of the palace, to go with the development of the Velia (New Basilica and the rebuilt Temple of Rome and Venus), though the suite of **baths** (19) may be all that there was to show before his untimely end. Imperial interest is then assumed to have waned since Constantine moved the real centre of power to Constantinople (Istanbul), but alterations and repairs certainly continued to be made. Several C5 emperors of the West (Honorius, Valentinian III, Lucius Severus) and the Goths (Odoacer and Theodoric) based themselves in Rome for long periods, living on the Palatine. The Byzantine garrison was still appointing a 'Keeper of the Palatine Palaces' in the late C7. Part of a sizable **C5–C7 cemetery** has been excavated at the south end of the platform (7). Some sectors show signs of abandonment well before that, however, and the summit was probably deserted soon after, never to be seriously occupied again. The southern half in particular was attacked for building materials and is riddled with tunnels and deeper-level mines for volcanic sand (*pozzolana*), which contributed in no small measure to the destruction of the buildings above. In the C16 and C17 the hilltop was parcelled out among the Farnese, Spada, and Barberini families, who converted its crumbling terraces into elegant gardens and vineyards. The Farnese project was especially stylish and its surviving elements are architectural monuments in their own right.

Major excavations started along the northern wing of the Domitianic palace in 1720–6, directed by Conte Suzzani for the Farnese Duke of Parma, basically looking for works of art to enrich his museum at Parma. A second extensive campaign, directed by Pietro Rosa for Napoleon III, cleared much of the area towards the SW corner in 1861–5 and, in 1866–8, the northern approach. The **House 'of Livia'** was explored in 1869, the 'Hippodrome' garden in 1870. The central zone of the Domitianic palace was uncovered in 1926–8 and somewhat arbitrarily restored in a lightning operation during 1934–6 together with superficial clearances along the southern and eastern slopes in readiness for Hitler's state visit. Since then, most attention has been focused in and around the early buildings at the far SW corner.

Visit: One of the pleasures of the Palatine is that it is a park where you wander at will. On the other hand, it is a large park, without signposts or labels, so for the first-time visitor the following description embodies an itinerary. It makes a complete circuit anti-clockwise beginning at the mouth of the Via Nova just up from the Arch of Titus (to reach the same point from the Via di S. Gregorio entrance take the path to the right, round the eastern corner of the hill).

Farnese Gardens

A short distance along the Via Nova (or if that is closed the modern path parallel to it higher up), an elegant C16 staircase, incorporating a subterranean grotto beneath a moss-laden 'nymphaeum', leads up to the **aviary** at the NE corner of the **Farnese Gardens**. The terrace between the two pavilions looks directly across to the New Basilica and also gives an excellent sense of the rest of the hill. The gardens extending to the rear were famous in the early C17 for their rare botanical specimens, collected by

Cardinal Odoardo Farnese, but their present layout was made for Napoleon III in the 1860s, and much of the planting is actually the work of Giacomo Boni, the excavator of the Forum, who lived in the aviary from 1907 to his death in 1925 and is buried in the adjacent flower garden— Boni's reconstruction of what the ancient Romans meant by a *viridarium*. Past Boni's garden, the northern corner of the terrace provides another impressive view, down into the House of the Vestals and the Forum, and across to the Quirinal hill. The massively artificial nature of the platform at this corner, dating from the late C1–early C2, is demonstrated by the flight of stairs in the middle and the precipitous vaults at the edges. Further back, under the central area of the gardens, ranges the earlier platform built by Nero after AD 64. Little is known of the buildings it carried beyond the likelihood that they were arranged around a large central courtyard. The blocked-off staircase leading down into the ground in the eastern sector is ancient and connects with the cryptoporticus which runs the length of that edge, one in a network of subterranean links between one part of the palace and another.

The balcony at the far SW angle of the gardens is a good vantage point from which to look across at the Capitoline hill, down into the Forum Boarium (see map p. 242), and over the excavations beside the Temple of Great Mother (the concrete structure with several large trees growing out of it) on the lower terrace (Fig. 51) at the end of the hill. Much of the western edge of the terrace has fallen away, and the surviving elements, gutted by C15–C18 stone-robbing, are reduced to their foundations or lower, but it is possible to discern the outline of an open court beside the temple with a range of rooms on the west. The lower terrace can be reached by the stairs nearby or, if they are closed, by another set of steps (partly ancient) further along, beyond the oval basin (an ancient fishpond) at the SE corner. The basin and barrel-vaulted rooms along this edge of the platform date from the early C2 AD. They replaced previous buildings in much the same position, dating from the early C1 AD, presumed to be additions made to the Augustan palace by Tiberius.

Precinct of Victory. Fig. 51

The promontory at the SW corner, overlooking the Tiber, is one of the few areas of the Palatine yet excavated extensively in depth, thanks largely to the activities of C15–C18 stone-robbers, who created various 'windows' through the superimposed buildings. The robbers were not interested in concrete, so the core of the podium of the **Temple of Great Mother** survives, as does the podium of the small **Temple of Victoria Virgo** beside it, but the podium of the **Temple of Victory**, mostly built of squared tufa blocks, they removed almost entirely, thus exposing wells and cisterns and other fragmentary remains of the C6 and C5 BC. An artificial platform immediately in front of the temples (B) was also gutted, for

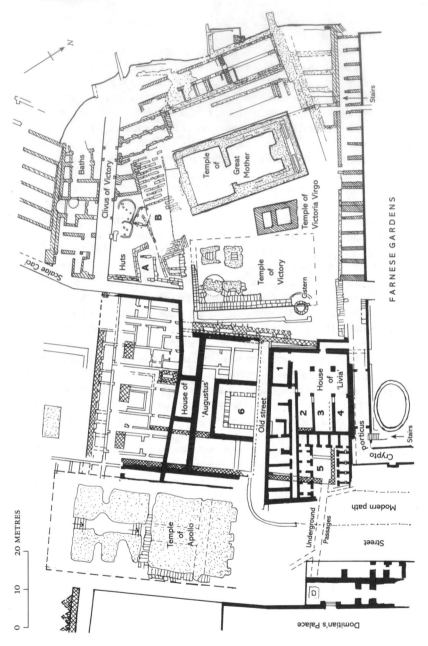

▲ **Fig. 51.** Palatine. SW corner. Site plan

▲ **Fig. 52.** Palatine. Reconstruction of Iron Age huts

it was supported on ribs of solid stone blocks, whereas the ruins of later extensions and reinforcements in brick-faced concrete were ignored. And since the stone ribs were set down on to the natural bedrock of the hill, the gutting has permitted modern excavators to reach considerable areas of the bedrock itself, which is pitted with the floors and post-holes of **Iron Age huts** dating from the C9 and C8 BC. The largest hut plan measures 5 × 3.5 m., a slightly oval rectangle; the spaces between the wall posts were probably filled with wattle and daub, and the roof thatched with reeds; there was a small porch in front of the door. The huts were destroyed by the late C7 (to be replaced by more substantial structures of which we know little) but the memory of early settlement on this particular corner of the hill endured in the legends which surrounded it. The steep stepped street which led directly up the slope in front (the *Cermalus*) was known as the *Scalae Caci* (Stairs of Cacus, a local monster defeated by Hercules). Somewhere at the foot of the slope was the shrine of the *Lupercal*, the cave where the she-wolf had suckled Romulus, the future founder of the city, and his twin Remus when they were first washed ashore. The top of the slope was the site of the house where Romulus and Remus had been brought up by the shepherd Faustulus, and where the omens choosing Romulus as king had been read in the passage of wild birds. The '**House of Romulus**', a modest reed hut which the priests carefully preserved and replaced as need be, was reportedly still in existence in the late C4 AD. Possibly its location is marked by the rectangular enclosure (A), which belongs to a general transformation of the area in the C4 and C3 BC following the construction of the **Temple of Victory (Victoria)**. Paid for by Lucius Postumius Megellus out of the fines he collected as public magistrate and his share of the booty from the wars against the Samnites of central Italy, the temple was begun in 307 BC and dedicated in 294 BC. Victoria was rapidly becoming a very important goddess for the Romans as their armies moved to conquer the rest of Italy and her cult was soon connected with the Lupercal and the mythical origins of Rome. The project involved a new street, the *Clivus* of Victory, which ran in from the north to join up with the old *Scalae Caci* just below the putative house of Romulus. The front half of the temple podium remains as four masses of (later) concrete infill with the imprint of tufa blocks; its eastern flank can also be made out, in the rows of tufa blocks running up to (and once incorporating) a C6 cistern. The platform originally measured 33 × 19 m. (112 × 64 RF), but nothing remains in elevation. Fragments of Corinthian capitals and entablature in stuccoed travertine show that it was rebuilt or restored in the early C1 BC, probably after a major fire of 111 BC. Then at least, if not before, it was a *peripteros sine postico*, with a column height of 11.2 m. (38 RF). A fragmentary inscription records some rebuilding or renovation by Augustus.

The Hut of Romulus

They [Romulus and Remus] lived the life of shepherds, depending on the labour of their hands, and building the mountain huts made—roof and all—out of sticks and reeds. Now there was one of these, even in my own times [late C1 BC], on the slope of the Palatine hill towards the Circus. Those in charge of it maintain it as a holy place: they must not embellish it at all: but if by weather or lapse of time it is damaged in any way, they repair it as closely as possible to the original condition.

(Dionysius of Halicarnassos, *Roman Antiquities* 1. 79. 11)

The **Temple of Great Mother of the Gods** (*Magna Mater* or *Mater Deum*) was introduced in 205 BC, during the final years of the Second Punic War, when the Romans were facing crises on all fronts. Their traditional oracle, the Sibylline Books, told them that they should seek 'the Mother' and bring her to Rome. The Mother was interpreted as the goddess known to the Greeks as Cybele and ambassadors were sent to her sanctuary at Pessinus in Phrygia (central Turkey), then under the control of the Attalid empire, to ask for her sacred image, a silver statue with a piece of black stone set in place of the face. Taken to Rome by sea (an altar in the Capitoline Museums shows the scene, with the Vestal Virgin, Claudia Quinta, pulling the ship to land by her girdle), she was lodged provisionally in the Temple of Victory during the thirteen years it

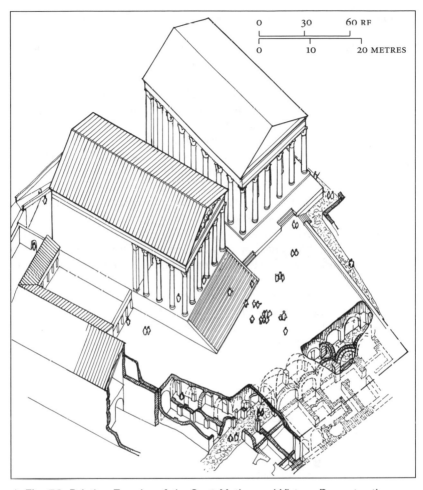

▲ **Fig. 53.** Palatine. Temples of the Great Mother and Victory. Reconstruction, c. AD 200

took to build her new temple, dedicated by Marcus Junius Brutus in 191 BC. Annual theatrical games, the *ludi Megalenses*, for which the playwrights Plautus and Terence wrote some of their best comedies, were held on her feast day (11 April), performed on a temporary stage erected in front of the temple. The audience sat on the (now missing) temple steps, which spread out on both sides to embrace a wide forecourt. Almost all trace of the original temple has gone, but its tufa podium was about the same size as the concrete one we see now (33 × 17 m.; 112 × 58 RF). Most of the concrete of that, standing 4.46 m. (15 RF) high, dates from a rebuilding after a fire in 111 BC, as do the *peperino* tufa column drums, capitals and pieces of cornice which are lined along the eastern flank, some preserving thick white stucco coating. On their evidence, there were two orders, Corinthian 38 RF high for the porch and a smaller Ionic inside the cella. A second rebuilding, following another fire (in AD 3), was presumably paid for by Augustus and mainly affected the cella: the upper level of the podium and the outer walls were reconstructed, in quasi-reticulate tufa and concrete; the interior colonnade was converted to Corinthian and refashioned in marble, perhaps on two storeys. The relaid floor was paved in red/white *breccia rosa*, black slate, and pink-grey Chian marble. Both rebuildings involved the forecourt as well, which eventually extended into a huge level platform, with the old *clivus* of Victory passing in a tunnel beneath it (see Fig. 53). Like Victory, who came to be seen as the guardian of Empire, Magna Mater developed during the C1 AD into a major state deity. She was venerated as the protectress of the city not only in Rome but elsewhere in Italy and the West until well into the late C4 AD. A headless marble statue, showing her seated on a throne flanked by two lions, was found near the Palatine temple and is exhibited in the Palatine Museum (see p. 404).

The smaller concrete podium between the two larger temples, to be identified as the shrine of **Victoria Virgo** (Maiden Victory), is dated by brickstamps to the middle of the C2 AD and relates to a correspondingly higher ground level. Excavations have shown that it overlies two earlier buildings, one of which is probably the original shrine, dedicated by Marcus Porcius Cato in 193 BC.

Houses of 'Livia' and 'Augustus'—Temple of Apollo. Plan, Fig. 51

House of 'Livia'. Backing on to the narrow space (once a street) to the east of the Temple of Victory is a small aristocratic house which underwent numerous alterations but whose basic structure in concrete faced with quasi-reticulate tufa dates from about 75–50 BC. The attribution to Augustus' wife Livia, already doubtful when the house was first excavated in 1869, is now purely conventional. However, it has a reasonable chance of being the house, previously owned by the orator Hortensius, which Augustus had acquired in 41/40 BC and began in 36 BC to develop into his main residence. Its principal entrance faced east, fronting onto what was to become the forecourt of the Temple of Apollo. As in the houses near the Arch of Titus (Fig. 45), the basement under its atrium (Fig. 51: 5, not accessible) was filled with small cells for the household slaves.

The equivalent level at the rear of the house formed a sunken dining-court, which can be reached by an ancient entrance at the north corner (if closed, ask custodians). The entrance was made at the time that the court-yard and its suite of dining rooms were modified and redecorated with advanced 'Second Style' (see p. 49) wall paintings, probably in the early Augustan period (about 30 BC). Though they have deteriorated considerably over the past 130 years, the paintings were of fine quality and the differing schemes employed reflect a hierarchy in the spaces they decorate. In the room in the right-hand corner (Fig. 51: 1) each wall was given an elaborate design of illusionistic architecture, in which a large picture of a rural sanctuary in a landscape was set in the centre of a richly veneered panel scheme, with a colonnade of delicately ornamental columns in front. By contrast, the walls out in the courtyard (which had real columns supporting its portico roof) were treated in a relatively simple scheme of imitation veneer, alternating wide black and narrow green panels framed in red in the middle zone, bordered above and below by yellow bands. Of the three tall rooms opening off to the rear the two side ones (Fig. 51: 2, 4) are both treated as if they had an internal colonnade in front of their veneered walls. The scheme in the right-hand room (Fig. 51: 2) is the better preserved, with luscious garlands of fruit and flowers looping between its golden plant-like columns, set off against a background of white panelling. The yellow frieze which runs along the top of the panelling was filled with Egyptianizing landscape scenes. Above that are fragments of a further set of panels, with winged female figures (Victories?) whirling on filigree brackets. The same figured panels appear in the upper zone of the left-hand room (Fig. 51: 4), which did not have the garlands and was predominantly red where the other is white. The central room (Fig. 51: 3) was the most richly decorated of all, in a scheme possibly inspired by the displays of Greek art in temples and public buildings. Each wall had a large mythological picture in the middle, set in a large columnar frame with screen walls to either side pierced by architectural vistas with figures. The mythological picture on the back wall, now totally illegible, showed a theme popular among Augustan poets, the story of the monster Polyphemus and his jealous love of the sea-nymph Galatea. Its companion on the other wall is still partly visible; Io, fatefully beloved by Zeus, was seated on a rock in front of a sacred column, with her guardian-herdsman Argus leaning on his spear at the right and Hermes (Mercury) hovering behind her to the left. The smaller picture painted as part of the screen to either side represents an antique Greek panel painting (a *pinax*), highly prized and protected by little folding doors. The *pinax* on the left of the long wall shows two women, one standing, the other seated, and between them a goat being brought to sacrifice on the shoulders of a boy. That on the right of the back wall is a similar three-figure composition, of a noble woman and her hand-maidens.

The three lead water pipes mounted on the left-hand wall of room (3) are stamped respectively with the name of Domitian, a certain Julia Aug[usta] (who could be any one of several Imperial ladies), and L. Pescennius Eros, an agent of the Severan emperors. They were found connected to each other in the underground passageways which ran between the basement at the eastern end of the house and the basement of the Neronian and then Domitianic palace.

The passageways are not the only evidence that the house remained part of the Imperial palace until Late Antiquity, though its upper levels were radically altered in the course of time, in part already within the later Augustan period (probably after the fire in AD 3 which also damaged the Temple of Magna Mater) and even more substantially in the middle and then the late C1 AD (after the fire of AD 64 and then as part of the new Flavian palaces). A brick foundation was built down the length of the sunken court (its position is marked by the scar in the floor and up the back wall of room (3) and another runs across the back wall of room (2). Both align with similar foundations set down in the atrium end, and those in turn must relate to sizeable brick structures built in the area to the south, beside the Temple of Apollo, over the top of the varying levels in a large house which is also likely to have formed part of the House of Augustus.

House of 'Augustus'. Visible over the tufa wall mid-way along the other side of the street which runs along the southern edge of the House of 'Livia', are some fragmentary traces of the upper terrace of a fine house of the C1 BC, built on the site of an earlier house, of about 100 BC, and itself much built into and over in later times. The main feature discernible from afar is the floor level of a small tufa peristyle (Fig. 51: 6), its western angles marked by the two fragments of fluted columns.

Excavations since 1961 have exposed a complicated series of rooms arranged on a lower terrace (†permit required), which runs under the podium of the Temple of Apollo. The situation fits the written sources which tell us that the temple was founded on a part of the site which Octavian (Augustus) had bought intending to extend his own house but which was then struck by lightning, an omen that the space was to be used for religious purposes. Once the temple was built, the remnant of the property on the side towards the Temple of Victory was connected at the level of its upper terrace with the House of 'Livia' across the way (either abolishing the street between them or reducing it to a corridor; its present level is arbitrary and its western end is blocked by a wall which clearly linked the two properties together). Later, with the building of Domitian's palace to the east if not before, the upper terrace was extended out over the rooms on the lower terrace, which were filled in and new lower terrace laid out on the hillside in front at a higher level.

The rooms trapped under the podium of the Temple of Apollo preserve some exceptionally fine Second Style wall-paintings of pre-Augustan date; those and others in the western sector, perhaps early Augustan, are conserved on site; some have had to be reconstructed from thousands of fragments and are on show in the new Palatine Antiquarium.

Temple of Apollo. Vowed by Octavian at the battle of Naulochos against Sextus Pompey in 36 BC, the temple was dedicated on 9 October 28 BC and stood until AD 363. Its podium measured approximately 24 × 45 m. (80 × 150 RF) but almost all the tufa blocks which faced and reinforced it have been quarried away; the NE side is marked by the mound of rough concrete. The top and bottom half of a Corinthian capital, a piece of fluted column shaft and a fragment of cornice, displayed on the wall beside the laurel hedge, are the sole survivors of the temple elevation, which was of solid white Italian marble and (judging by the capital) had columns almost 15 m. (50 RF) high.

The temple is generally assumed to have faced out from the hill, for the SW side of the podium gives the impression of a staircase, but the steps were made in the C19 and it is worth entertaining the contrary view. The NE half has barrel-vaulted passages in its core, which suits the lighter weight of the front porch, whereas the voids in the SW half argue for more solid tufa construction, to bear the weight of the cella. Written sources suggest that the temple façade made a tremendous visual impact, more understandable if it commanded the top of the street leading up to the entrance to Augustus' house, rather than facing out over the valley of the Circus Maximus. Statues in Parian marble by the archaic Greek sculptors Bupalos and Athenis of Chios decorated the pediment, surmounted by a statue of the sun-god Helios in his chariot. The temple doors were inlaid with antique ivory reliefs, and the cella housed three cult images: Apollo, his twin sister Artemis (Roman Diana) and their mother Leto (Latona), all by famous Greek sculptors of about 360 BC. Apollo, in his guise as patron of poetry and music, wearing a long robe and playing the lyre, was the work of Scopas, perhaps taken from the sanctuary at Rhamnous, near Athens; Diana was the work of Timotheus, with her head restored by C. Avianus Evander; Latona was by Cephisodotos.

Ancient descriptions also mention a portico of Numidian yellow marble columns with statues of the fifty Danaids, the daughters of Danaus (son of Io and ancestor of the Greeks) ready to kill their fifty cousins, the sons of Danaus' brother Aegyptus (Egypt). Where the portico was in relation to the temple is not stated and has not been identified with any certainty on the ground; it could have been down on the lower terrace, or on the upper terrace over to the west, or simply on three sides of the temple itself. In the Palatine Antiquarium are two Danaids in black Greek marble and one in red Greek marble (which could have formed pairs between the columns) and sets of brightly painted terracotta reliefs with Danaids and other mythical figures (which may have decorated the portico entablature) turned up in the ruins of the podium. Augustus' enclave reportedly also included a library, large enough to hold Senate meetings (perhaps replaced in due course by the two large apsidal rooms on the new Flavian terrace beyond the temple (see Fig. 54). A shrine of Vesta was added in 12 BC when Augustus took over as chief priest (*pontifex*

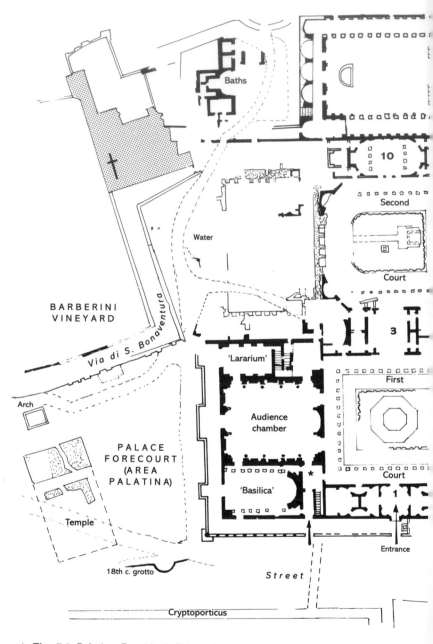

▲ **Fig. 54.** Palatine. Domitian's Palace. General plan

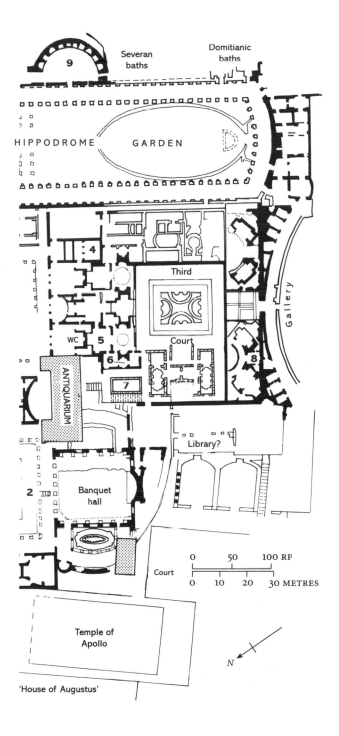

Severan baths

Domitianic baths

9

HIPPODROME GARDEN

Gallery

4

Third

WC

5

6

Court

7

8

ANTIQUARIUM

Library?

2

Banquet hall

Court

0   50   100 RF

0   10   20   30 METRES

Temple of Apollo

N

'House of Augustus'

▲ **Fig. 55.** Palatine shrine of Vesta on a coin of Tiberius, c. AD 22–3

maximus) and moved the public residence required of the priesthood away from its traditional location near the Regia (and its original shrine of Vesta) to his Palatine house, which already enjoyed public status. No trace of the shrine has been found but it appears on coins in company with the two famous statues of cows which stood in front of it, works by the Greek sculptor Myron (*c*.460 BC).

To the east of the Temple of Apollo the considerable rise in ground level and a dramatic change in scale and technique from tufa to red brick announce the western front of the Domitianic palace. Its construction respected the temple forecourt and turned the street which led up to it (*clivus Apollinis*) into a wide colonnaded avenue.

Domitian's Palace. Fig. 54

Built between 81 and 92 AD, the palace was designed by Rabirius, one of the few Roman architects we know by name. It has not yet been fully excavated (and is especially vague in the NE sector towards the convent of S. Bonaventura) but what there is to see covers more than 3 hectares. The main body (taking its orientation and some of its features from an earlier palace which Nero had built on the same site) is composed around two peristyle courtyards. The entrance on the west side (in line with the old front door of the House 'of Livia'), leads first into an **octagonal vestibule** (Fig. 54: 1), with an extraordinary sequence of curvilinear waiting-rooms (?) on either side. Then comes the **first court**, which apparently went by the name of 'Sicily' (cultured Romans enjoyed identifying parts of their houses with suitably famous places; Augustus had a private study at the top of his house which he called his 'Syracuse'). Once enclosed on all four sides by a portico of the fluted columns of Numidian yellow marble whose fragments are scattered here and there, the open area of the court was almost entirely occupied by a pool as big as a lake, with a large octagonal island in the middle, where fountains will have played water down steps and channels. Everything (the island, the floor and sides of the pool, the surface of the courtyard and the back walls of the colonnades) was once veneered in marble.

Water and coloured marbles, both in enormous quantities, were two themes which ran throughout Rabirius' design; a third was a lavish use of gold, and a fourth, which impressed his contemporaries even more, was sheer height and space. Grandeur on quite such a scale was the prerogative of the gods. In keeping with the increasing absolutist character of his regime, Domitian was flaunting the concept of his own divinity (he frequently compared himself with Jupiter the Best and Greatest, and was assassinated four years after the palace was finished).

Something of the vertical dimension we have mentally to restore to the buildings which soared up to either side of the first courtyard survives in the NW corner of the '**Basilica**'. Its present height of 16.3 m. (55 RF) is only the equivalent of the first floor. The 'basilica' (its plan resembles a basilical church) is one of two smaller reception or council halls flanking a huge central one known as the 'Aula Regia' or **Audience Chamber**. Excavations under the floor have shown that Nero had built a hall of similar character, though considerably smaller, on precisely the same spot. Domitian's version, 38 m. long by 31 m. wide (128 × 104 RF), had walls 3 m. thick, articulated on the inside into bays containing niches for eight large statues. Two of the statues, one representing Hercules, the other Bacchus with a Satyr, both 12 RF high (3.5 m.), were found in the C18 and are now in the museum at Parma. They are carved in metallic green Bekhen stone from the eastern desert of Egypt. Phrygian purple columns projected on plinths in front of the niches, and were surmounted by further colonnades, taking the ceiling about 30 m. (100 RF) above the floor. The roofing will have been of wood, its span requiring beams at least 26.5 m. (90 RF) long, probably of cedar, imported from the Lebanon. The whole suite was principally orientated towards a monumental porch along the north front (one of the columns, in green-grey Carystian marble, has been set up at the west end). From the porch, which looked directly down on the palace forecourt (*area Palatina*), the emperor would appear to the people in the *salutatio*, the traditional Roman morning ceremony when the rich and powerful formally received their friends and dependants. The 'reception' suite has its own entrance on the west, behind the basilica, at the same point that a staircase (*) comes up from a subterranean corri-

---

House of the Griffins—Aula Isiaca

Wealthy houses of the late C2–C1 BC are preserved to first floor level beneath the northern side of Domitian's palace. Under the 'Lararium' is the House 'of the Griffins' (†permit required) decorated with very early Second Style wall-paintings of about 100 BC, most of which remain in place; some are in the Palatine Antiquarium. Under the 'Basilica' was discovered the 'Aula Isiaca', a room with walls and ceiling painted in the Egyptianizing style of about 30 BC, now rehoused in a suitable space over to the SE of the second court (Fig. 54: 4).

dor connected with the *cryptoporticus* in front of the so-called *Domus Tiberiana* on the other side of the street. The corridor (usually accessible and worth a detour) is spacious and was surely not intended only for servants; it allowed anyone to cross over to the other part of the palace without going outside. Near its junction with the *cryptoporticus* the floor has subsided unevenly, over buildings buried still deeper in the subsoil.

Returning to the first courtyard, on the SW side is the **Banquet Hall** (*cenatio*). Traces of two previous dining-halls, both built by Nero, one before and one after the fire of AD 64, have been excavated beneath its floor. The staircase (Fig. 54: 2) was part of the pre-AD 64 hall: it leads down to a small sunken court (permit required) with a *triclinium* of dining-couches under a columned pavilion against the back wall, flanked by fountain rooms to either side and facing a fountain in the form of a theatrical stage building, everything veneered in coloured marbles. Its Domitianic successor repeats the same basic formula, but on a monster scale.

The height of the hall has been estimated as equal to its length, 31.60 m. (106 RF). It was entered through a colonnade of grey Egyptian granite columns 36 RF high and the interior was lined with three super-imposed orders of columns. None of the column shafts have survived, but Statius' poem thanking Domitian for a dinner party (see box p. 138) implies that the lowest were of Numidian yellow, the middle of Phrygian

▼ **Fig. 56.** Nero's dining court of pre-AD 64 (preserved beneath Domitian's Banquet Hall)

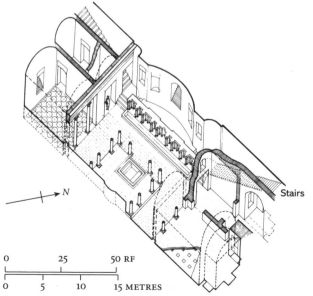

purple, and the uppermost of pink-grey from Chios or the greenish Carystian. Once inside the hall the guests could look back out through the grey granite colonnade to the peristyle court, its island-fountain filling the scene in the distance. They could also look out through large picture windows which opened between the columns of the interior order to a

▼ **Fig. 57.** Domitian's Palace. Reconstruction of the great Banquet Hall and its fountain courts

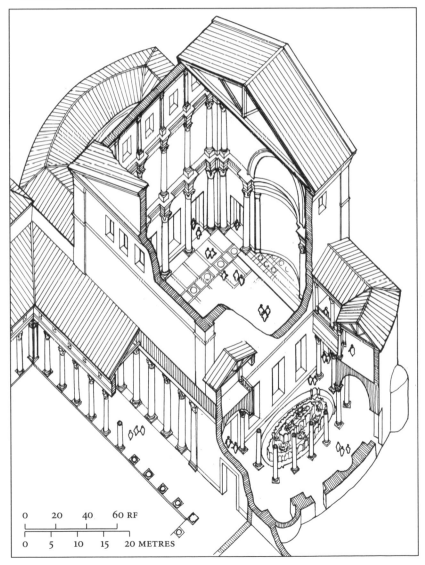

Jupiter's dining room

I think I am dining with Jupiter in mid-heaven...An edifice august and huge; magnificent not with a hundred columns but as many as could support heaven and the gods were Atlas eased of his burden. The neighbouring house of the Thunderer [i.e. Temple of Jupiter on the Capitoline] views it with awe, and the powers rejoice that you [Domitian] are lodged in a like abode...the vast spread of the building, and the reach of the far-flung hall, more expansive than a plain, embracing beneath its shelter a vast expanse of air, and only lesser than its lord; he fills the house and gladdens it with his mighty spirit. Libyan mountain [Numidian yellow] and gleaming Illian [Phrygian purple] stone are rivals there, and much Syenite [Egyptian granite] and Chian and the rock that vies with the grey-green sea [Carystian]; and white [Italian] Luna also, but only to carry the columns. The view travels far upward, the tired vision scarcely reaches the summit and you could think that it was the golden ceiling of the sky. Here...Caesar has bidden the Roman elders, and the ranks of equites recline together at a thousand tables...(Statius, *Silvae* 4. 2. 18–31 (AD 93/4))

fountain court on either side. Only the western court has been uncovered completely (the eastern one runs under the Antiquarium). Originally surrounded by Numidian yellow colonnades on two storeys, the tiered oval fountain has been reconstructed in brick to give some idea of its elaborately curvilinear profile but it ought to be clad in coloured marbles. The marble pavement now visible in the bottom of the pool, however, belongs to the preceding palace built by Nero after AD 64; more of the same floor level has been excavated to the west, as far as the foundations of the curving back wall of the Domitianic court. The swirling design of stylized flowers and looping tendrils is the most remarkable example of the art yet found, executed in red and green porphyry, with minute details inset in Numidian yellow and red limestone, against a background of Phrygian white/purple. The plinths of a colonnade can be seen on the north, set off from the floral design by a border of equally beautifully cut panels of pink-grey Chian framed in strips of green porphyry. Almost as extraordinary as the quality of the floor itself is the fact that the Flavian builders made no attempt to lift it but hacked their foundations through it and simply buried the rest where it lay.

The windows between the Banquet Hall and the fountain courts were glazed and heating installed under the hall floor in the AD 120s (reign of Hadrian), but the surviving pavement undulating over the collapsing hypocaust on the NE side of the Hall dates from the early C4 AD (Maxentius or Constantine). A border set between the column bases along the wall consists of orange alabaster, Lucullan black, and Carystian green;

then comes a wider border of large panels of Numidian yellow and pink-grey Chian separated by strips of grey granite. The principal design was composed of grey granite roundels set in Numidian yellow squares alternating with Phrygian purple rectangles framed in Lucullan black. In the shallow apse in the back wall the pattern changes to a combination of geometric and curvilinear shapes in red and green porphyry, Phrygian purple, Numidian yellow, and Chian pink, all recycled from elsewhere and rather roughly laid, perhaps commissioned by one of the emperors who sometimes used the palace in the C5 AD.

For the **Antiquarium** see p. 403.

If the first court and its great banquet hall were primarily designed for grand public feasts with thousands of guests (who probably overflowed into the peristyle colonnades), the **second court** was possibly intended for more select occasions, though the intermediary block had rooms facing both ways and there was ready access (Fig. 54: 3) between the two. The second pool was as large as the first and also presented a seascape, perhaps evoking some scene from Greek mythology: a narrow causeway led to a small island (off-centre) with at least one sculpture set in the open water on the west. On the NE side, where both the pool and the associated colonnade had rounded corners, the court backs up against the foundation of a massive wall, beyond which some further foundations are partly exposed (according to plans drawn in the C16, the area was once occupied by another trio of huge halls like the tripartite 'reception' suite of the first court, facing northwards). By contrast, the equivalent block on the SW side of the court (to the left of the Antiquarium) is standing to a considerable height, having been incorporated into the Villa Mills (ex-Convent of the Visitation), assisted by some zealous 1930s reconstruction. The side facing the second court contained a suite of rectangular rooms centred on a semicircular hall, all with wide doorways giving them a clear view of the pool. One of the rooms on the east (Fig. 54: 4) houses the Second Style wall- and ceiling-paintings from the 'Aula Isiaca', of c.30 BC, found in excavations below the floor of the 'Basilica'. Passing through the tall central archway (which should probably have been restored as a large window rather than a door) the other side of the block looks out over a **third court**, which has two levels and a quite different, more private character. The **upper level** on the NE consisted of three sets of rooms, placed back to back with those facing the second court, with small forecourts which let light into the rooms on the lower level. The middle of the outer edge of the terrace has fallen in, revealing the underlying room, one of three octagonal rooms with walls composed of alternately semicircular and rectangular niches, supporting umbrella-shaped concrete domes. This suite and the rest of the **lower court**, 10 m. deep, were apparently created as an afterthought, hollowed out of a court at first constructed on a level with the rest of the palace. It was a world of its own, reached only by the staircase (Fig. 54: 7) which descends around an apsidal fountain court in the north corner. The suite on the NW side is an exotic juxtaposition of variously sized rectangular rooms, light-wells and pools of water; even the island in the middle of the peristyle pool consists of an unusual design of *peltae* (curvilinear shields). The best view is from the far west corner of the upper terrace (Fig. 54: 8), which contains a small suite of rooms arranged in a half-circle. This is also the one point from which you can approach the SW edge of the hill and look across to the Aventine and down into the circus Maximus. On the Palatine side, the long curving wall in the immediate foreground below you belongs to a sort of external corridor along the palace façade, a colonnaded or arcaded gallery linking the two wings which project beyond it. The impression that the gallery connected with the sunken court behind is false; the doorway was made in the 1930s; also modern is the door from the sunken court to the sunken 'stadium' on the east.

Crossing back to the main block, do not miss the **little octagonal room** (Fig. 54: 6), an illustration in miniature of what the western vestibule (Fig. 54: 1) must have looked like. The **marble roof tiles** displayed on top of the wall at (Fig. 54: 5) apparently come from the palace, another indication of its temple-like status.

Along the SE extends the great sunken garden, nicknamed the '**Stadium**' or '**Hippodrome**' from its resemblance in plan to a racetrack. Its depth is the same as the adjacent sunken court, 10 m. below the main palace, and was created by cutting back into the slope of the hill on the near side and building up the other three. Domitian, who also built Rome a real stadium on the campus Martius (Piazza Navona, p. 209), obviously had a particular fondness for the form; he had another version in his great country villa near the Alban Lake (Castelgandolfo), which set a trend. Pliny the Younger describes one he planted in his Tuscan villa around AD 100, with plane trees, cypress, bay, fruit trees, and acanthus plants. What the Palatine garden contained, beyond the two semicircular fountains at either end, we do not know. Round the inner perimeter (a distance of some 355 m. or 1200 RF) ran a two-storey portico, 6 m. (20 RF) wide, carried on slender piers of brick-faced concrete. The upper level, connecting with most of the surrounding palace, was both a balcony and a corridor. The lower level (a short stretch of which has been reconstructed at the northern corner) is not open to the public, but was essentially a promenade from which to enjoy the garden, sheltered from the sun or rain. Stairs led down to it from the main palace at three points on the western side and it was also accessible from the baths at the south corner. The piers of the colonnade were shaped on the outside as half-round columns (Tuscan on the lower level, Corinthian on the upper), all veneered in coloured marble (the surviving column bases are of pink-grey Chian); the underside of the concrete barrel vault was richly coffered. Height and comparative slenderness took their toll on the brick piers, which had to be reinforced with arches in the early C3 AD, when the terrace at the NE end was also remade, producing a series of rooms perhaps intended to look like starting gates. In the centre of the east side, the **semicircular exhedra** (Fig. 54: 9, closed) was constructed on three levels, one for the garden, one opening off the upper gallery and one a belvedere on top of its concrete semi-dome. Its outer wall once rose as a huge semicircular tower in the centre of a bastion-like façade towards the Caelian hill, but was later reduced to a quarter circle when the C3 Severan emperors built large new baths between it and the original Domitianic baths at the far south corner. Later still, the garden court itself was invaded by the **elliptical structure** at the SW end, apparently the arena of a private amphitheatre. When first excavated (in the 1870s) its side walls were standing rather higher, and there were radial walls between it and the piers of the portico. It seems to date from the late C3 or early C4 AD, signifying Diocletian, Maxentius, or Constantine, but could be somewhat later. That someone should install an amphitheatre in the Palatine palace even in the late C4 or C5 is not impossible; by then gladiatorial games were becoming rarer, but wild beast fights, aquatic shows, and public executions of criminals were to continue well into the C7 and emperors ever since Domitian had been known to stage such events at home, with or without a purpose-built arena. (The Sessorian palace, one of the many alternative Imperial residences in Rome, near S. Croce in Gerusalemme, had been provided with its own amphitheatre in the early C3.) Footings of other additional brick structures in the northern half of the Palatine garden (possibly arches or small pavilions) can be dated to the late C4 or early C5, and stamped bricks attest constructions or repairs by the Ostrogothic kings, Theodoric and his successor Athalaric, in the early C6.

A set of **baths** on the terrace to the NE is attributed to Maxentius (AD 306–12). Only parts of lesser rooms in the north half of the complex are still standing, its central hall and hot rooms on the south side will have extended almost as far as the 'Hippodrome'. Huge cisterns lie beneath the adjacent **convent of S. Bonaventura**, outside the archaeological zone. To the left of the convent the boundary wall of the **Barberini vineyard** runs along the outer edge of the great rectangular platform (see on site map, Fig. 50: 7), most of which is also outside the archaeological zone. Laid out along the natural ridge at the same time as Domitian's palace, on a level with the suite of halls on the north side of the second peristyle, the platform may have carried mainly porticoes and gardens, the latter perhaps planted in pots and called the *Adonaea* or Gardens of Adonis. Various parts of the substructures began to collapse in the C2, however, probably because of unsuspected voids (ancient tufa quarries) in the underlying bedrock, and much of the original scheme was rebuilt around AD 160–70. The rebuilding included a solid rectangular terrace in the middle, on which the emperor Commodus (AD 180–92) then installed a large temple (parts of the podium can be seen if you can gain access to the church of S. Sebastiano). Facing west and approached by a wide staircase leading directly off the upper Via Sacra, which deity the temple housed is debated, but circumstantial evidence suggests some form of Jupiter, and it is possible that the C2 building simply replaced an earlier one, vowed to **Jupiter Victor** by Quintus Fabius Maximus Rullianus in battle against the Samnites in 295 BC. As such, it might also be the same temple which the eccentric emperor Elagabalus (AD 218–22) rededicated to his own god Sol Invictus Elagabalus, but was restored to Jupiter ('Ultor') by his successor Alexander Severus (AD 222–35).

Passing through the gap between the SW corner of the platform and the northern façade of the Domitianic palace, the ground level in the roughly triangular area beyond drops steeply away as a result of extensive excavations and subsidence. The exposed concrete foundations of the porch along the palace façade show how much of the Imperial forecourt has disappeared. Some distance further down the slope, on the left-hand (west) side of the path, the modern basalt-and-concrete plinth (7 × 8 m.) marks the position of one pier of the **palace gateway**, a **monumental arch** (the other pier lies under the modern boundary wall to the east),

▼ **Fig. 58.** Five Flavian buildings on a relief from the tomb of the Haterii family (Vatican Museums, ex-Lateran collection)

Key:

1 Entrance to the Iseum on the Campus Martius	4 Palatine palace gateway (?)
2 Stadium of Domitian	5 Temple of Jupiter Stator
3 Arch of Titus	

1   2

built by Domitian, possibly on or near the site of the Mugonia Gate, the original gate to Romulus' ancient Palatine city. The concrete lumps sinking into the grass some 15 m. away to the west (one tipping at an odd angle) are parts of the front of the podium of a **temple** (Fig. 54), which originally measured at least 24 by 47 m. (80 × 160 RF). It, too, was built by Domitian, at the same time as the new palace, and faced east, towards the arch, but it incorporates a much earlier predecessor. When first excavated in 1866 it was identified as the temple of **Jupiter Stator**, an idea rejected soon afterwards but now back in favour. Romulus himself, so the story goes, vowed the temple in a battle against the neighbouring Sabines, when the Romans had been driven out of the Forum up to the Mugonia Gate but then successfully stood their ground (hence the epithet 'Stator', stayer). The place was made sacred but no temple was actually built until 294 BC, when Marcus Atilius Regulus made a similar vow at the battle of Luceria against the Samnites (distant relatives of the Sabines). For Domitian, who clearly regarded himself as the equal of Jupiter, to have Jupiter guarding his doorstep could not be more appropriate (if the temple in the middle of the Barberini vineyard was also in existence by this time and dedicated to Jupiter then the palace approach was doubly honoured). Both the arch and the temple could be among the buildings represented on the Haterii relief (Fig. 58: 4 and 5 respectively).

Through the small door in the boundary wall on the right a bridge leads over the Via di S. Bonaventura to the north corner of the Barberini vineyard platform (plan, p. 100, fig. 36). To the rear of the guard hut beside the Arch of Titus exit is a large concrete foundation (partly cut through by

4   **5**

the road), which used to be identified as the Temple of Jupiter Stator (Fig. 36: 46) but has since been demonstrated not to be a temple at all but the base of some honorific monument of the C2 AD (possibly Hadrianic), later used as the foundation for a medieval tower (*Torre Cartularia*). Further along, occupying the space between the substructures of the Palatine platform and the street, is a long rectangular **insula** building (Fig. 36: 47), constructed in the late C2 or early C3 with shops on the ground floor and stairs to apartments above, arranged around a central courtyard. In the late C3 or early C4 the shops at the western end were converted into a small bath-suite and then some time after that an apsidal fountain building (*nymphaeum*) was installed in the western half of the courtyard. The plan of the *nymphaeum* has suggested a church (and an identification as S. Maria de Metrio) but there is no real evidence. Rather, it probably signifies that the *insula* was made into a wealthy **Late Roman house**. Around the corner of the hill some rooms of another such house (Fig. 50: 20) were excavated in 1990. Built in the late C3 or early C4 (that is, around the same time as the adjacent Arch of Constantine), it was still occupied, after a fashion, in the C7. Traces of other walls and terraces poke out from the slopes all along this side of the hill, awaiting excavation.

The path beyond the Via di S. Gregorio entrance leads up to the five surviving double arcades of the **aqueduct** which supplied the huge quantities of water required for the palace fountains and baths. An extension of the Aqua Claudia (whose source lay 61 km. away in the mountains beyond Tivoli), which Nero had led along the spine of the Caelian hill in AD 64, the present structure is Domitianic (c. AD 90), with its arches reinforced by Septimius Severus in about AD 200. It never had more than the two superimposed arcades: to reach the top of the Palatine, the water must have crossed the valley in a siphon (i.e. contained in lead pipes), disgorging into a higher-level distribution tank. The far south corner of the hill is not normally open to the public, but some of the scale of the substructures under the Severan extensions can be appreciated from a distance.

Leaving by the Via di S. Gregorio entrance (whose C16 portal previously stood at the entrance to the Farnese Gardens on the north slope), it is well worth walking round the outside to look back at the hill from the Circus Maximus. En route, the empty area fenced off on the corner of Via di S. Gregorio and Via dei Cerchi contains the foundations of the **Septizodium**, a great freestanding façade 90–95 m. (300–350 RF) long, dedicated by Septimius Severus in AD 203. A sizeable portion of the elevation, composed of three superimposed Corinthian colonnades, survived until the C16, but was demolished in 1588–9 for its white and coloured marble (104 blocks of greyish-white Proconnesian were used to restore the Column of Marcus Aurelius). The name refers to the seven planetary gods, who may have appeared in the midst of a rich array of statues of the emperor and members of the Imperial family, a sort of billboard at the

▲ **Fig. 59.** Septizodium in a print by E. Du Pérac (1575)

foot of the Severan palace above. Crossing over to the far side of the Circus Maximus, the view of the Palatine terraces can be magnificent, especially when caught in the late afternoon/evening sun.

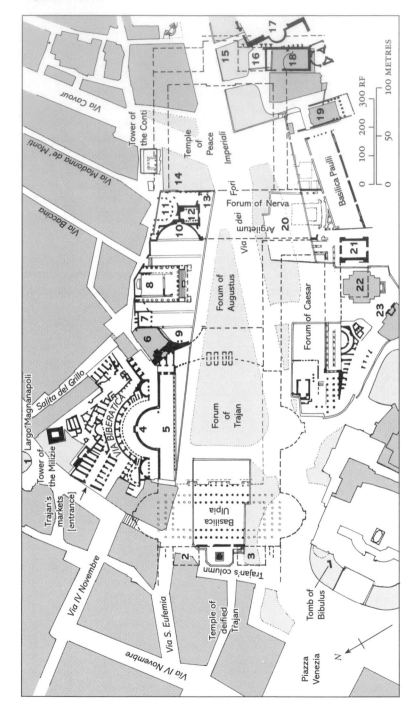

Via Cavour

Tower of the Conti

Temple of Peace

Fori Imperiali

Basilica Paulli

Forum of Nerva

Via dei Argileto

Via Madonna de' Monti

Via Baccina

Largo Magnanapoli

Salita del Grillo

VIA BIBERATICA

Tower of the Milizie

Trajan's markets [entrance]

Forum of Augustus

Forum of Caesar

Forum of Trajan

Via IV Novembre

Via S. Eufemia

Basilica Ulpia

Trajan's column

Temple of deified Trajan

Tomb of Bibulus

Piazza Venezia

N

100 METRES

300 RF

0   100   200   300

0   50   100

Imperial Forums (Map: Fig. 60)

The modern Via dei Fori Imperiali, 'Street of the Imperial Forums' (previously 'of Empire'), was made in 1932–3 to provide a wide avenue for Fascist military parades from the Colosseum to the Piazza Venezia. It ploughed not only through C16 and later housing but also through the hillside behind the New Basilica of Maxentius/Constantine and left in its wake one of Rome's most tantalizingly incomplete archaeological zones. Exposed in irregular wedges on either side of the main road are elements of five enormous colonnaded squares, known collectively as the Imperial Forums, which must join up with one another but almost every critical point of contact is currently invisible. The excavation of some of the missing links on the south side is now in progress, and extensions to the excavated areas in other sectors may be possible in the near future but the road seems set to remain for some time to come, a physical barrier easy to escape on paper but a real challenge on the ground. The map (Fig. 60) attempts to show how what is actually visible (in solid black) possibly combines with what is not (dotted lines) to produce coherent units, but bear in mind that some of the dotted parts are very doubtful, especially the junctions in the centre between the forums of Caesar, Augustus, and Trajan.

The Imperial Forums were constructed in fairly rapid succession from about 50 BC to about AD 115, not to some master plan but none the less in an organic sequence and with such lavishness in materials and workmanship that they could still impress an emperor in AD 357, when Constantius visited from his Eastern Empire. First came the **Forum of Caesar**, put into action by Julius Caesar in 54 BC but advocated for some time before, which was intended simply to enlarge the old Roman Forum, to provide a second, equivalent space as close as possible to the republican Comitium and Senate House (not the Senate House you see now, which

◄ **Fig. 60.** Imperial Forums. General site plan

Key:

1 Republican city gate	14 Park (North angle Temple of Peace)
2–3 Trajan's Libraries	15 Site of main hall (Temple of Peace)
4 Exhedra of Trajan's Forum	16 Hall of Marble Plan
5 Porticus of Trajan's Forum	17 New Basilica
6 House of the Knights of St John	18 SS Cosma e Damiano
7 Hall of colossal statue	19 Temple of Divus Antoninus
8 Temple of Mars Ultor	20 New excavations (1996+)
9–10 Exhedras of Augustus' Forum	21 Senate House
11 *Porticus Absidata*	22 SS Luca e Martina
12 Temple of Minerva	23 *Carcer* ('Mamertine' Prison)
13 'Le Colonnacce'	

belongs to the imperial period, but its predecessor, called the *Curia Hostilia*, which stood in a different position, orientated due north–south, somewhere under the church of SS Luca e Martina). The valley bottom so near the original Forum was already thickly built up with wealthy houses and other commercially valuable properties and the project cost millions of sesterces in land purchases alone. The site chosen had a new alignment, probably determined by the main street in the area, the *Argiletum*, which led into the old Forum from the valley between the Esquiline and Viminal hills (its line is reflected in the Via Madonna dei Monti and continues as the later Forum of Nerva).

In 46 BC Caesar was authorized to move the Senate House itself to its present site, architecturally integrated with his new Forum. All the subsequent Forums were similarly oriented, starting with the **Forum of Augustus** (*c.*25–2 BC) laid out on the same side of the street as Caesar's, cutting into the foot of the Viminal hill, followed by the **Temple of Peace** (AD 71–5) off on the other side, as far as the SW flank of the Esquiline hill, and the **Forum of Nerva** (AD 97) which monumentalized the Argiletum itself. Lastly came the **Forum of Trajan** (AD 106–13 and after), a huge project to the NW, which involved cutting back into the Quirinal hill on one side and the Capitoline on the other, also rebuilding the Forum of Caesar in the process. The final touch was added by Hadrian in the AD 120s when he built the **Temple of the Deified Trajan** in a further court to the NW. By the end, the complex was more than 200 m. wide and over 600 m. long, filling the whole inner valley bottom, uniting the old Forum with the Field of Mars round the Capitoline hill in a continuous sweep of colonnaded spaces.

Visit: The public is not generally allowed down into the various excavated sectors, but for an overview the street level is better anyway. The sequence followed here starts from the Forum of Caesar, beside the church of SS Luca e Martina, and takes in the other elements on the south side of the Via dei Fori Imperiali, before crossing the road at the junction with the Via Cavour and moving back along the north side to the Column of Trajan. From there you can make another loop up the hill to Trajan's Markets (which also contain a Museum of the Imperial Forums) and the Republican wall at Largo Magnanapoli and down again round the back of the Forum of Augustus to the Porticus at the north end of the Forum of Nerva.

Forum of Caesar. Map, Fig. 60, and plan, Fig. 61 ★

Comune (†lower level)

Only two areas of the Forum have been excavated: a small part of its south corner (a palimpsest of concrete foundations and traces of marble pavements) where it communicated with the imperial Senate House, and a

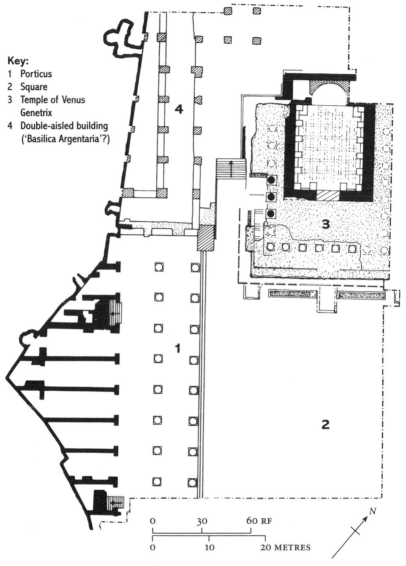

Key:
1 Porticus
2 Square
3 Temple of Venus
  Genetrix
4 Double-aisled building
  ('Basilica Argentaria'?)

▲ **Fig. 61.** Forum of Caesar. NW sector, plan

larger area (Fig. 61) which contains the other end of the SW **porticus** (1), some of the open expanse of the **Forum square** (2) and most of the podium of the **temple** (3) which dominated the NW short side. Relatively little of what is visible belongs to the Caesarian building: the travertine paving of the square (in slabs 30–45 cm. thick), the tufa and concrete core of the temple podium and the lower level of the structures terracing the

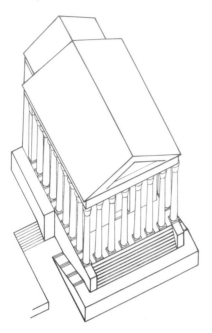

▲ **Fig. 62.** Forum of Caesar. Temple of Venus Genetrix. Reconstruction, c. AD 110

hillside behind the porticus, distinguished by the arcaded wall of brown tufa blocks with keystones and imposts in white travertine. The porticus colonnades and the temple superstructure were replaced, together with the upper levels of the buildings behind the porticus, when the whole hillside to the NW was remodelled in the early C2 AD as part of the construction of the Forum of Trajan. Everything also underwent major repairs and alterations after the fire of AD 283.

The basic scheme, however, remained that started by Caesar in 54 BC and finished off by Augustus in 29 BC. The square evidently took its elongated shape if not its precise dimensions from the old Roman Forum, tidied into a proper rectangle of approximately 124 × 45 m. and given a double-aisled porticus (16 m. wide) down each long side. The **temple** (Fig. 62) was introduced at a slightly later stage, having been vowed by Caesar the night before the Battle of Pharsalus in 48 BC, during his civil war with Pompey, to win over Pompey's favoured goddess *Venus Victrix*, though when inaugurated in 46 BC (while still unfinished) it actually honoured Venus as **Venus Genetrix**, 'universal mother', from which Julius Caesar's family (and thus all the emperors from Augustus to Nero) claimed descent. Her cult statue was a new creation by Arcesilas, a leading sculptor of the period, and Caesar also endowed her temple with valuable antique paintings, collections of engraved gems, a gold statue of Cleopatra, a corselet of British pearls, and other *objets*. Closely related in design to that of Castor on the Roman Forum, the temple had eight columns across the front but only eight down the sides, since for lack of space the rear of the original cella was embedded in the bedrock of the hillside. The front of the 5 m. high podium, like that of Castor, incorporated an orators' platform, but modified so that the steps on both sides led up from the rear (a measure of protection against angry crowds). The three Corinthian columns and section of entablature which have been reerected on the temple podium belong to the exterior order of the Trajanic rebuilding, which was dedicated in AD 113 (on the same day as the Column of Trajan, see p. 164). The marble is Italian (Luna) and the column height 12.87 m. (43½ RF; shaft

▲ **Fig. 63.** Temple of Venus Genetrix. Fragment of the frieze from the interior of the cella. Erotes and the spoils of war. (Palazzo dei Conservatori, Braccio Nuovo)

36 RF); the frieze is noted for its elaborate acanthus-plant scroll carved in high relief. Inside the cella, the side walls were lined with two superimposed colonnades (24 and 18 RF high respectively), the frieze of the lower (composite?) order decorated with reliefs showing Venus' baby companions, *erotes*, playing with the spoils of war (Fig. 63). The entrance to the apse at the rear was framed by two larger columns and pilasters whose ornate composite capitals were possibly reused in the porch of the Lateran Baptistery in the C5 (see p. 348).

Set into the paving of the square along the front of the temple podium (which is missing all its white marble facing) is an arrangement of two low brick-and-concrete walls on either side of a larger square central element, with footings of two fountains at the extremities and holes for a metal fence in front. Brickstamps in the walls indicate that the assembly dates from AD 123 or later; presumably it held a display of statues, perhaps reinstating a set of nymphs, the *Appiades*, which are mentioned in connection with the temple façade by the Augustan poet Ovid but had been transferred by the AD 70s to the Hall of Liberty, which in its turn had possibly fallen victim to Trajan's new Forum and Basilica (see p. 163). Other statues in Caesar's forum included two of Caesar himself in military dress, one standing, and one on horseback (the horse was Alexander the Great's famous steed Bucephalas, portrayed in bronze by Lysippus). A colossal figure of Tiberius was donated by fourteen cities in Asia Minor (now Turkey) to which he had sent relief after they were struck by earthquakes in AD 17, 23, and 29. Inscribed pedestals attest to one erected by the

North African city of Sabratha to Hadrian's wife Sabina in AD 138, and another by the prefect of Rome to the emperor Arcadius in about AD 408.

The three steps leading up to the higher pavement level of the **porticus** are restorations of 1934, as are the columns of its double colonnade, in arbitrary combinations of fragmentary granite shafts and Corinthian capitals, some of which which may reflect genuine repairs of the early C4 (when the Senate House we see today was also rebuilt, see p. 70), others may not actually belong to the Forum at all. But their foundations are those of the Caesarian colonnades as rebuilt in the early C2; whether there was another storey on top is not clear.

Between the porticus and the street called **clivus Argentarius** ('the bankers' rise') which ran round the Capitoline hill at a higher level, Caesar's builders had constructed a series of parallel tufa walls and concrete barrel vaults forming ten deep rooms accessible from the new Forum at the lower level but capable of supporting further floors which would have opened in the opposite direction, towards the **clivus**. The upper levels were rebuilt in brick-faced concrete in the early C2, incorporating a large public latrine set in a semicircular exhedra and two broad staircases leading from the street down to the Forum level. The **double-aisled building** (Fig. 61: 4) prolonging the Forum porticus on a higher level to the NW, approached by a new flight of steps beside the temple podium, also dates from the early C2, when the hillside into which the temple of Venus Genetrix had been built was destroyed to make the space for the Forum of Trajan. Where the additional colonnades led, except around the newly exposed (and restructured) rear of the temple, is not known but they reveal several phases, including a marble pavement of C6 or later date. The building might be one known in late Roman/early medieval sources as the *Basilica Argentaria*, sharing the epithet with the street which ran just above it.

While in the vicinity you can also visit the **Carcer** or 'Mamertine' Prison (Map, Fig. 60: 23), down the steps in the porch of S. Giuseppe dei Falegnami (an offering is expected of you at the turnstile). The wall of travertine blocks beside the stairs was restored according to the inscription by M. Vibius Rufinus and M. Cocceius Nerva sometime between 39 and 42 AD. The church crypt of the Crucifix is built over two ancient cells which lie behind the travertine wall, lower in the ground, one on top of the other. The upper cell, trapezoidal in shape, was probably one of several which stretched back into the hill at the same level, exploiting old subterranean stone quarries. The lower cell, now reached by a modern staircase, previously by an irregular hole in the roof, was originally circular (diam. 7 m.). This was the death cell, where convicted enemies of the State (such as Jugurtha and Vercingetorix) were strangled and others were detained awaiting execution by being thrown off the Tarpeian Rock (a cliff on the Capitoline hill). The Roman writer Sallust described the cell in about 40 BC: 'in the prison there is a place called the *Tullianum* . . . about twelve feet deep, closed all round by strong walls and a stone vault. Its aspect is repugnant and fearsome from its neglect, darkness, and stench.' The name Tullianum could be derived from *tullius*, meaning a spring of water, since water drained through it.

New Excavations. Map, Fig. 60: 20

In 1996 a large site was opened in the space between the Via dei Fori Imperiali and the limit of the Roman Forum excavations, from the back of the Senate House to the Basilica Paulli (Aemilia). The area covers the lower end of the Argiletum—that is, the Forum of Nerva, the entrances to the Forum of Caesar and the Temple of Peace—and will undoubtedly transform our picture of the Imperial Forums and their development but also reveal much-needed insights into their early medieval history. Among the first discoveries was a stretch of a medieval paved street with a substantial C9 house beside it, which had reused tufa blocks from the Forum of Nerva to create an imposing arcaded street front. Deeper down, it is now clear that the street already had a colonnade down the SE side by the mid C1 AD, that is, a precursor of the monumental Forum of Nerva.

Temple-Forum of Peace. Map, Fig. 60: 14–18

Passing the entrance to the Roman Forum, to the gardens at the higher level beyond, you come to the church of **St Cosmas and Damian**, founded by Pope Felix in AD 527. It occupies a large audience hall which was once part of the Temple of Peace (Map, Fig. 60: 18), at the end of a suite of halls ranged along the SE wing of the temple precinct. The excavation outside the church entrance (Fig. 60: 16), in front of the ancient brick wall on the left of the ramp, has exposed the floor level of the next hall in the line, the hall of the **Marble Plan**. The brick wall, peppered with clamp holes, was once completely veneered with large rectangular slabs of Proconnesian marble on which was incised in AD 203–11 a great map of Rome, drawn at a scale of 1:240 with north at the bottom (Fig. 64). Only small patches of the map survive, about 10 per cent of the whole, broken into over a thousand fragments which have been retrieved in the area on various occasions since 1562 (and are currently in store at the Museo di Roma). Both halls were newly built at the time the map was made, the whole temple complex having been badly damaged by fire in AD 191. Although there is nothing else to be seen above ground, by a nice coincidence much of its larger plan is among the surviving fragments of the Marble Plan. It consisted of an open square, literally square in shape (*c.*108 × 108 m.), which will have been the *templum* proper, with a large altar set towards the rear and surrounded by colonnades on all four sides. The precinct was ten times the size of the Augustan altar of Peace (see p. 185). The original building, dedicated by the emperor Vespasian in AD 75, had been paid for by the spoils of the Jewish War (AD 70–1) and had contained both the treasures from the Temple at Jerusalem, numerous other works of art, and a large library, presumably installed in the range of halls behind the colonnade on the SE side. What other functions the square had, and how the hall of the Marble Plan fits in with them are interesting questions. The building was always called 'Templum', until the late Empire, when it began to be called 'Forum', and had probably taken the place of a large food market, the **Macellum**, attested since the C3 BC and rebuilt in 179 BC, then not heard of after the mid-C1 AD. Elsewhere *macellum* signifies a square court custom-built as a market, with provision for covered shops on all four sides and a round building in the middle, also filled with stalls and shops. An enigmatic feature of the Marble Plan's representation of the

▼ **Fig. 64.** Hall of the Marble Plan. Reconstruction of original veneer panelling scheme. Surviving fragments which have been identified so far are marked in black (The map is upside down in modern terms, with south at the top)

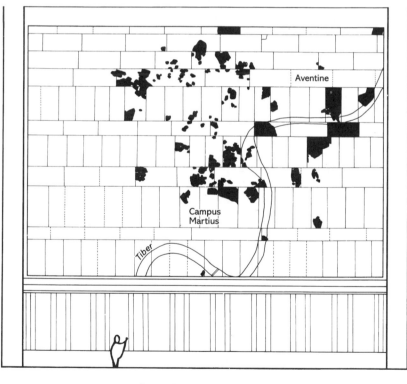

0   5   10   15 RF

0   1   2   3   4   5 METRES

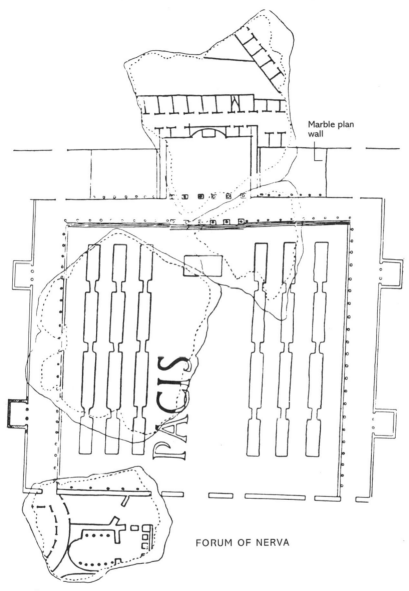

▲ **Fig. 65.** Temple of Peace. Plan reconstructed on the basis of fragments of the Marble Plan (AD 204)

courtyard are the interlinked rectangles, usually interpreted as a garden of flower beds or large shade-trees but one wonders whether they might not have been stalls. The answer may soon be provided by the New Excavations, which could reach the west corner of the square.

Beyond St Cosmas and Damian rears the great bulk of the **New Basilica**, built by Maxentius and Constantine in the early C4 (see p. 115). The angled buttress at its north corner marks the point at which it once made contact with the back wall of the (by then) Forum of Peace.

Crossing over the Via dei Fori Imperiali and its junction with Via Cavour, you come to the small park beside the stump of the C13 **Tor dei Conti** (Map, Fig. 60: 14), corresponding to the north angle of the Temple of Peace. A battered Corinthian capital and fragment of pink Egyptian (Aswan) granite shaft set up in the park probably come from the colonnades of the temple square, as rebuilt in the late C2/early C3. The tower, one of the marvels of medieval Rome until its upper two storeys were brought down by an earthquake in 1348, stands on top of one of the alcoves in the temple's outer wall. The wall of tufa blocks along the NE edge of the park is the party wall between the temple square and the Forum of Nerva, only excavated to its full depth on the other side.

Forum of Nerva. Map, Fig. 60: 12–13   ★

Comune (†lower level)

The upper part of the two Corinthian columns and their superstructure just beside the street (Fig. 66) have always been visible, nicknamed *Le Colonnacce* 'those ugly columns'. The fluted shafts are of Phrygian purple marble and the frieze on the entablature is carved in relief with scenes of women engaged in various domestic occupations (spinning, weaving, childbirth). On the attic storey the surviving sculptured panel in the recess shows the goddess Minerva; the plain surfaces on the projections to either side have dowel holes for metal appliqués, and more holes on top of the uppermost cornice probably anchored a series of bronze statues or trophies. As the excavations in front and northwards have shown, the columns belonged to a much longer 'engaged' colonnade, of perhaps twenty columns, which lined the SE side of the Forum of Nerva, framing the entrances to Vespasian's Temple of Peace. There was presumably a similar colonnade down the other side, off which lay entrances to the Forums of Caesar and Augustus. The elongated square, of similar size and proportions to that in Caesar's Forum, measured 117 × 39 m.

At the north end, as in Caesar's and Augustus' forums, there was a **temple** (Map, Fig. 60: 12), which was quite well preserved until 1606 but is now reduced to the lower levels of its concrete and tufa podium. Although inaugurated by Nerva in AD 97, the Forum had actually been built by his predecessor Domitian, son of Vespasian, and the temple was dedicated to Domitian's favourite goddess Minerva, one of the Capitoline triad, goddess of both craftsmanship and war, a rival to Mars. The Forum was also known as the ***Forum Transitorium*** (the passage-way forum), presumably because, in addition to forming a vestibule to the buildings on

▲ **Fig. 66.** Forum of Nerva, colonnade

either side, it remained a thoroughfare from end to end, having transformed but not abolished the major street called the *Argiletum*. To the right of the temple of Minerva, where the street ran through an arch, the ruts of wheeled traffic (probably in late antiquity) are evident in the stone paving. To the left, the temple was built tight against the tall curving wall of grey tufa blocks belonging to the SE exhedra of the Forum of Augustus.

Forum of Augustus. Map, Fig. 60: 7–10 ★

Comune (†lower level)

The modern street runs at an oblique angle across the temple end of the Forum, allowing you to see the whole of the **SE exhedra** (10) and the **temple** (8), just over half of the **NW exhedra** (9) but little of the rest of the forum square, which must stretch back under the Via dei Fori Imperiali to meet the Forum of Caesar. The great wall of grey *peperino* tufa (from Gabii) which rises in the background to its original height of 30 m., with horizontal bands and capping of white travertine, was calculated to protect the Forum within it from the ever present risk of fire from the densely inhabited hillside behind. Although Augustus bought up (at vast expense) all the available properties from the Forum of Caesar as far as the foot of the Viminal hill, apparently there were some he could not, so the boundary wall is not straight and the entrances to the Forum from the rear are not in equivalent positions on either side of the temple. Given the overall constraints on the length of the site, and the size of the temple which had to be accommodated, the courtyard was shorter and wider than Caesar's but probably matched it in actual area (8,000 m²).

The **temple**, dedicated to the war-god **Mars Ultor** ('the Avenger'), had been vowed by Octavian in 42 BC at the battle of Philippi which saw the defeat of the assassins of Caesar. It was consciously related in design to the Temple of Venus in Caesar's Forum, but one and a half times larger, and the front steps were normal (though flanked by fountains like the Venus temple). The exterior order, all in white Italian (Luna) marble (as were the steps, the facing of the podium and the cella walls and the pediment) was canonical Corinthian, the columns 17.8 m./60 RF high with

▼ **Fig. 67.** Forum of Augustus. Temple of Mars Ultor and porticoes. Reconstruction view

shafts of 50 RF, eight across the front and eight down the sides. The three still standing on the right side still support the coffered ceiling slabs which covered the aisles, decorated with large gilded rosettes. In the front porch and the cella the floor was paved in Numidian yellow, Phrygian purple, and 'Lucullan' red/black marbles. The medieval brick and tufa wall supporting some courses of marble blocks stands more or less beside the cella doorway. Inside the cella the walls had Phrygian purple pilasters framing statue niches behind a row of six free-standing columns down either side. The pilaster and column capitals had the winged horse Pegasus instead of volutes (an example can be seen in the museum in Trajan's Markets). In the apse, approached by five steps veneered in Egyptian alabaster and flanked by the legionary standards lost and then regained in the wars against Parthia (Iran), stood the cult statue of Mars, whose colossal marble torso may be that, with restored head, arms and legs, now in the Capitoline Museum (at the foot of the staircase to upper floor). The temple was the ceremonial focus of military politics and foreign policy: Augustus decreed that the Senate should meet in it when considering wars and claims for triumphs (the space was as large as the Senate House proper); military commanders setting off for the provinces officially took

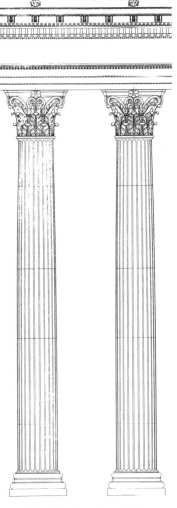

▲ **Fig. 68.** Temple of Mars Ultor. Corinthian order

their leave there; it was the setting for the ceremony in which high-born Roman boys assumed the adult toga, coming of military age.

The **porticoes** down the long sides were intended as venues for courts of justice, especially the public prosecutors. Made longer by curving them into the two great **exhedras**, and paved with Italian grey, Numidian yellow and 'Lucullan' red/black marbles, they had numerous statue niches built into their walls, providing for an ever expanding gallery of Rome's great and good. The larger central niche of the exhedra was occupied on the one side by a group showing Aeneas, ancestor of the Julian family, fleeing Troy with his father and son, and on the other by Romulus, founder of Rome, with a spear and the *spolia opimia* 'spoils of honour' he had won by killing an enemy general in battle. Each was flanked by statues of their respective descendants: Julio-Claudians on one side, the Great Men of the Republic (*summi viri*) on the other. Inscriptions on the statue plinths gave the names and distinctions of each person, and a marble panel on the wall beneath the niche carried a brief eulogy of their deeds. Some of the original series portrayed personifications of the peoples conquered by Augustus, and the provinces of the Empire later donated others—the inscribed base of one from Spain declared that it had used 100 pounds of gold. There were supposed to be strict rules for the award of a new statue but Augustus' successors often abused the system and the space was soon full—one of the functions of Trajan's later forum was to accommodate the overflow.

At the end of the NW porticus there was space for a separate room (Fig 60: 7), its entrance formed of two Phrygian purple marble columns and containing a statue base covered in Phrygian purple marble veneer, cut out around one foot of the statue, which was presumably of metal (bronze, gilded bronze or silver), standing, about six times life-size (9–10 m. high). It is likely to have portrayed either the Deified Julius Caesar or, posthumously, Augustus himself. The walls of the room were veneered with more Phrygian purple, Numidian yellow, 'Lucullan', and white Greek (Pentelic) marble, combined with inlaid panels in other materials. Two of the panels might have been famous paintings by Apelles, court painter to Alexander the Great, one showing Alexander with Castor, Pollux, and Victory, the other with an allegorical figure of War. The emperor Claudius later had Alexander's portrait changed to Augustus'. On the façade of the porticus towards the square, the Corinthian colonnades had shafts of Numidian yellow marble and the upper (attic) storey consisted of columns in the form of handmaidens (known as *Caryatids*), representing the enslavement of a vanquished people, framing shields with heads of the ram-horned Jupiter Ammon (Fig. 69) or barbarian kings.

The whole enterprise took more than twenty years to build (by Roman standards an inordinate length of time) and the temple was still not quite finished when inaugurated in 2 BC. Much then survived, however, in excellent condition until well into the early Middle Ages; its present ruinous and despoiled state was largely the product of the late C16 and after. A scale model reconstruction is displayed, together with various fragments of architecture and sculpture, in the museum in Trajan's Markets.

The **C12–C15 house** perched above the NW exhedra of the Forum of Augustus (Map, Fig. 60: 6), headquarters of the Knights of St John of Jerusalem, has its chapel in the basement, installed in the courtyard of a

▲ **Fig. 69.** Forum of Augustus. Caryatids and shield from the attic storey of the *porticus*

Roman house, and its elegant arcaded loggia is resting on a massive piece of ancient buttressing. The latter was apparently constructed by the emperor Domitian in the early 90s AD in preparation for a new Forum, halted by his assassination in AD 96. To what extent the project anticipated the eventual scale and layout of Trajan's Forum (see below) is debated but it is very possible that Domitian did most of the work of clearing the site.

Forum of Trajan. Map, Fig. 60: 4–5

Via Alessandrina. Comune (accessible from *Trajan's Markets)

The curving façade of warm red brickwork against the hill to the left of the Domitianic buttress belongs to the complex of buildings known as **Trajan's Markets** (see p. 170), where the side of the Quirinal hill and its streets had been cut away to accommodate the enormous new Forum of Trajan. At the foot of the Market hemicycle runs the basalt-paved street which separated it from the *peperino* tufa perimeter wall of the Forum, whose **NE exhedra and porticus** lie in the foreground (Fig. 60: 4–5 and Fig. 76). Both are reduced to their floor level and only a short stretch of the perimeter wall is still standing more than one block high, to the left of the exhedra; you have to imagine it rising to about the same height as that of the Forum of Augustus, a great barrier to protect the forum and its costly marbles and statuary against fire.

The Forum square, dedicated in January AD 112, was paid for *ex manubiis*: from Trajan's share of the spoils from the conquest of Dacia (Romania) in AD 106 and was of powerfully triumphal character. Its architect was Apollodorus of Damascus, an accomplished military engineer who had designed a remarkable bridge across the Danube which launched the Dacia compaigns. The two long **porticoes**, evidently modelled on those in the Forum of Augustus, were 112 m. (380 RF) long and 14.8 m. (50 RF wide), the floor raised three steps (of Numidian yellow marble) above the level in the open square and paved in Numidian yellow and Phrygian purple. The back wall was enlivened with pilasters in Numidian yellow marble framing other marble panelling. The opening to the **exhedra** was screened by ten columns of Numidian yellow; the interior of the exhedra was two storeys high, lined with a two-storey freestanding colonnade (with Phrygian purple shafts below, Numidian yellow above), framing ten niches which once contained over-life-size marble statues. The alcove in the centre of the exhedra's rear wall was framed by two columns of grey Egyptian granite (one has been reerected). The porticus colonnade along the forum square had cable-fluted shafts of Phrygian purple with composite bases and Corinthian capitals of white marble, 9 m. (30 RF) high, three of which have been reconstructed from fragments. On the upper storey, where Augustus' scheme had placed Caryatids, Trajan's had barbarian captives carved in Phrygian purple (with heads and hands inserted in white). Between them, carved in white Italian marble, large rectangular panels showing captured Dacian arms and armour alternated with shield-portraits of past emperors and empresses (among them Nerva and Agrippina the Younger). The façade was capped by a parapet wall in which pedestals projected naming the Roman legions which had fought in Dacia, with their standards reproduced in bronze above. The square itself was paved in huge blocks of Italian marble. In the centre stood a colossal statue of Trajan in military dress on horseback. The SE limit of the square is unexcavated except for a short section of a massive foundation exposed in the corner of the present excavation which shows that it curved outward towards the Forum of Augustus. It probably incorporated a monumental triumphal arch (shown on coins) and a wealth of carved ornament. The opposite side of the square was filled by the great Basilica Ulpia, the central section of which can be seen in the excavation (carried out by the French in 1811–13) in front of the Column of Trajan, marked by the forest of grey granite columns.

Basilica Ulpia. Map, Fig. 60

Comune (†lower level)

Inaugurated on the same day as the Forum in January 112 but paid for by Trajan out of his own money (rather than the proceeds from the sale of booty which had financed the Forum square), the Basilica was the largest which had yet been built in Rome. Its primary purpose, like the Basilicas Paulli and Julia in the old Roman Forum, was to provide prestigious covered space for law courts, but it was also the venue for distributions of imperial largesse, and other official acts of generosity such as the cancelling of public debts. Marcus Aurelius held an auction of imperial valuables there to raise money for his wars. According to the Marble Plan, the apse at the NE end may have taken over some of the ceremonial functions of the old *Atrium Libertatis* (Hall—or Court—of Liberty), concerned with the records of the Roman citizenship and the freeing of slaves (see p. 240).

With five aisles and a large semicircular apse at either end, the basilica measured 600 RF long and 200 RF wide (176 × 59 m.), the central nave 300 × 85 RF (88 × 25 m.). The ground-floor colonnades, all with shafts of grey Egyptian granite, were 36 RF high, an upper colonnade (30 RF) around the central nave had shafts of Carystian green marble; with their respective entablatures, the height of the nave ceiling is estimated at almost 25 m. (84 RF), the height of its pitched roof was perhaps a round 100 RF (29.6 m.). All that remains on the site now, apart from the reconstructed granite columns, are the centre of the great concrete platform on which the building stood, some patches of its marble flooring (Numidian yellow, Phrygian purple, and 'Lucullan' red/black) and various loose chunks of the architectural superstructure. On the side facing the Forum square the Basilica was approached by a flight of five steps of

▼ **Fig. 70.** Basilica Ulpia. Reconstruction of interior (Gatteschi 1924)

▲ **Fig. 71.** Basilica Ulpia on a coin of Trajan, AD 112–14

Numidian yellow (a few fragments survive) at the top of which a columnar porch stepped forward in three parts, the central one with four columns, the lateral ones with two, all with shafts of Numidian yellow marble, white corinthian capitals and bases and an architrave decorated with an elaborate frieze of baby *eros* figures springing out of acanthus plants. Above was an attic storey of Dacian prisoners and shields, like those on the porticus façades. The porch roofs were flat and, according to the coinage struck to celebrate the building (Fig. 71), supported large groups of statues. In the bays between the porches three large statues of Trajan were set up in his honour by the Senate; parts of one showing him as a general and another as magistrate in the toga are in the museum in Trajan's Markets. The third probably portrayed him as chief priest.

The other long side of the Basilica has entirely vanished but consisted of a strong wall of travertine and tufa blocks, which, together with the apses buttressing from the ends, will have given the otherwise entirely columnar structure its essential stability. The wall was pierced by four doors on the ground floor and (no doubt) windows above, lighting the gallery over the side aisles. Two of the doors led to staircases up to the gallery level, the other two gave access to a small colonnaded courtyard in the rear, which had the **Column of Trajan** in the middle and a **Library** to either side (Fig. 60: 2–3). Nothing can be seen of the Libraries from above, but that on the west (25) has been excavated, underneath the park beside the Column.

Column of Trajan. Map, Fig. 60 ★★

†State

128 RF (38 m.) high, composed of twenty-nine huge blocks of white Italian marble (eight for the base, nineteen for the column, two for the pedestal on top) the Column once bore not the statue of St Peter which it has now (placed there in 1588) but a 16-foot bronze statue of Trajan in military dress, taking the structure to an overall height of 144 RF. Free-standing columns were traditional victory monuments in ancient Rome and much of the decoration is appropriately triumphal: the reliefs on the base portray piles of captured Dacian arms and armour, surmounted by

▲ **Fig. 72.** Trajan's Column frieze
(*left*) Trajan and his officers, (*right*) Soldiers foraging

garlands carried in the beaks of four imperial eagles; the torus of the column base is carved in the form of a victor's laurel wreath. But the inscription on the SE side of the base (facing the Basilica Ulpia) says that the Senate and People of Rome erected the column in honour of Trajan in AD 113 for a specific purpose: *ad declarandum quantae altitudinis mons et locus tantis operibus sit egestus* (to show how high a mountain—and the site for such great works—had been cleared away). How it was meant to do this is not immediately obvious, but the door beneath the inscription leads to a **spiral staircase**, a virtuoso feat of engineering carved out of the solid stone, which rises inside the shaft, lit by forty narrow windows, and out to the platform on top of the capital 35 m. (118 RF) above ground, on the side facing the Quirinal hill. There was a metal fence round the edge so that people (twelve to fifteen at a time) could move around for a panoramic view in all directions, the primary one no doubt being over the top of the Basilica Ulpia (whose roof tiles shimmered in gilded bronze) down the length and breadth of Trajan's Forum (and all the earlier forums). The Column was still famous for this view in the C4 AD (and was again from the 1550s, when the little C9 church of S. Nicola de Columna, which had used it as its bell-tower, was demolished and the Column became papal Rome's first official archaeological monument). The Column is principally admired these days, however, for the **helical frieze** minutely carved in low relief on the outside of the shaft. 200 metres long,

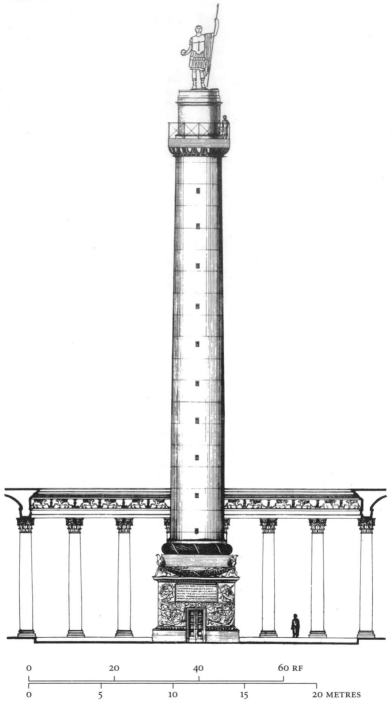

it relates the story of the two Dacian Wars (AD 102–3; 105–6) in a continuous sequence of 155 scenes, containing over 2,600 figures at about two-thirds life-size. Conveniently unwound in drawings and plaster casts (there is one set in the Museo della Civiltà Romana at EUR and another is partially reassembled in the Victoria and Albert Museum in London), the frieze has become an important document for the history of Dacia, the study of Roman military tactics and equipment, and Roman narrative art. Its message was strongly ideological, a pictorial edition of Trajan's *Dacica* (his own lost account of the campaigns) and his vision of imperial power, intended as a

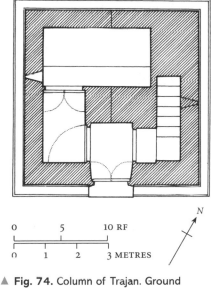

N

▲ **Fig. 74.** Column of Trajan. Ground plan

symbol for posterity. In fact, it is possible that the shaft was originally plain, marked only by the windows lighting the internal staircase (Fig. 73), and that the frieze was carved on it only after Trajan's sudden death in AD 117, when by special dispensation of the Senate the Column became Trajan's tomb. The care lavished by the sculptors on detail which can hardly be seen from more than a metre away suggests an act of piety, commissioned not by the Senate but by someone who did not have to count the cost, namely Trajan's successor Hadrian, who claimed to have been adopted by him on his death bed.

Hadrian was certainly responsible for the final addition to the whole grand scheme, the **Temple of the Deified Trajan**, dedicated sometime between AD 125 and 128, which lies somewhere (probably on axis with the Column) under the late C16 Palazzo Valentini immediately to the NW. It honoured both Trajan and his wife Plotina (who had died in about AD 122 and had also been deified) as Hadrian's adoptive parents, and was the only one of Hadrian's many buildings in Rome on which he inscribed his own name (unlike, for example, the Pantheon, p. 201). The huge Corinthian capital and grey Egyptian granite shaft lying on the ground behind the Column, belonging to an order 60 RF (17.7 m.) high, come from the temple porch. Three key scenes in the Column frieze are arranged on the vertical axis on the NW side towards the temple, whose front steps probably provided the best view of the shaft:

◄ **Fig. 73.** Trajan's Column without the frieze

(2nd band, just below the window slot) *Omen of Victory*: at the start of the first campaign a man falls backwards off his mule watched by Trajan and his officers, above right.

(12th band) *Victory* writing on a shield, which signals the division between the two Dacian wars.

(22nd band) *Suicide* of the Dacian king Decabalus: the end of the war.

Both Hadrian's successor Antoninus Pius and *his* successor Marcus Aurelius were commemorated by huge column monuments set up beside the Field of Mars, though they were not actually buried in them. Marcus Aurelius' column, while obviously a close imitation of Trajan's, strikes interesting contrasts in several respects (see p. 193).

Although the Column is now the only component of Trajan's Forum which has withstood time, the rest probably remained fairly intact until the great earthquake of AD 801 if not later; numerous honorary statues were added in the C4 and C5; public recitations were still being held in the Library in the early C7 and although the Byzantine emperor Constans II appropriated some of the bronze statuary and other ornaments in AD 663,

---

Tomb of Bibulus. Piazza Venezia, Map, Fig. 60

In the grassy area to the left of the front steps of the Vittorio Emanuele Monument is one wall of an important funerary monument, dating from the first half of the C1 BC, which stood on the right-hand side at the beginning of the Via Lata/Flaminia, just outside the Porta Fontinalis of the republican city wall. Constructed of tufa faced with travertine, the design resembles a Greek hero-shrine in the contemporary monumental style, with a tall doorway flanked by four Tuscan pilasters supporting an entablature decorated with a frieze of garlands and bulls' skulls, above which there will have been a wide protective cornice. The rough edge on the blocks down the west side indicated that it once abutted another monument. On the podium, below the doorway, is inscribed: *C. Poplicio L.f. Bibulo aed. pl. honoris virtutisque caussa Senatus consulto populique iussu locus monumento quo ipse postereique eius inferrentur publice datus est* (for Gaius Poplicius Bibulus, plebeian aedile, in recognition of his worth and valour, by decree of the Senate and People the site for a tomb for him and his descendants has been given at public expense). Traces of a similar inscription can be seen on the stump of the left-hand wall. Since the man was probably C. Publicius Bibulus, tribune of the plebs in 209 BC, the present tomb is presumed to be a rebuilding of the original monument, undertaken by his family to stress the honour for subsequent political advantage. Public burial within the religious boundary of the city (*pomerium*) was a rare distinction, and might imply that Bibulus had died in office (see the tomb of Hirtius p. 214).

the buildings were still admired a hundred years after that. The entrance arch on the SE side of the Forum square stood propped up by medieval walls until largely demolished by the street commissioners in 1526.

Climbing the steps (the Gradinata di Via Magnanapoli) to the Via IV Novembre and continuing uphill on the right-hand side of the street, you come first to an excellent view down into an ancient street, whose name by AD 1003 if not before was **Via Biberatica** (probably deriving from *biber*, Latin for beverage, which may have been the principal commodity sold by the shops on either side). The street forms part of the site known these days as Trajan's Markets.

▼ **Fig. 75.** Tomb of Bibulus. Front and left hand side

0   5   10 RF

0   1   2   3 METRES

Trajan's Markets. Map, Fig. 60 and Fig. 76 ★★

*Via IV Novembre. *Comune*

The complex acquired the label 'Trajan's Markets' at the time it was excavated in the 1920s and 1930s. Built in AD 107–10—at the same time as Trajan's Forum—and predominantly commercial in character, the name is not completely off the mark, but is misleading in that it suggests a unified structure with a single function. In reality the buildings constituted several independent units and operated on three separate street levels, which at various points interconnected by staircases as they did in any hillside quarter of the city. The project basically reconstructed the hillside terracing and redirected its network of roads around the outside of the new Forum, replacing all the old buildings with new ones. It employed the latest expertise in brick-faced concrete construction and is easily the best illustration of what Roman urban architecture could achieve in the capital in the heyday of the middle Empire. In the first half of the C2 AD many quarters in the city were redeveloped in the same radical fashion, but the other surviving instances are modest by comparison (such as the apartment block on the side of the Capitoline hill, see p. 232). You can fill in some of the picture by a visit to ancient Ostia, Rome's harbour city at the mouth of the Tiber which was almost entirely rebuilt in the same period, but it lies on the flat, involving none of the challenges set by the hillside sites of Rome.

The modern bridge brings you in under a huge brick arch to a broad passage lined with shop units (Fig. 76: 1), roofed by an extraordinary concrete vault raised on piers, both covering and allowing air and light into the central space yet integrated with a second level of shops on an upper terrace. The merits of the roofing system are best appreciated from the upper level (reached by the staircase through the last door on the left-hand side). Short roofs, set between the arches buttressing the outside of the central vault against the upper shop-fronts, sheltered the shop doorways. The high-level walkway across the south end of the hall is modern (the shops on the west side had their own staircase at the opposite end). Returning to the ground floor, there are two exits at the south end. Only the passage on the right is original—the continuation of the street as a staircase, down to connect with the Via Biberatica. The doorway on the left should be simply to a shop, but a corridor has been broken through into the adjacent unit (Fig. 76: 2), a large building on at least three floors, with its principal face turned towards the hill behind. Reoccupied and extensively restructured in the Middle Ages when it became part of the hilltop fortress focused on the immensely tall C12–C13 Torre delle Milizie (inaccessible), the building now hosts the **Museum of the Imperial Forums**, exhibiting fragments of the decoration of the Forums of Augustus and Trajan.

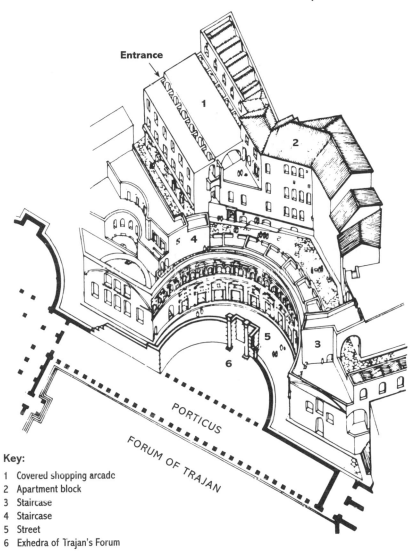

Entrance

Key:

1 Covered shopping arcade
2 Apartment block
3 Staircase
4 Staircase
5 Street
6 Exhedra of Trajan's Forum

▲ **Fig. 76.** Trajan's Markets. Axonometric reconstruction

Descending the stairs to the Via Biberatica you can explore the street in both directions. Uphill to the left most of the shops which lined the far side have been reduced to their floor level; only the last unit, which contains a staircase, stands to any height (Fig. 76: 3). Its roof terrace, reached by the steps off to the left before the tall arcading, gives a fine view. In the other direction, an entrance at the right-angled bend (Fig. 76: 4) leads to a rather labyrinthine sequence of landings and stairs which eventually takes you down to the bottom level, to the street which curves round the tufa wall delimiting the porticus and semicircular exhedra of Trajan's Forum (Fig. 76: 5). *En route*, at the first intermediary level, a corridor heads off into the dark unexcavated recesses of the hill, round the back of one of three concave walls incorporated into the design apparently to give added strength where the terracing projected forward of the central hemicycle. On the next level down you can walk along the middle gallery of shops round the hemicycle, behind the arcade with its smart façade of decorative brickwork, in which brick pilasters with travertine bases and capitals frame the archways, supporting an entablature created out of sets of specially shaped bricks. The space above the entablature, between that and the travertine string course higher up, is filled with alternately triangular and round-headed pediments flanked by broken pediments, also of moulded brick. The red colour of the brickwork of the pilaster shafts was once enhanced with red paint; the entablatures and pediments may have been similarly treated, to stand out against the rest of the background brickwork coated in white stucco.

The lowest level of shops, around the foot of the hemicycle, are little more than alcoves, their unequal depths reflecting the constraints of the bedrock against which they are constructed. One of the shop-fronts has been restored to show how the travertine frames of their doorways were set forward of the front wall to give a little extra space, with a small window boxed in over the lintel. At this level you can also examine at close quarters the remnants of Trajan's Forum beyond the tufa wall (see p. 161). The modern tunnel at the west end (barred) connects with the excavation in front of the Basilica Ulpia.

Republican City Gate. Map, Fig. 60: 1

Largo Magnanapoli

Continuing up the Via IV Novembre from Trajan's Markets, amidst the palm trees on the traffic island in the middle of the junction at the top of the hill, two courses of blocks of Grotta Oscura tufa mark the course of the republican city wall of the early C4 BC and possibly one of its gates, the *Porta Sanqualis*. The wall rose up from the valley on the line of the Via della Salita del Grillo and then ran along the edge of the Quirinal (from Via XXIV Maggio to Largo S. Susanna).

Turning right into the Via della Salita del Grillo ('the cricket's hop'), down the hill, on the right-hand side you come first to further Roman buildings to the rear of Trajan's Markets, and then the continuation of the Via Biberatica, intersected by the later street. Beyond the bend at the bottom looms the great **Fire Wall of the Forum of Augustus**, its vertical mass relieved by the horizontal bands of white travertine and the 'rustication' (sunken joints) of the tufa masonry. The medieval windows and C16 doorway are remnants of the many later buildings which exploited the massive shelter of the wall; the arched entrances, however, are original. The staircase leading up inside the house at the corner (Fig. 60: 6, owned by the Knights of St John of Jerusalem) is laid on top of an ancient one; the chapel to the left of the foot of the staircase occupies the ground floor of a house nestling in the angle beside the NW exhedra of Augustus' forum, the stairs led to its upper storey.

Beyond the fire wall, tangential to the curve of the SE exhedra of Augustus' Forum is the curve of the **Porticus Absidata** (Map, Fig. 60: 11), a monumental marble porch set at the point where the street coming down the valley bottom (more or less where the Via Madonna de' Monti runs now) turned the corner to enter the Forum of Nerva. It was built at the same time as the Forum (c. AD 95–7) and although reduced to its foundations the surviving elements indicate a two-storey Corinthian arcade, 19 m. (65 RF) high, which will have masked the rather cramped rear of the Temple of Minerva as well as providing a suitable pivot to direct the traffic to the left.

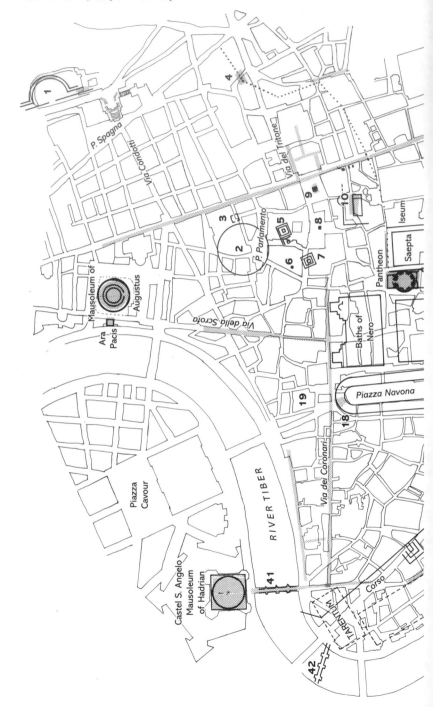

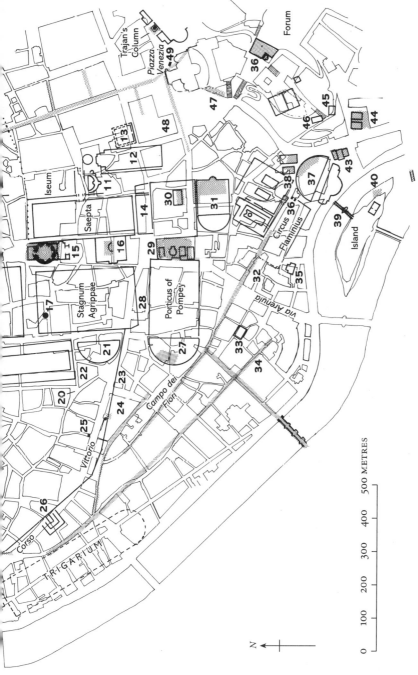

▲ **Fig. 77.** Field of Mars. General site plan

Key to figure 77 on pages 174–5

1 Gardens of Lucullus (Trinità dei Monti)
2 Augustan Sundial (site of)
3 Original site of Ara Pacis
4 Aqua Virgo (Via del Nazareno)
5 Altar to deified Marcus Aurelius (site of)
6 Column of Antoninus Pius (site of)
7 Altar to deified Antoninus Pius (site of)
8 Augustan Sundial Obelisk (Piazza Montecitorio)
9 Column of Marcus Aurelius (Piazza Colonna)
10 Temple of Hadrian (Piazza di Pietra)
11 *Serapeum* (site of)
12 *Porticus Divorum* (site of)
13 Altar of Mars ? (site of)
14 *Diribitorium* (site of)
15 Basilica of Neptune (Via della Palombella)
16 Baths of Agrippa (Via della Ciambella)
17 *Labrum* from Baths of Nero (Via dei Staderari)
18 Stadium of Domitian substructures (Piazza di Tor Sanguigna)
19 Palazzo Altemps (Museum)
20 Piazza del Pasquino
21 Odeum (site of)
22 Palazzo Braschi (Museum of Rome)
23 Palazzo Farnesina ai Baullari (Barracco Museum)
24 Palazzo della Cancelleria
25 Tomb of M. Pansa (site of)
26 Large altar enclosure (site of)
27 Theatre of Pompey (Via di Grotta Pinta)
28 Abbot Luigi (Largo Vidoni)
29 Republican temples (Largo Argentina)
30 Temple (Via delle Botteghe Oscure)
31 Theatre of Balbus (Via Caetani)
32 Via dei Calderari
33 Temple of Mars ? (S. Salvatore in Campo)
34 Via di S. Paolo alla Regola
35 Temple of Castor and Pollux (site of)
36 Entrance porch of Porticus of Octavia
37 Theatre of Marcellus
38 Temple of Apollo Medicus Sosianus
39 Pons Fabricius (Ponte Quattro Capi)
40 Travertine ship's prow
41 Pons Aelius (Ponte Elio)
42 Pons Neronis (site of)
43 Three temples (S. Nicola in Carcere)
44 Two temples (S. Omobono)
45 Temple, site of, possibly *Fides* (Public Trust)
46 Temple, site of, anonymous
47 Roman apartment building (Via Giulio Romano)
48 Madam Lucretia (Piazza S. Marco)
49 Tomb of Bibulus

Field of Mars (*Campus Martius*)
(Map: Fig. 77)

All the low-lying flood plain within the large loop of the Tiber north of the Capitoline hill but west of the Via del Corso (the ancient Via Lata/Via Flaminia) is often still called by its ancient name *Campus Martius* ('Campo Marzio' in Italian), meaning the field consecrated to Mars, the god of war. It is the one part of Rome which continued to be quite densely inhabited after the C9 AD, becoming the centre of the late medieval and Renaissance city, and is still densely inhabited today, an extraordinary blend of past and present even for Rome. The Stock Exchange occupies a Roman temple, the boiler-rooms of the offices of the Senate are set in the ruins of Roman thermal baths; a modern theatre nestles in the shell of a Roman theatre. Many of the streets are on the lines of ancient streets, and the walls of the buildings on either side of them are often balanced directly on top of Roman walls. Some buildings are actually the upper storeys of Roman buildings whose lower storeys are buried deep under the mud of centuries of Tiber floods and the debris of human occupation (e.g. the outer walls of the Crypta Balbi (p. 220) and the buildings at the corner of Via di S. Paolo alla Regola and Via del Conservatorio (Map, Fig. 77: 34). The 'hills' which feature in the local place names beginning with 'Monte', as in Montecitorio, Montevecchio, Monte Giordano, Monte Cenci, Monte Brianzo, Monte della Farina, are all man-made. Most grew up over the collapsed remains of large buildings or are medieval rubbish dumps; Monte Secco, behind the Tiber wharves near the Ponte Margherita, was a smaller version of the amphora-mountain of Testaccio below the Aventine (see p. 367). It is best not to worry about how everything fits together and simply enjoy the variety of the landscape, as one relic of antiquity after another pops up out of the ground or out of the side of a building. On the other hand it is useful to have some broad picture of the changing nature of the ancient subsoil in mind.

During the Republic (C5–C1 BC), the Campus was truly an expanse of flat open grassland, rather marshy in the middle, used for military training and exercises, with particular areas set aside for horse and chariot races. It was also the place where the male citizens of Rome would assemble for public meetings, where the census was taken every five years and where they would vote in their 'centuries' (groups of 100), the same units in which traditionally they were organized for battle. In the southern sector, close to the foot of the Capitoline hill, was an area designated the Flaminian fields, later the **Circus Flaminius**, whose position is known (roughly between the Theatre of Marcellus and the Via Arenula), and another called the State or People's Farm (*Villa Publica*), extent unknown, on whose lands there was a building or complex of buildings which housed the census records and served as a headquarters for army levies and the inspection of arms. The Villa was also a place where foreign ambassadors were received and where a victorious general would wait to hear whether he was going to be granted a triumph, whose parade would start from the adjacent Circus Flaminius. In the course of the C3 and C2 a host of victory-temples was set up around the Circus, and in a line to the north of it (partly excavated in the Largo di Torre Argentina) which may represent the route to the Campus, beside the Villa Publica. Through the area of the Villa and the Circus ran an early ritual boundary in the form of a stream called the *Petronia*, which rose from a spring on the west slope of the Quirinal hill (Via Panetteria) and wound in diagonal course to join the Tiber above the Tiber Island (Ponte Garibaldi). Somewhere convenient both to the Villa and Mars' Field was a great **Altar of Mars**, with an associated temple, and in various places there were tombs which had been erected by special dispensation of the Senate to public benefactors (mainly generals who had died in battle). At the far western extremity of the Field (near the river end of the modern Corso Vittorio Emanuele), there was a place called **Tarentum** or **Terentum**, where sulphur emerged from a fissure in the ground, believed to be the entrance to the Underworld and marked by an altar to the appropriate deities, Dis and Proserpina. Nearby there was a training/racing track for horses and chariots, called the **Trigarium**, which is thought to have been located along the line of the modern Via Giulia. Shipyards and their associated workshops and stores lined the riverbank on the west, but habitation tended to keep to the higher ground over to the east, on the other side of the causeway of the Via Lata (Via del Corso), since the Tiber regularly overflowed its banks at the upper bend, flooding the plain under several metres of water.

During the Empire, however, the perennial flood-risk notwithstanding, the open space of the republican Campus practically disappeared, its various functions translated into ever more ambitious public buildings. The process had already started in the C2 BC when the victory-temples which clustered in the southern sector began to be given monumental roofed colonnades (***porticus***), either on one side, or two, or all four (forming a square). They provided shade from the sun and shelter from the rain, and also, with their pavements raised on platforms, offered a measure of protection against floods. (By the C2 AD the Campus was famed for having so many *porticus* that it was possible to walk from the Forum of Trajan to the Aelian bridge in front of the Mausoleum of Hadrian continuously under cover.) The next development had been to set the temples not only within porticoes but in association with a permanent theatre. Ever since the late C3 BC dramatic performances in the Greek tradition had become part of various Roman religious rites and festivals, and several sanctuaries outside Rome had theatres incorporated into their design for the purpose, but inside Rome it was the custom that theatres should be wooden and temporary, erected for the occasion and then dismantled. Then in the space of fifty years three stone theatres were built in celebration of victories, all on the Campus and in close proximity to one another – the first by Pompey in 55 BC, embodying five temples (p. 214), to which Julius Caesar immediately planned a rival, eventually dedicated in memory of Augustus' nephew Marcellus in 13 BC (p. 243), and the third by L. Cornelius Balbus in the same year (p. 220). Rome's first stone amphitheatre was built on the Campus in the same period, by T. Statilius Taurus after his triumph of 34 BC, and dedicated in 29 BC (destroyed in the fire of AD 64, it was then supplanted by the Colosseum and its location is unknown).

Julius Caesar also launched grandiose plans for the Villa Publica and its traditional roles, including a permanent voting enclosure (**Saepta**) in the form of two monumental porticoes, completed by Augustus' henchman Agrippa in 26 BC. What other rebuilding may have been involved is not known, but to the west of the Saepta and on the same alignment, right in the centre of the Campus, Agrippa then built the first version of the **Pantheon** (27–25 BC), a **Porticus** (or a **Basilica**) dedicated to Neptune (Map, Fig. 77: 15), and a **Laconicum** (an early form of heated bath usually associated with a running track or exercise ground for youths). With the aid of a new aqueduct, the **Aqua Virgo** of 19 BC, the Laconicum developed into the more elaborate *thermae* or **Baths of Agrippa** (Map, Fig. 79: 16), set beside large **Gardens** with a **Lake** (the **Stagnum of Agrippa**) from which a street canal named the **Euripus** (the 'Straits') led west across to the western tip (emptying into the Tiber upstream of the modern Vittorio Emanuele bridge). East of the Saepta (i.e. near the church of S. Ignazio) two temples to the Egyptian gods **Isis** and **Serapis** were dedicated in 43 BC, perhaps another of Julius Caesar's initiatives. Augustus may also have been following in Caesar's footsteps with his great family **Mausoleum**, finished in 28 BC, dominating the skyline at the other end of the Campus, 800 m. to the north. Caesar's family tomb has not been located, but was on the Campus side of the Via Lata/Flaminia, perhaps between the Mausoleum and two later Augustan additions to the scene, the **Altar of Augustan Peace** (Map, Fig. 77: 3) and a great **Sundial** (Map, Fig. 77: 2).

One of Julius Caesar's aborted plans in 45 BC had been to solve the problem of flooding altogether by diverting the Tiber through the valley behind the Vatican. As it was, the general ground level on the Campus rose at least 4 m. in the course of the last three centuries BC and the C1 AD, during which seventeen major floods are recorded (there were probably many more). Some of the temples founded on the old ground level had their superstructure demolished and their podium heightened to take them up to the new level; others simply sunk lower as the ground level rose around them. Embankment works in the course of the C1 and C2 AD did a lot to contain the river, and another major rise in level took place not because of floods but a huge **fire in** AD **80** which swept in a great swathe from the Pantheon to the Theatre of Marcellus, devastating many of the buildings on either side. In the great rebuilding programme Domitian added the **Stadium** (Piazza Navona) and **Odeum** (Map, Fig. 77: 21) on the west side of Agrippa's gardens and replaced the temples of Isis and Serapis on a monster scale, attaching to them a temple to his favourite goddess Minerva and also a **Porticus Divorum** (Map, Fig. 77: 12)—dedicated to his deified father Vespasian and brother Titus in commemoration of their triumph in the Jewish War.

In the C2 AD, after the emperor Hadrian had rebuilt the Pantheon and the Saepta following another fire and added a large temple to his deified mother-in-law and sister in front of the north end of the Saepta, his successors Antoninus Pius, Marcus Aurelius, and Commodus created a whole block of dynastic monuments alongside the Via Lata/Flaminia: Antoninus Pius set up a **Temple of Deified Hadrian** (Map, Fig. 77: 10), approached through an arch in honour of Antoninus' own heirs-designate Marcus Aurelius and Lucius Verus, and Marcus Aurelius then erected an **altar** (Map, Fig. 77: 7) and a **Column** (Map, Fig. 77: 6) celebrating the **Deification of Antoninus Pius**. Marcus' son Commodus trumped that with a **Column** (Map, Fig. 77: 9), an **altar** (Map, Fig. 77: 5) and a temple (unlocated) to his parents, **Deified Marcus Aurelius and Faustina**. Thereafter, no more large-scale changes took place although the Severan emperors carried out various repairs and improvements, the most substantial of which were rebuildings of the **Baths of Agrippa** and the **Baths of Nero** (on the north side of Agrippa's Gardens), which changed their name in AD 227 to the **Alexandrine Baths** in recognition of major works by Alexander Severus.

All around the fringes, and in amongst the great buildings, there were houses, shops, clubs, workshops. To the west of the Piazza Navona (Domitian's Stadium), between the Via dei Coronari and the Via del Governo Vecchio as far as the Chiesa Nuova, was the **marble-workers' quarter**, cutting and polishing veneer, making architectural and figurative sculpture. A thick layer of quartz sand and marble dust lies in the subsoil and when deep foundations are laid unfinished statues are often found, such as the Barbarian Prisoner in the Vatican Museums (ex-Lateran collection).

In the course of the C4–C7, as the population and resources of greater Rome declined, and society itself was transformed, the public buildings on the Campus became increasingly obsolete in function if not in fabric. Their massive structures began to accommodate a proliferation of smaller and alternative installations (churches, welfare centres, hostels, taverns, merchants' houses, markets, manufacturing and industrial operations of one kind or another) and the pattern of continuous use was set whereby so many of them are still standing today.

The *Ludi Saeculares* or Secular Games were held on the Field of Mars, not always precisely on the centenary. After the first in 348 BC, the next were organized in 249 and 146 BC; plans for a celebration in about 45–42 came to nothing. Augustus staged them afresh to launch his New Age in 17 BC, with three nights and three days of sacrifices and scenic games followed by another seven days of theatrical shows and chariot-races. The poet Horace composed a festival hymn, the *Carmen Saeculare*, for the occasion. It was decreed that the official cycle should be 110 years, but Claudius celebrated the 800th anniverary of Rome in AD 47; Domitian chose AD 88 and Septimius Severus AD 204. Philip the Arab staged the last, for the millennium in AD 248.

Visit: the sequence here starts at the north with the Mausoleum of Augustus and the Altar of Peace, since the Altar is generally only open (and is anyway best seen) in the morning. The itinerary ends at the Porticus of Octavia and the Tiber Island. All the other monuments can, after a fashion, be seen from the street, and the Pantheon interior has very long hours.

Mausoleum of Augustus. Map, Fig. 77 ★

Piazza Augusto Imperatore. Comune (†interior)

The great tomb is now a huge circular ruin of concrete and tufa reticulate, planted with cypresses, and artificially situated in a hollow. Steps lead down on three sides of the hollow to the original ground level, partly excavated in 1937 when the structure was 'liberated' of medieval and later buildings and the surrounding piazza of undistinguished Fascist architecture was created. In antiquity the Mausoleum was set in a sacred precinct which stretched between the Via Flaminia (Via del Corso) and the river bank, with groves and promenades open to the public. The original entrance, and principal modern approach, is on the south side (towards what was previously the open space of the Field of Mars).

Among Augustus' earliest building projects, completed during his sixth consulship in 28 BC, the Mausoleum was, and remained, the largest tomb in the Roman world, subsequently only matched—carefully not surpassed—by that of Hadrian on the other side of the Tiber (Castel S. Angelo, see p. 369). In ground plan (Fig. 79) the outer diameter measured 300 RF (*c.*89 m.) and the outermost wall was 40 RF (*c.*12 m.) high. Its facing of white limestone (travertine) has been robbed, exposing the tufa rubble and concrete core, reinforced with large blocks of travertine. Inside there are further concentric concrete walls. The second and third, rising to greater heights, are bonded to the outer wall by massive semicircular buttresses and radial walls to form a single structure 25 m. thick, penetrated only by the narrow passage which leads from the

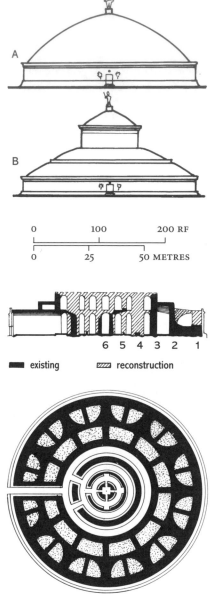

▼ **Fig. 78.** Mausoleum of Augustus.
Two alternative reconstructions of
elevation

A

B

| 0 | | 100 | | 200 RF |

| 0 | 25 | | 50 METRES |

6 5 4 3 2 1

■ existing   ▨ reconstruction

▲ **Fig. 79.** Mausoleum of Augustus.
Section, actual state, and plan

entrance to a circular, vaulted corridor between the third wall and the fourth. The fourth wall was faced inside and out with travertine and has almost entirely disappeared as a result. Two doors opened through it to another vaulted corridor surrounding the **burial chamber** itself, enclosed by the fifth wall, also lined on both faces with travertine. The chamber consists of a circular hall around a central concrete pillar. The door was on axis with the entrance passage and the walls contained rectangular recesses for cinerary urns on the other three principal axes. The central pillar contains a square inner chamber, where Augustus' own urn may have been deposited.

Given the ruinous state of the structures at its core, the original elevation and external appearance of the building are uncertain. Strabo, who saw it in 7 BC, describes it as a great mound (a *tumulus*) on a high foundation of white stone, thickly covered with trees. The description can be taken to imply a mound of earth rising unbroken to the summit (Fig. 78A), filling the voids between the outer three walls and continuing over the vaulting of the inner three. Alternatively, the relative strength of the fourth concentric wall has suggested a stepped profile (Fig. 78B), with a second higher drum emerging from the first. Whichever type of reconstruction is favoured, the overall height is usually reckoned to have been about half the diameter, i.e. 150 RF (40–45 m.). Its maximum present height is about 100 RF (30 m.). What type of trees Strabo saw and where they were planted, depending on the profile chosen, are open questions. He adds that the top bore a bronze statue of Augustus.

The differing views of the original appearance influence (and are influenced by) differing views of its significance in Augustan political ideology. On the one hand, a simple earth mound recalls the shape of a tumulus of Etruscan or Asiatic Greek type, perhaps calculated to evoke the tumuli of the princes of Troy, which the Augustan version of the Trojan myth claimed as the ancestors of the Julian family. On the other hand, the Mausoleum was built before Augustus took the title Augustus, that is, well before an 'Augustan' ideology as such can be identified. The name *mausoleum* was used of it from the start; this, and a stepped profile of more or less monumental architectural character, might imply a straight-forward rival to the great dynastic tombs of the Hellenistic kings and specifically the tomb of King Mausolos of Caria at Halicarnassus, one of the Seven Wonders of the ancient world. An attractive compromise between all the options, at least in theory, is that Augustus' model was actually the *mausoleum* of Alexander the Great in Egypt, whose shape is not known but might have been an architecturally elaborate version of a *tumulus* in the tradition of the Macedonian kings.

Many members of Augustus' family could have been buried in the Mausoleum; those known are: first, his nephew Marcellus, who died in 23 BC, followed in 12 BC by his life-long friend (and son-in-law) Marcus Agrippa, then Drusus the Elder (9 BC), Lucius and Gaius Caesar (AD 2 and 4), and Augustus himself in AD 14, when two bronze plaques bearing the text of his *Res Gestae*, his own record of his achievements, were affixed to either side of the entrance (a modern copy is transcribed in bronze on the flank of the nearby building housing the Altar of Peace). Thereafter came Drusus the Younger, Livia, Tiberius, Agrippina, mother of Caligula (her urn was used in the Middle Ages as a corn measure and is now in the Capitoline Museum), Nero and Drusus (brothers of Caligula), Poppaea (wife of Nero). The last definite burial is that of the emperor Nerva in AD 96, though he was not related to the Julian family. It is possible that the ashes of Julia Domna (wife of Septimius Severus) found at least a temporary resting place there in AD 218. By the C4, if not before, the entrance was flanked by two obelisks of red Aswan granite (one now stands in front of S. Maria Maggiore, the other is part of the Horse fountain on the Piazza del Quirinale).

In the C2 AD the smooth **level pavement** around the Mausoleum was used as an architect's planning floor: lines incised on the western side seem to be the project drawings for the design of the pediment of Hadrian's Pantheon (see p. 203).

During the Middle Ages the Mausoleum was converted by the Colonna family into a fortress, which was destroyed in 1167 and then quarried for building materials. In the C16 the Soderini family bought the site and laid out an ornate garden within the enclosure formed by the

▲ **Fig. 80.** Mausoleum of Augustus when it was occupied by the Soderini gardens, shown in a print by E. Du Pérac (1575)

upper part of the ruins (Fig. 80). In the C18 this became an arena for bull-fights, and in the C19 was used for circus and theatrical performances. From 1907 until 1936 it was occupied by the 'Augusteo', a concert hall with seating for 3,500, the internal staircases and some of the supporting walls of which still survive.

Altar of the Augustan Peace (*Ara Pacis Augustae*). Map, Fig. 77 and Fig. 81 ★

*Lungotevere in Augusta. *Comune*

Reconstructed in 1938 from hundreds of fragments, the **altar** is the most famous example of Augustan monumental sculpture in Rome. It consists of an altar proper, surrounded by a high enclosure, all made of white Italian (Luna) marble and elaborately carved in relief by some of the best sculptors of the day. It was decreed by the Senate on 4 July 13 BC to celebrate Augustus' return after three years' absence in Spain and Gaul settling matters in the western Empire and was situated not where it is now but 450 m. away (Fig. 77: 3 and box p. 190), facing the Via Flaminia (Via del Corso), the road by which Augustus had re-entered the city. (Six years earlier, his return from a similar mission to the eastern Empire had also been marked by an altar, dedicated to *Fortuna Redux*—'Fortune who brings you home'—on the Via Appia, just outside the Capena Gate.) The work took 3½ years, and was dedicated on 30 January 9 BC, which happened by chance or design to be Augustus' wife Livia's birthday. *Pax*, the goddess of Peace, was almost unknown before 13 BC but central to Augustus' later political ideology, and the word soon became synony-mous with the Roman Empire at large, which was often called simply the

Pax Romana. Nero portrayed the altar on his coinage of AD 64–7 as a symbol of imperial peace (Fig. 83) and Vespasian inaugurated a whole temple-forum in honour of Pax in AD 75 (see p. 153).

The modern installation reproduces the original situation, where the **altar platform** (40 × 36 RF), built of tufa and travertine blocks capped with marble, stood against the embankment of the Via Flaminia, its east front on a level with the road. The west front, which is that towards the modern entrance, originally faced the Field of Mars, whose level was

▼ **Fig. 81.** Altar of Augustan Peace. Ground plan including later (Hadrianic) precinct

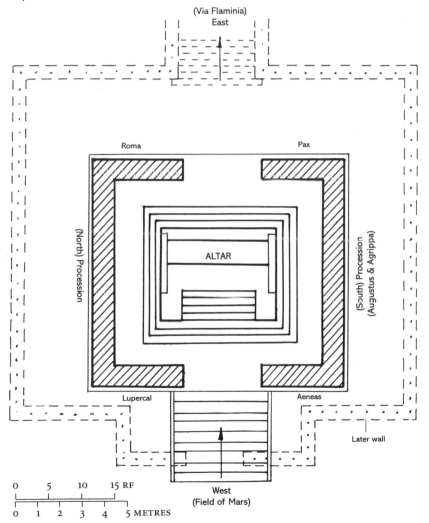

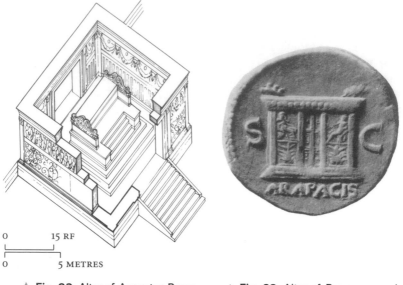

0   15 RF

0   5 METRES

▲ **Fig. 82.** Altar of Augustan Peace.
Axonometric view

▲ **Fig. 83.** Altar of Peace on a coin
of Nero, AD 66

about a metre lower, hence the steps. Around the edge of the platform, with a wide doorway in the middle, rises the enclosure wall, which was composed of two courses of tall rectangular slabs (some weighing over ten tons) with a narrower horizontal course between them. The upper cornice is entirely invented and has accordingly been left plain, but it ought to be richly ornamented and, according to the coin images (Fig. 83), surmounted by large flame-like palmettes at the four corners. Otherwise the reconstruction is fairly reliable; the missing parts are integrated in plaster, where possible using casts taken from the surviving marble parts. The great unknown, as always, is the original colour; all the reliefs will have been enhanced with brightly painted detail and have to be thought of in both dimensions.

The **enclosure** was carved, inside and out, in imitation of a light columnar palisade. On the **exterior**, delicately wrought acanthus plants, the indispensable ingredients of Augustan imagery, extend up the columns and fill the lower zone, where their complex symmetrical scrolls are entwined with vines and ivy and pairs of alighting swans. In the upper zone, above a crossbar decorated with a Greek meander motif, are sculptured panel paintings. On the Field of Mars (modern entrance) side they refer to the mythical founders of Rome, Romulus and Aeneas. What little survives of that to the left of the door shows Mars on the left, Faustulus the shepherd on the right; between them is a fragment with a bird perched in a fig-tree—presumably that which grew at the entrance to the *Lupercal*, the cave where the wolf suckled Romulus and Remus. The right-hand relief shows Aeneas (with his mantle over his head) sacrificing to the Penates (household gods he had brought from Troy) who are sitting in their temple at Lavinium (top left). Below, two attendants (*camilli*) bring the white sow who had farrowed thirty piglets, and other offerings for the sacrifice. Leaning on a staff behind Aeneas is his son Ascanius–Iulus (the ancestor of the Julian clan).

On the **inside** of the enclosure wall, around the altar itself, the column shafts are plain and the lower zone is rendered as a series of vertical slots, probably meant to reproduce the slats of a wooden fence. Hanging from the upper crossbar are sacrificial dishes (*paterae*), with traces of a red undercoat for gilding, and bulls' skulls strung with garlands of fruit and flowers. The **altar**, mounted on a stepped podium measuring 6 × 7 m. (20 × 24 feet), stands over 3 m. tall. Its U-shaped counter, approached by steps, appears to have been a calculated anachronism, reviving a Hellenistic type quite common in Rome and Latium in the C4–C3 BC (similar to the one under the Black Stone on the Forum see p. 74). The left-hand wing, capped by large acanthus-scroll volutes supported on crouching sphinxes, carries a small frieze showing the sacrificial procession destined for the altar—two bulls and a sheep, with their attendants, accompanied by magistrates and priests and (on the inner face) the Vestal Virgins. Fragments of two other friezes of different sizes exist but have not been included in the reconstruction. One showing personifications of the provinces may have decorated the podium.

The side of the enclosure which was turned towards the Via Flaminia was the altar's principal public face. In the panel relief on the right the goddess *Roma* was seated on a pile of armour between *Honos* and *Virtus*, the personifications of bravery in battle and its due reward, both particularly associated with Augustus. The relief on the left (restored in 1784 by Francesco Carradori) shows another seated female who ought to be *Pax*, though her iconography is complex and much discussed. With the two children in her lap she strongly resembles Venus Genetrix, mother of the Julian family, while the figures of the Sky and Sea to either side suggest that she may represent Land (*Terra*) or Mother Earth (*Tellus*), or Italy, or Empire. The answer is probably that she is all these things, that Pax was a multiple concept, and portraying her for the first time was a considerable challenge. The acanthus scrolls on this side are especially finely worked, and if you look closely among the leaves from which the plant emerges you can find worms, a frog and a scorpion, a lizard and a cicada. More lizards, a frog, and a snake attacking a little nest of birds lurk in the undergrowth of the acanthus on the 'north' (Lungotevere) side.

It is the **processional friezes** carved in the upper register on the 'north' and 'south' (Mausoleum) sides for which the altar is most famous nowadays. Along each side, some forty or fifty figures, executed at three-quarters life-size, move slowly in a public parade. The most important

AUGUSTUS

HERALDS AND ATTENDANTS

▲ **Fig. 84.** Altar of Augustan Peace. South processional frieze

people appear on the **'south' side** (Fig. 84), which (unlike the 'north') is also fortunate in preserving its original heads: the front third of the procession, at the left end, is very fragmentary but clearly contained heralds and attendants, signifying the presence of priests and magistrates, perhaps also senators. In the middle third comes first Augustus, with the *rex sacrorum* (a high priest) close behind him, then the next four figures wearing leather helmets with spikes on top are the major *flamines* (chief priests) of the four State cults: Mars, Quirinus, Deified Julius Caesar (in the background), and Jupiter (the one with the stick). Their attendant (*lictor*) follows, with his axe over his shoulder. After him is Augustus' henchman and fellow magistrate Agrippa. Both he and Augustus have their togas drawn up over their heads in their capacity as presiding magistrates and are distinguished by their greater height. The child with a torque round his neck could be one of the many foreign hostage-princes being educated in Rome. The veiled lady is probably Augustus' wife Livia, followed by various other members of the imperial family, with their children and servants. Everyone is dressed in their best, the men and boys in the new Augustan official form of the toga, and high-laced patrician boots, the women in all-enveloping mantle and stola. The precise identities of the figures have evoked much scholarly concern, but many of the images, and indeed the whole procession, could be purely symbolic. In the **'north' frieze** the same occasion is viewed literally from the other side: more magistrates and attendants in company with the ordinary citizens of Rome. The figure in the centre and another towards the front carry a box of incense and flask of wine. Those offerings, and the general air of informality, with people chatting to each other, the laurel wreaths on their heads and twigs of laurel in their hands (those with scrolls are wrongly restored), are most suited to a *supplicatio* or festive thanksgiving, either for Augustus' return or more generally for the Augustan Peace.

AGRIPPA

HIEF PRIESTS   IMPERIAL FAMILY

In 13 BC, the site on the Via Flaminia was open ground, midway between Augustus' Mausoleum and the built-up area of the southern Field of Mars, possibly coinciding with the *pomerium* (the sacred boundary of the city where soldiers had to lay aside their weapons) or with the point where the Senate officially greeted Augustus on his arrival, or both. In 10 BC the great Augustan sundial was laid out close by to the west (see overleaf). By the early C2, however, the ground level had risen almost 3 m. and most of the sundial disappeared, but the altar was preserved, set off by brick retaining-walls capped with stone coping and a metal fence. The upper zone, with the panel reliefs and the processional friezes, will have been even more visible than before, conveniently at spectators' eye level, and may have been slightly retouched and repainted for the occasion. Augustus and Agrippa and several other figures in the procession on the south side have the pupils and/or irises of their eyes and eyebrows incised, a practice most unlikely before the C2.

On the south side of the church of S. Rocco, across the Via di Ripetta from the Altar of Peace, a tall marble panel records the levels of major **Tiber floods** in the days before the Lungotevere embankment was built in the late 1880s.

The recovery of the Ara Pacis

- 1568 ten large fragments dredged up by chance when building the Palazzo Peretti (later Fiano-Almagià) whose SE angle on the Via in Lucina was unwittingly sited over the western half of the altar.
- 1859 another seventeen fragments retrieved when trying to repair severe cracks which had appeared in the palazzo walls owing to its precarious foundations
- 1903 major excavations identified the precise site of the altar and retrieved another fifty-three pieces of it but were stopped by flooding and concerns for the stability of the palazzo.
- 1937–8 the Fascist regime, fired by its great exhibition celebrating Augustus and the Roman Empire, sponsored a new campaign, a technological wonder in its day. The palazzo was underpinned and the area of the altar isolated within a wall of frozen earth, inside which the ground water could be drained and the lower levels excavated to the required depth. Seventy-five substantial pieces and hundreds of chips were found and the exact plan of the monument was established. It was then reconstructed in the form we see now, which incorporates all the earlier finds, previously scattered in collections in Rome, Naples, Florence and Vienna (though the Louvre still has one panel from the north processional frieze, substituted in the reconstruction by a cast).

Augustan Sundial (*Horologium Augusti*).
Map, Fig. 77: 2

In 10 BC, the twentieth anniversary of the conquest of Egypt, and evidently in close association with the Altar of Peace (in its original location, Map, Fig. 77: 3), Augustus dedicated an enormous sundial, which new work by German archaeologists has been able to reconstruct on paper (Fig. 85) even if there is not much to see on the ground. It occupied most of the area between Piazza di S. Lorenzo in Lucina and Piazza del Parlamento and was designed by the mathematician Novius Facundus. The dial was inlaid in bronze on a vast expanse of travertine paving, over which a shadow was cast by a vertical pointer, 100 RF (30 m.) high. This was appropriately composed of the traditional Egyptian offering to the Sun, an obelisk, with a spiked bronze globe on top, mounted on a tall pedestal.

By the AD 70s, however, when Pliny the Elder wrote about it in his *Natural History*, it had not been working properly for thirty years: despite immensely deep foundations the pointer had probably shifted off mark. In the late AD 70s or 80s, after the general ground level was raised over a metre, at least the central part of the dial was relaid. A short section of the meridian line (Fig. 86) was discovered at the higher level by German excavations in 1979/80, which dug deep below the cellar floor of no. 48 Via di Campo Marzio (permit required). The cross bars and signs of the zodiac written alongside them in Greek (the customary language of ancient mathematics and astrology) show how the meridian also functioned as a calendar, indicating the day of the month by the precise length of the shadow cast at noon; the smaller Greek annotations say that the trade winds stop before Virgo, and summer begins during Taurus. Only one other part of the dial floor has ever been recorded, 500 years ago, when sinking the foundations for the chapel of St Philip and James on the west side of S. Lorenzo in 1463.

▼ **Fig. 85.** Augustan sundial. Site plan

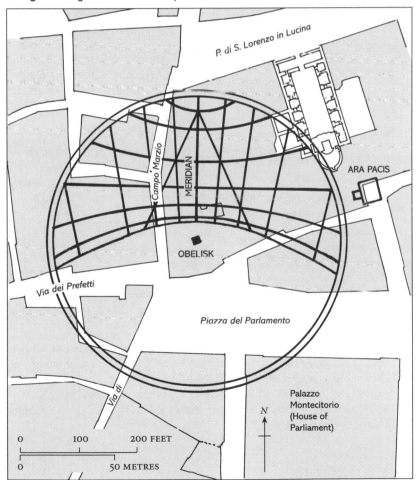

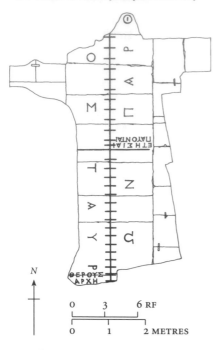

N

0   3   6 RF

0   1   2 METRES

▲ **Fig. 86.** Augustan sundial. Plan of part of the meridian excavated under Via di Campo Marzio, 48

The **obelisk** pointer fared rather better; it stood, a famous feature of the landscape, throughout antiquity. When it finally fell (sometime between the C8 and C12) it broke into five pieces. A barber digging a latrine in the time of Pope Julius II (1503–13) 70 m. SW of S. Lorenzo hit the pedestal and, although it was then reburied, the memory remained and eventually in 1748, when building the house which is now Piazza del Parlamento no. 3, with a tremendous effort (commemorated in the plaque over the doorway), all five fragments of the shaft were brought to the surface. The pink Aswan granite needed to restore it was provided by the shaft of the Column of Antoninus Pius (see box).

In 1792 the obelisk was set up in the **Piazza di Montecitorio** (Map, Fig. 77: 8) and has stayed there ever since. The (restored) inscription repeated on two sides of the pedestal (now facing north and south but previously east and west) reads

IMP. CAESAR.DIVI.F.	Imperial Caesar, son of Divus (Julius)
AUGUSTUS	Augustus
PONTIFEX MAXIMUS	chief priest
IMP. XII COS XI TRIB. POT XIV	in 10 BC
AEGUPTO IN POTESTATEM	Egypt under the will of
POPULI ROMANI REDACTA	the Roman People having been brought
SOLI DONUM DEDIT	gave this as a gift to Sol (the Sun)

The obelisk, made for Psammetichus II (594–589 BC), was one of two which Augustus had carried off to Rome from the great temple at Heliopolis soon after the annexation of Egypt in 30 BC. The other was the one now in the Piazza del Popolo, which was also re-erected by Augustus in 10 BC and dedicated with an identical inscription, in the Circus Maximus (see p. 264).

Column of Antoninus Pius. Map, Fig. 77: 6

Set up in commemoration of the emperor, who died in AD 161, near the altar celebrating his deification (Map, Fig. 77: 7), the Column was of unknown order, probably Corinthian, with a monolithic 50-foot shaft of Aswan granite (which had been quarried in AD 106 for one of Trajan's great projects but never used). Six metres of it stuck out of the hillside of the Monte Citorio until 1703, when excavations around the base exposed its richly sculpted pedestal made of a single huge block of Italian marble (28 m³), now one of the showpieces in the Vatican Museums (it has a courtyard to itself, beside the upper entrance). The front (Fig. 87) shows Antoninus Pius and his wife Faustina (who had died and been deified twenty years earlier) being carried heavenwards by a winged figure, with Roma waving them off from the bottom right, and the personification of the Field of Mars reclining at the left, holding the sundial obelisk to set the scene. On each side a relief in a completely different style (Fig. 88) shows the ritual cavalry parade which encircled the pyre three times in the course of the funeral. The shaft of the column, damaged by fire in 1789, has disappeared, recycled into the repair of other Aswan granite monuments (such as the sundial obelisk).

Column of Marcus Aurelius and Faustina.
Map, Fig. 77: 9 ★

Piazza Colonna. State

Designed as a funerary monument in conscious emulation of that of Trajan (p. 164), the Column was built with an internal **spiral staircase** to be climbed for a panoramic view from the top. Precisely when it was erected is unknown but it is assumed to have been set up by the emperor Commodus after the death of his father Marcus Aurelius in AD 180 (Marcus' wife Faustina, daughter of Antoninus Pius and Faustina, had died in AD 175). In the summer of AD 193, the first year of the reign of Septimius Severus, one of his freedmen called Adrastus, who had been appointed custodian (*procurator*) of the Column, applied for and was granted permission to build himself a little hut on public land nearby so that he could carry out his duties more efficiently. The inscribed stone on which he proudly recorded the tale has survived (Vatican Museums) and also tells us that the Column was nicknamed 'Centenaria'—the hundred-footer. That (29.6 m.) is exactly the height of the Doric column (torus base, shaft and capital), not the overall height of the monument, which was much greater. The present height above ground is 39 m. but the figure stated in the C4 Regionary Catalogues is 175½ RF (51.95 m.), part of which can be accounted for by whatever stood on top (presumably a

▲ **Fig. 87.** Column of Antoninus Pius. Sculpted pedestal, front side (Vatican Museums)

▲ **Fig. 88.** Column of Antoninus Pius. Pedestal, right hand side (Vatican Museums)

▲ **Fig. 89.** Marcus Aurelius' Column frieze
(*Top*) Barbarian mother and child flanked by Roman auxiliaries
(*Bottom*) Emperor receiving submission of barbarians

statue of Marcus Aurelius), the rest by what lies below ground. A further 3.8 m. of its pedestal are currently invisible and below that—never seen— is probably a huge stepped base reaching another 3 m. down to the ancient ground level. The present profile of the pedestal was created to suit the ground level in 1589, when (as the inscriptions on every face attest) Pope Sixtus the Fifth ordered extensive repairs and set the bronze statue of St Paul on top. Renaissance drawings show that the old profile was inter- rupted half-way up by a projecting band of relief sculpture (the remnants were chiselled off in 1589), in which winged victories were holding garlands on three sides and the emperor received the submission of barbarians on the fourth. Weathered, struck by lightning, rocked by earth- quakes, its sculpture (in much higher relief than on Trajan's Column) had suffered considerable damage by the C16. So much so, that the restorers filled the gaps with the coarser and greyish Proconnesian marble (from the Septizodium, see p. 144), rather than the fine white Italian of the orig- inal. Although the shaft was anyway less refined in profile than Trajan's, being a straight cylinder, only 14 cm. narrower at the top than at the bottom, the drums have also shifted far out of position at two points to produce some unsightly kinks (as on Trajan's Column, the dowels pinning the drums together were robbed in the Middle Ages leaving them free to move independently of each other).

Unless you have remarkable eyesight or powerful binoculars the reliefs are best looked at in books (or the plaster casts in the Museo della Civiltà Romana at EUR), but their general theme is easily grasped. They tell the story of Marcus Aurelius' wars north of the Danube, against the Marcomanni in 172–3 and the Sarmatians in 174–5 (his wife Faustina accompanied him on both campaigns, dying at the end of the second). Starting at the bottom with the Roman army crossing the Danube and moving upwards in twenty-one spirals, the two campaigns are divided, as on Trajan's Column, by a figure of Victory writing on a shield (ten bands up on the side facing the Via del Corso). The artistic style, however, is that of the later C2, much more powerful than that of Trajan's Column. Compare the details illustrated in Fig. 89 with those from Trajan's (Fig. 72, p. 165). The carving is bolder, the content of the scenes greatly simplified, with fewer figures and less circumstantial detail; the action is almost continuous battle, the conflicts between Roman and Barbarian far more violent and cruel.

The architectural setting of the Column in antiquity, presuming it had one, is a complete blank. The entrance to the internal staircase was on the Via del Corso side, facing the main road, but a temple to the Deified Marcus and Faustina could lie behind (matching the Temple of Trajan and Plotina in a similar position behind the Column of Trajan). Under the offices of the newspaper *Il Tempo*, between the Piazza Colonna and the Piazza di Montecitorio, fragments of coffered marble ceiling suitable for a temple were retrieved when building a paper chute in 1960. Incidentally,

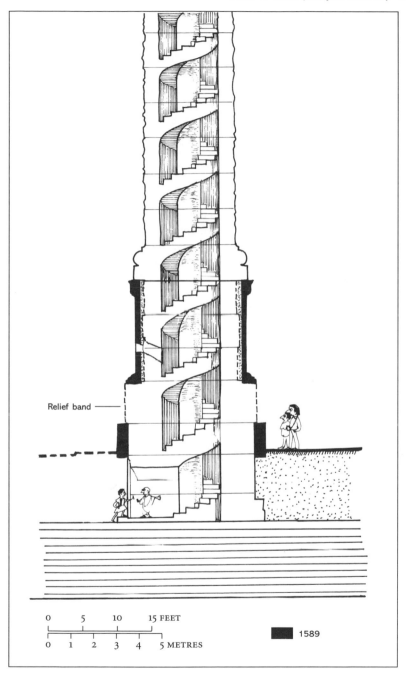

Relief band

0   5   10   15 FEET

0   1   2   3   4   5 METRES

1589

▲ **Fig. 90.** Column of Marcus Aurelius. Ancient and modern profiles of the pedestal

the Ionic columns of the colonnade along the front of the *Tempo* building are ancient, but come from a Roman villa at Veii (14 km. north of Rome).

The **fountain basin** in front of the Column was designed by Giacomo della Porta in 1577 and constructed of huge blocks of ancient pink/grey Chian marble. The water comes from the **Aqua Virgo**, the aqueduct first built by Agrippa in 19 BC to supply his new baths near the Pantheon. Since its destination was so low-lying, the 20.8 km. long channel from the Via Collatina (Salone) ran mostly underground and has never ceased to operate, though it was reduced to a trickle during the Middle Ages by lack of maintenance at its principal source. Pope Nicholas V reactivated it without too much trouble in 1453, to feed an early version of the famous Trevi fountain and it was extended to the Piazza Navona by the 1570s. The last kilometre, where it emerged from the Pincian ridge (above the Piazza di Spagna), was carried in antiquity on arches and has had numerous modifications made to it in the course of time. One of its Roman arches can be seen if you make a short detour up the Via del Tritone.

Aqua Virgo. Map, Fig. 77: 4

Via del Nazareno. Comune (†lower level)

Crossing the Via del Corso to the Via del Tritone, Via del Nazareno is the fourth street on the left going up the hill towards the Piazza Barberini. Behind the railings at no. 14, deep below the present street level, is one of the arches which carried the Aqua Virgo across a side street. The arch was constructed in travertine (to contrast with the general run of arcading in *peperino* tufa) in the exaggeratedly rusticated style favoured by the emperor Claudius (other examples can be seen on the Porta Maggiore and Temple of Deified Claudius on the Caelian). An inscription on the architrave dates it to AD 46 and explains that Claudius had to rebuild a long stretch of the arcading because his predecessor Caligula had demolished it to get stone for an amphitheatre (probably a rebuilding of that of Statilius Taurus, see p. 179). The small round-headed doorway in the wall on the opposite side of the street is the ghost of the *specus*, the water channel, which still exists, running through the building behind. In its Roman heyday the aqueduct could supply just over 100,000 m³ of water every 24 hours. A view of the arch can also be had from the window at the back of the Bar Accademia on the Via del Tritone.

You may return to the Field of Mars by way of the Aqua Virgo's most famous modern fountain, the **Trevi** (down the street just across the Via del Tritone from the Via del Nazareno), which gives you some idea of the amount of water the aqueduct carried (the Trevi can disgorge 80,000 m³ a day). The Via delle Muratte takes you back to the Via del Corso, across which is the Via di Pietra (Fig. 91), where there was once a monumental triple archway, probably dedicated in the names of Antoninus Pius' sons Marcus Aurelius and Lucius Verus, leading from the Via Lata (the Corso) into the precinct of the Temple of Hadrian. The foot of one pier of the arch survives in the basement of the shop at the corner.

Temple of Deified Hadrian (*Hadrianeum*).
Map, Fig. 77: 10

Piazza di Pietra

Eleven columns and the cella wall of one side of the temple are still standing, built into a C19 *palazzo* (designed by V. Vespignani) which houses the Rome *Borsa* (Stock Exchange). The order is Corinthian, 50 RF (14.8 m.) high, constructed entirely of Proconnesian marble with its distinctive grey/white horizontal bands. Only the lower part of the entablature is original but the rest is recorded in C16 drawings. Behind the railing, a deep excavation in front of the colonnade has exposed the original ground level of the temple precinct, 5 m. below the present square, and the flank of the high podium of *peperino* tufa, which was once faced with white marble to match the columns above. Although both ends and the other side of the temple disappeared long ago, traces of the vaulting under the front steps have been found under the Via dei Burrò, showing that it faced east (towards the Corso) and probably had eight columns across the

▼ **Fig. 91.** Temple of Deified Hadrian. General site plan

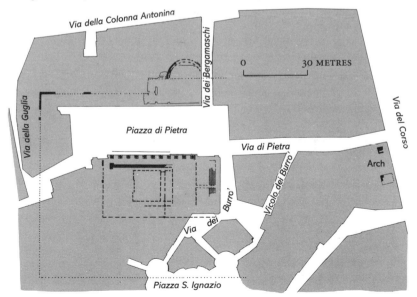

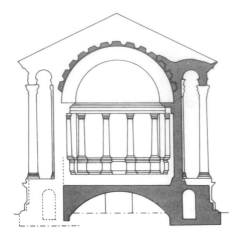

▲ **Fig. 92.** Temple of Deified Hadrian. Restored cross-section. Shading indicates surviving structures

front, with thirteen down the sides. Parts of the interior of the cella, which was lined with an engaged order 36 RF high and had a coffered concrete barrel vault, survive inside the Borsa building. Excavations in 1878 and recent explorations in the cellars of the buildings on the other sides of the Piazza di Pietra have identified the line of a monumental enclosure wall, with a large curving exhedra at the back of no. 43.

There is no inscription to identify the temple as that of Hadrian (who died in AD 138 and was buried in his new mausoleum across the Tiber, see p. 369), but one was dedicated to him by his successor Antoninus Pius in AD 145 and is listed in the Regionary Catalogues in a crowd of Hadrianic and later dynastic monuments between the Pantheon and the Via del Corso. The Piazza di Pietra temple can confidently be dated in the late Hadrianic or early Antonine period on the basis of its architectural style, and the location is appropriate.

To the west, under Via dei Pastini and the Piazza Capranica, there was apparently another major temple precinct, perhaps that of Matidia and Marciana, Hadrian's mother-in-law and her mother, Trajan's elder sister, both of whom were deified after their deaths.

▼ **Fig. 93.** Province and Trophy reliefs from Piazza di Pietra (Naples Archaeological Museum)

The 'Province' reliefs

Over the centuries a series of marble pedestals and panels have been found in the vicinity of the temple and are generally believed to have formed part of its decoration (ten are on display in the courtyard of the Palazzo dei Conservatori Museum, five others are in the Naples Archaeological Museum; there are twenty-four all told). Carved in relief with personifications of cities and peoples of the Roman Empire alternating with military and naval trophies, the marble is Proconnesian and the scale compatible with the exterior order of the temple, but whether they actually belong to it is questionable. They could come from some other large public building of the mid–late C2 in the surrounding area.

Pantheon. Map, Fig. 77   ★★

Piazza della Rotonda. Comune (*interior) free

Erected by the emperor Hadrian in AD 118–25, the Pantheon has now stood for almost 1,880 years, one of the most magnificent architectural monuments of antiquity. Even today its domed interior space (the Rotunda) inspires a special awe, not just because of its size (the dome held the world record for a concrete span until the CNIT building in Paris in 1958) but also the quality of the light, the colour and sound.

The building owes its survival partly to the fact that it was converted into a church in AD 608 (St Mary of the Martyrs) but even more to the extraordinary strength and stability of its construction. It was the third 'Pantheon' on the site. The first, built by Marcus Agrippa in 27–25 BC, was destroyed in the great fire of AD 80. Replaced by Domitian, it then was struck by lightning in AD 110 and burned again. Hadrian (as was his practice in all the buildings he restored or rebuilt in the city, with the exception of the Temple of Deified Trajan) did not dedicate the new Pantheon in his own name but in that of the original dedicant: thus the bold inscription on the front: M. AGRIPPA L. F. COS TERTIUM FECIT (Marcus Agrippa, son of Lucius, made this in his third consulship). Faintly legible beneath is a two-line inscription in small letters which refers to renovations by Septimius Severus and Caracalla in AD 202: *pantheum vetustate corruptum cum omni cultu restituerunt* (with every refinement they restored the Pantheum, worn by age) but it seems that no rebuilding was involved.

The structure comprises two distinct parts: the front porch and the circular drum, which share the same low plinth (1.3 m., 4½ RF high) but are architecturally in strong contrast—even conflict—with each other. The **porch** belongs firmly in the Classical tradition of monumental entrances, its pedimented front supported on Corinthian columns with monolithic shafts of Egyptian granite and bases and capitals of white

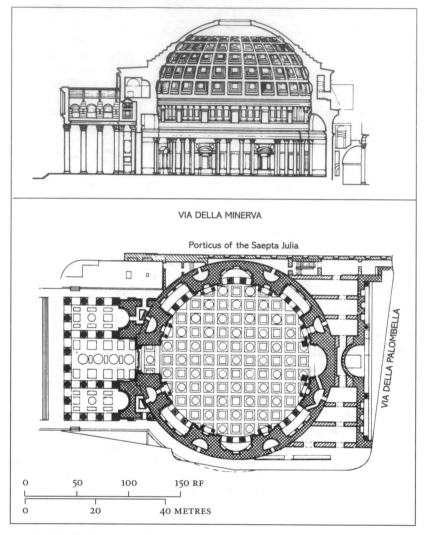

VIA DELLA MINERVA

Porticus of the Saepta Julia

VIA DELLA PALOMBELLA

| 0 | 50 | 100 | 150 RF |
| 0 | 20 | | 40 METRES |

▲ **Fig. 94.** Pantheon. Plan and section

Greek (Pentelic) marble, its exterior also once clad in white marble. The design of the **Rotunda**, on the other hand, although once coated in white stucco to look like a marble building on the outside, comes from the purely Roman world of concrete bath-buildings and palatial halls.

The contrast was not meant to be as marked as it is today, for the columnar porch once occupied the end of a long colonnaded forecourt (which you may imagine stretching further back than the present piazza, perhaps even beyond the Piazza della Maddalena, with a clear view north-

▲ **Fig. 95.** Pantheon. Reconstruction of façade and flanking porticoes

wards across the Field of Mars to the Mausoleum of Augustus), while most of the curving mass of the Rotunda was not visible, being hemmed in by the Saepta Julia on the east and embraced by another large building (the 'Basilica of Neptune') from the rear.

None the less, the physical connection between the porch and the Rotunda is decidedly awkward. If you stand to one side, you can see that a sort of transitional block rises between them, with a second pediment on the front, whose outer corner is on a level with one of the moulding courses on the outside of the Rotunda wall, whereas the pediment over the front porch coincides with nothing. It seems that the design originally envisaged a porch as wide and deep as the present one but with columns 60 RF high (50-foot shafts) instead of the actual 48 RF (40-foot shafts)—which would have taken the front pediment as high as the present second pediment. What forced the change in plan could be simply that the monolithic column shafts had to come all the way from Egypt and for some reason a complete set of the larger size was unobtainable (lost in a shipwreck, damaged in transit, needed elsewhere). The smaller columns were also not as thick, with the result that the spaces between them are wider than normal, and the pilasters which continue the colonnade on the back wall of the porch are curiously unbalanced, being narrower on the front than on the sides.

Intrinsic shortcomings apart, the **porch** is also missing various elements which will have made it a rather more coherent building than it appears now. It was approached from the front by four wide steps of Numidian yellow marble. The blank pediment should be filled with gilded bronze appliqué, which the pattern of holes suggests may have been an eagle and wreath (the attributes of Imperial Jupiter). All eight columns across the front and the two down the outsides should be of grey granite, only the four in the middle the rose-pink of Aswan, but the left flank was badly damaged during the Middle Ages and its columns (including the capitals and entablature) were restored in the C17, using pink Aswan shafts. That at the corner was brought from Domitian's villa at Castelgandolfo in 1626; the other two came from the Baths of Nero, in 1666. The 1626 operation was the work of Pope Urban VIII Barberini, who also took the opportunity to remove the original truss of massive bronze girders which had supported the porch roof (eliciting the famous pasquinade *quod non fecerunt barbari, fecerunt Barberini*: where the barbarians failed, the Barberini succeeded. Most of the 200 tons of metal went to make 80 cannon for Castel Sant'Angelo). To require such strong support, the original roof tiles were presumably of white marble. All the rest of the porch, inside and out, was veneered in marble. The exterior panelling, in white Greek (Pentelic) marble, survives best on the right-hand (west) flank: the horizontal bands between the pilasters were carved in relief with instruments of sacrifice (dishes, jugs, incense boxes, sacrificial axes) above garlands looping between ornate candelabras. The door in the corner leads to a staircase in the triangular space between the porch and the Rotunda, matched by one in the other angle, which serve rooms located at the top of the transitional block and in the upper level of the Rotunda wall, and continue up to the Rotunda roof. The outside doors around the base of the rotunda lead into small semicircular voids in the thickness of the wall, perhaps used for storage.

The interior of the porch, a space 34 m. (115 RF) wide and 20 m. (67½ RF) deep, is divided by the four inner columns of rose-pink granite into three aisles, the central wider one leading to the Rotunda, the outer two ending in tall apsidal recesses (the door in the left-hand apse is modern). Much of the pavement of grey granite rectangles and discs set in white marble (or travertine) is a modern restoration but reasonably authentic. Although the veneer on the inside of the alcoves and their surrounding wall surfaces has gone, the brickwork is studded with holes from its attachment. The **horizontal panels** between the pilasters framing the main doorway repeat the sacrificial objects cum garland-and-candelabra motif of the exterior. Grey granite and red porphyry panels were recorded in the lower zone of the wall to the left of the doorway in the C16 and a fragment of 'Lucullan' black/red marble survives between the pilaster capitals in the topmost register. To the bottom right of the doorway is a little inscription of 1270 referring to the erection of a bell-tower on top of the porch roof. The other inscriptions celebrate the restorations by Urban VIII and clearance work by Pius IX in 1853. The **bronze doors** are ancient and were in place by the C15 but are unlikely to be the originals. They are far too small for the marble door frame (which provided for doors 12 m./40 RF high and 7.5 m./25 RF wide), and the threshold (a single block of 'Lucullan' red/black) has been deeply recut.

The **Rotunda** has an internal diameter of 150 RF (44.4 m.), which is the same as the height from the floor to the circular oculus in the roof; its dome is a perfect hemisphere. Quite capable of letting in rain and birds as well as light and air, the oculus measures 30 RF (8.8 m.) in diameter and still preserves a decorative frieze of sheet bronze round its inside edge. (The outside of the dome was originally entirely covered with large sheet bronze tiles, but they were removed by order of the emperor Constans II in 663 and it is now protected by sheet lead, some of which may date from the C8). It is possible that the inside of the dome, with its five rings of twenty-eight coffers of diminishing size, was also clad in sheet bronze. There is no trace of paint or stuccowork or other finishing, but (under the modern rendering) the concrete is peppered with dowel holes.

The wall of the Rotunda is 6 m. (20 RF) thick, embodying seven large **alcoves** at ground level, alternately rectangular and semicircular in shape. The alcove on axis with the door (adapted to the altar and apse of the later church) is semicircular and open to the full height of its semi-domed ceiling (the mosaic is C18). It once contained a low podium, not unlike the one that supports the modern stalls, and its special status is further emphasized by the way in which the red porphyry frieze and heavy cornice which divide the drum wall into two horizontal zones are drawn in around the recess and project forward of it to either side, supported on Corinthian columns, with cable-fluted shafts of Phrygian purple. The same order, 36 RF (10.6 m.) high, was applied to the other six alcoves, whose openings are screened by two columns set between matching corner pilasters, using Numidian yellow marble for the four rectangular alcoves and Phrygian purple for the two semicircular ones on the cross axis. Now variously transformed into chapels and tombs (those on the cross axis contain the kings and queens of the short-lived Italian monarchy, 1870–1946), each alcove originally had three shallow rectangular niches for statues in the back wall, to which extra light filtered down from a window set above the cornice. Further rectangular niches are set between one alcove and the next, each with an aedicula projecting in front. The aedicula pediments are alternately triangular or curved, their columns alternately fluted Numidian yellow or unfluted red porphyry or grey granite, but they have undergone many alterations and, like the veneer on the surrounding wall surfaces, much has been restored in alien stones or in paint. Under the third aedicula on the left is the tomb of the great Renaissance painter Raphael (1483–1520), exhumed in 1833 and re-buried in an ancient Roman sarcophagus donated by pope Gregory XVI. The oval niches flanking the left-hand aediculas were intended for portraits of the 'Virtuosi al Pantheon', an academy of arts founded in 1543, whose archives still occupy the rooms over the porch. The original decoration of the upper zone was removed in 1747, in the belief that it was an inferior restoration by the Severan emperors in the early C3 AD (viz. the inscription on the façade) and would be improved upon by the scheme which now replaces it. However, a short stretch of the original is reconstructed over the first alcove and aedicula to the right of the main altar: on a high dado of Phrygian purple, the fourteen 'windows' centred alternately over the alcoves and aediculas were interspaced with sixty-four pilasters of red porphyry with white marble capitals set in groups of four (echoing the four columns of the alcove openings below) and framing panels and discs of red porphyry and Numidian yellow bordered in Phrygian purple and white. The **pavement** has been variously patched (and may have been completely relaid at some stage) but is apparently the original: bands of Phrygian purple 3 feet wide form a grid of 10-foot squares, filled alternately in red porphyry and Numidian yellow and containing either smaller (7-foot) squares in Phrygian purple or roundels in red porphyry or grey granite.

Exceptional structure that it is, no one really knows what **function** the Pantheon served. The name, in conjunction with the form and decoration of the porch, has generally been taken to signify that it was a temple, either a temple 'of all the gods' (though the cult is not otherwise attested at Rome), or, more plausibly, some kind of ruler-cult. The city of Rome (unlike the Empire at large) never took kindly to the idea of worshipping emperors as gods during their lifetime but it is possible that the Pantheon provided a setting—not a temple in the conventional sense—in which the living emperor would appear in company with the gods (including his own deified predecessors). Located on the edge of the Field of Mars, where the people might be called to assembly in the adjacent *Saepta*, also alongside Agrippa's public park, lake, basilica, and baths, joined later by Nero's baths, always in sight of Augustus' Mausoleum, its possible uses as a ceremonial space could be many. Of the first Pantheon it was said that Agrippa originally intended to honour Augustus, by naming the building after him and setting up his statue in it, but Augustus refused the honour and his place was taken by a statue of his deified father Julius Caesar; statues of Augustus and Agrippa were set up in the porch. Two other statues are mentioned, a Mars and a Venus (who was famous for her earrings, made by cutting in half the pearl that Cleopatra did not eat when she bet Mark Antony she could spend 10 million sesterces on a meal). In AD 59 the Arval Brethren, the college of twelve priests who made regular vows for the well-being of the imperial family, met there, perhaps in the porch (they normally met in the porch of the Temple of Imperial Harmony on the Forum, see p. 77). Hadrian's later Pantheon was one of the places (in addition to the Forum and the Palatine Palace) where the emperor held court, seated on a public tribunal, hearing petitions and giving judgements. And we hear of an imperial edict being read out *in Pantheo* in AD 368 or 370.

Excavations around the porch in 1891 traced the outline of an earlier building, presumably Agrippa's, coinciding closely with the present porch, with its entrance possibly (but by no means certainly) on the opposite side (i.e. facing south). The same campaign identified another coloured marble pavement 2.5 m. below the rotunda floor.

The straight brick wall with rectangular niches in it running along the eastern flank, parallel with the Via di Minerva, probably constitutes the western limit of the **Saepta Julia**, restored or rebuilt by Hadrian at the same time as the Pantheon. The Saepta were the voting halls of the old republican system, which had been rebuilt by Agrippa in 26 BC to a scheme originally planned by Julius Caesar in 54 BC, but under the Empire were hardly ever used for voting. Gladiatorial shows were staged there by Augustus, Claudius, and Caligula; Nero held a gymnastic display. They were also one of the venues for the Secular Games. According to its fragmentary depiction on the Marble Plan in the early C3, the building was essentially a huge rectangular court (310 × 120 m.) open to the north, with a *porticus* down each long side and a great roofed hall (Map, Fig. 77: 14), called the *Diribitorium* (the counting house) across the south end. The Diribitorium was famous, until they perished in the fire of AD 80, for the hundred-foot beams of larch in its roof.

Attached to the back of the Pantheon's Rotunda (Map, Fig. 77: 15 and Fig. 94) is another Hadrianic building, or rebuilding of some earlier structure, a large rectangular hall (46 × 19 m.) now transected lengthways by the Via della Palombella, with its other half buried under the building on the other side of the street. The marble frieze which ran beneath the cornice on top of its internal columns, decorated with leaping dolphins, mussel-shells, and tridents interspersed with acanthus leaves and palmettes, has suggested its identification with the **Basilica of Neptune**, a previous version of which had been dedicated by Agrippa in 25 BC and destroyed in the fire of AD 80. Its function is unknown but it lies immediately to the north of—and was possibly in its Hadrianic reincarnation incorporated into—the **Baths of Agrippa**, also damaged in AD 80 and reconstructed by Hadrian.

In the Piazza della Minerva, the Aswan granite obelisk carried by the statue of the elephant (carved in 1667 to a design by Bernini) is ancient, made in Egypt in the C6 BC. It was found in 1655 on the site of the **Iseum or Temple of Isis**, rebuilt by Domitian after the fire of AD 80, which lies under the buildings on the other side of the church of S. Maria sopra Minerva (see Map, Fig. 77). To the right of the church, a slight detour up the Via del Pie' di Marmo takes you to another fragment probably from the temple: the colossal **marble foot** which gave its name to the street (it now stands on the corner of the third street on the right, the Via S. Stefano del Cacco). The form of sandal the foot is wearing suggests a male cult statue, perhaps Isis' consort Serapis.

Back-tracking to the Piazza della Minerva and continuing down the Via dei Cestari to the Via dell'Arco della Ciambella, between nos. 13 and 16 on the right-hand side, with later buildings nestling within its shell, is a segment of the curving wall and dome of a **large circular hall** (about 23 m. in diameter) in brick-faced concrete (Map, Fig. 77: 16). The brick

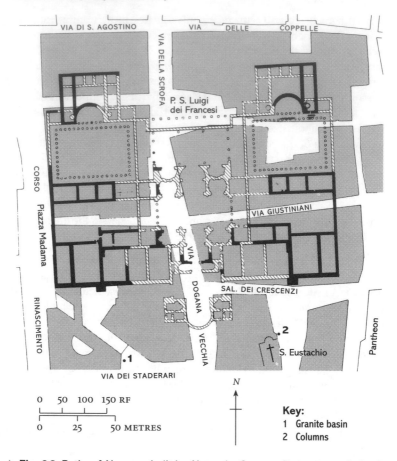

▲ **Fig. 96.** Baths of Nero – rebuilt by Alexander Severus. Reconstructed plan in relation to modern streets

ribbing in the vault is characteristic of the late Severan period (AD 230s) but could be earlier. A lot more of the building was visible, and its plan drawn, in the C16 from which it is clear that it formed part of a large set of public baths, presumably those of Agrippa in one of their later rebuildings. The Baths extend beyond the Via della Rotonda–Via della Torre Argentina to the west, where they will have fronted onto a huge park containing an artificial lake, the **Stagnum**, also part of Agrippa's original scheme. The exact size of the park surely changed over the years but you may imagine it filling the whole area as far as the Corso del Rinascimento and northwards to the Piazza di S. Eustachio, at which point the space was invaded in the AD 60s by the **Baths of Nero**, subsequently rebuilt on a gigantic scale by Alexander Severus in AD 227, and renamed in his honour the **Thermae Alexandrinae**. Their site (Fig. 96), measuring about 200 × 120 m., is marked by a considerable hill, readily visible when you look north up the Via della Dogana Vecchia from the Piazza S. Eustachio. Both the C16 Palazzo Madama (now the Italian Senate) and the church of S. Luigi dei Francesi on the left and the Palazzo Giustiniani and other palazzi on the right almost as far as the Via di S. Agostino–Via delle Coppelle make use of the walls of the Baths, which have recently been discovered to be still standing four storeys high in the palazzo at Piazza Rondanini no. 33. Columns of Egyptian grey and pink (Aswan) granite have been pulled up from the subsoil for centuries, two being used to restore the porch of the Pantheon in 1666 (see p. 204). Two found in 1934 under S. Luigi dei Francesi have been set up on the flank of the church of S. Eustachio (Via di S. Eustachio). Others still lie in the boiler rooms of the Palazzo Madama and more have been sighted in other cellars all around. In the Via dei Staderari (Fig. 96: 1), newly installed as a fountain, is a **great basin (*labrum*)** of Aswan granite which probably comes from the *caldarium* (hottest room) of the Baths.

Continuing westwards, the Corso del Rinascimento marks the eastern side of the Stadium of Domitian, out of which the Piazza Navona has evolved into one of Rome's most wonderful urban spaces.

Piazza Navona—Stadium of Domitian. Map, Fig. 77 ★

Designed for athletic contests in the nude Greek fashion (which the Romans never really took to), the Stadium was inaugurated by the emperor Domitian sometime before AD 86, when the first of new games in honour of Jupiter Capitolinus (the *Certamen Capitolinum Iovi*) were held there. It was used for various other types of event, such as public executions, substituting for the Colosseum as a venue for gladiatorial games when that was struck by lightning in AD 217, and was renovated by Alexander Severus in AD 227, at the same time as he rebuilt the adjacent Baths of Nero.

The shape of the piazza, curved at the north end and straight at the south, preserves very closely that of the ancient running track (192 m./450 RF long, 53 m./180 RF wide). All the buildings around are built on top of the seating, which took the outer dimensions of the building to over 275 m. long (probably 1,000 RF) and 106 m. (360 RF) wide. A sizeable sector of the substructures was exposed when the buildings in the centre of the northern end of the piazza were demolished in 1936–8 in a scheme to open a vista to the river. The scheme was aborted, but the excavations were left accessible under the new building and can be seen from the street if you take the Via Agonale out of the Piazza and turn left (Map, Fig. 77: 18). There were two tiers of seats, capable of holding about 30,000 spectators, supported on travertine and brick-faced concrete ribbing, very similar in construction and in the architectural style of the outer elevation to

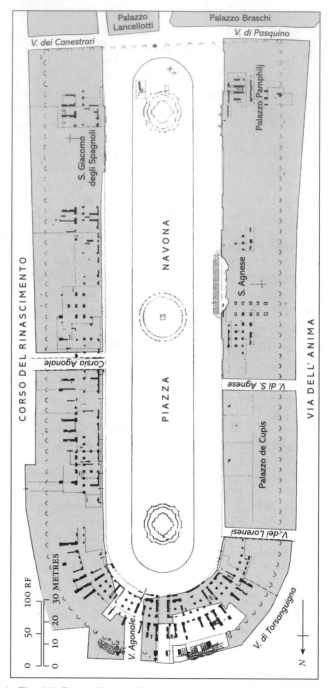

▲ **Fig. 97.** Piazza Navona (Stadium of Domitian). General site plan

The **obelisk** on Bernini's Four Rivers fountain (1651) in the centre of the square has nothing to do with the Stadium, but *is* connected with Domitian. Of Aswan granite, 16.54 m. high, it was found in the Circus of Maxentius on the Via Appia (see p. 336), having been carried there in the C4, but that was not its first location. The hieroglyphs on the shaft were cut by Roman, not Egyptian, stonecutters and offer a hymn to Domitian and the deified Vespasian and Titus, possibly referring to something being restored. It was long thought to have come from the huge Temple of the Egyptian gods Isis and Serapis to the east of the Saepta (Map, Fig. 77: 11), rebuilt by Domitian in AD 80, but that is now doubted; an alternative might be the temple which Domitian built on the Quirinal hill to celebrate his family cult—the *Gens Flavia* (p. 350).

its near-contemporary, the Colosseum (p. 276). The arcades (*fornices*) were notorious hang-outs for prostitutes of both sexes, a reputation which has coloured the story of St Agnes, whose martyrdom in the Stadium in AD 304(?) is commemorated in the huge Baroque church (Borromini 1657) on the west side of the square.

Beyond the Piazza di Tor Sanguigna, the museum in the C16 **Palazzo Altemps** (Map, Fig. 77: 19, entrance in Via di S. Apollinare) houses amongst other things the **Ludovisi marbles**, an important collection of ancient statuary assembled by the Ludovisi family in the course of the C16–C18 and acquired by the Italian state in the late C19 (see p. 401).

The street leading out of the Piazza Navona at the far SW corner, the Via del **Pasquino**, takes you to the little Piazza del Pasquino (Map, Fig. 77: 20), named after the fragmentary marble statue mounted on the pedestal at the angle of the Palazzo Braschi. The best known of Rome's talking statues, origin of the word *pasquinade*, meaning a satirical protest in verse or prose, 'Mister Pasquin' was found during roadworks in 1501 at the corner of the Via della Cuccagna, having probably decorated the Stadium. It is a work of the C2 AD, thought to portray an episode from the *Iliad* of Homer, where the Spartan king Menelaus defends the corpse of Achilles' companion Patroclus. In its second life, on the feast of St Mark (25 April) it used to be dressed up as a pagan god—Venus, Janus, or Apollo—and epigrams were pinned on it in the course of competitions held in the square. How it got the name *Mastro Pasquino* is unknown but variously supposed to refer to a tailor, barber, or schoolmaster of the neighbourhood.

The street at the opposite (SE) corner of the Piazza Navona, the Via della Posta Vecchia, leads into the little Piazza dei Massimi at the rear of the Palazzo Massimo (Map, Fig. 77: 21), where a large column shaft of Carystian green marble (8.6 m., missing its lower collar) has been set up. It comes from the lower order of the stage-building of the **Odeum**, which lies on this spot, partly excavated in 1936–7 on the site of the adjacent building which fronts on to the Corso del Rinascimento. A roofed theatre

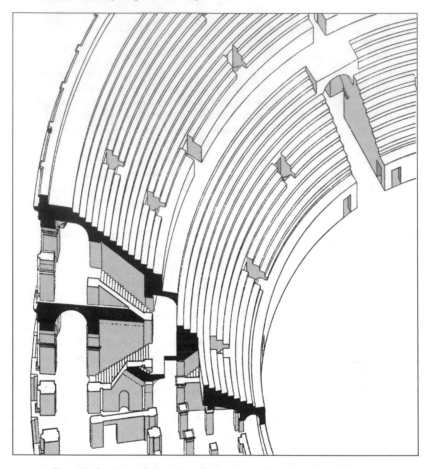

▲ **Fig. 98.** Stadium of Domitian. Reconstructed section of seating

for musical performances and competitions, with a seating capacity of 10,600, the Odeum was another of Domitian's Greek-style additions to Rome's cultural scene, to complement the Stadium. It faced east towards the park and lake of Agrippa. Apparently still unfinished when Domitian was assassinated in AD 96, it was completed early in the reign of Trajan (AD 98–117). The curving shape of the auditorium can be followed in the street pattern, from the curving façade of the Palazzo Massimo (designed by Baldassare Peruzzi in 1532–6) on the Corso Vittorio Emanuele round into the Piazza di S. Pantaleo. Two museums face each other across the Corso at this point: the **Museo di Roma** in the Palazzo Braschi (Map, Fig. 77: 22), though mainly a museum of medieval and modern Roman life often has exhibitions of prints, drawings and photographs relevant to the study of the ancient city.

Excavations in the cellars under the palazzo which houses the **Museo Barracco** (p. 402) across the way (Map, Fig. 77: 23) have uncovered a street and part of the columned courtyard of a late Roman (C3–C4) house (sometimes visible, ask at the Museum entrance). Excavations in 1988–93 under the courtyard and cellars of the **Palazzo della Cancelleria** (Map, Fig. 77: 24, *†permit Vatican) have traced some remnants of the great C4 basilica-church of St Laurence built by Pope Damasus (AD 366–84). Under the far NW corner of the Palazzo, close to the Corso Vittorio Emanuele, excavations in the 1930s found the **Euripus**, the canal which flowed out of the Stagnum of Agrippa to the Tiber, and

▼ **Fig. 99.** Stadium of Domitian. Restored exterior elevation

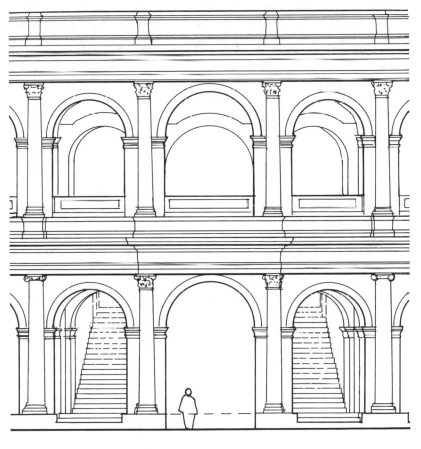

```
0        5       10      15 FEET
|_____|_____|_____|

0    1    2    3    4    5 METRES
```

the **tomb of Aulus Hirtius**, consul in 43 BC, who died in the battle of Modena and was awarded a State funeral, with the right of burial on the Field of Mars. Marble-sculptors had set up shop in the neighbourhood by the C2 and among the scrap marble stored against the tomb were the 'Cancelleria reliefs', two panels from a large imperial monument of the late C1, showing the emperor setting out and returning from campaign (Vatican Museums, ex-Lateran collection).

Between the eastern end of the Campo de' Fiori and the Largo di Torre Argentina lies the **Theatre** (Map, Fig. 77: 27) **and Porticus of Pompey**, Rome's first permanent theatre, built by Cn. Pompeius Magnus, powerful rival to Julius Caesar, as a victory monument following his triple triumph in 61 BC. The complex, completed by 55 BC, was laid out immediately behind a whole line of earlier republican victory temples (see opposite) and somehow incorporated five temples (or shrines) into its structure, perhaps ranged around the upper edge of the theatre seating (the principal temple was dedicated to Pompey's favourite goddess *Venus Victrix*, the others to *Honos*, *Virtus*, *Felicitas*, and a deity whose name began with V). There is hardly anything structural to see except inside the restaurants 'Costanza' (Piazza del Paradiso) and 'Pancrazio' (Piazza del Biscione), both of which are built into the radiating concrete vaults and walls, faced in fine tufa *opus reticulatum*, which supported the seating. Evocative of the height and shape of the auditorium are the curving profiles of the buildings on the Via di Grotta Pinta (Map, Fig. 77: 27), reached through the Passetto del Biscione (or if that is closed round the outside by the Piazza del Paradiso and Largo dei Chiavari). Attached to the theatre proper was its **porticus**, known from fragments of the Marble Plan to have been a great rectangular precinct (180 × 135 m.), laid out on the same east–west axis, with porticoes down the north and south long sides (on the line of the Via del Sudario and Vicolo dei Chiodaroli–Via di S. Anna respectively). The eastern end, which once contained an annex where Senate meetings were sometimes held and where Julius Caesar was murdered on 15 March 44 BC, lies under the Via di Torre Argentina. Its back wall projects into the excavated **area of the Largo Argentina**, behind Temple B (see Fig. 100).

The **Abbot Luigi**, in the Largo Vidoni (Map, Fig. 77: 28) on the eastern flank of the church of S. Andrea della Valle, is another of Renaissance Rome's speaking statues (like the Pasquino). Once the portrait of a Roman official dressed in a toga, he used to stand round the corner, nearer the church in Via del Sudario, taking his name for his resemblance to one of its sacristans. He has repeatedly 'lost his head' in one cause or another, the last time in 1985 (the present one is a cast of it made of concrete).

Republican Victory-Temples. Map, Fig. 77: 29 and Fig. 100 ★

Largo di Torre Argentina. Comune (†lower level)

The area was created by extensive demolition work in 1926–8, intended to widen the streets and allow for new development, but in the event preserved as an archaeological site. All that was retained of the medieval quarter at the higher level is the C12 tower-house (called Torre del Papito or dell'Olmo) at the SE corner. The principal components at the ancient level are the eastern end of the **Porticus of Pompey**, down the western margin (Fig. 100: 1, 3), beyond which are **four republican temples** set side by side, all facing east, but built at different times and variously modified or rebuilt on later occasions. Unfortunately, the whole area was excavated in great haste in 1929 and although further investigations have been made since, the chronology of the temples is still far from clear. Nor, although theories abound, is there any hard evidence to show which deities they were dedicated to—they are commonly called by the letters A to D.

Temple A is the rectangular one with standing columns at the north end, surviving rather better than the others because the church of S. Nicola dei Cesarini or Calcarari (the lime-burners) was built into it in 1132. The two apses in the rear were part of the church. The large tufa podium (15 × 27.5 m.) and series of tufa columns, which once ran all the way round the cella—nine down the sides and six across the front and back (and were once completely coated with white stucco to look like marble)—apparently date from the mid–late C1 BC. Soundings under the cella and the forecourt have found two earlier phases. In the first (C3 BC), built on the natural clay when the general ground level was about 3 m. lower, the temple was only the size of the later cella (9.5 × 16 m.), set on a podium 4 m. high, approached by 18 steps. Later, a large rectangular platform (12.5 × 14 m.) was constructed over the foot of the old staircase in order to raise the temple's altar 1.5 m. higher, presumably to keep it out of the way of floods. By the early C1 BC the whole area had been repaved in tufa at the higher level. The white travertine paving that you see in front of the temple today belongs to a second repaving, a metre higher still, following the great fire of AD 80, in which all the temples were damaged and had to be extensively repaired (among the repairs to Temple A were the two travertine columns, front right).

Temple B, the circular one with parts of six columns standing, is definitely the youngest of the four, with its foundations set at the level of the tufa repaving and probably dating shortly after 100 BC. Originally it had eighteen Corinthian columns, with tufa shafts and travertine bases and capitals, finished in white stucco, free-standing around a small cella 9.3 m. (30 RF) in diameter, on a podium 2.5 m. high. Inside was a solid base for a colossal cult statue (probably the goddess whose marble head, right arm

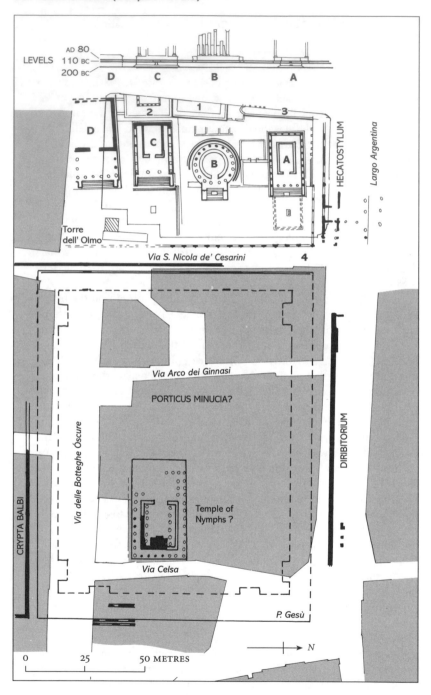

LEVELS
AD 80
110 BC
200 BC

D C B A

2 1 3

D

C B A

HECATOSTYLUM

Largo Argentina

Torre dell' Olmo

Via S. Nicola de' Cesarini 4

Via Arco dei Ginnasi

PORTICUS MINUCIA?

Via delle Botteghe Óscure

DIRIBITORIUM

CRYPTA BALBI

Temple of Nymphs ?

Via Celsa

P. Gesù

N

0 25 50 METRES

and a foot were found in the area between B and C, now in the Palazzo dei Conservatori, Braccio Nuovo). Two long bases were provided on either side of the front steps for more statues. Later, around 50 BC, the small cella was demolished and the gaps between the columns walled up with slabs of tufa, resulting in a cella with a diameter of 15.5 m. (52 RF); the podium was also enlarged, by adding an outer ring of tufa (*peperino*) slabs. After the AD 80 fire the tufa infill between the columns was faced with brick so that the columns became invisible, the cella floor was raised and a new staircase and porch built at the front, together with the brick altar (veneered in marble). Temple B is the only one whose identity is reasonably assured as **Fortuna Huiusce Diei** (Good Fortune on This Day), known to have been round, vowed by Q. Lutatius Catulus at the battle of Vercellae on 30 July 101 BC. In the days of Pliny the Elder (AD 70s) a crowd of antique Greek statues stood in front of or under the porch (seven bronze nude youths and an old man by Pythagoras of Samos) and there were three by Pheidias inside.

Temple C preserves its original podium of solid tufa blocks (17.1 × 30.5 m.) decorated along the sides with heavy upper and lower mouldings characteristic of the early C3 BC. Contemporary with or slightly older than the first phase of Temple A, it was initially approached by twenty steps from the old ground level of the Field of Mars, and like Temple A its altar was later raised on a large rectangular platform, which was then eliminated by the repaving of the precincts in tufa at the end of the C2 or early C1 BC and subsequently buried under the higher-level travertine pavement after AD 80. The old altar—still in place underneath the travertine paving in front of the temple (Fig. 101)—is inscribed: 'In accordance with the law proposed by Plaetorius, [this altar] was restored under the supervision of the joint magistrate [in charge of dedicating temples] Aulus Postumius Albinus, son of Aulus, grandson of Aulus.' Which Postumius Albinus he was is not certain; the consul of 151 BC, a legate in 110 BC, even the consul of 99 BC are all possible. The floor of the temple cella and what remains of the superstructure belong to the period after AD 80, as does the colossal head of a matronly-looking goddess, possibly from its cult statue, found nearby (set up in the far NW corner of the site).

Temple D, the largest of all (23.5 × 37 m.), is mostly hidden under the modern road (Via Florida) at the south. Its podium has at least two phases, one before and one after the surrounding area was repaved in the late C2/early C1 BC. Both podiums were made of concrete, so even the first is not likely to date earlier than the C2 (but excavations are needed in

◀ **Fig. 100.** Republican victory-temples in Largo Argentina. General site plan

Key:

1 '*Curia*' (Porticus of Pompey)	3 Public latrine (Porticus of Pompey)
2 Peristyle court (C3–C2 BC)	4 *Statio Aquarum* (?)

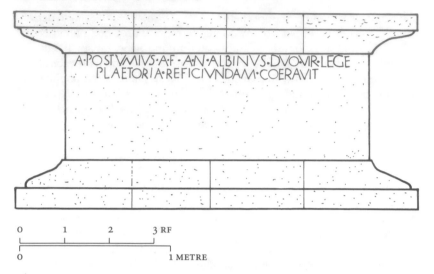

A·POSTVMIVS·A·F · AN·ALBINVS·DVO·VIR·LEGE
PLAETORIA·REFICIVNDAM·COERAVIT

| 0 | 1 | 2 | 3 RF |
| | | | 1 METRE |

▲ **Fig. 101.** Altar in front of Temple C, Largo Argentina

greater depth); the later one is faced with travertine; the cella walls, which occupy the full width of the podium, with columns only at the front, were reconstructed in brick-faced concrete, probably after AD 80.

Ancient written sources provide six potential contenders for temples **A**, **C**, and **D**: *Juturna, Feronia, Juno Curitis, Jupiter Fulgur, Nymphs, Lares Permarini*. **Temple A** is possibly that of the watery goddess *Juturna* (see also p. 95), built by a Lutatius Catulus, probably the consul of 241 BC, after his victory against the Carthaginians at sea; the likely connection of the neighbouring Temple B with a later Lutatius Catulus strengthens the possibility. In a poem Ovid wrote in about AD 2 Juturna is juxtaposed with the end of the *Aqua Virgo* by which he might have meant the Baths of Agrippa, not far to the north. **Temple C** could be identified with *Feronia* (an Italic earth-goddess of Sabine origin related to Juno) whose temple on the Field of Mars certainly existed by 217 BC and may have been built as early as 290 BC. For **Temple D** we then have *Juno Curitis, Jupiter Fulgur*, the *Nymphs*, or the *Lares Permarini*. These last ('Guardians of Seafarers') had their temple vowed by L. Aemilius Regillus at the naval battle of Myonnesos (Syria) in 190 BC, dedicated in 179 BC and later enclosed in the *Porticus Minucia*, built as another victory monument in 110 BC. Efforts have been made to argue that the *Porticus* is the colonnade which runs down the east side of the Largo Argentina area (hidden underneath the modern street) rebuilt after AD 80 on the line of an earlier one, but the colonnade's principal face is turned to the east, suggesting that it related primarily to something in that direction (a street, or another adjacent precinct). If the *Porticus Minucia* is elsewhere then the temple of the *Lares Permarini* has to be elsewhere as well (for one possibility see below). We know nothing of the early history of the temple of the *Nymphs* except that it was burned and rebuilt *c*.57 BC, held the records of the censors in charge of the corn ration, and was near the *Villa Publica* (which could cover a wide area). *Juno Curitis* (Juno as protectress of spearmen) and *Jupiter Fulgur* (Lightning) had their anniversary on the same day and are likely to have formed a pair, but since Jupiter's is said to have been an altar in an open enclosure, they are usually both ruled out, unless we make Temple D that of Juno, and Jupiter lies in the unexcavated area further to the south.

The nature of the **other buildings** which subsequently clustered in between and behind the temples is poorly understood. That in brick between temples A and B (no. 4 on plan) comprises two rooms opening off the temple court, the inner one once richly decorated with marble; it could be another shrine of some kind. An alternative suggestion (heavily dependent on the identification of the precinct as the *Porticus Minucia* and Temple A with Juturna) is that it was the **Statio Aquarum**—the headquarters of the curators of the water supply. The rest are apparently small workshops and hovels exploiting the otherwise unused space between the temples and the boundary wall at the eastern end of the Porticus of Pompey. The long marble-lined **public latrine** at the NW end (Fig. 100: 3) belongs to the Porticus, not the temple area. The seats faced west, looking out through a colonnade towards the Porticus gardens.

Temple—Via delle Botteghe Oscure.
Map, Fig. 77: 30, and Fig. 100

Discovered in 1938 when digging the foundations for a new building which was then never built, the main elements visible from the street are two fluted Corinthian columns 10.6 m. (36 RF) high, which were re-erected in 1954. The shafts are composed of travertine drums, the capitals made in two halves, with a coating of white stucco. They stand on a podium of concrete faced with travertine and the cella wall behind them is of brickfaced concrete. More of the plan of the temple is known from the Marble Plan (see Fig. 100). It was very large (*c*.40 × 27 m.), with columns on all four sides, eight across the front and back, twelve down the sides. The cella had an internal colonnade and a substantial base for the cult statue(s). Most of what is visible seems to date from a restoration of the late C1 AD (after the fire of AD 80), but the column bases may have been recycled from an earlier version (mid-C1 BC) and there is possibly an earlier (concrete) podium within the later one. The Marble Plan indicates that the temple was set, somewhat off centre, in a monumental porticus which filled the whole space between the other side of the Via delle Botteghe Oscure and the Corso Vittorio Emanuele, bounded by the Via

Celsa to the east and of uncertain extent to the west (perhaps only as far as the Via Arco dei Ginnasi). It has been suggested that the fragmentary inscription on an adjoining fragment of the Marble Plan (. . . MINI) could refer to the *Porticus Minucia* of 110 BC, in which case the temple is probably that of the *Lares Permarini* (see p. 218). If the Porticus is not the Minucia, however, there are other possible candidates, such as the temple of the *Nymphs*, if that is not to be identified with Temple D in the Largo Argentina (see p. 219).

Theatre and Porticus ('Crypta') of Balbus.
Map, Fig. 77: 31

Via Caetani

Inside the buildings along the south side of the Via delle Botteghe Oscure runs the northern boundary of another enormous Porticus. Nicknamed 'the Crypts', it was part of Rome's third theatre (after those of Pompey and Marcellus) which L. Cornelius Balbus the Younger was allowed to construct in celebration of his victory over the Garamantes (in Libya) in 19 BC. The complex was finished in 13 BC (the day of its inauguration coinciding with a major Tiber flood, so the celebrants had to arrive by boat) and included small columns of Egyptian onyx (alabaster), a rarity at the time. The Theatre building is completely buried under the block on the west side of the Via Caetani (under the Palazzo Caetani and Palazzo Mattei), but a large area of the Porticus was the focus of major archaeological excavations in 1981–8 in the grounds of the ex-convent of S. Caterina dei Funari to the east of the Via Caetani (the excavations are currently suspended and not accessible to the public).

The site is providing some extraordinary insights into Rome's later urban history, especially the 'Dark Ages' of the C6–C9, when the shell of the old porticus was a hive of industrial activity (including bronze- and glass-working). Older ground levels have only been examined in a few places, but the gutting of the buildings along the Via delle Botteghe Oscure and the stripping of the plaster from those on the Via dei Delfini side have revealed that the outer perimeter walls of the Porticus (as rebuilt after the fire of AD 80) are still standing within the fabric of the later city to heights of more than 12 m.: starting with eleven courses of tufa blocks capped with one of travertine and another of tufa they continue in concrete and brick (a part of the brickwork can be seen from Piazza Lovatelli, high up to the right of the façade of S. Caterina). In passing, the courtyard of the **Palazzo Mattei di Giove** (Via Caetani no. 32), which houses the State Record Library (Discoteca) and other institutions, has a fine array of ancient reliefs and statues incorporated into its design (by Carlo Maderno, 1598–1611).

Turning right from the Via Caetani, along the Via dei Funari, you come to the **Piazza Mattei** (where the shells at the four corners of the delightful fountain 'of the Turtles' (1658) are made out of recycled ancient black/red 'Lucullan' marble), south of which the Via della Reginella and the Via dei S. Ambrogio both lead to the **Via del Portico d'Ottavia**.

The zone between the Via del Portico d'Ottavia and the Tiber, and from the Theatre of Marcellus as far west as the Via Arenula, roughly corresponds to the **Circus Flaminius**. Laid out by C. Flaminius Nepos in 220 BC on public land bearing his family name, the *Prata Flaminia*, it was not a proper circus for chariot-racing in the sense of the Circus Maximus; it had no seating, nor starting gates, nor was it necessarily even circusshaped, though it could be used for horse-racing. During the last two centuries of the Republic it was a large, general purpose open space, where public meetings, markets, banking, and funerary orations could take place, where the Taurian Games (which included horse-races) were held every five years on the occasion of the Census, and it was also one of the venues for the sporadic Secular Games. Its most prestigious function was as the point of assembly and departure for military triumphal processions, and in the course of time no less than **eleven victory-temples** are recorded around its margins, variously honouring *Vulcan, Neptune, Juno Regina, Hercules Custos, Hercules Musarum* (of the Muses), *Jupiter Stator, Fortuna Equestris, Mars, Castor and Pollux, Diana*, and *Pietas*. Only four are firmly located: **Juno Regina** (the podium, with two composite columns 48 RF high still standing, is buried in the midst of the block of houses between Via S. Angelo in Pescheria and Via Tribuna di Campitelli), **Jupiter Stator** (under S. Maria in Campitelli), **Hercules of the Muses** (the podium was found in 1980–1 in the cellars to the east of the Via di S. Ambrogio), and **Castor and Pollux**, represented on a fragment of a marble plan which can be positioned at the corner of Via delle Cinque Scole and Via S. Bartolomeo de' Vaccari (Map, Fig. 77: 35). Another two, Hercules Custos and Mars, were probably at the western end of the Circus. Mars, built by D. Junius Brutus in 138 BC, using a Greek architect Hermodorus of Salamis and imported Greek marble, could be the temple which lies under the church of S. Salvatore in Campo, Map, Fig. 77: 33. Diana and Pietas were probably at the eastern end, near the temples of Apollo and Bellona (Fig. 77: 38), but were sacrificed to build the Theatre of Marcellus in the late C1 BC (see p. 243) and replaced by smaller shrines incorporated into the design of the theatre or its porticus. Fortuna Equestris also vanished by the early C1 AD. Vulcan and Neptune were both very early and long-lived, but we are in the dark as to their precise whereabouts. The temples on the north side were enclosed in monumental porticoes, the entrance to the **Porticus of Octavia** which gives the modern street its name being one visible remnant (Map, Fig. 77: 36). The arcade on the **Via S. Maria dei Calderari** (Map, Fig. 77: 32) perhaps represents the porticus of a temple at the west end. Sometime during the C1 AD what remained of the Circus's open space was paved in travertine; by the early C3, when it appears on a fragment of the Marble Plan, that space was probably reduced to the area between the Via delle Cinque Scole and the Theatre of Marcellus.

Porticus (?) Via S. Maria dei Calderari no. 23B.
Map, Fig. 77: 32

Two travertine columns with Tuscan capitals, buried to half their original height under the street level, support a wide architrave built partly in travertine, partly in brick. The large brick archway in the wall between the columns currently spans the shop doorway, possibly an earlier window, below which there may have been a door. More of the structure has been visible and recorded on various occasions in the past, including a little-known reconstruction and plan by Thomas Burgess in 1830 (Fig. 102). Plans drawn in the C16 indicate that it extends under the whole of the present block and northwards over the next street to the block beyond. In 1896 the wall above the archway was stripped of its modern plaster and found to be faced with *opus mixtum* (tufa reticulate and courses of brick). Identical walling has been traced in the cellars of the palazzo to the west, facing Via Arenula, and in the shop at no. 18 Via di S. Maria del Pianto there are some similar architectural elements in travertine. When there was more to see, the structure was believed to be a major public building, either the Porticus of Philippus or the 'Crypta' of Balbus; now that both of those are known to have been located elsewhere, the building is unidentified. Some would like it to be the *Porticus Minucia Frumentaria* (not to be confused with the older *Porticus Minucia* referred to above, p. 219–20), the distribution centre for public grain rations set up in the C1 AD, probably in the reign of Claudius (AD 41–54), but it is probably not big enough for that, though the location would be convenient for deliveries of grain by river.

Gateway to the Porticus of Octavia. Map, Fig. 77: 36★

Via del Portico d'Ottavia (S. Angelo in Pescheria)

Adapted in the C8 as the atrium of the church (now S. Angelo in Pescheria, i.e. 'in the Fish Market', previously St Paul 'in the Circus'), the double-sided columnar porch was known in the Middle Ages as 'Severus' temple'. The inscription on the architrave records the names and titles of the emperors Septimius Severus and his son Caracalla in the year AD 203 and, in the bottom line, explains that they had restored [the building] as the result of a fire: *incendio corruptam rest*(ituerunt). The marble of the architrave is Greek (Pentelic), different from that used for the Corinthian columns, which are of Italian (Luna), and has had an earlier frieze

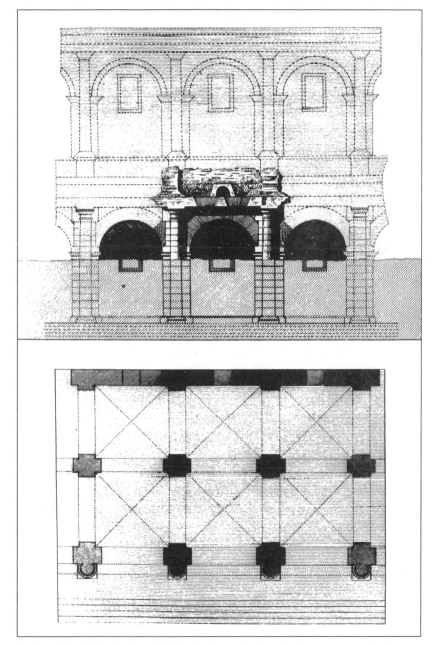

▲ **Fig. 102.** Via S. Maria dei Calderari. Travertine façade. Plan and elevation by
Thomas Burgess (1830)

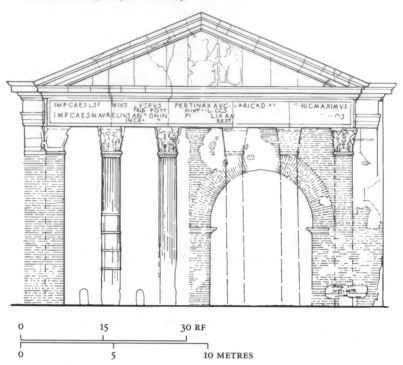

0   15   30 RF

0   5   10 METRES

▲ **Fig. 103.** Gateway to the Porticus of Octavia

chiselled off to make way for the inscription. If you look up at the rear of the pediment which faces the other way, you can see that its blocks have all been recycled from an earlier building—including sections of fluted column shafts and pieces of cornice, possibly dating from the late C1 BC. In fact AD 203 was the third time that the building had been rebuilt or repaired, and the second time because of fire.

The gateway marks the main entrance to the **Porticus of Octavia**, a lot more of which is known from the Marble Plan (Fig. 104). It stretched 50 m. to right and left (a few fragments of columns have been re-erected to give the idea) and 140 m. backwards almost as far as the 'Crypta' of Balbus (the NW corner was found in 1987–9 under the Palazzo Patrizi Clementi, between the Via dei Delfini and the eastern end of the Via dei Funari), enclosing the victory-temples of Juno Regina (founded in 179 BC) and Jupiter Stator (131 BC). Its earliest version had been called the Porticus of Metellus, having been built, together with the Temple of Jupiter Stator, by Q. Caecilius Metellus with the proceeds from his victory in Macedonia in 146 BC. When Metellus' porticus was replaced, in about 27–25 BC, it was renamed after Octavia, sister of the emperor Augustus and mother of Marcellus (see p. 243), and incorporated a library in memory of

Marcellus, schools and meeting rooms (all apparently on the north side). Quantities of antique Greek statuary and paintings were displayed in it, the most famous being a great composition in bronze by Lysippus portraying Alexander the Great on horseback with his twenty-five cavalry-companions who had died at the battle of the Granicus in 334 BC. Metellus had taken the group from the sanctuary at Dion in Greece to Rome as part of his spoils of war, rededicating it in his original Porticus and it bore a charmed life, surviving the fire of AD 80 and that which occasioned the reconstruction of AD 203, as well as the sack of Rome by the Goths in AD 410.

Since the closing of the pedestrian street through to the Via del Teatro di Marcello there is not much to be seen, from this angle and distance, of

▼ **Fig. 104.** Porticus of Octavia. Evidence of the Marble Plan in relation to modern topography

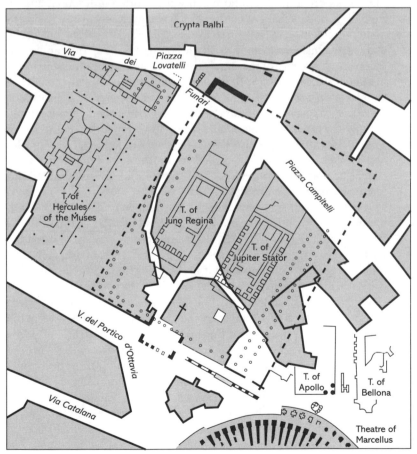

the **Theatre of Marcellus** (Map, Fig. 79: 37) nor the **Temple of Apollo Sosianus** (Map, Fig. 77: 38), so they are to be found in the Circus Flaminius–Circus Maximus section (see pp. 243–7). The Via del Portico d'Ottavia, however, continues down to the Lungotevere, where the Tiber Island is just over the road.

Tiber Island. Maps, Fig. 77 and Fig. 112   ★

A ridge of alluvial sand formed by the river itself, not a rock, the island measures only 280 × 70 m. at its widest, and has had a curious history, always distanced from the city, either as a place of ill omen or, equally appropriately, an isolation hospital (there is a large hospital on it now, run by the Fatebenefratelli since 1548). The ancient Romans, who simply called it 'island' or *inter duos pontes* (between the two bridges), crowded it with temples, the earliest and most important being one to Aesculapius, the Greek god of healing, whose cult was imported to Rome in 291 BC from his main sanctuary at Epidauros following a plague. The decision to build the temple on the island, so the story goes, was made by one of the god's sacred snakes who jumped off the boat as it came up river and swam ashore there. No trace of the temple has been found but it almost certainly lies under the church of St Bartholomew, at the downstream end. Other temples or shrines were erected in the C2 BC to rather odd or archaic kinds of gods, such as *Jupiter Jurarius* ('guarantor of oaths') and *Faunus* (an old Italic god who spoke oracles and protected boundaries, grandson of Saturn). Later there were also *Veiovis* (a relative of Jupiter), *Gaia* (oracles and another witnesser of oaths), *Tiberinus* (the god of the river Tiber), *Bellona* (a war goddess), and at least a statue of the multivalent and untranslatable *Semo Sancus Dius Fidius*.

Although there may have been earlier wooden bridges to the island, the present stone bridge across from the Field of Mars (left bank), the **Pons Fabricius** (Map, Fig. 77: 39), dates from 62 BC. The two marble pillars (herms) with four heads set in the parapet were not originally part of the bridge, but were moved to it in the 1840s from the adjacent river-bank, where they are recorded in the vicinity of the church of S. Gregorio (Monte Savello) since the C14. The heads apparently portray different aspects of Janus, god of boundaries and gateways; slots in the sides of the pillars suggest they supported the angles of a metal fence around some sort of square or rectangular enclosure, perhaps associated with the Temple of Janus near the Theatre of Marcellus (see p. 249). The bridge was built by one Lucius Fabricius in his capacity as commissioner of roads, recorded by the inscriptions engraved in the stone below the parapet on both sides. The smaller inscriptions underneath were added in 21 BC to the effect that the consuls had checked the work and found it satisfactory, possibly after repairs (there was a huge flood in 23 BC). It is now the last

▲ **Fig. 105.** Tiber Island. Travertine prow

working Roman bridge in Rome. That on the other side of the island, the **Pons Cestius**, originally built a few years after Fabricius', was also very long-lived, having been rebuilt in the C4 and repaired in the C11 but then fell victim to the new Tiber embankment in 1886–9; only the central arch preserves some of the ancient structure.

With the two bridges sticking out on either side the island looks even now rather like a gigantic ship with oars and evidently struck the same visual chord in Roman minds. Around the mid-late C1 BC someone had the genial notion of modelling the downstream end of the island, on the side facing the Field of Mars, literally in the shape of the **prow** of an ancient trireme, constructed in blocks of travertine and tufa (Map, Fig. 77: 40, Fig. 105). Carved in relief under the prow is the head of Aesculapius, his healing staff entwined with a snake beside him. On the thwart is a bull's head.

For a better view of both the Pons Fabricius and the prow, it is possible to walk on the travertine counter at the water's edge: take the steps which lead down off the square in front of the hospital on the south (Trastevere) side. From the downstream end you can also see what remains of the **Pons Aemilius**, the Ponte Rotto (Broken Bridge). The footings of its oldest piers, probably laid in conjunction with the construction of the Via Aurelia (the road to Etruria) in the mid-C3 BC and subsequently remade in 179–142 BC, have been identified in the Tiber bed slightly further upstream and on a different angle. The present structure, in travertine with a core of tufa and concrete, was apparently a complete rebuilding by Augustus (late C1 BC) and once consisted of six large arches with two smaller ones carrying the approach ramps at each end. Damaged and repaired in about AD 280, again in 1230 and once more in 1557, its eastern half was carried away in 1598 and two of the remaining three arches were demolished in the 1880s.

Capitoline Hill (Map: Fig. 106)

Since its transformation during the C16–C17 into Rome's palatial centre of local government (the 'Campidoglio') and even more so since the imposition of the monster Vittorio Emanuele Monument at the north end in 1911, the Capitoline hill has not only lost much of its original shape but also turns its principal faces in the opposite directions from those which prevailed in antiquity.

Measuring only 480 m. by 200 m., smallest of the hills of Rome, it was once a natural fortress, with rocky cliffs on all sides and two tree-covered crests on top, one smaller and slightly higher than the other: the northern one, where the church of S. Maria in Aracoeli stands today (48 m. above sea level), was called the *Arx* (citadel). The southern crest (45 m. a.s.l.), mostly covered now by the Palazzo dei Conservatori (1568) and Palazzo Caffarelli (1584), formed a high promontory towards the Tiber and went by the name of *Capitolium*. (Both terms are often used interchangeably by ancient and modern writers to mean the whole hill.) The lower saddle between the two crests (38 m. a.s.l.), corresponding more or less with the actual Piazza del Campidoglio, was described as *inter duos lucos* (between the two groves) or *Asylum*, an area where, according to Roman legend, Romulus, in his efforts to found the new city, had declared a sanctuary to attract foreign refugees. Pottery found in the excavations at S. Omobono, at the foot of the south corner (see p. 250), suggests that the river end of the hill was already a focus of settlement in the Bronze Age (C14–C13 BC) and later Roman tradition placed a 'House of Romulus' on the Capitolium, like that on the Palatine (see p. 125). Traces of Iron Age huts dating from the C9 and C8 BC have been found in the Asylum area and fragments of tufa walling typical of the C6 BC outcrop at various points around the hill. By the C4 BC we hear of aristocratic houses on the *Arx*, and others were probably located along the more accessible slopes on the side overlooking the Forum valley.

The *Arx* was a place of augury, where the omens were read in the flight of birds, from the **Auguraculum**, a point with a clear view to the Alban Mount (now Monte Cavo), 27 km. to the SE of the city. It also held a **Temple of Juno** (goddess of fertility and the sanctity of marriage) famous for its sacred geese, who had raised the alarm when the Gauls tried to attack the citadel one night in 390 BC and were thereafter looked after at State expense, carried each year on litters with purple and gold cushions in a ceremony at which dogs were crucified as a terrible reminder of the guard dogs who had failed to bark.

The Capitolium end was reserved exclusively for religious purposes from a very early period, becoming the centre of the State cult and desti-

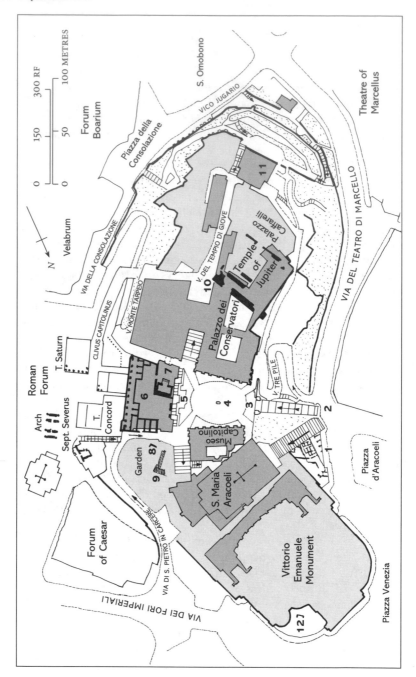

nation of the Roman military triumphal procession. A small temple for Jupiter Feretrius, bringer of victories, was said to have been founded there in Romulus' day (and still existed in the C1 AD). It was joined in the C6 BC by a huge **Temple of Jupiter the Best and Greatest** (*Juppiter Optimus Maximus*), the largest of its kind ever built, and in due course by several other temples and shrines, such as *Fides* (Trust), and *Ops*, a goddess of abundance, associated with Saturn, whose temple stood just below the hill, beside the Forum (see p. 80). Gigantic stone buttressing added to the cliff-faces on the west and south sides to level and extend the Capitolium precinct once counted among the wonders of Rome (but has all long since collapsed or been quarried away). Another massive substructure, which goes by the name of the 'Tabularium', was built in the late C2 or early C1 BC across the Forum end of the saddle to support some significant building (or group of buildings) where the Palazzo Senatorio rises today. By contrast, the equivalent structures which rose against the cliff face on the other sides of the hill during the C1–C3 AD consisted mainly of multi-storey apartment blocks (*insulae*); many were destroyed when building the Vittorio Emanuele Monument; one sample has been preserved beside the steps up to S. Maria in Aracoeli.

In time several staircases and stepped streets led up from the Forum side, both to the saddle and separately to the *Arx* (the Stairs of Gemonia) and the Capitolium (the *Clivus Capitolinus*), and a stair of a hundred steps (*Centum Gradus*) is mentioned, probably at the Tiber end. There were surely various ways of getting down on the Field of Mars side, although probably nothing so convenient as the present gentle slope of the *cordonata*, the monumental ramp designed by Michelangelo in 1560–2.

After the late C6 AD (when the Temple of Jupiter was still standing but being stripped of its statuary and roof-tiles) the history of the hill is pretty much a blank until the C12 (when the Roman people formed their own government in opposition to the papacy and built the initial nucleus of the Palazzo Senatorio). A monastery of St Mary is recorded on the *Arx* in AD 882 and 955, presumably the predecessor of S. Maria Aracoeli, whose present structure, however, dates from the mid-C13/early C14.

Visit: visible remains of Roman date are scarce, consisting principally of the 'Tabularium' on the Forum side and the Insula on the NW side, some traces of tufa walls in the garden of the Aracoeli and some glimpses of the

◄ **Fig. 106.** Capitoline Hill. Site map

Key:

1 Five-storey *insula*	8 Part of the *Auguraculum* (?)
2–3 Michelangelo's ramp (*cordonata*)	9 Temple of Juno Moneta (?)
4 Piazza del Campidoglio	10 East corner of Temple of Jupiter
5 Stairs to Palazzo Senatorio	11 Villa Caffarelli
6 Palazzo Senatorio ('Tabularium')	12 Tomb of Bibulus
7 Temple of Veiovis	13 Temple of Vespasian and Titus

podium of the Temple of Jupiter. A walk on the far end of the hill towards the river is pleasant, and gives a sense of scale and location, but much of the wider view is restricted by trees. The main attractions, therefore, in addition to their monumental Renaissance and later architectural settings, are the contents of the **Capitoline and Palazzo dei Conservatori Museums** (see p. 378) and the remarkable pieces of Roman sculpture on display outside.

The description here starts from the Piazza d'Aracoeli (to the right of the Vittorio Emanuele Monument coming from the Piazza Venezia) but if coming from the direction of the Forum or Via dei Fori Imperiali, the quicker route is by Via di S. Pietro in Carcere, which can also be reached by the steps behind the Arch of Septimius Severus. The only other routes are steep footpaths at the southern end, from Vico Jugario on one side and Via del Teatro di Marcello on the other, which connect with the Via del Monte Caprino. The connection between Via della Consolazione and Via del Monte Tarpeio is currently blocked.

Madam Lucretia

In the corner of the square in front of S. Marco, beside the Piazza Venezia (Map, Fig. 77: 48) is the upper half of a colossal female statue of the early C3 AD wearing the costume of the Egyptianizing goddess Isis, possibly the cult statue from her temple on the Field of Mars (see p. 207). The figure has been in its present position since about 1500, often painted and dressed up on special occasions. On May Day 1701 she was hung with carrots, onions, garlands, and ribbons as if she were going to be married, and she has been known to 'speak', most famously in 1799 when she fell forwards on her face and someone wrote on her back 'I can't stand (it) any longer' (the first major attempt to oust the papacy and form an independent republican government had just failed).

Shops and Apartment Building on Five Levels (*Insula*). Map, Fig. 106: 1

Via Giulio Romano (Piazza d'Aracoeli). Comune (†interior)

Although it is set back from the road, partly hidden by trees and the steps to S. Maria in Aracoeli to the right, a fair amount of the *insula* can be seen from the street. It was discovered in 1927 when the church of St Rita (C17) was demolished, exposing the remains of a predecessor, S. Biagio 'of the Market', which had been installed on the second and third floors of the Roman building in the C12–C13. The bell-tower and one of the frescoed chapels of the earlier church have been preserved in the restoration of the Roman façade.

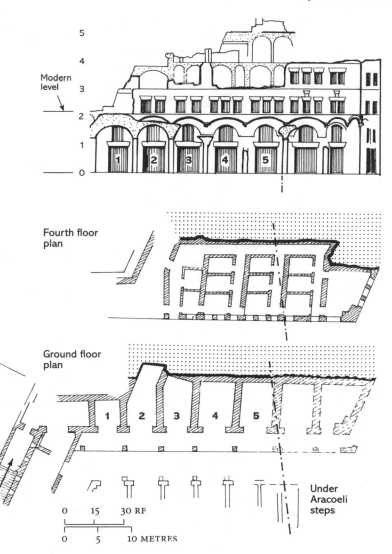

▲ **Fig. 107.** Apartment block beside Aracoeli steps. Elevation and plans of two floors

The *insula*, constructed of brick-faced concrete on at least five storeys, dates from the early C2 AD, contemporary with Trajan's Markets (p. 170) and not dissimilar from them in function though more modest in scale. Rising from the ancient ground level, 9 m. below the modern pavement, the first three storeys comprise single shop units stacked against the near-vertical face of the hillside behind, the second storey is a mezzanine, the third had a balcony in front, reached by the staircase/ramp at the NE (left) end. On the fourth level the hillside stepped back, and the plan changed to form eleven cell-like rooms separated by narrow corridors, reminiscent of the slave-quarters under the wealthy aristocratic houses on the Palatine (see p. 112) and may have served the same purpose: a large apartment on the next level up turned at right angles and extended onto the saddle below the *Arx*.

S. Maria in Aracoeli. If you are feeling fit and energetic the 125 steps up to the front of the church, whether or not the church is open, afford a magnificent view. The church façade dates from a complete rebuilding in the late C13 or early C14 and the steps were made in 1348, voted by the people of Rome in thanksgiving for deliverance from a plague. If the church is open, you do not have to come back down again: it has another entrance on the south side, where stairs lead down to the Piazza del Campidoglio. Among the many notable features of the church interior is the assortment of twenty-two ancient columns on either side of the central nave, the third on the left, of Aswan granite, bearing a curious inscription at the top of the shaft: *a cubiculo Augustanorum* (referring to the office of the Imperial Chamberlain?).

At the foot of the ***cordonata*** (Map, Fig. 106: 2), the great graded ramp constructed in 1559–66 leading up to Piazza del Campidoglio, the two **crouching lions in black granite** were made for a sanctuary somewhere in Egypt in the early Ptolemaic period (late C4–C3 BC) and probably brought to Rome in the reign of Domitian (AD 81–96) to embellish the Temple of the Egyptian Isis on the Field of Mars (see p. 207). Although nothing of the temple is visible, many items from its rich collection of Egyptian sculptures survive, having been highly prized during the Middle Ages and later (the majority are now in the Egyptian Museum in the Vatican, but the Capitoline Museums also have some important pieces). These two lions were already known in the C13 and were set up in the square in front of the palace at St John Lateran by the C15, at the feet of the equestrian statue of Marcus Aurelius (see opposite). They followed him to the Campidoglio in the mid-C16 and were adapted to fountains when piped water was brought to the hill in 1587–8.

The **Colossal statues of Castor and Pollux with their Horses** standing at the top of the *cordonata* were found in fragments in 1561 on the site of the Temple of Castor and Pollux beside the Circus Flaminius (see p. 221 and Map, Fig. 77: 35). Originally monoliths of Greek (Pentelic) marble, 5.5 and 5.8 m. high respectively, they were probably not the cult statues of the temple proper, but stood in front of it, on the wings of the front steps. Since the heads are restored (one completely, the other in nose, chin and hair) it is impossible to be sure, but they might have portrayed Augustus' grandsons Gaius (who died aged 24 in AD 4) and Lucius (who died aged 19 in AD 2). Both youths were already identified with Castor

and Pollux during their lifetime and became more so after
their deaths.

On the balustrade to right
and left of Castor and Pollux
are two famous marble compo-
sitions known since the Middle
Ages (and still commonly
referred to) as the 'Trophies of
Marius': 'trophy' meaning the
display of captured enemy
arms and armour mounted on
a wooden framework which
was carried as part of the
triumphal procession. The
association with the Roman
general Marius, who defeated
the Cimbri (German tribes
who had invaded northern
Italy) in 101 BC, is pure fiction.
They were made for one of the
triumphal monuments of the
emperor Domitian in the late

▲ **Fig. 108.** The emperor Marcus
Aurelius. Portrait head on his bronze
equestrian statue (Capitoline
Museum)

C1 AD or Trajan in the early C2 (the shields and equipment are very like
those on the base of Trajan's Column) but were subsequently reused in the
early C3 to decorate a great fountain building on the Esquiline hill (see
p. 297). When they were moved from there to their present positions in
1590 an inscription was seen on the underside of one indicating that the
marble had been quarried in the reign of Domitian.

Pendants to the Trophies on either side are two **statues of emperors in military dress**, taken from the Quirinal hill in 1635, where there
had originally been four of them: a dynastic group of **Constantine the
Great** (here on the left) and his sons **Constantine II** (on the right),
Constantius II (now in the porch of St John Lateran) and Constans (lost),
set up in the Baths of Constantine, probably to celebrate the thirtieth year
of his reign in AD 336. At the far ends of the balustrade are two **milestones** from the via Appia, that on the right marking the first mile
(headed **I**), with an inscription recording repairs under Nerva in AD 97,
that on the left the seventh (**VII**), inscribed with the name and titles of
Vespasian in AD 76.

The **bronze statue of the emperor Marcus Aurelius on horseback** standing on the pedestal in the centre of the square is an excellent
modern replica (1997). The original, which had stood on the
Campidoglio since 1538 and is still a potent political symbol to modern
Romans, miraculously survived a bomb attack in 1979 but was then

discovered to be deteriorating rapidly from atmospheric pollution. Carefully restored in 1981–9, it is now kept under cover in the adjacent Capitoline Museum (the building on the left). The statue has been known since the late C8, when it stood near St John Lateran and was believed to represent the emperor Constantine the Great; subsequently political expedient changed this to the Roman knight Marcus Curtius (see p. 85) or the Ostrogothic king Theodoric the Great, but by the C15 his true identity was recognized from the portraits on coins. Twice life-size and originally gilded to look like solid gold, the statue may have been produced after the emperor's death in AD 180, when he was deified. It shows him with the beard of a philosopher (Fig. 108), but in military tunic and cloak, and military boots, his right arm outstretched in a gesture of clemency. Under the raised right hoof of the horse there was once a small figure of a kneeling barbarian.

Marcus Aurelius, the philosopher-emperor

Born Marcus Annius Verus in AD 121 (in a house near the Lateran), of a Spanish family related to the emperor Hadrian, by the age of 8 he was already being groomed as a possible future Roman emperor, educated by the best teachers in rhetoric, grammar, philosophy, and law. In AD 138 when Hadrian adopted Antoninus Pius as his successor, Antoninus Pius adopted Marcus, who took Antoninus' family name Aurelius, and succeeded him as emperor in AD 161. He spent most of his reign trying to defend the frontiers of the Empire, dying while on campaign across the Danube in AD 180, but is best known for his *Meditations*, jotted down (in Greek) during the last ten years of his life, full of his preoccupation, influenced by the Stoic school of philosophy, with the meaning of world-order and man's relationship to it; the necessity for moral effort and tolerance of one's fellow human beings; his disillusion and despondency in the face of the real world in which he lived.

In front of the staircase up to the Palazzo Senatorio (Map, Fig. 106: 5) are three more showpieces from the public museum which was assembled on the hill in the C16. The two colossal bearded males reclining semi-nude and holding *cornucopiae* ('horns of plenty') personify rivers, the **Nile** on the left, leaning on a sphinx, and the **Tiber** on the right (with wolf and twins). They came in 1518 from the Quirinal hill, where they had decorated the Baths of Constantine (*c.* AD 315). The seated statue in the central alcove portrays **Roma**, which the inscription on the base records was purchased by the Comune in 1593. Both her body of red porphyry (originally a statue of Minerva) and her head of white marble are ancient but did not previously belong together. Her arms and the attributes they hold are also C16 restorations.

If your tastes run to seeing many more famous and not so famous Roman statues, inscriptions, and other works of art, the two parts of the Capitoline Museums on either side are packed full of them (p. 378). The courtyard of the **Palazzo dei Conservatori** (on the right) is free, and contains among other things the head, hands, and foot of the colossal statue of Constantine the Great from the New Basilica (see p. 116) and the 'Province' reliefs, which may have decorated the Temple of Hadrian (see p. 221). Among the best-known works in the galleries upstairs are the five ancient bronzes donated by Sixtus IV which started the municipal collections off in 1471: the **Capitoline wolf,** a colossal **head of Constantius II,** a colossal **hand holding a globe,** the **Camillus** and the **Boy extracting a thorn from his foot.**

To the rear the Palazzo dei Conservatori is built against the flank of the massive podium of the **Temple of Jupiter Best and Greatest Capitolinus,** a solid wall of grey tufa blocks, which can be seen at the end of the long corridor on the second floor of the museum (†more remains are preserved in the museum garden). At the centre of Roman State religion and poli-

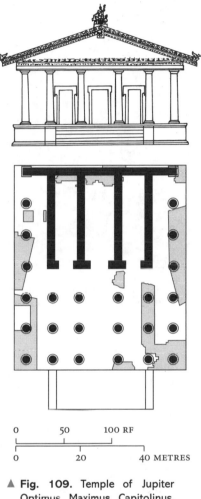

▲ **Fig. 109.** Temple of Jupiter Optimus Maximus Capitolinus. Restored ground plan and front elevation of C6 BC phase

tics (the incoming magistrates began their year of office with sacrifices at the altar in front of it and the Senate held its first meeting of the year inside it), the temple was said to have been vowed by the fifth king of Rome Tarquin the Elder (616–576 BC) during the war against the Sabines, and completed by his (grand?)son the last king Tarquin the Proud (534–510 BC), though it was not dedicated until the first year of the Republic, 509 BC. It was of Etruscan type and exceptional size (Fig. 109), the podium almost square, 53 × 62 m. (180 × 210 RF). Eighteen huge stone columns formed the porch, behind which were three cellas, one each for the 'Capitoline

▲ **Fig. 110.** Temple of Jupiter Optimus Maximus Capitolinus. Marble relief (from the Basilica Ulpia) showing a sacrifice in front of the temple

triad': Jupiter in the middle, in his role as god of the Roman State ('best of all the Jupiters'), his wife Juno Regina on the left and their colleague Minerva on the right. Burned down in 83 BC, again in AD 69 and once more in AD 80, each rebuilding kept the same foundations and the original plan, but instead of the original Tuscan order the final rebuild, dedicated by Domitian in AD 89, was Corinthian, in Greek (Pentelic) marble. A fragment of a fluted column has survived, 2.1 m. in diameter, which could signify an astonishing height of 21.3 m. (72 RF). Domitian exceeded even his own excessive standards by gilding all the bronze roof-tiles, gold-plating the doors, and commissioning a new cult statue of Jupiter in ivory and gold, to rival Pheidias' famous statue of Jupiter's Greek counterpart Zeus, at Olympia. A fragment of a lost relief from Trajan's Forum which had the temple as part of the background (Fig. 110) shows the pediment crammed with more statues, Jupiter, Juno, and Minerva seated in the centre, flanked by the chariots of the Sun and Moon, Vulcan forging Jupiter's thunderbolts to the right. More chariot groups, and Mars and Venus, stood on the gable. Given its height and exposed position, it was struck by lightning on several occasions but was still largely intact in the late C6 AD, though despoiled of all its gold. It was still recognizable, though in ruins, in the C12. In 1545 several of the Pentelic marble column drums and capitals were dug out and recycled for other purposes, one capital was carved into a great lion for the Villa Medici at S. Trinità dei Monti, the rest went to make statues for the chapel of Federico Cesi in S. Maria della Pace.

'Tabularium'.
Map, Fig. 106: 6

Palazzo Senatorio (the seat of modern Rome's city council) Via S. Pietro in Carcere. Comune (†interior)

Both flanks of the Palazzo Senatorio coincide with the side walls of the ancient building, whose blocks of dark grey *peperino* tufa (from the Alban hills) are especially evident on the south— Via del Campidoglio—side. It starts from the Forum level as a solid buttress through which a **vaulted staircase** runs up the hillside behind, connecting the area of the Temple of Saturn beside the Forum directly with the area in the saddle between the two crests of the hill (the door at the foot of

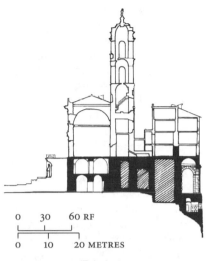

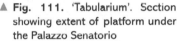

▲ **Fig. 111.** 'Tabularium'. Section showing extent of platform under the Palazzo Senatorio

the stair can just be seen, later blocked by the Temple of Vespasian and Titus). The line of windows in the tufa wall marks a sequence of small **underground chambers** (used until the last century as a city gaol), reached by an internal staircase at the northern end. Above those are the tufa arcades, all but two blocked in, of an open gallery which ran the full width of the façade, providing a high level passage from one crest of the Capitoline hill to the other. The piers of the arcades are decorated on the exterior with Doric half-columns, their capitals and architrave in white travertine limestone, capped by a Doric frieze of metopes and triglyphs. The roof of the gallery was powerfully constructed as a series of arches with concrete cross-vaults between them. Fragments found at the foot of the hill indicate that there was once a second arcaded gallery above the first, of the Corinthian order, entirely in travertine, which will have risen almost to the height of the second row of modern windows. By the time it reached the level of the saddle on the hill behind, the structure extended over some 3,000 square metres in a trapezoidal shape which broadly coincides with that of the present Palazzo Senatorio. In the core is a **massive platform** constructed of tufa, concrete and earth, providing the foundation for a substantial building or series of buildings on top, whose western limit coincided with the front of the present Palazzo, but was stepped back at the corner in a large re-entrant to accommodate the Temple of Veiovis (see below), beside which the vaulted staircase emerged.

The modern name 'Tabularium' comes from an inscription (seen in the cellars in the C15 but now long lost) recording that the consul of 78 BC

Quintus Lutatius Catulus had supervised the building of a *substructio* and a *tabularium*. A second inscription of the same type but not specifying the building concerned was found in the debris on the Forum side in 1845 and has been set up as the keystone of a doorway on the north side (facing the Via di S. Pietro in Carcere: (Q. Lu)TATIVS Q. f. Q. n. C(atulus Consul) | (de s)EN SENT(entia) FACIVNDV(m) | EIDEMQUE(p)ROB(avit). Neither inscription need necessarily refer to the structures under the Palazzo Senatorio, but since those do constitute a substantial substructure and could well date from the 70s BC (though they could also be fifty years earlier or fifty years later) the temptation to make the association is strong. Any or all of the chambers in the depths and along the northern flank of the substructure could qualify for the role of *tabularium* (literally a place, a room, or cupboard for storing *tabula* or writing tablets, i.e. an archive) and it is customary to imagine the superstructure constituting a huge Public Records Office, though as far as we know ancient Rome had no such thing; each office or institution had its own *tabularium*, keeping its own records. One suggestion is that the building on top was the Hall of Liberty (*Atrium Libertatis*), which housed the office of the Roman censors. The office regulated admission to the Roman citizenship for non-Romans and ex-slaves, held the records of public lands, displayed the texts of laws and maintained a library of other documents. The Hall of Liberty will have needed several *tabularia* and was restored in lavish form by Gaius Asinius Pollio with the spoils of his victory over the Illyrians in 39 BC to include two libraries, space for numerous works of art (see pp. 325) and perhaps a basilica. However, although the Hall must have been somewhere in this vicinity, the written sources suggest that it was located somewhat further round the edge of the hill, closer to the Forum of Caesar.

The remains of the **Temple of Veiovis** (Map, Fig. 106: 7; special permit †*Comune*) were excavated in the cellars under the SW corner of the Palazzo Senatorio in 1939–42. Veiovis (who also had a temple on the Tiber Island, see p. 226) was in origin a sort of anti-Jupiter (Iovis), the prefix Ve- having a negative or diminutive value, but he shed the dark side of his character in time and became more of a young Jupiter, iconographically linked with Apollo or Mercury. The temple was vowed by an unknown benefactor in 196 BC and dedicated in 192, before the 'Tabularium' was built, but then rebuilt in the C1 BC after the 'Tabularium' had enclosed it on two sides. To increase the size of the cella despite the confined space the rebuilders placed it sideways (like the Temple of Concordia Augusta on the other side of the 'Tabularium', see p. 77). Soundings in the core of the podium showed that the first temple had a rectangular plan typical of the C2 BC, with four columns across the front, six down the sides, none at the back. The original cult statue of cypress wood lasted almost 300 years, but probably perished in the fire of AD 80, to be replaced by a marble version, whose headless body was found in the excavations and stands at the foot of the access stairs. In the late C1 AD the cella walls were reinforced with brick piers, perhaps to support a concrete roof.

Across the Via di S. Pietro in Carcere, in the **small garden** beside the lateral stairs up to **S. Maria in Aracoeli**, two low walls of *cappellaccio* tufa blocks can be seen on the right (Map, Fig. 106: 8). The tufa is characteristic of the C6 BC, and the structure has been tentatively identified as one corner of the ***Auguraculum***, the augurs' precinct. To the rear of the garden, other larger tufa structures on the same orientation extending back under the stairs (Map, Fig. 106: 9) possibly belong to the **Temple of Juno Moneta** ('who warns'), vowed by L. Furius Camillus in 345 BC in battle against the Aurunci (about 100 km. to the south of Rome). It was built on the site of what had previously been a private house and was associated with the early Roman mint; 'moneta' then acquired its alternative meaning, 'money'.

The park at the other end of the hill top can be reached by the matching stairs on the opposite side of the Piazza del Campidoglio, which lead up to the Via del Tempio di Giove. On the right, when you come out into the Piazza Caffarelli (Map, Fig. 106: 10) is the front corner of the podium of the Temple of Jupiter (see above). (If the route is closed, return to the Piazza del Campidoglio and take the Via di Villa Caffarelli on the right-hand side of the Palazzo dei Conservatori instead.) From the far end (Via di Monte Caprino) trees permitting, the panorama on the left includes the west flank of the Palatine, the lower end of the Forum valley (the Velabrum), and on the right the Theatre of Marcellus.

Circus Flaminius to Circus Maximus (Map: Fig. 112)

(via the Vegetable and Cattle Market and Tiber Port)

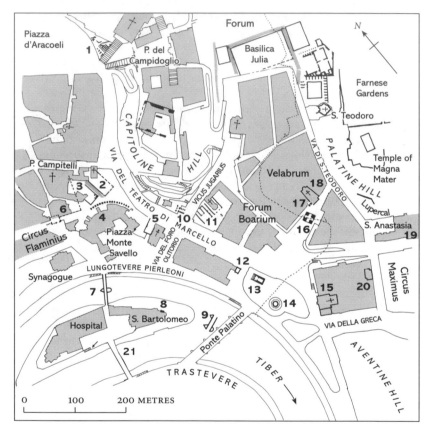

▲ **Fig. 112.** Circus Flaminius to Circus Maximus. General site map

Key:

1. Five-storey *insula*
2. Temple of Bellona
3. Temple of Apollo Medicus Sosianus
4. Theatre of Marcellus
5. S. Nicola in Carcere
6. Porticus of Octavia
7. Pons Fabricius
8. Prow
9. Pons Aemilius (Ponte Rotto)
10. Triumphal Way Arcades
11. S. Omobono
12. House of Crescenzio
13. Temple of Portunus
14. Round temple
15. S. Maria in Cosmedin
16. Arch of Janus
17. Arch of the *Argentarii*
18. S. Giorgio al Velabro
19. S. Anastasia
20. Mithraeum
21. Pons Cestius

Theatre of Marcellus. Map, Fig. 112: 4   ★

Via del Teatro di Marcello. Comune (†enclosure)

Fortified in the C11–C12 by the Pierleone family as part of their stronghold between the Tiber Island and the Capitoline hill, the site then passed in 1368 to the Savelli, who later employed Baldassare Peruzzi in 1519 to create the *palazzo* that still rises out of the ruins today, with additions in 1712 when the property was taken over by the Orsini family (it is now subdivided into several smaller apartments).

The theatre was first planned by Julius Caesar as a rival to that of Pompey (see p. 214) but left unfinished at his death in 44 BC. Augustus took over the project and completed it in the name of Marcellus, his sister Octavia's son, who was to have been his heir but died in 23 BC. The Secular Games of 17 BC were partly staged there but its formal inauguration did not take place until 13 or 11 BC. Set in a prime position between the Circus Flaminius (see p. 221) and the Temple of Apollo (see below) it was by far the most important of Rome's three theatres, capable of holding 20,500 people. In association with a new law which Augustus passed governing the order in which the various social groups who composed the audience were to be seated, it became the model for a contemporary rash of theatre-building throughout Italy and the western Empire.

The curving façade of **two superimposed arcades** which you can see from the Via del Teatro di Marcello represents just under a third of the outer perimeter of the theatre's semicircular banks of seating (the *cavea*). It has always been visible, but was made more so by demolitions and restorations in 1926–32, when the whole neighbourhood from the theatre to the Circus Maximus was destroyed to make a new road route out of the city to the sea (Via del Mare). Shopkeepers were ejected from the theatre arcades and the footings were cleared down to the ancient ground level (the high tide of the latest ground level is marked by the severe damage which starts about half-way up the bottom piers). The lower archways led to the lowest tiers of seating and to staircases which led to the middle tiers and a higher-level corridor, behind the upper arcade, from which further stairs led to the highest tiers. The façade is constructed entirely of travertine and embellished by framing each arcade in an architectural order of semicolumns: Doric on the ground floor, the more delicate Ionic on the next level up (Fig. 113). Something of the original effect is reconstructed in the last two arcades on the right, recreated in 1926–7. The Romans clearly considered the style highly appropriate to supporting structures. It is found earlier in the 'Tabularium' (p. 239) and was later applied in a grand manner on the Colosseum (p. 282). There must have been an attic level (where the modern apartment windows appear now), probably a plain wall without arcades and simply decorated with flat pilasters in keeping with the fact that the uppermost seating will have been of wood.

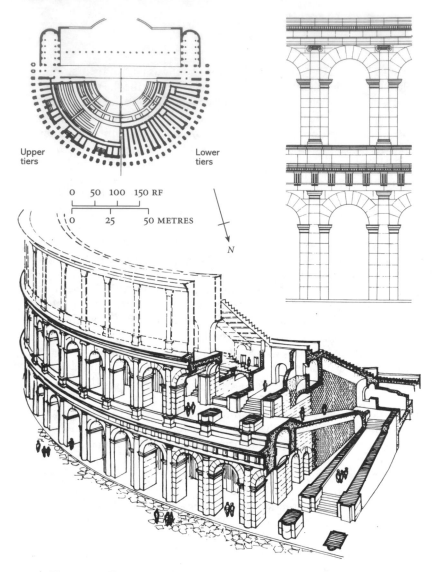

Upper tiers

Lower tiers

0   50   100   150 RF

0   25   50 METRES

N

▲ **Fig. 113.** Theatre of Marcellus. Reconstructed plan, section of seating (*cavea*), and outer elevation

Although other parts of the *cavea* survive in the private apartments of the Palazzo Savelli-Orsini, the plan of the stage front and rather cramped porticus which lay between it and the riverside is known mainly from the Marble Plan. The porticus (which probably contained the temples of Piety and Diana displaced by the building of the theatre) was already being demolished in AD 365–70 to use the stone for repairs to the nearby bridge of Cestius on the Tiber Island (p. 227). The stage building seems to have lasted at least until AD 421 when the city prefect Petronius Maximus set up some statues in it; the colonnaded hall at its south end was still standing in 1575 but is now reduced to one travertine pier and a Doric column beside the palazzo gate.

Temple of Apollo Medicus Sosianus. Map, Fig. 112: 3 ★

Three white marble columns raised on a modern travertine and tufa base a few metres to the right of the theatre arcades mark the front right-hand corner of the temple that the Theatre of Marcellus was built to serve. Actually the columns were excavated (in 1926–8) at the other end of the temple front, and the base is no guide to the podium's original form, but the restored height is approximately correct. Apollo, a very Greek god, was introduced to Rome at an early date; there was already a shrine for him somewhere outside the city boundary in the late C6 BC. After a plague in 433 BC a temple was vowed to him as Apollo Medicus (the healer), dedicated in 431 by Cn. Julius, ancestor of Julius Caesar. Restored or rebuilt after the Gallic sack in 353 BC, the temple was possibly rebuilt again in 179 BC, when the construction of a theatre in front of it is mentioned. The *Ludi Apollinares*, a festival of theatrical and other games in honour of Apollo Medicus, had been instituted since 212 BC and soon became an annual event, lasting nine days in July. The surviving temple, however, like the surviving theatre, was built in the late C1 BC.

Beautifully carved in Italian (Luna) marble, **the temple porch** had six columns across the front and another two at the sides, beyond which a further seven were attached to the cella wall as semi-columns and made of travertine finished with stucco. The order is Corinthian, 50 RF high, enriched with rope-like decoration on the bases and alternately wide and narrow

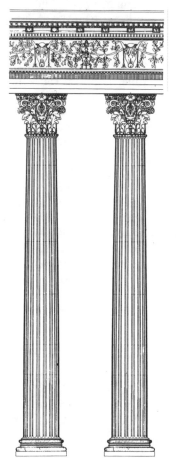

▼ Fig. 114. Temple of Apollo Medicus Sosianus. Corinthian order

fluting on the column shafts (Fig. 114). The capitals have sprigs of laurel (attributes of Apollo) and elaborate flowerheads under the volutes, the entablature has a frieze of laurel branches strung between bulls' skulls and candelabra with tripod bases. To save marble, the capitals were made in two halves, the lower half using a smaller block than the upper, and of the entablature only the cornice blocks were solid marble, the rest was a veneer applied to beams of travertine. More pieces of the temple front are stored under the theatre arcades, including the apex of its tall triangular pediment, which was once filled with antique Greek statuary—numerous fragments came to light when the temple podium was excavated in 1937–8 and have recently been reassembled (†Capitoline Museums). Dating from about 450–425 BC, they show the goddess Athena in the midst of battling Greeks and Amazons.

The scant remains of the cella belie the evidence for its **richly decorated interior**, once awash with coloured marbles: Phrygian purple, Numidian yellow, and 'Lucullan' red/black were combined in the floor, the walls were lined with a two-storey Corinthian colonnade, the shafts on both levels monoliths of 'Lucullan' red/black, their white marble capitals incorporating tripods entwined with snakes, framing statue niches which were themselves framed between colonnettes of Numidian yellow and Chian pink/red. The temple is known to have housed a large collection of marble statues, all relating to Apollo: the children of Niobe by Scopas or Praxiteles (C4 BC); an Apollo by Philiskos of Rhodes (C2 BC); Apollo, Latona and Diana, and the nine Muses; Apollo with a lyre by Timarchides of Athens (C2 BC). Between the upper and lower interior orders a sculptured frieze depicted scenes of battle and a triumphal procession (Fig. 115).

Who built the temple is much discussed. The epithet *Sosianus*, which was still being used of it by Pliny in the AD 70s, should refer to Gaius Sosius, who had been one of Julius Caesar's lieutenants and could easily have vowed to rebuild the temple when he was awarded a triumph for his victory in Judaea in 34 BC, holding the consulship in 32 BC. The act would have had strong political overtones, for Sosius was an opponent of

▼ **Fig. 115.** Temple of Apollo Medicus Sosianus. Frieze from interior order of the cella, showing a triumphal procession (Palazzo del Conservatori, Braccio Nuovo)

Octavian (later Augustus), who was in the process of building an entirely new temple to Apollo on the Palatine hill at the same period (see p. 131). But the surviving sections of the internal frieze show a battle against northern barbarians, not Jews, and the enemy arms being carried in the procession are also of northern type. This, together with the wealth and particular range of marbles in the interior (contrasting with the relative economies on the outside), has led to speculation that if Sosius began the temple someone else may have finished it, namely Augustus, giving it his own triumphal stamp (he celebrated a triple triumph in 29 BC, one for victories over various German peoples). Like many other temples in the vicinity Apollo's anniversary was changed during Augustus' reign to Augustus' own birthday (23 September). That Augustus would dare to usurp Sosius' project, or that Sosius would agree to modify his project to honour Augustus' victories instead of his own, is not entirely implausible given the volatile politics of the age. Although Sosius sided with Mark Antony and shared the defeat at Actium in 31 BC Augustus pardoned him and by 17 BC he was in a privileged enough position to preside over the Secular Games; no wonder the temple continued to bear his name.

A second podium excavated in 1938–9 to the east (right) of the Temple of Apollo (Map, Fig. 112: 2) is identified as that of the **Temple of Bellona**, a warrior mother-goddess, personifying battle-frenzy. It was vowed in battle against the Etruscans and Samnites by Appius Claudius Caecus in 296 BC and continued thereafter to bear a special connection with the Claudian family, in due course therefore also with the imperial family of Augustus and his successors. Only parts of the podium's core of concreted tufa rubble survive; all the squared stone has been robbed. A few loose fragments of marble and travertine architecture found nearby, such as a colossal Corinthian capital decorated with a breastplate and palm frond (stored in the theatre arcades), are attributed to the temple elevation, probably rebuilt in the late C1 BC.

Republican Victory-Temples (in the Vegetable Market). Map, Fig. 112: 5

S. Nicola in Carcere
Via del Teatro di Marcello no. 46

The medieval church of St Nicholas 'in the Prison' was consecrated (or reconsecrated) in 1128 and remodelled with the addition of the ornate façade in 1599. Its bell-tower was previously a fortified tower belonging to the Pierleone family (matching that beside their C11 mansion across the road). The rest is built into the remains of three ancient temples, once tightly grouped together in the midst of the *Forum Holitorium*—the Vegetable Market—which occupied the space between the south tip of the Capitoline hill and the river bank, where produce could be delivered

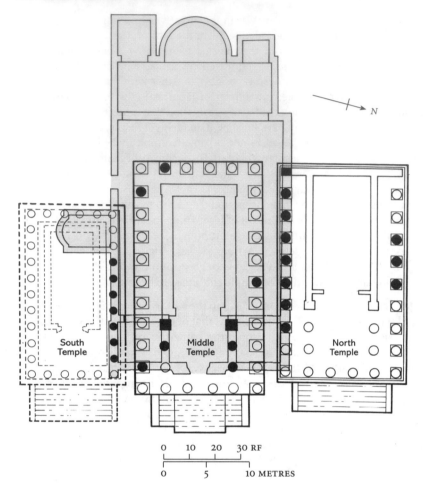

▲ **Fig. 116.** Temples at S. Nicola in Carcere. Reconstructed ground plans

conveniently by boat (there was still a vegetable market in the Piazza di Monte Savelli until this century).

The church covered the middle temple completely and incorporated the lateral colonnade of the adjacent temple on each side, so there are Ionic columns in *peperino* tufa on the north (right) flank of the church, but Doric columns in travertine on the south (left). All three temples in their actual states date from the C1 BC and early C1 AD, with repairs in brick-work after a fire during the reign of Hadrian (AD 117–38). They were in origin much older. Two must be the temples of *Janus* and *Spes*, both founded in the mid-C3 BC, and the other has to be *Juno Sospita*, of the early C2 BC. Like those in the Largo Argentina (see p. 218) it is not absolutely certain which temple is which, but the **north temple** is the best candidate for **Janus** (god of gates and beginnings, closely associated with the Tiber). Vowed by C. Duilius after the Roman victory off Mylae (Sicily) against the Carthaginians in 260 BC, it was restored by Augustus and rededicated by Tiberius in AD 17. The podium and two column shafts were exposed by demolitions in 1932; the cella walls which should rise up between the two sets of columns have disappeared. There were once six *peperino* columns across the front and eight down the sides (none at the back) with their fluting and other detailed finishing applied in white stucco (traces remain on those embedded in the church wall); the tufa blocks sticking out at right angles over the entablature are the remnants of the ceiling which connected the colonnade and the cella wall. The frieze of the entablature (travertine at the front, tufa towards the rear) is riddled with small dowel holes for appliqué decoration, presumably in metal, in a garland motif similar to that in stucco on the Temple of Portunus (see Fig. 119). The podium, of travertine around a concrete core, was designed so as to leave a series of small chambers down the sides (like the Temple of Castor in the Roman Forum, see p. 91). The modern restoration on the north side shows the chambers walled up (as they were when found), but the other side is well-preserved under the church floor and demonstrates their original cell-like form. Although possibly the 'prison' referred to in the name of the church, that is not likely to have been their intended function in antiquity. They are only 1.5 m. high, which rules out offices or shops, but could have been useful for storing equipment in connection with the nearby vegetable market.

The **south temple**, the smallest, is most likely that of **Spes (Hope)**, vowed by A. Atilius Caiatinus during the wars against the Carthaginians in Sicily sometime between 258 and 249 BC. It was struck by lightning in 218 BC, burned down in 213 BC and again in 31 BC and was rededicated by Germanicus in AD 17. To judge from the flank walled into the church its last rebuilding used travertine for everything in elevation except the core of the podium (presumably of tufa blocks, all robbed). The Doric order is properly Greek, with no column bases, and there were originally eleven columns down the sides, six across the front and back, all surfaces and details refined in white stucco.

The **middle temple**, directly under the church, was the largest and probably that vowed to **Juno Sospita** (the Saviour) by C. Cornelius Cethegus in 197 BC in the course of the war against the Insubrians (in northern Italy), dedicated in 194, and rebuilt in 90 BC, by L. Julius Caesar. It had the same plan as the south temple, with six columns across the front and back, eleven down the sides, but the order was Ionic and the stone *peperino* tufa, like the north temple. The column on the left of the church façade belongs to the second row under the temple porch, not its front. The podium and lowest courses of the cella walls are preserved under the church floor; as on the north temple, the podium walls had small chambers set between the footings of the columns. They had concrete barrel vaults, and ran across the back as well as down both sides. The fourteen columns dividing the interior of the church into three aisles are ancient but have been assembled from various other buildings, not from the temples.

Arcades along the Triumphal Way. Map, Fig. 112: 10

Along the edge of the paved market area in front of the temples ran the Triumphal Way, the route taken by triumphal processions, which set off from the Circus Flaminius, passed through the Porticus of Octavia and between the Temples of Apollo and Bellona and then headed for the Vicus Jugarius, by way of the Carmentis (or Triumphal) Gate in the republican city walls (more or less where the modern road junction is now). At least the first part of the course as far as the Gate seems to have been roofed over, the roof carried on arcades which ran along the street on either side. Two adjoining sections of double arcading survive on the other side of the Via del Teatro di Marcello, beside the junction with the Vicus Jugarius. That in travertine (on the left) was more monumental but is very fragmentary, reduced to the stumps of its piers. The other, mostly in *peperino* with only footings in travertine, preserves two arcades on one side and three on the other. The arches are framed on the outside with Tuscan semi-columns supporting a horizontal entablature and a heavy cornice, repeated with flat pilasters on the inside. The materials and style are characteristic of the C1 BC.

Archaic and Republican Temples (S. Omobono). Map, Fig. 112: 11

Vico Jugario–Via del Teatro di Marcello. †Comune

The site was scheduled for redevelopment as government offices in 1937 when soundings to set reinforcements into the subsoil around the apse of S. Omobono pulled up large fragments of terracotta statues and architectural decoration (†Capitoline Museums) belonging to the roof of a temple (or perhaps two temples) of the archaic period (C6 BC). The find was quickly identified with the temples of the fertility goddess **Fortuna** and **Mater Matuta** (goddess of the dawn, new growth and hence childbirth), whose construction later Roman tradition attributed to the sixth king of Rome Servius Tullius (578–534 BC). Further investigation exposed the corner of a temple podium, 4 m. below the surface, and a preservation order was placed on the whole area. Additional small-scale excavations in depth during 1959–64 and others in 1986 traced a sequence of occupation starting with Iron Age huts in the second half of the C7 BC and continuing down to the building of the present church in AD 1482 (then known as

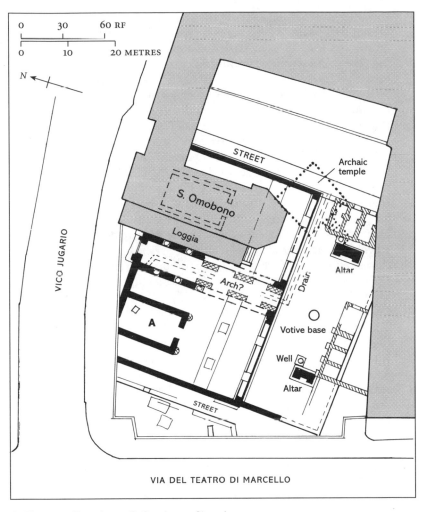

0   30   60 RF
0   10   20 METRES

N ←

STREET

Archaic temple

S. Omobono

Loggia

VICO JUGARIO

Arch?

Drain

Altar

A

Votive base

Well

Altar

STREET

VIA DEL TEATRO DI MARCELLO

▲ **Fig. 117.** Temples at S. Omobono. Site plan

St Salvator in the Porticus, or 'of the weighing scales'; its dedication to
St Homobonus, patron saint of tailors, dates from AD 1700).

The archaic temple is still very poorly known since it is not only
trapped under a mass of later structures but also lies below the water table.
It was apparently destroyed towards the end of the C6 BC—coinciding
neatly with the traditional date for the expulsion of the kings and the
beginning of the Republic—and subsequently vanished under huge
deposits of earth and rubble which made a new terrace at the foot of
the Capitoline hill, about 6 m. above the older level. On this terrace, and
on a new alignment, a solid platform 47 m. (160 RF) square was then

constructed of the local tufa (*cappellaccio*), perhaps quarried from the hill behind, to support two new temples on a single podium, with their altars on a lower level in front. The operation is credited to Camillus, the legendary general who led the Romans to their first great military success, capturing the Etruscan town of Veii (12 km. north of Rome) in 396 BC.

From the perimeter wall along the modern Vico Jugario, the rectangle delineated by two courses of tufa blocks that you see in the foreground (Fig. 117: A) is the cella of the western of the two C4 temples (its pair lies under the church). The visible structure (with later repairs in travertine) belongs to a rebuilding after the fire of 213 BC (the same fire that destroyed the temple of Spes, on the south side of S. Nicola in Carcere). The altars in front of the temples (marked by the low roofs) are of the U-shape characteristic of the C4–C3 BC and—curiously—faced east (at 90° to the temples). They represent an intermediary phase, dated by the circular base on axis between them which records a votive donation by Marcus Fulvius Flaccus, who defeated Volsinii (Orvieto) in 264 BC. The spoils carried off to Rome included 2,000 small bronze statues, some of which may have been among Flaccus' gifts to the sanctuary.

Major changes were made in the early C2 AD, possibly caused by the same fire which required repairs to the temples under S. Nicola in Carcere. The temples were reduced to their cellas (which were repaired in travertine and brick and given new façades) and the passageway that had always lain between them, with a gate towards the Vicus Jugarius, was converted into a colonnaded porticus. The foundations of the old front porches were reused to form another broad colonnaded porticus which met the other in a T-junction. All the patches of travertine paving that survive here and there are associated with this phase. Optimists have argued that six concrete foundations at the intersection are the footings of a monumental marble arch. The shops around the margins of the old altar forecourt date from AD 200–400. How early a church was founded on the site is not known; possibly not before the C12, but the area continued to be densely inhabited in the early and later medieval period.

The **streets** alongside the S. Omobono temple precinct were heading for Rome's oldest **river port** and the *Forum Boarium* (the Cattle Market), which gave its name to the whole of the river end of the Velabrum valley as far as the Circus Maximus. The 1930s' Anagrafe building (Registry Office) across the road covers a substantial block of Roman warehousing behind the Tiber wharves, the southern end of which is marked by the medieval **House of Crescenzio** (Map, Fig. 112: 12). Dating from about AD 1100, the inscriptions over the front door (whose archway is formed of a cornice from an ancient circular building set sideways) name one Nicolaus Crescens, son of Nicolaus and Theodora, a member of one of Rome's most powerful families in the C10–C12. The accompanying verses declare Nicolaus' pride in his ancient ancestry and his desire that his house should recall the grandeur of ancient Rome. It occupied one of the family's towers, guarding the approach to the ancient Aemilian bridge over the Tiber (now the Ponte Rotto: see Map, Fig. 112: 9 and p. 227). Only the ground floor and the beginning of an upper storey with an arcaded loggia survive. The mock temple effect on the south flank (Via del Ponte Rotto) combines roughly moulded brickwork of the C11 (for the semi-columns and pilasters and their capitals) with fragments of ancient marble entablature and console brackets (supplemented at the angle with a wonderfully medieval-looking copy of the griffins and candelabra frieze). The blocks forming a strip of rosettes higher up the wall come from the ceiling of a Roman public building.

Temple of Portunus. Map, Fig. 112: 13 ★

Via del Ponte Rotto. Comune (†interior)

How this temple managed to last two millennia almost intact, whereas all those just up the road did not, can be explained by the fact that it was converted into a church of St Mary at a very early date (in AD 872 or shortly after), while it was still in good condition. The columns at the front were blocked in, some windows were opened in the cella walls and the interior was decorated with frescoes, but little else was touched. Then in the mid-C16 (by which time if not before it was known as St Mary of Egypt) it was given to an order of Armenian monks, who built up against it but kept it in reasonable repair, making no major changes to the structure. Its present isolation results from the sweeping demolitions of the 1930s, when all trace of the church was removed from the exterior (though fragments of C9 frescoes remain inside).

▼ **Fig. 118.** Temple of Portunus. Axonometric reconstruction

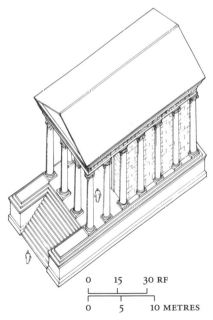

Long known to the many Renaissance and later architects who studied it in detail as the Temple of Fortuna Virilis, the alternative attribution to the harbour-god **Portunus** is now generally accepted. In antiquity it stood just inside the harbour area, set back from the approach to the Aemilian bridge, within a colonnaded precinct which housed a

| 0 | 15 | 30 RF |

| 0 | 5 | 10 METRES |

▲ **Fig. 119.** Temple of Portunus. Entablature

market for flowers and garlands. The bases of two statues set up in 2 BC in honour of Augustus' grandsons Gaius and Lucius Caesar, as *principes Juventis* (the equivalent of 'Crown Princes') were dug up in the area of the front steps in 1551 (now in the Capitoline Museums). More recent excavations in front of and beside the podium found traces of an earlier temple, dating from the late C4 or C3 BC, raised on an extremely high podium (6 m.) to keep it clear of Tiber floods. The present temple is a replacement of about 80–70 BC, following a general rise in the surrounding ground level, a modest construction, the same width but somewhat shorter than its predecessor, on a much lower podium faced in travertine. The order is Ionic, with a column height of 28 RF (8.24 m.), those in the porch and at the four corners of the cella in travertine, the semi-columns and the cella walls in Anio tufa; both types of stone were coated with stucco to give the effect of white marble, refining the detail on the column capitals and bases and adding fluting to the shafts. Most of the decoration moulded in stucco on the frieze of the travertine entablature has been lost but can be reconstructed on the basis of Renaissance architects' drawings (Fig. 119). The combination of garlands and three forms of support (erotes, candelabra, and bulls' skulls), where we should normally expect two at most, suggests a fancy restoration in the late C1 or C2 AD.

Round Temple. Map, Fig. 112: 14 ★

Piazza Bocca della Verità. Comune (†interior)

Popularly known as the Temple of Vesta (simply because of its circular shape) the actual deity to which it was dedicated is unknown, although some form of Hercules, demigod of victory and commercial enterprise is likely. At least three different Hercules temples, possibly four, and other lesser shrines are known to have been located in this area, between the Cattle Market, the Circus Maximus, and the Tiber, associated with an important altar (see below, S. Maria in Cosmedin). Like the Temple of Portunus the Round Temple owes its survival to being converted into a church, though it is not recorded as such until AD 1132, when it was known as St Stephen 'of the carriages'. By that time it had already lost its original roof and marble entablature and also the upper third of the cella wall, which was replaced in the C12 in brick-faced concrete incorporating tall arched windows. Further restorations (and a fresco over the altar) were made in 1475. In the C17 the church was rededicated to St Mary 'of the Sun' but then deconsecrated at the beginning of the C19, when the ground level around it was lowered to expose the podium and the standing structure restored by Valadier in 1809/10.

50 RF (14.8 m.) in diameter, with Corinthian columns 36 RF high (if one includes the top step of the podium), the temple dates from the late C2 or early C1 BC. It was an extremely costly commission for that period, a Greek design, probably by an eastern Greek architect, using Greek (Pentelic) marble—then a very rare commodity in Rome—for all the exterior finish: the colonnades and their entablature and the outer face of the cella wall, the surviving lower zone of which still preserves its decora-

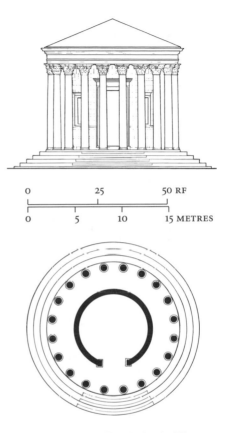

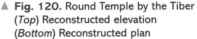

Fig. 120. Round Temple by the Tiber (*Top*) Reconstructed elevation (*Bottom*) Reconstructed plan

tive effect of finely drafted Greek-style masonry (the inner face was lined with tufa, stuccoed to give the same effect). The two rectangular windows to either side of the doorway were part of the original structure. Peculiar features indicative of its relatively early date are the flat ends to the fluting on the column shafts, the carving of the foot of the shaft in one block with the base and the plinths, and the fact that these do not stand on top of, but are integrated with, the uppermost step. In the mid-C1 AD the north side of the temple colonnade was badly damaged: ten complete columns were replaced in white Italian (Luna) marble, together with one of the capitals on the south side. The new capitals, like the old, were in two halves but were made recognizably different in the details of their design (Fig. 121).

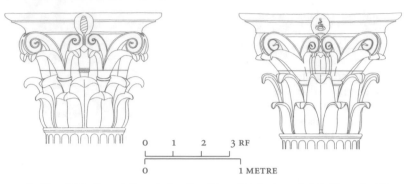

▲ **Fig. 121.** Round Temple by the Tiber. Original capital (*left*), early C1 AD replacement (*right*)

Roman Buildings — S. Maria in Cosmedin.
Map, Fig. 112: 15

Piazza Bocca della Verità. * *Church*

Across the road from the Round Temple, the church of St Mary 'in Cosmedin' (apparently referring to Constantinople) has been associated with the Greek community in Rome since the C8, and perhaps even earlier. The elegant bell-tower and present layout belongs to a major rebuilding in the C12. Mounted on the wall at the left end of the entrance porch is the *Bocca della Verità* (the mouth of Truth), a large marble disc, originally a fountainhead, with the head of a river god in low relief, who will bite off the hand of those who tell lies.

The church stands on the site of—and has absorbed into the front part of its structure—an unusual Roman building of the late C4 AD: a possibly unroofed arcaded enclosure raised on a platform, approached by steps on three sides. Inside the church, the wall on the left coincides with the NE short side; you can see the brick corner piers and three reused columns of fluted white marble (two with composite capitals, an Ionic one in the middle); of the seven columns on the longer NW side two flank the main door and others are embedded in the bell-tower, the side chapel, and the sacristy (all have composite capitals and mainly date, like those on the short side, from the C2 AD; one is earlier). The fourth side of the enclosure had no arcades, for it abutted another platform, constructed of large blocks of Anio tufa, which extends under the altar end of the church and beyond (a small part is exposed in the C8 crypt, if you are lucky enough to find it open). The tufa platform measured at least 21.7 by 31.5 m. and was more than 4 m. high; not suited to a temple podium, one idea is that it supported the **Great Altar (*Ara Maxima*) of Hercules Invictus,** known to have been located somewhere between the Cattle Market and the starting gates of the Circus Maximus. Roman legend ascribed the altar to the remotest past, spinning a tale whereby Hercules was passing through Rome on his way back to Greece with the cattle he had stolen from Geryon (the eighth of his famous Labours) when some were driven off and hidden in a nearby cave by a local monster called Cacus, but Hercules found them and killed the monster, his victory commemorated by sacrificing some of the bulls. Initially a private cult, run by two families, it became part of the

▼ **Fig. 122.** S. Maria in Cosmedin. Plan showing earlier Roman structures

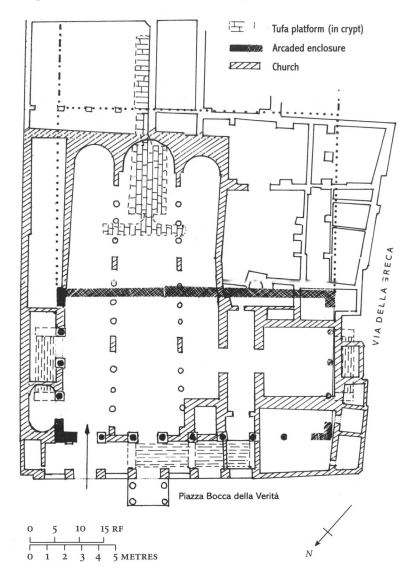

Tufa platform (in crypt)

Arcaded enclosure

Church

VIA DELLA GRECA

Piazza Bocca della Verità

0   5   10   15 RF

0   1   2   3   4   5 METRES

N

State religion in the late C4 BC and public sacrifices (of bulls) continued well into the C4 AD. Both women and dogs were excluded from the rites. What function the front arcaded precinct could have had, if indeed it abutted the altar of Hercules, is obscure. On the basis of some inscriptions found nearby (actually dedications to Hercules Invictus and to Ceres, whose temple lay further towards the Aventine) it is commonly identified as the *statio Annonae*, the headquarters of the officials in charge of the public grain supply, but no such connection need be made. In the C6 a sizable aisled hall was built across it, probably to serve as a Christian oratory attached to a *diaconia* (welfare centre).

Whilst in the church, the nave and choir enclosure preserve a fine **cosmatesque floor**, so-called after the Cosmati brothers who made many similar floors in the churches of Rome and Lazio in the C12–C13. This one dates from AD 1120–3; all the marble derives from earlier Roman pavements and wall veneer, predominantly red and green porphyry and Numidian yellow with an admixture of white or grey. The design centres on a choice selection of large roundels (previously in floors like that in the Pantheon) framed and linked together by bands of mosaic, and surrounded by panels filled with a rich variety of geometric patterns.

'Arch of Janus'. Map, Fig. 112: 16   ★

Via del Velabro

A massive marble structure 16 m. high, 12 m. wide, the four-way arch stands with its piers astride the Great Drain (*Cloaca Maxima*) which runs down the valley to the Tiber beside the Round Temple. Possibly an 'Arch of the Deified Constantine' which is listed in this area in the Regionary Catalogues, it must date from the early C4 AD (the quadripartite concrete vault over the crossing incorporates terracotta storage jars in a technique typical of the period) and probably replaced an earlier one on the same spot. It seems not to have been a triumphal arch but a *Janus* of the boundary-marker type found in the Roman Forum (which may also have coincided with the Drain, see p. 69). Much of the marble shows signs of having been reused, but the rather rough appearance and squat proportions are misleading. The holes at every joint were made in the Middle Ages to extract the iron dowels which held the blocks together and all four façades have also been robbed of the small free-standing colonnades which projected in front of the niches on both levels (see Fig. 123). Whether the niches were intended to contain statues is uncertain but their semidomes are elegantly carved in the form of scallop shells. A figure of Minerva is carved on the keystone of the archway on the north (left) side; Roma appears on the east. A doorway in the SE pier led up to a suite of chambers and corridors in the upper reaches; the arch must have had an attic storey, which some would restore as a pyramid but is more likely to have been rectangular, echoing the podium-like footings. A substantial super-structure in brick-faced concrete, shown in C16–C18 drawings, was removed in 1830 in the belief, perhaps mistaken, that it was the remnant of C13 fortifications by the Frangipane family.

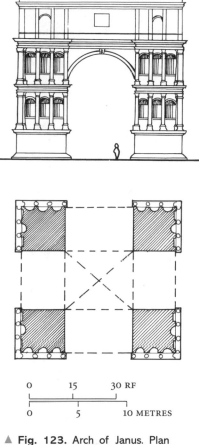

Arch of the *Argentarii*.
Map, Fig. 112: 17 ★

Piazza di S. Giorgio al Velabro. Comune
Even without one end embedded in the side of the church of St George in the Velabrum and the bottom of its rectangular piers buried in the ground, the 'arch' was always an unusual shape, better described as a gateway. It was originally 23⅓ RF (6.9 m.) high and free-standing (Fig. 124), although the back is not decorated, marking one of the entrances to the Cattle Market. Up to well above head height the piers were of plain travertine, presumably because they were likely to be rubbed up against by the cattle (and other animals), but thereafter the structure is of greyish white Proconnesian marble slabs on a concrete-and-rubble core.

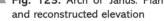

| 0 | 15 | 30 RF |
| 0 | 5 | 10 METRES |

▲ **Fig. 123.** Arch of Janus. Plan and reconstructed elevation

The long inscription on the architrave records that it was dedicated in AD 204 by the *argentarii et negotiatores boari huius loci* (the cattle merchants and their bankers of this place—i.e. the Cattle Market) in faithful devotion to the divine will of the emperors Septimius Severus and Caracalla, his younger brother Geta, the empresses Julia Domna and Plautilla, and probably also Plautilla's father Gaius Fulvius Plautianus. The names of Plautianus (disgraced in AD 205), Plautilla (also exiled in AD 205 and murdered in AD 211), and Geta (murdered in AD 212) were subsequently erased. Flanking the inscription on the left is Hercules, whose image symbolized the Cattle Market area, with his club and the skin of the Nemean lion; on the right is a semi-nude figure holding a cornucopia, probably representing the Roman People. The more important associa-

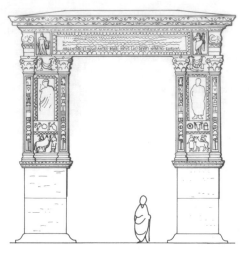

▲ **Fig. 124.** Arch of the 'Argentarii'. Reconstructed elevation

tions of tradesmen (*collegia*) quite often set up honorific monuments to the reigning emperor and his family in return for (or hoping for) special favours, and this is a very large gesture of the sort. Possibly, Septimius Severus had granted the cattle-dealers exemption from public taxes in recognition of the public service that their trade represented.

Every inch of the upper marble surface was crammed with carved ornament, conveying a rather confused message of military might and imperial piety mixed with some local colour. Each pier face (except on the back) had three figurative panel reliefs, one large one in the middle, smaller ones above and below, framed between pilasters with composite capitals. On the **front** faces the pilaster shafts were decorated with Roman legionary standards, capped with imperial eagles, and pairs of eagles held garlands in the panel between the pilaster capitals. In the main panel on the left pier the figure was male, wearing a toga, but is otherwise unrecognizable (he could be one of the two emperors, or the two chief magistrates of the year, less likely one of the tradesmen themselves). The panel below shows a bull being brought to sacrifice. On the **outer left** side, not much remains of the lower panel but it apparently showed cattle being driven by herdsmen: the *boarii* doing their job, providing sacrificial meat for Rome (and the army?). The middle panel showed two soldiers with two prisoners (only the legs of one survive), probably Parthians, very similar to the panels on the pedestals at the foot of the Arch of Septimius Severus on the Roman Forum (see p. 75). Under their feet ran a small frieze of sacrificial instruments (axes, mallets, knives) and in the upper panel, between the pilaster-capitals, four sacrificial attendants carry an incense burner. The pilaster shafts are decorated with imperial eagles perched on top of an acanthus scroll. **Inside** the archway the reliefs are better preserved: in the main panel on the right is Septimius Severus, his toga drawn up over his head as chief priest, pouring a libation over a pine-cone and pear on a tripod altar. Beside him is his Syrian wife Julia Domna, holding a herald's staff (*caduceus*), apparently symbolic of her role as 'Mother of the Military Camps'; her badly carved arm and the blank space beside her are due to the obliteration of the memory of their second son Geta, murdered by Caracalla in his mother's arms in AD 212. The facing panel on the left is even more lacunose: Caracalla survives very well, together with the altar at which, like Septimius Severus, he was making an offering; but both his father-in-law Plautianus and his wife Plautilla have been chiselled off. Beneath both main scenes, the frieze of sacrificial objects (vessels, helmets, fly-whisk, etc.) continues and below that, the bull sacrifice takes place. In the upper register are Victories holding palm fronds and garlands.

S. Giorgio al Velabro. Map, Fig. 112: 18

Badly damaged by a terrorist bomb in 1993, the porch dated from the C13, the bell-tower resting on the Arch of the Argentarii from the C12, and the rest of the church from the C9, taking its irregular shape from various earlier buildings. The arcades which divide the interior into three aisles are supported on ancient columns and capitals combined from different sources: the first two columns on the right have shafts of Phrygian purple, the next two of white marble, but all the others are of granite; the capitals are a mixture of Ionic and Corinthian, mostly imperial Roman (C1–C3), but the fifth on the left dates from the C5 and the two Ionic ones opposite it on the right are also early Christian (C4). There was a *diaconia* (church welfare centre) on the site by AD 640 and Pope Zaccaria (AD 741–52) is said to have endowed it with the relic of the head of St George, which he had found in the Lateran. One of the most popular and enduring soldier-saints (though the Catholic Church now denies him saintly status), George was martyred in Palestine in about AD 303, and became very important in the Eastern Greek church in the C6, which would fit in with the generally Greek enclave in the Forum Boarium (see S. Maria in Cosmedin, S. Anastasia). He was already known in England in the C7–C8, long before England adopted him as patron saint in the C14 (as did Venice, Genoa, Portugal, and Catalonia).

Roman Buildings—S. Anastasia.
Map, Fig. 112: 19

Via di S. Teodoro. †Church

Excavated under the nave and side aisles of the C17–C18 church in 1857–63, on the same alignment but 10 m. lower in the ground, are parts

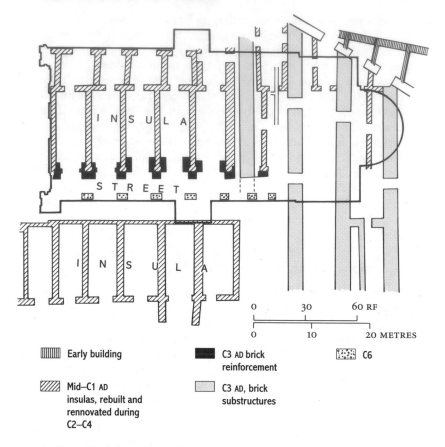

Early building

Mid–C1 AD insulas, rebuilt and rennovated during C2–C4

C3 AD brick reinforcement

C3 AD, brick substructures

C6

▲ **Fig. 125.** S. Anastasia. Plan of earlier Roman buildings beneath the church

of two insula buildings of the mid-C2 on opposite sides of a street, which ran along the foot of the Palatine terracing (see p. 120). A church was installed on the site in the C4 by a lady called Anastasia. It was later associated with the saint of the same name, who was martyred at Sirmium in AD 304 and whose cult became very important at Constantinople in the C5, being exported to Rome in connection with the Byzantine garrison on the Palatine in the C6. In the C7 the church ranked third after the Lateran and S. Maria Maggiore.

Mithraeum. Map, Fig. 112: 20

Via dell'Ara Massima di Ercole. †Comune

Although often called the Mithraeum of the Circus Maximus, the two were actually separated, as they are now, by a road. The structure in which the Mithraeum was installed dated from the C2 AD and consisted of five barrel-vaulted chambers, preserved in places to a height of 5 m., which had been adapted to support—and were presumably once surmounted by—two wide staircases on the side facing the Circus. The stairs (made in two phases) suggest a substantial building with a public function, but what that could have been is unknown. The Mithraeum was created in the late C3, laid out crosswise through three of the chambers, with entry from the street on the staircase side. Its inner sanctum, paved in reused slabs of coloured marble, still preserves many votives made by the worshippers (mainly ex-slaves) and some of the cult reliefs: Mithras slaying the bull, watched by the torchbearers of day and night, the Sun and the Moon, and the crow; Mithras carrying the bull on his shoulders, dedicated by one Tiberius Claudius Hermes, *Deo Soli Invicto Mithrae* (To Mithras, the

▼ **Fig. 126.** Mithraeum near the Circus Maximus. Axonometric view, actual state

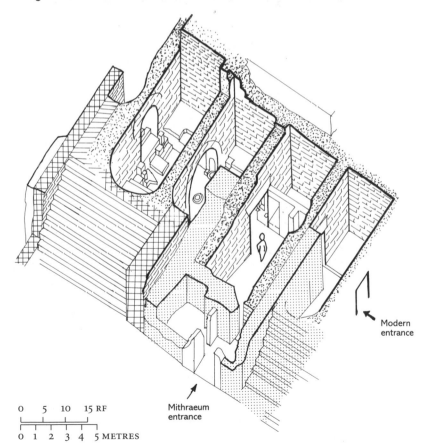

0   5   10   15 RF

0   1   2   3   4   5 METRES

Mithraeum entrance

Modern entrance

invincible Sun God) in accordance with a vow. Not far away, under the modern buildings to the NW, lies the site of a round temple of the invincible Hercules (*Invictus*), demolished in the time of pope Sixtus IV (1471–84). A colossal gilded bronze statue of Hercules found nearby was given to the Capitoline collections (Palazzo dei Conservatori).

Circus Maximus

Via dei Cerchi–Via del Circo Massimo

Occupying the whole length of the valley between the Palatine and Aventine hills, the Circus was Rome's oldest and largest public space, reputed to have been founded by the first kings in the C6 BC. It was basically a race-track for chariots but could accommodate all manner of other spectacles, including public executions, gladiatorial contests and wild animal hunts. The oldest events staged in it were the Roman Games (*Ludi Romani*), a festival of chariot-races and military displays held annually for fifteen days in September in honour of Jupiter the Best and Greatest, but about twenty of the other annual games which had been instituted by the imperial period included at least a day in the Circus.

By the late C1 AD it could hold 250,000 spectators. The track measured about 540 m. long and 80 m. wide, the banks of seating round the outside 30 m. wide and 28 m. high, of concrete and stone up to the second tier, of wood at the top. Excavations (1930, 1979–88) have examined parts of the seating which are still standing at the rounded eastern end (†Comune). They date mainly from the reign of Trajan (*c.* AD 103) but show signs of extensive rebuilding already under Vespasian and Domitian (AD 70–80s), based on earlier (late C1 BC and mid-C1 AD) footings which differ slightly in plan from one side to the other. The twelve starting gates at the west (Tiber) end, partly excavated and then reburied in 1908, were laid out in a shallow arc so as to give each charioteer an equal start.

Of the track itself and the richly ornamented *spina*, the central barrier around which it turned, nothing is known on the ground (they lie about 9 m. below the present ground level), but detailed representations appear in mosaics and reliefs (Fig. 127). The great Aswan granite **obelisk** dating from about 1280 BC which Augustus took from Heliopolis in Egypt and erected at the eastern end of the *spina* in 10 BC was dug up on the orders of Pope Sixtus V in 1587 and can now be seen in the **Piazza del Popolo**. The **obelisk** in the centre of the *spina* was also found in 1587 and now stands in the **Piazza S. Giovanni in Laterano**. At 32 m. high, weighing 522 tons, the largest surviving of its kind, it was quarried under Thutmosis III (1504–1450 BC) for the temple of Amon at Karnak. Destined by Constantine in AD 330 for Constantinople it then lay on the docks in Alexandria for twenty-five years until Constantius II decided to bring it with him on the occasion of his visit to Rome in AD 357. An inscription in

▲ **Fig. 127.** Circus Maximus. Relief showing a chariot race in the Circus (Vatican Museums)

verse on the base dedicated it to the city of Rome, recalling how Constantine would have taken it to Constantinople instead and how Constantius had restored unity to the Empire.

The Circus continued in regular use until well into the C5; the last official races were organized in AD 549 by the Ostrogothic king Totila. During the Middle Ages the site reverted to fields and by the C19 was covered with various industrial enterprises, including the gasworks. After tentative beginnings in 1911, the whole area was cleared in the 1930s and designated a public park. The park layout was intended to recall that of the Circus arena, but for a better idea of the real thing you should visit the Circus of Maxentius out along the Via Appia Antica (see p. 336).

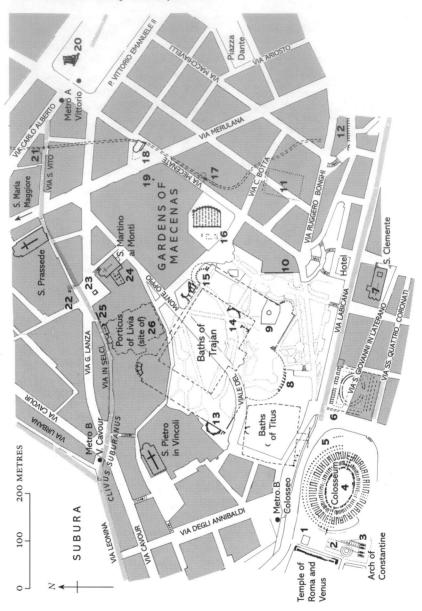

▲ **Fig. 128.** Colosseum Valley and Esquiline Hill. General site map

Colosseum Valley and Esquiline Hill (Map: Fig. 128)

The Colosseum is situated in a natural depression, at the end of what was once a much deeper valley between the Caelian and Esquiline hills, blocked to the west by the Velia (which joined the Palatine and Esquiline hills until sliced through by the Via dei Fori Imperiali in 1932–3). A stream ran along the valley bottom from the east (along the line of the Via Labicana) and turned, somewhere under the Colosseum, to run down the valley between the Caelian and Palatine (Via di S. Gregorio). Recent excavations near the Meta Sudans (see p. 271) indicate that such ground waters were probably already canalized by the C6 BC (in drains like the Cloaca Maxima which drained the Forum valley). By the end of the C2 BC the valley bottom was densely inhabited and housing also crowded the lower slopes of the surrounding hills. In the course of the late C1 BC and the C1 AD the luxury 'vegetable gardens' (*horti*) of the wealthy claimed large tracts of the higher ground on the Esquiline, preeminently those created by the Etruscan nobleman Maecenas along and across the line of the old republican city walls leading up to the Esquiline Gate (Map, Fig. 128: 18–19). Willed to Augustus in 8 BC, Maecenas' gardens were cherished by the imperial family as their private property for several generations. In contrast, another sumptuous estate on the hill which Augustus had inherited in 15 BC, the house of his one-time adviser Vedius Pollio, was razed a few years later and the site made into a public resort, the Porticus of Livia (Map, Fig. 128: 26).

Key to Fig. 128

1. Base of Colossus
2. *Meta Sudans*
3. Arch of Constantine
4. Colosseum
5. Boundary stones
6. *Ludus Magnus*
7. S. Clemente
8. Exhedra of Trajan's Baths and (modern) entrance to *Domus Aurea*
9. Upper level of *Domus Aurea* octagon
10. Eastern limit of *Domus Aurea*
11. Large colonnaded precinct (site of)
12. Terrace wall in reticulate (C1 AD)

13–15. Parts of Baths of Trajan
16. Cistern (Sette Sale)
17. Republican city wall
18. 'Auditorium' of Maecenas
19. Site of tower of Maecenas (?)
20. Nymphaeum of Alexander Severus
21. Esquiline Gate
22. Compital shrine
23. Tower of the Capocci
24. Loggia
25. Basilical hall, Via in Selci
26. Porticus of Livia

Nero's New Palace

The entrance hall was designed for a colossal statue, 120 RF high, bearing Nero's head. So vast were the grounds that triple colonnades ran for a mile. There was, too, a sea-like lake, surrounded by buildings made to look like cities. The parklands contained fields, vineyards, pastures, and woodlands; there was a great variety of animals, domestic and wild. Some parts of the palace were overlaid with gold and studded with jewels and mother-of-pearl. The dining rooms had ceilings of ivory, with sliding panels, to allow flowers and perfumes to be showered down on the guests. The ceiling of the main dining room was a rotunda, which revolved slowly, day and night, like the very vault of heaven. There were baths with a lavish supply of both sea-water and sulphur water. When the palace was completed on this sumptuous scale, Nero's approval as he dedicated it was confined to the remark: 'At last I can begin to live like a human being!'

(Suetonius, *Nero* 31)

After the great fire of AD 64 (which he watched from a tower in the Gardens of Maecenas) the emperor Nero seized much of the area for his personal domain, as the centre of a new palatial complex called the *Domus Aurea* or **Golden House**, an outrageous extravagance not yet finished at the time of his suicide in AD 69 and soon obliterated by his successors. It survives in brief written descriptions (see box) which can be tied to isolated elements on the ground (sketch map, Fig. 129). The complex extended from the Palatine to the Velia (where a forecourt containing a colossal statue of Nero dominated the skyline) and along the south flank of the Esquiline to join up with the Gardens of Maecenas, back down into the valley and across to the western end of the Caelian hill. There it incorporated a large platform previously intended for a temple of the Deified Claudius (see p. 312), converting one flank into a monumental fountain (*nymphaeum*) which was fed by a new branch of the *Aqua Claudia*. The water then flowed down to an artificial lake (a **stagnum**, like that on the Field of Mars), set in the bottom of the valley, surrounded by pavilions, gardens and porticoes. More water flowed down from the Esquiline side, where another aqueduct must have supplied a long **new wing** built facing due south from the hillside (see p. 290), full of dining rooms and fountains, probably accompanied by the exotic salt- and sulphur-water baths which Suetonius also mentions.

Under the Flavian emperors Vespasian and his sons Titus and Domitian, the twenty years from AD 70 to 90 saw the area transformed once more. Nero's dining wing was abandoned (Vespasian preferred to live in the Gardens of Sallust at the other end of town and Domitian moved back to the Palatine in state) but its baths were apparently remod-

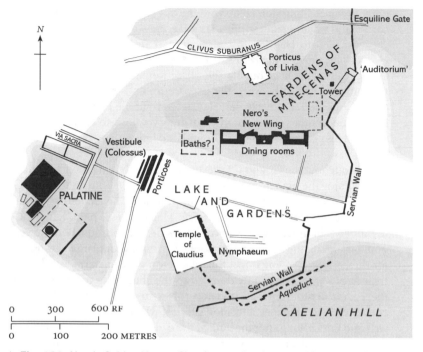

▲ **Fig. 129.** Nero's Golden House. Sketch map showing possible extent of the palace and grounds

elled for public use as the **Baths of Titus** (Map, Fig. 128); the temple of Claudius project was revived and completed. The porticoes and gardens in the valley bottom were abolished and the street system restored, and the Colosseum (known simply as **Amphitheatrum**) took the place of the lake. Four gladiatorial schools—the **Ludus Magnus**, *Matutinus*, *Dacicus*, and *Gallicus*—were constructed in the zone immediately to the east, together with a gladiatorial armoury (*Armamentarium*) and the *Castra Misenatium*—barracks for sailors from the imperial fleet at Misenum (on the Bay of Naples) who operated the amphitheatre awnings. The imperial **mint** was transferred from the Capitoline hill to a new building somewhere in the valley (possibly the building under the church of S. Clemente).

Following another fire in AD 104 the Esquiline quarter was the focus of another major imperial benefaction, the **Baths of Trajan**, for which an enormous artificial platform was constructed on the hillside overlooking the Colosseum valley, absorbing a large part of Nero's abandoned dining wing into its foundations. They were the first imperial *thermae* to be built away from the Field of Mars in a prime residential sector of the city (four other quarters were to be similarly endowed by the C4 AD). The baths' outer precinct almost joined up with the old Porticus of Livia at the north corner and whatever still survived of Maecenas' gardens to the east.

It was left to Hadrian to cancel the last remnant of Nero's Golden House folly, moving the colossal statue out of the vestibule on the Velia and spreading the huge double Temple of Roma and Venus in its place, a monumental bridge between the Colosseum and the Via Sacra. Recent excavations (1992) indicate that Hadrian rebuilt the Baths of Titus at the same time, another of his anonymous interventions to bring the monuments of his predecessors up to date and into line with his own yet grander schemes.

Throughout the C2 and C3 the *horti* of the rich and powerful continued to enjoy the high ground outside the Esquiline Gate. In the mid-C3 the Gardens of the Licinii family (who produced the emperors Valerian and Gallienus) spread as far as the Porta Maggiore (see p. 357). In the C4 the inner Esquiline, always a favoured residential location, became very popular among the senatorial aristocracy, who laid out large new houses for themselves, stepping down the hillside on artificial terraces. Many of their sites were subsequently donated to the church (in the same way as the earlier aristocracy had donated theirs to the emperor) and were converted into churches and monasteries, which flourished on the hill well into the C9, long after the bulk of the ordinary population had moved down closer to the river, on the field of Mars and around the Vatican.

For the next thousand years the hilltop reverted mainly to farms, vineyards, and country villas, until 1870, when Rome became the capital of the newly reunified Italy. Then it was radically redesigned as a huge new residential quarter, taking its orientation mainly from the new railway line into Termini Station. So radical and so rapid was the new development that most of the archaeology has vanished without trace; only the site of the Baths of Trajan was spared, together with a few other monuments which were considered of special interest and could be fitted into the new plan.

Visit: the proposed itinerary begins at the Piazza del Colosseo, in front of the Colosseo metro station, and moves east along the Via di S. Giovanni in Laterano as far as S. Clemente, then crosses over the via Labicana to the public gardens (Parco Oppio) and up to the top of the Esquiline hill at Piazza Vittorio Emanuele, then turns back down the far side of the hill into the valley of the Subura, ending at the Argiletum. There is no pressing reason why you should follow the same order, in full or in part. Only the Colosseum (interior), S. Clemente, the 'Auditorium of Maecenas' and S. Martino have fixed hours, but especially in summer, as long as you avoid Sundays and Mondays, they are generally open (or reopen) in the later afternoon. Unfortunately, Nero's Golden House may not be accessible at all.

Base of the Colossus. Map, Fig. 128: 1

The square area of grass in the paving beside the street in front of the platform of the Temple of Roma and Venus marks the location of an extraordinary gilded bronze statue of the sun-god Sol (Helios), reportedly
102½ or 120 RF (30.3 or 35.5 m.) high, the rays of his radiate crown
23½ RF (7 m.) long. Originally made *c.* AD 64–6 for the emperor Nero by
a Greek sculptor called Zenodorus who specialized in colossal works, the
statue had at first portrayed Nero himself, nude, as Sol/Helios, and was set
up on the crest of the Velia, at the entrance to his Golden House. After
Nero's death the head and attributes were changed to those of Sol but it
remained in its original position until Hadrian needed the site for the
Temple of Roma and Venus. Moving the statue in AD 126–8 was such a
major feat of engineering that we know the name of the architect,
Decrianus, and that he contrived to haul it standing upright, using twenty-
four elephants. The base, measuring 60 × 50 RF (17.6 × 14.75 m.), was
excavated in 1828 and again in 1986. Traces of three parallel walls
approaching it at an oblique angle from the west were seen during the
1828 excavation and may have been the remains of a ramp by which the
figure was manœuvred into its new position. Hadrian had a scheme to
commission a companion colossus of the moon-goddess Luna to stand in
front of the other corner of the temple platform and so form a pair of
doorkeepers appropriate to the residence of the goddess Roma Aeterna
(Eternal Rome), but it came to nothing. During the reign of Commodus
Sol's attributes were changed to those of his favourite god Hercules, but
they were changed back by the Severan emperors, under whose influence
Sol became an increasingly important symbol of the permanence of
empire and imperial authority, and the Colossus acquired magical
powers. In the C8 the Venerable Bede (AD 673–735) could quip 'quandiu
stat Colisaeus, stat et Roma; quando cadet Colisaeus, cadet et Roma.
Quando cadet Roma, cadet et mundus' (as long as the Colossus stands
Rome stands too; when the Colossus falls, Rome will fall. When Rome
falls, so falls the world). When the Colossus fell is not recorded (probably
pulled down for its metal) but by the C11 the Romans, pragmatic as ever,
had simply transferred its name—and its powers—to the nearby
amphitheatre instead.

Meta Sudans. Map, Fig. 128: 2

The area fenced off between the Colossus base and the Arch of
Constantine was the focus of new excavations in 1981–3 and 1986–9. The
circular foundations in the centre represent the **Meta**, a monumental
fountain dedicated by the emperor Domitian sometime between AD 89
and 96, that is, not long after the Colosseum. *Meta* normally refers to a
circus turning post, and indeed the fountain took the shape of a tall cone

on a cylinder, whose concrete core still stood over 9 m. high until demolished in 1936. The epithet *sudans* ('sweating' or 'dripping') implies that the water flowed down the sides of the cone, whose full height is estimated to have been at least 17 m. (58 RF). The pool around its base was 16 m. (54 RF) in diameter and 1.4 m. (5 RF) deep. It not only marked the point where the Triumphal Way turned to ascend the Velia to the Via Sacra, but also the intersection between at least four city wards (regions II, III, IV, and X, perhaps also I). The outer ring of shallow foundations (25.5 m. in diameter) are probably the footings of a colonnade erected around the fountain in the C4 AD, perhaps in association with the construction of the Arch of Constantine. Underneath and around the Meta on all sides are the razed remains of porticoes which had been built by Nero as part of his Golden House: they constituted the western margin of a park containing a great artificial lake (a *Stagnum* like that in the centre of the Field of Mars), where the Colosseum stands now. A deep excavation in one of the rooms to the north of the Meta identified a paved tufa surface, with a large drain beneath it, 6 m. below the present level, associated with pottery of the C6–C5 BC.

Arch of Constantine. Map, Fig. 128: 3 ★

Dedicated on 25 July AD 315, the tenth anniversary of Constantine's reign, the arch spanned the Triumphal Way, just before that turned left at the Meta junction, climbing the slope of the Velia to meet the Via Sacra (at the Arch of Titus). A lengthy inscription repeated on both faces (the lettering once inlaid in gilded bronze) explains its purpose:

IMP(eratori) CAES(ari) FL(avio) CONSTANTINO MAXIMO
To the emperor Flavius Constantine, the Great,

P(io)F(elici) AUGUSTO S(enatus) P(opulus)Q(ue)R(omanus)
pious and fortunate, the Senate and People of Rome,

QUOD INSTINCTU DIVINITATIS MENTIS
because by divine inspiration and his own great spirit

MAGNITUDINE CUM EXERCITU SUO
with his army

TAM DE TYRANNO QUAM DE OMNI EIUS
on both the tyrant and all his faction

FACTIONE UNO TEMPORE IUSTIS
at once in rightful

REM PUBLICAM ULTUS EST ARMIS
battle he avenged the State,

ARCUM TRIUMPHIS INSIGNEM DICAVIT
dedicated this arch as a mark of triumph

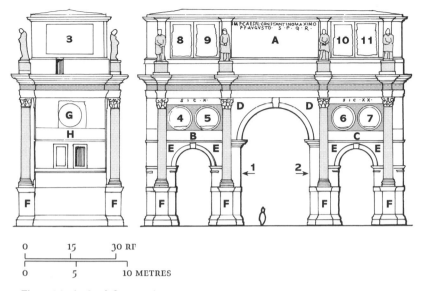

▲ **Fig. 130.** Arch of Constantine
Key:

Spolia:
1–3. Great Trajanic Frieze
4–7. Hadrianic roundels
8–11. Panel reliefs of M. Aurelius

Constantinian:
A. Dedicatory inscription
B. Siege of Verona

C. Battle of Milvian Bridge
D. Victory
E. River Gods
F. Victories and captives
G. Roundel: Sun (East) and Moon (West)
H. Departure from Milan (West), entry into Rome (East)

The 'tyrant' was Maxentius, who had ruled Rome from AD 306 until defeated and killed by Constantine's troops at the Battle of the Milvian Bridge (on the Via Flaminia just north of the city) on 28 October AD 312.

Although the arch is similar in size and design to the Arch of Septimius Severus on the Roman Forum (p. 75), standing almost 21 m. (70 RF) high and 25.6 m. (87 RF) wide, the hundred years' difference in date shows immediately (especially after recent cleaning) in the range of materials employed. The bulk of the Constantinian structure, like the Severan one, is of greyish white Proconnesian marble but it is all recycled (a lot came from one particular arch) and towards the top is mixed with other grey and white marble from other sources. Another novelty characteristic of the late date is the extensive use of colour. The four fluted Corinthian columns on each face, with pilasters behind them to match, were originally made for a Flavian building (late C1 AD) and have Numidian yellow shafts (the last on the right on the Colosseum side was removed and replaced with one of Phrygian purple by Pope Clement VIII c.1597 because he needed a yellow one for a door at St John Lateran, see

p. 349). The background around the roundels was veneered with purple-red porphyry; the frieze on the main entablature was also faced with some different stone, perhaps green porphyry; the pedestal bases carrying the statues of Dacian prisoners on the attic are of Carystian green; the prisoners' bodies are of Phrygian purple.

The Dacian prisoners are so like examples found in Trajan's Forum that it is widely believed they were taken from it, but there is no evidence to suggest that any part of the Forum had been, or was being, dismantled by the early C4, quite the contrary (see p. 161). More likely the figures came from some other Trajanic monument, or rather, from one which had already been dismantled for some reason, perhaps long before, but whose marbles had been kept in the expectation that they could be reused (like the reliefs found under the Palazzo della Cancelleria, see p. 213). Three other groups of such material, carefully selected for their subject-matter, are incorporated into the Arch's decoration (numbered 1 to 11 on Fig. 130, the arrangement is identical on both faces):

1–2 (in the central passage) two sections from a continuous panel relief, in white Greek (Pentelic) marble, known as the **Great Trajanic Frieze**. That on the left (Palatine) side, under the Constantinian caption *liberator urbis* (liberator of the city), shows an emperor—with his head recut as Constantine—charging into battle on horseback against barbarians. On the opposite wall, labelled for Constantinian purposes *Fundator quietis* (founder of calm), the emperor appears in battledress but on foot, being crowned by Victory and greeted by two females, probably personifications of Honour (in Amazon dress with a crested helmet) and Virtue (in battledress with lion-skin boots). **3** (on the short sides of the attic) are two more sections of the same frieze, with more of the battle scene. The length of the original is estimated to have been at least 18 m. (other fragments have survived, two in the Villa Borghese, p. 404). Opinion is divided as to the identity of the original emperor; both Domitian and Trajan are equally possible on grounds of style and iconography, but the use of Pentelic marble and the fact that the reliefs were available for reuse at all could tip the balance in favour of Domitian (whose memory and monuments were annulled following his murder in AD 96).

4–7 eight circular reliefs known as the **'Hadrianic roundels'**, mounted in pairs, two pairs on each side (Fig. 131). All in white Italian (luna) marble and surely all from one monument, they show alternately scenes of hunting (bear, boar, and lion) and sacrifices to appropriate deities (Silvanus, Apollo, Diana and Hercules). On the roundels on the south (Circus Maximus) side the portrait of the principal figure in the sacrifice scenes has been recut into Constantine; in those of the hunt to his co-emperor Licinius (or perhaps his father Constantius Chlorus); on the north side the pattern is reversed. Who the original protagonists were, and what the

▲ **Fig. 131.** Arch of Constantine. North side, left half. Roundels showing a boar hunt and sacrifice to Apollo. Panel beneath has a scene set in the Roman Forum

previous architectural setting of the roundels was, are unsolved puzzles. Sculptural style and technique suit a date in the first half of the C2 AD; a connection with Hadrian is favoured by the possible identification of one of the background heads as his favourite companion Antinous, who drowned in the Nile in AD 130, on the basis of which it has been argued that the reliefs come from an arch erected in his memory. However, since the youthful Antoninus Pius also seems to have been present, with rather greater prominence, the monument may have promoted a vision of Hadrian with his intended successor(s) which never took place, perhaps suppressed before completion (several of the reliefs are decidedly unfinished).

8–11 framing the inscription on the attic are the **panel-reliefs of Marcus Aurelius**, eight tall rectangular reliefs in Italian (Luna) marble. The four on the south (Circus Maximus) side show the emperor at war; on the north side he is engaged in civilian duties. In every relief the emperor's portrait has been recut into that of Constantine but three other panels of the identical size and related character are known, in which the emperor is clearly Marcus Aurelius, probably celebrating his triumph in AD 176

(Palazzo dei Conservatori museum, main staircase). The Conservatori three were brought to the museum in 1515 from the church of SS Luca e Martina (near the arch of Septimius Severus); opinion is divided as to whether they and those on Constantine's arch were originally set up on one or two separate arches.

All the rest of the decoration was carved by Constantinian workmen and is keyed in Fig. 130 by letters. Their most ambitious contributions were the roundels on the short sides (G), and the panel frieze which runs below (B, C, H). In the roundels Sol and Luna appear respectively driving chariots, symbols of the eternity of Rome and the Empire which Constantine had just saved. The panel frieze starts on the short west (Palatine) side with Constantine and his army setting out from Milan. On the south side the left-hand scene (B) shows his army besieging Verona, on the right (C) is the Battle of the Milvian Bridge. On the east end, Constantine makes his triumphant entry into Rome, and on the north side left (B) he addresses the Roman people from the rostra on the Forum (Fig. 25, p. 82) and on the right (C) hands out gifts of money. The figure style and proportions are those favoured by contemporary sarcophagus makers, some of whom may have been among the workforce for lack of other local expertise. The pedestal bases (F) had a winged Victory with palm frond on front, Roman soldiers and barbarian prisoners on the sides. More Victories fill the spandrels of the central archway (D) and pairs of disgruntled-looking river gods recline in the spandrels of the lateral archways (E).

Colosseum (*Amphitheatrum*)   ★★

State (*ground level (free); *upper level (ticket))

Begun in AD 70 by Vespasian and completed up to the third storey before his death in AD 79, the top level was finished off by his son Titus and the whole building inaugurated in AD 80. It is by a considerable margin the largest amphitheatre in the Roman world, 189 m. (640 RF) long, 156 m. (528 RF) wide, and 48 m. (163 RF) high. When intact the outer perimeter measured 545 m. (1,835 RF), and is estimated to have required 100,000 cubic metres of travertine, with 300 tons of iron clamps holding the blocks together. Equally vast amounts of tufa and brick-faced concrete were employed in the radial ribs and vaults which supported the seating. Although never matched in scale nor in the refinements of its architectural style the basic design was emulated by many amphitheatre builders throughout the Empire.

After a major fire in AD 217, which affected the uppermost level of seating and the arena (both largely constructed of wood), the amphitheatre was not fully operational again until about AD 240. Further repairs are mentioned in 250 or 252 and in 320, after which come those under

EAST

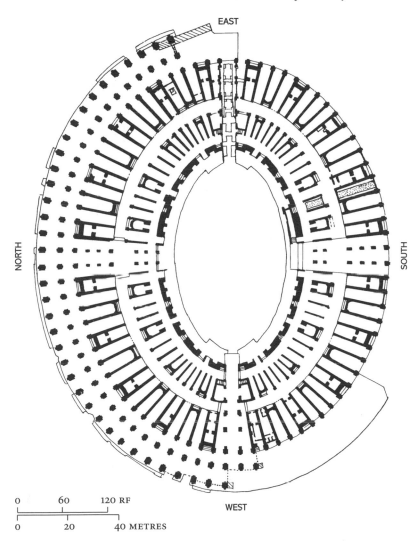

NORTH

SOUTH

0   60   120 RF

0   20   40 METRES

WEST

▲ **Fig. 132.** Colosseum. Ground plan, actual state

Theodosius and Valentinian (recorded in a lengthy inscription, see below), probably as the result of a serious earthquake in AD 443; more followed in 484 and 508. Gladiatorial contests are last mentioned in 434/5 but animal hunts went on until at least AD 523. By the later C6, however, a small church had been installed, using the arena as a cemetery, and the multiplicity of vaulted spaces were being taken over as housing and work-shops; they were still being rented out in the C12. About 1200 the Frangipane family took over the whole pile and for about a century it was strongly fortified (some traces survive in the NE sector). By 1362 (perhaps in the earthquake of 1349) the outer south side had collapsed in great heaps of stone which went in the next four hundred years to building numerous palaces, churches, hospitals, and repairing bridges, roads and the Tiber wharves. From the mid-C14 until the early C19 the northern third belonged to a religious order and continued to be inhabited. By the end of the C18 the stone robbing stopped and efforts turned instead to preservation; the great triangular wedge reinforcing the tail end of the façade on the SE side was built in 1807; a similar intervention on the NW side dates from 1827. Reinforcements were made to the interior in 1831 and 1846 and in the 1930s, at which time the arena substructures (already partly excavated in 1810–14 and 1874) were fully exposed. However, long-term conservation and maintenance of both sub- and superstructures is now an increasing challenge.

Entering by the **main entrance** (on the west), note first the large marble block lying on the ground on the right-hand side of the passage-way. It bears a long inscription referring to the restoration of various parts of the amphitheatre in the reign of Theodosius II and Valentinian III (AD 425–50) but is riddled with holes from the inlaid bronze letters of a previous inscription, which has recently been reconstructed as having read: IMP · CAES · VESPASIANUS · AUG | AMPHITHEATRUM · NOVUM | EX · MANU- BIIS ..... FIERI · IUSSIT (The emperor Vespasian ordered this new amphitheatre to be erected from his general's share of the booty . . .). It was not the principal dedicatory inscription, which will have run round the parapet of the arena, but a shorthand version which was probably repeated at various other significant points around the building. The block was found in 1813 at the arena end of the eastern entrance, where it could have formed the lintel of the doorway. The new reading not only confirms that the amphitheatre was essentially Vespasian's project, but adds the information that he built it as a triumphal monument in the Roman tradition, from his spoils of war (presumably the Jewish triumph of AD 70, which brought some 50,000 kg. of gold and silver from the Temple at Jerusalem).

The **interior** of the Colosseum is a world unto itself, with its own microclimate; enthusiastic botanists in the C19 counted some 420 different species of flowers and other plant-life (all eradicated in 1871 as a threat to the masonry, vegetation still thrives wherever it gets a chance). In antiquity it was a theatre of ritual death, witnessed by the emperor, Vestal Virgins, and senators, in company with a segregated microcosm of the rest of male Roman society. According to the Calendar of AD 354 the **seating** could hold 87,000 people, though modern estimates prefer to reduce the figure to 50,000 (still double the capacity of any of Rome's theatres, yet only a fifth of the Circus Maximus). As in the theatre, the spectators were dressed and seated in accordance with their status and profession. The emperor and the Vestal Virgins faced each other across the arena in special

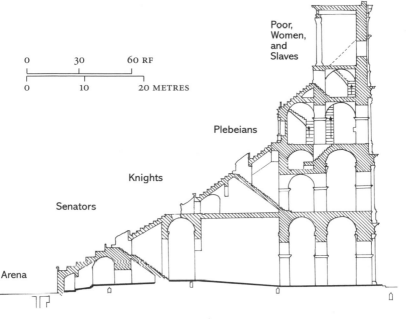

▲ Fig. 133. Colosseum. Reconstruction of seating zones

boxes on the central short axis (where the Christian crosses have been placed). Ranged around at the same level, on broad platforms to which they brought their own chairs (*bisellia*) sat the senatorial class, all in white togas with red borders. Above the senators came the knights (*equites*), above them the ordinary Roman citizens (the *plebs*), all in their togas too. Boys who were not yet of age sat with their tutors in a specific sector, as did serving soldiers on leave, scribes, heralds, foreign dignitaries, public slaves, some of the colleges and priesthoods, and a probably whole range of other categories (some were banned, notably gravediggers, actors and anyone who had fought as a gladiator). The middle three zones had built-in stone seating, some of which was replaced in marble in late antiquity (however, the wedge of marble seating low down at the east end is an erroneous piece of reconstruction done in the 1930s). Inscriptions specified the length of seating reserved for particular groups (in the C5 some seats were carved with the names of individual senators). At the very top, 40 m. above and almost 50 m. away from the arena, was a gallery for the common poor, slaves, and whatever women dared to join them. There it was standing room only, or very steep wooden benches.

The **parallel walls** which fill the centre of the scene nowadays were, of course, not normally visible in antiquity, being capped off with wooden planking and covered with sand. The **arena** thus formed, like the amphitheatre around it, was the largest in the Roman world, an oval (not

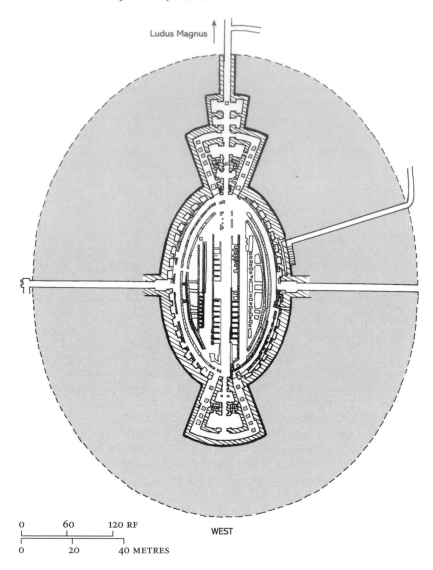

Ludus Magnus

0   60   120 RF
0   20   40 METRES

WEST

▲ **Fig. 134.** Colosseum. Plan of subterranean levels

an ellipse) 83 m. long and 48 m. wide (280 × 163 RF). It must have been able to handle enormous numbers of animals and men, in the most elaborate stagings, and to judge by the fact that at least twelve different phases can be seen in the substructures, ideas and arrangements were constantly changing. The system of eighty vertical shafts in the four parallel walls dates from about AD 300, with repairs in the C5; it apparently raised animals in cages to just below the arena floor, where they were released through trap doors. What the initial installations consisted of is not at all clear; accounts of Titus' first games in AD 80 refer to the arena suddenly being filled with water for a display of horses and bulls (who had been trained to swim), and the re-enactment of a famous sea battle between Corcyreans (of Corfu) and Corinthians (mainland Greeks). The supply of sufficient water is no problem, since an aqueduct had previously filled a great lake on the site (see p. 268 and Fig. 127) and there is evidence for major hydraulic lifting mechanisms at either end of the subterranean network (see Fig. 134). But no one can see how the present arena could be made watertight nor how there could be enough space for warships to move around. Either the reports have the wrong location or the design of the original arena was much simpler (perhaps a single—and rather wider—channel down the longer axis).

Tunnels allowed the animals and other performers to be brought in directly underground. An extension of the tunnel at the eastern end also connected with the main gladiators' barracks, the **Ludus Magnus**, to the east (Map, Fig. 128: 6). Separate underground passages were provided beneath the main entrances on the short axis for the emperor and Vestal Virgins to reach and leave their boxes without necessarily passing through the crowds.

From the *upper level** (up the stairs to the left of the main entrance) you gain first an excellent view outwards over the **Temple of Roma and Venus** (see p. 113 and Fig. 47) and can then explore more of the amphitheatre interior and its system of stairs and corridors. The miscellany of blocks and column drums visible on the

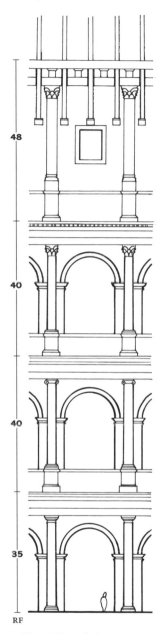

▲ **Fig. 135.** Colosseum. Exterior elevation with reconstruction of uppermost level. Heights of levels are in Roman feet

inner face of the wall round the top of the cavea represent repairs, probably after the fire of AD 217.

The **outer elevation**, well preserved all along the north side, is a very elegant example of Roman trabeated arcading (Fig. 135). It consists of three superimposed arcades, each archway framed by semi-columns supporting horizontal entablatures, and a fourth, attic storey where the arcades become small windows and the semi-columns are reduced to flat pilasters. The lowest order is a sturdy Tuscan, which was evidently considered more appropriate for an amphitheatre than the Doric; the next (unusually) is Ionic; the top two are both a simplified Corinthian; the shafts have almost no taper, and the width of the piers and archways is constant from bottom to top. The manner in which the architect married the façade design to the internal complexities of the building and its circulation systems is extraordinarily skilful.

At ground-floor level all the eighty archways on the outside were public entrances giving access to different sectors of the seating and seventy-six of them were numbered (those surviving run from XXIII to LIV), so that spectators could be directed to use a particular entrance to reach their designated sector. The numbering started from the first arch to the right of the axial entrance on the south (Caelian hill) side. All four axial entrances were richly decorated with painted stucco reliefs (several fragments survive in the north entrance).

The stone brackets above the windows on the top storey, with corresponding sockets through the upper cornices, held wooden masts which projected above the outer wall at regular intervals, 240 of them in total. They supported the rigging whereby sailors from the imperial fleet were able to manœuvre the 'sails' or awnings which cast shadows to prevent the spectators, especially those on the lower terraces, boiling in the sun of a hot day (though cold was more likely to be the problem during the annual games, which took place in the middle of winter).

A series of **tall stone bollards** was set around the perimeter, at a distance of 18 m. from the main building, five of which are in place on the east side (Map, Fig. 128: 5). They either formed a religious boundary, or an outer barrier where tickets were checked, or functioned as anchors for the rigging apparatus (perhaps they could serve all three purposes at once).

Gladiatorial shows were called *munera* (dutiful gifts) and were always given by individuals, not by the State. By the time the Colosseum was built they were being held as a regular public event, in December, as part of the New Year ritual, coinciding with the yearly political cycle, when they would be paid for by the incoming magistrates. At other times they could accompany the funerary rites for major public figures, or could be held on the anniversaries of past deaths. They were also staged in celebration of military triumphs. Such was their popularity that from the reign of Domitian it was decreed that in Rome they could only be given by the emperor; and elsewhere they required his sanction. The daily programme was usually divided into three parts: wild animal hunts (*venationes*) in the morning, public executions at midday, and gladiatorial contests in the afternoon; shows could run for many days depending on the available number of animals and gladiators. Trajan is said to have celebrated his Dacian triumph in AD 107 with 11,000 animals and 10,000 gladiators in the course of 123 days. Gladiators were a mixture of condemned criminals and prisoners of war (who were generally expendable), and career professionals (slaves, freedmen, or free volunteers), mostly men but occasionally women, specialized in different types of armour and weaponry: the heavily armed *Myrmillo* (named after the fish on his helmet) and the Samnite both had large oblong shields and swords; the more lightly armed Thracian, a round shield and curved scimitar; the *Retiarius* only a net and a trident. Others fought from chariots (*essedarii*), or on horseback. The fights were often staged in elaborate sets, with moveable trees and buildings; the executions might involve complicated machinery and torture; some acted out particularly gruesome episodes from Greek or Roman mythology. Animals for the *venationes* came mainly from Africa and might include rhinoceros, hippos, elephants, and giraffes, as well as lions, panthers, leopards, crocodiles, and ostriches.

Ludus Magnus. Map, Fig. 128: 6 ★

Via di S. Giovanni in Laterano. †Comune

Found in building operations in 1937 but not fully excavated until 1957–61, the visible remains represent slightly less than one half of the practice arena and its enclosing barracks; the rest lies under the street and buildings on the other side. The **Magnus**, as its name implies, was the principal of the four gladiatorial schools set up by Domitian in the AD 80s (the others were called the **Dacian**, the **Gallic**, and the *Matutinus* or **Morning** School, which presumably trained combatants for the animal-hunting shows). The barracks around the outside of the building were probably on three floors; the central courtyard had a Tuscan colonnade on all four sides, and fountains at each corner, but its open space was almost entirely filled by the arena. At 63 m. long by 42 m. wide (210 × 140 RF), the arena is 25 per cent smaller than the Colosseum's but quite normal for amphitheatres outside Rome, where the gladiators would do a lot of their fighting. Most of the surviving structure is a rebuilding under Trajan, in the early C2, when the ground level and the seating was raised, though the arena remained at its initial level. Watching the gladiators train was a popular pastime; the seating provided for about 3,000 spectators. On show-days the gladiators could transfer directly to the Colosseum by an underground passage.

The building naturally lost its function as soon as gladiators were no longer needed and by the C6 was being used for burials. Soundings under the arena found (at a depth of 2 m.) the floor level of an elegant house of the C1 BC; the east wing overlies a modest commercial building of the early C1 AD. Further structures now hidden under the adjacent bank building have been tentatively identified as the **Armamentarium**, the gladiatorial armoury.

S. Clemente. Map, Fig. 128: 7 ★★

*Via di S. Giovanni in Laterano. *Lower levels*

The Irish Dominicans, who have owned the church and its monastery since 1677, started investigating the archaeology of the site in the mid-C19 and the work continues as and when funds are available. The present church dates from AD 1108 (with a remarkable mosaic in the apse and many other original features) but the marble panels forming the choir enclosure come from its even larger predecessor of the C5, which has been excavated beneath the nave. And beneath that, 11 m. underground, lie two Roman buildings, separated by a narrow alleyway, both dating from the late C1 AD. One constitutes the basement floor of a courtyard-style house, with a **mithraeum** installed in it in the late C2 AD; the other is a large and strongly built structure of *horrea* (warehouse) type.

The entrance to the subterranean levels is through the sacristy (ticket office and shop), down a broad staircase. On the first landing is displayed a cast of the **altar of Mithras**, from the mithraeum, with Mithras killing the bull on one side and the figures of the torch-bearers Cautes and Cautopates and a large snake, symbol of regeneration, on the others. According to its inscription it was set up (*posuit*) by Caius Arrius Claudianus, who had reached the highest grade in the cult (*Pater*, 'Father'). He was probably a freedman of the same branch of the Arria family to which the emperor Antoninus Pius had belonged.

The floor level in the vestibule ahead of you at the bottom of the staircase is that of the **C5 church**, a three-aisled apsidal basilica, whose size and position relative to the upper one and to the older buildings below is illustrated in Fig. 137. The walls on both sides of the vestibule were originally free-standing colonnades, that on the left belonging to a peristyle forecourt, that on the right forming the basilica entrance. Their column shafts, bases and capitals, as customary for a building of the late Empire, were *spolia* from older buildings, but of high quality and carefully disposed. The column shafts on the entrance side (now only three but originally four) were of the rare Carystian black at each end, and Chian pink/grey in the middle. Progressive blockings were made to reinforce

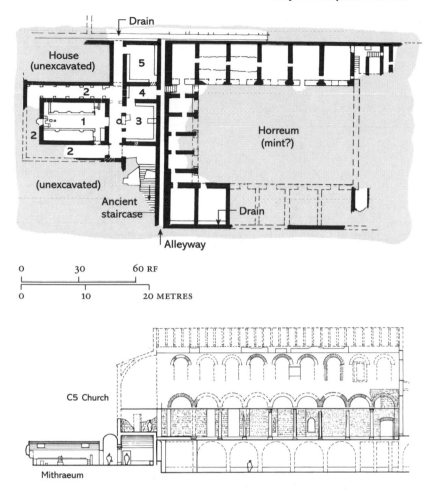

▲ **Fig. 136.** S. Clemente. Plan of Roman buildings at lowest level and long-section with reconstruction of C5 basilical church above.

them in the C9–C12 (the frescoes on the right date from the end of the C11 or early C12, just before efforts to keep the old church on its feet were abandoned and the new, narrower, church was built on top). Similar blockings around the **nave colonnades** are mostly the foundation work for the upper church but two on the left-hand colonnade date from the C11 and have contemporary frescoes; the patches of marble and tessellated pavement in front are rare examples of a style current in the late C6 or early C7. Five columns are visible on this (south) side of the nave, once a series of four select pairs (the survivors are of two kinds of shelly dark

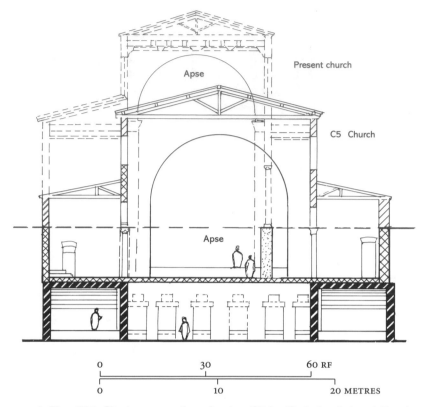

Present church

Apse

C5 Church

Apse

0   30   60 RF

0   10   20 METRES

▲ **Fig. 137.** Short cross-section showing C5 basilical church in relation to present church

grey breccia and a fine black marble). Those of the right-hand (north) colonnade are a more motley crowd, probably in origin four nicely matching pairs but the second, third, and fourth in line from the east end (a veined Italian and two large cable-fluted Carystian green respectively) are substitutes made in the C7 or C8. The seventh is a beautiful monolith of purple/white and yellow marble breccia from Skyros. Together with the missing eighth it may have been taken over from an earlier building on the spot, dating from the late C3 AD, whose outer walls the basilica reused as the footings for its own perimeter; C3 painted wall plaster imitating marble veneer can be seen along the base of the north wall.

The entrance to the **earlier Roman levels** (plan, Fig. 136) is at the far end of the left-hand (south) aisle. The staircase by which you descend (partly obstructed by foundation piers from the upper church) is ancient and originally communicated between the ground floor of a large Roman house and its semi-subterranean basement. Dated by brickstamps in the steps of the stairs to *c*. AD 90–6, late in the reign of Domitian, the house

formed part of the redevelopment of the Colosseum valley after the aboli-
tion of Nero's Golden House. The part of the basement which has been
excavated consists of a central room (1), with a low barrel-vaulted roof,
surrounded by a corridor on all four sides (2), off which there were further
rooms on each side, though only those on the east are visible (3–5). The
corridor ceilings rose higher than the roof of the central room, with
windows slanting up to draw light and air in from an open courtyard
which must have lain above. The central room originally had a door at
each end and two on the north side and the ceiling was decorated with
pumice stone and mosaic in imitation of a watery rocky cave or grotto. It
was probably designed as a summer dining room, or simply a cool retreat,
together with the room on axis at the east (3) and that to the north (5)
which both have elegant late C1 AD stucco work on their vaults. Around
AD 200, however, the central room was converted into a **mithraeum**; its
existing decoration was perfectly suited to simulating Mithras' cave; only
the doors had to be blocked and broad masonry dining couches
constructed on either side where the initiates of the cult (all male) would
share a communal meal. The door at the west end became a niche where a
shaft of sunlight would be directed to strike the cult image, in front of
which stood Arrius Claudianus' altar (see above). At the same time, the
two marble pillars (their composite capitals unfinished) were set to
embellish the doorway of room 3. Benches were installed around the walls
of both it and rooms 4 and 5. Room 5 also had new frescoes painted on the
walls above the benches; the two better preserved fragments show a man
and a woman. Traces of later flooring and the two piers inserted to shore
up the apex of the vault of room 3 indicate that although the mithraeum
was probably walled up by the end of the C4 (the cult was officially
suppressed in AD 392), the basement was still being used long afterwards,
perhaps until the C10.

A small (original) door from (4) leads to the narrow alleyway between
the house and a large **horrea or warehouse**, whose outer walls were
made of large blocks of Anio tufa. The door into the tufa building was
made in modern times but the small barrel vault over the alley is apparently contemporary with the house—slightly later than the tufa building.
Inside its protective tufa walls the other building consisted of a series
of evenly-sized rooms set around a courtyard—of uncertain length.
The design is normally associated with Roman granaries and other warehousing, but that would not exclude other commercial or industrial functions. The proposal that it accommodated the workshops of the imperial
mint (*Moneta Caesaris*), which should lie somewhere in the neighbourhood, is attractive but runs up against a problem, in that as far as we know
the moneyers continued to operate into the C4, probably on the same site,
whereas this building under S. Clemente was rebuilt from first-floor level
in the second half of the C3, into a building of quite different character.
The level we see had already had its floors thickened, and the walls lined

with waterproof cement (perhaps in an effort to counter the rising damp in the valley bottom); the building that replaced it merely used the lower floor as a platform, filling it solid with earth. And although on its new higher level (which was then to become the level of the C5 church) the C3 building was also organized around a courtyard, the inner surfaces of its walls were painted in imitation of marble veneer, matched by real marble columns. The latest theory is that the new building was in fact the wealthy private house in which the church of St Clement (fourth pope of Rome, exiled to the Crimea and martyred in about AD 100) was founded sometime in the C4 by a Christian of the same name.

From S. Clemente the ground rises to the Via Labicana, on the other side of which extends the **Parco Oppio**, made into an 'archaeological zone' in the 1930s to protect the sites of the Baths of Titus and Trajan and the Esquiline wing of Nero's Golden House. Very little of any of the three appears on the surface and the park's design has absolutely nothing to do with what lies beneath, least of all the main road (Viale del Monte Oppio) which runs on a diagonal through the middle. However, with some dedication (and caution, since the gardens are not the most salubrious) it is possible to track down some substantial but widely separated parts of the Baths of Trajan and a small area of the first floor level of the Esquiline wing of Nero's Golden House.

Baths of Trajan. Map, Fig. 128: 8, 13–15

Parco Oppio

Built in AD 104–9, the baths were designed by Trajan's favourite architect Apollodorus of Damascus, designer of his Forum (see p. 161). Although only a few isolated elements stand above ground, the larger plan can be put together from fragments of the Marble Plan and drawings made by architects in the C16 when more was visible (Fig. 138). How revolutionary the concept and its design was for its day is difficult to tell, since none of its possible prototypes (Baths of Agrippa, Nero, and Titus) have survived in their original shape, but the model was later emulated in four other quarters of the city, first by Caracalla beside the Via Appia (see p. 319), then Decius on the Aventine, Diocletian on the Viminal (p. 352) and Constantine on the Quirinal.

The main bath block, measuring approximately 190 × 140 m., with the hot rooms oriented SW so as to take maximum advantage of the afternoon sun, was set within a very much larger colonnaded precinct (c.300 × 220 m.), presumably filled with gardens, around the outside of which blossomed semicircular halls (exhedras) in great variety, all laid out on a vast artificial platform. There was a grand entrance on the NE, where most of the bathing clientele will have come from, but other lesser entrances were provided from all directions. Every inch of the space offered by the

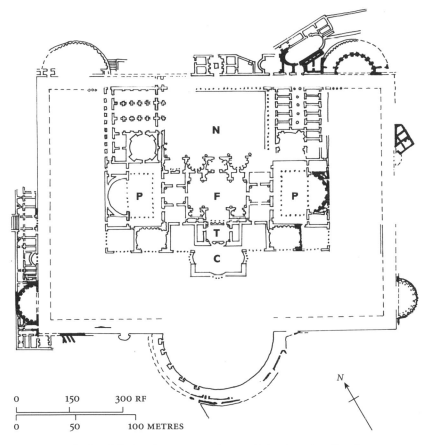

▲ **Fig. 138.** Baths of Trajan. Reconstructed ground plan based on Renaissance drawings. Elements visible today are indicated in black

substructures of the platform and the gaps between the exhedras was used for shops, storage, and no doubt living accommodation for the army of slaves who operated the baths and tended the gardens and other amenities. The parts you can see are:

- The semicircular terrace projecting from the SW side of the platform (Map, Fig. 128: 8), two storeys high, in brick-faced concrete with a balcony along the upper edge supported on travertine brackets (mostly 1930s restoration). The hemicycle on top was probably fitted with concentric rows of seating, for people just to sit and chat or to watch sporting or other events held in the adjacent space. Running through the substructures of the semicircular terrace and the southern corner of the precinct, at an angle of about 30°, are the precarious remnants of the lower level of the Esquiline wing of Nero's Golden House (see overleaf).

- A large semicircular exhedra in brick-faced concrete at the western corner of the outer precinct (Map, Fig. 128: 13), lined with statue niches on two levels, missing its semi-domed roof. The large rectangular sockets indicate that a free-standing columnar façade projected in front of the niches, framing their contents in coloured marble; the smaller holes pockmarking the walls show that they, too, were lined with marble veneer.

- Two walls of the central bathing block (Map, Fig. 128: 14). The straighter one belonged to one of the secondary hot rooms beside the main caldarium (Fig. 138: C). The semicircular one was a large exhedra beside the palaestra courts (Fig. 138: P); the springing of its semi-dome concrete roof survives, with part of the first row of square coffers which decorated the ceiling.

- A large semicircular fountain house (nymphaeum) at the eastern corner (Map, Fig. 128: 15). The whole exhedra floor was a large water basin, filled by fountains set in the row of alternately round-headed and rectangular niches around the lower zone of the enclosing wall. The semi-dome had hexagonal coffering on its ceiling and the walls were lined with coloured marble veneer. A corridor runs on two levels round the outside, probably connecting with a two-storey colonnaded gallery which ran right round the outside of the precinct.

Nero's Golden House. Modern entrance: Map, Fig. 128: 8

Via della Domus Aurea. †State

Buried in the SW sector of the platform of the Baths of Trajan is a length of 220 m. of the Esquiline wing of the palace which Nero built after the fire of AD 64 (see pp. 15 and 268). His architect and engineer were Severus and Celer, noted for their skills in large-scale projects and ingenious machinery. 142 rooms, with immensely high ceilings (10–11 m.) are known in whole or part (Fig. 139). In his later, madder years, Nero was a fanatical banquet-giver and the entire lower floor of his new wing seems designed for the purpose, with triple and quintuple suites of dining rooms in many shapes and sizes. There are fifty around a rectangular peristyle court (A) which backs against the hillside at the west end; those on the south side form two parallel sets interleaving back to back, one set looking inwards to the court, the other outwards through the valley façade. In a large hall on the east side (N), its 13 m. high barrel vault decorated to evoke a cave with pumice stone and a mosaic (showing an archetypical cave monster, the one-eyed giant Polyphemus), the diners were surrounded by fountains pouring down the walls and into pools in the adjacent rooms. Another fifteen rooms were grouped in matching sets around a pentagon-

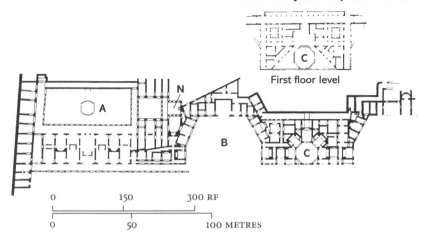

First floor level

▲ **Fig. 139.** Nero's Golden House. Esquiline wing. Plans of ground floor and of first floor over octagonal court

al court (B), and a remarkable set of five, with a cascade of water running down the back, looked into an octagonal court (C) (Fig. 140), whose concrete dome represents a major advance in Roman architectural development. The octagon apparently marks the centre of the wing and we should imagine the western half of the plan repeated on the east. The beginning of a colonnade which probably ran in front of the entire façade (perhaps on two storeys) survives at the far western end. The irregularities to the rear reflect the nature of the site on which the building was laid out, partly cut into the living rock, partly into—and over—earlier houses and warehouses which had also been terraced against the hillside. After Nero's death all the main rooms were stripped of the marble which had veneered the floors and walls; a few still retain their (once famous but now decayed) polychrome stuccowork on the vaults. The relatively modest 'Fourth Style' wall paintings which decorated the service corridors and oddly-shaped intermediary rooms around the dining suites were left in situ, but are under constant threat from the tremendous humidity, which caused the site to be closed to the general public in 1983, for an indefinite period.

On the outside, an island on the terrace in the Parco Oppio (Map, Fig. 128: 9) contains an area of the upper storey of the Golden House, located above the Octagonal court (Fig. 139, inset). The plan bears little relation to

▼ **Fig. 140.** Nero's Golden House. Sectional view of the octagonal dining court and its concrete vaulting

that of the floor below (other than the light well for the Octagon) and comprises a long ornamental pool with a colonnade along one side, off which open two small peristyle courts containing fountains. Everything was richly decorated and lightly built. At this level, the wing was on a par with the hillside behind and may have extended much further back (it is noticeable that various elements on the NE side of the Baths of Trajan have the same alignment).

'Sette Sale' Cistern. Map, Fig. 128: 16

Via delle Terme di Traiano. Comune (if closed, ask at the 'Auditorium of Maecenas')

The cistern (whose medieval nickname simply means 'Seven Rooms') has the same cardinal orientation as the Esquiline wing of Nero's Golden

▼ **Fig. 141.** Sette Sale cistern. Plan and reconstruction of western façade by Pirro Ligorio (c.1550)

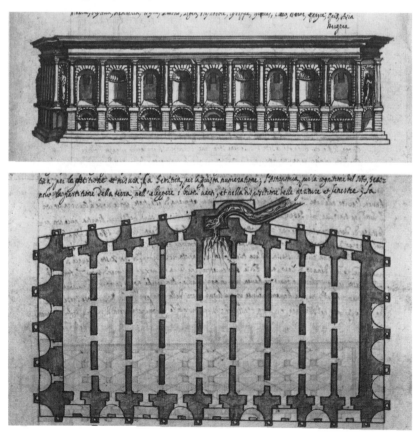

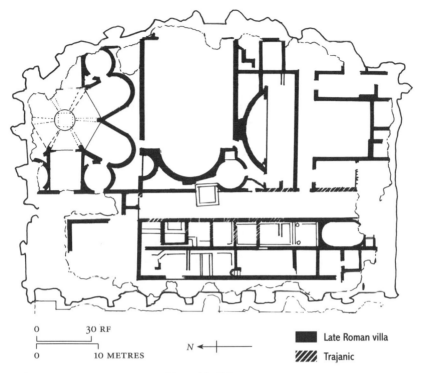

| 0 | 30 RF |
| 0 | 10 METRES |

N ←—|—

■ Late Roman villa

▨ Trajanic

▲ **Fig. 142.** Sette Sale cistern. Plan of buildings on top

House but is contemporary with the Baths of Trajan (AD 104–9). Massively constructed in brick-faced concrete, its curved side was set into the hill behind but the rest stood free, high enough to produce the pressure required to distribute the water (in lead pipes) to all parts of the bath-building and its precinct (and possibly other properties in the area). It had a capacity of 8 million litres, stored on two levels, the interior space divided by eight parallel walls into nine compartments, with staggered openings from one to the next. The water came from branches of the Aqua Julia and Claudia. There are traces of a rectangular block of rooms on the ground in front of the western façade and another block on the roof terrace (which was paved with coarse black mosaic), presumably for the maintenance/operating staff and their equipment. In the C4 AD, however, when the Esquiline became the focus of ever more extensive Imperial and aristocratic residential estates, someone appropriated the cistern roof for a **villa-pavilion**, converting the earlier rectangular block on the west side into a small range of baths and laying out a suite of exotically shaped reception/dining halls, richly decorated with coloured marble. The suite faced east, towards the Servian wall and whatever had become of the Gardens of Maecenas.

Servian Wall. Map, Fig. 128: 17

Via Mecenate

Long sections of the defensive tufa wall which had enclosed the republican city since the C4 BC (see p. 6) remained a feature of the later city, at any rate on the hills, and much of its course over the Esquiline was found during the redevelopment of the area in the late C19. The modern Via Mecenate runs almost parallel with a fairly straight stretch, which still stands several courses high in the garage workshop on the east side of the street.

'Auditorium of Maecenas'. Map, Fig. 128: 18 ★

Via Merulana/Via Leopardi. *Comune

Now isolated in a small park and covered with a modern roof, the building was discovered when laying out the Esquiline quarter in 1874. It is but one element of a much larger residential complex which was cleared at the time (and then destroyed). The connection with the Gardens of Maecenas is supported by the likely date of the original concrete walling, faced with tufa reticulate of late C1 BC type, and the fact that it intersects with the republican city wall (visible on the Via Leopardi side). Also, a lead water pipe stamped with the name M. Cornelius Fronto was found close by.

Gaius Maecenas, an Etruscan nobleman and Roman knight, probably from Arezzo, was one of Augustus' best friends, a trusted deputy and confidante. A poet himself, his name became a byword for inspired patronage of others: the literary circle he gathered around his dining couches included Virgil, Horace, and Propertius. He spent most of the last fifteen years of his life in semi-retirement in his *horti* on the Esquiline, the first of their kind on the hill, laid out in the 30s BC over the old republican city wall and the burial pits of the poor which lay outside. At his death in 8 BC Maecenas left the *horti* (together with all his other property) to Augustus. Tiberius took up residence in them in AD 2. Nero is said to have gloated over the Great Fire of AD 64 from **Maecenas' tower**, presumably a belvedere located at the highest point in the gardens (which may coincide with the cinema across the road, see map, Fig. 128: 19). Their fate after the débâcle of Nero's Golden House is uncertain. By the mid-C2 AD they were owned by M. Cornelius Fronto, famous orator and consul of AD 143, tutor and friend to the young Marcus Aurelius.

The ramp by which you descend inside the building is ancient, its floor of herring-bone brickwork (*opus spicatum*) contemporary with the original structure, as is the mosaic floor of the landing at the bottom and the door to the 'auditorium' on the left. There was once also a door straight ahead, leading out to a terrace, on to which the 'auditorium' also opened. 'Auditorium' is the name given to the room by its excavators in 1874, who saw the seven concentric steps in the rounded, apsidal end as the seats of

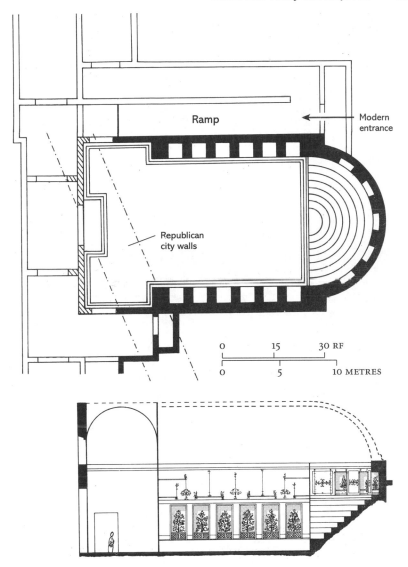

▲ **Fig. 143.** 'Auditorium' of Maecenas. Plan and reconstructed elevation

a miniature theatre, where Maecenas' protégés would recite their latest works. Alternatively, given that the holes around the second step down from the top seem to have carried water pipes, the installation could have formed a cascade (though what happened to the water once it reached the bottom of the steps is not clear). Either way, the room was essentially a setting for dinner parties: the couches would be arranged in front of the

▲ **Fig. 144.** 'Auditorium' of Maecenas. Wall painting in side niches as recorded in 1873

apse, facing the transept at the other end, where entertainments would be staged. The present solid wall closing the SE side was made in 1876; it should either be open or at least have a wide door, giving access to a front terrace, from which there will have been a view to the Alban hills in the distance. All trace of the roof has gone: it was probably of wood, not concrete.

A small patch of the original mosaic floor of minute white tessera, with two red bands round the margins, has been exposed to the left of the apse. The marble floor laid on top, and all the other traces of decoration in the hall, belong to a refurbishment in the late Augustan or early Tiberian period (*c.* AD 5–20). Marble veneer was applied to the lower zone of the walls, the steps in the apse, the ledges and frames of the niches above. *Trompe l'oeil* paintings in the niches (sadly decayed) gave the impression of windows looking out onto *horti*-like gardens—of tall trees, fountains, and birds (Fig. 144). The remaining wall surfaces were painted with costly red cinnabar (natural mercuric oxide from Spain) enlivened with small friezes showing Bacchic and miniature garden scenes on a black background. At some later point (mid-C1 AD?) the brick wall was added to the front of the apse steps, and later still the doors on either side at the other end of the hall were blocked up. The fragments of stucco, terracotta and marble mounted on the walls do not belong to the 'auditorium' but were found in the vicinity and include some fine Augustan architectural ornament, especially the capitals decorated with dolphins and sphinxes.

Nymphaeum of Alexander Severus. ★
Map, Fig. 128: 20

Piazza Vittorio Emanuele

A monumental public fountain, now believed to have been supplied by a branch of the Aqua Claudia or Anio Novus (not the Julia as was long assumed), the nymphaeum was built by the emperor Alexander Severus (reg. AD 222–35), who issued special coins to celebrate the event in 226. The 18 m. high mass of brick-faced concrete which is all that is left today was completely revetted in marble and adorned with numerous pieces of sculpture. Thomas Burgess's plans and reconstruction of 1830 (Fig. 145) give the general idea. The water arrived at the rear of the building, from the right, about 10 m. above ground, and divided into two streams, which then subdivided into five, three to the front and two to the sides. They flowed into an upper basin, from which the water was collected into pipes and fed through a series of fountain niches, five on the front and two on the sides, with two pipes spraying out of each, down to a basin at ground level, where people would be able to draw the water. The fountain stood in the fork of two main roads (the ancient *Via Labicana* and *Praenestina*), at a multiple junction just outside the Esquiline Gate. In the late Middle Ages

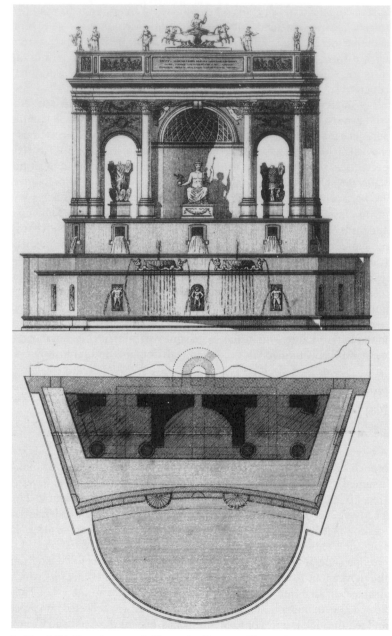

▲ **Fig. 145.** Nymphaeum of Alexander Severus. Plan and reconstructed elevation by Thomas Burgess (1830)

the ruins became known as the Temple or Trophy of Marius, after the two marble sculptures which stood in the upper arches until the late C16, when they were moved to the Capitoline hill (see p. 235).

Esquiline Gate (Arch of 'Gallienus'). Map, Fig. 128: 21

Via di S. Vito

Now squashed between the church of S. Vito and apartments on the other side of the street, the gate is one of the original gates of the republican city

▼ **Fig. 146.** Esquiline Gate ('Arch of Gallienus') with the Nymphaeum of Alexander Severus beyond, in a mid-C19 photograph

wall, rebuilt in the time of Augustus (27 BC–AD 14). There should be a smaller pedestrian arch on each side but they were demolished in the late C15. The surviving part, made of solid blocks of travertine, is 8.9 m. (30 RF) high and the same wide and 3.4 m. (11½ RF) deep, with the voussoir archway framed by Corinthian pilasters supporting a horizontal entablature. In the mid-C3 the Augustan inscription on the entablature frieze was chiselled off and thin slabs of marble were applied to carry a new inscription, which continued in two lines on the fascia mouldings below. The inlaid panels have gone, but the remainder of the text reads: 'GALLIENO CLEMENTISSIMO PRINCIPI, CUIUS INVICTA VIRTUS SOLA PIETATE SUPERATA EST, ET SALONINAE SANCTISSIMAE AUGUSTAE | AURELIUS VICTOR, V(ir) E(gregius), DICATISSIMUS NUMINI MAIESTATISQUE EORUM' (to Gallienus, most clement prince, whose invincible courage is only outdone by his piety, and to her imperial highness Salonina, Aurelius Victor [a high-ranking official in the imperial household], in complete devotion to their majesties' will [made this]). The missing section probably named Gallienus' father, the emperor Valerian, who (to the horror of the Roman world) was captured and executed by the Persians in AD 260.

Continuing down the Via S. Vito and crossing over the Via Merulana to the Via S. Martino ai Monti, you are following the track of the ancient street which led up to the Esquiline Gate from the Forum valley. The early medieval church of **S. Prassede** on the right-hand side (entrance in Via di S. Prassede) has some fine C9 mosaics on its apse, triumphal arches and in the chapel of St Zeno.

Compital altar. Map, Fig. 128: 22

Via S. Martino ai Monti no. 8

Discovered in 1888, when the apartment block was being built, the altar was left *in situ* in the basement. It consists of a travertine altar raised on a high base, with a platform of tufa blocks in front (once veneered in marble) approached by steps at the sides. To the rear are various travertine blocks and column drums of uncertain destination. The altar was a *compitum*, a shrine at a crossroads, where offerings were traditionally made to the *Lares*, the little deities who presided over crossings of all kinds (thresholds and boundaries). After Augustus' reorganization of the city wards in 7 BC, each neighbourhood (*vicus*) was expected to elect local magistrates (usually freedmen) who would tend the compital shrine and form a local 'watch' to fight fires and petty crime. In addition to the Lares, the magistrates were allowed to make offerings to the emperor, but only in the more abstract form of his *Genius* (loosely translated as his 'spirit'). Other individual gods would be honoured as well. According to the inscription on a marble base set in front of the altar this shrine once possessed a small statue of Mercury, god of circulation and movement (of people and goods) donated by Augustus in 10 BC from the money he received from the people of Rome as New Year gifts (about the time that he was building the Porticus of Livia just across the way, see p. 303).

In the square on the other side of the modern crossroads are the excessively renovated twin C13 towers of the Capocci (Map, Fig. 128: 23), behind which rises the C9 church of S. Martino ai Monti, supported on a high platform. The tufa blocks forming the foundations of the platform, visible under the apse and up the side along the Via Equizia, were possibly taken from the republican city walls.

S. Martino ai Monti. Map, Fig. 128: 24

Piazza S. Martino ai Monti-Viale Monte Oppio. *Crypt

A church may have existed on the site since the early C4, when St Sylvester (pope AD 314–35) is said to have set up an oratory in the *titulus* (meeting house) run by a Christian called Equitius. In the early C5 pope Symmachus then built the first version of the larger basilical church, dedi-

▼ **Fig. 147.** S. Martino ai Monti. Roman structures beside later church

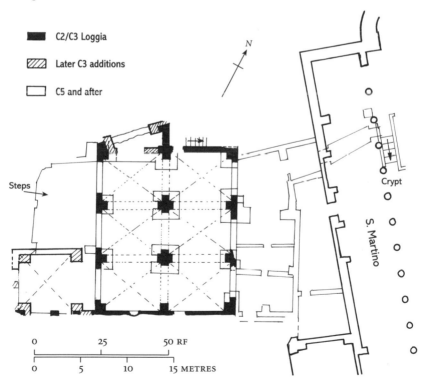

cated to St Martin of Tours, which was replaced in the C9 by the present one (interior and façade remodelled in the Baroque style in the C17). The twenty-four columns in the nave colonnades are supposed to have come from the C5 church, but if so, it had nothing of the quality of that, for example, at S. Clemente (see p. 284). Two shafts are of Carystian Green, five Phrygian purple, six dark grey (Teos?) and the rest white (Thasian) marble; the capitals of the first four columns on either side are Composite, the others Corinthian, all probably ancient but heavily restored in the C17.

Underneath the monastery buildings to the west, 10 m. below the level of the C9 church and reached by way of its crypt, is an unusual **Roman building** of the late C2/early C3 (Fig. 147), much altered by later adaptations and reinforcements (the fragmentary wall-paintings date from the C8–C9). Although traditionally identified with the house of Equitius, the original Roman structure, in brick-faced concrete, was architecturally more akin to a loggia: a rectangular hall, 17.6 m. × 14.2 m. (60 × 50 RF), with one blind side against the hill, but open on the others. The concrete ceiling, 6 m. (20 RF) high, was formed of six cross-vaults supported with the aid of two quadripartite piers in the centre. There was a small porch at an oblique angle on the NW and (at least in a later phase) a larger one on the SW. By a lucky chance, the building can be identified on a fragment of the Marble Plan, from which it appears that steps led up on the SW from a narrow street which ran along that side. Signs of a staircase beside the NW porch suggest that the upper level was accessible, either as an open terrace or covered with an upper storey (perhaps Equitius' house after all).

Returning to the Piazza S. Martino, the **Via in Selci** which snakes steeply downhill to the left reflects the course of the ancient *Clivus Suburanus*, a busy street that started in the lower valley at the Argiletum and rose up through the densely-populated quarter known as the *Subura*, possibly all the way to the Esquiline Gate. The name 'in selci' refers to the basalt blocks of its Roman paving, and in fact the level we walk on is more or less the late Roman level. The street front of the first building on the left as you begin to descend (Map, Fig. 128: 25) displays a palimpsest of different periods (Fig. 148), but from pavement up to roof height it is essentially the flank of a large **late Roman building**, perhaps one of the basilical halls characteristic of aristocratic residences on the hill in the C4/C5. It was raised on a platform parallel with the hillside, using the undercroft beside the street for a row of shops. Five rather roughly built travertine piers at ground level represent the shop doorways, which once all had flat brickwork lintels like that on the far left as well as the semicircular 'relieving' arches which spring from one pier to the next. The brickwork inside the arches is mostly part of the same build but the doorways have since been blocked with all sorts of different materials at different times (large brown tufa blocks, small grey tufa blocks, bricks, rubble, concrete), replaced by smaller door-

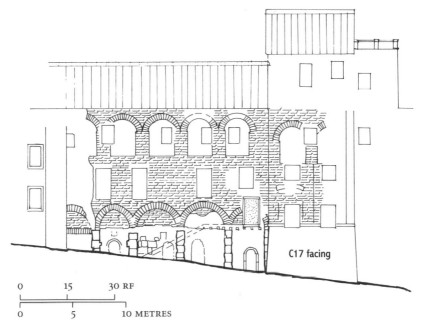

C17 facing

```
0        15        30 RF
├────────┴─────────┤
0         5        10 METRES
├─────────┬─────────┤
```

▲ **Fig. 148.** Via in Selci. Late Roman basilical hall over arcaded shop fronts

ways, and at one stage partly obscured by a staircase leading to a now blocked door opened at a higher level. The upper brick arches are a row of large clerestory windows, subsequently blocked in and replaced by smaller ones, which will have lit the interior of the basilica, but nothing more is known of the structure (the building has long housed the convent associated with the adjacent church of S. Lucia).

Thanks only to the Marble Plan and references in ancient writers we know quite a lot about another, even larger building a bit further down the street, the **Porticus of Livia**, which must extend over the hillside between the church of S. Lucia and the Baths of Trajan (Map, Fig. 128: 26); hardly anything has been pinned down on the ground. The Porticus was built by Augustus in 15–7 BC on the site of the house and grounds which he had inherited from one of his early advisers, the extremely wealthy freedman Publius Vedius Pollio. Dedicated in the name of his wife Livia in celebration of the success of their marriage, it contained a shrine or altar to *Concordia* (the same deity later honoured with a major temple on the Forum, see p. 77), and was a cleverly judged and highly popular benefaction, giving the inhabitants of the Subura their own equivalent of the private garden-estates (*horti*) which were otherwise taking over large tracts of the upper Esquiline. There were gardens and fountains surrounded by shady colonnades entwined with a famous vine, and a gallery of paintings (though nothing very valuable). Excavations in 1984 identified relative ground levels in the pre- and post-Augustan phases, 10 and 6 m. below the actual ground level in the point chosen (towards the Via di Sette Sale) and found evidence for continued use into the C5, followed by burials in the mid C6.

Crossing over the Largo Venosta (the junction of the modern Via Lanza and Via Cavour) and down the steps to the Metro station on the other side you can pick up the line of the *Clivus Suburanus* again, and follow its descent to the Forum valley, along the Via Leonina and the Via Madonna di Monti, to join the Argiletum at the Porticus Absidata of Nerva's Forum (see p.156). The character of the modern street is not unlike its ancient ancestor, lined with craftsmen's workshops and tall tenements, narrow, noisy, hot, and dusty in the summer.

Key to Fig. 149

1. Nymphaeum	7. Caelian Antiquarium
2. Aqueduct	8. SS Nereo ed Achilleo
3. S. Stefano Rotondo	9. Baths of Caracalla (site entrance)
4. Caelian Gate	10. Tomb of the Scipios
5. Temple of Claudius platform	11. Tomb of Pomponius Hylas
6. 'Library of Agapetus'	12. Museum of the Aurelianic walls

Caelian Hill and the Via Appia
(Map: Fig. 149)

▼ **Fig. 149.** Caelian Hill and urban stretch of the Via Appia. Site map

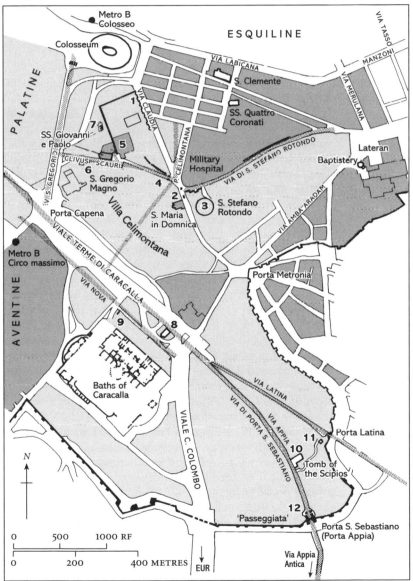

The hill has lost some of its prominence since the valleys which define it on three sides have filled up with the debris of centuries of occupation (the level in the valley between it and the Palatine on the west has risen about 10 m.; between it and the Esquiline to the north over 6 m.; that to the south almost the same), but it still preserves much of its ancient shape. The Romans distinguished two parts, a major and minor, the major being the higher (and larger) area at the west end, the minor a bulge on the north flank, now commanded by SS Quattro Coronati; a small valley lay between them (currently defined by the Via Claudia and Piazza Celimontana). There were three lesser spurs round the slopes of the major Caelian: the Temple of Deified Claudius took advantage of one, the church of S. Gregorio marks another, and the Villa Celimontana (previously Villa Mattei) occupies the third. To the east the spine of the hill blended into the wider plain; whether the Lateran counted as part of it is not known. In the valley along the southern edge ran the Via Appia (Viale delle Terme di Caracalla), starting from the Capena Gate at the east end of the Circus Maximus. Along the top, from the Caelian Gate out to the Porta Maggiore, ran the *Via Caelimontana* (Via di S. Stefano Rotondo–Via D. Fontana), its route followed in due course by branches of four aqueducts (the Appia, Marcia, Julia, and Claudia).

Apart from the name *Caelius*, which tradition connected with the Etruscan general Caele Vibenna of Vulci, whose army had camped there as the first step to making Servius Tullius Rome's sixth king in 578 BC, it was not a hill with many stories to tell. An older name for it was *Querquetulanus* (forested with oak); no early temples or sanctuaries are recorded but it was densely inhabited by the C2 BC and remained predominantly residential thereafter. Under the Empire it acquired the **Temple of Deified Claudius** and a monumental food market, the *Macellum Magnum* built by Nero in AD 59 (location unknown), and a local fire station (under S. Maria in Domnica). In the early C2 AD sizeable areas were commandeered for two large **military barracks**. The *Castra Peregrina* were for provincial soldiers seconded to Rome for special duties (recent excavations indicate they run under as well as to the east of S. Stefano Rotondo). The *Castra Equitum Singularium*, further along the plateau to the east (beyond the Lateran, in the region of Via Tasso), housed a new mounted bodyguard, the *Equites Singulares* or Emperor's Horse, recruited mainly from Germany and Pannonia (the Balkans). 500-strong to start with, in the early C3 Septimius Severus increased the Equites corps to 1,000 and built an additional set of barracks for them near by (partly excavated under St John Lateran). During the C4 a number of wealthy senatorial families built mansions in the Lateran area; others concentrated on the S. Gregorio spur, and both areas subsequently became the focus of major churches and monasteries.

Visit: the Caelian part of the route makes a circuit from the Colosseum, up the Via Claudia to the Via di S. Stefano, then over to SS Giovanni e

Paolo and the Caelian antiquarium on the side facing the Palatine. The Via Appia part starts at the Circus Maximus and follows the road all the way out to its sixth milestone (a distance of almost 9 km.). On Sundays only, the first 5 km. are served by the 760 bus, with stops at the Baths of Caracalla, half way along the Via di Porta San Sebastiano, the Porta San Sebastiano and various points as far as the tomb of Caecilia Metella.

Nero's Nymphaeum. Map, Fig. 149: 1

Via Claudia

Exposed when the present street was made in 1880, the massive ruin of brick-faced concrete 167 m. long and over 11 m. high constitutes the core of a monumental fountain, built by Nero after the fire of AD 64 as part of the gardens of his new Golden House (see p. 268 and Fig. 129). To the rear it rested against a great artificial platform which had been intended to (and did eventually) support a temple of the deified emperor Claudius (see p. 312); to the front it looked over a small valley and could be seen from Nero's new wing on the flank of the Esquiline across the way. The design of seven alternately curving and rectangular niches is not unlike the fountain in Nero's earlier dining court on the Palatine (see Fig. 56, p. 136), just twelve times larger, and presumably made similar play with coloured marbles in an elaborate columnar façade. Enormous quantities of water came along the spine of the hill on a new aqueduct (see below), at a level easily high enough to give the fountain an upper storey, perhaps with cascades like the installation on the Palatine. Although what we see of the structure was evidently spared when the temple of Claudius project was re-activated after Nero's death, whether any of it continued to function as a fountain is not clear. Recent excavations in the vacant plot a bit further up on the other side of the Via Claudia suggest that the area immediately in front was densely built-up again by the later C1 AD. At some

▼ **Fig. 150.** Nero's Nymphaeum. Plan

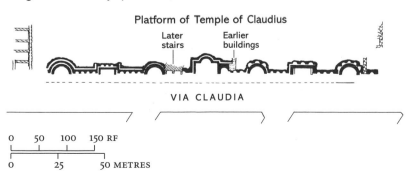

stage a staircase was inserted to the left of the central niche and the apse of the niche when first cleared in 1881 had traces of Christian paintings.

At the top of the Via Claudia the multiple junction between the Piazza Celimontana, Via di S. Paolo della Croce, Via della Navicella and Via di S. Stefano Rotondo was an equally complicated intersection in antiquity, around the Caelian Gate in the republican city wall.

Nero's Aqueduct. Map, Fig. 149: 2

Via di S. Stefano Rotondo

At the junction of the Via di Navicella (straight ahead) and Via di S. Stefano (to the left) the tall brick pier with the stumps of arches on two sides belongs to the Caelian extension of the Aqua Claudia, more of which appears along the Via di S. Stefano Rotondo, at first on the right (south) side, then a longer stretch on the left (north). Built by Nero after the fire of AD 64 the aqueduct branches off its parent at the Porta Maggiore (see p. 357) and runs along the spine of the hill through the gardens of the Villa Wolkonsky (residence of the British Ambassador), past the Lateran, along the Via di S. Stefano Rotondo (ex-*Via Caelimontana*), over the Caelian Gate and on to the south side of the platform of the Temple of Claudius, where there was a large collecting tank (recorded in the C16). Further extensions were then made from there across to the Palatine (see p. 144) and over to the Aventine (no trace).

Three phases can be seen in the surviving structure, for the original Neronian arcades were very tall and slender and soon required strengthening: Vespasian in the later C1 AD added an inner lining and sometimes intermediary arches, then much more solid infillings were made by order of Septimius Severus in AD 201; by the C3 and C4 many of the arcades were completely closed. Repairs are recorded still being made in the C8.

S. Stefano Rotondo. Map, Fig. 149: 3   ★

*Via di S. Stefano Rotondo no. 7. *Interior*

Consecrated during the reign of Pope Simplicius (AD 468–483) to commemorate the protomartyr St Stephen (d. *c.* AD 35) and perhaps housing a relic, the building has changed a lot in the course of the past 1,500 years but is still a wonderful example of C5 architecture, which has no precise equivalent anywhere in the Late Roman world. Indeed, it was long thought that the church had taken over an earlier, non-Christian building (a round temple or perhaps Nero's missing market), but conservation works in progress since 1960 have explored every detail of the fabric and excavated various areas of the subsoil, confirming the C5 date

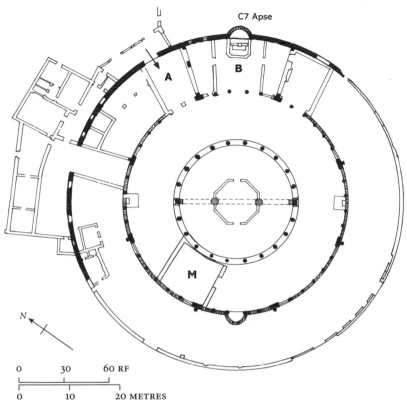

C7 Apse

A B

M

N

0	30	60 RF

0	10	20 METRES

▲ **Fig. 151.** S. Stefano Rotondo. Plan. Actual state

and the nature of the original plan and elevation, reconstructed in Fig. 152.

It is best to start from the middle and move outwards. The tall central cylinder, 22 m. (75 RF) high and the same in diameter, stands on a ring of twenty-two columns, whose recycled grey granite shafts came in slightly different lengths (19–21 RF) and with a variety of older bases, but were evened up by travertine plinths and new C5 Ionic capitals. The marble architrave was also new, largely carved *in situ*, with some very odd profile mouldings. Light filtered into the central space through twenty-two clerestorey windows, probably glazed with thin panels of coloured alabaster. Mentally remove the arcaded wall supported on two 28 RF pink Aswan granite shafts which currently divides the central void in half; it is a reinforcement inserted in the C12. The choir enclosure in the middle has to go as well; there was none until the C8.

Around the outside of the central hall is an ambulatory formed by a second concentric cylinder, 150 RF in diameter, originally pierced

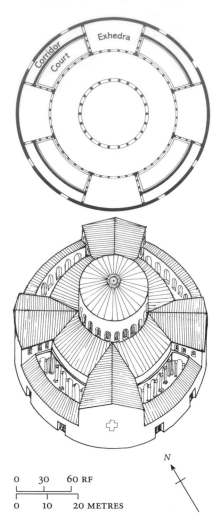

0   30   60 RF

0   10   20 METRES

▲ **Fig. 152.** S. Stefano Rotondo. Original C5 plan and reconstruction in elevation

by forty-four arcades standing on eight masonry piers and thirty-six columns, beyond which there was a yet larger circle, 225 RF in diameter. The space between the outer two rings was divided into eight parts: four exhedras on the cross axes, open courts on the diagonal axes. Corridors behind the courts linked the exhedras to external doors. Only the NE exhedra (B) is still on its feet (though subdivided by later walls), having been given an apse and an altar and converted into a chapel by Pope Theodorus (AD 624–49) for the relics of the martyr saints Primus and Felicianus (retrieved from a cemetery 15 miles outside Rome on the Via Nomentana). Much of an original C7 mosaic showing the two saints survives in the conch of the apse. The other three exhedras and the internal courts were all demolished in the C12, leaving only the perimeter wall standing to a height of about 6 m. The building basically shrank to the second ring, whose intercolumniations were blocked to form an outside wall (the horrendous scenes of martyrdom which decorate the blockings date from 1582). The circular windows are part of the C12 works; the original lighting effect was much more varied, alternating between the bright courts and the darker exhedras. The spacing and height of the arcades and columns varied too, partly on purpose, to emphasize the rhythm of alternate types of space beyond them, partly because the reused column shafts and the capitals and bases were not all the same size. The exhedras had four columns bearing five arcades, with noticeably taller shafts (averaging 18 RF) and Corinthian capitals (arcade imposts 23 RF). The courts had seven arcades on five smaller columns (shafts 13–15 RF) with Ionic capitals (imposts 19 RF). Primus and Felicianus' chapel has granite shafts, with plain-leafed capitals; but its counterpart on axis at the SW was distinguished by a set of fluted marble shafts with matching fully carved Corinthian capitals.

Other differences in status within the internal spaces, despite the non-hierarchical plan, were probably emphasized by the decoration of the floors and walls, which was apparently carried out some fifty years after the building was consecrated, in marble and mosaic donated by Pope John I and Felix IV in AD 523–30. Although almost every scrap was lost during C15 renovations if not before, enough signs have been found to indicate that the central hall and the exhedras were paved with large slabs of white or grey marble; the courts had coarse mosaics of large marble tesserae (predominantly white or grey with a sprinkle of other colours); the floors in the outer annular corridors were of simple concrete. The floor in the second ring was the most elaborate, either entirely of coloured marble *opus sectile* (triangles forming squares around smaller squares) or possibly divided into eight zones, *opus sectile* in front of the exhedras, marble slabs in front of the courts. The walls of the central hall and the exhedras, up to window height, and those at the back of the courts were panelled with marble veneer topped off with moulded stucco-work. The original roofs, like their existing replacements, were of tiles supported on wooden beams, and probably had stucco ceilings suspended on the underside; that over the central hall could have been a semi-dome or faceted cone, that over the ambulatory was surely flat, those in the exhedras perhaps barrel-shaped.

An excavation under the floor of the ambulatory on the west side in 1973–5 (plan: M) discovered an intact **mithraeum**, installed in about AD 180 in a room belonging to the **Castra Peregrina** (the barracks for provincial soldiers on assignment in Rome, guarding the corn supply, etc.), which extend under the church and off to the east. Enlarged at the end of the C3 to include the neighbouring room, the mithraeum was violently suppressed about a century later and sealed up with all its marble and terracotta altars, statuettes and reliefs, preserving extensive traces of their paint and gilding (Museo Nazionale Romano).

Returning to the Via della Navicella, the **marble ship** decorating the fountain in the middle of the road in front of the church of S. Maria in Domnica was made in 1513 (the base bears the name and arms of the Medici pope Leo X), copying an ancient one which had been on the site at least since the time of Sixtus IV (1471–84) and was said to have come from the ruins of the Castra Peregrina across the way. **S. Maria in Domnica**, whose present structure dates from the early C9 with renovations in the C16 and C19, stands on the site of the headquarters (*statio*) of the Fifth Cohort of the *Vigiles* (a police and fire brigade, one of the seven created by Augustus each looking after two regions of the city). Inside, the eighteen grey granite columns with Corinthian capitals which divide the nave from the side aisles are all ancient spolia.

Caelian Gate (Arch of Dolabella). Map, Fig. 149: 4

Via di San Paolo della Croce

Trapped under the brick-faced concrete superstructure of Nero's aqueduct which steps across it in a dog-leg, the gate is made of large travertine blocks and bears a faint inscription on the east (external) face, just below the top cornice, recording that it was built by order of the senate by the consuls of AD 10, P. Cornelius P. f. Dolabella and C. Iunius C. f. Silanus (who was also *flamen Martialis*, high priest of Mars). Some of the tufa blocks of the republican city wall in which it was set are just visible down the right-hand margin (the further course of the wall to either side has been demolished). The arch's present squat proportions are due to the fact that the street level has risen over 2 m.; the passage was originally 6.5 m. (22 RF) high.

Continuing along the Via di San Paolo, the aqueduct arcades can be seen over the wall on the right, heading in the direction of the Temple of Claudius. The street then opens into the Piazza di SS Giovanni e Paolo, which is surrounded by remnants of Roman buildings.

Temple of Deified Claudius. Map, Fig. 149: 5

*Piazza dei SS Giovanni e Paolo. *Arcades*

Set in hand after his death in AD 54 by Claudius' niece and widow Agrippina the Younger, mother of Nero, work on the temple stopped when Nero had her killed in AD 59 and was not taken up again until after his death in AD 68, to be dedicated by Vespasian in the early AD 70s. An enormous rectangular terrace (175 × 205 m.) was built out from the crest of the hill to support the temple at a level on a par with the top of the Palatine and is still a major feature of the landscape (though secluded in the private gardens of the monastery of the Passionist fathers attached to SS Giovanni e Paolo). Its eastern side was temporarily converted by Nero into a monumental nymphaeum (see above p. 307). No trace of the temple itself has yet been found, but from fragments of the Marble Plan we know it faced west, towards the Palatine, set slightly to the rear on the shorter axis of the platform, in a precinct which the Plan shows filled with narrow parallel strips, perhaps representing trellised gardens.

On the western (Palatine) side a wide set of steps led up from the valley on axis with the temple (the *casino* of the Caelian antiquarium, Fig. 149: 6, is built on part of their substructures) and the terrace bastions were given a monumental **travertine façade** in an exaggerated rusticated style dear to Claudius' antiquarian tastes (Fig. 153). A small part of the upper arcading and the return of the SE corner of the platform can be seen at the foot of the (C12) bell-tower on the north side of the square; to see the section shown in Fig. 153, which lies just inside the gate, enquire in the sacristy of SS Giovanni e Paolo. The driveway is on the line of an ancient street whose original level has been excavated (6 m. below ground), exposing the full height of the façade. On the lower level the openings are rectangles instead of arches, infilled with brick rather than travertine. The rustication, which is essentially a normal state of unfinish exaggerated to aesthetic effect, gives a good demonstration of how Roman masons will have gone about carving an elaborate architectural façade, like that on the Theatre of Marcellus or the Colosseum (Figs. 113, 135). The blocks forming the façade were first assembled in part-worked state, with the architectural detail (cornice profiles, capitals, shafts, and bases) only finely drafted at essential points. Keystones, friezes, anything to be carved in high relief would be left as solid lumps. Once everything was safely in position, the final dressing would start, working from the top downwards, taking the scaffolding down as they went, so that the workmen could

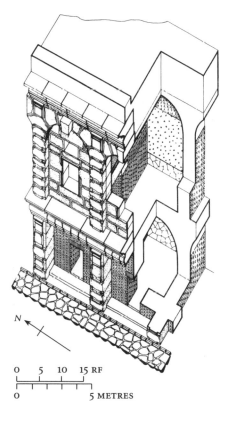

▲ **Fig. 153.** Temple of Deified Claudius. Rusticated travertine arcading on east side of platform (at SS Giovanni e Paolo)

see what they were doing and had room to manœuvre. The difference between the Claudian rustication, which may have been meant to evoke the monuments of Rome's archaic past, and an unfinished building, is the sheer amount of excess stone (the keystones are too large, the undressed blocks too bulging) and the regular pattern of finish versus unfinish.

SS Giovanni e Paolo. Map, Fig. 149 ★

*Piazza di SS Giovanni e Paolo. *Earlier Roman levels*

Founded by the Roman senator Pammachius in the early C5, possibly with money he left on his death in AD 410, the basilica stands on the site of

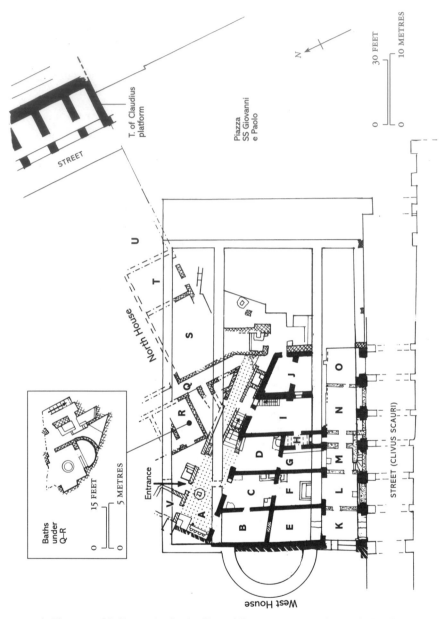

▲ **Fig. 154.** SS Giovanni e Paolo. Plan of Roman structures beneath the church and its monastery

an earlier *titulus* owned by a certain Byzans, commemorating Saints John and Paul (about whom nothing is known for certain but supposedly two brothers, martyred during the reign of the anti-Christian emperor Julian in AD 362). Although the church interior was completely redecorated in the C18, when the large piers lending support to the lateral colonnades were inserted, the building has not lost its basic C5 form. The central nave is 50 RF wide and 150 RF long, ending with an apse 20 RF in diameter at the west end; the side aisles are 25 RF wide, separated from the nave by arcades borne on twelve columns with black granite shafts (16 RF) and Corinthian capitals. A change in planning during construction left no windows in the outer side walls, so the aisles were dark, but in contrast the nave must have been extraordinarily light and airy. It had four tall windows in the apse, thirteen in a clerestory down the long sides, with another thirteen circular (*oculus*) windows set above them, and the east wall was almost entirely open, with five arcades on two storeys (the upper arcades can be seen on the outside). The present porch was added in the C12, but there will have been an earlier porch or forecourt.

Excavations made under the church in 1887–94 and 1913 found not only the pre-C5 *titulus* they were looking for, but a sizeable slice of Caelian hillside life in the C2–C4 AD (Fig. 154). Access is through the door at the far end of the right-hand aisle. The modern stairs bring you down through the foundations of the north outside wall of the C5 church, facing those of its north colonnade, at the end of a narrow courtyard (A) which has a **fountain (nymphaeum)** with a large **mythological painting** (3 × 5 m.) filling the whole west wall. Probably dating from the mid–late C3 AD, the subject of the painting is much discussed. It could be Proserpina (Libera) returning from the Underworld at the beginning of Spring, resting on a small island in company with her mother Ceres and brother Bacchus; alternatively, giving the erotes playing in boats to either side a more than anecdotal significance, she is Venus in her role as protectress of sailors. The rooms to either side (V) and (B) were also richly decorated, probably to serve as dining rooms (V has a mosaic floor; for B, see below).

As can be seen on the plan, though it is difficult to follow on the ground, courtyard (A) was in origin a narrow alley running between the backs of three or four different properties. Rooms Q–U belonged to the upper floors of a wealthy house dating from the AD 120s which was terraced down a steep slope to the north and aligned with the street in front of the platform of the temple of Claudius. Rooms B–J, together with the portico K–O, constituted the ground floor of a fairly smart apartment block, built around AD 200, fronting onto the street on the south side of the church (*Clivus Scauri*), where its façade, flanked by parts of two others, survives to a height of three storeys (Fig. 155). Its principal apartments were on the first floor, reached by a common staircase in the centre (G–H), which is also legible in the placing of the windows on the façade. The adja-

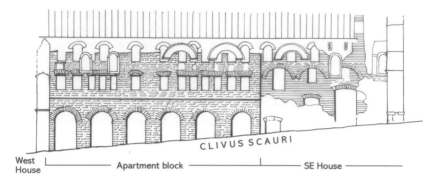

CLIVUS SCAURI

West House | Apartment block | SE House

▲ **Fig. 155.** SS Giovanni e Paolo. Elevation towards the Clivus Scauri

cent property to the east although visible in the street front has only been excavated in small part; it was built about the same time as the north house. Remnants of the house to the west, which lies outside the area covered by the church, have been traced down the hillside; it too dates from the early C2 AD.

From the courtyard (A) you come first into (C), one of the back rooms of the south apartment, off which the room to the right (B) has fine white-ground **paintings** on the upper part of the walls (a frieze of winged genius-like figures surrounded by garlands and various types of large bird) and on the ceiling (erotes harvesting grapes, with more birds). The decoration is close in date and theme to that on the fountain wall in (A), to which the room once opened. The lower zone of the walls was apparently panelled with something perishable (wood) or worth removing (marble, like the floor). In Rooms C–D, F–G, however, the decoration is of very different character and belongs to a later phase, c.300–350, with painted imitations of polychrome marble veneer on the walls and figures in panels on the vaults, best preserved in Room D. There some of the imagery—a praying woman, male figures holding scrolls, pairs of sheep—indicates that by this stage the householders were Christians. The room lies between the stairwell (H) and the courtyard at the back, where a second staircase had been installed. In the second half of the C4 the back staircase was converted into a **martyrs' tomb**: three bodies were buried under it at the east end, the door from room D to the back stair was narrowed and heightened, the stairs were veneered in marble, and a **confessio** made on the landing (P). The paintings around the confessio walls are divided on two registers; on the facing wall, to either side of a small window (which looked out over the tomb), are male figures, both unfortunately headless, wearing the Greek-style *pallium*; beneath, curtains drawn back to either side reveal a youthful Christ in a long tunic, with his hands outstretched in prayer, while two figures prostrate themselves at his feet. On the right-hand wall the upper scene showed the martyrdom, probably by beheading, of three kneeling figures, two men and a woman, blindfolded with their hands bound behind their backs; the corresponding panel on the left wall apparently showed their arrest. They are presumed to be Crispin, Crispianus, and Benedicta, who, according to the legend of St John and St Paul, were also martyred in the reign of Julian, and buried in the house of a Christian named Byzans. Various other modifications were made to the ground floor of the building at about the same time (e.g. extra rooms under the arcaded portico, possible extensions into the neighbouring property to the SE); any predecessor to the C5 church, however, must have been located in the larger apartments on the first floor. When the C5 church was built the location of the confessio under the nave was marked by a well-shaft and an altar, and one of the rooms on the older ground level on the south side was actually accessible by stairs down from the south aisle (Fig. 154: M), having been left as a sort of crypt. It has wallpaintings from the C11/12.

From room I a modern passage returns you to the eastern end of courtyard (A) dividing the south building from the north house, and thence to a corridor (Q) which led between the rooms on the upper level of the north house. Little can be seen of the latter (reportedly decorated with stucco and wall-mosaics) but the corridor leads to a steep staircase down to the basement level of the house and part of a small private **bathhouse** (Fig. 154, inset plan). More was found in 1856 but has been reburied.

Leaving the church, on the east side of the piazza, beside the gates to the Celimontana public park, is another large **Roman building** of the C3 AD, represented by a series of brick-faced concrete walls supporting barrel vaults, apparently the undercroft of a substantial rectangular platform, the main building being laid out on top.

Clivus Scauri

The street down the flank of SS Giovanni e Paolo, spanned to picturesque effect by seven brick arches, once ran straight down to connect with the main road in the valley bottom (part of the Triumphal Way, now Via di S. Gregorio), forming an important link between it and the Caelian Gate. Although its name (Scaurus' Rise) is only attested in medieval sources, that could be ancient too. Scaurus was a quite common Roman surname during the Republic (like many it refers to a physical defect, in this case having swollen ankles). Alongside SS Giovanni e Paolo, whose south wall incorporates much of the C3 street front (Fig. 155), the street front on the other side of the street is also preserved, although both are difficult to see because of the arches. Except possibly the last in line, which may be of C3 date, the arches were added in the Middle Ages (C12), buttressing the south wall of the church.

'Library of Agapetus'. Map, Fig. 149: 6

Just beyond SS Giovanni e Paolo, on the opposite side of the Clivus Scauri, the curving wall starting in brick at the bottom, changing to block-and-brick above, is the apse of a large basilical hall, about 22 m. wide and of unknown length, built at about the same time as SS Giovanni e Paolo or somewhat earlier (late C4). The apse originally had five tall windows, 6 m. (20 RF) high, all since blocked, and traces of similar windows survive in the short section of side wall which still stands on the south. It is possible that the hall later became the library of the monastery of St Gregory, which possessed a valuable collection of Christian texts formed by Pope Agapetus I (AD 535–6), for there are traces of a high-level passage connecting it to the oratory on the slope beyond. Its original function, however, was probably a grand reception/audience chamber in a Late Roman mansion (like that on the Via in Selci, see p. 302), possibly belonging to the Anicii Petronii, the senatorial family of which Pope Gregory was a descendant. He founded his monastery in AD 575 in his own house, which is described as having a courtyard, a nymphaeum and a *triclinium*.

The present church of **S. Gregorio Magno** dates from the C12 (completely remodelled outside in 1629–33, inside in 1725–34); it and its monastery were relocated at the same time, from the slope above and to the east of the 'Library', where they had initially been associated with a church or oratory of St Andrew. Between the library and the present church there are considerable remains of C2 and C3 apartment buildings, and even part of some republican structure (C2 BC), but nothing of the Late Roman or early medieval period.

Down the steps at the bend opposite S. Gregorio, and round to the right, you come to the Via del Parco del Celio, on the right-hand side of which at no. 22 is the **Caelian Antiquarium** (Map, Fig. 149: 7), small but well worth the detour (see p. 403). To the rear the *casino* which houses part of the collections is built on the substructures of the steps which led up to the Temple of Claudius.

Back-tracking to the south of S. Gregorio, the woods beyond the church obscure a valley between it and the Villa Celimontana spur. Wooded in Roman times as well, it contained a grove (*lucus*) and spring (*fons*) inhabited by local water-goddesses called the *Camenae*, and especially sacred to the nymph Egeria, who had consorted with Numa, the first king of Rome, giving him wise counsel. The Vestal Virgins used to come daily to draw their water from the spring, and the grove was still a place of religious cult in the late C4 AD. There were springs all along the slopes on this side of the hill; one was tapped as the source of a small aqueduct, the *Aqua Mercurii* (of Mercury), which ran alongside the Circus Maximus to fill two fountains at the SW corner of the Palatine (near S. Anastasia).

The Beginning of the Via Appia

Piazza di Porta Capena

The modern road junction around the east end of the Circus Maximus was a major intersection in antiquity too, where the republican city wall ran down from the Caelian and over to the Aventine, pierced by the **Capena Gate**, which marked the start of the **Via Appia**. Named for Appius Claudius, the censor who undertook its first metalling as far as Capua in 312 BC, the Via Appia was the oldest and most prestigious of Roman roads, the one on which its armies marched down to Campania and from there the length of South Italy, to the conquest of Sicily, North Africa, and eventually (from Brindisi) the whole of the eastern Mediterranean. Roman generals setting off for war, governors to their provinces, and emperors on state tours were for ever being seen off and welcomed back along it. Almost as soon as the road was made, the first mile or so began to fill up with monuments—temples, altars, honorary arches, and especially tombs, of all shapes and sizes. None of the temples mentioned by ancient writers has been found—there should be one to *Honos* and *Virtus*, possibly dating from 304 BC (just outside the Capena Gate), one to the *Tempestates* (vowed by one of the Scipios in a storm off Corsica in 259 BC and perhaps located near their family tomb, see p. 328), and one to *Mars* (over a mile out, beyond the Aurelianic Walls). There was also an altar to *Fortuna Redux*, celebrating Augustus' safe return from travels in the eastern empire in 19 BC, set up in its own precinct or in that of Honos and Virtus. Few of the tombs at the start of the road have been found either, but they were soon stacked several rows deep and (judging by their successors which spread ever further out from the city) they got more and more extravagant in architectural, eye-catching style as time went by. In AD 203 an enormous billboard—the three-storey **Septizodium** (see p. 144 and Fig. 59)—was placed just beyond the point where the road entered the city gate, at the corner of the Palatine palaces. And in AD 211 Caracalla set about giving the Via Appia its largest show-piece of all, the great thermal baths which were to serve the densely populated slopes of the Aventine and the Caelian on either side.

So as you walk down the Viale delle Terme di Caracalla, which has taken its place, forget the modern (1930s) park-avenue; the Via Appia was only 4 m. wide, its endless stream of travellers submitted to a constant barrage of street-side advertisements.

Baths of Caracalla. Map, Fig. 149: 9 ★★

*Via delle Terme di Caracalla–Via Antonina. *State*

Since the Via Appia frontage was so crammed with monuments of one sort or another, the Baths were actually laid out on a parallel street created

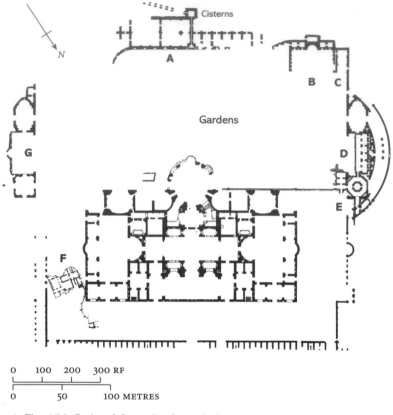

▲ **Fig. 156.** Baths of Caracalla. General plan

specially for the purpose (and literally named New Street). They were the second of the really big Imperial *thermae* of Rome after those of Trajan (see p. 288), capable of accommodating perhaps 10,000 people at once, and are by far the best preserved. Their platform (covering an area of approximately 100,000 m²), the cisterns (with a capacity of about 8.2 million litres) and the central block were built by the emperor Caracalla between AD 211 and 216. The structures around the outer precinct (A–C, D) and (G) were completed somewhat later, though probably before the death of the last Severan emperor Alexander Severus (AD 222–35). The design is based on the same principles as the Baths of Trajan, with the Olympic-sized swimming pool (*natatio*), cold hall (*frigidarium*) and hot room (*caldarium*) all aligned on the central axis, and a series of secondary rooms, including the exercise courts (*palaestrae*), duplicated in a symmetrical arrangement on either side. The principal innovation was the circular shape of the now vanished *caldarium*.

Sheer scale was a major part of the fun. It has been estimated that the project employed on average 9,000 workmen a day for five years, variously engaged in producing the raw materials, transporting them to the site, and the building itself. Right at the back the supporting platform reflects the original ground level but the rest is artificial, in places raised over the top of demolished buildings (part of an early C2 house has been excavated on the SE flank of the central block (F) (inaccessible)). The foundations involved excavating 150,000 m³ of earth, refilled with stone and mortar; the substructures required 280,000 m³ of tufa and mortar, over 15 million pieces of brick, and over 330,000 m³ of landfill; the walls and vaults 210,000 m³ of concrete, 5.6 million pieces of brick and 815,000 complete bricks. The interior was elaborately enriched with architectural schemes requiring 6,300 m³ of marble and granite, including 252 column shafts, sixteen of which were 40–42 RF long, weighing about 50 tons each.

Once built the whole complex continued to function into the C6. Diocletian made some repairs around AD 300 and a little later Constantine added an apse to the great *caldarium*. In the early C5 there were reportedly still 1,600 seats available for bathers. Brickstamps attest further restoration work under Theodoric (AD 493–526). Although it is often assumed that the baths ceased to function after their aqueduct (the *Antoniniana*, a special branch of the Claudia/Marcia) was cut by the Goths in AD 537, it is more likely that they fell gradually out of use in the C6. By the C7 the eastern corner of the precinct was used as a cemetery, probably associated with the adjacent church of SS Nereus and Achilleus, which is first recorded in AD 595. In the Middle Ages the ruins became a quarry for marbles and other materials (there were 100 tons of iron in the vaults alone); some of the Harpocrates capitals from the outer precinct were used in S. Maria in Trastevere in the 1130s, while others, decorated with winged thunderbolts, from the palaestras of the central block, are to be found in the Duomo at Pisa. The worst depredations took place under Pope Paul III (Farnese 1534–49) who removed all the remaining columns and some gigantic pieces of statuary, which became the showpieces of the Farnese palace: the Farnese Bull, the Farnese Hercules (now in Naples). In the early C17 the site became a summer retreat for the students at the Collegio Romano, who used to play ball in the *natatio*. From the 1930s until 1994 the summer season of the Rome opera house was performed on a vast stage set between the two standing piers of the *caldarium*.

Visit: To the rear of the church of SS Nereus and Achilleus a set of modern steps leads up on to the precinct level (now a car park), through the collapsed vaults of the front of the terrace towards the street, which was lined with shops and bars. The great concrete wall facing you belongs to the central block of the baths. It had four entrances (all now barred), once framed by columned porches, some traces of which survive above the second entrance from the right. The outer two entrances led through a tripartite hall into the colonnaded courts of the *palaestra*. The inner two each opened into a vestibule with the swimming pool (*natatio*) on one side and the dressing rooms (*apodyteria*) on the other, and the main axis of the baths ahead.

The **modern entrance** is to the right of the main block. Given the current programme of conservation most of the hot rooms along the SW side of the main block may be out of bounds. From the west corner, Fig. 157 (1), where the outer angle of the room is missing, you come in to the **palaestra** (2), originally open to the sky but surrounded on three sides by porticoes of Corinthian columns (25 RF high) which had grey Troad granite shafts and capitals decorated with winged thunderbolts. The flat portico roofs formed a promenade terrace and were paved in black and white mosaic with sea monsters and dolphins (fragments are propped against the walls). Under the porticoes the ceiling was lined with glass mosaic and the walls with marble veneer. The floor was decorated in a fish scale pattern mosaic, of alternating red and green porphyry, Numidian yellow and various grey marbles. The open court was also paved with mosaic in the same coloured stones in geometric shapes imitating marble slabs, with a border of acanthus scrolls in green porphyry on a white background. The suite of three **exhedras** (3–5) had their walls veneered in

▼ **Fig. 157.** Baths of Caracalla. Restored plan of central bath-block. a. Farnese Hercules. b. 'Latin' Hercules. c. Farnese Bull

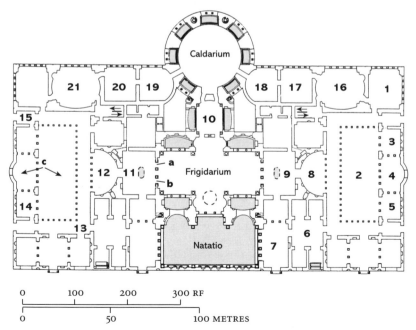

marble up to the springing of their concrete cross-vaults, of which the scars are visible. Either in the court or the central exhedra there was once a large statue group composed of a marble island, a ship and figures. Through the door in the east corner, room (6) is the dressing room (*apodyterium*), once roofed with a double cross-vault about 20 m. high, lit by windows set above the vaults of the rooms on either side, all paved in black mosaic with white geometric designs. The staircase in the north corner led to roof terraces above and over the tripartite hall to the west. Room (7) was one of the main entrance halls. Its concrete cross-vault, best preserved on the NE/NW sides, was lined with tiles and decorated with mosaic, once attached by large iron rods, robbed in the Middle Ages, leaving a regular pattern of holes. The very coarse mosaic of green porphyry cubes on the floor belongs to a later C3 or C4 restoration. The travertine plinths on the east side of the hall mark the positions of four columns 36 RF (10.6 m.) high, beyond which steps led down into the open-air swimming pool (*natatio*). The pool was about a metre deep and overlooked by a great stage-like façade on the NE wall, designed in a typically extravagant Severan manner, with five different sizes of architectural order. Four 42 RF columns with grey Egyptian granite shafts divided the whole into three vertical bays. Each bay contained six statue niches within two superimposed orders, the lower probably with Carystian green shafts, the upper in Numidian yellow. The niches in their turn were framed by small aediculas (all lost). On the opposite side two large semicircular bays, framed by giant grey Egyptian granite columns, flanked the principal entrance to the pool.

Returning to the palaestra, the semicircular exhedra (8) formed an elegant vestibule to the main cold halls. It had glass mosaics on the vault (the impressions of the tesserae can just be made out), marble panelling on the walls and an elaborately coloured mosaic on the floor, now in the Vatican, ex-Lateran collection (Fig. 158), showing athletes, boxers, discus throwers, wrestlers, and their trainers. The first room in line beyond (9) had a large fountain in the centre in the shape of an oval wine vat, 6 m. long, made of grey Egyptian granite (it and its pair from room (11) are now fountains in the Piazza Farnese). In the north corner, about half-way up the wall is a small piece of fluted Numidian yellow marble, the only survivor from the upper registers of veneer. Two 36 RF columns with grey granite shafts once stood in the doorway to the great cold hall, the *frigidarium*. Measuring 59 × 24 m. (200 × 82 RF) and 34 m. (116 RF) to the crowns of its three cross vaults, the hall had three bays on either side, marked by four columns with 40–42 RF grey granite shafts, those at the four corners occupied by plunge baths, fed by fountains pouring from the niches around them. The entrance to each pool was decorated with two columns with red porphyry shafts and figured composite capitals representing Hercules (Fig. 159), Bacchus, Venus, Mars, and others. The central bay on the north side has a circular pool in the middle of it, beyond which

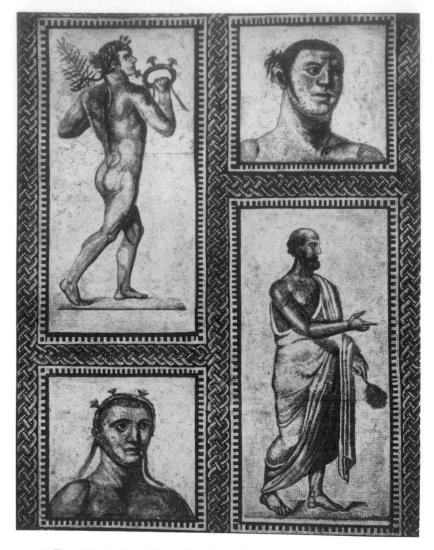

▲ **Fig. 158.** Baths of Caracalla. Mosaic floor (detail) with athletes and their trainer (Vatican Museums, ex-Lateran collection)

two red porphyry columns stood at the entrance to the natatio. One of the shallow recesses in the bay possibly housed a colossal gilded marble statue of Aesculapius, the god of healing, whose head is now in the Museo Nazionale Romano, ex-Planetarium (see p. 400). The corresponding bay on the other side led to the intermediary warm room, the *tepidarium* (10), its entrance marked by the two small, heat-retaining doorways, with a fountain niche set in the wall between them. At the SE end of the frigidar-

ium, before room 11, once stood two colossal statues of Hercules, one now
in the Naples Archaeological Museum (Fig. 160). The plan and decoration
of the whole SE side mirrors that on the NW: more of the mosaic floor
under the palaestra colonnades can be seen at the north corner (13),
where a section of the marble architrave and frieze of plant scroll and
erotes has been restored. A small area of richly painted stuccowork
remains high up on the NE wall of room 14. Placed in the centre of the
palaestra court, or in the central exhedra, was a famous marble statue
group, known nowadays as the **Farnese Bull** (Fig. 161), showing Zetos
and Amphion, sons of Antiope, tying Dirce to the horns of a raging bull in
revenge for her cruelty to their mother. Carved, reputedly out of a single
block, by two virtuoso sculptors called Apollonios and Tauriskos for an
unknown commission on Rhodes in the late C2 or C1 BC, it stood 3.7 m.
(12½ RF) high and was fitted out as a fountain, so that water bubbled up
out of the rocky ground and ran down the sides of the base. Taken from
Rhodes to Rome, it entered the collection of Asinius Pollio (76 BC–AD 4)
and was first put on public display in the Hall of Liberty (see p. 240).

▼ **Fig. 159.** Baths of Caracalla. Composite capital with figure of Hercules

▲ **Fig. 160.** Baths of Caracalla. The 'Farnese Hercules' (10 RF high) from the Frigidarium (Naples, Archaeological Museum)

An exhibition installed in room 15 (previously a side entrance) contains wall paintings from the early C2 house buried under the eastern corner of the precinct (see Fig. 156: F).

Retrace your steps to room 1 and take the first possible turn to the left along the façade of the main block. The hot rooms to either side of the great circular caldarium (16–21) offered a range of different kinds of dry heat. Their missing front walls were composed almost entirely of glass, taking advantage of natural solar energy. The surrounding surfaces on the outer façade wall were finished with coloured glass mosaic, so that the

▼ **Fig. 161.** Baths of Caracalla. The 'Farnese Bull': colossal statue group from the eastern palaestra (now in Naples, Archaeological museum)

whole block will have shimmered in the afternoon sun. All that survives of the caldarium proper (which equalled the Pantheon rotunda in height and was three-quarters its diameter) are two piers of brick-faced concrete 35 m. high. It contained seven plunge baths and the domed ceiling was probably lined with gilded sheet bronze.

In line with the caldarium on the SW side of the precinct (in front of the cisterns) was a stadium-shaped structure with tiered seating (A). A stade long (178 m. = 600 RF) it may actually have served for foot-races and other athletic events. The (heavily restored) rectangular hall lined with niches to the right (B) may have been a library; the broad staircase beside it (C) was another main entrance to the baths from the Aventine hill behind. Along the NW side of the precinct lies a suite of three halls with a shallowly curving promenade on the outside. Apart from being a richly decorated retreat the central hall (D) was designed to display a large statue in its apse, perhaps a colossal image of the emperor. Over the railing to the right of the hall you can catch a glimpse down into one end of a large subterranean *mithraeum* (E), installed soon after the baths were constructed, in part of their great network of underground passages. Another installation nearby was a watermill, for grinding grain, making use of the abundant supplies of water.

On the other side of the modern intersection between the Viale delle Terme di Caracalla and the Via Druso, the line of the Via Appia survives as the Via di Porta San Sebastiano, from which the Via Latina (now the Via di Porta Latina) forks off at an oblique angle to the left. The Via Latina, like the Via Appia, went to Capua, but took a more inland route. It, too, attracted large numbers of tombs (a particularly interesting group which survives 6 km. out, at its fourth milestone, has been turned into an archaeological park, a short walk from the metro Line A, Arco di Travertino). For the first 500 m. after the two roads fork, the whole area between is riddled with tombs.

Tomb of the Scipios. Map, Fig. 149: 10

*Via di Porta San Sebastiano no. 9. *Comune*

Dating from the C3 and C2 BC and containing the burials of six generations of the *Cornelii Scipiones*, one of the most powerful aristocratic families in mid-late republican Rome, the tomb was first discovered in 1614 and explored further in 1780 and 1926–7. Although it probably had some suitably visible structure on top, where the C17 farmhouse stands now, it did not actually front on to the Via Appia but on to a side road linking the Appia and the Via Latina, where it could take advantage of an outcrop of tufa (*cappellaccio*), perhaps exploiting an earlier stone quarry. A main gallery down the centre has three branches on either side, which connect

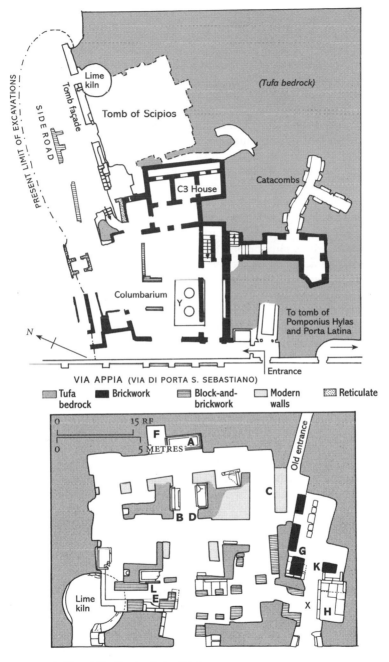

▲ **Fig. 162.** Tomb of the Scipios.
(*Top*) General site plan   (*Bottom*) Plan of interior of tomb

with two outer galleries parallel to the first. Four internal piers, subsequently invaded by cuttings for further burials, were left to support the bedrock above. On the west side is another gallery, at a slightly different angle, with a separate entrance. The Cornelii Scipiones were unusual (and rather pretentious) not only in choosing to have their tomb rock-cut in the Etruscan manner but also in preferring inhumation in stone sarcophagi when most of their contemporaries practised cremation.

The earliest burial is the sarcophagus at the far end of the main gallery (A), which contained Lucius Cornelius Scipio Barbatus, consul in 298 BC. Made of *peperino* tufa (that on display, like all the others, is a replica, the originals are in the Vatican, Chiaramonti Museum), the sarcophagus is the only one to be decorated, with an ornate Doric frieze along the top of the box and Ionic volutes at either end of the lid, modelled on sarcophagi fashionable in the Greek cities of South Italy and Sicily. An inscription in verse added on the box in the early C2 BC extols his virtues: 'a brave and wise man, whose physical beauty was equal to his valour, he was consul, censor, and aedile amongst you. He captured Taurasia and Cisauna in Samnium (central Italy); he subdued the whole of Lucania (South Italy) and brought back hostages.'

In the gallery immediately in front of Barbatus were buried his son (B) also called Barbatus (bearded), who conquered Corsica, becoming consul in 259 BC and censor in 258, and a great-great grandson (D), who died at the age of 20, in the 150s BC. The latter's mother, Paulla Cornelia, wife of (Scipio) Hispallus, was buried in a makeshift sarcophagus squeezed into the wall above and behind (A); her inscription has been mounted on the wall of the recess to the left, which contained (F) Scipio Asiagenus Comatus, aged 16, named after his uncle Scipio Asiaticus/Asiagenus who had won a great victory in Asia Minor in 189 BC. (F)'s father, L. Cornelius Scipio, quaestor in 167 BC had died aged 33 in 160 BC and was buried at the other side of the tomb (E). While (A) and (B), the earliest, were hewn out of solid stone, the others were constructed out of four slabs. The slab mounted on the (modern brick) wall at the far right (C) belonged to the front of the sarcophagus of P. Cornelius Scipio, son of Scipio Africanus (defeater of Hannibal): 'you wore the spiked helmet of the *flamen Dialis* (high priest of Jupiter); death made all your achievements short-lived: honour, fame, valour, glory, and genius. If you had lived longer, you would easily have outdone the glory of your ancestors. So the earth willingly takes you to her bosom.' He was *augur* in 180 BC and is known to have composed speeches and stories in Greek. Of poor health, as his epitaph makes clear, he died young, but his adopted son Scipio Aemilianus (second son of L. Aemilius Paullus) went on to become a hugely successful general in the 150–130s BC.

Although Aemilianus' own burial is not attested, he was probably responsible for a major remodelling which took place in about 140–130 BC. The tomb was getting very crowded by then: although only eight sarcophagi have survived, the cuttings around the walls and into the piers add up to about thirty. The subsidiary gallery was opened to the right (X), where a very large sarcophagus (H) was installed for C. Cornelius Scipio Hispanus, who was praetor in 139 BC and probably died shortly before 130 BC. After listing his public offices (praetor, curule aedile, quaestor, military tribune, juridical and religious magistracies) his epitaph reads: 'I incorporated the virtues of my family in my own behaviour. I fathered sons and I equalled the deeds of my father. I gained the praise of my ancestors, who were proud of having produced me. My public honour has ennobled the lineage.' The size of sarcophagus perhaps provided for other members of the family to be added later. Of another large sarcophagus on the opposite side of the gallery (G) we know only that it was made towards the end of the C2 BC, for the wife of a Scipio.

At this time the tomb also acquired a monumental tufa façade, whose podium survives, with an arch framing the entrance (or vent) to the subsidary gallery, which was probably matched for the sake of symmetry by another on the far side of the central entrance. The podium wall is covered with several layers of plaster with traces of paintings on military themes. Of the upper register, only the footings of some semicolumns survive; one reconstruction proposes niches between the semicolumns, to contain three statues which are mentioned by ancient writers: Scipio Africanus the Elder, his brother Publius and their favourite poet Quintus Ennius (239–169 BC).

According to Cicero, who was a great admirer of Scipio Aemilianus in particular, the Scipios ceased to bury in the tomb at the beginning of the C1 BC. By the early C1 AD their line was extinguished anyway and another branch, the Cornelii Lentuli, appear to have taken over care of the monument, some of whom had their cremated remains deposited there (L) and (K). Between the tomb and the main road a large **columbarium** (dovecote) tomb (Y) was discovered in 1926. It is a type of tomb common in the zone between the Via Appia and Via Latina, mostly made in the early C1 AD for the huge slave (and ex-slave) families of imperial and other wealthy households. This one is quite well preserved, with five levels of semicircular niches, each containing two pottery cinerary urns, with more around the two masonry columns which supported the roof, providing for 470 burials. Unfortunately they are all anonymous, so there is no way of telling whether it was connected with the Cornelii Lentuli family.

By the C3 AD, in any event, both the Scipios' tomb and the columbarium were apparently forgotten; a three-storey house in brick-faced concrete was built on the hill above, with an entrance leading off the main road. Traces of black-and-white mosaic floors and simple wall paintings are preserved in the rooms at ground level. Under the pressure of population in the city (still growing apace in the C3) and with the attraction of the Baths of Caracalla not far away many more such properties probably spread along the main road filling any available space in amongst the older cemeteries. Under the adjoining property to the south there is a small catacomb.

Before leaving, ask the custodians if you can visit the **Columbarium of Pomponius Hylas**, which lies in the public gardens behind the Scipios' tomb, close to the Porta Latina (Map, Fig. 149: 11). Found in 1831, the superstructure has gone but the small subterranean burial chamber is exceptionally well-preserved, its elaborately architectural interior brightly decorated in glass mosaic and painted stucco. It dates from around AD 20 and takes its name from the inscription in mosaic beneath the niche in the wall over the foot of the stairs: *Cn. Pomponius Hylas* and his wife *Pomponia Cn. l. Vitale*, but was probably initially built for the two people whose ashes were deposited in the central niche in the apse, named in the marble plaque beneath: *Granius Nestor* and *Vinileia Hedone*. Eighteen other depositions are identified, from which it seems that the tomb was one of the burial clubs run by subscription among friends or professional colleagues or as a commercial enterprise by a speculator. The niche on the left-hand wall was remade in the later C1 AD.

Even if the columbarium cannot be seen, it is worth walking over to the **Latina Gate** and the stretch of the **late imperial city walls** to the north and south of it, either before or after visiting the Appia Gate (Porta San Sebastiano). Of lesser status than the latter, the Latina Gate has kept much of its original shape, contemporary with the first phase of the walls (AD 271–5), a single passageway, faced in travertine or simply brick, set in a blank brick-faced wall and flanked by two semicircular towers. Under Honorius in AD 401–3, when the whole circuit was extensively remodelled and doubled in height, the passageway was reduced in size, lined and framed on the exterior with marble (its keystone bears one of the Christian monograms typical of Honorius' builders), and the wall above it was heightened in travertine with the addition of five windows. The line of the earlier passage can be made out in the stonework. The semicircular tower on the left is largely of the late C3, with no windows, only arrow-slits; that on the right was completely rebuilt in AD 402 and then repaired several times since. A square foundation around the foot of the right-hand tower may represent an aborted Honorian project to sheath the lower part in stone (as on the Appia Gate). The blocking of all the windows probably took place during the Gothic siege in AD 537–8. Slots at the outer end of the passageway were to guide an iron portcullis which could be brought down in front of the gates themselves—double doors which opened inwards—with a fortified court and a second gate on the inside (demolished in the C18). Between the Latina and Appia Gate, there should be twelve towers spaced at fairly regular 30 m. (100 RF) intervals but the fourth is missing. Most of those which are still standing were rebuilt, together with large sections of the facing of the curtain wall, in the C15 and C17; the older brickwork survives in places in the lower zones.

Appia Gate and Museum of the Walls. ★
Map, Fig. 149: 12

Via di Porta San Sebastiano. Comune (*museum)

Renamed in the Middle Ages after the important extra-mural church of St Sebastian which lies about 2.4 km. further out (see p. 412), the gate is the finest of the entire circuit, as refashioned by Honorius in AD 401–3. The two 28 m. high towers, square for the first 18 m., round for the upper floors, were previously thought to represent two phases (the square bastions being reinforcements to towers which were originally round right down to the ground) but are now believed to be of a single build, together with the curtain wall between them. All three components are faced to an equal height with solid blocks of marble, mostly obtained from dismantled tombs. The small round bosses which appear on some of the blocks were left to show how much dressing had been required to adapt the stones to their new setting; they should all have been removed in the final finishing, but often were not (especially on the eastern face of the eastern tower); some were carved into little crosses in relief. Passing to the inside of the gateway, the keystone of the arch bears an inscription in Greek thanking saints Conon and George and God's mercy for the (temporary) defeat of the Goths in AD 403. The walling on the right flank of the gateway belongs to the earliest phase of the gate, when it had two passages, one for the Via Appia and one for a pedestrian side track which ran parallel to it.

A second arch about 20 m. behind the gate goes by the name of the '**Arch of Drusus**' but was actually built in the early C3 AD, embellishing the point at which the *Aqua Antoniniana*, the aqueduct supplying the Baths of Caracalla, crossed over the Via Appia. An arch in honour of Drusus (father of the emperor Claudius) was set up on the Via Appia after his death in 9 BC, however, and may have stood very close by, for the foundations of another arch, of suitable date, were seen during roadworks in 1931 about midway between the existing arch and the gate (see Fig. 163). This intermediary arch was later incorporated into the Honorian gate as part of an inner court

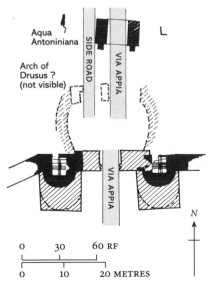

▼ **Fig. 163.** Appia Gate. Plan. Aurelianic phase in black, Honorian hatched

protecting the gate from the rear and therefore was probably still standing in the C8, when a series of inscriptions were transcribed, naming Drusus several times over. Two other arches are recorded on the Via Appia, honouring the deified emperors Trajan (died AD 117) and Lucius Verus (died AD 169). Their locations are not known, but all may have been in this vicinity, close to a temple of Mars whose site is also uncertain, but may lie on the left just outside the Appia Gate.

A **museum** installed in the western tower and the gallery over the gate has models and other information illustrating the development of the walls. The round tower room once contained the winches to operate the portcullis. Windows on this level and along the gallery over the gate were designed for catapults and the roof formed a platform for major artillery (*ballistae*). An interesting collection of plaster casts displays the variety of decorative motifs found in the C3 and C5 brickwork: circles, loops, diamond patterns, arrows, Greek and Latin crosses, chi-rho monograms. They are builders' marks—the 'signatures' of the many different gangs of workmen employed in building the walls. The black-and-white mosaics set in the floors of the tower rooms and corridors are not ancient; like the spiral stairs and lift-shaft at the entrance to the museum, they date from 1942–3, when the secretary of the Fascist party made the gate into his private office.

Entry to the museum entitles you also to the **'Passeggiata'**—a 380 m. walk along the walls themselves, as far as the Viale Cristoforo Colombo. The walkway you walk along, well-preserved between the first

▼ **Fig. 164.** Aurelianic Walls. Restored view showing original and Honorian phases

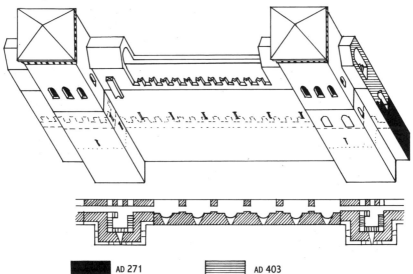

AD 271   AD 403

six towers and again between the eleventh and twelfth, dates from Honorius' rebuild of AD 401–3, like the Appia gate. Its floor level coincides with the parapet level of the initial Aurelianic phase (AD 271–5), when the walls were only 7.6 m. (26 RF) high, with a simple crenellation on top. Honorius heightened the wall, with proper arrow-slits for bowmen on the first level, and a gallery roof on top, where stone-throwing artillery (*onagri*) could be mounted. Upper floors were added to the towers as well, with catapult platforms on top. As now, there was an empty zone behind the wall to allow the troops to move from one position to another as quickly as possible. Unfortunately, it is no longer permitted to walk on the very top, or to ascend the twelfth tower, but the view over the gardens and fields inside gives a good idea of what most of the area inside the walls looked like from the Middle Ages until the late C19.

Via Appia Antica. Map, Fig. 165

Beyond the Gate the ancient Appian Way continued to be lined with tombs spreading further and further out from the city into open countryside, in front of great villas, market gardens and farms, intermingled with staging posts and taverns. These days, however, a walk along the first 2.5 km. of the Via Appia Antica is not recommended. There is little to see except high boundary walls, and since there is no pedestrian sidewalk the continuous traffic is a menace to life as well as lungs. If you do not have a car, there is a fairly frequent bus service on Sundays which can be caught at the Porta San Sebastiano and will take you all the way to the 'Villa di Massenzio'. There are earlier stops if you want to visit the **Catacombs of St Callistus** (p. 410) and/or those of **St Sebastian** (p. 412), from which you can then proceed on foot. On other days, take the 218 bus, which goes along the Via Ardeatina, getting off at the Largo Fosse Ardeatine (Catacombs of Domitilla) and then cross over to the Via Appia along the Vicolo delle Sette Chiese, which joins the Via Appia just before St Sebastian.

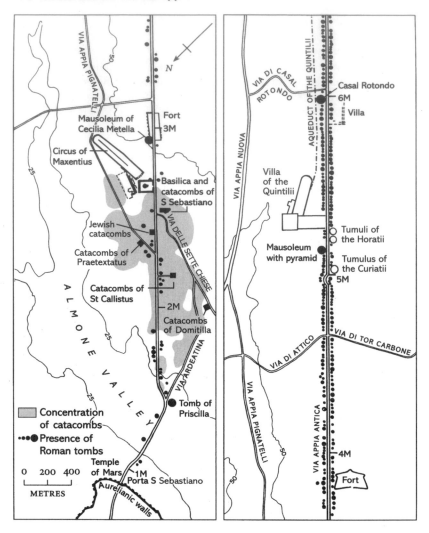

▲ **Fig. 165.** Via Appia. Site map from the Porta S. Sebastiano to Casal Rotondo
(6th milestone)
(*Left*) The first 4 km. (*Right*) The next 4 km

Villa and Circus of Maxentius. Fig. 166 ★

*Via Appia Antica, 3 km. *Comune*

In the dip between the church of St Sebastian and the tomb of Cecilia
Metella which commands the crest of the hill beyond, the whole of the
area on the left-hand side of the road belonged at the beginning of the

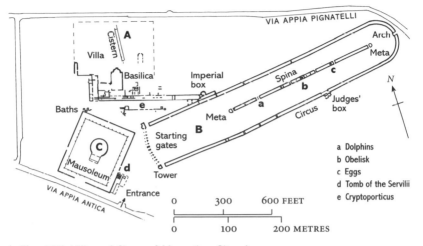

▲ **Fig. 166.** Villa and Circus of Maxentius. Site plan

C4 AD to the emperor Maxentius, who rose to power in AD 306 but was defeated by Constantine in AD 312. On a slight hill about 100 m. away from the road there is a suite of palatial-style buildings on a terrace (A), connected by a long corridor to a full-scale circus for chariot racing set in the valley beside it (B). In front, a mausoleum occupied the centre of a large precinct laid out beside the Via Appia (C).

The **Circus** is oriented almost exactly east–west, with twelve starting gates at the west end, flanked by the two tall towers which face you as you enter the site. Constructed, like the rest of the complex, in concrete faced with block-and-brickwork (*opus vittatum*) and three storeys (16 m.) high, the towers contained the mechanism for raising the gates, which were set out on a curve between them, six to either side of a central arch. Each starting box was wide enough to hold a chariot-and-four. The track, excavated in 1825 and in 1960 (at the time of the Rome Olympics), is among the largest known, 503 m. long and varying in width from 75 to 79 m.: almost as large as that of the Circus Maximus in Rome (see p. 264), but that could take six-horse and other exceptional teams (such as camels or elephants). The barrier down the middle (the *spina*), once veneered in white marble, is precisely 1,000 RF (296 m.) long. The outer walls of the track are not straight nor parallel with it, being carefully designed so that the track was no wider at any point than it need be (ideally 30 m. wide for twelve teams) but gave a bit more space at the starting line and after the first turn. The spina has been extensively restored—but on reasonable grounds—and is our best evidence for the appearance of that in the Circus Maximus as well. On the rounded platforms at each end, where the chariots turned seven times in the course of the normal three-mile race, were the *metae*, three tall cones with marble eggs on top (see Fig. 127 on p. 265). In the centre (b) was an **obelisk** (removed in 1648 to adorn the Four Rivers' fountain in the Piazza Navona, p. 211). The two halves of the rest of the length contained a water channel (the *euripus*) divided into four sections, where each faction stationed attendants who would scoop up water to throw over their teams in the course of the race. Set on columns at (a) and (c) there were the **dolphins** and the **eggs**, both means of counting the laps, the eggs being removed one by one as the laps were completed, the dolphins (of bronze) were apparently pivoted, turning tail up or tail down. Statues of various kinds stood or sat at other points, and on the edge of the basins. The excavators found pieces of figures of Hercules, Victory, Venus, Bacchus and an Amazon.

Three-fifths of the way down the right-hand track, is the **judges' box**, which overlooked the finishing line. The **imperial box** (*pulvinar*) had the best view of the race as a whole—the start, the sprint down the left-hand track and the crashing turns at the east end. The rest of the seating, capable of holding about 10,000 spectators, was supported on a single continuous concrete vault, a quarter-circle in cross-section. Most of the vaulting has collapsed, perhaps because it was very lightly built, incorporating globular terracotta storage jars in a technique characteristic of the early C4 (best seen to the right of the triumphal arch at the far east end). Under the archway is an inscription recording the excavations by Antonio Nibby in 1825, and a facsimile of the **inscription** which he found, probably from a statue base, identifying the site with Maxentius (it had previously been attributed to Caracalla): 'to the Deified Romulus, of most noble memory, twice consul, son of our lord Maxentius, invincible and perpetual Augustus, grandson of the deified Maximian the Elder and the deified Maximian the Younger, twice Augustus.' Romulus died, aged 4, in AD 309; one of the Maximians was Maxentius' father and rival, who committed suicide in AD 310; the other was Galerius who died in AD 311.

Of the **villa** on the hill overlooking the left-hand side of the circus, partly explored in 1963–5, very little can be seen because of the vegetation. It took over the platform of a late republican villa, re-developed and greatly enlarged in the mid C2 AD, with a two-storey cryptoporticus along the SE front, which the Maxentian builders retained and extended to the east to meet up with the circus. The central component in the new buildings was a **basilical hall** (A), 112 × 66 RF (33 × 19.5 m.), with an apse at the far end, central heating ducts in the walls, and an outer hall across the entrance forming a vestibule or ante-chamber. Such halls were a feature of late Roman aristocratic residences (as on the Esquiline, p. 302 and the Caelian, p. 318), used for ceremonial purposes of one kind or another (official duties, audiences, receptions, banquets etc.).

Beside the side entrance to the precinct of the mausoleum (d) are the remains of an older **tomb** (named since the C16 'of the *Servilii*'), in the form of a cylindrical drum on a square base (Fig. 167). It was stripped of all its outer facing stones and used as a lime-burners' kiln in the Middle Ages but inside still preserves its cruciform mortuary chamber surrounded by an **annular corridor** (stuccoed and painted), not unlike the arrangement at the core of the mausoleum of Augustus (see p.181) with which it is broadly contemporary (end of C1 BC). The corridor had a ritual function in the Roman cult of the dead, related to the circumambulation performed at funerals, especially those of military leaders (see box, p. 193, and Fig. 88). Those visiting the tomb to pay their respects would walk round the corridor in one direction when entering, and walk round in the opposite direction before leaving. Not all tombs had such corridors; they are a particular feature of the Augustan period and possibly a mark of consular rank.

The huge **mausoleum** which Maxentius sited alongside 300 years later was also essentially a circular tomb (Fig. 168). The plan suggests a Pantheon-like superstructure, of which nothing remains and in fact may never have been built, but is possibly featured on Maxentius' coinage (see p. 110, Fig. 44). A C19 farmhouse obscures the front steps and floor of the porch but the vaulted interior of the burial chamber behind (long used as

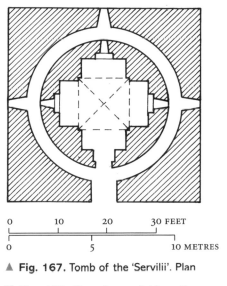

0   10   20   30 FEET

0   5   10 METRES

▲ **Fig. 167.** Tomb of the 'Servilii'. Plan

▼ **Fig. 168.** Mausoleum of Maxentius. Plan of basement level.

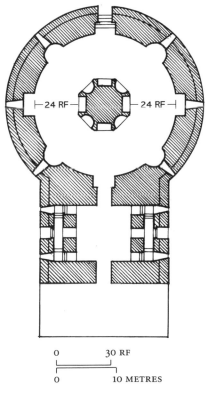

├─24 RF─┤   ├─ 24 RF ─┤

0   30 RF

0   10 METRES

stabling) is largely intact and a very impressive space. 23.6 m. (80 RF) in internal diameter, it consists of an annular corridor 24 RF wide around an octagonal pier 32 RF wide (each face 12 RF long), with alternately semi-circular and rectangular niches to contain sarcophagi round the pier and the outer wall. It had an entrance at the rear. No trace of a floor, nor any decoration survives, reinforcing the likelihood that the building was never finished. The cloister-like precinct enclosing the tomb also shows signs that work was interrupted: neither the walls nor the surviving fragments of the cross-vaults which covered the porticoes had yet been plastered. Its fourth side, towards the road, may have been half open, to allow access to the construction site.

Maxentius' reasons for choosing this location, and how the circus fits into the picture, are not easily explained, but it is possible that the function of the entire complex was primarily funerary. Inscriptions and other finds suggest that the site either adjoined or actually formed part of an estate which had once belonged to Annia Regilla, a relative of the emperor Marcus Aurelius and wife of the Greek millionaire Herodes Atticus. When Regilla died in AD 160, her husband consecrated the whole estate to the gods of the underworld and her memory, renaming it *Triopion*, and making elaborate arrangements for her funerary cult to be celebrated in association with a sanctuary dedicated to the goddess Ceres and the deified empress Faustina. We do not know whether the mausoleum Maxentius built was intended specifically for Romulus in AD 309 or Maximian in AD 310 or more generally for the whole family; a mausoleum of very similar type was built in *c*. AD 300 at a large villa belonging to the family of the Gordians (briefly emperors in AD 238–44) on the Via Praenestina (Tor de'Schiavi) and around AD 326 another, at the heart of a great Imperial estate on the Via Labicana (Tor Pignattara), where Helena, mother of Constantine was buried in a great porphyry sarcophagus in *c*. AD 330. Interestingly these other two are both associated not with circuses but circus-shaped funerary basilicas (like S. Sebastiano). Circus-games had strong dynastic connotations; several emperors built full-scale circuses at their birthplaces (the Julian family further along the Via Appia at Bovillae, Nero at Antium, Antoninus Pius at Lorium). The ritual associ-ation of chariot-racing with cycles of life and death is also bound up with the worship of the Sun (amongst many other gods), but it is not likely that Maxentius was emulating the young emperor Elagabalus (reg. AD 218–22), whose palatial summer residence near the Porta Maggiore (see p. 21) had included a huge circus. Elagabalus identified himself with the Syrian sun-god of the same name and his circus (together with an adjacent temple) had been for his own fanatical self-worship.

Tomb of Caecilia Metella ★

*Via Appia Antica. *Castle and interior (free)*

The Via Appia's best-known landmark, dominating the skyline just before its third milestone, the tomb consists of a cylindrical drum on a square base 29.64 m. (100 RF) in diameter and 11 m. high. Mentally remove the crenellated brick wall from the top, which was added when the tomb became but one tower in a large fortress built across the road by the Caetani family in the late C12. The original roof was probably a shallow stone cone.

Most of the travertine facing blocks have been robbed from the base, exposing its rough concrete core, but are well preserved on the drum, with their edges drafted in the Greek manner, up to and above a cornice moulding which protects a decorative frieze carved in blocks of Greek (Pentelic) marble with a motif of bulls' skulls and garlands. On the side towards the road, the frieze is interrupted by a larger relief panel showing military trophies, surmounting the dedicatory inscription 'CAECILIA Q(uinti) CRETICI F(ilia)

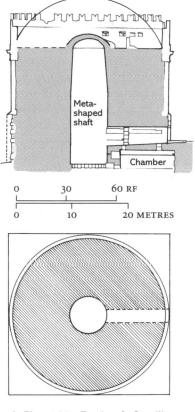

Meta-shaped shaft

Chamber

0   30   60 RF

0   10   20 METRES

▲ **Fig. 169.** Tomb of Caecilia Metella. Plan and section

METELLA CRASSI' (Caecilia Metella, daughter of Quintus Caecilius Metellus Creticus, wife of Crassus). The location and size of the tomb argue for her high social status; the design, materials and artistic quality suggest a date in the last quarter of the C1 BC. Her father was probably the consul of 69 BC, who celebrated a triumph in 62 for his victories in Crete (hence his surname); her husband, who presumably built the tomb, may have been Marcus Licinius Crassus, who sided with Octavian (Augustus), was consul in 30 BC and awarded a triumph in 27 BC. His grandfather of the same name, a powerful contemporary of Sulla, Caesar and Pompey, had made a huge fortune in the 80s BC and the family remained exceedingly rich.

Inside, the core of the podium and drum is solid except for a narrow passage leading to a tall central shaft, tapered in shape like a circus turning-post (*meta*) and capped with a small domed vault. The fine brickwork lining the shaft walls is among the earliest examples of the technique in Rome, made of very thin tiles, sawn into shape and with their edges ground smooth. Off the bottom of the shaft in the podium of the tomb, underneath the entrance passage, lies the mortuary chamber proper.

The fragments of inscriptions and sculpture set in the walls of the castle courtyard and displayed in the small **antiquarium** were brought in for safe keeping from all along the Via Appia. The **panoramic view** from the tomb roof is spectacular: north over the circus of Maxentius and towards the walls of Rome, east to the Via Latina and the aqueducts still marching across the plain through the suburbs of modern Rome; haze allowing, you may also see the Sabine hills around Tivoli and Palestrina.

Further along the Via Appia

Continuing along the Via Appia Antica, past the junction with the Via di Cecilia Metella (where the 660 bus runs across to the Via Appia Nuova and the metro line A Colli Albani station) a short stretch of old basalt paving survives, and about 400 m. further on the road finally acquires the picturesque character for which it was so famous in the C18. For the next 4 km. as far as the sixth milestone at Casal Rotondo, the roadsides are open, lined with pines and cypress trees and the ruins of tomb after tomb in all shapes and sizes. Most took the form of towers or houses or small temples, but there are some more cylindrical monuments of the Servilii/Caecilia Metella type. Considerable restoration work was done in the C19 and early C20, not all of it very reliable; some of the little monuments which pop up here and there supporting pieces of reliefs and inscriptions were the work of Antonio Canova in 1808–12, and Luigi Canina in the 1860s.

Just before the **fifth milestone** (400 m. after the crossroads with the Via di Attico/Via di Tor Carbone) the road makes a detour to the left, as it crossed a slight dip before a ridge, associated with a sequence of four large earthen mounds of archaic *tumulus* type, all on the right-hand side of the road, the first just before the bend, the second just after it, and another two, 250 m. further on. By tradition the fifth milestone coincided with the *fossae Cluiliae*, an ancient boundary between the territory of Rome and that of the Latins of Alba Longa (in the Alban Hills) where, in the early C7 BC, three Roman brothers, the Horatii, fought three Latin brothers, the Curiatii. Two Horatii were killed first but the third Horatius then killed all three Curiatii, after which Rome's supremacy in Latium was unchallenged. According to the Roman historian Livy, writing in the late C1 BC, the dead were buried where they fell, the two Romans close together, nearer Alba Longa, the Latins more spread out, closer to Rome. Since the surviving *tumuli* are built using concrete, tufa, travertine and marble they cannot be the genuine archaic article, however, and are most probably

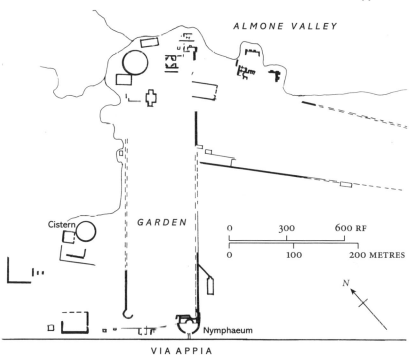

ALMONE VALLEY

Cistern

GARDEN

| | 0 | 300 | 600 RF |
| | 0 | 100 | 200 METRES |

N

Nymphaeum

VIA APPIA

▲ **Fig. 170.** Villa of the Quintilii. Site plan

rebuildings of the original tombs as historical monuments, contemporary with Livy's account, celebrating the heroes of early Roman tradition. Other large tombs cluster in the vicinity, including (on the left) one clearly shaped like a pyramid, although now reduced only to a huge mass of concrete.

Immediately after the pair of *tumuli* attributed to the Horatii, off in the distance on the left are the ghostly shells of the **Villa of the Quintilii**, one of the great country villas which ringed the outskirts of the city in the C2 and C3 AD. Names stamped on lead water pipes found in 1828 identified it as having belonged to two brothers Quintilius Condianus and Maximus. They rose to prominence in the reign of Antoninus Pius, serving as joint consuls in AD 151, and were famed in equal measure for their culture, military ability, brotherly relationship, extraordinary wealth, and the tragedy of their fate. Their success aroused the envy of the emperor Commodus and in AD 183 he had them killed on a trumped up charge of conspiracy, confiscating all their property, including the Via Appia estate, which he was especially jealous of and which remained in imperial hands until the C6 AD. Its lands stretched from the Appia to the Via Latina (now the Via Appia Nuova) and perhaps met up with the estate of Annia Regilla towards Rome. The residential nucleus, on which construction started around AD 125, lay 300 m. away from the Via Appia, terraced down the hillside overlooking the valley of the Almone, towards the Via Latina. The Via Appia frontage consisted of a great rectangular enclosure, presumably filled with gardens, at the corner of which is the **nymphaeum** which marks the modern entrance to the site. Fed by the villa's aqueduct, it was not in origin an entrance at all, but a streetside fountain intended to impress (and for the use of) passers-by; it has another fountain at its back, towards the garden. Much of the older structure is confused by its conversion into a small fortress in the C12–C13. The standing buildings in the distance were the focus of extensive excavations at the end of the C18, yielding enormous quantities of statuary and coloured marbles (Vatican Museums). New survey and excavations began in 1985–9 to investigate the detailed layout and history of the complex, but it has since become heavily overgrown again.

From the Villa of the Quintilii to the **Casal Rotondo** (the largest circular tomb on the Via Appia) just before the sixth milestone, is another 1 km. Large tombs get fewer, small republican tomb enclosures increase. About 300 m. before Casal Rotondo, on the right, are the ruins of an ancient inn or posting station, with a small set of baths. Behind lies another very large country villa, which extends alongside the road all the way to the Casal Rotondo. The name comes from a medieval farmhouse (*casal*) once installed on top of it (since replaced by a modern villa). Stripped of its outer stone facing, the drum currently measures about 27 m. in diameter; its original dimension was probably 100 RF; the podium on which it stood is buried below ground, but is reportedly 35 m. (120 RF) across. There is nothing to say whose tomb it was, but the materials and form suggest the Augustan period (late C1 BC). Of the same period, but probably unrelated, are the fragments of a circular marble shrine mounted on a modern wall built for the purpose beside it. Only 4 m. in diameter, the monument can be reconstructed as a small round

▼ **Fig. 171.** Via Appia, Casal Rotondo. Reconstruction of fragments of a circular marble shrine

temple (Fig. 171) which will have capped a tall tower tomb and is dateable on the basis of the capitals, garlanded candelabras and masks to about 30 BC (the style is very similar to the Temple of Apollo Medicus Sosianus, p. 245). The name Cotta inscribed on one fragment might refer to a member of the family of Aurelii Cottae who wielded considerable power in the early–mid C1 BC. After Casal Rotondo the Appia can be followed as far as the outer ring road (Raccordo Annulare) but gets increasingly squalid. The Via di Casal Rotondo to the left leads over to the Via Appia Nuova (1 km.), where there are buses which will take you back into Rome.

Some Other Sites

THE LATERAN

Chosen by Constantine in AD 312/13 for the site of the first cathedral and residence of the new Christian patriarchy of Rome, the area had already attracted some Imperial and other aristocratic residences since the late C1 AD. By the early C2 it included the garden estate (*horti*) of Domitia Lucilla, birthplace and childhood home of the emperor Marcus Aurelius, and the house of his father's family (the Annii Veri), and the town house of the Quintilii brothers (for their huge estate on the Via Appia, see p. 343). In the early C3 the emperor Septimius Severus presented his general T. Sextus Lateranus with a town house (alongside the Annii Veri) which was still in existence in the late C4 and seems to have been the source of the toponym 'Lateran'.

▼ **Fig. 172.** St John Lateran. Plan of church and baptistery showing locations of features mentioned in text

Key:

1. Lateran Baptistery
2. Entrance porch
3. Oratory of St John the Baptist
4. Oratory of St John the Evangelist

5. North door
6. Altar of the Holy Sacrament
7. Bronze doors from the Senate House
8. Statue of Constantius II

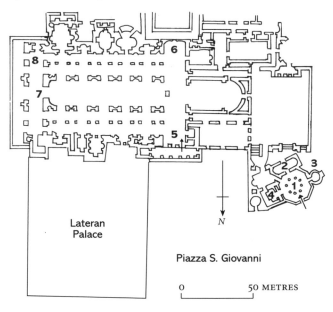

Lateran Baptistery.
Map, Fig. 149 and Fig. 172: 1

Piazza S. Giovanni in Laterano. *Interior*

A baptistery (the ceremonial setting for the rite which admitted a person to membership of the Christian Church) will have formed part of Constantine's initial Lateran scheme in *c.* AD 315 and excavations have demonstrated that the relatively slender walls of the present octagonal building stand on the wide foundations of a previous circular structure, dating from the beginning of the C4. The older foundations provided for eight engaged columns where the inner corners of the octagon are now (see the plan in Fig. 173) and suggest a building with a concrete roof (a dome or octagonal vault).

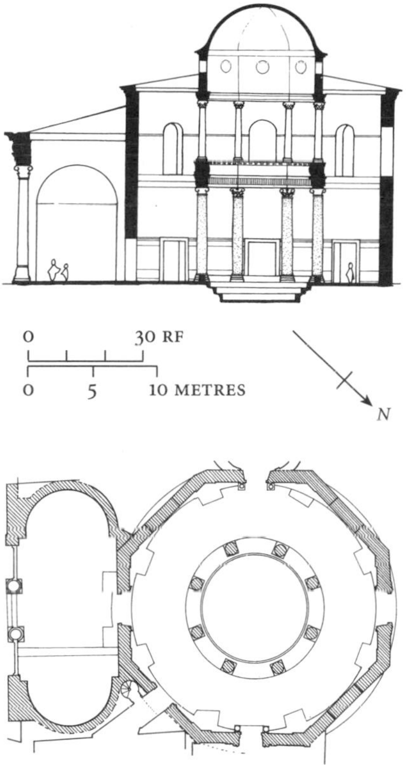

The actual octagonal walls, with wooden roofing, are possibly the work of pope Sixtus III (AD 432–40), though the Book of Pontiffs credits him only with the eight porphyry columns and the verses inscribed on their entablature around the font. The exterior brick-

▲ **Fig. 173.** Lateran baptistery. Ground plan showing earlier circular building foundations and reconstruction of original elevation

work, exposed in 1971, reveals that there was originally a wide doorway in each wall of the octagon, except perhaps the one where the modern entrance is now. The doorways were matched by large windows higher up the wall (later reduced to the present smaller ones). Pope Hilarus (AD 461–8) attached the oratories of St John the Baptist and St John the Evangelist to either side. Various other interventions have affected the appearance of the building. The inside was extensively restored and redecorated by Urban VIII Barberini in 1637 and Innocent X in 1646–9 and further altered by Alexander VII Chigi in 1657–61 when Borromini replaced the roof, because it was collapsing, and added the stucco frieze round the outside (the keys and tiara symbolize the papacy, the hills and oak-trees are emblems of the Chigi family).

The entrance on the side facing the Piazza S. Giovanni was created in 1575; the original approach was from the opposite side, facing the church, where there is a monumental **porch** (Fig. 172: 2), also of the C5. It is the best place to start, going through the Baptistery and out to the yard beyond, if that is permitted. The red porphyry column shafts which frame the porch doorway were artificially lengthened by joining two shafts together; their elaborate Composite capitals, with three rows of acanthus leaves and fluting on the body of the *kalathos*, come from some major public building of the early C2 AD (smaller versions of the same design have been found in the Forum of Caesar, probably belonging to the Trajanic rebuilding of the Temple of Venus Genetrix, see p. 150, from which the Lateran pair is therefore sometimes assumed to have been taken). The ornate bases decorated with acanthus, laurel-leaf, oak-leaf, *anthemion*, plaited motif and vine scroll, date from the late C1 AD (Flavian). The pilasters to either side have Phrygian purple shafts and Corinthian capitals of fine Augustan workmanship (they closely resemble examples from the Basilica Paulli on the Forum, see p. 67). The architrave which runs acoss the top dates from the mid-late C2 AD (it is very like that on the Temple of Hadrian, see p. 199). The lintel of the door is an architrave block of the late C2/early C3 placed on its side so that the ornament shows. The great marble slabs (old paving stones) which wall up the lateral openings were not part of the C5 scheme, whose door (originally of bronze) should be free-standing, with at most a metal grille to either side. (The unfinished medieval inscription at the top left-hand corner of the slab to the right of the doorway was addressed to Henry VI of Swabia in 1191.) Inside the porch, the mosaic in the right-hand (NE) apse dates from the C5, a beautiful design of tendrils in gold and green on a deep blue background. High on the wall to the left another precious survivor is a section of the original C5 **coloured marble panelling** (*opus sectile*), in green and red porphyry with intricate scrollwork in Numidian yellow.

Moving back into the Baptistery proper, whose walls were once lined with the same type of marble panelling, the pool in the centre was originally rather deeper (the early rite was generally for adults and involved total immersion as in a bath). The eight red porphyry columns (on average 6.4 m, *c.*19 RF, high) set around it are those which the Book of Pontiffs says were installed by Sixtus III, but had been assembled by Constantine (perhaps they are the eight which had lined the outer wall of the earlier circular building). Their reused capitals form pairs, two sets of Ionic (of mid-C2 AD date) on the main axis, Corinthian (early C1 AD) on the NE and Composite (early C3 AD) on the SW. When they were all refurbished in 1637 the flowers on their abacuses were replaced by bees (symbol of the Barberini family of Urban VIII). The architrave blocks probably came from the same building as those on the front porch; the eight Latin verses added by Sixtus III recount the significance of the baptismal rite. The **Oratory of St John the Baptist** (on the west, Fig. 172: 3) built by pope Hilarus (AD 461–8) has been refashioned inside but still has its original entrance: two red porphyry columns with (very unusually) green porphyry capitals and bases stand on red porphyry pedestals and support an architrave of Phrygian purple. The bronze doors, decorated with *peltae* (shield) designs, are also original (though probably reused). The **Oratory of St John the Evangelist** on the opposite side, also built by Hilarus, had its bronze doors replaced in 1196, but the mosaic on its cross-vault dates from the C5, with the Lamb of God in the centre, surrounded by animals in panels framed in candelabra designs.

Excavations in greater depth under and around the Baptistery area have traced the foundations of a C1 AD house, supplanted in about AD 140 by a bath-building, which was damaged in AD 191 and rebuilt, but partly converted back into housing. The tall, squarish structure with large arches in brick-faced concrete some 20 m. south-west of the Baptistery (on the other side of the entrance to the Pontifical University) is a remnant of the rebuilt baths.

St John Lateran (S. Giovanni in Laterano) was built by Constantine on the site of the barracks of the Imperial Guard (the *Equites Singulares*, which he abolished in AD 312) and several wealthy houses (probably Imperial property). Initially dedicated to St Salvator, it was completely rebuilt, on the same basic plan, in the C14 and remodelled in the mid-C17; the east façade dates from 1733–5. Despite the heavily Baroque overtones its huge five-aisled space (102 × 60 m.) gives some idea of what one of the late Roman basilicas, especially the Basilica Julia on the Forum (see p. 89) will have felt like.

The church houses several significant relics of Imperial Rome. Supporting the organ loft over the inside of the north door (Fig. 172: 5), designed by Valsoldo in 1598, are two **Numidian yellow marble columns**, one removed from the Arch of Constantine (see p. 272). At the opposite end of the transept, framing the altar of the Holy Sacrament (Fig. 172: 6) are four **gilded Corinthian columns**, extraordinary reminders of a vanished form of luxury architecture. 24 RF tall, they are cast in bronze of considerable strength. All the shafts and the capital on the outer left-hand column are ancient, dating from the early C2 AD (period of Trajan or Hadrian), presumably made for a temple or other public monument. They were apparently reused first in the old Constantinian basilica, perhaps incorporated into the *fastigium* (pedimented screen before the altar) and then moved to various other positions. The column bases and the other three capitals were made when installing them around the altar in 1597–8. The **bronze doors** in the main entrance at the east end of the church (Fig. 172: 7) were taken in 1660 from the Senate House on the Roman Forum (see p. 70). At the south end of the entrance porch (Fig. 172: 8) stands a **colossal marble statue** of an emperor in military dress trans-ferred here in the belief that it portayed Constantine but actually of his son Constantius II, one of a family group probably set up in the Baths of

Constantine on the Quirinal hill, of which two others can be seen on the Capitoline hill (p. 235).

The **Obelisk** in the Piazza S. Giovanni came from the Circus Maximus (p. 264).

The Viminal. Map, Fig. 174

The plateau joining the Esquiline and the Quirinal hills—these days the area between the Termini railway station and the Via XX Settembre—was the highest of the high ground along the eastern side of the city. Its ancient name *collis Viminalis* may refer to willow trees, a natural characteristic (like the oaks on the Caelian), or its own local deity, a form of Jupiter called Viminus, who was worshipped at an altar, possibly located on the south edge of the Piazza dei Cinquecento. Its reputation as a hill (*collis*) probably depended on a short extension at that point, between the two valleys now followed by the Via Nazionale and the Via Urbana. Like the Quirinal and Esquiline, the area was thickly populated by the C2 BC and continued to be a desirable residential district until late antiquity. Remains of substantial houses dating from the C2–C4 AD were levelled in the C19 and 1950s when building (and then rebuilding) the railway station and its forecourt. The western margin, where the hill merged with the Quirinal, saw a lot of new development in the late C1 AD, when the emperor Domitian decided to convert his birthplace, the house of his uncle Flavius Sabinus on the Quirinal, into the *templum Gentis Flaviae*, a large funerary monument celebrating the whole of the Flavian dynasty. The site has not been located for certain, but may lie under and to the south of S. Susanna (Fig. 174: 15). Fragments of some exceptionally fine sculptural reliefs which could come from the temple's decoration, in Greek (Pentelic) marble, were found during building operations in the late C19 between the Via E. Orlando and Via Torino (Museo Nazionale Romano-

---

Key to Fig. 174

1. Museum Aula X (= vestibule of baths)
2. Museum court IX (= *apodyterium:* undressing room)
3. Museum court VIII (= portico beside swimming pool N)
4. Museum Aula V–IV–I (antechambers to frigidarium F)
5. Museum entrance wing
6. Small Cloister (ex-Ludovisi collection)
7. Great Cloister
8. 'ex-Planetarium' (hot room of baths)
9. S. Isidoro (small room beside palaestra)
10. S. Bernardo alle Terme (west pavilion)

11. East Pavilion
12. Exhedra
13. Site of temple of *Quirinus* (?)
14. Republican city walls (Largo S. Susanna)
15. Site of temple of the *Gens Flavia* (?)
16. Site of temple of *Salus* (?)
17. Republican city walls (Stazione Termini)
18. Retaining wall of *agger*
N. *Natatio*
P. *Palaestra*
F. *Frigidarium*
C. *Caldarium*
M. Metro station

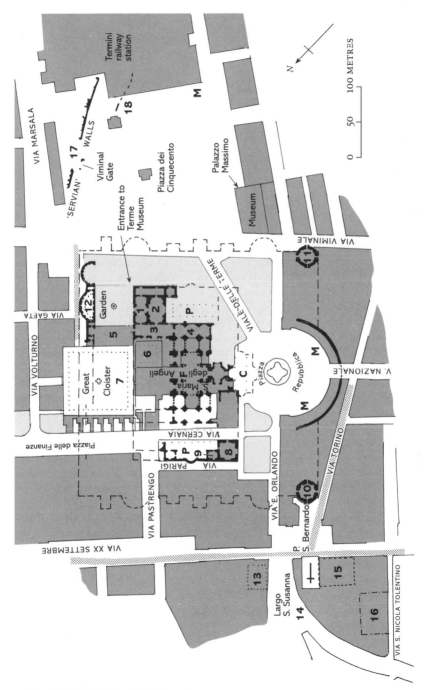

▲ Fig. 174. The Viminal hill. Site plan

Palazzo Massimo; others are in the Kelsey Museum in Ann Arbor). The other major development, which still dominates the modern scene, were the great Imperial Baths of Diocletian.

Baths of Diocletian. Map, Fig. 174 ★

Piazza della Repubblica

At least four inscriptions have been found dating the dedication of the Baths to the period between 1 May AD 305 and 25 July AD 306 and crediting Diocletian's co-emperor Maximianus with having purchased the land for their construction, probably when he visited Rome in AD 298. The complex, like its predecessors built by Trajan (p. 288) and Caracalla (p. 319), consisted of a huge artificial platform, 356 × 316 m. (1200 × 1060 RF), an area of 11 hectares, with a range of pavilions, fountain buildings, alcoves, and other accessory facilities around the outer margin. In the centre were the baths themselves, contained in a rectangular block, 244 × 144 m. (825 × 485 RF), composed in accordance with a design canonical since those of Trajan if not earlier. A large open-air swimming pool (*natatio*), huge covered cold hall (*frigidarium*), small intermediary warm room (*tepidarium*) and huge hot hall (*caldarium*) were set in a linear sequence down the middle, flanked symmetrically to either side by two sets of secondary rooms (undressing rooms, lounging rooms etc.) arranged around two open courts (*palaestrae*). The water came from the *aqua Marcia*, which was augmented for the purpose, and collected in a vast cistern (under Piazza dei Cinquecento). Serving a thickly populated zone the baths continued to function until the C6 AD. In the early C5 they are still described as having seats for three thousand (whereas Caracalla's

▼ **Fig. 175.** Baths of Diocletian. Reconstruction

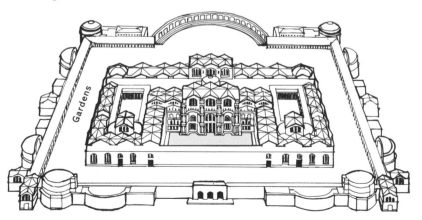

Baths were down to about half that number); the total number of people they could accommodate could have been as many as three times that.

Substantial sectors of the bathing block and its precinct can be seen in seven separate places:

- The great semicircle of the **Piazza della Repubblica** (built together with the Via Nazionale in 1896–1902) is set on top of a semicircular terrace of even greater size which projected from the SW side of the outer precinct (like that on the Baths of Trajan, see p. 288), commanding a panoramic view over the city from the head of the valley (down which the Via Nazionale runs now).

- **S. Maria degli Angeli**, on the NE side of the Piazza della Repubblica, was designed in 1563–6 by Michelangelo to exploit the nucleus of the central bathing block, which was still standing to vault height (though mining in the subsoil for the local volcanic sand (*pozzolana*) had brought about the collapse of much of the SW front, including the bulk of the *caldarium* (Fig. 174: C)). The concave wall in which the entrance to the church is set previously constituted an apsidal recess in the *caldarium*'s NE wall; the first hall inside the church door occupies the intermediary warm room (*tepidarium*); the main basilica occupies the *frigidarium* (F) and its adjacent smaller halls at either end. Although extensively refashioned in 1749 by Vanvitelli (who turned the orientation of Michelangelo's church through ninety degrees, building the choir and apse on the NE side, out into what had previously been the *natatio* or open air swimming pool), the interior spaces are still essentially those of the C4 building. The **frigidarium** was 53 × 22 m. (180 × 75 RF); it has lost some of its height (30 m./100 RF) because the floor level has been raised (the bases of the columns are fakes), and in width is missing the four plunge pools which opened off to either side, but the cross-vaulting and the eight massive Composite columns with shafts of pink Egyptian (Aswan) granite 48 RF high have not moved since antiquity (the columns in the vestibules on the cross axis are Vanvitelli additions, made of brick, plastered and painted to look like granite). Through the door labelled Sacrestia is a small chamber made out of one of the frigidarium plunge pools (with its original vault), housing an exhibition on the history of the Baths and the church, beyond which you come out into the area of the **natatio**, with a section of its theatre-like back-drop visible to the full height. All the columns and capitals have been robbed but many of the corbel and entablature blocks remain, mostly carved in rather faulty Greek (Pentelic) marble. From the sacristy take the side exit to the Via Cernaia (if closed simply go back through the church and round the outside).

- **Via Cernaia** runs through the middle of the western *palaestra* court of the bath-block. Demolitions and excavations on both sides of the street have exposed the original floor levels. On the east side there is a large gap, where a whole suite of halls flanking the palaestra has disappeared, exposing the scars of vaults and roof terraces. The mosaic in the foreground belongs to the palaestra court, using the same design as in the Baths of Caracalla, of overlapping scales in red and green porphyry, Numidian yellow and grey marble. On the west side of the street run the footings of the palaestra colonnade, behind which is a large apsidal exhedra. On the **Via Parigi** you can follow the exterior wall of the bath block, whose broad projecting cornice was not just decorative but provided a walkway for maintenance staff to clean roof gutters, hot air vents and windows.

- The **ex-Planetarium** (Fig. 174: 8), between the Via Cernaia and Via Parigi, was once an octagonal hall at the western corner of the bathing block; its concrete dome is still intact, but all the interior finishing has gone. The cast-iron frame under the dome is a relic of the old Planetarium. In 1986 it was taken over as an **annex of the Museo Nazionale Romano** (*State) and now displays a selection of marble statuary from the Baths of Diocletian and Caracalla as well as two remarkable bronze statues from the Quirinal (see p. 400). Excavations under the floor have exposed a street and buildings of the late C1 AD (Domitianic), levelled in order to build the baths. Sometimes accessible is an exhibition in the small church of St Isidore (Fig. 174: 9), installed in another room of the baths.

- **S. Bernardo alle Terme**, the church in the piazza of the same name (Fig. 174: 10), occupies one of the two circular pavilions at the S and W corners of the outer precinct of the Baths. The outside is completely masked by later building but the interior, a small version of the Pantheon rotunda, 22 m. (75 RF) diameter, still preserves its original shape, including the octagonal coffering on the ceiling.

- The matching pavilion at the south corner is also still standing (and currently housing a restaurant), the exterior brickwork of its drum (once coated with white stucco in imitation of dressed masonry) sticking out into the **Via del Viminale** (Fig. 174: 11).

- Eleven halls of the eastern side of the central bath-block and part of the NE angle of the outer precinct are embodied in the old **Museo Nazionale Romano delle Terme** building (entrance from Piazza dei Cinquecento). At the time of writing, because of the reorganization of the museum (see p. 398) and building repairs, little is accessible except the garden court, on one side of which is the shallow exhedra (Fig. 174: 12) of the outer precinct and on the other the entrance wall of the bathing block, with the door to the vestibule (1). The exhedra had an internal colonnade framing statue niches in the walls and the floor is paved with a mosaic of black, red and white tesserae, in a radiating geometric design of hexagons and rhomboids framed in plaited borders. The hexagons contain stylized rosettes. The external face of the exhedra and its flanking rooms can be seen from **Via Gaeta**.

Republican City Walls. Map, Fig. 174: 17

Piazza dei Cinquecento

Over 100 m. long and in places seventeen courses (9 m.) high, the stretch of walls to the left of the Termini Station forecourt is by far the best preserved in the city. The blocks are almost all of Grotta Oscura tufa, characteristic of the original construction, which was set in hand in 378 BC by the censors Spurius Servilius Priscus and Quintus Cloelius Siculus. The blockwork on the side facing the station forecourt is irregular because it represents the inside of the wall, which was once reinforced with a great earthen rampart (the *agger*), 42 m. wide, retained by a lower wall to the rear (Fig. 174: 18). Many of the blocks bear quarry-marks (single letters, using the Greek alphabet) which suggest that the expertise to build the wall was brought in from Greek southern Italy or Sicily. On the outside there was a 36 m. wide ditch, 15 m. deep, which, like the rampart, accompanied the wall all the way across the Quirinal–Viminal–Esquiline plateau, otherwise without natural defence.

The C4 walls were not Rome's first fortifications; like most other cities in Latium it had a complete circuit by the C6, traditionally associated with the sixth king Servius Tullius (578–535 BC), but little is known of their nature and course—the C4 rebuilding employed quantities of *cappellaccio* tufa, likely to derive from the earlier circuit. The C4 walls in their turn underwent numerous repairs and modifications in the course of the C4–C1 BC, the last during the Civil Wars in 87 BC (to which the reticulate-faced concrete wall along the outside of the Termini Station stretch probably belongs). By the late C1 BC, however, they were clearly regarded as obsolete and large tracts were built over, or demolished, as need be. The gates tended to be kept, since most marked administrative boundaries, and during the reign of Augustus were rebuilt in more monumental form (see pp. 299 and 312). The gap in the Termini Station sector, between the tall stretch and a shorter, lower section to the north probably coincides with a city gate (completely destroyed for its stone). How the rest of the Termini Station sector came to survive could be due to the attractions of the internal rampart, whose south-facing slopes made excellent vineyards, or pleasant garden promenades (the bank survived until the C19).

A small section of the return of the walls along the far side of the Quirinal ridge can be seen in the Largo S. Susanna (Fig. 174: 14).

'Minerva Medica'. Fig. 176

Via Giolitti (at east end of Via P. Micca). Comune (†interior)

Unfairly marooned in a sort of wasteland beside the railway tracks is the shell of an exceptional building dating from about AD 300. Constructed of

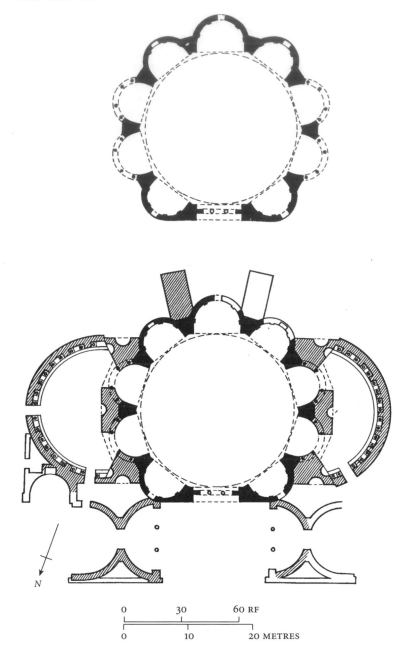

▲ **Fig. 176.** 'Temple of Minerva Medica'. Restored ground plan showing the two phases

brick-faced concrete, in its initial phase it consisted of a free-standing decagonal hall, 24 m. (80 RF) in diameter covered with a concrete umbrella-shaped dome, 33 m. (112 RF) high. At ground level, it started as nine tall and deeply semicircular alcoves (the tenth forms the entrance), above which the walls supporting the dome rose straight but pierced by ten round-headed windows. The four alcoves on the cross-axis opened outwards through colonnades. The dome was not the heavy, inert mass of Pantheon-style tradition, requiring a central oculus, but a bold new departure, apparently set as thin, lightweight panels infilling an armature of brick ribs which came together in a point. The full arcs of the ribs were still standing, without their infill, until 1828, when the centre collapsed, leaving the present profile. The lightness of the structure was evidently rather too daring: about twenty years after it was built, large wedge-shaped buttresses were stacked against the east and west sides, reducing the openings of the colonnaded alcoves to one intercolumniation in each, and further buttressed by an outer semicircular exhedra; two large rect-angular buttresses were also placed against the south wall, and the entrance side was given a porch. There was underfloor heating in the main hall (and in the porch); the walls were lined with marble veneer, the underside of the dome with glass mosaic (subsequently replaced by painted plaster). Numerous statues filled the niches in the side-courts, which may also have contained fountains.

Commonly known as the '**Temple of Minerva Medica**' (a mis-understanding which arose in the late C16) it has also been mistaken for part of a bath-building. It is much more likely, however, to have been a **dining pavilion** in a very wealthy late Roman residence, for which a suit-able candidate presents itself in the **Gardens (*horti*) of the Licinii**, the family of the emperor Gallienus (ruled AD 253–268), who was accus-tomed to take his entire court there in summer. The property seems to have extended from near S. Bibiana (Via Cairoli) perhaps as far as the Porta Maggiore, and was in due course included within the Aurelianic Walls to the east (on the far side of the railway tracks). More late buildings are known to exist in the subsoil and it is very possible that the palace continued to thrive until the C6 AD, counting among its later occupants two high-ranking Imperial officials, whose over-lifesize portrait statues dating from about AD 400 were found in fragments in medieval walls blocking niches in the pavilion (Palazzo dei Conservatori Museum).

Porta Maggiore. Map, Fig. 177

Piazza di Porta Maggiore–Piazzale Labicano

In antiquity the zone was an even more complicated intersection than it is now, with the fork of the Via Labicana and Via Praenestina coinciding with the intersection of a whole series of aqueducts all converging on the

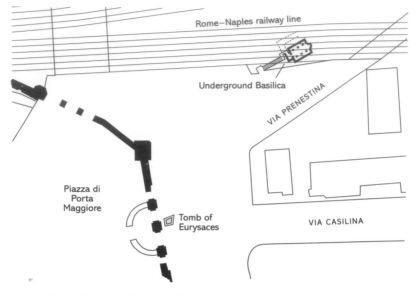

▲ **Fig. 177.** Porta Maggiore. Site plan

same point: the *Anio Vetus* of 272 BC, which ran underground; the *aqua Marcia* (144 BC), the *aqua Tepula* (125 BC) and the *aqua Julia* (33 BC), followed by the *aqua Claudia* and the *Anio Novus* (both started by Caligula in AD 38, finished by Claudius in 52). The arches supporting the latter two, stacked one on top of the other, as they crossed over the two roads, constitute what is now called the Porta Maggiore, though it only became a real gate with the building of the Aurelianic Walls in AD 271–5 (which are still connected to it on either side).

The travertine masonry of the arches and their superstructure, surviving to its full height at 19 m., is all in the 'rusticated' style of exaggerated unfinish typical of Claudius (see pp. 313 and 198), best seen on the inside face. The low curving walls behind the side piers are the foundations of an inner court built behind the gate by Honorius in AD 401–3 (as on the Ostia Gate and the Appia Gate). Honorius' outer defences (semicircular towers on square bases), which formed two separate gates (*Porta Praenestina* and *Porta Labicana*) were demolished in 1834–8, revealing the exterior face of the Claudian arches in their entirety (Fig. 178). Claudius' inscription appears on the top register with a characteristically archaic spelling of Caesar: TI CLAUDIUS DRUSIIF CAISAR AUGUSTUS GERMANICUS PONTIF(ex) MAXIM(us) | TRIBUNICIA POTESTATE XII COS V. IMPERATOR XXVII PATER PATRIAE | AQUAS CLAUDIAM EX FONTIBUS QUI VOCABANTUR CAERULEUS ET CURTIUS A MILLIARIO XXXXV | ITEM ANIENEM NOVAM A MILLIAR LXII SUA IMPENSA IN URBEM PERDUCENDAS

▲ **Fig. 178.** Porta Maggiore. Exterior face

(Tiberius Claudius, son of Drusus, Caesar, Augustus, Germanicus, Chief Priest, with Tribunician Power for the twelfth time, five times Consul, twenty-seven times Imperator, Father of his Country, saw to the construction at his own expense of the Claudian Water from the springs called Caeruleus and Curtius 45 miles distant and the Anio Novus from 62 miles.)

The inscription in the middle zone was added by Vespasian in AD 71, after he had carried out repairs, and below that is one from Titus, recording further work in AD 81.

In front of the pier between the two arches is the exotic **Tomb of the baker Eurysaces** (Fig. 179), built in about 30 BC, that is, about eighty years before the aqueduct came along. Carefully respected at that time, the tomb was subsequently incorporated into the central tower of the Aurelianic–Honorian city gate and exposed when that was demolished in the C19. The west end—towards the Porta Maggiore—is only missing the roof; the east end was truncated by the tower-builders and was an oddly pointed shape anyway, apparently fitting a trapezoidal plot determined by the surrounding road system. Raised on a podium of tufa blocks (which compensated for the fact that the level of the Via Praenestina on the north side was about 3 m. higher than that of the Via Labicana on the south), the upper part of the tomb is made of travertine around a concrete core, forming a very curious structure. A lower zone consists of pairs of cylinders

0   6 RF

0   1   2 METRES

▲ **Fig. 179.** Tomb of Eurysaces. North side

interspaced with rectangular piers forming a sort of platform for the upper zone, where pilasters at the corners support an elaborate entablature across the top of three rows of hollow circles. On the plain band between the two zones an inscription repeated on each side declares: EST HOC MONIMENTUM MARCEI VERGILEI EURYSACIS PISTORIS, REDEMP-TORIS, APPARET (This is the tomb of Marcus Vergilius Eurysaces, baker, contractor, he serves. . . . [possibly some minor public official]). A freed-man (ex-slave) who probably made a fortune supplying bread for the public ration in the mid-C1 BC, he was immensely proud of the source of his wealth. The frieze on the entablature shows his bakery in operation: (south side) grinding and sieving the flour, (north side) mixing and kneading the dough, shaping the round loaves and placing them in a domed pizza-type oven, (west) stacking the loaves in baskets and carrying them to be weighed. The cinerary urn containing the ashes of his wife Atistia (Museo Nazionale Romano) took the form of a *panarium* (bread basket). A marble relief which was probably set on the east face (now in the Capitoline Museums, Museo Nuovo) portrayed him and Atistia in formal Roman dress (toga for him, stola for her). No satisfactory explanation has yet been found for the cyclinders and circles; the circles could be more cylinders laid on their sides, but the only cylindrical objects appropriate in the context of the baker's trade would be tubes for measuring grain, blown-up to a monster scale.

Underground Basilica. Map, Fig. 177

Via Prenestina. †Comune (frequently closed for conservation)

Across the junction outside the Porta Maggiore, on the left-hand side of the Via Prenestina, the entrance to the site is in the angle of the wall beside the Rome–Naples railway line. Discovered by accident in 1917, the subterranean chamber lies about 10 m. below the modern surface, hollowed out of the friable natural tufa bedrock, consolidated with concrete rubble. It

▼ **Fig. 180.** Underground Basilica at Porta Maggiore. Plan

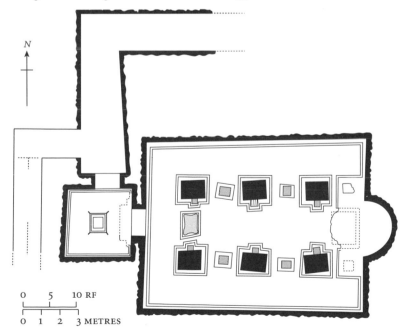

comprises a near-rectangular hall (11.5 × c.9 m.), divided into three aisles by six rectangular piers which support three concrete barrel vaults, 7.25 m. high. At the east end is a small apse; at the west a small vestibule, to which a staircase led down from the east (the ancient entrance and the ancient ground level above the basilica have not been explored). Light and air came down a shaft to the vestibule but the inner recesses of the basilical space must have been lit by lamps.

Elaborate white stucco-work with figurative scenes moulded in low relief covers the walls, piers and vaults, datable to the first half of the C1 AD. Around the upper zone of the walls is a set of figures standing on small bases, presumably meant to be statues. On the piers (where panels have been cut out) are candelabras and Victories; the one surviving panel shows a seated Hercules receiving the golden apples from one of the Hesperides (daughters of Night and Darkness). On the central vault the subject-matter in the square panels is a miscellany of scenes from Greek myth or drama (especially Euripides), the smaller rectangular panels show cult objects of various kinds, athletic games, rural life, rustic sanctuaries, pygmies; the intervening spaces are filled with Medusa heads, palmettes, victories, erotes, candelabras. On the lateral vaults diamonds and rectangles alternate down the middle, containing Nereids (sea-nymphs) and Medusa heads (the Gorgon whose image turned people to stone), surrounded by smaller scenes from mythology and religious cult. In the apse is a **painting** depicting the Greek poetess Sappho throwing herself off a cliff into the embrace of the sea-goddess Leucothea and Triton (a merman), watched by Apollo and Phaon, the beautiful young boatman who had rejected her love.

Despite the variety of the decoration on the walls and ceiling none of the imagery is sufficiently specific to determine the function of the chamber. The floors are of white mosaic with a simple black border; no furniture or other objects were found. At one extreme it has been interpreted as a secret meeting place for followers of neo-Pythagoreanism, one of the philosophical mystery cults (with a doctrine of reincarnation and the transmigration of souls), suppressed in the 50s AD. At the opposite extreme, it was simply a cool underground dining room associated with a country villa (what lies above is unknown). A sort of compromise between the two would see it as part of a tomb—a place for ritual dining (perhaps with specific cult associations) in remembrance of the dead.

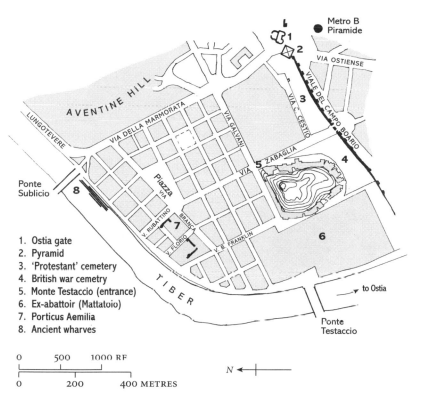

1. Ostia gate
2. Pyramid
3. 'Protestant' cemetery
4. British war cemetry
5. Monte Testaccio (entrance)
6. Ex-abattoir (Mattatoio)
7. Porticus Aemilia
8. Ancient wharves

▲ **Fig. 181.** Pyramid-Testaccio. Site map

PYRAMID-TESTACCIO

Ostia Gate (Porta S. Paolo) and Museum of the Via Ostiensis. Map, Fig. 181: 1

Piazza S. Paolo-Ostiense. State, Ostia Superintendency (*museum)

Similar in size and shape to the Appia Gate (see p. 333) and almost as well preserved, the Ostia Gate (*Porta Ostiensis*) has the added distinction that it is the only gate with its inner court still standing (albeit hastily rebuilt in AD 1410). The city walls on either side were demolished, reducing the gate to a traffic island, in the 1920s. When first built, as part of the Aurelianic walls of AD 271–5, the semicircular towers were only one storey high, and there were two passages through a low curtain wall between them. Under Honorius (AD 401–3), the towers were heightened, with a gallery level running across over the gates, and the inner court was constructed, with

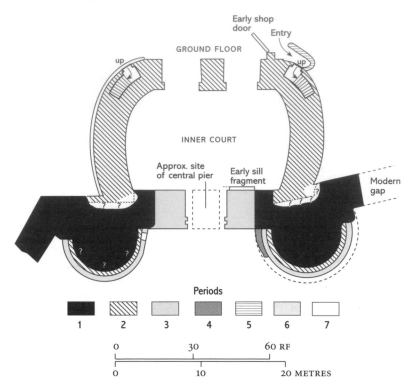

▲ **Fig. 182.** Ostia Gate. Plan

two inner archways matching the two on the outside. In a third phase, the outer archways were reduced to a single passage; yet another storey was added to the towers. Like the Appia, the road it commanded (*Via Ostiensis*) was a much-travelled route, which connected Rome and her sea-port Ostia, at the mouth of the Tiber. The gate's modern name, already used in the C6 AD, refers to the great church of St Paul 2 km. down the road. In the **museum** installed in the towers and gallery are exhibited models of the ancient town of Ostia and the harbours at Portus, plaster casts of funerary reliefs and inscriptions which have been found along the way, and the wall paintings from a rock-cut tomb of the early C3 AD discovered near the apse of the church of St Paul.

Pyramid of Cestius. Map, Fig. 181: 2 ★

Piazzale Ostiense. Comune (†interior)

Three hundred years older than the Ostia Gate and 4 m. beneath it in ground level, the pyramid is a monumental tomb, built *c.*18–12 BC (during the reign of Augustus) in the fork of the *Via Ostiensis* and a road which ran across to the Tiber (approximately where the Via della Marmorata does now). Its dedicatory inscription, repeated on both the east and west face so as to be legible from both roads, reads C CESTIUS L F POB EPULO PR TR PL | VII VIR EPULONUM: Gaius Cestius Epulo, son of Lucius, of the voting tribe Poblilia, praetor (chief magistrate), tribune of the *plebs*, one of seven state priests in charge of public banquets (*epulones*) in honour of Jupiter (and other religious festivals). Several members of his family made similarly successful public careers in the mid C1 BC but nothing else is known about him, except his remarkable tomb.

On the east side a smaller inscription beneath records that the tomb was built in accordance with Cestius' will, taking only 330 days (OPUS APSOLUTUM EX TESTAMENTO DIEBUS CCCXXX | ARBITRATU | PONTI P F CLA MELAE HEREDIS ET POTHI I.(F)). It was constructed of concrete faced with blocks of white Italian (luna) marble and measures 100 RF (30 m.) square at the base, 125 RF (36.4 m.) high. Pyramids of similar size and proportions had been built for private individuals in Upper Egypt during the New Kingdom, but in Cestius' day were especially characteristic of Nubia (Sudan), suggesting that possibly Cestius had served in the province (annexed in 24 BC). Though unusual, his choice was not

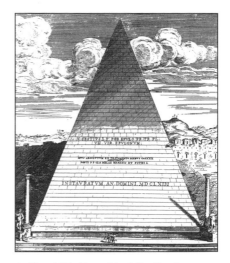

▲ **Fig. 183.** Pyramid of Cestius in a print by Pietro Santi Bartoli (1697)

▼ **Fig. 184.** Marble statue base naming Cestius' heirs. With fragments of the bronze statue which stood on top (Bartoli, 1697)

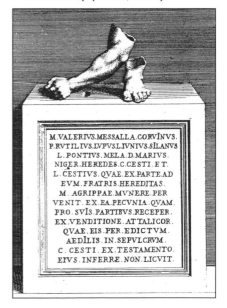

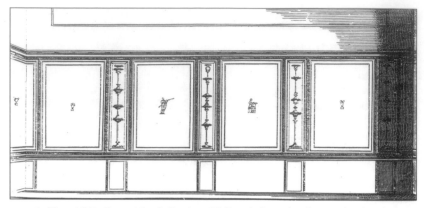

▲ **Fig. 185.** Pyramid of Cestius. Wall paintings in the tomb chamber as recorded in a print by Pietro Santi Bartoli (1697)

unique; another of its kind, which stood between the Vatican and the Mausoleum of Hadrian, was demolished in the C15–C16.

The larger lettering 'Instauratum an domini MDCLXIII' refers to restorations by Alexander VII in 1663, following excavations on the west side in 1660–2, which found two marble bases for bronze statues (Fig. 184) with inscriptions explaining that they were set up by Cestius' heirs (Marcus Agrippa among them), paid for by the sale of valuable tapestries (*attalici*), which could not be deposited in the tomb as Cestius had wished, because of recent legislation against luxury. The same excavations also found the two columns which have been re-erected in their original positions at the corners of the base of the pyramid on the west side (visible from the 'Protestant' cemetery), and tunnelled into the centre of its concrete core to find the funerary chamber. This is a simple rectangular void, 5.85 × 4 m., with a barrel vault, and when discovered still had fine 'Third Style' paintings on the walls (Fig. 185), though it had been despoiled of any other contents (earlier robbers had broken through by another route; apparently no access was left in antiquity).

When the Aurelianic walls came to be built in the late C3, the pyramid was incorporated on its diagonal, so as to form a triangular bastion. The walls along the Viale del Campo Boario once continued straight down to the riverside, where they turned back upstream to protect a vast area of docks and warehousing known in antiquity as the **emporium**, now called 'Testaccio' after its most prominent landmark.

Monte Testaccio—the Amphora Mountain.
Map, Fig. 181: 5

Via Zabaglia–Via Galvani. †Comune

The triangular hill (whose Italian name derives from the Latin, meaning made of brick or pottery) covers an area of 20,000 m² at its base and is 35 m. high; it was probably once considerably higher. As far as we know it is entirely what its name implies, composed of millions upon millions of **broken amphoras**, the heavy pottery containers in which the Roman world was accustomed to transport wine, olive oil, fish sauce, and various other liquid, semi-liquid, and dry commodities. Located to the rear of a ring of large warehouses which lined the wharves of Rome's main river-port, it symbolizes the 'consumer city', swallowing the produce of its mighty empire in a one-way trade, throwing away the 'empties' in a heap to one side.

Nothing about the hill is quite so simple, however, for on the surface, at any rate, it consists almost entirely of olive-oil amphoras: the hefty globular ones from Baetica (Spain), which weighed 30 kg. and held 70 kg. of olive oil, or the thinner, lighter ones from Tripolitania (Libya) and Byzacena (Tunisia). And although many carry painted labels including dates, none earlier than AD 144 has yet been found in archaeologically-excavated levels (though AD 138 is attested on some loose finds) and nothing later than the mid-C3. It is assumed (but has yet to be proven) that a core of older material must lie deeper in the hill. The overwhelming preponderance of oil amphoras, when numerous other types must have passed through the port, also demands some explanation. Perhaps (unlike most other commodities) the oil was decanted into bulk containers upon arrival and the amphoras could not be reused, not because there were simply too many of them, but because the oil they had contained was believed, rightly or wrongly, to render them unusable. Certainly, the latest excavations (1991) indicate that the construction of the hill was not a haphazard, free-for-all dump but a reasonably disciplined operation, raised in level terraces with retaining walls (also built of amphora sherds). The amphora were carried up whole, probably in batches of four, by donkeys or mules, and smashed on the spot—again, with a degree of organization; the rocky layers produced by the tough Spanish

▼ **Fig. 186.** Monte Testaccio. Spanish oil amphora (left), North African oil amphora (right). Scale 1:40

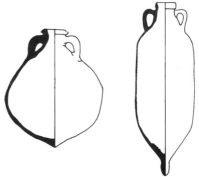

▲ **Fig. 187.** Monte Testaccio. Diagram showing terraced construction

amphoras were stabilized by packing them with the smaller debris of the North African forms, and then everything was liberally sprinkled with powdered lime to neutralize the stench of rancid oil.

Most other amphoras when emptied of their first contents could be washed out and used again for the same or another product, or if damaged could be recycled for different purposes, depending on their shape. Those with long tubular bodies could be turned into water-, drain- or ventilation-pipes, by knocking the neck and handles off the top and the carrying peg off the bottom; the handles and pegs could serve as aggregate in concrete walls; if not used as tubing, the body could provide flat sherds ideal for backing marble veneer on floors and walls. More bulbous shapes could become flower pots or the like. Fragments of all kinds could be further pounded into chips (as were bricks) for *opus signinum*—a waterproof concrete used for industrial flooring, roofing and cistern lining. All else failing, the waste could simply be used as landfill.

Porticus Aemilia. Map, Fig. 181: 7

Via Branca–Via Vespucci

The **emporium** or commercial riverport behind which Monte Testaccio rose had been a development of the late C3/early C2 BC, as the old river harbour at the bend beside the Tiber Island (see p. 252) was no longer adequate to the needs of a rapidly expanding city. The broad plain to the SW of the Aventine Hill offered a much larger site, with a km. of river frontage. An integral part of the new facilities was the ***Porticus Aemilia***, a vast roofed space, 487 × 90 m. (1600 × 300 RF) where goods offloaded from new stone wharves along the riverbank could be taken into safe-keeping, checked and sorted as in a modern customs shed. First erected in 193 BC by the consuls M. Aemilius Lepidus and L. Aemilius Paullus, perhaps in mud brick and timber, it was rebuilt in concrete in 174 BC and is still standing in places at the Via Florio, Via Rubattino, and Via Benjamin Franklin (Map, Fig. 181: 7). It is the oldest surviving example of concrete construction in Rome, its outer walls 1.4 m. thick faced with small irregular nodules of tufa (*opus incertum*). The roof was also of concrete, apparently as a series of fifty parallel barrel vaults, staggered in four sections as the floor sloped towards the Tiber, supported on 294 internal piers (Fig. 188).

A section of the **riverbank wharves**, as raised and redesigned on three levels in the early C2 AD, has been excavated and preserved as an

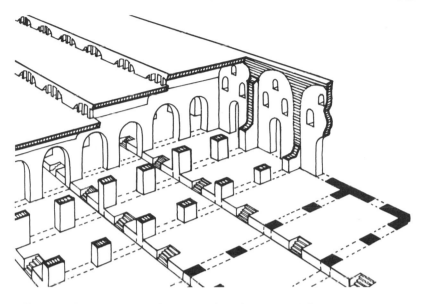

▲ **Fig. 188.** Porticus Aemilia. Reconstruction of concrete roofing

archaeological site along the Lungotevere Testaccio (Map, Fig. 181: 8), south of the (modern) Ponte Sublicio (if closed, a good view can be had from the bridge). From the finds in the earthen debris filling the rooms to the rear the wharves did not go out of operation until the late C5 or C6 AD.

Mausoleum of Hadrian—Castel S. Angelo. ★
Map, Fig. 77

*Lungotevere Castello. State (*interior)*

An artificial mountain over 50 m. high, commanding a major bridgehead, the Mausoleum was incorporated into the Tiber defences from the late C3 AD and became ever more strongly fortified as time went by—with the result that most of what can be seen from the outside is not ancient. The upper half of the circular superstructure, the palace and the statue of the archangel Michael on top, the round bastions at the four corners of the podium, the curtain wall, the ditch and the triangular outworks, date variously from the C13–C16. However, a lot of the ancient structure survives at the foot of and inside the circular drum, and the upper battlements offer excellent views in all directions. The castle, which was only decommissioned in 1901, also contains an art collection, exhibition space, and a military museum.

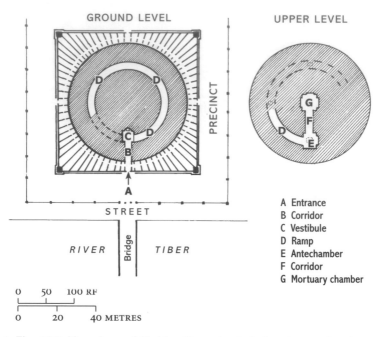

GROUND LEVEL   UPPER LEVEL

PRECINCT

STREET

RIVER   Bridge   TIBER

0   50   100 RF

0   20   40 METRES

A Entrance
B Corridor
C Vestibule
D Ramp
E Antechamber
F Corridor
G Mortuary chamber

▲ **Fig. 189.** Mausoleum of Hadrian. Reconstructed plan at ground and upper level of drum

The Mausoleum was started by Hadrian in the AD 120s and was not quite ready when he died aged 63 in AD 138, but was quickly completed by his successor Antoninus Pius in AD 139. The ashes of Hadrian and his wife Sabina (who had died a year or two before him) were the first to be deposited, together with those of Aelius Caesar, Hadrian's first adopted son and heir, who had also died in AD 138. They were followed by most of the Antonine and Severan emperors, and their wives and immediate families, the last recorded deposition being Caracalla in AD 217.

Hadrian's choice of site—separated from the bulk of the city on the far side of the river—was eccentric but had various advantages, especially since the project included the **bridge** in front, the *Pons Aelius* (Hadrian's family name), completed in AD 134. Now called Ponte S. Angelo after the castle, the access ramps, road bed and parapets were remade several times in the course of the C14–C19 (the statues of St Peter and St Paul at either end date from 1530; the ten angels and their bases were designed by Bernini in 1668, carved by pupils and followers), but the central three arches are original. In later times bridgehead and Mausoleum constituted a dead end; in antiquity, however, as now (since 1892), the bridge connected with a road along the riverbank, an important artery in a newly developed sector of the city, in which imperial interests were strong. The land used for the tomb was part of the Gardens of Domitia, which had been imperial property since the C1 AD (the Domitia in question was either Nero's aunt or Domitian's wife) and were kept up by the emperors until at least the C4. They were Aurelian's preferred residence when in Rome (early AD 270s).

By virtue of the bridge, the tomb could also be considered part of the Campus Martius, a desirable association from the funerary point of

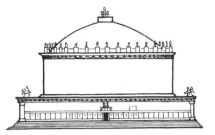

▲ **Fig. 190.** Mausoleum of Hadrian. Reconstruction

view (see p. 178), not least in the comparisons which would be drawn with the Mausoleum of Augustus, 800 m. away to the NE (see p. 181). The two monuments shared the same orientation (north–south) and also their greatest dimension, the width of the base of Hadrian's tomb equalling the outer diameter of Augustus', at 300 RF (c.89 m.). But Hadrian probably aimed to outdo the older tomb in every other respect, though with all the stone robbing, tunnelling and rebuilding that has gone on over the centuries many of the details are blurred.

The design was essentially a traditional type, a solid cylinder set in a square base, like the tombs of the Servilii or Caecilia Metella on the Via Appia (pp. 338, 341, Figs. 167, 169), except wrought on a huge scale: the cylinder was 225 RF in diameter, 72 RF high (or higher), rising out of a base 300 RF wide, 40 RF high. The quality of exterior finish was also in another league. Architects' sketches made before the last remnants were stripped at the end of the C15 show that the base was completely encased in white Italian (luna) marble, with an elaborate cornice and a frieze of bulls' heads and garlands along the upper edge and a large pilaster with an acanthus-scroll capital at each angle (Fig. 191). The rest of the wall surface was divided into two horizontal zones, with tall marble panels

▼ **Fig. 191.** Mausoleum of Hadrian. Reconstruction of the architectural order decorating the podium

0   3 RF

0   1 METRE

▲ **Fig. 192.** Mausoleum of Hadrian. Frieze from the cornice of the drum(?) (Castel S. Angelo museum)

below, six courses of drafted blocks above, separated by a projecting horizontal band. On the side facing the river, flanking the entrance to the tomb, the lower panels were inscribed with the names of the dead. Over the entrance itself was a large panel naming Hadrian and Sabina. The cylinder was presumably sheathed in white marble, too; surviving sections of a larger frieze of bulls' heads and garlands (in the Castle museum) suggest that it was crowned with an entablature to match that on the base. Procopius, in describing the defence of the mausoleum (by then a fortress) against the Goths in AD 537, mentions colossal figures of men and horses in bronze at each corner of the base and marble statues being hurled from above, where they were presumably located on the parapet. Excavations when making the embankment in 1892 found the footings of an outer enclosure, consisting of a low tufa wall with travertine posts at intervals, which may have supported a bronze fence surmounted by large gilded bronze peacocks (symbols of immortality) of which two survive, now in the Vatican Museums (Cortile della Pigna).

▼ **Fig. 193.** Mausoleum of Hadrian (Castel S. Angelo). Section, showing the original parts of the structure (hatched)

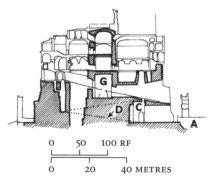

0   50   100 RF

0   20   40 METRES

To see the inside, the **modern entrance** is from the park on the east side, across the ditch and through the C16 curtain wall. This brings you into the mausoleum's base, which was originally hollow, constructed around the central cylinder as a series of radial barrel-vaulted chambers (see Fig. 189). All the vaulting connecting with the cylinder has since been demolished to form a circular street and the truncated chambers converted into stores. What function the chambers had in antiquity (other than structural, as a way of lightening the weight on marshy ground) is not known. There were doors in the centre of each side, and between the chambers, but only the main entrance on the south side (A), on axis with the bridge, gave access to the funerary chamber in the core of the central drum, which was constructed of concrete with tufa and marble aggregate combined with tufa and travertine blocks. The **first radial corridor** (B), from which the marble lining has been removed from the walls and floor exposing its travertine underlay, leads to a **vestibule** (C), similarly stripped of its marble, with a large niche in the back wall for a colossal statue of Hadrian (the head could be that in the Vatican Museums, Sala Rotonda). Off to the right starts an **annular corridor** (D), a feature of high-ranking funerary ritual since the late Republic but in this case taking in the form of a **helical ramp**, 20 RF (6 m.) high and 10 RF (3 m.) wide, rising at a gradient of 1/10. The brickwork of the walls has holes for the attachment of marble veneer and the floor was once paved in mosaic. The ramp makes a complete turn inside the drum, with vents in the ceiling at four points, and now connects with a ramp made by pope Alexander VI in 1492 which rises across the diameter of the cylinder in a straight line where previously there was an anteroom (E) and a **second radial corridor** (F), situated directly over the first (and 12 m. higher up) leading to the principal **funerary chamber** (G), 8.5 m. square and 10.2 m. high. Alexander VI's ramp crosses the upper reaches of the funerary chamber (it once did so as a drawbridge) and continues straight on upwards through the core to the far side of the drum, where a C16 staircase to the left rises to the 'Courtyard of the Angel' and the rest of the castle on top. Roman concrete walling forming two further chambers above the principal chamber can be traced up the centre of the later superstructure (see section Fig. 193), but how the higher chambers were reached, how high the cylinder walls rose, and the nature of the original roof are all open questions. The debate is similar to that concerning the Mausoleum of Augustus: some like the idea of a second smaller drum; others prefer a tumulus-type earthen mound (see Fig. 78). In either case there was a figure of Hadrian (supposedly in a four-horse chariot) at the pinnacle, and it is possible that, as today, visitors to the tomb could climb right up to the top for a **panoramic view**.

Among the many interesting things to see in the papal apartments, is the **bathroom of pope Clement VII** (1523–34), stuccoed and painted in the antique manner by Giulio Romano. From the topmost battlements you get a bird's eye view of the **Passetto**, a high level escape route between the Vatican and the Castle, built in 1277 along the top of a C9 fortification wall which still stands for most of its length, along the Via dei Corridori.

Mausoleum and Circus-Basilica of 'St Constantia'. ★
Fig. 194

*S. Agnese fuori le Mura, Via Nomentana 2 km. *Church*

Situated at the third milestone on the ancient Via Nomentana (easily accessible by any bus which runs along the modern road of the same name), the complex of church, catacombs, mausoleum, and funerary basilica makes a very pleasant excursion. The present **church** (3) dates from the C7, built by Pope Honorius I (AD 625–38), unique in having a women's gallery over the central nave. The columns down the nave are

▼ **Fig. 194.** S. Agnese, S. Costanza and catacombs beneath. General site plan

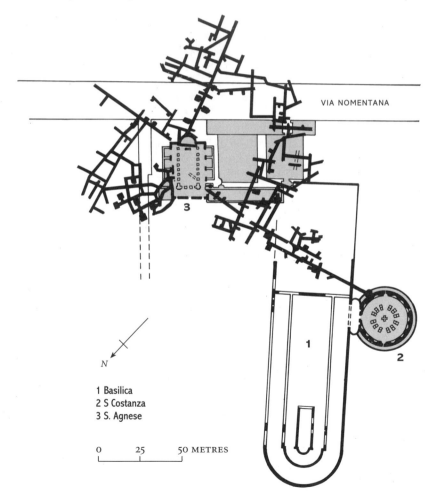

VIA NOMENTANA

3

N

1 Basilica
2 S Costanza
3 S. Agnese

0   25   50 METRES

1

2

ancient, with a pair of Chian pink/grey shafts at the altar end and another pair in the centre of each side, preceded by two of fluted Phrygian purple. The mosaic and marble panelling in the apse is of the C7; the marble candelabra beside the altar was previously in the Mausoleum but is a work of the C2 AD. The gallery of inscriptions (mostly funerary epitaphs) displayed up the staircase on the south side are finds from the vicinity— a major suburban cemetery from the C1 AD onwards. The **catacombs** below the church are believed to contain the grave of St Agnes, martyred in the Stadium of Domitian (Piazza Navona) in the reign of Diocletian. On the hill above

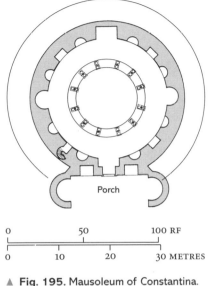

▲ **Fig. 195.** Mausoleum of Constantina. Original plan

S. Agnese stand the **Basilica** (1) and circular **Mausoleum** (2) built by Constantina, elder daughter of the emperor Constantine. The basilica (now the walled garden off to the right of the Mausoleum entrance) was constructed first, in about AD 337–57, when Constantina was living in Rome, perhaps in a villa close by. It honoured St Agnes, but like others of its kind (e.g. St Sebastian on the Via Appia; Villa of the Gordians on the Via Praenestina), it was not set up directly over the martyr's grave. It measures 98 m. (330 RF) long, 40 m. (135 RF) wide, shaped like a circus; the outer ambulatory was roofed; whether the central nave was also, is not certain. The **Mausoleum** which Constantina built for herself (subsequently mistakenly identified with a non-existent St Constance) probably dates from AD 351–2. It has lost the apsidal porch (similar in form to that at the Lateran Baptistery) which joined it to the basilica but otherwise is wonderfully well preserved, an excellent example of a Late Roman central-ized plan. The external diameter is c.29 m. (100 RF), internal 22.5 m. (75 RF), with alternating round and rectangular niches symmetrically disposed around the walls. An inner colonnade, 48 RF in diameter composed of twelve pairs of granite columns, 12 RF high, surmounted by arcades, supports a clerestorey, pierced by twelve windows, rising to the concrete dome. The ceiling of the ambulatory between the outer and inner ring, roofed with a concrete barrel vault, is lined with the original C4 **mosaics**, much restored in the C19, executed in brilliant colours on a white ground. There were eleven panels, corresponding radially with the inner colonnade, starting with geometric designs close to the door and getting more elaborate and figurative as you progress round to the burial niche on axis at the rear wall. The third panel along on either side shows erotes harvesting grapes; the central portrait medallion shows Constantina (on the right) and her first husband Hannibalianus (on the left). The last two panels contain a still-life of flowers, fruit, birds and amphoras. The mosaics in the larger semicircular niches on the cross-axis, with representations of St Peter and St Paul are later (C5 or C7). Constantina's imperial red porphyry sarcophagus in the niche in the rear wall is a replica, the original is in the Vatican Museums (p. 389).

A walk around the north side of the site, down the Via di S. Agnese (turn left outside the entrance) to Piazza Annibaliana and back up Via Bressanone (thence the Via di S. Costanza takes you back up to the Via Nomentana) gives a rare view of its hilltop position and the great buttresses retaining the outer wall of the basilica.

Museums

Written jointly with Judith Toms

The collecting and public display of art works and curiosities has a longer history in Rome than anywhere else in Europe, reaching back to the Hellenistic kingdoms of the C4 and C3 BC from which the Romans adopted and developed the practice of collecting. Much of the material was war booty, originally used as religious dedications in celebration of military triumphs, but other kinds of public display soon became popular. Major collections of sculpture were displayed in public spaces such as porticoes, temples, and forums; the porticoes of Octavia and Livia had fine displays of sculpture, and one of the greatest collections was in the Temple of Peace (pp. 153–5); it included many masterpieces from Nero's Domus Aurea (looted from Greece) and the temple treasures of Jerusalem. The relationship between art collecting and the process of government, which is such a feature from the Renaissance onwards, started early, for example the Temple of Concord contained many religious dedications but was also the place where the Senate met.

In the later Roman and medieval periods many monuments—now classed as pagan and thus open to suspicion—suffered from deliberate destruction and looting. However, there were attempts to protect them, for example statues were gathered for safe keeping into the Basilica Julia in the C4–C5, and some remained intact and above ground because they could serve the spirit of the times, such as the great bronze equestrian statue of Marcus Aurelius, mistaken for the Christian emperor Constantine, and the She-wolf, which became an emblem of Rome's legendary past. Many of the ancient monuments on show in Rome were located by seats of government—in front of the papal palace of the Lateran and on the crest of the Quirinal. There were also some pieces around the Pantheon and elsewhere in the streets of Rome. And thus the habit of associating art—especially art of an earlier time—with public spaces, and the role of art in legitimizing government, continued from the Roman period.

It is not surprising then that there was a frequent return to the past for present political needs: we see it in the C12 with Cresenzio (p. 252), and in the mid-C14 when Cola di Rienzo praised Rome's great past in his attempt to rouse church and populace against the powerful aristocratic families. Nor is it surprising that the popes of the C15 believed that their status and temporal power were enhanced by the collecting and display of works of art. They and their successors gave works of art to the city council of Rome, thus developing the great state collections of the Capitoline museums, and created the vast collections of the Vatican. Princes and rival powers (often closely linked with the church) formed another group of collectors in the C14–C16. Wealthy private individuals also played an important role as many of the great private collections were eventually sold or donated to the Church or State. After 1870 the new Italian state and the local comune divided responsibility for the city's museums and, as the expansion of modern Rome brought many new discoveries, also created new museums such as that of the Terme.

The following guide includes the main museums with collections of ancient art and artefacts, summarizing for each the origin and development of the collections, the architectural setting, and the contents and their arrangement. Given the vast quantity of material, it is only possible to mention a selection of pieces, chosen mainly for their relevance to the archaeology of Rome: because they have been unearthed in Rome or its environs, are famous in the history of Rome, such as the She-wolf, or are particularly interesting examples of the eclectic and distinctive nature of Roman art. There are many other pieces which are well known, for example the numerous marble statues, carved in the Roman period in the Greek manner, which have influenced artists and art historians from the Renaissance period onwards. The idealized Greek-style nudes and divine statuary types (Apollo, Venus, satyrs, etc.) were often used to decorate Roman public buildings such as baths, theatres, and temples.

Most of the museums listed are in the city centre, but there are also three at EUR (Esposizione Universale di Roma—the site of the Universal Exhibition of Rome planned for 1942 and subsequently converted into a new suburb, 2 km. SW of the city walls; see Fig. 200). The museums are almost all housed in buildings of architectural and historical interest, including Renaissance palaces which have been adapted over the centuries but still retain much of their original character.

Musei Capitolini (Capitoline Museums).
Map, Fig. 106, p. 230

*Piazza del Campidoglio. *Comune*

The Capitoline Museums constitute the oldest public collection in the modern world and one of the finest in Rome. There are some 1,300 works, the great majority being marble statues, including some of the prime examples of the Roman taste for statuary in the earlier Greek tradition. The long and complex history of the collections can be reconstructed from papal and state records, inventories, and guide-books—these last being written as early as the 1600s.

The collections: The municipal collections of ancient sculpture in Rome began in 1471 when pope Sixtus IV decided to move five ancient bronzes from the Lateran to the keeping of the Conservators (the city council), whose palace on the Campidoglio had recently been rebuilt.

The bronzes thus restored to the Roman people 'by whom they had been produced' (as the commemorative inscription accompanying the donation declared) included the She-wolf, the Spinario (boy picking a thorn from his foot), and the colossal bronze head of Constantius II. The She-wolf was placed above the main entrance of the Palazzo dei Conservatori as a symbol of Rome's mythical past. Soon after, other major pieces arrived such as the gilded bronze Hercules from the Cattle Market, and under Innocent VIII (1484–92) the fragments of an acrolithic statue of Constantine from the New Basilica on the Velia. It is clear that the Campidoglio at this time had become the natural home for monuments of historical significance for Rome, while the papal museum in the Belvedere of the Vatican, inaugurated by Julius II, contained masterpieces of ancient art.

Acquisitions drifted in during the 1500–1600s, including the *Fasti* from the area of the Regia (p. 99), and the bronze bust said to be Lucius Junius Brutus (given in 1564 by Cardinal Pio di Carpi). In 1566 Pius V ordered the removal of some 'pagan' statues from the Vatican to the Campidoglio, and by doing so changed the overall feel of the museum to one concerned mainly with ancient art, especially Roman.

The second main period of acquisition was in the 1700s. In 1720 Clement XI purchased for the Campidoglio the remnants of the Cesi collection, and in 1733 Clement XII bought the Albani collection of sculptures (most found in Rome or the environs) from his nephew Cardinal Alessandro Albani, one of the most important collectors of the C18. Clement XII inaugurated the Capitoline Museum in 1734, and in the mid-1700s Benedict XIV added ancient sculptures and also founded the picture gallery section of the Capitoline Museums with the Sacchetti and Pio collections. With this he aimed to increase the study of fine art and protect the artistic wealth of Rome by avoiding the dispersal of these two important private collections. Other material came from the many contemporary excavations in Rome.

During the French occupation of Rome (1798) Napoleon I removed twenty-one pieces from the Campidoglio to Paris, but they were returned in January 1816 after the Congress of Vienna ordered restitution. Their return gave an opportunity for a complete rearrangement of the Capitoline Museums in 1816. The final phase of acquisition took place after 1870 when the main sources of new material were the excavations during building work in Rome, and the Castellani gift of Greek, Etruscan, and Italic vases.

The **architectural setting** is mostly the work of Michelangelo who, in 1536, was commissioned to redesign the space, turning it into the first planned piazza in Rome. He redesigned the two existing buildings—the Palazzo Senatorio and the Palazzo dei Conservatori, and designed a third—the Palazzo Nuovo—and the main entrance ramp; it took some 120 years to complete the project. The result is harmonious and elegant.

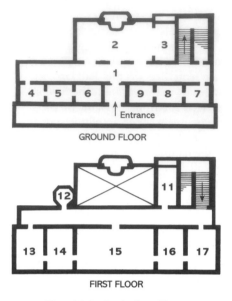

GROUND FLOOR

FIRST FLOOR

▲ **Fig. 196.** Capitoline Museum. Plans of ground and first floor

A **visit** can start in either of the palazzi to left and right; a ticket covers both.

The **Palazzo Nuovo (Museo Capitolino)** to the left contains many sculptures, most acquired during the C18. **Room 3** houses the recently conserved gilded bronze **statue of Marcus Aurelius on horseback**; a copy replaces it in the Piazza del Campidoglio (Fig. 108, p. 235). At the rear of the **courtyard (2)** is the colossal reclining river-god statue known as **Marforio**, probably dating C2 AD, of a type usually associated with Roman bath-houses and fountains. It was first recorded in the C8 near the arch of Septimus Severus beside the Forum, then was moved in 1588 to Piazza S. Marco, and to its present position by 1595. In the late Middle Ages it became one of Rome's 'speaking statues' (for others see pp. 211, 214 and 232). The two statues in Luna marble of **satyrs** holding baskets on their heads (probably C2 AD) were known from at least 1490 and became famous elements of the Della Valle collection of antiquities, housed in their palace near Piazza Navona. They had probably adorned the façade of a building in the Field of Mars. Also in the courtyard are items from the Egyptian collection; almost all come from the Temple of Isis and Serapis (Iseum) in the Field of Mars (p. 207). The fragments of **three columns** in grey Egyptian granite were found in 1883 and formed part of the great porticoes of the temple. The relief scenes at their feet represent the ceremonies of the cult of Isis carved in the Roman imitative manner: priests of Isis hold sacred vases and poles topped with models of gods and the sacred lotus flowers. The **basalt sphinx** also came from the Iseum but is a genuine Egyptian piece, made for Amasis II (569–525 BC).

Rooms 4–6, which may not be open to visitors, contain statues, reliefs, and inscriptions relating to the oriental cults of Mithras, Cybele (Phrygian mother goddess), and some Syrian divinities which became popular in the West in the C2 and C3 AD. In (4) is the relief of the Vestal Virgin Claudia pulling the ship bringing the Great Mother (Cybele) to Rome in 204 BC (see p. 126). At the foot of the stairs to the first floor is a colossal marble statue of **Mars** found in the early C16 near the Forum of Augustus, and possibly the cult figure of the Temple of Mars Ultor. It is a work of the late C1 or early C2 AD. Only the torso and head (except for the helmet crest) are original; the arms and legs are ebullient C16 restorations. **Rooms 7–9** contain various Roman sculptures, including the Attic **sarcophagus of 'Alexander Severus'** dating to *c.* AD 230, and carved in Greek Pentelic marble. Found in 1582 in the Monte del Grano, an Imperial mausoleum about three miles outside Rome near the Via Tuscolana, it reputedly contained the Portland vase (now in the British Museum). The figures reclining on the lid in the form of a dining couch portray a man and wife, not likely to be Alexander Severus, the emperor (AD 222–35) and his wife, but two younger members of their family. This style of lid has its origins in the Etruscan culture as far back as the C6 BC (e.g. the sarcophagus of the married couple, Villa Giulia museum, p. 296). The reliefs depict episodes from the life of the Greek hero Achilles who died young, shot in the heel by an arrow whilst fighting in the Trojan War. *Front*: he is trying to escape his fate by hiding on Skyros (Achilles centre wearing woman's clothing); the scene continues on the left end with his host King Lycomedes of Skyros enthroned, and his young warriors. *Back*: Achilles' reconciliation to the death of his friend Patroclus at the hands of Hector by the ransoming of Hector's body (Trojans wear trousers and 'Phrygian' caps). On the right end is the Greek general Agamemnon with Odysseus, Achilles, and attendants.

The **first floor** houses a large and varied collection, mostly sculptures in stone, but also some reliefs, inscriptions, and mosaics. Most are of Roman date, and in the Greek Classical or Hellenistic manner. The **Hall of the Doves** (**11**) has Roman portrait herms, busts, and sarcophagi, also the fine polychrome **Dove mosaic** in various marbles cut into tiny tesserae, found in 1737 forming the centrepiece of a floor in Hadrian's Villa at Tivoli. The **masks mosaic** in marble and alabaster was found in 1824 on the Aventine at the site of the Baths of Decius (AD 252). The case below the far window contains the best preserved fragment of a *tabula Iliaca*—a slab with representations in miniature of tales from Homer's *Iliad*—in finest 'Palombino' limestone. The friezes are numbered to correspond with the books of the epic and most of the people and scenes are labelled. The outlines and details were added in colour. The fashion for illustrating whole books started in the Hellenistic period; this example probably dates to the C1 AD and was a Roman collector's piece. It was found around 1683 in a large villa near the road to Marciano. The octagonal room (**12**) is dedicated to the famous **'Capitoline' Venus**, whose reputation rests largely on her appeal to C19 tastes. Found on the SE flank of the Quirinal hill *c.*1675, probably in a bath building, she is a good example of a Venus type popular in the C2 AD. The **Hall of Emperors** (**13**) has 65 busts of Roman emperors and their families in chronological order, starting from the left of the door. Most came from the Albani collection and were restored and/or adapted in the post-Medieval period. The **Hall of Philosophers** (**14**) contains a series of 79 portraits of Greeks celebrated in the fields of politics, science, and literature, many not identified, dating to the late Republican and Imperial periods. At the centre of the **Great Hall (15)** is the **colossal baby Hercules** in green basalt (a rare stone from Egypt), found on the Aventine, probably on the site of the Baths of Decius (AD 252), and bought by the Conservators for the collection in 1570. A costly piece, surely made for the Imperial court, it is a good example of the Roman taste for the unrestrained and camp. The **two centaurs** are companion pieces, found in 1736 in the domed hall of the small palace at Hadrian's Villa and date around AD 130. They are carved in black marble which probably comes from Tunisia, but are signed by Aristeas and Papias, two sculptors from Aphrodisias in SW Turkey—a major school of sculpture. The **Hunter** (*Cacciatore*) was found in 1747 in a tomb on the Via Appia and probably dates to the C3 AD. It is a life-size funerary statue of a man holding a hare and a spear; an inscription on the left side of the plinth reads POLYTIMVS.LIB. It is not clear whether Polytimus a freedman set up the statue in honour of his patron, or if Polytimus is the artist. The head is a portrait and the body is of a classical athlete type, while the hare and the tree are in the Hellenistic style—a typically eclectic Roman mixture. Made from one block of marble, it is also an example of the late Roman delight in huge monolithic sculpture.

Room 16 is named after the red marble statue of a **Faun**, or young satyr, campanion of Bacchus, the god of wine. Found in 1736 in the small palace of Hadrian's Villa and heavily restored, it was probably carved in the same workshop as the two centaurs in the Great Hall. The wine-red stone was surely chosen on purpose to evoke its subject. **Room 17** is named after the **Dying Gaul, or 'Gladiator'** found shortly before 1623 in the area of the Gardens of Sallust on the Pincian. Carved in Greek marble, in the very expressive late Hellenistic style which continued to be popular for certain subjects in the C1 AD, it is a work of exceptional quality. After its rediscovery the piece quickly entered the 'musée imaginaire' of educated Europe. From 1638 onwards it was reproduced countless times, greatly influencing the development of Baroque sculpture and penetrating to other areas of the arts—for example it features in Byron's poem *Childe Harold* (1818).

On the other side of the piazza is the **Palazzo dei Conservatori** containing the rest of the Musei Capitolini. It is divided into five main sections: the Sale dei Conservatori (the Halls of the Conservators), the Museo del Palazzo dei Conservatori (the Museum of the Palace of the Conservators), the Braccio Nuovo (New Wing), the Museo Nuovo (New Museum), and the Pinacoteca (Picture Gallery). The **courtyard** contains the **colossal head of Constantine** and other fragments from the high acrolithic statue, almost 15 m. high, found in the New Basilica (p. 115). In various qualities of white marble, it is a powerful work of the C4 AD (the head was apparently reworked from one of Hadrian). On the walls of the **staircase to the first floor** there are various sculptures and inscriptions.

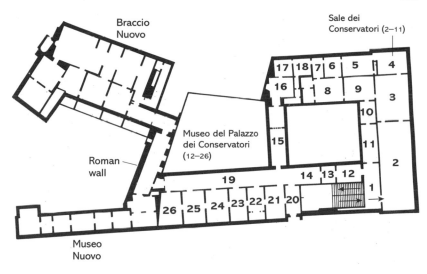

Braccio
Nuovo

Sale dei
Conservatori (2–11)

Museo del Palazzo
dei Conservatori
(12–26)

Roman
wall

Museo
Nuovo

▲ **Fig. 197.** Palazzo dei Conservatori. First floor plan

The **Panel reliefs of Marcus Aurelius** in Luna marble show scenes from the wars fought by Marcus Aurelius on the Danube: his triumph (he rides in a chariot drawn by four horses with a Victory and a temple behind), the submission of the barbarians (the emperor, on horseback, wears military costume, barbarians kneel before him), and Marcus Aurelius sacrificing before the temple of Jupiter Capitolinus (his head is veiled and he sacrifices over a small tripod). These panels came from a triumphal arch, possibly the same one which produced the reliefs now on the Arch of Constantine (p. 272).

The **Halls of the Conservators (2–11)** are a set of rooms occupying half of the first floor of the original palazzo. Mostly of interest for their lavish Baroque decoration they contain only a few, though important, sculptures and inscriptions. The great hall, the **Sala degli Orazi e Curiazi (2)**, once used for sittings of the Public Council, has frescoes painted between 1595 and 1640 by Cavalier D'Arpino (Giuseppe Cesari) and Cesare Rossetti depicting scenes from the history and mythology of Ancient Rome.

Room 4 has the remarkable **bronze portrait head**, possibly of the C3 BC, inserted into a C16 bust and said to be of Lucius Junius Brutus, legendary founder of the Roman Republic in 509 BC. The bronze **Spinario** (boy picking a thorn from his foot) was first mentioned in the C12, and was in the Lateran Palace before its transfer to the Campodoglio in 1471. Probably made in the C1 BC, it will have adorned a Roman house or garden. Another fine bronze is the small figure in a short tunic, a

Camillus or acolyte who assisted at sacrifices. Its provenance is unknown, but it may be dated to the C1 AD and was much admired and reproduced during the Renaissance. The Hellenistic **bronze crater** with flutings below a chased frieze of lotus flowers inlaid with silver, is likely to have been looted from the eastern Mediterranean. It was found in the early C15 in Nero's seaside villa at Anzio (ancient Antium).

Room 5 contains the **She-wolf** probably of Etruscan manufacture and dating to the early C5 BC; it was recorded in the C10 at the Lateran, and was moved to the Campidoglio in 1471. From early on this bronze was adopted as a symbol of Rome's mythical origins, coming to represent the she-wolf which suckled Romulus and Remus; the twins were added to the bronze by Antonio del Pollaiolo around 1509. From the end of the C17 it was widely believed to be the statue said by Cicero to have been on the Capitol and struck by lightning in 65 BC, but this now seems unlikely. Set in the left wall are fragments of the **Consular and Triumphal Fasti** found near the Regia (p. 105), originally belonging to the Regia or a nearby arch. The Consular Fasti are the list of consuls, decemvirs, consular tribunes, censors, and dictators from the foundation of the Republic to the Augustan Period. The Triumphal Fasti do the same for Roman generals honoured with triumph, from Romulus to Augustus. **Room 6** contains an **Egyptian hunting dog** in green serpentine—a rare marble—found near the 'Auditorium' of Maecenas (p. 294). **Room 8** is the throne room with C18 tapestries with scenes from Roman legends of the Republican period. **Room 9** has frescoes painted in 1508–13 by the Bolognese painter Jacopo Ripanda, relating tales from the Punic Wars (Rome's struggle against Carthage in the C3 BC).

The **Museum of the Palace of the Conservators (12–26)** consists of two long galleries overlooking the garden and a series of adjoining rooms. **Rooms 16–18** can be approached from room 7. They contain two portrait statues of **late Roman officials**, over life-size, in togas, found at 'Minerva Medica' (p. 355), part of a late Roman palace. Of Parian marble, they date about AD 400, when portraiture of such high quality is almost unknown in Rome, though the art was still thriving in the Eastern Empire, especially at Aphrodisias. They were probably carved by Aphrodisian sculptors. From the steps of room 16 there is a good view of this end of the **Lamian Gardens Gallery (15)** which contains sculptures discovered on the Esquiline and Viminal hills when laying out the new quarters of the city after 1870. The **bust of Commodus**, deified as Hercules, in Italian marble on a pedestal of oriental alabaster, was found in 1874 in the debris of a building of the time of Alexander Severus. The **Esquiline 'Venus'**, a young nude girl binding her hair, in Parian marble, dating from the late C1 BC or early C1 AD, was found close by. Who she is has been much discussed, the question being complicated by the Egyptianizing elements on the vase beside her. The **coloured marble floor** once paved a long corridor in a palatial dining suite of the mid-

C1 AD. It combines large squares of gold and brown alabasters from Egypt and western North Africa, with triangles of 'Lucullan' black and strips of Phrygian purple.

The **Gallery** (**19**) is lined with statues, most recovered during building operations in Rome after 1870. **Rooms 20–21** contain sculpture, sarcophagi, and inscriptions from the early Christian period. **Rooms 23–24** house objects from the **Castellani collection**; Greek and Etruscan painted vases, and Etruscan terracottas and bronzes. Large ancient bronzes rarely survive to the present day; **room 25** contains a notable collection including the **colossal head** of Constantius II (emperor AD 337–61), a fine example of late Imperial portraiture. It was in the Lateran in the Middle Ages together with the **colossal left hand** (mentioned by Benjamin de Tudela around 1170) which must be part of the same statue. One of the **two globes** with spikes belongs with the hand (damage to the hand shows where it was attached). The other was originally on the top of the Vatican obelisk from which it was removed in 1586. Most of the pieces in **room 26** were found on the Esquiline in the area of the gardens of Maecenas (p. 267). The **Hanging Marsyas**, which originally belonged to a larger sculptural group, is of Phrygian purple marble which vividly suggests the swollen veins of the tortured body of the satyr awaiting his punishment for challenging Apollo to a musical contest— Marsyas lost and was flayed for his impertinence. The emotional intensity and contorted body made this subject very suitable for treatment in the Hellenistic style.

Rooms 27–33 form the **New Wing** and **35–46** the **New Museum**. Both sections, created in the 1920s and 1930s, have been closed for many years but can be visited with a permit. The **New Wing** contains sculpture for the most part found during the 1930s. From the far end of the gallery (**19**) is a good view of a section of the tufa block podium of the **Temple of Jupiter Capitolinus** (p. 231), now incorporated as one side of the passage (**34**).

The **New Museum** was founded in 1925 with sculptures from excavations carried out after 1870, and was later enriched with other sculptures which subsequently came to light. It has important public inscriptions, sculptures, sarcophagi, and architectural fragments mostly of Roman date.

The **Picture Gallery** is located on the second floor and contains Renaissance and later paintings, especially Italian. In the central niche of **room 7** is a **colossal gilded bronze statue** of a youthful **Hercules**, from a round temple in the Cattle Market (p. 254). It is probably a work of the C1 AD.

Musei e Gallerie Pontifiche (Vatican Museums).
Map, Fig. 200

*Viale del Vaticano. *(Vatican City).*

The papal museums in the Vatican City are justly renowned for the quantity, wealth and importance of their collections, assembled in the course of a complex process of papal patronage from the Renaissance to modern times. From the medieval period to the 1500s the church possessed some notable sculptures including the equestrian statue of Marcus Aurelius and the She-wolf which were kept in the Patriarchy at the Lateran (the former papal residence). There were few important antiquities at the Vatican although some spolia had been reused in the building of St Peter's Basilica, and the bronze pine cone and two bronze peacocks stood in its forecourt.

The **collections** began in earnest when Julius II moved the statue now known as the Apollo Belvedere to the Vatican in 1503. This was soon followed by other ancient sculptures, including the Laocoon. They were set up in the Belvedere Courtyard (architecturally improved by Bramante) and many artists and writers gathered here to discourse upon the arts and to study the sculpture.

That first collection was largely dismantled under Pius V (1566–72) in the period of the Counter-Reformation when more than 60 works were removed to the Campidoglio or into the hands of the Medici family, and the Vatican remained largely depleted of ancient works for most of the C17, while great collections were amassed by members of the major aristocratic families.

The 1700s saw a return to collecting, due not only to the antiquarian interests of the popes but also to their desire to document the early history of the church and some of the main collections on view today were created. A major source of acquisitions was the great private collections which were partly or wholly sold when their owners suffered in the financial crises of the period. As a result Rome became the centre of the antiquities trade in Europe. To feed the growing market many commercial excavations were undertaken, for example those at Ostia and the Villa of the Quintilii (p. 343, Fig. 170) in the late 1700s. By law the Vatican had first choice of one-third of all finds from excavations and the option to purchase more. So many ancient art works were taken away from Italy (many on the Grand Tour wished to return with sculpture, paintings, and ancient vases) that Clement XIV (1769–74) restricted the export of antiquities. He also acquired many items for the Vatican, employed a large band of sculptors and marble-workers to restore the sculptures and, like other C18 popes, refurbished, altered, and built large parts of the Vatican complex to display the collections. He and his successor Pius VI (1775–99) created the **Museo Pio-Clementino**.

At the end of the 1700s the Vatican collections suffered under French Rule: Napoleon ordered the removal of many works of art and in 1798 famous pieces such as the Apollo Belvedere and the Laocöon were paraded through the streets of Paris in triumph.

The collections were reconstructed and extended in the 1800s, notably under Pius VII and Gregory XVI. Pius VII (1800–23) acquired a large number of works, created the **Museo Chiaramonti** and the **Braccio Nuovo**, banned the export of art works from the Papal State, and appointed Antonio Canova as Inspector General of Fine Arts in 1802. He also presided over the return from Paris in 1816 of many of the looted works. This was not without incident—the Laocöon was damaged when the sledge carrying it slipped in heavy snow on the Mont Cenis pass. Gregory XVI (1831–46) formed the **Etruscan and Egyptian Museums**. With the creation of the Kingdom of Italy in 1870 the Papacy could no longer claim a third of all antiquities found in Latium, and the flow of ancient artefacts into the Vatican was much reduced.

The C20 saw the creation of three new museums of ethnography, history, and modern religious art. There were some acquisitions of antiquities but the main changes to the archaeological collections were in the nature of reorganization and refurbishment. The **Lateran museums** were dismantled and moved to the Vatican under John XXIII (1958–63).

The **architectural setting** for the collections consists of a complex set of halls and galleries, many custom built. The architecture and rich decorations are of great interest; especially notable is the Museo Pio-Clementino, housed in a series of rooms, most built under the popes Clement XIV and Pius VI in the later 1700s. Simonetti was the architect of the whole project, designing a number of new rooms and a monumental stairway (Fig. 198, nos. 2–8). While each space is different in form, all share the use of classical elements—columns, capitals, etc., and are sumptuously decorated with paintings, mosaics, reliefs, and exotic stones. Inspiration for the form of some rooms was drawn from classical architecture—the Sala Rotonda (room 4) for example has a cupola largely inspired by that of the 'Temple of Minerva Medica' (p. 355).

A **visit** to the Vatican Museums requires stamina and map-reading skills. Due to the volume of visitors a one-way system has been in place for some time, and a choice of routes is given. This, combined with changes in which sections may be open or closed at any time, make it difficult to plan a visit in detail. The plan (Fig. 198) shows two main complexes of buildings some 300 m. apart and linked by series of galleries and courtyards. Inside the entrance on Viale Vaticano is a ticket office for tour parties. The monumental double staircase, built in 1932 with ascending and descending spirals cut into the hill to connect the street level with that of the museums, leads up to a ticket hall for individual visitors (there are also lifts). The **vestibule** has **mosaics** from Hadrian's Villa. Outside is the **Cortile delle Carrozze** with the **base of the column of Antoninus Pius** (see

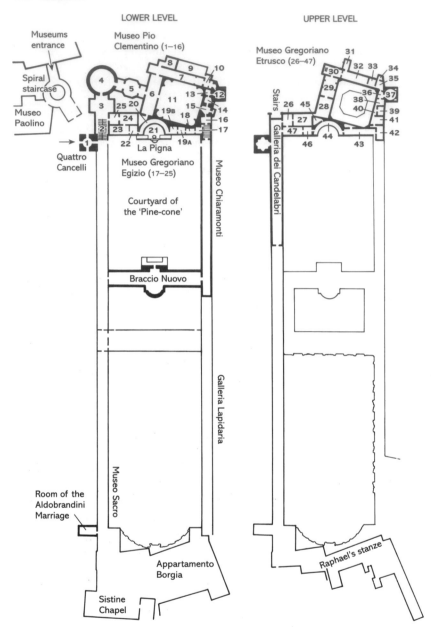

▲ **Fig. 198.** Vatican Museums

p. 193), which might not be visible as this area is under renovation in preparation for the Millennium celebrations.

A **vestibule** (**1**) leads to the other collections. The **Museo Pio-Clementino** (**2–16**), created in the later C18 by Clement XIV and Pius VI, mainly of Roman sculptures, is housed in a series of lavishly decorated spaces. The **Room of the Greek Cross** (**3**) has **two red porphyry sarcophagi** (C4 AD), the one on the left, decorated with large acanthus scrolls and erotes treading grapes, belonged to Constantina, daughter of Constantine the Great, and was found in her mausoleum on the Via Nomentana (p. 375). That on the right is of Helena, Constantine's mother, and comes from the mausoleum she built beside the catacombs of St Peter and Marcellinus on the Via Labicana (now Casilina, at Tor Pignattara) in about AD 320. Found in the early C17 and extensively restored (in porphyry) in an operation lasting nine years, it bears scenes of Roman cavalrymen slaughtering barbarian captives. The *Rotonda* (**4**), Simonetti's great circular gallery with cupola, has in the centre a massive **porphyry basin** (4.76 m. or 16 RF in diameter) first recorded in the C16 in front of the Senate House on the Forum, where it seems to have been set up as a public fountain in the C4 or C5. It will have been made originally for one of the great imperial *thermae*. The **mosaics** on the floor are from baths at Sacrofano and Otricoli; they portray mythical subjects including sea monsters and tritons. The **Room of the Muses** (**5**) contains the **Belvedere Torso**, in marble, dating around 100 BC and signed by Apollonius, son of Nestor, from Athens. The subject is much debated but might be Hercules. Unusual in never being restored, it was known at least by the 1430s, and had a great influence on Renaissance artists, including Michelangelo. The **Hall of the Animals** (**6**) contains a variety of sculptures of animals, both of the Roman period and also many wholly or in part (completing some ancient fragments) by Francesco Antonio Franzoni (1734–1818) who was employed at the Vatican as sculptor and restorer. The decorations of the **Cabinet of the Masks** (**8**) include eight columns and eight pilasters from an alabaster quarry near Terracina. In the floor are **four mosaics**, three representing comic masks, found around 1780 on the north side of Hadrian's Villa. A mosaic on the wall, from the same site, represents the Nile. The satyr in red marble also comes from Hadrian's Villa. All the statue bases are ancient altars. The **Octagonal Courtyard** (**11**), built after a design by Bramante and altered by Simonetti who added the octagonal portico in the Ionic style, is a showcase for famous pieces. The **Laocöon** statue group, found in 1506 near Sette Sale (p. 292), is a work of the C1 BC in the 'baroque' style of the day. Reputedly cut from one block of marble (but actually in seven pieces), it depicts Laocöon, the priest of Apollo at Troy, and his sons being suffocated by two snakes. The **Apollo Belvedere** is another early find, known since the 1490s, much admired and copied by Renaissance and later artists. It probably came from a villa near Grottaferrata, and was set up in the Belvedere Courtyard (from which it derives its name) by 1511. One niche holds statues made by Canova after 1797 when Napoleon removed so many of the Belvedere treasures to Paris. The vats and tubs made of hard Egyptian stones (including granite, serpentine, and diorite) are of Imperial Roman date, and were once fountains and basins in Roman baths. **Room 13** opens onto **Bramante's staircase** of the early C16. It is a heliocoidal ramp with granite columns in the four orders and provided the inspiration for the C20 entrance ramp. **Room 15** contains the **'Apoxyomenos'**, an athlete cleaning himself with a strigil, carved from a single block of marble, found around 1849 in Trastevere. The small **room 16** contains the **sarcophagus of L. Cornelius Scipio Barbatus**, in peperino, found in 1780 in the tomb of the Scipios (p. 328) near the via Appia.

The **Museo Chiaramonti (26)**, occupying part of a 300 m. long gallery designed by Bramante, was founded by Pius VII (1800–23) of the Chiaramonti family. It contains a fine collection of portrait busts of the Imperial period, sarcophagi, altars, and decorated architectural fragments. On the right is a series of funerary inscriptions and monuments including (section X, no. 26) the **tomb monument of the miller** P. Nonius Zethus, probably an ex-Imperial slave. Dating to the C1 AD, it is decorated with the tools of his trade, and has spaces for eight cremation urns, one still in place. It is interesting to compare the differences in **styles of portraiture** through the Imperial period. The female portraits often have complex coiffures which are datable to the reigns of particular emperors, for example the Trajanic style with a high crest of curls over the forehead, which contrasts sharply with the simpler Severan chignon. The busts show many restorations, especially the noses—almost none of which are original.

The **Galleria Lapidaria** (Gallery of Inscriptions) at the far end of the gallery (permit required, though occasionally visitors are routed this way) has more than 5,000 pagan and Christian inscriptions, many from tombs and catacombs beyond the city walls of Rome.

The **Braccio Nuovo** was built in 1817–22 by Raffaele Stern primarily to display statuary. The C19 frieze of stucco reliefs decorating the upper wall includes references to various antique statues in Rome at the time. The black-and-white Roman **mosaics** set into the floor come from a Roman villa near the third milestone of the via Ardeatina. **Ancient columns** incorporated in the decoration of the gallery include two of Numidian yellow from near the tomb of Cecilia Metella on the via Appia (p. 341), and two of oriental alabaster found in a Roman villa near Acqua Traversa. Most famous among the works displayed here is the enigmatic statue of **Augustus** in a niche on the right, found in 1863 in the villa of his wife Livia at Prima Porta near the eighth milestone of the via Flaminia. He is wearing military armour with his hand raised in speech but his bare feet indicate he is dead. The decoration on his breastplate refers to what he considered his greatest triumph—the return, in 20 BC, of the legionary standards lost to the Parthians in 53 BC. The colossal statue of a reclining bearded god on the left in the centre of the gallery represents the **Nile**, found together with one of the Tiber (Louvre) in 1513 near the church of S. Maria Sopra Minerva (the site of the Iseum, p. 207).The river-god is accompanied by 16 much restored baby *erotes* (referring apparently to the 16 cubits the Nile can rise during the rainy season), a sphinx, cornucopia, and crocodile. On the edges of his rocky couch are relief scenes including other Nilotic plants and animals.

The **Museo Gregoriano Egizio** (Gregorian Museum of Egyptian Antiquities) (**17–25**) was founded by Gregory XVI in 1839. Interest in Egyptian antiquities grew after the discoveries of Jean-François Champollion (1790–1832) and his decipherment of the Rosetta Stone in 1822, and major collections were established in 1824 in Turin and Florence, soon followed by that in the Vatican. **Rooms 17–18** contain a selection of material from Mesopotamia including some important Assyrian reliefs; **room 19a** has objects from Egypt dating from the C4 BC to the C15 AD. **Rooms 20–23** are of principal interest in the context of Rome: **room 20** contains three **pink (Aswan) granite statues** found in 1714 in the area of the imperial Gardens of Sallust on the Pincian hill, where they had occupied an Egyptian-style pavilion built by the emperor Caligula, following the death of his favourite sister Julia Drusilla in AD 38. Two, which Caligula had brought from Heliopolis, portray the Hellenistic rulers of Egypt in 284–246 BC, Ptolemy Philadelphus and Arsinöe (his sister and wife); the third represents Drusilla, with whom Caligula's relationship had probably been incestuous. This room opens onto the terrace of the **bronze pine cone (21)**, which was made for a monumental fountain (the water sprayed out of the tips of the leaves) located on the Field of Mars, either in the Baths of Agrippa or the Iseum. It is signed by Publius Cincius Salvius. The huge marble capital on which the cone is mounted comes from the Baths of Alexander Severus (p. 208). The **bronze peacocks** to either side once stood on the railings around the Mausoleum of Hadrian (p. 369). **Room 22** has fragments of columns from the Iseum, and a river-god statue with a cornucopia and crocodile in highly polished grey-blue marble. **Room 23** recreates part of the **Canopus of Hadrian's Villa at Tivoli** to display the Egyptian and Egyptianizing statues found there in the 1740s. Notable for its typically Roman blend of sculptural styles is the statue of Hadrian's 'favourite', the Bithynian youth **Antinous dressed as a Pharaoh.**

From Simonetti's staircase (**2**) a 300m. long corridor leads to the complex with the Sistine Chapel, although visitors are not always sent along this route. The corridor contains the antiquities belonging to the **Vatican Library Museum**: note the small ivories in custom-built cabinets in the first room. The **Room of the Aldobrandini Wedding**, if open, is well worth seeing. Its namepiece is a large panel from a **Roman wall**

painting, of the C2 AD, discovered in 1601, near the Esquiline Gate (p. 299). For over 150 years until the excavations at Pompeii and Herculaneum, it was the most celebrated example of ancient Roman painting, seen and copied by many artists including Van Dyck. The subject is still disputed but a key element seems to be a bride seated on a bed. Also in this room are two cabinets of **gold glass** dating from the C3–C4 AD. Mainly found marking tombs in the catacombs, the glass discs formed the bottoms of drinking cups.

The first floor can be reached via various routes including a staircase at **2** or via Bramante's famous stairway (**12** and **38**). The **Galleries of the Candelabra** were created when open loggias were closed in under Pius VI (1775–99) and are named after the elaborate Roman **marble candelabras** set at intervals down their length. They also contain many sculptures from old aristocratic collections.

The **Museo Gregoriano Etrusco** (Gregorian Museum of Etruscan Antiquities)—rooms **26–47**—was founded by Gregory XVI in 1837. Interest in Etruscan antiquities had developed since the early C18 and received a new impulse from major discoveries in the territory of the Papal State to the north of Rome and in the neighbouring Grand-Duchy of Tuscany. Many of the objects come from excavations carried out in south Etruria between 1828 and 1836 and others are from private collections such as that of Giacinto Guglielmi, acquired in 1989 (material from the site of Vulci). There are also a small number of pieces from Rome and other Latin sites.

Room 26 contains pottery and bronzes, mostly from tombs of the Early Iron Age (generally dated C9–C8 BC but probably starting in the C10). The material to the left is from Etruria and includes a group of pottery biconical cremation urns (C10 to earlier C8) found in 1776–8 at the Casal di Lanza cemetery of Vulci, and two similar urns in sheet bronze (C8 BC). To the right, the reconstructed **chariot** (*c.*550 BC) with its iron and sheet-bronze fittings was found at 'Roma Vecchia' (south of Rome) and acquired in 1804. The other objects date from the C10–C7, and come from Rome and Latin sites at Castelgandolfo and Palestrina. The pottery cremation urns shaped like huts (C10–8) are useful in reconstructing the appearance of huts found in excavations, such as those on the Palatine (see Fig. 52, p. 125). Note also the amber, which came by trade from the Baltic area, decorating bronze jewellery of the C8 and C7 BC.

Room 27 exhibits C7–C6 material found in Etruscan tombs at Cerveteri in 1836. Note in the cases to the left some fine-walled **bucchero cups**, one of which had been covered with silver sheet. On the right is the vast array of objects from the **Regolini–Galassi tomb** (named after its finders, a priest and an army general), one of the wealthiest 'princely' tombs yet found of the Orientalizing period (end of C8–C7), when Etruscan contacts with the eastern Mediterranean were particularly wide-ranging and intense. There were three separate burials, two in the corridor and one in an alcove, all dating to the first part of the C7 BC. The body at the end of the corridor, probably that of a woman, was accompanied by bronze, gold, and silver vessels, including a great bronze cauldron decorated with six lions' heads, and elaborate gold jewellery worked in repoussé and exquisite granulation—particularly splendid are the pectoral, the two arm-rings with figures of women, and the enormous brooch (*fibula*) with lions on the catch-plate and a series of tiny ducks in 3D on the leaf-shaped bow. The second burial in the corridor was of a man laid out on a funerary bed and surrounded by a rich panoply—note the eight bronze shields, a chariot with iron and bronze fittings, firedogs, sets of bronze and pottery vessels including 15 large storage jars, and a large wheeled bronze container—possibly an incense burner. Goods with the alcove burial included two gilded silver figured Cypro-Phoenician bowls.

Room 28 has a large collection of **Etruscan bronzes**—household items such as candelabra, mirrors, incense burners and *cistae* (cylindrical toilette boxes), as well as armour and sculptures. The Etruscans were famed in antiquity for the quality of their bronzes, and the Romans took thousands of statues and other bronzes as booty during their expansion into Etruria in the C4–C2 BC. The near life-size statue of a youthful warrior, the **'Mars'** found at Todi, dating to the C5 BC, was probably made at Orvieto. An inscription on the skirt of his breastplate reads (in Umbro-Latin) *Ahal Trutitis dunum dede*—Ahal Trutitis gives this as a gift—presumably to the sanctuary of his favourite deity. **Room 29** is filled with sarcophagi, grave markers (*stelai*), and tomb 'guardians' (animals and other figures) dating from the C6–C2 BC, carved in various local stones. Upstairs from **room 30** are a couple of rooms with jewellery (mostly from Vulci), small bronzes, and terracottas, including heads and large-scale pedimental sculptures. Note the **sheet-gold diadems** which were used as funerary wreaths. **Rooms 31–33** and **35–36** house a collection of **cinerary urns** of the C4–C2 BC from northern Etruria (Chiusi and Volterra) in local stones such as alabaster, with complex figurative scenes in relief drawn from Greek and Etruscan myth, sometimes combining both. **Rooms 39–40** show the **Antiquarium Romanum**—an eclectic mixture of bronzes, ceramics, architectural terracottas, ivories, and glass ranging in date from Etruscan to Roman. **Rooms 44–47** contain the important collection of painted **Greek, Italian, and Etruscan vases**, mainly excavated from south Etrurian tombs during the earlier C19. Note the many imported black- and red-figure vases of Athenian Greek manufacture and their Etruscan equivalents.

Just before the exit from the Vatican Museums, in the **Museo Paolino**, is the **Museo Gregoriano Profano** (Gregorian Museum of Pagan Antiquities) founded by Gregory XVI (1831–46), moved here from the Lateran by John XXIII, and opened in 1970. It contains mostly Roman sculpture, much in the Classical Greek style, and some early Greek works. It also has the **mosaic of the 'unswept floor'**— a *trompe l'oeil* scene of banquet debris signed by Heraclitus, from a house on the Aventine. The **Cancelleria reliefs** (p. 214) are two large reliefs of the Flavian period (AD 70–96) showing the return of Vespasian to Rome and the departure of Domitian (recut into Nerva). The sculptures from the **tomb of the Haterii,** found on the Via Casilina in 1848, carry funeral scenes and one of building a tomb with the aid of a huge slave-driven crane. One relief shows five major imperial monuments (see p. 142, Fig. 58) suggesting that the family were building contractors in the late C1 AD. See also the unfinished statue of the **Barbarian Prisoner** from the marble-working area of the Field of Mars (p. 180), and a **funerary statue** (*c.* AD 210–20) of a woman dressed as Hercules' companion Omphale. She is nude but for the animal skin over her head with the paws neatly knotted in front, holds a club, and also wears a fine curled wig as befits a Roman woman of some rank.

Museo Nazionale di Villa Giulia.

*Piazzale di Villa Giulia 9. *State*

The Villa Giulia museum houses the most important and comprehensive collection of Etrusco-Italic antiquities (other major collections include those in the Vatican and Florence Archaeological Museum). The Villa Giulia Museum was set up by law in 1889 as the Museum of later prehistoric antiquities from Latium—north and south of the Tiber; (new discoveries from Rome itself went to the Terme museum). In 1909 the area of its jurisdiction was reduced to Southern Etruria, that is, northern Lazio.

▼ **Fig. 199.** Villa Giulia Museum. Plans of ground and first floors

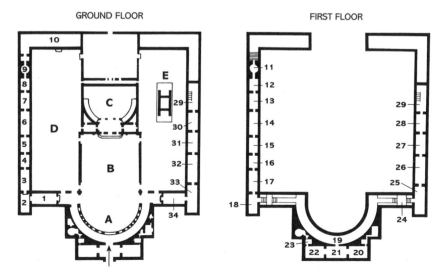

Official excavations in Southern Etruria during the C20 have yielded large quantities of finds. A feature of the museum is the topographical sections in which material from the same context—tomb, sanctuary, votive deposit, is displayed as a whole unit, thus contributing greatly to the study of the cultures to the north and south of the Tiber in the first millennium BC. A major reorganization was undertaken in the late 1950s by the Superintendent, Enrico Bartoccini, and the present installation mostly dates from the 1950s and 60s.

The **architectural setting** is the Villa Giulia, an elegant late Renaissance villa designed by Vignola for Pope Julius III (1550–5). Set in lands which extended from the hills of Parioli to the Tiber at the Milvian Bridge, the villa was linked to the river by a canal. Today only the main casino (A) and the nymphaeum (C) designed by Vasari remain of the original complex. The two-storeyed casino has a Renaissance façade and a hemi-cycle at the back which anticipates the Baroque. The marbles and sculptures which originally decorated the niches of the atrium and nymphaeum have long gone, dispersed to various collections including that of the Vatican. Also largely lost are the fine stuccoes of the cortile (B), loggia, and nymphaeum, destroyed through neglect and architectural alterations. However, some sections of stucco and painted decoration remain; the vault of the portico at the rear of the casino is painted as a pergola supporting a riot of vegetation, birds, and cupids.

On the ground floor, **rooms 1–10** form part of the topographic section. The artefacts almost all came directly from official excavations and are arranged according to site. With the exception of Tarquinia there are finds from all the main Etruscan sites of Southern Etruria—Vulci, Bisenzio, Veii, and Cerveteri. **Room 1** has early Etruscan stone sculptures: note the later C6 tomb statues from Vulci of the hippocamp with rider and the centaur. **Room 2** contains C10–C8 BC finds from Vulci belonging to the proto-Etruscan **Villanovan** cultural group including cinerary urns in the form of model huts and biconical vases, bronze weapons, and jewellery. **Rooms 3– 4** have finds from Vulci mostly dating to the C7–C6, especially of pottery, both imported Greek figured ware and local Etrusco-Corinthian. A basement room, reached from **room 5**, contains a reconstruction of an **Etruscan chamber tomb** from Cerveteri, with two chambers and the tomb goods. **Room 5** has finds from Vulci dating to the C4 and Hellenistic period, including three unusual models—of a temple, a stoa, and what might be a tower or lighthouse, and the terracotta anatomical votives of Hellenistic date—hands, breasts, and internal organs. **Room 6** contains Villanovan to Archaic period material from the inland site of **Bisenzio**—noted for its profusion of local pottery with painted geometric decoration, and a bronze biconical urn (*c.*710 BC) and wheeled object both with a series of cast bronze figures and animals engaged in possibly ritual activities. **Room 7** exhibits the famous late C6 **polychrome terracottas**, found between 1916 and 1939, which decorated the roof of the Portonaccio temple at Veii. Most striking are the life-size figures which stood on the roof ridge—probably representing the myth in which Hercules (with lion's skin) carries off the Ceryneian hind (sacred to Diana, sister of Apollo) and is challenged by Apollo (the almost complete striding figure). Also present are Hermes (with hat) who may be acting as intermediary, and a woman carrying a child—possibly Leto (mother of Apollo). They might be by the school of Vulca, the sculptor who is credited with the terracotta decorations of the original Temple of Jupiter Capitolinus in Rome (p. 231). The **maenad, gorgon, and Acheloos antefixes** are mounted on the wall to show their original position on the building. **Room 9** contains another fine example of large-scale painted terracotta sculpture—the **sarcophagus of the married couple** from Cerveteri, dated to the late C6. Acquired in 1893, this depicts a man and woman reclining on a banquet couch, their garments modelled in exquisite detail. They originally held objects of ritual significance—perhaps an egg (his right hand), a perfume flask, and a piece of fruit (her right and left). **Room 10** has a large collection of pottery from Cerveteri, dating between the C7 and C2 BC, including many imported black- and red-figure pieces. The great majority of vessels were used for the consumption of wine in the exclusive social contexts of the banquet and drinking party.

Upstairs in the north wing is the **Antiquarium (rooms 11–17)** which contains finds mostly not acquired from official excavations, and consequently lacking secure provenances. The material comes from various sources: from the Kircherian Museum which was broken up in 1913 and distributed amongst the four state museums of Rome, from acquisitions, and donations. There are many Etruscan bronzes (C7–C3 BC)—personal tools and ornaments, household equipment such as the well-known and finely crafted **candelabra and mirrors** (especially in room **14**), and **votive figurines** including the elongated figures which so influenced the C20 sculptor Giacometti. **Room 18** contains the Etruscan two-wheeled chariot from a C6 BC tomb at Castro, where it was found beside the bodies of two horses. Carefully excavated in 1967 and restored, this is a rare example of such a vehicle with its iron bound wheels and figured sheet-bronze decoration.

The hemi-cycle **(19)** contains the **Castellani collection** of Greek and Etrusco-Italic pottery (C8–C1 BC), donated by Augusto Castellani to the state in 1919, and installed in the Villa Giulia by 1923. There are some particularly fine Attic black- and red-figure vases, many signed. Almost all the main classes and periods of pottery are represented.

The small rooms 22–23 house material from Pyrgi, one of the ports of Cerveteri. **Room 22** displays a reconstruction model of temple A, and various architectural terracottas from both temples A and B; see the large terracotta plaque (*c.*460 BC) from Temple A bearing a scene in high relief of the Seven Against Thebes (at the centre Tydeus bites the head of

Melanippos), antefixes from the 'cellae', and an Acheloos acroterion found in 1996 in the South Area—the Apollo sanctuary belonging to building B and dated to the late C6. **Room 23** has copies of the **Pyrgi tablets**—three sheet-gold plaques, found in 1964 and dating to around 500 BC, recording in both Etruscan and Phoenician the dedication of the sanctuary at Pyrgi to the goddesses Uni (Etruscan) and Astarte (Phoenician) by Thefarie Velianas a ruler of Cerveteri. This cultural mixing in a sacred context underlines the cosmopolitan nature of this thriving port. Also on display are votive inscriptions on pottery and bronzes, and coins—silver tetradrachme from Syracuse, Messene, Leontinoi, and Athens, dating to the C5.

The **South wing** contains more of the topographical section of the museum, with material from the other major sites north and south of Rome—most of the material is from tombs and sanctuaries. At the time of writing, rooms 25–30 containing material from the Faliscan area north of Rome (sites of Falerii Veteres, Capena, and Narce) are closed for refurbishment. Room 29 has architectural terracottas from the **temples of Falerii Veteres.** To the right are terracottas from the Temple of Apollo at Lo Scasato (C4–C2 BC), and to the left terracottas from the pediment and entablature of one or both temples near Sassi Caduti. These include sculpted figures which filled the pediment. Rooms 30–3 contain material from the Latin cultural area south of the Tiber—from the sites of Nemi, Lanuvium, Velletri, Gabii, Satricum, and Praeneste.

Room 33 is dedicated to the Latin site of Praeneste and its environs. The Barberini collection, acquired in 1908 by the state, consisted of goods from various C4–C2 BC tombs, and the rich Orientalizing (late C8–C7) **Barberini tomb**, which is displayed alongside items from the similarly rich C7 **Bernardini tomb**. These trench tombs contained a variety of prestige goods which reveal wide cultural contacts with Greece and the Near East. Note the Cypro-Phoenician **gilded silver plate** with repoussé figured decoration. Also characteristic of the period are the large **gold fibulas**, the bronze throne, the ivories, and the bronze cauldron with cast figures and animals peering over the rim. Also in this room are the contents of **C4–C2 BC tombs**: note the many bronzes, especially the toilet items, mirrors, strigils, spatulas, and cistae (toilette boxes). The **Ficoroni cista** (late C4 BC), found in 1738, is the largest and finest known example. A cylindrical sheet-bronze vessel with cast feet and handle, it bears engraved scenes from the legend of Jason and the Argonauts, with an inscription naming the maker as Novios Plautios. **Room 34** has finds from the Etrurian and Umbrian sites of Terni, Todi, and Nocera Umbra, mostly from tombs.

In the garden is a full-size reconstruction of the **Temple at Aletrium** (Alatri) (E) by Count Adolfo Cozza (1891) based on the archaeological remains and Vitruvius' description of the Tuscan temple type. It is complete with painted terracotta decorations.

Museo Nazionale Romano (delle Terme).
Map, Fig. 174

Via delle Terme. *State.

One of Italy's great national collections, the National Roman Museum was founded in 1889 along with the Villa Giulia museum, to hold state collections of antiquities from Rome and neighbouring areas. It was housed at first in parts of the Baths of Diocletian in the expectation that the whole site would eventually become available. Unfortunately, that has not been the case, the collections have vastly outgrown the space, and the building itself developed major structural problems, with the result that much of the museum has been closed for decades. At present small selections of material are on show in four locations—at the original building, the ex-Planetarium/Aula Ottagonale, the Palazzo Massimo, and the Palazzo Altemps.

The **collection** consists largely of objects found in Rome and the environs after 1870, and also material from older Roman collections: part of the Kircherian museum, broken up in 1913, and the Ludovisi-Boncompagni collection acquired by the state in 1901.

The older display focussed almost exclusively on 'fine art'—statues and other sculpture, wall paintings and mosaics, but the new reorganization is bringing the many other categories of material out of store: inscriptions, architectural fragments, brick stamps, measuring devices and weights, coins, medals, and jewellery.

Terme Building. Map, Fig. 174: 1–7

Via delle Terme

The Terme museum took its name from its location—within the imperial Baths of Diocletian (p. 352), including sections of the convent of the Certosini of S. Maria degli Angeli, built into the *natatio* and side halls of the baths in 1563–6.

Parts of the Terme building open to visitors at present are the front **garden** with tombstones, inscriptions, and architectural fragments, one small room, and the Great Cloister. The small room, in the wing between the garden and the cloister contains the two famous statues of a **discobolus** (discus-thrower) from Castelporziano and from the Lancellotti collection. They face each other, allowing comparison of form and technique (C2 AD).

The **Great Cloister**, built in 1565 (wrongly ascribed to Michelangelo), is filled with sculptures, sarcophagi and other funerary monuments, architectural fragments, and inscriptions. Parts may be inaccessible due to building work.

Palazzo Massimo. Map, Fig. 174

Piazza dei Cinquecento

Across the road from the Terme site, this palazzo was designed in 1883–7 by Camillo Pistrucci to house the Collegio Massimiliano Massimo. It has recently been restored to be the main seat of the Museo Nazionale Romano. It will contain the finer and more famous pieces of Greek and Roman sculpture in the museum's collection, as well as some mosaics, wall paintings, coins, medals, and jewellery. At the time of writing the ground floor is open and the other floors are in preparation.

The ground floor houses mainly sculpture. A small room by the ticket office contains what was probably a cult statue—a twice life-size **Minerva** dating between the late C1 BC and the beginning of the C1 AD, found in Rome in 1923 near via Marmorata. Her dress is of Numidian yellow with details in black marble, her feet in white Italian (Luna) marble, the face is a modern cast from an Athena statue. **Rooms 1–2** contain marble sculpture from the time of Sulla to Augustus (*c.*100 BC–AD 14), the *fasti antiates maiores*, fragments of an ancient calendar from Antium (Anzio) probably dating to 84–55 BC, male portraits from Palestrina and Mentana in various styles, and a statue—the **Tivoli General**—datable about 70 BC from the sanctuary of Hercules Victor, the ageing face contrasting with a youthful athletic body. It was carved out of eleven pieces of marble. **Room 3** has sculpture of the Julio-Claudian period. Note the **two bronze heads**, one of the imperial prince Germanicus, brother of Tiberius, dating to the earlier C1 AD and found in the Tiber, and that of L. Cornelius Pusio dating to the mid to late C1 AD found on the Quirinal (via IV Novembre). The latter is accompanied by an inscription on bronze dedicated to Pusio (the name means 'pretty lad') by the centurion M. Vibius Marcellus. **Room 4** at present has a display of bronze, gold, and silver **coins** from the C7 BC to the late C1 AD, in chronological order. **Room 5** has a **painted frieze** from a columbarium on the Esquiline, dated mid C1 BC, and depicting scenes from the Trojan wars and the legendary origins of Rome. Also the famous togate statue of the emperor **Augustus as Pontifex Maximus**, dating about 20 BC, found in the via Labicana. Only its fine portrait head and hands were carved in best white Greek (Parian) marble, the body in Italian (Luna). **Room 7** contains antique Greek statues found in Rome. The most well-known is the **Dying Niobid** from the Gardens of Sallust, dated *c.*440 BC. In Greek myth she is one of the daughters of Niobe, and was shot with an arrow which she is trying to remove. **Room 8** contains examples of the so-called 'neo-Attic' style of sculpture characteristic of sculptors from Athens working for Roman patrons from the end of the C2 BC to the early imperial period. Much of their repertoire was drawn from the classical past. An altar (end of the C1 BC) found 22 km. down the via Nomentana, is decorated with figures of muses and maenads relating to the cult of Dionysus (the Roman

Bacchus or Liber Pater). A basin decorated with marine figures, dated to *c*.100 BC, was found in the area of the hospital of Santo Spirito, near the Vatican. It will have decorated a bath or garden.

It is anticipated that the arrangement of the other floors will be along these lines: **First floor**—sculptures from the Imperial villas, including Hadrian's villa at Tivoli, and Nero's villa at Subiaco. **Second floor**—wall paintings and mosaics from the Republican period onwards: the **garden paintings from the Villa of Livia at Prima Porta** are masterly frescoes from a subterranean dining room of about 40 BC; they were detached and restored in 1952–3 to save them from decay. The room (*c*.6 by 12 m.) has been reconstructed; all four walls carry paintings of a garden with a low fence in front of a meadow, with trees and shrubs beyond. Various species of plants and birds are identifiable. The **Farnesina stuccoes and wall paintings** come from a huge riverside villa destroyed when building the Tiber embankment in 1879. The villa dated from about 20 BC and may have belonged to Augustus' colleague Marcus Agrippa. The decorations represent volutes, vegetation, landscapes, figures, and Bacchic scenes. Many Second and Third style paintings were found in the same building—these include figured scenes of mythological subjects, landscapes, theatrical masks, and many and varied architectural structures.

The **basement** will contain coins, medals, and jewellery, and other Greek and Roman sculptures.

Ex-Planetarium or Rotunda Diocletiani or Aula Ottagonale. Map, Fig. 178: 8

Via Parigi

This is the hall at the west corner of the central block of the Baths of Diocletian (see p. 352). The interior is octagonal with a completely conserved cupola. In the C19 it was converted into a Planetarium and now displays Roman statues and busts, mostly C2–C3 AD, and from the great Imperial Baths of Caracalla and Diocletian.

Two exceptional bronze statues are the showpieces, both chance finds from the flank of the Quirinal hill in 1885. One is an over life-size **statue of a man** portrayed in heroic nudity, variously believed to be a late Hellenistic Greek ruler or a Roman general, dating from *c*.100 BC. The other bronze is a **seated boxer**, still wearing his heavy leather boxing gloves (*caestus*). Also a work of the C1 BC, the lips and the injuries on face, arms, and legs are inlaid with copper, and the cauliflower ears, broken nose and dazed expression are all vividly rendered. The rock seat is modern. It was thought to be signed by Apollonios, son of Nestor, of Athens, the sculptor who made the Belvedere Torso (Vatican, p. 389), but recent cleaning has not confirmed this.

On the left half of the hall all the sculptures (3–12) come from the Baths of Caracalla (p. 319). The two herms (5–6) with heads of young and old Apollo in archaic Greek style were found in the garden precinct; the nude statues (an athlete, Hercules, Mercury, Apollo, and Venus) will have stood around the rooms of the central bathing block. The huge bearded **head of Aesculapius** (12), god of healing, came from a statue almost 4 m. (13½ RF) high, which stood in the great cold hall (*frigidarium*) in company with others of its size. When discovered (in 1901) there were still traces of gilding on its face. An **Aphrodite** (13), in Parian marble, found in the Baths of Diocletian near the external large niche of the NW arm of the church of Santa Maria degli Angeli in 1932, dates to the early Imperial period. This was found together with a **male torso** (15) in the Classical Greek manner, dating C1 AD. Also from the Baths of Diocletian are the head of an athlete (16), a herm (17), and a togate figure (19).

Palazzo Altemps. Map, Fig. 77: 19

*Via S. Apollinare. *State*

Just north of Piazza Navona, this new outpost of the Museo Nazionale Romano principally accommodates the Ludovisi collection acquired by the state in 1901. The collection was formed in the early C17 by Cardinal Ludovico Ludovisi, nephew of pope Gregory XV (1621–3) and originally housed in his great villa on the Pincian hill (rebuilt in 1890 the villa is now the American Embassy). The sculptures were extensively restored by contemporary sculptors, as was the fashion of the time, many by Alessandro Algardi (1595–1654) and others by Gian Lorenzo Bernini (1598–1680).

The Palazzo Altemps is a fine Renaissance palace begun for Girolamo Riario c.1480, then refashioned after 1578 to the design of Martino Longhi the Elder. It has a courtyard with portico and loggias, Ionic pilasters, and a simple façade on three floors. The palazzo was acquired by the state in 1982 and has been restored. The chapel on the first floor has frescoes by Pomarancio and Ottavio Leoni (1604–17). At the time of writing, opening hours have not yet been fixed and the Palazzo may not be consistently open to the public.

One of the notable pieces is the **Ludovisi throne**, in Greek (Aegean) marble, a work of the C5 BC, probably brought to Rome from a sanctuary in Greek southern Italy after the conquests of the C3 BC. It was found in 1887 in the grounds of the Villa Ludovisi—the area of the Imperial Gardens of Sallust. The low relief scene carved on the back shows the birth of Aphrodite who rises from the sea flanked by attendants. The left side shows a naked girl seated and playing the double flute, and the right a clothed woman burning incense on a brazier.

Museo Barracco. Map, Fig. 77: 23

*Corso Vittorio Emanuele 168. *Comune*

The **collection** was created by Baron Giovanni Barracco and consists of some 380 pieces of ancient sculpture and some pottery, mosaics, and smaller items. It not only illustrates the history of sculpture in the Mediterranean and Near East up to the medieval period, but is a record of one man's life as a collector in the later 1800s.

Born in 1829 to a wealthy family in southern Italy, Barracco studied classics and archaeology and soon after 1860, when he moved to Rome to take up a career in politics, began collecting antiquities choosing fine examples where possible, advised by Wolfgang Helbig, the director of the German Archaeological Institute, and Ludwig Pollack another distinguished scholar. After 1870, intensive building work in Rome uncovered a great profusion of archaeological sites and finds, and the antiquities market flourished. Barracco displayed his acquisitions in his home on Via del Corso.

In 1904 Barracco donated his collection to the Comune of Rome who allocated a plot on Corso Vittorio Emanuele on which Barracco then built a museum to house it. Designed by Gaetano Koch, the museum had a Neoclassical façade, spacious well-lit rooms, and mobile stands but was demolished in 1938 and the collection moved to the Capitoline Museums. There it remained in store until 1948 when it was put on display at its present location.

The small **Renaissance palace** in which the collection is installed was designed by Antonio da Sangallo the Younger in 1523 for the Breton prelate Thomas le Roy. The string courses are carved with his heraldic device—Farnese lilies—which gave the building its name of La Farnesina ai Baullari. The style has parallels in Florentine Renaissance architecture, with the small cloister, internal loggias on first and second floors, and string courses in travertine. Some C17 frescoes remain on the first floor.

The exhibits are arranged on three floors. The **ground floor** has a few examples of Greek and Roman statuary, including an Apollo seated on a rock, in Pentelic marble (head is missing). It was found in the Gardens of Caesar in Trastevere and was probably carved originally for a temple pediment.

On the **first floor** there is a small collection of Egyptian antiquities in **room 1**. These include some fine pieces of sculpture such as the **lion's head** in wood of the 18th Dynasty, a bust of a bearded man, in diorite, dating to the Roman period in Egypt, and the **stele of Nofer** from Giza, dating to the 4th Dynasty (2640–2520 BC). Nofer was scribe and treasurer to the Pharaoh, and is shown in the usual position—seated before an offering table. **Room 2** has Sumerian and Assyrian pieces: note the Assyrian reliefs from Nimrud and Nineveh. **Room 3** has Etruscan material, including three **grave markers** from Northern Etruria dating to the early C5 BC. The largest is a base in local stone carved in low relief with funeral scenes including dancing and lamentation. Traces of red and black paint are visible.

The **second floor** houses Greek, Roman, and medieval antiquities. A number of the Roman sculptures are in the Classical Greek manner. The Greek sculpture includes some fragmentary Attic grave stele. A good example, and probably the oldest Greek piece in the museum, is the **stele** in Parian marble with horse and rider in **room 5**, dating to *c*.520 BC. **Rooms 7–8** contain Hellenistic period works including the marble sculpture of a **greyhound** licking her wounds, signed by Sosikles, and also Greek and South Italian pottery. In **room 9** there is a mixture of Italic, Roman, and medieval material. Note the **bust of a child** of the Julio-Claudian family (C1 AD), and a fragment of polychrome **mosaic** (end C1 AD) of two partridges at a water bowl, both from Livia's villa at Prima Porta.

On request visitors will be shown the **Roman remains** which were uncovered below the palace in 1899 (see p. 213), and wall paintings (now in a separate part of the palazzo) from the late imperial building—fragmentary panels of landscape scenes with people and animals.

Caelian Antiquarium

*Via del Parco del Celio 22. *Comune*

Opened in 1995, the Antiquarium's main theme is 'Daily Life in Imperial Rome', including pottery, glass, as well as mosaics (the Harbour at Portus), and wall paintings (from under S. Crisogono in Trastevere). Set up in the garden on the left of the entrance is an interesting selection of funerary monuments and various architectural elements, such as the ceiling panels from the temple building behind the Column of Marcus Aurelius (see p. 193).

Museo Palatino (Palatine Antiquarium)

*Palatine Hill (see Map, Fig. 50). *State (timed groups of 25 every 30 mins, no extra charge beyond the cost of the ticket to the Palatine)*

The **collections** began in the later C19 with the finds made by Pietro Rosa (see p. 122) but in 1882 were then transferred to the newly created Museo Nazionale Romano at the Terme. Re-opened on a small scale in the present building in 1936 (converted from part of the Convent of the Sisters of the Visitation) it was then closed from 1984 to 1997 for structural repairs, renovation, and reorganization.

The **ground floor** documents the history of settlement on the Palatine from the Palaeolithic (100,000 BC) to the end of the Republic (mid C1 BC). The Iron Age (C10–C7 BC) is mainly represented by the finds from the Precinct of Victory at the SW corner of the hill (p. 123), including models of its hut village and the 'House of Romulus', and material from tombs. Rome's expanding empire in the mid-Republic is reflected in the splendid terracotta statues of Jupiter and Apollo and other architectural terracotta decorations dating c.300 BC, possibly from the Temple of Victory in its earliest phase (pp. 123, 126).

The **first floor** is devoted to the Imperial period from Augustus (31 BC–14 AD) to the C4 AD. Room V displays elements from the Temple of Apollo (p. 131): **Danaïds in black and red Greek marble**, brightly painted **terracotta panels**, a fresco showing the seated Apollo against a blue background, and a remarkable statue of a **young athlete in black Egyptian basalt** found in the area to the east of the temple. Room VI has decorations from parts of the palace built by Nero before the fire of AD 64, including **figurative panels in coloured marble** and frescoes using gold and blue glass paste. Rooms VII-VIII are peopled with Imperial portraits from Nero to the Tetrarchs together with a taste of the wealth of marble veneer, architectural ornament, and sculptural reliefs which adorned the **Palace of Domitian** and its successors. Room IX hosts statues in best quality white marbles which filled the niches and colonnades of the palace halls and courts and a selection of others from around the hill. The seated statue of **Magna Mater** was found near her Palatine temple (p. 126). The '**Aura**', personifying a gentle breeze, was found built into a medieval tower near the Arch of Titus but is apparently a work of about 400 BC, which will have been taken from the pediment of a Greek temple and, presumably, reused in a Roman one (as both Augustus and Sosius did for their temples of Apollo, see pp. 131 and 245).

Galleria Borghese

*Villa Umberto I, Piazzale del Museo Borghese. *State*

This gallery is best known for its collection of Renaissance and later paintings and sculpture, including Bernini's greatest early sculpture and works by Titian, Caravaggio, and Canova, but it also contains some significant antiquities from Rome.

The history of the antiquities collection is complex, though largely in the hands of one family—the Borghese. Scipione Borghese (1576–1633), the most prominent collector in the family, was appointed cardinal in 1605 by his uncle Pope Paul V (Camillo Borghese), and with the income began to collect antique statues. They came from other collections and from unofficial excavations and accidental finds. The sculpture was initially kept in his residences, the Palazzo Campeggi and a summer residence on the Quirinal, but was moved in 1625 to his new country villa on the Pincian hill—the Casino (or Villa) Borghese which was built for him by Giovanni Vasanzio in 1613–15. The sculpture moved to the Casino Borghese (it took 200 loads) also included antiquities collected by Giovanni Battista (1554–1609) another of Scipione's uncles. Prince Marcantonio Borghese (1601–58) was responsible for the elaborate Neoclassical frescoes on the ceilings of the Villa Borghese and other decoration of the rooms of the ground floor and some of the rooms of the upper floor in the late 1700s. He adapted the interior in 1782 to a museum and gallery. To the collection of antiquities were added the paintings which had been housed in the Palazzo Borghese.

The Borghese antiquities collection was purchased in 1807 by Napoleon Bonaparte, brother-in-law of Camillo Borghese (1775–1832) who had married Pauline Bonaparte and become a Prince of the French imperial family. By this time the collection consisted of some 523 pieces, including many famous sculptures. All but a few went to Paris and still remain in the Louvre. The collection was later rebuilt by Luigi Canina with new acquisitions and sculptures found in excavations on Borghese property in Italy.

The villa with its contents was purchased by the state in 1902. Closed, wholly or partly, since 1983 for repairs (the building rests unstably over a network of tunnels, some natural, some cut in antiquity) it was finally reopened in the summer of 1997 but as a precautionary measure the number of visitors is restricted to 300 on the ground floor and 90 on the first floor at any one time. Visitors must book tickets ahead of their visit, preferably some days beforehand; they will then be admitted at a set time, for two hours.

In the **portico** are fragments of **reliefs of the Praetorians** belonging to the 'Great Trajanic frieze' (p. 274), in marble, built into the C4 triumphal arch 'Arco di Portogallo' on the via Lata (via del Corso) demolished in 1527. Other panels were similarly reused on the Arch of Constantine (p. 272). The whole relief was over 30 m. long, and a reconstruction in plaster can be seen in the Museo della Civiltà Romana (p. 407). The **salone** has colossal heads from cult statues of Hadrian, Antoninus Pius, and two deified empresses; set in the floor are five fragments of spectacular **gladiator and wild animal hunt mosaics**, from a villa of the C3 AD near the Via Tuscolana at Torrenova in 1834. **Room 2** (room of David) has more reliefs and two sides from a sarcophagus with reliefs of the labours of Hercules and the birth of Apollo and Diana, of the mid-C2 AD. **Room 3** (room of Apollo and Daphne) has a marble amphora—carved in the 'Neo-Attic' style of the late C1 BC with a scene of Bacchic dance. **Room 4** (gallery of the Emperors) has a series of C17 busts of Roman emperors with heads in red porphyry on busts of alabaster, a large Roman burial urn in red porphyry from the mausoleum of Hadrian, and a copy in bronze of the **Farnese Bull**, by Antonio Susini. **Room 5** (room of the Hermaphrodite) has a Roman mosaic of a fishing scene, and a Roman version of the famous Hellenistic statue of the **sleeping hermaphrodite**. **Room 7** (the Egyptian room) has a black marble statue of Iris dating about AD 150. **Room 8** (room of the faun) contains the **Borghese satyr** (also known as the dancing faun, and the Marsyas), the hands wrongly restored, a Roman sculpture in the Greek manner, found in 1824 at Monte Calvo (Sabina), and a bust of Tiberius dating to C1 AD.

Museo Preistorico ed Etnografico 'Luigi Pigorini' (Luigi Pigorini Museum of Prehistory and Ethnography)

*Via Lincoln 1, EUR. *State*

This is one of the main collections of its type in Europe, and is the Italian national collection of prehistory and ethnography. It gathers together a wealth of prehistoric artefacts from Italy and elsewhere in Europe, and also a fine ethnographic collection from many parts of the world. There are some 170,000 items.

The **collection** was built up in different phases. In the late C17 the priest Athanasius Kircher began a collection of antiquities and ethnographic artefacts in the Collegio Romano, and these then formed part of the Museo Preistorico del Nuovo Regno d'Italia founded in 1876 (later the Museo Kircheriano). From the early 1870s the prehistorian Luigi Pigorini developed the collection, and was responsible for the principles that underlay the founding and growth of the museum. The ethnographic material was largely provided by Italian explorers, also by gifts and acquisitions from many private collections. The Kircher collection was broken up in 1913, with the ethnographic section remaining at the Collegio Romano and the rest being dispersed to other Roman museums. Also in 1913 the collection of Enrico Giglioli, some 17,000 objects, was acquired. The prehistoric collection covers the Neolithic, Bronze, and Early Iron Ages, and while concentrating on Europe also has some material from Asia Minor, Russia, North Africa, and the Americas. The museum was moved to the **Palazzo delle Scienze** at EUR by 1962.

Generally, only a limited number of rooms are open and it is impossible to predict which these will be. Most relevant for the archaeology of Rome is the material from **Late Bronze and Early Iron Age cemeteries in Rome** and the environs, especially the contents of the tombs from the Forum and the Esquiline—evidence of the earliest stages of the development of the Roman civilization.

Museo della Civiltà Romana (Museum of Roman Civilization)

*Piazza Agnelli, EUR. *State*

This is an unusual museum in that the exhibits are mostly not actual ancient artefacts but models, casts, plans, and maps. Documenting the history of Rome and various aspects of Roman civilization across the empire, all areas of life and culture are covered, especially technology, agriculture, building types, towns, and cities. Various artefacts such as sculptures, reliefs, and frescoes are reproduced at full-size, and there are many models of buildings and settlements. The casts were mainly made for a great archaeological exhibition held at the Baths of Diocletian in 1911, and the Augustan Exhibition of Roman Culture in 1937.

The museum is located in an imposing building paid for by FIAT and donated to the city of Rome.

Principle attractions are the **scale model of the city of Rome** at the time of Constantine (the scale, 1:250, is almost the same as that of the Marble Plan, see p. 153); the complete series of casts of the **Columns of Trajan** (Fig. 72, p. 165) **and Marcus Aurelius** (Fig. 89, p. 195); and a reconstruction in plaster of the '**great Trajanic frieze**' (p. 274).

Museo dell'Alto Medioevo (Museum of Early Medieval Antiquities)

*Piazza Marconi, EUR. *State*

Located on the first floor of the Palazzo delle Scienze, the same building which houses the Museo Pigorini, this small collection was established in 1967 and contains Italian material dating from the fall of the Roman empire to the C10 AD. There is late C5 AD material from the Palatine— sculpture including a Byzantine emperor and empress, and jewellery; C7–10 church reliefs and friezes; C7 glass; and C5–C8 coptic materials and fabrics.

Catacombs (Map: Fig. 200)

By Judith Toms

Catacombs are complex networks of underground passages and rooms used for burial found in many places around the Mediterranean, but the most famous and extensive are those of Rome. They lie beyond the Roman city walls and near main Roman roads in places with suitable deposits of soft volcanic tufa and date from C1 to C5. Multiple burials in underground chambers were common in the first millennium BC in central Italy (e.g. the chamber tombs of the Etruscans, and Roman *columbaria*) and the catacombs may be seen as a continuation of this ancient practice. Earlier burials were generally cremations, but the rite changed to inhumation in the early C2 AD. The term catacomb was first applied, by 354, to the catacombs of St Sebastian and by the C9 was extended to the others. It derives from the Greek *katà kymbas* (near the hollows), probably referring to the pozzolana quarries at the St Sebastian site. The catacombs were mainly used by Christians, though some also contain earlier pagan burials, and a few were reserved for Jews. Some of the earliest catacombs seem to have been located on private land, but ownership and management soon passed to the Church. In spite of a commonly held belief it is unlikely that catacombs were much used for refuge.

The full extent of the catacombs is not known but must total hundreds of kilometres. They were excavated by skilled grave-diggers—the *fossores*, sometimes starting from old pozzolana quarries (*arenarie*). The galleries vary in height—they can be over 20 feet high as a result of lowering the passages to make room for more burials, are generally about a metre wide, and are arranged on as many as five superimposed levels. Shafts (*luminaria*) bring in light and air. The most common tombs are the *loculi*–rectangular niches in tiers. The body was wrapped in a sheet and the *loculus* closed with tiles or marble slabs sealed with lime. Some were inscribed (many in Greek as well as Latin, reflecting the cosmopolitan nature of Rome's population) with the deceased's name, and sometimes also a date and Christian phrases. Others were not inscribed but could be recognized by artefacts such as a cup, plate, oil lamp, jewel, or toy attached to the tomb. A more lavish tomb type is the *arcosolium*, a niche topped with an arch and often decorated. They generally occur in the so-called *cubicula*, small rooms used as family vaults and for the burial of leading figures—popes and martyrs. The cubicula may have architectural decoration, niches for lights, and shelves for offerings and funerary meals. Many catacombs still contain frescoes and stucco-work decoration—some images are clearly of biblical subjects, but others are harder to interpret. Some scenes might be either pagan or Christian, for example banquet or

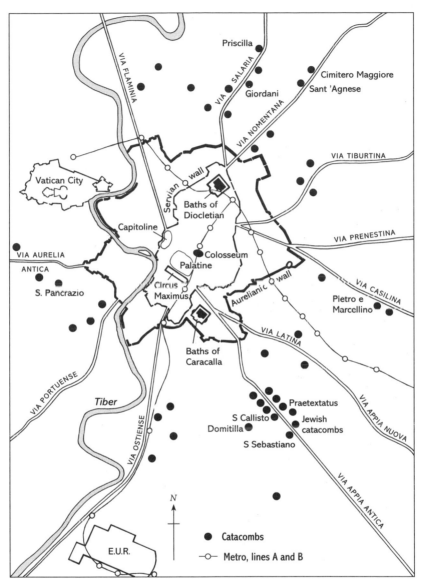

▲ **Fig. 200.** Map of Rome and environs showing main Roman roads and cata-combs

wedding scenes, as at this early period Christian iconography, which drew to some extent on earlier traditions, was still crystallizing.

Many catacombs became places of devotion and pilgrimage with basilicas being built above ground in the C4–C7 to accommodate the increase in visitors. Guides for pilgrims to Rome were being compiled as early as the C7. Many relics were transferred to churches in the C8–C9 and the catacombs were largely forgotten by the C12. They began to be rediscovered in the C15, and with increasing interest and energy in the late C16, especially through the efforts of Antonio Bosio (1575–1629) who explored 30 sites and was a pioneer in his attempts at careful recording. In the C17 and C18 many inscriptions, sarcophagi, and remains were removed to museums and churches or collected as souvenirs, and it was not until the mid-1800s that systematic recording resumed, principally by the archaeologist G. B. De Rossi (1822–94).

Of the catacombs open to the public, those of St Sebastian, St Callistus, and St Domitilla form a group by the Via Appia Antica and are the most frequently visited, but can be crowded with large groups. The catacombs of St Agnes on the Via Nomentana and St Priscilla on the Via Salaria tend to be quieter and are equally interesting. A good range of sites can be visited, but it is not possible to explore the catacombs at will—all visits are guided, and the itinerary is not always the same. A number of the catacombs not open to the public may be visited with special permission. The catacombs are not to everyone's taste—they are damp, humid and chilly, the passages can be uneven and cramped, there are some steep stairs, and the lighting can be poor.

Catacombs of St Callistus (S. Callisto).
See also Map, Fig. 165

Via Appia Antica 110

First investigated in 1849 by De Rossi, over 20 km. have been explored so far, but much more remains. In use from the C1 to C4, and built on five levels, this was the official burial place of the popes of Rome for most of the C3. They are named after St Callistus, who died in 222 after a short-lived and controversial papacy. He was apparently born a slave, and after serving time as a convict in the mines on Sardinia was placed in charge of these catacombs by pope Zephyrinus (199–217) whose papacy introduced some organized management of the Christian catacombs under the control of the Church. The complex of St Callistus began as a series of separate independent burial areas, some pagan, which were eventually linked together by the C4.

The **basilica** of SS Sixtus (pope and martyr, d. 258) and Cecilia contains a small three-apse building. Pope Zephyrinus is generally thought to have been buried in the central apse; he was later commemorated (on insufficient grounds) as a martyr. The building is now a museum exhibiting inscriptions and fragments of sarcophagi, and a bust of De Rossi. A staircase (AD 380) leads to the second level of the catacombs—the tour usually stays on this level.

Documents indicate that fourteen popes were buried in the complex of St Callistus, in various parts of the catacombs, and one in the basilica above ground. Although Callistus was linked with these catacombs he was buried in a cemetery on the via Aurelia. The **crypt of the popes** is a rectangular hall with twelve *loculi* and four niches; it was discovered in 1854 in a poor condition and substantially reconstructed. It was the burial place for the early bishops from Pontian (230–35) to Miltiades (died 314) with the exceptions of Marcellinus (died 304) and Marcellus (died 309). Original inscriptions in Greek have been found for five of them—Pontian, Anterus (235–6), Fabian (236–50), Lucius (253–4), and Eutychianus (275–83). Pope Damasus (366–84) refurbished the crypt and set up two inscriptions in honour of the popes and martyrs, the first is now at the end of the crypt. There are also remains of the base of an altar and a seat.

Adjoining is the so-called **crypt of St Cecilia**, one of the most venerated martyrs of the early Roman church and patroness of church music, but almost nothing is known of her life for certain. Her great popularity is largely due to her apocryphal acts (C5) in which she was a young Christian patrician betrothed to Valerian—a pagan. She refused to consummate the marriage and was martyred in 230 in her house in Trastevere. Her acts claim that she was buried in these catacombs, however her supposed relics were found in the catacombs of Praetextatus by Paschal I (817–24) who moved them to the church which bears her name in Trastevere. Maderno sculpted a life-size marble statue of her as she was supposed to have looked in death, with three cuts on her neck, and a copy of this was placed in the crypt around 1600. There are also C7 and C8 Byzantine frescoes showing St Cecilia, St Urban, and Jesus Christ. In another chapel near the crypt of the popes is a painted ceiling with a representation of Orpheus.

Further on is the **'gallery of the sacraments'**—a gallery with six small *cubicula* decorated with early C3 frescoes. Many have interpreted the series of *cubiculi* as representing the sacraments, but it might be better to see each as a separate unit. A frequent image is of a banquet, interpreted by some as the Eucharist, but by others as a funerary banquet drawing on iconography which stretches far back into the first millennium BC in Italy, Greece, and the Near East. Other scenes have been more easily identified with biblical stories such as Moses striking water from the rock, Jonah, and the sacrifice of Isaac.

In another part is the **crypt of St Eusebius** martyred in 310 (exiled to Sicily by Maxentius) with a C6 copy of an inscription by St Damasus. In an adjoining *cubiculum* is the funerary inscription of pope Gaius (283–96) and in another *cubiculum* is an inscription (AD 298) in which the bishop of Rome is called 'pope' for the first time. Another cubiculum has two sarcophagi with mummified remains.

Further on is the oldest part of the catacombs—the **crypts of Lucina** with paintings dating from early C2 to C6, the **tomb of Cornelius**

(251–3) has a contemporary Latin inscription (in contrast with other popes' inscriptions in Greek) containing the title 'martyr', and fine later C6 Byzantine frescoes of Sixtus II, Cornelius, and Cyprian.

There are also many tombs on the surface which date from the C1 BC onwards—both pagan and Christian.

Catacombs of St Sebastian (S. Sebastiano). See also Map, Fig. 165

Via Appia Antica

This is the only early Christian cemetery which has always remained open. Sadly, this has contributed to the poor condition of some parts, especially the first level. There are four levels and the guided visits tend to concentrate on the second. The term 'catacomb' was first applied to this site—probably referring to the stone quarries of the area—and then extended to the other cemeteries. The site is named after St Sebastian, martyred during Diocletian's persecutions in the late C3 and buried here. According to C5 legend he was a soldier, and the first attempt to kill him with arrows failed, so he was clubbed to death. Earliest representations of him are as an elderly bearded man holding a crown. The familiar image of him as a youth shot with arrows was popular from the C15.

The site has a very complex history. The events in the area occupied by the basilica of S. Sebastiano have been reconstructed as follows. Late Republican tombs were built in an underground stone quarry cut into the sharply sloping hill. Over time a series of structures were built above the quarry—a double line of Roman *colombaria* (chambers holding many cremation burials) dating from the late C1 BC to the early C2 AD, and two buildings known as the 'small villa' and the 'large villa' of imperial date. The quarry collapsed and an open hollow (the 'piazzuola') was then created to the south-east. Three above-ground chamber tombs were built here, and then in the mid-C3 the hollow was filled in and the 'triclia' was built. At the beginning of the C4 the area was covered by the foundations of the large funerary basilica, and this was flanked by various mausoleums which were being built as late as the C9 AD.

The C4 **basilica**, first dedicated to the apostles Peter and Paul who were temporarily buried here, was originally very like those at S. Lorenzo and S. Agnese. But when restored and adapted in 1609–12 under Scipione Borghese, it was reduced to the central nave. Stairs lead down to the catacombs. The **crypt of St Sebastian**, which housed the body of the martyr, originally dates to the early C4 and has been much remodelled. The **'large villa'** built in the C1 or the beginning of the C2 (and in use until the C4) consists of rooms around a courtyard paved with white mosaic, with paintings dating to the end of the C1 to the beginning of the C2 including a fine marine scene in the main room. The **'small villa'** is represented by a small courtyard with covered portico and black and white mosaics. Below this is a large room with C3 wall painting and a bench around the walls—it may be a meeting room for religious purposes. The set of **colombaria** is one of the most notable in Rome demonstrating the developments in funerary architecture and decoration (paintings and stucco) from the C1 to the beginning of the C2. The **'triclia'** is a courtyard porticoed on three sides with rooms off, and many painted graffiti (including invocations to the Apostles Peter and Paul), dating to the mid-C3, used for meetings and funeral banquets in honour of the apostles.

On a lower level (13m. below the church floor) built in the **'piazzuola'** are three pagan *colombaria* of the C1 which became inhumation tombs in C2. They have brick façades and rich painted and stucco decoration with both pagan and Christian subjects. On the right is that of **M. Clodius Hermes** (named in a marble inscription) with a fresco above the door lintel with banquet scenes, a flock of sheep with a shepherd, and other groups of figures. Inside are niches for cremations and *loculi* for bodies, and paintings of early C2 and of C3 date. These include scenes of birds, fruit and grapes in a glass bowl, and a scene often interpreted as Jesus before a crowd but which might equally be a heroized image of the deceased. The tomb of the **'Innocentiores'** (centre)—a guild or funerary club—has stucco decoration including a peacock—symbol of immortality, and painted decoration of various dates. Some early Christian symbols, such as a fish, scratched into the walls of the lower cell might indicate that these tombs were taken over by Christians in the later phase of their use. The **tomb 'of the Axe'** (left) is named after an image of an axe on the exterior, and is also richly decorated with stuccoes including vines growing from vessels standing on fake pilasters.

Under the exterior of the basilica is the **'platonia'**—the later C4 tomb of St Quirinus, the **chapel of Honorius III** with C8 paintings, and a *cubiculum* which seems from a graffito 'domus Petri' to have been the temporary **tomb of St Peter.**

Catacombs of Domitilla (or of SS Nereus and Achilleus). See also Map, Fig. 165

Via delle Sette Chiese 282

These are amongst the most extensive catacombs in Rome, dug on three levels, and they also began at an early date. They contain various early paintings and also a mosaic with a Christian theme. The earliest burials on the site were pagan, arranged in discrete groups which were later surrounded and absorbed by the Christian catacombs, and the different zones were joined together during the C4. The eponymous Domitilla was a Roman matron of the C1 AD probably related to the Flavian emperors' imperial family. She was regarded from the C4 as a Christian martyr but this is open to doubt even though the 'Coemeterium Domitillae' ('cemetery' i.e. 'catacombs' of Domitilla) has Christian burials dating back to the end of the C2.

The entrance leads down to the underground **basilica of SS Nereus and Achilleus**, built at the end of the C4 over the tombs of these saints, supposed martyred in Rome in the C2. The cult of their relics in these catacombs is very ancient and well testified. According to the late C4 inscription by Pope Damasus on the tomb they were soldiers who converted to Christianity and were martyred for it, but their legendary acts make them eunuchs in Domitilla's household who shared her exile and martyrdom. The basilica, rediscovered in 1874 and then restored, has three naves, eight columns with ancient capitals, and remains of a *schola cantorum*.

To the left of the basilica is the earliest part of the catacombs with the **tomb of the Flavians** (the family of Domitilla), found in 1865, pagan, dating to the C1 or C2. Cut into a hill and with a fine brick façade, this tomb had a separate entrance onto the ancient Via Ardeatina. Later a vestibule and a room for funerary banquets were added. At the end of the banquet room is the small **cubiculum of Eros and Psyche**, named after the Roman wall paintings, now poorly preserved, which show Eros and Psyche gathering flowers surrounded by flowers and birds. The main burial chamber with its few original tombs was used in the C4 for many Christian loculus and arcosolium burials. Nearby are other early tombs, some also pagan, some Christian. One has painted scenes including Daniel among the lions, and a fisherman, and another has inscriptions which name two of the dead as Ampliatus and his wife Aurelia Bonifatia.

Down a wide stairway is the largest and best-known zone—that of **'the Good Shepherd'**, which developed around a long gallery with early pagan burials. Smaller galleries and large rich *cubiculi* open onto the gallery; some *cubiculi* were originally lined with marble. This zone also includes galleries and chambers on the lower level; one is the *cubiculum* of 'the Good Shepherd' after a painting at the centre of the ceiling of a shepherd carrying a lamb on his shoulders, probably dating to the C3. This image was originally pagan and was then adopted into the Christian repertoire.

Another area dating to the C3 and C4 has paintings of the veiled Madonna seated holding a child accompanied by the four Magi, Jesus, and the Apostles. In the same room are scenes of the grain market in Rome —storerooms, boats on the Tiber, and a bakery.

Catacombs of Priscilla

Via Salaria 430

Around 2.5km. from the centre of Rome, these large and interesting catacombs, on two levels, have been the subject of scholarly debate—whether
or not they contained the body of the St Priscilla of Christian tradition,
and how to interpret and date the painted scenes. There are three main
zones—the area of the Acilii, the area of the 'Greek chapel', and the
'arenario'; all three became linked together at a later stage of the
catacomb's development. In the C1 or C2 AD there was a Roman villa
on this site, probably belonging to the senatorial family of the Acilii
Glabriones. Then, probably not until the late C3, Christians started using
the site for burial. The Acilii and 'Greek chapel' zones occupied parts of
the villa.

The largest room in the **Acilii zone** is a cistern of the villa; it has been
wrongly identified as the tomb of the Acilii and of St Priscilla on the basis
of inscriptions mentioning members of the Acilii family (including a
Priscilla) which are probably intrusive from upper levels of the villa building. St Priscilla, also 'Prisca', was an early Christian convert mentioned in
the New Testament. But, in spite of traditions dating back to the C9, there
is no evidence to link her either with the Priscilla of these catacombs on
the Via Salaria or with the Prisca who gave her name to the church on
the Aventine.

The 'Greek chapel' area includes a cryptoporticus (in tufa and brick
with cross-vaulting) and a nymphaeum (octagonal room with semicircular niches) both part of the Roman villa. The main burial room is
called the **'Greek chapel'** after painted Greek inscriptions. It has three
chambers off the main room, stuccoes and frescoes. These include a scene
of Moses striking water from the rock at the entrance, the Madonna and
child and Magi on the arch which divides the room, and at the end of the
room is a banquet scene (above the apse), Daniel among the lions, the
resurrection of Lazarus, the sacrifice of Isaac, and Noah. The banquet
scene has usually been interpreted as the breaking of bread in the
Eucharist, but is has also been suggested that it represents a funerary
banquet scene and not necessarily a particular Christian scene. It is clear
that elements of Christian iconography were derived from previous pagan
traditions and some were probably still being defined at this relatively
early period, thus making interpretation sometimes difficult. The date
of the paintings has been estimated variously from the later C2 to the
early C4.

The oldest zone is that of the **'arenario'**—probably a pozzolana
quarry. It may have begun in the early C3. Notable here is the **cubiculum
of the 'veiling'**, with a series of painted and stucco scenes, some recognizably representing Old Testament stories such as Jonah, and the sacrifice
of Isaac. At the end of the room an arcosolium has a painted scene of a

standing woman with her head partly veiled, flanked on one side by a seated woman with a child, and on the other by two men, the older handing a veil to a seated woman. Some interpret this as the consecration of the Virgin and the Madonna and child, others as a scene of maternity and of teaching or a wedding ritual.

Pope Sylvester built a basilica on the site and was one of the many popes buried there between 309 and 555.

Catacombs of St Agnes (Sant'Agnese). Fig. 194

Via S. Agnese 3, off the Via Nomentana

These catacombs are not only well preserved, but together with the related buildings—the church of St Agnes, the mausoleum of Constantia (Fig. 194, p. 374), and a huge ruined Constantinian basilica—form one of the great early Christian complexes of Rome. The catacombs are entered from the left nave of the church. Found in 1865–6, they date from the C3 to the early C4. The oldest zone is to the left of the church, and two later zones stretch towards the basilica and towards and beyond the Via Nomentana. There are no paintings but many inscriptions may be seen and a number of the loculi remain intact.

Agnes was venerated as a virgin in Rome from the C4, but early legends of her martyrdom vary considerably, and nothing certain is known about the date or manner of her death. The earliest evidence for her cult dates to AD 354.

Some Catacombs which can be visited with a Permit

Apply to the Pontificia Commissione di Archeologia Sacra (the Pontifical Commission for Sacred Archaeology), 1 Via Napoleone III. Only recommended for visitors particularly interested in the catacombs as the office can only process a limited number of permits at any one time. It is advisable to apply in Italian, and some time in advance to allow for the necessary arrangements to be made: the paperwork, and staff need to be sent to the site to open it and act as guides.

Catacombs of Praetextatus (Pretestato)

Via Appia Pignatelli 11

These catacombs are of great interest but much work remains to done, both excavation and research. The eponymous Praetextatus might have been the landowner. Burial, both Roman and Christian, at the site dates from the C1 to the C4. It seems that in the C3 the unusually spacious central gallery (*spelunca magna*—'great cave', which probably began life as a cistern), the adjoining area and the part above ground, were used for the burial of Roman aristocrats including the emperor Balbinus (238), many of whom might not have been Christian. It seems likely that many of the Christians later buried here were also of high social rank.

In the large entrance (1932) is displayed a C1 AD marble funerary monument shaped like a temple and decorated with architect's tools, and various sarcophagi of C2–C3 date including the oldest from the catacombs (*c.* mid-C2) with a relief of the legend of the Argonauts, and the sarcophagus of the emperor Balbinus—he and his wife are sculpted on the lid.

The **spelunca magna** is flanked by large complex cubicula containing aristocratic and wealthy burials, both pagan and Christian. Notable are those of the various martyrs such as the deacons Felicissimus and Agapitus who were martyred with pope Sixtus II in 258. The crypt said to be attributed to **St Janvier** has remains of marble veneer and fine well-preserved wall paintings of the four seasons, birds, vases, and vegetation (*c.* mid-C2 AD). Another cubiculum has remains of coloured marble wall veneer in *opus sectile* and mosaic, and three large arcosolium tombs (C4).

The arcosolium **tomb of Celerina** has a vivid painting of the biblical Susanna as a lamb being persecuted by the elders (identified by the painted inscription—SENIORIS) in the form of two wolves.

Jewish Catacombs on the Via Appia Antica

Via Appia Antica 119A

There are extensive Jewish catacombs around Rome. This set was excavated in 1859, and contain tombs dating from the C3 to the C6. A Roman building in reticulate masonry (end of the C1 BC) was reused for funerary rituals and as the entrance to the catacombs. The tomb types are *formae*—cut into the floor, and loculi cut in the walls and mostly closed with bricks. The painted inscriptions are almost all in Greek. Some arcosolium tombs occur and also some oven-shaped ones. There are a few painted images—subjects include the *menorah* (the seven-branched candlestick), the cornucopia (plenty), and the palm-leaf (victory).

Catacombs of St Pancras (S. Pancrazio or Ottavilla)

Via S. Pancrazio (near the Via Aurelia Antica)

The catacombs date to the C4 and are of interest not only as the burial place of St Pancras, said to be from Phrygia (Central Turkey) and martyred at the age of fourteen under Diocletian in 304, but also because the sector of the catacombs known as 'di Botrys' has yielded a number of burial inscriptions of people of oriental origin—yet more confirmation of the cosmopolitan character of Rome at this period. Pancras was buried in a cemetery which dates back to the late Republican period, around which the catacombs developed.

Pope Symmachus (498–514) built a small basilica over the tomb of the saint. Honorius I (625–38) replaced it with the present building, remodelled in the C12 and C17. A small museum contains some sculpture and Christian and pagan inscriptions.

Catacombs of the Cimitero Maggiore

Via Asmara 6 (beyond Sant'Agnese)

This contains the tomb of S. Emerenziana who shared a wet nurse with St Agnes. There is an underground basilica with rock-cut seats, which also occur in some cubicula in these catacombs and might be for funerary banquets. There are good quality wall paintings (C4): images include Daniel among the lions, Jonah, Adam and Eve, and a veiled praying woman with a child who might be the Virgin Mary, and Moses (with a rod) and Aaron attacked by their countrymen.

Catacombs of SS Peter and Marcellinus

Via Casilina 643 (near Tor Pignattara)

Dating to the C3–C4, these are the catacombs with the richest collection of wall paintings. There are various scenes from both the Old and New Testaments, such as Moses striking water from the rock, Noah in the ark, Daniel and the lions, the Jonah cycle, and the marriage at Cana. A banquet scene includes servants labelled as Irene (Peace) and Agape (Love). Another painting, probably of the C5 and therefore added after burial had ceased here, shows Christ enthroned between SS Peter and Paul with below a sheep and other saints.

Helena, mother of Constantine the Great, chose the site as the location for a grand mausoleum, a large part of which is still standing beyond the modern entrance of the catacombs.

Catacombs of the Giordani

Via Salaria (at the corner with Via Taro)

These are the deepest catacombs in Rome, cut on five levels. There is a fine C4 painting of a praying woman, and a series of biblical scenes including Jonah under the pergola, Daniel, and Abraham sacrificing the ram in place of Isaac.

Chronological Table

753 BC   Foundation of Rome (traditional date)

Regal period: the seven kings (traditional dates)

753 BC   Romulus
715   Numa Pompilius
673   Tullus Hostilius
642   Ancus Marcus
616   Tarquinius Priscus
578   Servius Tullius
535   Tarquinius Superbus

Republic

509 BC   Republic founded
451   Roman law encoded in the Twelve Tables
421   Plebeians begin to win equal rights
396   Defeat of Veii
272   Taranto falls
270   Overseas expansion begins
202   End of second Punic war
197   First victory in Greece
146   Sack of Corinth; Carthage razed
133   Capture of Numantia (Spain)
90–88   Social or Italian War
88–82   Civil war between Marius and Sulla
49–45   Civil War between Pompey and Julius Caesar
48–44   C. Julius Caesar dictator
44–31   Civil War between Octavian and others

Roman emperors

(**Bold** type indicates the name they are usually known by)

48 BC   C. **Julius Caesar**
31   C. Octavius Caesar (Octavian) **Augustus**   ⎤
AD 14   **Tiberius** Claudius Nero Caesar   │
37   Gaius Caesar **Caligula**   │ JULIO-CLAUDIANS
41   Tiberius **Claudius** Drusus Nero   │
         Germanicus   │
54   **Nero** Claudius Caesar Drusus Germanicus   ⎦
68–9   **Galba, Otho, Vitellius**
69   T. Flavius **Vespasian**   ⎤
79   **Titus** Flavius Sabinus Vespasianus   │ FLAVIANS
81   T. Flavius **Domitian**   ⎦
96   M. Cocceius **Nerva**

98	M. Ulpius **Trajan**	
117	P. Aelius **Hadrian**	
138	T. Aelius Aurelius **Antoninus Pius**	
161	**Marcus Aurelius** Antoninus	ANTONINES
180	L. Aurelius **Commodus**	
193	**Pertinax, Didius Julianus, Pescennius Niger, Clodius Albinus**	
193	L. **Septimius Severus**	
211	M. Aurelius Antoninus **Caracalla**	
217	**Opellius** Macrinus	
218	M. Aurelius Antoninus **Elagabalus**	SEVERANS
222	M. Aurelius **Alexander Severus**	
235	C. Julius Verus **Maximinus**	
238	**Gordian I** and **II, Balbinus, Pupienus, Gordian III**	
244	M. Julius **Philip 'the Arabian'**	
249	G. Messius Quintus **Trajan Decius**	
251	C. Vibius **Trebonianus Gallus**	
253–60	P. Licinius **Valerianus** and	
253–67	P. Licinius Egnatius **Gallienus**	
268	M. Aurelius **Claudius Gothicus**	
270	L. Domitius **Aurelian**	
275	M. Claudius **Tacitus**	
276	M. Annius **Florianus**	
276	M. Aurelius **Probus**	
282	M. Aurelius **Carus, Carinus,** and **Numerianus**	
284	C. Aurelius Valerius **Diocletian** (East) M. Aurelius Valerius **Maximian** I (West)	
305	G. Galerius Valerius **Maximianus** (East) F. Valerius **Constantius** (West)	
306	M. Aurelius Valerius **Maxentius** (Rome) F. Valerius **Severus** (West)	
308	Valerius Licinianus **Licinius** (West)	
309/10	G. **Galerius** Valerius Maximinus (East)	

		POPES	
AD 312	**Constantine** (West) **Licinius** (East)	314	Sylvester
324	**Constantine**		
337	**Constantine II**	336	Marcus
	Constans I	337	Julius
	Constantius II	352	Liberius
361	**Julian**		
364	**Valentinian I**	366	Damasus
375	**Gratian**	384	Siricius
383	**Valentinian II**	399	Anastasius I
395	**Honorius**	401	Innocent I

423	**Valentinian III**	417	Zosimus
455	**Petronius Maximus**	418	Boniface I
455	**Avitus**	422	Caelestinus I
457	**Majorian**	432	Sixtus III
461	**Severus**	440	Leo I
467	**Anthemius**	461	Hilarius
472	**Olybrius**	468	Simplicius
474	**Julius Nepos**		
475	**Romulus** Augustulus		

Ostrogothic kings

476	Odoacer	483	Felix III
493	Theodoric	492	Gelasius
		496	Anastasius II
		498	Symmachus
		523	John I
526	Athalaric	526	Felix IV
		530	Boniface II
534	Theodahad	533	John II
		535	Agapetus I
536	Vitigis	536	Silverius
		537	Vigilius
540	Ildibad		
541	Erarich		
541	Totila		
552	Theia		

Byzantines

552–74	Narses	556	Pelagius
		561	John III
		575	Benedict I
		579	Pelagius II

Exarchs of Italy

584/5	Smaragdus		
589/90	Romanus	590	Gregory I
596/7	Callinicus		
603–8	Smaragdus		

Opening Times and Charges

Most sites, monuments and museums are operated either by the State or the Comune (Municipality of Rome) whose policies on opening and entry charges are becoming increasingly similar but not yet identical. Conservation work and staffing problems can cause frequent closures or alterations to opening hours.

Monday is generally closing day, except for the Forum and Palatine, Colosseum (ground floor), Pantheon, Baths of Caracalla, Tomb of Caecilia Metella (Via Appia), Vatican Museums.

Entrance to State and Comune sites and museums is **free** for those aged under 18 or over 60, but there are no student concessions. The Vatican and catacombs charge visitors of all ages, but offer student and group concessions.

Sites and monuments

NOTE: the sites marked †, all operated by the Comune of Rome, are normally closed; the days and times given are provisional (1997/8) and may be subject to change.

Summer season: May–September

Ara Pacis: Tues.–Sat. 9–16.30 (Summer 9–18.30); Sun. and holidays 9–13. L. 3,750

Auditorium of Maecenas: Tues.–Sun. and holidays 9–13 (summer 9–19). L. 3,750

Baths of Caracalla: Tues.–Sat. 9–16 (summer 9–18); Mon., Sun. and holidays 9–13. L. 8,000

Colosseum (upper level): Mon.–Sat. 9–15 (summer 9–19); Sun. and holidays 9–13. L. 10,000

† Insula P. d'Aracoeli: Wed. 14.30–16.30; Thur. 11.30–13.30. L. 3,750

† Mausoleum of Augustus: Tues. 14.30–16.30; Thur. 11.30–13.30. L. 3,750

Mausoleum of Hadrian: see Museums—Castel S. Angelo

† Monte Testaccio: (summer only) Tues. 9–13. L. 3,750

Nero's Golden House: closed for repairs (indefinitely)

Palatine Hill: Mon.–Sat. 9–15 (summer 9–18); Sun. and holidays 9–13. L. 12,000

Pantheon: Mon.–Sat. 9–18.30; Sun. and holidays 9–13. Free

'Protestant' Cemetery: 9–17 (summer); 9–16.30 (winter); closed Mon. L. 500

Roman Forum: Mon.–Sat. 9–15 (summer 9–18); Sun. and holidays 9–13. Free (1997)

† Stadium of Domitian: Wed. 11.30–13.30; Sat. 10–13

† Temples in Largo Argentina: Tues. and Wed. 14.30–16.30; Fri. 10–13. L. 3,750

† Temples at S.Omobono: (summer) Fri. 9–13. L. 3,750

† Theatre of Marcellus: Tues. 11.30–13.30; Sun. 10–13. L. 3,750
Tomb of Caecilia Metella (Via Appia): Tues.–Sat. 9–16 (summer 18.30); Sun., Mon., and holidays 9–13. Free
Trajan's Markets: Tues.–Sun. 9–16.30 (summer 9–18.30). L. 3,750
† Underground Basilica at Porta Maggiore: closed for repairs (1999)
Villa and Circus of Maxentius (Via Appia): Tues.–Sun. 9–17.30 (summer 9–19). L. 3,750

Museums

Alto Medioevo (EUR): Tues.–Sat. 9–14; Sun. and holidays 9–13. L. 4,000
Barracco: Tues.–Sat. 9–19; Sun. and holidays 9–13. L. 3,750
Capitoline: Tues.–Sun. 9–19; holiday (weekdays) 9–14. L. 4,000
Castel S. Angelo: Tues.–Sun. 9–20; extended opening (Aug.–Sep.) Tues.–Fri. 9–22; Sat. 9–23.30. L. 8,000
Civiltà Romana (EUR): Tues.–Sat. 9–20 (enter by 19); Sun. and holidays 9–13. L. 5,000
Nazionale Romano—Terme, Palazzo Massimo sections: Tues.–Sat. 9–14; Sun. and holidays 9–13. L. 12,000 (covers both sections)
Nazionale Romano—ex-Planetarium: Mon.–Sun. 10–13, 15–18 (summer 10–19). Free
L. Pigorini (EUR): Tues.–Sat. 9–14; Sun. and holidays 9–13. L. 8,000
Museo di Roma (Palazzo Braschi): closed for repairs (1997–2000)
Villa Borghese: Tues.–Sun. 9–19; timed groups at two-hourly intervals. L. 10,000 + 2,000 for reserved ticket
Villa Giulia: Tues.–Sat. 9–19; Sun. and holidays 9–14. L. 8,000
Walls (Porta S. Sebastiano): Tues.–Sat. 9–19; Sun. and holidays 9–13. L. 3,750
Vatican Museums: closed Sundays except last Sun. of the month, when open 8.45–13. and free (unless the Sun. coincides with a public holiday); Mon.–Sat. 8.45–16 (Aug.–Sept. and Easter); rest of year 8.45–13.45. L. 15,000, students L. 10,000.

Churches

Generally open every day and free but tend to close for 3–4 hours in the middle of the day (from 12.30 to 15 or later)

S. Agnese (Via Nomentana): 9–12, 16–18
S. Anastasia: closed for repairs (1997)
S. Clemente (excavations): 9 (Sun. 10)–12.30, 15–18.30. L. 4,000
S. Cosma e Damiano: 9–13, 15–19
S. Costanza (Via Nomentana): 9–12, 16–18; closed Mon. p.m. and public holidays
S. Francesca Romana (S. Maria Nova): 10–12, 15.30–18
S. Giorgio in Velabro: Tues. and Fri. 10–12.30, 16.30–19
SS Giovanni e Paolo: 9–12, 16–19; Roman remains: ask in the sagrestia
S. Giovanni in Laterano: 7–18.45
Lateran Baptistery: 9–13, 17.30–18.30
S. Maria in Aracoeli: 6.30–18

S. Prassede: 7.15–12.15, 16–18.30
S. Stefano Rotondo: Tues.–Sat. 9–13, 15.30–18; second Sun. of month 9–12

Catacombs

Standard charge is L. 8,000, or 4,000 for students/group concessions. All close one day a week, but the three large ones near the Via Appia Antica close on different days so there is always one open.

S. Agnese: 9–12, 16–18; closed Mon. p.m. and public holidays
S. Callisto: 8.30–12, 16–18; closed Wed.
Domitilla: 8.30–12, 14.30–17; closed Tues.
S. Pancrazio: closed for repairs (1997–?)
Priscilla: 8.30–12, 16–18 (summer); 14.30–17 (winter); closed Mon. and 5 Jan.– 2 Feb.
S. Sebastiano: 8.30–12.30, 14.30–17.30; closed Thur.

References and Further Reading

Compiled with the help of Tony Cubberley

Abbreviations

AJA	*American Journal of Archaeology*
ArchCl	*Archeologia Classica* (Rome)
ArchLaz	*Archeologia Laziale* (Quaderni dell'Istituto di Studi Etruschi ed Italici, Rome)
ARID	*Analecta Romana Istituti Danici* (Rome)
ArtB	*Art Bulletin*
BA	*Bollettino di Archeologia* (Italian Ministry of Culture, Superintendency of Antiquities)
BaBesch	*Bulletin Antieke Beschaving: Annual Papers on Classical Archaeology* (Amsterdam)
BC	*Bullettino della Commissione archeologica di Roma*
CIL	*Corpus Inscriptionum Latinarum* (Berlin)
Coarelli *FB*	F. Coarelli, *Foro Boario* (Rome, 1988)
Coarelli *FRI*	F. Coarelli, *Foro Romano. Il periodo arcaico* (Rome, 1986)
Coarelli *FRII*	F. Coarelli, *Foro Romano. Periodo repubblicano e Augusteo* (Rome, 1985)
InsIt	*Inscriptiones Italiae* (Rome)
JRA	*Journal of Roman Archaeology*
MAAR	*Memoirs of the American Academy in Rome*
MEFRA	*Mélanges de l'École Française de Rome. Antiquité.*
MonAnt	*Monumenti Antichi. Accademia dei Lincei* (Rome)
MPA	*RPA. Memorie*
NSc	*Notizie degli Scavi di Antichità. Accademia dei Lincei* (Rome)
PBSR	*Papers of the British School at Rome*
QISA	*Quaderni dell'Istituto della Storia di Architettura* (University of Rome)
QITA	*Quaderni dell'Istituto di Topografia Antica* (University of Rome)
RL	*Atti della Accademia dei Lincei. Rendiconti* (Rome)
RM	*Mitteilungen des Deutsches Archäologisches Instituts: Römische Abteilung*
Roma centro	*Roma. Archeologia nel centro* 2 vols. (Rome 1985)
Rome Papers	L. La Follette et al., *Roman Papers* (JRA Supplement 11, Ann Arbor, 1994)
RPA	*Rendiconti della Pontificia Accademia di Archeologia*

General works

Topographical dictionaries

E. M. Steinby (ed.), *Lexicon Topographicum Urbis Romae*, 5 vols. (Rome, 1993; in progress). Covers all buildings named in inscriptions and other ancient sources down to the C7, in alphabetical order, by name of deity in the case of temples and altars, name of saint in the case of churches, otherwise by Latin noun (aqua, arcus, basilica, curia, monasterium, porticus, etc.). Articles mainly in Italian, with full bibliographies.

L. Richardson Jnr, *A New Topographical Dictionary of Ancient Rome* (Baltimore and London, 1992). Less comprehensive than Steinby's Lexicon but handier to use and in English.

E. Nash, *A Pictorial Dictionary of Ancient Rome*, 2 vols. (2nd edn. London, 1968). Black-and-white photographs of all the major archaeological monuments.

D. Dudley, *Urbs Roma: A Sourcebook of Classical Texts on the City and its Monuments* (London, 1967).

Coins

P. V. Hill, *The Monuments of Ancient Rome as Coin-types* (London, 1989).

Marble Plan

G. Carettoni, A. M. Colini, L. Cozza, and G. Gatti, *La pianta marmorea di Roma Antica*, 2 vols. (Rome, 1960).

E. Rodríguez Almeida, *Forma Urbis marmorea: Aggiornamento generale 1980*, 2 vols. (Rome, 1981).

Antiquarian drawings and maps

A. Frutaz, *Le piante di Roma*, 3 vols. (Rome, 1962).

A. Bartoli, *I monumenti antichi di Roma nei disegni degli Uffizi*, 6 vols. (Florence, 1915–22).

G. Zorzi, *I disegni delle antichità di Andrea Palladio* (Venice, 1959).

Period studies

T. J. Cornell, *The Beginnings of Rome: Italy and Rome from the Bronze Age to the Punic Wars (c.1000–264 BC)* (London and New York, 1995).

A. Ziolkowski, *The Temples of Mid-Republican Rome and their Historical and Topographical Context* (Rome, 1992).

P. Zanker, *The Power of Images in the Age of Augustus* (Ann Arbor, 1988).

M. T. Boatwright, *Hadrian and the City of Rome* (Princeton, 1987).

R. Krautheimer, *Rome: Profile of a City, 312–1308* (Princeton, 1980).

R. Coates-Stephens, 'Housing in early Medieval Rome', *PSBR* 64 (1996), 239–59.

Aqueducts

T. Ashby, *The Aqueducts of Ancient Rome* (Oxford, 1932).

P. J. Aicher, *Guide to the Aqueducts of Ancient Rome* (Wauconda, Ill., 1995).

Catacombs

L. Hertling and E. Kirschbaum, *The Roman Catacombs* (rev. edn. London, 1960).

J. Stevenson, *The Catacombs* (London, 1978).

P. Pergola, *Guide with Reconstructions of the Roman Catacombs and the Vatican Necropolis* (Rome, 1989).

Roman art and architecture

J. H. Middleton, 'On the Chief Methods of Construction Used in Ancient Rome', *Archaeologia* 51 (London, 1888).

J-P. Adam, *Roman Building* (London, 1995).

M. Wilson-Jones, 'Designing the Roman Corinthian Order', JRA 2 (1989), 35–69.

—— 'Principles of design in Roman architecture: the setting out of centralised buildings', *PBSR* 44 (1989), 106–51.

R. Ling, *Roman Painting* (London, 1986).

Marbles

R. Gnoli, *Marmora romana* (Rome, 1971; 2nd rev. edn. 1988).

G. Borghini (ed.), *Marmi Antichi* (Rome, 1989).

J. C. Fant, 'Ideology, gift, and trade: a distribution model for the Roman imperial marbles' in W. H. Harris (ed.), *The Inscribed Economy* (JRA Supplement, Ann Arbor, 1993), 145–70.

H. Dodge and B. Ward-Perkins, *Marble in Antiquity. Collected papers of J. B. Ward-Perkins* (British School at Rome Archaeological Monograph 6, London, 1992); with extensive bibliography (Appendix 2).

R. Schneider, *Bunte Barbaren* (Worms, 1986). Symbolism of Numidian yellow and Phrygian purple marble in connection with barbarian figure-types.

Museums

C. Pietrangeli, *The Vatican Museums. Five Centuries of History* (Rome, 1993).

H. Stuart Jones (ed.), *A catalogue of the ancient sculptures preserved in the Municipal collections of Rome. The Sculptures of the Museo Capitolino* (Oxford, 1912).

—— *The Sculptures of the Palazzo dei Conservatori* (Oxford, 1926).

A. Giuliano (ed.), *Museo Nazionale Romano. Le sculture.* 12 vols. (1982–96).

Religion

M. Beard, J. North, and S. Price, *Religions of Rome*, 2 vols. (Cambridge, 1998).

Individual Sites and Monuments

Ancient authors (see pp. 32–6) are cited first.

ALTAR OF AUGUSTAN PEACE. Augustus, *RG* 12. Ovid, *Fasti* 1.709–22. Vergil, *Aeneid* 2.293–5, 8.81–5, 193–305. G. Moretti, *Ara Pacis Augustae* (Rome, 1948). M. Torelli, *Typology and Structure of Roman Historical Reliefs* (Ann Arbor, 1982). E. La Rocca, *Ara Pacis Augustae, in occasione del restauro della fronte orientale* (Rome, 1983). J. Pollini, *AJA* 90 (1986), 453–60. R. Billows, *JRA* 6 (1993), 80–92. D. Castriota, *Ara Pacis Augustae and the Imagery of Abundance* (Princeton, 1995). D. A. Conlin, *The Artists of the Ara Pacis* (Chapel Hill, NC, and London, 1997). APPIA GATE. L. Cozza, *JRA* 3 (1990), 169–71. APARTMENT BLOCK (INSULA) BENEATH ARACOELI. J. Packer, *BC* 81 (1968–9), 127–48. AQUA VIRGO. *CIL* 6.1252–4, 31564–5. Frontinus, *Aq* 1.4, 10, 18, 22; 2.70, 84. Pliny, *NH* 31.42. Suetonius, *Caligula* 21. L. Quilici, *QITA* 5 (1968), 125–60. Aicher, 68–74. ARCH OF THE ARGENTARII. *CIL* 6.1035. D. E. L. Haynes and P. E. D. Hirst, *Porta Argentariorum* (London, 1939). ARCH OF AUGUSTUS (Forum). *InsIt* 13.1–142, esp. 17–19, Dio Cassius 51.19.1, 54.8.3. E. Nedergaard, *BC* 96 (1994–5), 33–70. ARCH OF CONSTANTINE. *CIL* 6.1139. H. P. L'Orange and A. von Gerkan, *Der spätantike Bildschmuck des Konstantinsbogens* (Berlin, 1939). A. M. Leander Touati, *The Great Trajanic Frieze* (Stockholm, 1987). J. M. C. Toynbee, *The Hadrianic School* (Cambridge, 1934). E. Angelicoussis, 'The Panel Reliefs of Marcus Aurelius', *RM* 91 (1984), 141–205. ARCH OF GALLIENUS. See ESQUILINE GATE.

ARCH OF SEPTIMIUS SEVERUS. *CIL* 6.1033. *Historia Augusta, Sept. Sev. R.* Brilliant, *The Arch of Septimius Severus* (*MAAR* 29, New York, 1967). R. Nardi, *RPA* 55–6 (1982–4), 299–313. A. Claridge et al., *Roma centro* 1.34–40. R. Nardi, *Roma centro* 1, 41–55. ARCH OF TIBERIUS. (Forum). *CIL* 6.906, 31422, 31575. Tacitus, *Ann.* 2.41. ARCH OF TITUS. *CIL* 6.945. M. Pfanner, *Der Titusbogen* (Mainz, 1983). ARCHAIC CEMETERY (Roman Forum). G. Pinza, *MonAnt* 15 (1905), 273–314. 'AUDITORIUM OF MAECENAS'. V. Vespignani and L. Visconti, *BC* 2 (1874), 137–73. *L'archeologia in Roma Capitale tra sterro e scavo* (exh. cat., Rome, 1983), 225–52. 'AULA ISIACA' (Palatine). G. E. Rizzo, *Monumenti della pittura antica* III, *Roma* fasc II, 1936. G. Carettoni, *NSc* 1971, 323–26. BARBERINI VINEYARD. *La Vigna Barberini I. Histoire d'un site. Étude des sources et de la topographie* (Rome, 1997). BASILICA JULIA. *CIL* 6.1156, 1658, 9709, 9711, 31883, 31884–7. Pliny, *Ep.* 5.9.1. Cicero, *Att.* 4.16.8. Augustus, *RG* 20. Martial, *Ep.* 6.38.5–6. Quintilian 12.5.6. Statius, *Silv.* 1.1.29. Suetonius, *Aug* 29. Dio Cassius 56.27.5. G. Carettoni and L. Fabbrini, *RL* ser. 8.16 (1961), 53–60. Fabbrini *BC* 78 (1961–2), 37–54. BASILICA OF NEPTUNE. Dio Cassius 56.24. *Historia Augusta, Hadr.* 19.10. L. Cordischi, *BA* 5–6 (1990), 11–34. BASILICA NOVA—NEW BASILICA OF MAXENTIUS/CONSTANTINE. Aur. Vict., *Caes* 40.26. A. Minoprio, *PBSR* 12 (1932), 1–25. BASILICA PAULLI (commonly known as Basilica Aemilia). Plautus, *Curc.* 472. Cicero, *Att.* 4.16.8. Livy 26.27, 35.23, 40.51. Festus 258L. Varro, *LL* 6.4. Suetonius, *Aug.* 29.4. Pliny, *NH* 7.215, 35.13,

36.102. Tacitus, *Ann.* 3.72. Dio Cassius 49.42, 54.24. Plutarch, *Caes.* 29. G. Carettoni, *NSc* (1948), 111–28. M. Steinby, *Arctos* 21 (1987), 139–84. Frieze: A. Bartoli, *BdA* 1950, 289–94. H. Furuhagen, *OpRom* 3 (1961), 139–55. BASILICA-UNDERGROUND (Porta Maggiore). Ovid, *Ep.* 15.171–80. J. Carcopino, *La Basilique Pythagoricienne de la Porte Majeure* (Paris, 1937). S. Aurigemma, *La Basilica Sotterranea Neopitagorica di Porta Maggiore* (Rome, 1961). F. L. Bastet, *BaBesch* 45 (1970), 148–74. BATHS OF AGRIPPA. C. Hülsen, *Die Thermen des Agrippa* (Rome, 1910). E. Tortorici, in A. Cerasa-Gastaldo (ed.), *Il himillenario di Agrippa* (Genoa, 1990) 19–55. BATHS OF CARACALLA. J. DeLaine, *The Baths of Caracalla* (*JRA* Supplement 25, Rhode Island, 1998). M. Marvin, *AJA* 87 (1983), 347–84. D. Kinney, *ArtB* 68 (1986), 379–97. BATHS OF DECIUS. L. La Follette, in *Rome Papers*, 6–88. BATHS OF DIOCLETIAN. *CIL* 6.1130 [=31242], 1131. E. Paribeni, *Le Terme di Diocleziano e il Museo Nazionale Romano* (Rome, 1932). BATHS OF TRAJAN. *CIL* 6.1670, 8677–8, 9797. Dio Cassius 69.4.1. L. Cozza, *RPA* ser. 3. 47 (1974–5), 79–101. K. De Fine Licht, 'Untersuchungen an den Trajansthermen zu Rom' *ARID* suppl. 7 (1974); suppl. 10 (1983); suppl. 19 (1990). G. Caruso *et al. ArchLaz* 10 (1990), 58 ff. BLACK STONE (LAPIS NIGER). *CIL* 6.3640. Festus 184L. Horace, *Epod.* 16.13–14. Dion. Hal. 1.87.2, 3.1.2. R. E. A. Palmer, *The King and the Comitium* (Wiesbaden, 1969). Coarelli, *FRI* 161–99. CAELIAN HILL. A. M. Colini, *MPA* 7 (1944). CAPITOLINE HILL. A. M. Colini, *Capitolium* 40 (1965), 175–85. T. P. Wiseman, *Historia* 28 (1979), 32–50; *American Journal of Ancient History* 3 (1978), 163–78.

CATTLE MARKET [FORUM BOARIUM]. *CIL* 6.919, 31574. Varro, *LL* 5.146. Festus 271L. Livy, *Epit.* 16, 22.57, 24.47. Ovid, *Fasti* 6.477–8. Pliny, *NH* 28.12, 34.10. Tacitus, *Ann.* 12. 24. Plutarch, *Marcel* 3.4. Coarelli *FB*. CIRCUS OF MAXENTIUS. G. Pisani Sartorio and G. Calza, *La Villa di Massenzio sulla Via Appia* (Rome, 1976). CIRCUS MAXIMUS. J. Humphrey, *Roman Circuses* (London, 1986), 56–294. P. Ciancio Rossetto, 'Circo Massimo', *Roma centro* 1 (Rome, 1985), 213–23. CLOACA MAXIMA [GREAT DRAIN]. Livy 1.1.38, 1.56. Plautus, *Curc.* 476. Pliny, *NH* 36.104–8. Dio Cassius 49.43. *Roma sotterranea* 170–72. Coarelli *FRI* 83–86. COLOSSEUM, AMPHITHEATRUM FLAVIUM. *CIL* 6.32254–5, 32086–9, 32091–2, 32188–9, 32094, 32099–32248. Martial, *Spect.* 2. Suetonius, *Vesp.* 9; *Titus* 7. Dio Cassius 66.25. *Historia Augusta, Ant.* 8.2; *Comm.* 15.6; *Heliog.* 17.8; *Max. et Balb.* 1.3. Amm. Marc. 16.10.14. Cassiodorus, *Variae* 5.42. Theodoret 5.26. Bede, *PL* 94.543. J. C. Golvin, *L'amphitheatre romain* (Paris, 1988), 173–80. C. Panella, *BA* 2 (1990), 35 ff. G. Alföldy, *Zeitschrift für Papyrologie und Epigraphik* 109 (1995), 195–226. M. Wilson-Jones, *RM* 100 (1993), 391–442. COLOSSUS. Pliny, *NH* 34.35. Suetonius, *Nero* 31; *Vesp.* 18. Martial, *Ep.* 2. Cassius 66.15.1, 72.22.3. *Historia Augusta, Hadr.* 19.12–13; *Comm.* 17.9–10. Bede, *Collect* 1, III. C. Lega, *BC* 93 (1989–90), 339–78. COLUMBARIUM OF POMPONIUS HYLAS. *CIL* 6.5539-5557. T. Ashby, *PBSR* 5 (1910), 463–71. F. Coarelli, *Il sepolcro degli Scipioni a Roma* (Rome, 1988), 37–9. COLUMN OF ANTONINUS PIUS. *CIL* 6.1004. L. Vogel, *The Column of Antoninus Pius* (Cambridge, Mass., 1973). COLUMN

OF MARCUS AURELIUS. *CIL* 6.1585. Dio Cassius 71.8–10. G. Becatti, *La colonna di Marco Aurelio* (Rome, 1957). COLUMN OF PHOCAS. *CIL* 6.1200. F. M. Nichols, *Archaeologia* 52 (1890), 183–94. Ch. Hülsen, *RM* 6 (1891), 88–90. COLUMN OF TRAJAN. *CIL* 6.960. F. Lepper and S. Frere, *Trajan's Column, A New Edition of the Cichorius Plates* (Gloucester, 1988). A. Claridge, *JRA* 6 (1993), 6–22. M. Wilson-Jones, *JRA* 6 (1993), 23–38. COMITIUM. Varro, *LL* 5.155, 6.31. Cicero, *De amic.* 25.96. Livy 27.36.8, 45.24.12. Pliny, *NH* 19.23, 34.26. G. Boni, *NSc* (1901), 295–340. E. Gjerstad, *Opuscula Archaeologica* 2 (1941), 97–158. C. Krause, *RM* 83 (1976), 31–69. CRYPTA BALBI. D. Manacorda, *Archeologia urbana a Roma: Il progetto della Crypta Balbi 1* (Florence, 1982, in progress). CURIA. See SENATE-HOUSE. DECENNALIA BASE. H. Kähler, *Das Funfsäulendenkmal für die Tetrarchen auf dem Forum Romanum* (Berlin, 1964). DOMITIAN'S PALACE (Palatine). H. Finsen, *ARID* suppl. 5 (1962). G. Wataghin Cantino, *La Domus Augustana* (Turin, 1966). G. Carettoni, *NSc* (1971), 300–18; *ArchCl* 24 (1972), 96–104. L. D'Elia-S. La Pera Buranelli, *Roma centro* 1.176–78. M. G. Borghi et al. *BC* 91.2 (1986), 481–98, 526–34, 540–2. DOMUS AUREA [NERO'S GOLDEN HOUSE]. Tacitus, *Ann.* 15.42. Pliny, *NH* 34.84, 35.120, 36.111. Martial, *Spect.* 2.5–6. Suetonius, *Nero* 31, 39.2; *Otho.* 7; *Vesp.* 9. A. Boethius, *The Golden House of Nero* (Ann Arbor, 1960). L. Fabbrini, *ARID* suppl.10 (1983), 169–85 (includes bibiography). L. Fabbrini, *RPA* 58 (1985–6), 129–79. D. Hemsoll, in M. Henig (ed.), *Architecture and Architectural Sculpture in the Roman Empire* (Oxford, 1990), 10–38. L. C. Ball, in

Rome Papers (*JRA* suppl. 11, Ann Arbor, 1994), 182–254. ESQUILINE GATE. *CIL* 6.1106. E. Rodríguez Almeida, *BA* 9 (1991), 4–7. ESQUILINE HILL. M. Cima and E. La Rocca (eds.), *Le tranquille dimore degli dei: La residenza imperiale degli horti Lamiani* (exh. cat., Rome, 1986). C. Häuber, *Kölner Jahrbuch für Vor- und Frühgeschichte* 23 (1990), 11–107. FORUM OF AUGUSTUS. *CIL* 6.31606, 31611, 32354, 32359. *InsIt.* 13.3.1–36. *AnnEp* 1941.60. Pliny, *NH* 22.13, 35, 27, 35, 92–3, 36.102. Augustus, *RG* 21, 29. Suetonius, *Aug.* 21.2, 29.1–2, 31.5, 56.2; *Cal.* 24.3, 44.2; *Claud.* 33.1. Ovid, *Trist.* 2.296; *Fasti.* 5.549–96. Tacitus *Ann.* 13.8. Dio Cassius 55.10.2–5. P. Zanker, *Forum Augustum* (Tübingen, 1968); *Power of Images in the Age of Augustus* (Ann Arbor, 1988). H. Bauer, *Roma centro* I, 229–40. E. La Rocca, L. Ungaro, R. Meneghini (eds.), *I luoghi del consenso imperiale: Introduzione storico-topografico* (exh. cat., Rome, 1995). FORUM BOARIUM. See CATTLE MARKET. FORUM OF CAESAR [including TEMPLE OF VENUS GENETRIX]. Vitruvius 3.3.2, 4.1.8–10. Pliny *Ep.* 8.6.13. Suetonius, *Iul.* 26.2, 78.1. Pliny, *NH* 7.126, 9.116, 34.18, 35.26, 35.136. C. Ricci, *Il foro di Cesare* (Rome, 1932). C. M. Amici, *Il foro di Cesare* (Florence, 1991). R.B. Ulrich *AJA* 97 (1993), 49–80. FORUM HOLITORIUM. See VEGETABLE MARKET. FORUM OF NERVA [FORUM TRANSITORIUM]. H. Bauer, *RM* 90 (1983), 111–84. R. Meneghini, *Il Foro di Nerva* (Rome, 1991). E. d'Ambra, *Private Lives, Imperial Virtues* (Princeton, 1993). FORUM ROMANUM [ROMAN FORUM]. C. Hülsen, *The Roman Forum* (Rome, 1905). P. Zanker, *Forum Romanum: die Neugestaltung durch Augustus* (Tübingen 1972). Coarelli

FRI–II. Surdinus inscription: *CIL* 6.1468, 31662. Paving and associated monuments: C. F. Giuliani and P. Verduchi, *L'area centrale del foro romano* (Florence, 1987). Geology: A. J. Ammerman, *AJA* 94 (1990), 627–45. Subterranean tunnels: G. Carettoni, *BC* 76 (1956–8), 22–44. K. Welch, *JRA* 7 (1994), 69–80. FORUM OF TRAJAN. *CIL* 6.960, 987, 1710. Amm. Marc. 16.10.15. *Historia Augusta, Hadr.* 7.6–8; *Marc. Aur.* 17.4–5. Eutropius 8.5.7. C. M. Amici, *Il Foro di Traiano: Basilica Ulpia e Biblioteche* (Rome, 1982). P. Pensabene et al., *ArchCl* 41 (1989), *passim.* R. Meneghini et al., *Il Foro di Traiano* (Rome, 1990). J. Packer, *AJA* 96 (1992), 151–62. J. Packer, *The Forum of Trajan,* 3 vols. (Berkeley, 1997). FORUM TRANSITORIUM. See FORUM OF NERVA. FOUNTAIN AND POOL OF JUTURNA. Plutarch, *Aem. Paul.* 25, 2–3. Plutarch, *Coriolanus* 3.5. Valerius Maximus 1.8.1. Florus 1.28.15. Frontinus, *Aq.* 4. *CIL* 6.36807, 36951. G. Boni, *NSc* (1901), 41–144. E. M. Steinby, *Arctos* 21 (1987), 139–84. E. M. Steinby (ed.), *Lacus Iuturnae I* (Rome, 1989). GARDENS OF MAECENAS. Horace, *Sat.* 1.8, *Odes* 3.29.10. Dio Cassius 55.7.6. Suetonius, *Tib.* 15.1; *Nero* 38.2. Fronto 1.8.5. A. M. Colini, *RL* ser. 8.34 (1979), 239–50. R. C. Häuber, in *Roma capitale tra sterro e scavo* (exh. cat., Rome 1983), 204–22. GOLDEN HOUSE OF NERO. See DOMUS AUREA. HOROLOGIUM AUGUSTI. *CIL* 6.702. Pliny, *NH* 36, 72–3. Strabo 17.1.27. E. Buchner, *Die Sonnenuhr des Augustus* (Mainz, 1982). F. Rakob, *MEFRA* 98 (1987), 687–712. HORREA AGRIPP(IN)AE *CIL* 6.9973, 10026, 14.3958. G. E. Rickman, *Roman Granaries and Storebuildings* (Cambridge, 1971), 89–97. F. Astolfi, F. Guidobaldi et al., *ArchCl* 30 (1978),

132–46. HORREA VESPASIANI. *Chronogr.* AD *354,* 146. E. B. van Deman, *AJA* 27 (1923), 383–424. A. Carandini, *BA* 1–2 (1990), 159–65. HOUSE 'OF AUGUSTUS' (Palatine). Velleius, *Pat.* 2.81. Suetonius, *Aug.* 29.3, 57.2, 72.1. Dio Cassius 49.15.5, 53.16.4, 54.27.3, 55.12.4–5. Augustus, *RG* 34, 35. G. Carettoni, *Das Haus des Augustus auf dem Palatin* (Mainz, 1983). T. P. Wiseman, *MEFRA* 98 (1987), 393–413. HOUSE OF CALIGULA—DOMUS GAI (Forum). Suetonius, *Cal.* 22. Dio Cassius 59.28.5. H. Hurst, *ArchLaz* 9 (1988), 13–17. HOUSE OF 'THE GRIFFINS' (Palatine). G. E. Rizzo, *La Casa dei Grifi* (Monumenti della pittura antica III, Roma, Fasc. I, Rome, 1936). 'HOUSE OF LIVIA' (Palatine). Suetonius, *Tib.* 5. Lead pipes: *CIL* 15.7264–5, 7285. G. E. Rizzo, *La Casa di Livia* (Monumenti della pittura antica III, Roma Fasc. III, Rome, 1936). G. Carettoni, *NSc* (1953), 126–47. 'HOUSE OF TIBERIUS' (Palatine). *CIL* 6.8653–5. Tacitus, *Hist.* 1.27. Plutarch, *Galba* 24.7. Suetonius, *Vit.* 15.3. *Historia Augusta, Ant. Pius* 10.4; *Marc. Aur.* 6.3. Dio Cassius 71.35.4. M. A. Tomei et al., *BC* 91.2 (1986), 438–70. C. Krause et al., *Domus Tiberiana I* (Rome, forthcoming). HOUSE OF THE VESTALS—ATRIUM VESTAE, TEMPLE OF VESTA. *CIL* 6.1272. Festus 152L, 296L, 320L. Livy 5.40, 5.42; *Epit.* 19, 26.27. Aulus Gellius 1.12.9. Ovid, *Fasti* 6 *passim.* Pliny, *NH* 7.141. Suetonius, *Iul.* 46. Cicero, *De div.* 1.101. Dion. Hal. 2.66, 6.13. Plutarch, *Numa* 11.1. Dio Cassius 42.31, 72 [73].24. H. Bloch, *I bolli laterizi e la storia edilizia romana* (Rome, 1947), 67–85. G. Carettoni, *RPA* 51–2 (1978–80), 325–55. R. T. Scott et al., *ArchLaz* 9 (1988), 18–26. HOUSES (North slope of Palatine). A.

Carandini, *BC* 91 (1986), 263–71. *BA* 2 (1990), 159–65. T. Cornell, *The Beginnings of Rome* (London, 1995), 96–7. **LAPIS NIGER.** See **BLACK STONE. LATE ROMAN HOUSE** (NE slope of the Palatine). E. Hostetter et al., in *Rome Papers*, 131–81. **LATERAN BAPTIS-TERY.** Lib.Pont. G. B. Giovenale, *Il Battistero Lateranense* (Rome, 1929). G. Pelliccioni, *MPA* 12 (1973). **LUDUS MAGNUS.** A. M. Colini and L. Cozza (eds.), *Ludus Magnus* (Rome, 1962). **MACELLUM MAGNUM** (Nero). Dio Cassius 61.18.13. **'MARKETS OF TRAJAN'.** C. Ricci, *Il mercato di Traiano* (Rome, 1929). R. Meneghini, *Il Foro e I Mercati di Traiano* (Rome, 1995). L. C. Lancaster, *PBSR* 63 (1995), 25–44. **MAUSOLEUM OF AUGUSTUS.** Strabo 5.3.9. Suetonius, *Aug.* 100, 101; *Claud.* 1. Vergil, *Aeneid* 6.872–4. Tacitus, *Ann.* 1.8, 16.8; *Cons. Liv.* 67–74; *AnnEp* 1928.2. *CIL* 6.886. Pliny, *NH* 36.69–74. Dio Cassius 53.30.5. Aur. Vict., *Epit.* 12.12. Amm. Marc. 17.4.16. R. Cordingley and I. A. Richmond, *PBSR* 10 (1927), 23–35. G. Giglioli, *Capitolium* 6 (1930), 532–67. G. Gatti, *Capitolium* 10 (1934), 457–64; *L'Urbe* 8.16 (1938), 1–17. J. C. Reeder, *Classical Antiquity* 11.2 (1992), 265–304. L. Haselberger, *RM* 101 (1994), 279–308. H. von Hesberg and S. Panciera, *Das Mausoleum des Augustus: Der Bau und seine Inschriften* (Munich, 1994). **MAUSOLEUM OF HADRIAN** (Castel Sant'Angelo). Procopius, *BG* 5.22. *CIL* 6.984–995. Herodian 4.1.4. Dio Cassius 76.15.4., 78.9.1., 78.24.3. D. E. Strong, *PBSR* 21 (1953), 118–51, esp. 142–7 and fig. 6. M. T. Boatwright, *Hadrian*, 160–75. **MAUSOLEUM OF MAXENTIUS** (Via Appia). J. Rasch, *Das Maxentius-Mausoleum an der Via Appia in Rom* (Mainz, 1984). See also **CIRCUS** of Maxentius. **META SUDANS.** *Chronogr.*

AD 354 196.20. Cassiodorus 140.729. Excavations 1986–94: C. Panella, *BA* 1–2 (1990), 34–88. C. Panella (ed.), *Meta Sudans I* (Rome, 1996). **MITHRAEUM** under Baths of Caracalla. E. Ghislanzoni, *NSc* 1912, 319–25. M. Piranomonte et al., *BA* 23 (1994) (forthcoming). **MITHRAEUM** near Circus Maximus. C. Pietrangeli, *BC* 68 (1940), 143–73. **MONTE TESTACCIO.** E. Rodríguez Almeida, *Il Monte Testaccio* (Rome, 1984). **MUNDUS.** Plutarch, *Rom.* 11. Ovid, *Fasti* 4.819–836. Coarelli *FRI* 207–55. **NECROPOLIS** under St Peter's. B. M. Apollonj-Ghetti, A. Ferrua, E. Josi, and E. Kirschbaum, *Esplorazioni sotto la Confessione di S. Pietro in Vaticano* (Vatican City, 1951). J. M. C. Toynbee and J. B. Ward-Perkins, *The Shrine of St. Peter and the Vatican Excavations* (London, 1956). **NYMPHAEUM OF ALEXANDER SEVERUS.** T. Burgess, *Topography and Antiquities of Rome* (London, 1831), 201. G. Tedeschi Grisanti, *I trofei di Mario* (Rome, 1977). A. M. Liberati and G. Pisani Sartorio (eds.), *Il trionfo dell'acqua* (Conference Rome, 1987, Rome 1992), 59–72. **OBELISKS.** E. Iversen, *Obelisks in Exile* I. (Copenhagen, 1968). **PANTHEON.** *CIL* 6.896, 2041. Dio Cassius 53.27.2, 66.24.2, 69.7.1. Pliny, *NH* 9.58, 34.13, 36.38. Macrobius 3.17.17. *Chron.* 146. Orosius 7.12.5. *Historia Augusta, Hadr.* 19.10; *Ant.* 8.2. Amm. Marc. 16.10.14. K. De Fine Licht, *The Rotunda in Rome* (Copenhagen, 1968). W. L. MacDonald, *The Pantheon: Design, Meaning and Progeny* (London, 1976). P. Godfrey and D. Hemsoll, in M. Henig and A. King, *Pagan Gods and Shrines of the Roman Empire* (Oxford, 1986), 195–209. P. Davies, D. Hemsoll, and M. Wilson Jones, *Art History* 10.2 (1987), 133–53. **PLUTEI TRAIANA.** U.

Rüdiger, *Antike Plastik* 12 (1973), 161–74. PORTICUS ABSIDATA. H. Bauer, *RM* 90 (1983), 111–84. PORTICUS AEMILIA. Livy 35.10.12, 41.27.8. Gu. Gatti, *BC* 62 (1934), 135–44. PORTICUS MINUCIA VETUS and FRUMENTARIA. *CIL* 6.10223, 10224–5. Apuleius, *De mundo* 35. L. Cozza, *QITA* 5 (1968), 13–20. F. Zevi, *MEFRA* 105 (1993), 661–708. G. E. Rickman, *The Corn Supply of Ancient Rome* (Oxford, 1980); *ARID* suppl. 10 (1983), 105–8. PORTICUS OF OCTAVIA. Ovid, *AA* 1.69–70. Suetonius, *Aug.* 29.4. Pliny, *NH* 36.22, 28, 42. B. Olinder, *Porticus Octaviae in Circo Flaminio* (Stockholm, 1974) L. Richardson *AJA* 80 (1976), 57–64. H. Lauter, *BC* 87 (1980–1), 37–55. PRECINCT OF THE HARMONIUS GODS (DEI CONSENTES). *CIL* 6.102. Varro, *RR* 1.1.4. Livy 22.10. G. Nieddu, *Roma centro* 1.24–8; *BA* 71 (1986), 37–52. PYRAMID OF CESTIUS. *CIL* 6.1374–5. Cicero, *Phil.* 3.29. P. S. Bartoli, *Gli antichi sepolcri* (Rome, 1685). R. T. Ridley, *BA* 13–15 (1992), 1–30. REGIA. Solinus 1.21. Festus 278L. Servius, *Ad Aen.* 8.363, 8.3. Suetonius, *Iul.* 46. Festus 190L. Plutarch *Numa* 14.1. Pliny *NH* 34.48. Tacitus, *Ann.* 15.41. Aulus Gellius 4.6.1–2. Dio Cassius 44.17.2. Varro, *LL* 6.12, 6.21. Plutarch, *Quaest. Rom.* 97. *CIL* 6.511, 1301. Excavations: F. E. Brown, *MAAR* 12 (1933), 67–88; *Entretiens Hardt* 13 (1967), 47–60; *RPA* 47 (1974–5), 15–36; in L. Bonfante and H. von Heintze (eds.), *In Memoriam Otto J. Brendel* (Mainz, 1976), 5–12. S. B. Downey, *Architectural Terracottas from the Regia* (Ann Arbor, 1995). ROSTRA (Forum). Varro, *LL* 5.155. Livy 8.14.12. Dio Cassius 43.49. Lugli *Roma antica* 115–21, 140–4. Nash II.176–7. P. Verduchi, *RPA* 55–6 (1982–4), 329–40. Coarelli *FRII*

237–57. *Roma centro* 1.29–33. ROUND TEMPLE (by Tiber). Hercules Olivarius: *CIL* 6.33936. Hercules Victor: Livy 10.23. Macrobius 3.6.10–11, 17. Pliny, *NH* 10.79, 35.19. D. E. Strong and J. B. Ward-Perkins, *PBSR* 28 (1960), 7–32. F. Rakob and W.D. Heilmeyer, *Der Rundtempel am Tiber in Rom* (Mainz, 1973). Coarelli *FB*, 92–103, 108–204. A. Ziolkowski, *Phoenix* 42 (1988), 309–33. R. E. A. Palmer, *JRA* 3 (1990), 234–40. S. ANASTASIA. T. P. Whitehead, *AJA* 31 (1927), 405–20. G. Lugli, *Itinerario di Roma Antica* (Rome, 1970), 323–4. S. CLEMENTE. *CIL* 15.7192. F. Guidobaldi, *San Clemente. Gli edifici romani, la basilica paleocristiana e le fasi altomedioevali* (Rome, 1992). SS. GIOVANNI E PAOLO (IOHANNES ET PAULUS). V. E. Gasdía, *La casa pagano-cristiana del Celio* (Rome, 1937). Krautheimer, *CBCR I* (Rome, 1937), 265–300. S. MARIA ANTIQUA (and associated structures). R. Delbrück, *JdI* (1921), 8–32. S. MARTINO AI MONTI (Roman building). R. Krautheimer, *Corpus Basilicarum Christianorum Romae* III (Vatican, 1967), 97–108. S. OMOBONO, archaic and republican temples. A. M. Colini et al., *BC* 77 (1959–60), 3–143; *BC* 79 (1963–4), 3–90. E. Gjerstad, *BC* 78 (1961–2), 32–108. *La grande Roma dei Tarquini* (exhib. cat., Rome, 1990), 111–37. Coarelli *FB*, 205–442. S. STEFANO ROTONDO. C. Ceschi, *MPA* 15 (1982). F. Guidobaldi, *Pavimenti marmorei di Roma dal IV al IX secolo* (Vatican City, 1983), 142–9, 238–41. SAEPTA IULIA. *CIL* 6.32323.50, 15.7195. Cicero, *Att.* 4.16.14. Dio Cassius 53.23.2, 66.24.2. Pliny, *NH* 36.29. Martial, *Ep.* 2.14.5, 2.57.2, 9.59.1, 10.80.4. *Historia Augusta, Hadr.* 19.10. G. Gatti, *BC* 62 (1934), 126–8; *L'Urbe* 2.9 (1937), 8–23. D. Palombi,

QITA 10 (1988), 77–97. F. Castagnoli, *QITA* 10 (1988), 99–114. SENATE HOUSE—CURIA JULIA. Dio Cassius 44.5.2, 45.17.8, 51.22.1. Augustus, *RG* 19. Pliny, *NH* 35.27–8. *Chron.* 148. Herodian 5.57, 7.11. A. Bartoli, *Curia Senatus* (Rome, 1963). C. Morselli and E. Tortorici, *Curia, Forum Iulium, Forum Transitorium* (Rome, 1989), 1–263. SEPTIZODIUM. *Historia Augusta, Sept. Sev.* 19.5, 24.3–4; *Geta* 7.2. C. Hülsen, *Das Septizonium des Septimius Severus* (Programm zum Winckelmannsfeste 46, Berlin, 1886). I. Iacopi and G. Tedone, *BA* 1–2 (1990), 149–55; *BA* 19–21 (1993), 1–12. SETTE SALE. F. Castagnoli, *Le 'sette sale' cisterna delle terme di Traiano* (Val di Pesa, 1956). L. Cozza, *RPA* 47 (1974–5), 79 ff. K. De Fine Licht, *ARID* suppl. 10 (1983), 187 ff.; *Untersuchungen an den Trajansthermen zu Rom: 2. Sette Sale* (Rome, 1990). SPEAKING STATUES. P. Virgili, *BC* 95.2 (1993), 121–8. STADIUM OF DOMITIAN (Piazza Navona). Dio Cassius 75.16, 78.25.1–3. Suetonius, *Dom.* 5. *Historia Augusta, Heliog.* 26; *Alex. Sev.* 26. Amm. Marc. 16.10. A. M. Colini, *Lo Stadio di Domiziano* (Rome, 1943). 'TABULARIUM'. Lutatius Catulus inscription: *CIL* 6.1314. R. Delbrück, *Hellenistische Bauten in Latium* (Strasbourg, 1907–12), 23–46. N. Purcell, *PBSR* 61 (1993), 135–51. TEMPLE OF APOLLO (Palatine). Vell. Pat. 2.81.3. Suetonius, *Aug.* 29.3. Prop. 2.31.9–14. Ovid, *Trist.* 3.1.59–60. Dio Cassius 49.15.5, 53.1.3. Pliny, *NH* 3.24–25, 32. Augustus, *RG* 4.1. G. Pinza, *BC* 38 (1910), 3–41. H. Bauer, *RM* 76 (1969), 183–204. M. A. Tomei, *BA* 5–6 (1990), 35–48. TEMPLE OF APOLLO MEDICUS SOSIANUS (APOLLO IN CIRCO). Livy 4.25.3, 40.51.6. Pliny, *NH* 13.53. 35.99, 36.28, 36.34. A. M.

Colini, *BC* 66 (1938), 259–60; *BC* 68 (1940), 228–9. E. La Rocca, *Amazzonomachia: le sculture frontonali del tempio di Apollo Sosiano* (Rome, 1985). A. Viscogliosi, *Il tempio di Apollo in Circo e la formazione del linguaggio architettonico augusteo* (*BC* supplement no. 3, Rome, 1996). TEMPLE OF BELLONA. *CIL* 11.1827, 10.104. Cicero, *Verr.* 2.5.41. Livy 10.19.17. Ovid, *Fasti* 6.201–4. Pliny, *NH* 35.12. Plutarch, *Sulla* 7.6, 30.2–3. *Historia Augusta, Sept. Sev.* 22.6. F. Coarelli, *BC* 80 (1965–7), 37–72. G. Hafner, *RM* 94 (1987), 241–65. TEMPLE OF CASTOR (Roman Forum). Livy 2.20.12, 2.42.5. Cicero, *Verr.* 2.1.129–54. Suetonius, *Cal.* 22.2. Dio Cassius 59.28.5. Dion. Hal. 6.15. D. E. Strong and J. B. Ward-Perkins, *PBSR* 30 (1962), 1–30. I. Nielsen and B. Poulsen (eds.), *The Temple of Castor and Pollux I* (Rome, 1992). TEMPLE OF CASTOR (Circus Flaminius). M. Conticello de'Spagnolis, *Il Tempio dei Dioscuri nel Circo Flaminio* (Rome, 1984). E. Rodríguez Almeida, *JRA* 1 (1988), 120–31. TEMPLE OF CONCORD. *CIL* 6.89, 90–4, 2204–5, 3782–3, 8703, 30856–7. Cicero, *Cat.* 3.21. Ovid, *Fasti* 1.637–44. Livy 39.56.6, 40.19.2. Dio Cassius 56.25.1, 58.11.4. Suetonius, *Tib.* 20. Pliny, *NH* 34.73–37.4. Plutarch, *Cam.* 42.3; *C. Grac.* 17.6. C. Gasparri, *Aedes Concordiae Augustae* (Rome, 1979). TEMPLE OF DIVUS ANTONINUS AND DIVUS FAUSTINA. *Historia Augusta, Ant. Pius* 6.7., 13.4. *CIL* 6.1005. A. Bartoli, *MonAnt* 23 (1914), 949–74. TEMPLE OF DIVUS CLAUDIUS. Suetonius, *Claud.* 45; *Vesp.* 9. Tacitus, *Ann.* 12.69. A. M. Colini, *MPA* 7 (1944), 137–62. TEMPLE OF DIVUS HADRIANUS. *Historia Augusta, Verus* 3. H. Lucas, *Jahresbericht d. königl.*

Kaiser Wilhelms-Realgymnasium Berlin, 103 (1904), 1–27. V. Passarelli, 'Rilievo e studio di restituzione dell'Hadrianeum', Atti III Convegno Naz. di Storia dell'Architettura (1938). L. Cozza (ed.), Il tempio di Adriano (Rome, 1982). TEMPLE OF DIVUS JULIUS. CIL 6.2051. Vitruvius 3.3.2. Suetonius, Iul. 85; Aug. 100. Dio Cassius 47.18.4, 47.19.2, 51.19.2, 51.22.2, 51.22.4–9, 56.13.4. Augustus, RG 19. Appian 2.148.. Cicero, Att. 14.15.1; Phil. 1.5. S. Weinstock, Divus Iulius (Oxford, 1971), 385–401. M. Montagna Pasquinucci, MonAnt 48 (1973), 257–83. Roma centro 1.67–72. E. M. Steinby, Arctos 21 (1987), 147–56. TEMPLE OF GREAT MOTHER (MAGNA MATER) (Palatine). P. Romanelli, MonAnt 46 (1963), 201–330. P. Pensabene, in Roma centro 1.179–212; ArchLaz 1 (1978), 67–71; 9 (1988) 54–67; 11 (1993), 19–37; 12 (1994), 13–32. TEMPLE OF JANUS GEMINUS. Vergil, Aeneid 7.607–615. Ovid, Fasti 1.257–284. Livy 1.19.1–3. Plutarch, Numa 20.1. Macrobius 1.9.17–18. Pliny, NH 34.33. Varro, LL 5.165. Augustus, RG 42–5. Suetonius, Aug. 22. Dio Cassius 74.14. Procopius, BG 1.25.18–23. I. A. Holland, Janus and the Bridge (1926), 108–37. R. Staccioli, ArchCl 37 (1985), 283–9. Coarelli FRII, 187, 307. F. Castagnoli, BC 92 (1987–8), 11–16. TEMPLE OF JUNO REGINA (Porticus of Octavia). A. M. Palchetti-L. Quilici, QITA 5 (1968), 77–88. TEMPLE OF JUPITER STATOR. Cicero, Cat 1.11.33. Livy 1.13., 1.40.4, 10.36, 27.37.7. Ovid, Fasti 6.793–4; Trist. 3.1.31–2. Pliny, NH 34.29. Dion. Hal. 2.50.3. Plutarch, Cic. 16.3. M. A. Tomei, MEFRA 105 (1993), 621–59. 'TEMPLE OF MINERVA MEDICA'. G. Giovannoni, La cupola del c. d. tempio di M. M. (Rome, 1943). G. Carafa, La cupola della sala decagonale degli horti Liciniani (Rome, 1944). TEMPLE OF NYMPHS (?) (Via Botteghe Oscure). L. Cozza, QITA 5 (1968), 9–20. TEMPLE OF PEACE. Suetonius, Vesp. 9.1. Pliny, NH 12.94, 34.84, 35.102–3, 36.27. A.M. Colini, BC 62 (1934), 165–6. F. Castagnoli and L. Cozza, BC 76 (1956–8), 119–42. TEMPLE OF PORTUNUS. Varro, LL 6.19. J.-P. Adam, Le temple de Portunus au Forum Boarium (Collection École française de Rome 199, Rome, 1994). TEMPLE OF ROMA AND VENUS. E. Manieri Elia, QISA Nos. 1–10 (1983–7), 47–54. Roma centro 1.106–12. R. T. Ridley, Athenaeum 67 (1989), 551–65. A. Castella and S. Panella, ArchLaz 10 (1990), 52–4. 'TEMPLE OF ROMULUS'. CIL 6.1147. A. K. Frazer, Four Late Antique Rotundas (Ann Arbor, 1978). G. Flaccomio et al, 'Il tempio di Romulo', QISA 26 (Rome, 1981). TEMPLE OF SATURN. CIL 6.937, 6.1316; 10.6087. Livy 2.21.1–2, 41.21.12. Servius, Ad Aen. 2.116, 8.319. Tacitus, Ann. 2.41. Solinus 1.12. Suetonius, Aug. 29.5. Varro, LL 5.42, 5.183. Pliny, NH 15.32. Dion. Hal. 6.1.4. Dio Cassius 45.17.3. Macrobius 1.8.1–5. P. Pensabene, Tempio di Saturnio, architettura e decorazione (Rome, 1984). TEMPLE OF VEIOVIS (Capitoline). Livy 35.41. Ovid, Fasti 3.429–30. Vitruvius 4.8.4. Pliny, NH 16.216. A. M. Colini, BC 70 (1942), 5–56. TEMPLE OF VESPASIAN AND TITUS. CIL 6.938. P. Rockwell, RPA 60 (1987–8), 53–69. S. De Angeli, Templum Divi Vespasiani (Rome, 1992). TEMPLE OF VICTORY (Palatine). CIL 6.31059–60. Livy 10.33.9, 29.14.14, 35.9.6. T. P. Wiseman, Antiquaries Journal 61 (1981), 35–52; JRS 85 (1995), 1–22. P. Pensabene, BA 11–12 (1991), 11–51. TEMPLES (LARGO ARGENTINA). F.

Coarelli, in *L'area sacra di Largo Argentina* (Rome, 1981). A. Ziolkowski, *MEFRA* 98 (1986), 623–41. TEMPLES—VEGETABLE MARKET (S. Nicola in Carcere). Cicero, *De leg.* 2.28. Pliny, *NH* 7.121. Tacitus, *Ann.* 2.49. L. Crozzoli Aite, *MPA* 13 (1981). THEATRE OF MARCELLUS. *CIL* 6.1660, 32323.157, 32328.33, 33838a. Dio Cassius 43.49.2–3, 53.30.5–6, 54.26.1. Pliny, *NH* 7.121, 8.65. Martial, *Ep.* 2.29.5. Suetonius, *Iul.* 44; *Aug.* 29.4, 43.5; *Vesp.* 19.1. Augustus, *RG* 21. Plutarch, *Marc.* 30.6. P. Fidenzoni, *Il teatro di Marcello* (Rome, 1970). P. Ciancio Rossetto, *BC* 88 (1982–3), 7–49. THEATRE OF POMPEY. Plutarch, *Pomp.* 52.4. Tertullian, *De spect.* 10. F. Coarelli, *RPA* 44 (1971–2), 99–122. A. M. Capoferro Cencetti *Rivista di Archeologia* 3 (1979), 72–85. F. B. Sear *AJA* 97 (1993), 687–701. TIBER ISLAND (INSULA TIBERINA). Livy 2.5. Dion. Hal. 5.13. Livy 10.47. *Vir ill.* 22.1. Ovid, *Met.* 15.626–701, 736–44. M. Besnier, *L'Île Tibérine dans l'antiquité* (Paris, 1901). M. A. Brucia, *Tiber Island in Ancient and Medieval Rome* (Ann Arbor, 1991). TIBER RIVER. J. Le Gall, *Le Tibre, fleuve de Rome dans l'antiquité* (Paris, 1953). *ArchLaz* 7.2 (1986) (Il Tevere e le altre vie d'acqua del Lazio antico). TOMB OF BIBULUS. G. Boni, *NSc* 1907), 410–14. M Fischer, *BC* 88 (1982–3), 66–8. TOMB OF EURYSACES. *CIL* 6.1958. P. Ciancio Rossetto, *Il sepolcro del fornaio M. Virgilio Eurisace* (Rome, 1973). TOMBS OF THE SCIPIOS. *CIL* 6.1284–94. Cicero, *Tusc. Disp.* 1.13; *Arch.* 22; *De leg.* 2.57. Valerius Maximus 8.14. Livy 38.53, 38.56.

Pliny, *NH* 7.114, 187. Suetonius, *De poet.*, *Ennius* 8. F. Coarelli, *Il sepolcro degli Scipioni* (Rome, 1988). TULLIANUM [MAMERTINE PRISON]. Sallust *Cat.* 55.1–6. Varro *LL.* 5.151. Festus 490L. Propertius 4.4.3–14. Amm. Marc. 28.1.57. *CIL* 6.1539, 31674. J. Le Gall, *MEFRA* 56 (1939), 60–80. F. Coarelli, *FRII*, 64–76. VELIA. M. A. Tomei, *RM* 101 (1994), 309–38. VENUS CLOACINA. Plautus, *Curc.* 470–1. Pliny, *NH* 15.119. Livy 3.48.5. Coarelli *FRI*, 83–9. VIA APPIA. L. Quilici, *Via Appia de Porta Capena ai Colli Albani* (Rome, 1989). VIA DEI CALDERARI 23B. T. Burgess, *Topography and Antiquities of Rome* (London, 1831), 101. L. Attilia, *BA* 4 (1990), 76–82. WALL, AURELIANIC. *Historia Augusta, Aurel.* 21.9, 39.2. Zosimus 1.49.2. I. A. Richmond, *The City Wall of Imperial Rome* (Oxford, 1930). P. Romeo, *BC* 80 (1965–7), 151–183. L. Cozza, *BC* 91 (1986), 103–130; *BC* 92 (1987–8), 137–74; *ARID* 16 (1987), 25–52; *PBSR* 57 (1989), 1–6; *ARID* 20 (1992), 93 ff.; *ARID* 21 (1993) 81 ff.; *ARID* 22 (1994), 61 ff.; *ARID* 25 (1997); WALL, AURELIANIC: PORTA MAGGIORE [PRAENESTINA]. *CIL* 6. 1189, 1256–8. Richmond 205–17. WALL, REPUBLICAN. Livy 1.36, 1.44, 6.32, 7,20, 22.8, 25.7. Appian, *BC* 1.66. Cicero, *De div.* 1.45. Strabo 5.3.7. Juvenal 8.43. Dion. Hal. 4.13.5, 9.68.3–4. Horace *Sat.* 1.8.15. G. Säflund, *Le mura di Roma Repubblicana* (1932). E. Gjerstad, *Opuscula Romana* 1 (1954), 50–65. Coarelli *FB*, 35–59. 'WALL OF ROMULUS'. A. Carandini et al., *BA* 16–18 (1992), 1–18, 111–37.

Illustrations — Acknowledgements

Original photographs (reproduced by kind permission):

Biblioteca Apostolica Vaticana: 141
Brandt, R., Rome: 32
British School at Rome: 59, 80
British Museum, London: 43
Claridge, A., Oxford: 72, 89
Deutsches Archäologisches Institut, Rome: 6, 14, 15, 26, 58, 63, 87, 105, 115, 127
Fototeca Unione, American Academy in Rome: 12, 21, 33, 35, 37, 49, 55, 69, 71, 88, 192
Fratelli Alinari, Florence: 131
Heberden Coin Room, Ashmolean Museum, Oxford: 9, 10, 34, 44
Hunterian Coin Cabinet, University of Glasgow: 20, 44
Istituto Centrale per il Catalogo e la Documentazione, Rome: 31, 146, 159
Museo Nazionale Archeologico, Naples: 93

Reproduced from books:

66 from d'Ambra, *Private Lives*, fig. 1; **83** from Moretti, *Ara Pacis Augustae*, fig. 200; **108** from A. Melucco Vaccaro and A. M. Sommella (eds.) *Marco Aurelio* (1989), fig. 6; **158** from T. Kraus, *Römische Weltreich* (1967), fig. 352; **160** from P. Moreno, *Lisippo* exhib. cat. Rome 1990, 244.

Line drawings:

A. Claridge: A, C, D, E, F, G, 1, 13 (after Anon. Destailleur), 24 (after Lanciani *Ruins*), 27, 36, 38 (after Hülsen), 39 (after Ligorio), 45, 50, 51, 54, 60, 77, 79, 81, 84, 85, 90, 91, 100, 101, 104, 106, 107, 111, 112, 117, 122, 123, 124, 126, 128, 129, 130, 138, 142, 147, 148, 149, 150, 151, 152, 154, 155, 162, 163, 164, 166, 167, 168, 169, 170, 172, 173, 174, 175, 177, 181, 186, 189, 190, 191, 193
P. Connolly: 139
J. DeLaine: 157
S. Gibson: 2, 3, 4, 5, 7, 22, 25, 28, 29, 42, 46, 47, 48, 52, 53, 56, 57, 67, 76, 78, 82, 94, 95, 99, 103, 113 (plan and section), 118, 119, 120, 136, 137, 153, 176
H. Petter: 73
J. Toms: B, H, 8, 40, 61, 64, 74, 86, 109, 116, 125, 143, 165, 180, 194, 196, 197, 198, 199, 200
M. Wilson Jones: 23, 30, 41, 68, 113 (elevation), 114, 195.

Reproduced from books:

11 from Morselli-Tortorici fig. 26; **16-17** from Hülsen, *Roman Forum*, figs. 48–9; **18** from *Grande Roma dei Tarquini* (1990) fig. 3.1.39; **19** adapted from Coarelli, *Roma* (1974) p. 68; **62** from Amici, *Foro di Cesare* fig. 134; **65** from Colini (1934); **70** from Robathan, *Monuments of Ancient Rome* (1950) pl. 7; **75** from *NSc* 1907, fig. 39; 92 from Coarelli, *Roma* (1974) p. 265; 96 adapted from *Roma centro* II, 396; 97–8 adapted from Colini (1943); 102 from Burgess; 110 from *PBSR* IV (1907), pl. 29; 121 from Rakob and Heilmeyer, Beilage 16; 132 adapted from *LTUR* 1, fig. 14; 133 adapted from *Anfiteatro Flavio* (1988), fig. 7; 134 adapted from Golvin, pl. 37.1; 135 after Wilson Jones, RM 100 (1993), 430 fig. 30; 140 after Ward-Perkins, *Antiquity* 30 (1956), 218 fig. 3; 144 from *BC* 1874 pl. 16; 156 from Iwanoff and Hülsen (1898); 171 from von Sydow, *JdI* 92 (1977), 252 fig. 9; 178–9 from Ciancio Rosetti pls. IV, 1, XLII; 182 from Richmond, City Wall; 187 from Rodríguez Almeida (1984); 188 from F. Sear, *Roman Architecture* (1989) fig. 8.

Index

Note: in cases of multiple page references **bold** indicates principal entry.